LEGACY
TO POWER

LEGACY TO POWER

SENATOR RUSSELL LONG OF LOUISIANA

ROBERT MANN

Paragon House
New York

First edition, 1992

Published in the United States by

Paragon House Publishers
90 Fifth Avenue
New York, N.Y. 10011

Library of Congress Cataloging-in-Publication Data

Mann, Robert
    Legacy to power : Senator Russell Long of Louisiana / Robert Mann.
        p.   cm.
    Includes bibliographical references and index.
    ISBN 1-55778-467-1
    1. Long, Russell B.   2. Legislators—United States—Biography.
3. United States.   Congress.   Senate—Biography.   I. Title.
E748.L864M36   1992
328.73′092—dc20
    [B]   92-7890
                                                                  CIP

Manufactured in the United States of America

CONTENTS

ACKNOWLEDGMENTS

WHEN I BEGAN THIS PROJECT IN 1988, I hoped to write an authorized biography that would tell the story of Russell Long's life free of editorial control by the subject. However, as the work progressed, Long became increasingly curious about my treatment of his life. He insisted on reading the manuscript before permitting use of quotations from my interviews with him. Considering the critical way biographers and historians have portrayed his father, this was not an unreasonable condition.

Of the changes Long required, none were substantial or substantive, except in one area. Those involved passages about his battle with alcohol in the late 1960s. Long and I differed on several points in this area and the result was the exclusion of certain materials challenged by Long as inaccurate. I believe inclusion of this material would have painted a more complete picture of this extraordinary man's triumph over adversity and of his own human frailties. Nonetheless, Long did talk openly with me about his battle with alcohol and did not object to the vast majority of what I wrote about this period of his life.

Despite a few tense moments during debate over this portion of the manuscript, Long always remained cordial and very helpful. He phoned numerous friends, family members, and former colleagues to elicit their cooperation with my research. He gave freely of his time, more than fifty hours in formal and informal interviews over the course of my research. For this and other assistance, I will be forever grateful to Russell and Carolyn Long.

No book is the product of only the author. There are many friends, acquaintances, and colleagues who helped make my first book an exciting and rewarding experience. They opened doors and gave needed encouragement and invaluable assistance at crucial moments during my research and writing. In addition, this book would not have been possible without the cooperation of friends and colleagues of Russell Long (listed in the bibliography) who spent dozens of hours with me discussing their recollections of Long and his era.

For their special contributions to this book, those who have my deepest appreciation include Kris Kirkpatrick, for helping me sell this book to Russell Long; Kathy McClure, Karen Stall, Peggy Cassini, Kelly Kerr, and Arthur Worrell of the Long Law Firm, for their constant assistance; My agent, Clyde Taylor, of Curtis Brown, Ltd., for his invaluable counsel and steadfast belief in this book; Tim Wells, for introducing me and my book to Clyde Taylor, and Sally Lee, for introducing me to Wells.

Senator John Breaux, whom I served as press secretary throughout the writing of this book, was one of my most enthusiastic supporters; I thank him for his unfailing help and encouragement. At Louisiana State University's Hill Memorial Library in Baton Rouge, Merna Ford, Faye Phillips, Robert Martin, Lynn Roundtree (who has left LSU for other pursuits), and others on the library staff aided me immensely.

Several people helped me in editing this manuscript and, in the process, improved it greatly. John Copes offered me clear-headed insight and brutal honesty. My brother, Paul Mann, reviewed much of the book and helped me greatly in other respects. Karen Stall and Mike Stern, formerly of Russell Long's staff, applied their excellent criticism and legislative memory to a large portion of the text. At Paragon House, senior editor PJ Dempsey and Seymour Kurtz helped improve the work immensely. Rafael Bermúdez took on the unenviable task of smoothing over differences between Russell Long and the author regarding portions of the manuscript.

My parents, to whom I have dedicated this book, have given me a lifetime of love, support, friendship, and Christian example, and instilled in me a love of the written word. Finally, special gratitude to Cindy Horaist, whose constant and unselfish support kept me working through more-than-occasional periods of frustration, uncertainty, and fatigue. In her very special way, Cindy has brought exceptional love and happiness to my life.

Prologue

YOUR FATHER'S BEEN SHOT

$\mathcal{S}$TACCATO TELEPHONE RINGS SHATTERED the tranquility of the Long household shortly after ten o'clock the night of September 8, 1935. Russell—the polite, bashful sixteen-year-old son of Senator Huey P. Long—rushed to answer the call. Strain in the trembling voice of his mother's half brother, Gilman McConnell, was immediately apparent. His news was jolting.

"Russell, there's something bad that has happened here," said McConnell, superintendent of the state capitol building in Baton Rouge. "I hope it's going to be all right. But it's not good." McConnell blurted out his horrible news. "Your father has been shot. He's in the hospital. I believe it would be well for you and your mother and brother and sister to come up here."[1]

Russell numbly staggered to his mother's bedroom to deliver the awful message. Rose Long was stunned, but she steadied herself, betraying none of the fear that had crashed around her. She called for little Rose, her twenty-year-old daughter, and went to rouse her other son, twelve-year-old Palmer, who woke to his mother's voice and the incongruous admonition: "Don't get excited, but your daddy's been shot. Just take it easy." Calmly and quietly, Russell and the rest of the family dressed and packed. As they gathered enough clothes for several days, Lieutenant Governor

James Noe phoned from the hospital. His news was encouraging. Dr.
Arthur Vidrine, the attending physician, believed Huey's condition was not
serious. The information was a huge relief as they scurried around the
house.[2]

Until the moment the phone rang, the sultry New Orleans evening had
been no different than any other Sunday for the Longs. Russell spent most
of the day with friends, planning his campaign for freshman class president
at Louisiana State University. As usual, the family ate a light supper before
settling down for the highlight of Sunday night radio, the "Jack Benny
Show." As he was on most weekends, Huey Long was absent. This day,
he was in Baton Rouge to supervise a special session of the Louisiana
legislature summoned at his command by Governor Oscar K. Allen. Only
two days earlier, Huey left Rose with a kiss and the discomforting premonition "something" might happen to him. He told her, "I may not come
back, but I'll die fighting." In Louisiana's highly charged political atmosphere, the notion that Huey's life was in jeopardy was nothing new. The
front-page headline in the morning's *New Orleans Times-Picayune* offered
a clue of new enmities: "HUEY LONG STEAMROLLS 39 BILLS
THROUGH COMMITTEE."[3]

Although a United States senator, Huey Long dominated Louisiana like
no leader before or since. He was its undisputed potentate. His mighty
organization distributed all state patronage jobs and controlled virtually
every aspect of Louisiana government to the smallest local level. Governor Allen, a childhood friend whom Huey had handpicked, did his bidding
slavishly. Friends were rewarded handsomely. Enemies, of which he had
more than a few, were excluded and sometimes crushed. It was no
wonder the dreams of such a controversial man were filled with sinister
images of shadowy figures plotting to take his life.

Only a few weeks earlier, the forty-two-year-old senator rose dramatically in the U.S. Senate to alert his colleagues to an assassination conspiracy by a group of his Louisiana enemies. Reading from a secretly obtained
transcript of a July meeting at the DeSoto Hotel in New Orleans, Huey
shocked senators when he quoted one conspirator: "I would draw in a
lottery to go out and kill Long. It would only take one man, one gun, one
bullet." This was not the first time Huey had tasted the fear of assassination. Three years earlier, an unidentified gunman fired a shot into the
Longs' New Orleans home in a presumed assassination attempt. While the
bullet shattered a window and lodged in a book across the room, it left
Huey and his family frightened but unharmed.[4]

The morning of September 6—as Huey dressed and stuffed his pockets with his huge ring of keys, scraps of paper and his usual bundle of cash—Rose probably dismissed the premonition. As a politician's wife, she was accustomed to portrayals of Huey as a ruthless dictator. An assassination attempt on the man who ruled Louisiana with undisputed power, invincible at the polls, would surprise no one, not even his wife. Two days later, however, Huey's premonition would hold earth-shattering significance for Rose.

After Rose and the children finished packing, Russell calmly steered the streamlined DeSoto from the driveway of the Long's elegant Audubon Avenue home. Terrified by the situation awaiting them, they embarked on the eighty-mile drive up the newly constructed four-lane highway connecting New Orleans and Baton Rouge. The road paralleled the Mississippi River, carving a serpentine swath through the dense swamps and bayous between the two cities. Driving at high speed, they soon approached a detour sign diverting traffic around the Bonnet Carre spillway, a flood control project of the U.S. Army Corps of Engineers. They quickly concluded the detour would cost precious time, compared to the direct route afforded by the highway. Taking a gamble on the treacherous spillway road, Russell maneuvered the car off the pavement and onto the dirt and gravel. Driving cautiously through the darkness, he strained to see beyond the glow of the headlights. A wooden fence came quickly into view. As they drew closer, Russell saw heavy timbers and a gate, secured by a locked chain protecting the road from intruders. Russell and Palmer surveyed the situation before deciding to use the car's bumper jack to break the timbers. From the car, Rose and her daughter heard the crack of wood as the jack did its job. The lock was free. The gate swung wide. The two brothers quickly tossed the jack into the trunk and continued through the muggy Louisiana night.[5]

Not far behind them drove Dr. Urban Maes and his colleague, Dr. Russell Stone, two prominent New Orleans surgeons who received an urgent call from the Baton Rouge hospital where Huey was admitted. Huey wanted Maes and Stone to operate on his wound. Pulling up to the gate that Russell and Palmer had freed, the doctors forged ahead. Minutes later, their car slid off the road and into a ditch. They were stuck. Even worse, they did not arrive at the hospital until after Huey's operation was completed.[6]

* * *

About 12:15 A.M., the family raced toward Baton Rouge as doctors placed the ether cone over Huey's face to begin surgery. Not long afterward,

Russell wheeled the car into the parking lot of Our Lady of the Lake Hospital, less than a mile from the capitol. Quickly enveloped by friends—Governor Allen; Huey's secretary, Seymour Weiss; and others—Rose and the children first learned the details of Huey's shooting. A promising and popular young Baton Rouge physician, Carl Weiss (no relation to Seymour Weiss), shot him as he strode from the house chamber to the governor's office. The timorous Weiss—a devoted family man apparently enraged by a bill to engineer the defeat of his father-in-law, an anti-Long Louisiana judge—leapt from behind a marble column and pumped one bullet from his .38 caliber pistol into Huey's abdomen. Huey staggered away in pain. Meanwhile, his attacker scuffled with Huey's bodyguards, who threw him to the floor. They killed him, instantly, in a hail of fire from their guns.

Entering the hospital, the family went directly to the operating room, where they watched as doctors tried to locate the bullet and repair the damage. Several hours later, Dr. Vidrine pronounced Huey's condition "satisfactory." In truth, Huey was in grave danger. An inexperienced surgeon, Vidrine had not wanted to operate, but Huey's worsening state forced him to commence when Maes and Stone failed to appear. Without the guidance of more experienced surgeons, Vidrine committed a grievous error. While he repaired Huey's colon, he failed to probe for damage to the kidneys. When Maes and Stone finally arrived, the oversight shocked them. They inserted a catheter to determine if the bullet had struck a kidney. To their horror, Huey's bladder was full of blood, indicating damage to the kidney's renal duct. The organ was hemorrhaging. By this time, virtually nothing could be done to repair the damage. Another operation, they concluded, would surely kill him. They waited and watched.[7]

By 3:00 A.M., Huey was in shock. His blood pressure plummeted. There was no detectable pulse. In spite of this, Dr. Vidrine had issued the statement around 4:45 A.M. that claimed Huey's condition was "satisfactory." Not long after Vidrine released the announcement to reporters, Huey rallied. His blood pressure rose. Later in the morning he showed even more improvement, talking for abut ten minutes with Governor Allen. He was never entirely lucid, lapsing in and out of consciousness.[8]

As the day progressed, Huey's conditioned worsened. Doctors had given him one blood transfusion the night before. By noon, they prepared for a second. By day's end, he would receive four more, all with only temporary results. His fits of unconsciousness were more frequent by the afternoon. He was delirious much of the time, talking wildly about his plan to share America's wealth among all its people. Beyond the hospital, he imagined the huddled, poverty-stricken masses calling to him for help. Through his tears, Russell watched helplessly as his father cried out to his illusory populace. Sometime in the late afternoon, Huey suddenly asked: "Where are my children?" At once, Rose, Russell and Palmer were summoned. By the time they arrived, Huey once again lapsed into his coma. By midnight, he lost consciousness for the last time. A deathwatch enveloped the hospital.[9]

At 4 A.M., Huey faded. He had only a few precious minutes of life in him. The doctors told this to Mrs. Long as they ushered his children and friends into the room. As the group—including Lieutenant Governor James Noe; Seymour Weiss; the Reverend Gerald L.K. Smith; former aide, Earle Christenberry; and Huey's doctors—surrounded Huey's bed, many of them wept. The Reverend Gerald L.K. Smith prayed. "May the Lord have mercy on our souls, in the name of the Father, the Son, and the Holy Ghost." As Smith finished the short prayer, at 4:06 A.M., Huey Long died.[10]

While Huey's death was expected for more than a day, the last moment was devastating. Rose, Russell, and Palmer sobbed, but were stilled when their mother admonished, "No, children. He was brave. We must be brave, too." After a short prayer by Smith, the group filed slowly from the room. They accompanied Mrs. Long and the children downstairs to a waiting car, which whisked them to their hotel.[11]

Meanwhile, the task of informing the press of Huey's death befell Governor Allen. With Seymour Weiss standing beside him, biting his lip to maintain his composure, Allen fought off his own staggering grief to read a short statement: "This marks the death of Huey P. Long, the passing of the greatest builder of economics in the history of Louisiana in two hundred and twenty-five years. It also marks the passing of the greatest hero for the common right of all the people of America. His name will exist and be remembered in the annals of the state of Louisiana and the people of America."[12]

* * *

In his brief tenure as Louisiana's predominant political leader, Huey Long had secured his place in the hearts of generations of Louisiana citizens. As governor, he overthrew the elite Bourbons who ruled Louisiana as their private domain, with rank indifference to the concerns of common people. He built thousands of miles of roads and bridges and gave thousands their first chance for a real education. He taxed the oil companies who plundered Louisiana's natural resources, lowered utility rates, and hoisted Louisiana into the twentieth century. His enemies—the rich and powerful—vilified him as a tyrant and a thief. Average people, meanwhile, loved Huey as their champion and defender. To them, his death was a crushing blow.

Thousands of Huey's disciples flocked to Baton Rouge for his funeral on Thursday afternoon, September 10. Many were casual friends. Others were politicians, elected only because of their presence on the Long ticket. Some were appointees to the boards and commissions Huey controlled. Most, however, had never met the man who called himself the Kingfish. They voted for him and may have even heard him on the radio. But their first face-to-face meeting with the most important figure in Louisiana's history was the moment they filed past his open casket in the vast Memorial Hall of the capitol. There, they saw Huey's lifeless, tuxedo-clad body for the first and only time.

Mostly, the mourners came from rural places, flocking to Baton Rouge from the bayous of Acadiana or the red-clay hills of northern Louisiana. The men wore dusty, tattered overalls and the women, simple flowered cotton dresses. Some of the men wore their finest, ill-fitting suits. Hats clutched tightly in their hands and heads bowed, they shuffled past the casket, lingering for a moment to bid farewell to the man they had adored, but never met. "They were moved as deeply as those who knew him intimately," wrote one observer, who noted "tears streaming from the eyes of men and women alike." Muffled sobs filled the room as the mourning pilgrims ambled by, smothering the sounds of their grief by burying faces in soaked handkerchiefs.[13]

There were thousands of such moments. An estimated 175,000 people converged on the capital to pay their respects. At one point, the line that ended at the capitol building stretched down the steps toward the sunken gardens and encircled the huge park. Had the mourners stood single file, some believe they would have extended across the city and into the countryside. Their cars clogged every road leading into Baton Rouge. On the west bank of the Mississippi River, a line of cars four miles long waited to be ferried across into East Baton Rouge Parish.[14]

Huey's body laid in state from 2:00 P.M. Wednesday until 4:00 P.M. the next day. A mountain of floral arrangements, which continued to arrive up until the time of the funeral, enveloped his casket. At 3:00 P.M., the huge doors to Memorial Hall swung shut so workers could move the flowers to the grave site, just beyond the capitol steps. Finally, about 4:00 P.M., the hall was empty except for Huey's casket. On cue, his family and close friends filed past the bier for the final time. The last to approach the casket were Russell, his mother, little Rose, and Palmer; they remained for several minutes, gazing silently at Huey's ashen face. As they slowly pulled away, attendants lowered the cover and moved the casket across the hall toward the doors.[15]

Outside, the ninety-degree heat was stifling. The crowd waited impatiently for the funeral procession to begin. Some climbed trees or stood on housetops to get a better view. At 4:25 P.M., the majestic sight of Reverend Gerald L.K. Smith—a spellbinding preacher who had helped Long promote his Share Our Wealth program—silenced the murmuring throng. Leading the funeral procession, Smith stood atop the capitol steps for a moment, surveying the crowd. Then, as he began to descend the steps, the casket, borne by six pallbearers and several policemen, appeared. Behind the casket followed Rose Long, Russell, and other family members. Behind them were friends, U.S. congressmen and senators, and members of the state legislature. As the procession descended, the sounds of an organ from a neighboring church drifted over the capitol grounds and the hushed crowd. Mournful sounds of church bells tolling, only briefly, were heard in the distance. As the pallbearers approached the bottom of the forty-eight steps, the Louisiana State University marching band began playing "Every Man a King," Huey's campaign theme song. Normally, the tune was an upbeat melody. For this occasion, the band director arranged a slow, melancholy dirge in a minor key. When the procession reached the grave, Rose and her children sat in a row of chairs directly in front of the casket. There, they cried while waiting for the service to begin. Behind them, heads bowed, stood the rest of the family and other members of the funeral procession. After they had assembled, Smith approached the head of the casket.[16]

"The lives of great men do not end with the grave," said Smith, later notorious for his vehement anti-Semitism. "They just begin. This place marks not the resting place of Huey Long. It marks only the burial place for his body. His spirit shall never rest as long as hungry bodies cry for food, as long as human frames stand naked, as long as homeless wretches haunt this land of plenty." No one moved as Smith delivered a spellbinding sermon. "Oh, God, why did we have to lose him," he bellowed as he closed his remarks with one last rhetorical flourish. "He was the Stradivarius whose notes rose in competition with jealous drums, envious tom-toms. His was the unfinished symphony."[17]

When Smith concluded, Russell bowed his head as the attendants solemnly lowered the casket, adorned with a blanket of orchids and lilies, into the grave. By this time, the crowd was out of control, as thousands strained to catch a glimpse of the casket or snatch a flower from one of the arrangements. The police were helpless to control the throng. The family, hemmed in by the pressing mass of people, sat silently until police opened a path through the multitude. As they fought their way to a waiting car, the crowd continued pressing closer to the grave, trampling the flowers.[18]

As Russell and his family sped away, many in the crowd, and most of Huey's enemies, concluded they had witnessed the end of an era. The Kingfish was gone and, thus, his kingdom. What they could not have known was that Huey's death, and its profound impact on his elder son, marked both an era and a beginning. History would eventually record that Huey Long's martyrdom gave birth to one of the most enduring and celebrated political careers in American politics.

The Long era was not over. To the contrary, it had barely begun. From this day, Huey Long's aura would propel a host of Longs into Louisiana politics. They would serve as governor, congressmen, and state legislators. None of them, however, would serve with the single-minded intensity that tormented sixteen-year-old Russell, driving him toward no greater ambition than to complete his father's unfinished work. Whether he wanted it or not, Russell's birthright was power.

* * *

U.S. senator Russell Long was slightly superstitious. On this September day in 1985, as he surveyed the skies over Baton Rouge, he considered what, if any, meaning the dark, looming rain clouds might have for him. This was, he knew, a significant day. Unlike most among the gathering that waited to hear his speech at the Louisiana State Library, the clouds for Russell seemed portentous. For the moment, their interpretation would wait. He had something else to interpret: the earth-shattering incident which occurred exactly fifty years earlier in a corridor of the state capitol, which overshadowed the building he was about to enter.

Although the speech was to be delivered on the anniversary of the shooting, Russell, now 66, planned to focus on his father's momentous life. Therefore, he prepared remarks he hoped would stress the compassionate side of Huey Long, a man whose name seemed more comfortable preceded by words like *dictator, despot,* or *tyrant.* This, he knew, was one of his last opportunities to command the public attention needed to influence what historians and journalists might say about his father for years to come. For several months, he had labored over the speech, dictating remembrances of his father to an aide who transcribed the tapes and edited them into speech form. At first, he had prepared a stinging rebuke of his father's critics, a defensive diatribe aimed at those who faulted his father's harsh tactics or who doubted the motives behind his concern for the downtrodden. Gradually, as his staff and friends dissuaded him from this course, he came to believe a positive review of his father's life would yield better results.

Riding to the library, Russell was quiet, lost perhaps in thought about the events fifty years earlier which had dramatically changed the course of his sixteen-year-old life. As his car pulled up to the building, the clouds unleashed a torrent of rain, which confined him to the car for about ten minutes. Finally, with the downpour showing no sign of abating, he dashed for the building. When he arrived at the front door, he was soaked. Inside, he confronted a throng of about 150 friends, well-wishers, reporters and aficionados of Louisiana history. Clutching his speech notes, he made his way slowly through the crowd and took his place on the podium, where he waited, maintaining a tight, nervous smile as he was introduced.

For thirty minutes, he regaled the audience with stories of his father's legendary life. He told them how Huey paved the roads, built the schools, and tried to rid Louisiana of the corrupt elitists who disenfranchised the common man. He spoke of Huey's struggles to share the nation's wealth and his resulting enmity with President Franklin Roosevelt. Most of these stories had been learned from others, inherited from his mother or family members. Yet, he spoke with the enthusiasm and passion of a firsthand witness. When he was exhausted of anecdotes, he paused, and turned to the subject on everyone's mind—the assassination.

"Everyone has an opinion, I suppose, about my father's assassination. I don't believe it was an act of a single individual. In my judgment, there were likely other people involved in one respect or another." The statement flew in the face of evidence, long held as fact by historians, that Huey Long was the victim of a Baton Rouge physician, Carl Weiss, who acted on a personal grudge. To Russell, this simple explanation only cheapened the circumstances by which his father's life was taken.

"Keep in mind he was winning with fifty-five to sixty percent of the vote. But that was when the poor people couldn't vote because of that poll tax. It was only a dollar every year for the privilege of voting and a lot of poor people, never having voted, they couldn't see that it would make that much difference. They needed that dollar too much."

Huey, Russell noted, repealed the poll tax and doubled the number of eligible voters, most of them poor, uneducated, and ardent Long support-ers. In short, Russell said, his father was killed by opponents who would not allow the poor masses the chance to vote for Huey Long. His father did not live long enough to realize the benefit of an election without a poll tax.

Russell made an admission. He noted critics faulted Huey for his despotic tactics and his ruthless way of dealing with opponents.

He learned he had to fight fire with fire. And in doing that, some of the things he did could be criticized and some I'm sure were wrong. I have many times struggled with this moral question: Do the ends justify the means? Finally, I learned the answer to that question: It is a matter of degrees. In Huey's case, he was saying that this country was failing to provide a fair opportunity for people. People were poor, they were hungry, they were without homes and without warm clothing in the winter. And there were rich people holding onto their wealth for dear life. He wanted America to spread that wealth.

To emphasize the point, Huey's son concluded by reading a passage from his father's autobiography:

Then no tear-dimmed eyes of a small child will be lifted into the saddened face of a father or mother unable to give it the necessities required by its soul and body for life; then the powerful will be rebuked in the sight of man for holding that which they cannot consume, but which is craved to sustain humanity; the food of the land will feed, the raiment clothe and the houses shelter all the people; the powerful will be elated through the well being of all, rather than through their greed.

His speech was over. From the library, Russell led a procession two blocks away to his father's grave at the sunken gardens of the state capitol. There, in the steady Sunday afternoon drizzle, protected by a large umbrella, Russell placed a wreath at the base of the huge bronze statue of Huey Long that rests above his grave. Standing next to his brother, Palmer, Russell gazed silently at the grave for only a moment. Turning away, he made his way to the car, walking almost the same path he had taken fifty years earlier after his father's casket was lowered into the ground.

As the car pulled away, leaving the capitol behind, the son of Huey Long looked away from the other passengers, out into the dreary, rain-soaked streets. He was lost in thought as his wife, Carolyn, and his aides congratulated him on the speech.

Finally, he broke the silence. "That was for Dad," he said softly. "I owed him that."

To Mom and Dad

1

EVERY MAN A KING

*H*UEY LONG LOVED TO SPIN TALES of a hardscrabble childhood, telling more than one enraptured audience about his early years in a tiny log cabin in Winn Parish, Louisiana. That he was born in Winnfield in 1893 is the only portion of the story based in fact, the rest manufactured by Huey's populist imagination as evidence to voters that his were humble beginnings, like theirs. "Every time I hear of that cabin," one of his sisters once grumbled, "it gets smaller and smaller."[1]

In truth, Huey confessed in his 1933 autobiography that he was raised "in a comfortable, well-built log house. A year later we moved into a better house which was built on the same premises." Despite the image he conjured for his followers, Huey's was not a childhood of deprivation. His father, Huey P. Long, commonly known as Hu, was one of the largest landowners in the small north-central Louisiana town.[2]

The Long family's fortunes were further enhanced in 1900, when the Arkansas Southern Railroad extended one of its lines into Winnfield, building a depot on land owned by Hu. With the proceeds, he built a spacious house. Far from moneyed, the Longs were, essentially, land rich. Hu's only constant source of money came from the occasional sale of a hog or cow; the Longs grew and raised most of what they consumed. Nevertheless, they were an island of relative prosperity in a sea of rural poverty.

Those who knew Huey as a child remembered him as exceptionally bright, curious, outspoken, extremely self-confident, and always seeking

1

the limelight. "If he couldn't pitch, he wouldn't play," one of his childhood friends observed. His younger brother, Earl, remembered Huey was "nervous, curious about everything. Our father used to say that he'd jump in the well to see what it was like if it wasn't kept covered. He wouldn't stay still." Huey flouted the custom that dictated children were to be seen, not heard, and should speak only when spoken to. Childhood friends recalled he often interjected himself into conversations with elders, even to the point of offering strategic advice to old men playing checkers. "I can't remember back to a time when my mouth wasn't open whenever there was a chance to make a speech," he once told a reporter.[3]

At sixteen, Huey was expelled from school after circulating a letter attacking his high school faculty. "The teachers had it in for him," Huey's father once groused. "He dictated to them. They were a sorry bunch, some of them. Huey always had trouble with them." Free from Winnfield's confinements, Huey embarked on his new life as a traveling salesman. Still a mere teenager, he was not unprepared for what lay ahead. "When he left home at seventeen, [Huey] was probably more knowledgeable and perceptive than most southern college graduates at the time," wrote one historian. For the next three years, Huey would roam the South and Southwest selling cooking oil, packed foods, produce, and patent medicines to housewives. He was a natural, a fast talking, smooth-tongued drummer whose charms were difficult to resist.[4]

Brash and engaging, Huey had an almost innate ability to appraise customers and pitch the products tailored to their needs. When selling cooking oil, one biographer observed, "he was in the door one minute, in the farm wife's kitchen the next. He put on the apron, baked a cake, or prepared supper for the family." Despite all this success, his sales generated little financial reward as Huey quickly squandered his profits. He lodged in the best hotels and ate well. He was fired from one job for charging hefty bills on his expense account. Nonetheless, in the course of becoming a consummate salesman, Huey was learning to sell more than just cooking oil. He was learning to sell himself, honing valuable political skills that would pay rich dividends years later. Of politics, he said, "all I remember is that the first time I knew anything about it, I was in it."[5]

In the midst of a six-state odyssey—which led him as a salesman and sometimes as a hobo throughout Texas, Louisiana, Arkansas, Mississippi, Tennessee, and Oklahoma—Huey settled briefly in Norman, Oklahoma, where he took several part-time courses at the University of Oklahoma and supported himself selling produce. Huey soon grew restless again. This time, he cast his eyes east to Memphis, where a friend from

Winnfield arranged a sales job with the Faultless Starch Company of Kansas City. As director of sales for the Memphis region, Huey was a huge success, making more money than ever, as much as $125 a week. He directed sales in a four-state area and presided over a crew of salesmen that included his younger brother, Earl, whom Huey persuaded to move to Memphis. In December 1912, having been awarded a long Christmas break, Huey left directly for Shreveport. His mission was to persuade a young woman, Rose McConnell, to marry him.

Huey met Rose several years earlier in Shreveport when he was selling cooking oil, Cottolene. When the Fairbanks Company's New Orleans office instructed its Alexandria-area salesmen to organize cake baking contests—using Cottolene, of course, as a sales tool—Huey accepted the project with relish. Unfazed that salesmen were required to furnish the prizes themselves, Huey quickly organized a successful bake-off in Alexandria that proved so popular the company directed the sales team to move on to Shreveport and stage several more. One competition in which Huey served as judge included Rose and her mother. Walking down the line of women, Huey's eyes were drawn to the petite, blue-eyed, black-haired young woman, in whose cooking he took inordinate interest. "I bet you didn't make this cake," he said to Rose. "Yes, I did," she replied. Huey shot back, "How about having a date and proving it?" After courting for several weeks, Huey and Rose were infatuated. Rose had never met anyone with Huey's intellect, charm, and confidence. Huey, in turn, was completely enchanted by Rose, telling friends that not only was she the most beautiful woman he had ever met, but that he would marry her.[6]

Two and a half years later, after a long and sometimes stormy courtship, Huey returned to Shreveport to ask for Rose's hand, a question he had posed several times without an affirmative answer. Very much in love and eager to be married, Huey brought Rose to Winnfield to meet his parents. The family liked her, but worried that Huey, at nineteen, was too young for marriage. Huey dismissed their objections, but Rose, who sensed the family's displeasure and believed herself that Huey was not ready for marriage, refused to follow him to Memphis. Huey stormed back to Tennessee and only wrote and called her sporadically.

After a several-month hiatus, Huey launched a full-scale assault on Rose's heart. Worried that Huey was drinking heavily in her absence, Rose finally took the train to Memphis to rescue him. She found not a drunk, but a lovesick young man. Rose could not resist his charms any longer. They were married on April 12, 1913, the day she arrived in Memphis. After the Baptist minister administered the wedding vows,

Huey discovered he had no money for the preacher's fee, forcing Rose to dip into the eleven dollars she had brought with her.

Huey and Rose settled into a comfortable apartment, where they lived until financial difficulties forced Faultless to close its Memphis operation. The company's failure sent them packing for Winnfield to live with his family, where Huey sold for Faultless and later for a Tennessee medicine company, which finally released him in 1914 when the economy declined. This time, in desperation, he called on brother Julius, who advised him to resume his law studies. As an inducement, Julius promised to subsidize the couple if Huey enrolled in Tulane Law School in New Orleans. With the few hundred dollars he had saved and four hundred dollars borrowed from Julius, Huey and Rose set off for New Orleans and settled in a tiny apartment.

Instead of a methodical study regimen, Huey quickly settled on a shortcut to bar admission. As a law degree was unimportant to him, Huey took only four law courses, using the time left to study for a special bar exam administered by a lawyers' committee. In May 1915, at age twenty-one, he passed the committee's exam and was admitted to the bar. "I arrived at my old home town of Winnfield some few days after I had been admitted to the bar, ready for the practice of law," Huey wrote in his autobiography, noting the first few months "netted me no returns." What he neglected to say was he had returned to his hometown and joined his brother Julius's firm as a junior partner. After only a few months in Winnfield, he and Julius were embroiled in a feud, no doubt the result of Huey's usual impertinence. Huey, Julius revealed years later, was simply not deferential enough to his older brother or the rest of Winn Parish's small legal community. [7]

Finally, the feuding came to a head and the two brothers dissolved their relationship. Huey began looking for another job as a traveling salesman. Unable to find such work, he turned again to the law, locating a small anteroom over the Bank of Winnfield. He rented the room for four dollars a month and with his three law books and a white pine table for a desk, opened for business. "A shoe store opened on the street immediately next to the bank," Huey said, noting the owner "promised that whenever I was wanted at the telephone, he would call me." From every indication, the phone did not ring often for Huey. The "chip and wet-stone practice," as he called it, barely produced enough to pay the meager rent. Frustrated with his paltry income, Huey was forced to become a salesman again. This time, he found work selling kerosene oil for the Never Fail Company throughout north Louisiana. Rose kept the law office open, keeping Huey informed of the precious few clients who came to him for help.[8]

One such client approached Huey in 1916, a Winnfield widow who wanted to sue the Bank of Winnfield, owned by Huey's uncle George, for savings stolen by a bank employee. Huey accepted the case, but was rebuffed by the court when he was ordered to post a one-hundred-dollar bond to cover the court costs. Neither the widow nor her lawyer had anything close to that amount. Stunned by this move, Huey quickly requested an adjournment and spent the rest of the day searching the town for someone willing to loan him the bond money. Finally, in desperation, he approached state senator S. J. Harper. Although he served on the bank's board of directors, Harper was well known as a radical champion of the underdog. He loaned Huey enough money to appease the court.

The trial attracted considerable attention among Winnfield's citizens. The town's passions were inflamed by the widow's claim against the powerful bank, especially because she was forced to post bond money before her case was heard. In court, Huey attacked the bank so aggressively that the bank's vice president, B. W. Bailey, approached Huey's best friend, Harley Bozeman, imploring him to get Huey to soften his rhetoric. When Huey heard of the plea, he told Bozeman to "tell Uncle George and Mr. Bailey that they should feel complimented that Huey Long don't take out after topwaters [small fish] but after the big fish."[9]

Biographer T. Harry Williams said Huey was revealing a tactic he would employ time and time again during his political career: "If you want to attract popular attention and support, denounce the biggest, closest target at hand." Huey won his case. The court awarded the widow the full amount owed her by the bank. "I cleaned the hell out of them in that suit," Huey bragged afterward, "and after that I had all the law business I could handle." Huey was soon one of the most sought-after attorneys in the area, always seeming to find himself fighting for an underdog against some larger corporate interest. He was not getting rich, but he was certainly making more money than ever before. Huey bragged his practice grew to such proportions that his cases alone equaled those handled by every other member of the Winnfield bar combined.[10]

Unlike many other men of his time, Huey avoided service in World War I. True to the heritage of his Winn Parish forebears who had refused to fight in the Civil War, Huey received a Class IV deferment, given to men with dependents. "I did not go because I was not mad at anybody over there," Huey later explained. Safely protected from the draft, Huey applied himself to building his law practice. After only three years, he was

becoming something of a legal celebrity. The time had come, he concluded, to use his growing notoriety in another field of endeavor—politics.
In 1918, he made his move, declaring his candidacy for the north Louisiana
seat on the state's Railroad Commission, a moribund, three-member body
whose potential as a dynamic, aggressive institution had never been
fulfilled. Although they had extensive powers to regulate intrastate railroads, pipelines, and public utilities, the commissioners were lazy, slaves
to the state's wealthy interests and unwilling to exercise their authority. In
the commission, Huey saw potential. He suspected that if he could prod its
members to enforce the previously neglected laws regulating the state's
utilities, he could establish himself as a protector of the common man and
ride the ensuring notoriety into the governor's mansion. [11]

The commission's Third District encompassed twenty-eight parishes,
almost half the state, and was represented by veteran commissioner Burk
Bridges, who had served since 1912. Huey, confident as always, announced his intention to run against Bridges by telling a friend, "I can beat
that old man." From day one, Bridges underestimated Huey's potential.
Relying on his usual cronies and contacts, Bridges could not have foreseen
the kind of campaign this skinny upstart country lawyer would wage
against him. He soon found out—the hard way. [12]

Blazing a mad trail throughout north Louisiana, Huey nailed campaign
posters on virtually every fence post or telephone pole he could find.
Historian Harnett Kane noted that Huey "avoided all the courthouse
towns, the parish centers to which candidates usually gave their particular
attention." Instead, he focused his attention on the "scattered people of
the hills and hollows." Driving to almost every small town in the district,
Huey solicited the vote of every person he met, applying all the charm and
charisma he had acquired as a salesman. One of his most successful ploys
was a promise to the citizens of many small communities that he would
force the railroads to extend service to their towns. [13]

While Huey stormed the district, campaigning with an intensity never
before witnessed in Louisiana, Bridges continued to underestimate Huey's
populist appeal. On the day of the Democratic primary, the only election
that really mattered in Louisiana because of the party's dominance, Huey
ran less than two thousand votes behind Bridges. He edged out the other
three candidates for a runoff spot with the incumbent. In the second
primary, Huey beat Bridges by 635 votes. By virtue of no Republican
opposition, Huey Long, age twenty-five, was elected to his first public
office. The Railroad Commission was not Huey's goal. It was a means to
an end. The other two members of the commission, John T. Michel and

Shelby Taylor, did not realize that they would become two important puppets in Huey's quest for higher office. Their ignorance about Huey's intentions did not last long. The young commissioner would soon reveal his plans.

Those appalled by the power Huey Long eventually exercised over Louisiana would be well advised to examine the influence exerted in the state by Standard Oil of New Jersey when Huey arrived on the scene. The huge oil company pumped millions of barrels of oil out of the Louisiana ground each year. It employed hundreds of Louisiana citizens in its Baton Rouge refinery, reportedly the largest in the world, and generally had its way with the state's politicians. It operated as an unregulated entity, free to do what it wanted to whom it wanted; that is, until it crossed paths with Huey Long.

For years, Huey represented several Winnfield friends involved in oil drilling in Shreveport. Some paid him in oil stock. In time, several of these companies proved very successful and Huey began to believe he might soon be rich. Meanwhile, some of the larger oil companies, including Standard Oil, began pipeline embargoes to close the markets to the small independent oil companies. More than one hundred Shreveport-area oil companies, once encouraged by these same large companies to explore for oil at full tilt, were faced with extinction. "I had gone to sleep one night with transactions all ready to be closed for options and equities I had acquired which meant that I might some day be mentioned among the millionaires, to awaken in the morning to read that nothing I had was of value because the three pipeline companies said so," Huey recalled.[14]

The situation provided Huey with his first opportunity to awaken the commission from its slumber. While the commissioners usually conducted business in Baton Rouge, the February 1919 meeting was held in Huey's hometown of Shreveport. It gave him an excellent stage for the first confrontation with his newfound enemy, Standard Oil, whose representatives attended the meeting along with the pipeliners participating in the embargo against the local companies. "The faces of the Standard Oil group bore expressions of self-content," Huey wrote, adding "about these men there was that undefinable something that betokens freedom from money cares and anxiety as to the future." Of the independent oilmen, Huey told another story, noting on their faces were written "care, and in some cases, desperation." As the Standard Oilmen began to bully some representatives of other big oil companies, Huey had enough. "And this is a free country," he told them. "You've done this before and got by with it, but this time, go do it and see when you hear the last of it." With that, he stormed out of the meeting. True to his word, Huey soon engineered a commission ruling that declared the pipelines common carriers, placing them under commission jurisdiction for the first time. The ruling caused an uproar, sweeping Baton Rouge, Huey said, "like a hurricane." Huey had his cause.[15]

The next year, Huey assumed the rotating chairmanship of the commission and hit his stride. Described by one writer as "a restless St. George, [who] pierced one public utility dragon after another." To the delight of Louisiana voters, Huey relentlessly pursued the Cumberland Telephone and Telegraph Company, refusing to grant its requests for rate increases. Instead, he engineered a customer refund of almost $500,000. He canceled rate schedules that would have cost millions of dollars. In Shreveport, he sued the streetcar company when it raised its fare by a penny. Outraged by the rate hike, he refused to ride the trolley, walking to work until the case was settled in is favor. He fought for and won lower electric rates in Shreveport.[16]

While pursuing these and other cases, Huey never let his mind stray far from his archenemy, Standard Oil. In 1922, he persuaded the state legislature to cancel Governor John Parker's "gentleman's agreement" with Standard Oil on the severance tax by enacting a 3 percent tax. He also eliminated more than nine million dollars of value that Standard Oil claimed for rate-making purposes by its pipeline subsidiary. At one point, Huey responded by summoning company officials before the commission, demanding that they bring their books and records to the commission for public inspection. The company refused, charging into court to prevent Huey from seizing their books. The day before the judge's ruling, which Huey knew would be in favor of the company, he vented his frustration with a threat, on which he meant to make good. "We are going to see that the throats of every one of those double-decking politicians is cut from ear to ear."[17]

In the midst of these storms of controversy, Huey turned thirty in 1923. On his birthday, he made another bold move for which he was becoming famous: He announced his candidacy for governor in the next year's election. Huey had little money with which to mount a statewide race. His strength was in the rural areas, but he had no organization. He was young. He had little support in New Orleans. He did, however, have a plan. "I'll tell you how I'm going to win," he told one supporter. "In every parish, there is a boss, usually the sheriff. He has forty percent of the votes, forty percent are opposed to him, and twenty percent are in-betweens. I'm going to every parish and cuss out the boss. That gives me forty percent of the votes to begin with, and I'll hoss trade 'em out of business." Huey did exactly as he promised. He stormed into parish after parish, leaping to the stump and vilifying the local boss. Afterward, he retired to the town's hotel, where invariably many of the boss's political enemies arrived to offer assistance.[18]

Louisiana in the 1920s was composed of three disparate regions—New Orleans, Acadian south Louisiana, and north Louisiana—all loosely bound by economics and politics. To the people of Huey's north Louisiana, New Orleans was another world, the center of the state's commerce and politics. Dominated by wealthy bankers, lawyers, and merchants, the city boasted the nation's twelfth largest population and the second largest port. To the northwest of New Orleans—south of Alexandria from Baton Rouge to Lake Charles—was Acadiana, a rural region largely inhabited by Catholic descendants of French Nova Scotians expelled from Canada in the eighteenth century. Like Acadiana, north Louisiana was rural. Most similarities, however, ended there. Predominantly Protestant, the people of north Louisiana were a sober contrast to the easy, carefree life-style of the "Cajuns."

In the years since the Longs had migrated to Louisiana, the only real difference was that the men who ran the state had changed their names. The Bourbons, the state's ruling elite in the post-Reconstruction era, were replaced by wealthy New Orleans businessmen, the Old Regulars. They struck a loose alliance with the upriver cotton planters and had their way in state matters. In essence, this meant they elected the state's leaders, who, in turn, either did their bidding or left them alone. Whether the Bourbons or the Old Regulars, the abusive power of their wealth had not been threatened at the polls for decades. In the 1920s, the only path to statewide office was through the Old Regulars. If they liked you, they would steal the election. No one succeeded who tried to subvert the time-honored system—no one, not even Huey Long.

Huey's chief opponents for the Democratic nomination were Henry Fuqua, general manager of the state penitentiary, the anointed candidate of the Old Regulars. His other adversary was Hewitt Bouanchaud, Governor Parker's lieutenant governor, who derived much of his support from the antimachine factions in New Orleans and fellow Roman Catholic Acadians in south Louisiana. Huey's platform was simple: Standard Oil was the evil corporate giant whose domination of the state must be checked. He promised cheap natural gas for New Orleans from the Monroe fields in northeast Louisiana. He promised good roads for the farmers and better schools for children, including free textbooks. On top of this, he promised lower taxes. Huey's populist platform had its appeal. At the time, Louisiana was as backward a state as could be found in the nation. It ranked near the bottom in gross income and the value of its farm property brought up the rear. It was forty-fifth in the number of farms with electric power. In 1930, no individual in the state reported an income of more than one million dollars. Louisiana was next to last in the number of citizens who could read. More than 14 percent of white rural males had not spent one year in a classroom, and 40 percent had not advanced past the fourth grade.

The situation existed because the ruling elite allowed it. Dedicated to preserve its status, the state's upper class had no reason to share the wealth. "There was a state lying under the domination of the great white angels of feudal democracy," Huey said once. "The feudal state of America was the state of Louisiana. That is the way it has been run and had been allowed to be run and nobody dared gainsay any of them because the political organizations were so entrenched that no one tried to change it." Huey would try. Noted one historian: "He stirred to life something that had been dead for a generation."[19]

Huey showed Louisiana something new in campaigns. He took to the radio, delivering fiery speeches, entertaining and inspiring thousands of listeners in the process. He was one of the first American politicians to make use of the revolutionary new electronic medium. He mailed thousands of circulars throughout the state and tacked thousands more on telephone poles and fence posts in every corner of Louisiana. While his two opponents (Huey called them the "Parker Gold Dust Twins" for their ties to the incumbent governor) stayed above the partisan fray, Huey plunged into the campaign with relish. He attacked Fuqua and Bouanchaud for their disregard of the people. He shook every hand he could find.

Initially dismissed as a minor candidate, Huey soon persuaded most political observers that he was a force with a following. "As he plowed around the state, threading the rutted roads of mud or dust, buttonholing the farmers and the one-horse merchants, pushing on beyond the edge of decent roads by horseback into bayou settlements which never before had seen a candidate for governor, the wiseacres became aware that the commissioner was getting somewhere," one observer wrote.[20]

As election day passed, Louisiana was stunned. Huey did not win, but his third-place finish sent shock waves up and down the bayous, right to the steps of the state capitol. He was finally, and indisputably, a potent political force. Huey finished just seven thousand votes out of the runoff, behind second-place finisher Fuqua. He carried twenty-one parishes and led the pack in seven others, more than either candidate.

His loss has been analyzed in differing ways. Some, Huey included, maintained heavy rains in north Louisiana on election day kept many of his rural supporters home. Rain was not the only factor in Huey's loss. He did badly in New Orleans, where he finished a poor third. With the New Orleans vote excluded, Huey would have finished first. He also did poorly in south Louisiana with Catholic Acadians.

The votes had barely been counted before Huey cast his eyes to the 1928 election, knowing that to win he must become better known in south Louisiana and New Orleans. It did not require anything beyond simple arithmetic and a faint understanding of Louisiana politics to understand that Huey Long would be Louisiana's next governor. A road contractor in Alexandria, who had supported Fuqua, summed up the situation best when he declared, "we can't raise enough money to beat him again." Biographer Harnett Kane observed, "The next four years were preparation, the placing of his foot in the crack of more political doors, the making of more deals." Later that year, he was reelected overwhelmingly to his seat on the newly renamed Public Service Commission. The next year, Huey made his peace with several north Louisiana newspapers and then turned his attention to what had been his real stumbling block—New Orleans. This time he made his peace with the most powerful political figure in the city, *New Orleans States* publisher Robert Ewing, by supporting Ewing's candidate for mayor of New Orleans.[21]

The following year afforded another opportunity for Huey to mend fences with the state's political power structure. He campaigned for U.S. senator Edwin Broussard, a south Louisiana Cajun, in his race against former Governor J. Y. Sanders, whose political base lay in the state's northern parishes. Blanketing the state in twenty-one days, Huey and Broussard made as many as six appearances a day. They began their trek in south Louisiana, where Huey was the showcase of the troupe, delivering speeches in what one New Orleans paper called "unmistakable 'dynamite' English." He was a smash hit with the Acadians, who liked his freewheeling style and his energetic speeches. Although a Protestant from the hills of north Louisiana, his appearances with the immensely popular Broussard gave him much-needed credibility with skeptical Cajuns. Many of them concluded Huey was their kind of politician.[22]

By the time the governor's race of 1928 arrived, Huey's opposition was badly divided, unable to agree on a candidate to prevent him from his ascent to the governorship. One opponent was Governor O. H. Simpson, the lackluster lieutenant governor who became governor when Governor Fuqua died in the fall of 1927. Huey's other challenger was Eighth District congressman Riley Wilson, a fourteen-year congressman best known for his public feud with President Coolidge and Commerce Secretary Herbert Hoover over the allocation of costs for flood relief.

"Huey was young, slim, smiling and electrical, in 1928," wrote biographer Forrest Davis. "His impudence, his rashness, captured the plodding yokels." Huey, Davis noted, said exactly what the common folk would like to have said about the huge corporations and the big city machines "if they had thought of it—and if they had Huey's sharp wits." Huey became the most effective mouthpiece for the debilitating frustration and anger that had its genesis in the Populist movement of more than thirty years earlier. "He became the Karl Marx for the hillbillies," Davis declared. "He whipped up all their suppressed and ancient resentments and envies." Everywhere he went, these unwashed masses were drawn, almost mystically, to Huey. Standing in massive crowds in every corner of Louisiana, they cheered him on, shouting, "You tell 'em, Huey" or "Give 'em hell, big boy."[23] Nowhere was Huey so eloquent and spellbinding in this manifestation as in St. Martinville, where he spoke beneath a tree held sacred by the Acadians:

> And it was here that Evangeline waited for her lover Gabriel, who never came. This oak is an immortal spot, made so by Longfellow's poem, but Evangeline is not the only one who has waited here in disappointment.
>
> Where are the schools that you have waited for your children to have, that have never come? Where are the roads and the highways that you spent your money to build, that are no nearer now than ever before? Where are the institutions to care for the sick and disabled? Evangeline wept bitter tears in her disappointment. But they lasted through only one lifetime. Your tears in this country, around this oak, have lasted for generations. Give me the chance to dry the tears of those who still weep here.[24]

Such inspiration was not Huey's only rhetorical tool; he was a master of ridicule and soon had his audiences laughing hysterically at ridiculous descriptions of his opponents. Of Wilson's highly touted record of protecting Louisiana from floods, Huey played on passions still high from the disastrous flood earlier in 1927: "Wilson has been in Congress fourteen years, and this year the water went fourteen feet higher than ever before, giving him a flood record of one foot of high water a year." He dismissed Simpson for the way he had padded the state's Conservation Commission with cronies, calling the commission "a coon-chasin' and possum-watchin' brigade, that does its job cruising around in a fancy boat in the Gulf."[25]

Huey's most effective device, however, was his program. Launching his campaign with the theme "Every Man a King, but No Man Wears a Crown," Huey took dead aim at the hopes and aspirations of Louisiana's forgotten masses, those who had been promised much, but given very little. For them, Huey had an ambitious program: free school textbooks, thousands of miles of new paved roads, free bridges, and lower utility rates. He also promised, to the crowds' delight, to slap a five-cent-a-barrel tax on Standard Oil. The best response his two opponents could manage was to observe Huey's programs were ambitious and too costly. Huey's schedule was grueling. He cast a political blanket over the state with fire and brimstone, thousands of circulars, and regular radio addresses. "He was everywhere at once, his rivals believed," Harnett Kane wrote. "Sometimes they doubted reports that he had been in so many places in so short a time. Louisiana had never beheld a candidate with the ripsnorting energy, the determination of Huey." He was, Kane observed, "a one-man riot."[26]

Unlike four years earlier, election day in January 1928 was sunny. People flocked in droves to the polls. The first returns counted were in New Orleans, where Huey again finished a poor third. Heartened by his strong first-place finish in New Orleans, Wilson and his forces began celebrating victory, assuming Huey could not muster enough votes in the country parishes to overtake his lead. True to predictions, Huey swept north Louisiana in similar proportions to his 1924 victories in those parishes. That much the Wilson forces expected. What they could not have anticipated was Huey's tremendous success in rural south Louisiana, where in some French parishes Huey racked up astounding majorities of 60 to 70 percent. When the votes were counted, Huey had almost 127,000 votes to Wilson's 82,000 and Simpson's 80,000. Wilson, realizing the inevitability of Huey's victory, withdrew. Huey, thirty-four, won the Democratic nomination and became the youngest governor in the state's history.

The election returns revealed a Louisiana in the midst of a struggle among its differing classes. Huey maintained his support among north Louisiana voters and slightly increased his strength in New Orleans. His exploitation of the basic class struggle—the haves against the have-nots—cut through the heart of the traditional divisions in Louisiana politics. For the first time, a Protestant politician had successfully invaded predominantly Catholic south Louisiana. To say, however, that Huey won only by attracting the votes of Louisiana's poorest citizens, as some have maintained, is to overlook the poll tax and the disenfranchisement of the black citizen. Many poor whites could not afford the tax, and thus cast no vote at all. Blacks rarely were allowed to vote. In many cases, Huey's support came from the small independent farmers who, unlike many sharecroppers and tenant farmers, were not controlled by wealthy planters and landowners. Like the 1896 Louisiana governor's election, which Populist Party candidate John Pharr lost decisively, Huey had sought the office stressing many of the same issues that had once fueled Louisiana's failed Populist movement. Until Huey, generations of grievances had lain dormant, waiting for a leader to revive them. Like a phoenix, Huey raised them from the dead.[27]

2

THE KINGFISH

ONE OF HUEY'S BIOGRAPHERS OBSERVED that "the voters put a crown on his head, but hog-tied him hand and foot." Huey may have taken the governor's office by storm, but in the same election he simply could not manage to translate his popularity into support for his local and legislative candidates.[1] Yet, the people sensed this young man who issued such grandiose promises during his historic campaign was somehow different from the politicians of the past. They turned out in record numbers to his inauguration, which was described vividly by Forrest Davis:

> They came by special train, by motor car, by mule wagon and afoot. Fifteen thousand of them swarmed through the streets of horrified Baton Rouge; backwoodsmen, in to see one of their own elevated to the seats of the mighty. The men wore galluses, over their Sunday shirts, and black felt hats in the May heat; the women wore sunbonnets. They were quietly arrogant, impressed by the magnificence of the occasion to which they had been bidden as honored participants. Huey, with backwoods forethought, saw that there were frequent water buckets around the Capitol—with tin dippers. He had a large, outdoor dance pavilion with country musicians as well as the jazz band he preferred. He wanted them to feel at home.[2]

Huey moved quickly to seize control of every state office over which he had authority, firing every department head or officeholder under the governor's control. His motives were not as ruthless as they must have

15

seemed to some. To be effective, Huey knew his supporters must be placed in positions of authority. With a less-than-enthusiastic legislature, Huey needed to consolidate his power. Through sheer pressure and muscle, the new governor seized control of powerful, patronage-rich state commissions like the Hospital Board, levee boards, the Highway Commission, and the New Orleans Dock Board. He wrestled the Democratic State Central Committee from the hands of the New Orleans Old Regulars. He pored over the state constitution and legal codes to ferret out powers officially vested in the governor's office but long forgotten. As he soon discovered, he would need every ounce of authority he could muster.

In spite of the immense institutional resistance he encountered, Huey cajoled and pressured most of his program through the legislature. He provided free textbooks to all Louisiana schoolchildren. He won approval for a thirty-million-dollar bond issue to finance one of the most ambitious road construction programs in American history, replacing the antiquated "pay-as-you-go" system, which had allowed the state's precious few roads and bridges to crumble into a deplorable state. To enact his proposals, Huey employed nearly every trick in his bag.

More often than not, Huey got his way. A prime example was his determination to build a new governor's mansion to replace the decrepit, old, termite-infested building. When legislators balked at his request for funds to build a new mansion, Huey ordered the warden of the state penitentiary to send him a crew of prisoners. Leading them from the capitol to the mansion, Huey instructed the men to destroy the building, which they did to the legislature's horror. The demoralized opposition forces had no idea how they would stop this determined upstart. It was not long before Huey gave them their opening.

Early in 1929, Huey called the legislature back into special session to consider his proposed occupational license tax as a means to deal with the state's unexpected budget deficit. Officials of Standard Oil saw this tax of five cents on every barrel of oil refined in Louisiana as an all-out assault, a declaration of war. The tax proposal met with a storm of protest from businessmen around the state who feared that, once applied to the oil companies, an occupational license fee might be expanded to include almost every enterprise in the state. Most of those who supported Huey's road building and free textbook program did so with the understanding that someone else would foot the bill. Even before legislators arrived in Baton Rouge for the special session, the tax was dead. Some of Huey's most ardent allies had abandoned him, like "rats leaving a ship they think is fixin' to sink," he complained. Following defeat of Huey's tax proposal, emboldened legislators began talking of impeachment. They were handed their best chance shortly after the death of the tax proposal.[3]

It was called "Bloody Monday," one of the most dramatic and chaotic days in the Louisiana legislature's colorful history. As passions over the tax rose on the house floor, Shreveport representative Cecil Morgan sought recognition and was ignored by House Speaker John B. Fournet, a close Long ally. Fournet's action inflamed lawmakers on both sides, as Morgan shouted above the din: "I have in my hand an affidavit that the governor has tried to procure the assassination of a member of this House!" As order dissolved into disaster, Fournet entertained a motion by a Long ally to adjourn the session, meaning an end to the special session. The ensuing vote created an even greater uproar as the mechanical voting machine malfunctioned, showing the wrong votes alongside almost every name. Assuming the voting machine had been rigged by Long to forestall any impeachment moves, fights broke out all over the chamber. Ink wells and paste pots were hurled across the chamber, while the sergeant at arms and his assistants tried vainly to restore order like bouncers in a barroom brawl. By the time the representatives realized the voting machine was merely reflecting a previous vote that had not been properly cleared, it was too late. Passions were inflamed to the boiling point. There was no turning back.[4]

The next morning, readers of the *Baton Rouge Morning Advocate* were greeted with a front-page story headlined: "GOVERNOR LONG'S TYRANNY OVER LOUISIANA SHOULD END." That same day, the house listened quietly as the anti-Long forces introduced resolutions of impeachment against Huey, charging him with nineteen offenses and ordering his trial before the senate. The offenses included charges that Huey had attempted to bribe legislators; contracted illegal state loans; removed school officials for political reasons; carried a concealed weapon; used abusive language in public; engaged in immoral behavior at a New Orleans nightclub; usurped the powers of the legislature; and tried to employ someone to kill Representative J. Y. Sanders. The resolutions also included the accusation that Huey had intimidated the publisher of Baton Rouge's two newspapers, Charles Manship. Huey, Manship alleged, threatened to reveal publicly that his brother, Douglas, was a patient in a state mental institution. To keep this embarrassing family news a secret, Huey had allegedly told Manship and his paper to "lay off."[5]

The impeachment move chilled Huey to the bone. Brother Julius reported that when he arrived from Shreveport to offer support he found Huey lying in bed, sobbing uncontrollably. "They've got me," he told two of his supporters. His depression did not last long. With the help of his brother Earl, Huey emerged energized from his momentary depression and took his case directly to the people. He littered the state with hundreds of thousands of circulars and stormed across Louisiana, explaining to voters he faced impeachment only because he had dared to challenge Standard Oil, or, as he called it, the "Octopus." At a giant rally in Baton Rouge, he attacked Standard Oil viciously. "The buzzards have returned," he shouted. "They want to gloat and gulp at the expense of the poor and afflicted."[6]

After weeks of debate, the house finally voted, over a span of three weeks, to indict Huey on eight counts of misconduct, including charges that he had intimidated publisher Manship, attempted to bribe legislators, and misappropriated state funds. The sluggishness of the house in processing the charges, however, gave Huey a valuable tool for his defense. Of the eight charges against him, only the Manship charge was voted upon before the adjournment date specified in Huey's special session order. In other words, according to Huey, the only charge that had any legal standing was the first. After hearing testimony on the Manship case, the senate by a slim margin agreed with Huey's assertion that his threat to reveal Douglas Manship's mental illness had been made in a personal rather than official capacity. That vote gave Huey's forces the opening they needed. The next day, Huey revealed his hand.

For weeks, he had mounted an all-out, behind-the-scenes campaign to win the votes of at least fourteen senators, the minimum to prevent an impeachment conviction. While his opponents undoubtedly did their best to cajole and bribe legislators for votes for Huey's conviction, Huey campaigned even more effectively to save his political life. He offered to surface roads in lawmakers' districts. He dangled lucrative state jobs before them. He promised support if they sought higher office.

On the day the senate was to resume consideration of the charges, Huey sprung his surprise. As the prosecution prepared to call its first witness of the day, a Long supporter unveiled a motion to adjourn the trial. It was signed by fifteen senators, more than the one-third needed to defeat impeachment. The senators signing the document, known as the Round Robin, stated that because the charges against Huey were made after the special session's adjournment date, they would vote against impeachment regardless of the evidence. By noon, Huey's opposition forces were demoralized and in disarray. The senate adjourned. The impeachment threat was finished.

Although his administration was revived, Huey's friends noted the impeachment dramatically changed his attitude about politics. He became grim and more cynical, believing his enemies had perceived some weakness in him or a lack of resolve. He moved decisively to take control of every aspect of state government, seizing nearly every government position in the state. He rewarded his friends with those jobs and threw out his enemies. Even family members of his opponents lost their jobs. "I used to try to get things done by saying 'please,' " Huey said after his ordeal. "That didn't work and now I'm a dynamiter. I dynamite 'em out of my path."[7]

About this time, Huey adopted the nickname that soon became more than just an appellation: the Kingfish. Lounging around the governor's mansion, Huey and his friends enjoyed listening to the popular radio show "Amos 'n' Andy." Huey soon began calling one of his cronies "Brother Crawford," after one of the show's characters. In turn, Huey was dubbed "Kingfish," after the leader of the show's fictional lodge, the Mystic Knights of the Sea. The title stuck. Soon, Huey was known by almost every Louisiana citizen as the Kingfish.

Emboldened by his political stranglehold on Louisiana, Huey announced he would oppose Senator Joseph Ransdell for reelection to the U.S. Senate on July 16, 1930. The Long organization's newspaper, *The Louisiana Progress*, heralded Huey's candidacy with banner headlines and a cartoon of Ransdell, depicting him as a ridiculous, goateed old-timer. The caption labeled the seventy-year-old senator as "Louisiana's World Famous Archaeological Exhibit in Washington, D.C." Making Huey's candidacy even more audacious was that by electing him, Louisiana's voters would deny themselves representation in the Senate until Huey completed his term as governor, a full year after Ransdell's term expired. More important to Huey was ensuring Lieutenant Governor Paul Cyr, with whom Huey had parted political company, did not assume the governorship when he departed the state.[8]

Poor Senator Ransdell never had a chance. Huey gave no thought of building his campaign around the national issues on which Ransdell might have been able to debate. Instead, he ran for the Senate on a slate of state programs, which had little to do with the U.S. Senate. He unapologetically used his candidacy as a referendum for his ambitious state proposals. Earlier that year, during the legislature's regular session, Huey proposed a constitutional amendment authorizing a sixty-eight-million-dollar bond issue to finance the construction of three thousand miles of surfaced roads and a five-million-dollar bond issue for a new capitol building. He asked lawmakers to approve construction of more bridges and for a one-cent increase in the gasoline tax for port improvements. The impeachment, however, left him so politically weakened that he could not muster the two-thirds majority needed to place the bond issues on a statewide referendum.

Characteristically, Huey saw the setback as an opportunity. Announcing his candidacy against Ransdell, he proclaimed "in effect, my election will mean that the Legislature will submit my plan to the people, or those who refuse to accede to the publicly expressed stand of the voters will be signing their own political death warrant." To a friend he observed: "This campaign will have to do with what happened at the last session of the Legislature. That's going to be the issue."[9]

Huey deposed Ransdell handily, winning 57 percent of the vote and carrying fifty-three of the state's sixty-four parishes. As the Republicans had nominated no opponent, Huey was automatically elected. Even more important, at least momentarily, was the ringing endorsement the voters gave to Huey's legislative program. The Constitutional League, a fierce anti-Long organization that Huey dubbed "the Constipational League," disbanded the next day and the legislature met within a week of the election to begin enacting Huey's proposals. By December, even Huey's critics conceded the year had been wildly successful for him. He was still governor, but also a U.S. senator-elect. His legislative program was enacted and two thousand miles of road construction was underway. A new state capitol was rising from the banks of the Mississippi River, soon to be the tallest building in the South and a monument to the man who built it.

Huey also embarked on a mission to make Louisiana State University in Baton Rouge the premier school of higher education in the South. Once headed by General William Tecumseh Sherman before he left Baton Rouge to join the Union Army when Louisiana began its secession proceedings, LSU had been, at best, a second-rate university. In its history, the school had little to show in the way of academic achievements. Huey changed that, albeit by extremely suspect methods, diverting state highway funds to finance LSU's rebirth. Huey shrugged off attacks over his methods and delighted in calling himself "the official thief" for the school. By the time he finished, he had more than doubled the university's size. LSU had the finest physical plant of any school in the South. He had created a first-rate medical school. Enrollment increased from 1,600 to 4,000. "Huey's university" was one of the most respected public schools in the nation.

In spite of his repeated successes in Baton Rouge, Huey still reckoned with the problem of who would administer his domain when he left for Washington. While his plans for a successor were unclear, no one doubted Huey's determination to make sure Lieutenant Governor Cyr, formerly a loyal supporter, never got his hands on the governorship. In short order, Cyr handed Huey the key to a solution. In October 1931, Cyr was encouraged by some of Huey's enemies to challenge the governor's constitutional right to hold the governorship while a U.S. senator-elect. Cyr made his move in Shreveport, declaring himself governor after he was administered the oath of office by a local notary. Huey responded by sending national guard troops to the capitol. "I ordered that Cyr should be arrested as an impostor if he appeared upon the premises," Huey wrote. He then notified the lieutenant governor that his gubernatorial oath had not been properly administered by the secretary of state. Cyr, he declared, had effectively vacated the lieutenant governor's office, leaving the senate's president pro tempore, Allen O. King, as his successor. Huey was delighted by the opening presented him, noting in his autobiography, "with Brother Cyr suspended in mid-air about the Governor's chair, Senator King took the oath of office as lieutenant governor."[10]

Huey's only remaining task was to ensure that the state's government was in capable and, most important, loyal hands when he left for Washington. While he told friends that he planned to "push the boat away from the shore" and focus on national affairs, he had no intention of allowing anyone else to run Louisiana. To accomplish this, Huey needed to place the governorship in the hands of someone he could not only trust, but a man whom he could control. His old friend from Winnfield, a legislator named Oscar K. Allen, fit the bill. "He'll do anything you want," a friend told Huey when he was making up his mind. "Nobody else will." Allen was so servile to Huey that Earl Long joked: "A leaf once blew in the window of Allen's office and fell on his desk. Allen signed it."[11]

Allen was the perfect selection. With Huey constantly at his side during the campaign, Allen swamped his opponents, as did the rest of Huey's statewide ticket. Several months later, Huey also backed his friend, John Overton, in his challenge to his former ally, incumbent U.S. senator Edwin Broussard. In another demonstration of Huey's potency, Overton stomped Broussard, winning almost 60 percent of the vote. Departing for Washington in early 1932, Huey was confident. Although he no longer occupied any official office in state government, Louisiana was still firmly and completely under his control.

When Huey finally arrived in Washington to assume his Senate seat, he was already a national figure. The national press had long since taken

notice of his comic exploits and his utter domination of Louisiana government. Having checked into his hotel the night before, Huey received the
Washington press corps early the next morning, still wearing his lavender
pajamas while he shaved. "I'm a small fish here in Washington," he
announced, waving a cigar in one hand and his razor in the other. "But I'm
still the Kingfish to the folks down in Loozyanna." He hinted, however,
while smaller in stature than the Senate's bigger fish, he did not plan to
yield to their leadership. "There's too much concentration of wealth
among a few people," he told the reporters, who scribbled down his every
word. [12]

Those who believed Huey had been most appalling in Baton Rouge
quickly learned they had only seen a glimpse of his proclivity for disrupting
the status quo. "I had come to the United States Senate," Huey wrote,
"with only one project in mind, which was that by every means of action and
persuasion I might do something to spread the wealth of the land among all
the people." Harnett Kane said Huey was "everything that a freshman
Senator was not expected to be." That was an understatement. From the
very first day, Huey seemed to demonstrate he held the traditions and
folkways of the Senate in contempt. On the day of his swearing in, Huey
paraded down the middle aisle in the Senate chamber with a lighted cigar in
his hand, a flagrant violation of Senate rules. Senators watched in stunned
silence as he parked the smoldering butt on Majority Leader Joe Robinson's
desk as he received the oath of office. He then further turned the Senate on
its ear by roaming the chamber, glad-handing and slapping the backs of the
Senate's chagrined, stately veterans. [13]

Huey wasted little time before he proposed legislation to limit personal
incomes. His program, christened "Share-Our-Wealth," would create a
society, Huey said, in which "every man was a king, but no man wore the
crown." The Great Depression, he charged in a speech in March 1932,
had been brought about "because a handful of men in the United States
own all the money in this country." Shortly thereafter, he renewed his
attacks on the wealthy, warning that their tightly held fortunes might lead
to communism. "The country has been going toward communism ever
since the wealth of this country began to get into the hands of a few
people," he said. Huey maintained that the solution was to limit those
fortunes, tax the excess, and distribute the wealth to everyone. His
program could not wait, he said, as the nation's situation demanded fast
action. "I tell you," Huey declared to the Senate, "that if . . . I should see
my children starving and my wife starving, [our] laws against robbing and
against stealing and against bootlegging would not amount to any more to

me than they would to any other man when it came to a matter of facing the time of starvation."[14]

By April, Huey made known his utter disregard for Senate traditions, and Majority Leader Robinson, when he announced he was resigning his three committee posts. The next month, he attacked Robinson again, this time reading a list of clients of Robinson's Arkansas law firm, a list that included large power companies, banks, and railroads. Although Robinson was only then nominally connected to the firm, Huey made his point. He implied that Robinson was a pawn of the evil, wealthy interests that Huey believed controlled the country. He had fired his first salvo in his campaign to make the redistribution of wealth a national issue. Of his Share-Our-Wealth plan, Huey said sarcastically, "This bolshevistic, socialistic, communistic, radical, revolutionary resolution would not allow a man to have a net earning of more than one million dollars a year. What is a man to do with more than one million dollars a year?" In a matter of only a few months, Huey's performances had transformed him into a national figure and the Senate's leading progressive. One reporter for a national magazine observed that Huey "might be the leader of the revolution if and when." Although his efforts at enacting his wealth redistribution program stood little chance of passing at the time, he nonetheless gave a nationwide voice to the despair and hopelessness of millions of Americans, caught in the tight grip of the Great Depression.[15]

When Huey arrived in Chicago in June 1932 for the Democratic National Convention, he came in support of New York governor Franklin Delano Roosevelt, who he had been led to believe supported the concept of Huey's Share-Our-Wealth. Arriving a week before the convention began to help FDR's forces quell favorite-son candidacies in the southern states, Huey was a one-man tornado of activity for Roosevelt's cause. He roused the governor of Oklahoma from bed one morning and absentmindedly ate his breakfast while the governor shaved and listened to Huey's pitch for Roosevelt. He fought off his opponents' attempts to unseat his handpicked Louisiana delegation, announcing, "The Democratic Party in Louisiana? I am the Democratic Party in Louisiana. Who's got a better right to pick out a delegation?" He was most effective during the convention balloting, when he strong-armed the Mississippi and Arkansas delegations into holding fast for Roosevelt.[16]

Huey was as committed to Roosevelt during the fall campaign. Talking to reporters in New York, he praised Roosevelt, saying, "[H]e's one of the few men who knows about the government and the people of the United States and doesn't have to call in someone for information." Volunteering to campaign for Roosevelt, Huey said he preferred to be assigned to the most staunchly Republican states, possibly realizing that should he deliver one of those states for Roosevelt, his national star would shine even more brightly. "I think I'd like to speak in Vermont," he said. Roosevelt's people had other plans for Huey, shunting him off to relatively unimportant locations. Nonetheless, he tackled the assignment with characteristic enthusiasm, storming his way through North and South Dakota, Nebraska, and Kansas with sound trucks, attracting huge, enthusiastic crowds at every stop. He created such a sensation that by the end of his foray Democratic leaders in other states begged Roosevelt's campaign to send him to their states. On election day, Roosevelt won, defeating incumbent president Herbert Hoover. He had easily carried the states where Huey had campaigned, causing Roosevelt's campaign manager to speculate how much larger their margin of victory might have been had they made greater use of the senator from Louisiana. "We never underestimated him again," said one of Roosevelt's men. [17]

Roosevelt's aides should have known what to expect from Huey. Only two months earlier, Huey had clearly demonstrated his appeal was far greater outside of Louisiana than anyone might have imagined. When Arkansas senator Thaddeus Carraway died in November 1931, few in Arkansas cared that the governor appointed his widow, Hattie Carraway, to fill the remainder of his term. Even fewer expected that Mrs. Carraway, a quiet, dowdy woman, would seek the office in her own right. When she announced her plans to do just that, she sparked laughter in Washington and Arkansas. After all, she had virtually no money with which to campaign against six well-financed male opponents. When word of her dire political condition reached her in Washington, she turned to her friend, Huey Long, asking him to size up her political fortunes. In a few days, Huey encountered Hattie on the Senate floor and reported that the news she had received was correct: She had no chance of winning. After she thanked him for his help, Huey watched as Hattie returned to her desk, sat down, and started to cry. After a night of contemplating the matter, Huey went to Hattie the next day and volunteered to help. "Never mind about the campaigning," he said. "We can make that campaign in one week. That's all we need. That won't give 'em a chance to get over their surprise." [18]

True to his promise, Huey invaded Arkansas. He raced from one end of the state to the other, keeping a pace that exhausted almost everyone in the entourage but Huey. Making more than six speeches each day for a week, Huey framed the race as Hattie against the evil giants of Wall

Street. "Wall Street is gittin' after Hattie," he declared, defending her as a "brave little woman." Huey's road show attracted large crowds at every stop. In only a day, Huey's presence sent shock waves through the state's political establishment. A local politician, having heard one of Huey's first speeches on Hattie's behalf, wired friends in Little Rock: "A cyclone just went through here and is headed your way. Very few trees left standing." When he reached Little Rock, Huey attracted a massive audience of nearly thirty thousand, the state's largest political gathering ever. By election day, Huey had turned the state upside down. News of Hattie's political demise was premature. On election day, she crushed her opponents, beating her closest rival by nearly two to one.[19]

Shortly after Roosevelt's election, Huey ebulliently claimed that the new president's election was an endorsement of Huey's wealth distribution program. "The President-elect has not only been nominated, has not only been elected, but he has assumed the leadership of this nation in order that he might carry out the one great necessary decentralization of wealth in America," he said. Unfortunately, Huey soon discovered that he had overestimated Roosevelt's dedication to his Share-Our-Wealth program. "God damn it, Frank," Huey shouted to Roosevelt in a phone call shortly after the convention. "Don't you know who nominated you?" After being chastised by Huey for consorting with Wall Street bankers and other rich men, Roosevelt reportedly hung up and turned to a visitor, observing that Huey "is really one of the two most dangerous men in the country."[20]

Although they gave a different impression in the early days of the Roosevelt administration, the ties binding Roosevelt and Huey were never very secure. Roosevelt's men were glad to have Huey's assistance during the campaign, but tried to contain his involvement, evidenced by their insistence that he campaign for FDR only in insignificant states. Huey, meanwhile, supported Roosevelt for what he could get from the relationship—fame and a greater national forum for his program. The dissolution of their uncomfortable alliance came shortly after Roosevelt took office. As most members of Congress desperately lined up to follow the new president's leadership, Huey charted his own course. He had concluded that the new president was much too conservative and moved too slowly in light of the nation's dire economic conditions. He shouted in opposition to Roosevelt's proposed banking holiday, designed to stop the alarming number of bank failures. He said that the bill would save the big banks, but "the little banks in the counties and in the parishes and in the States are most in need of protection." His amendment to allow local

banks to become eligible for increased government assistance by joining
the Federal Reserve System was soundly defeated after Huey nearly
came to blows with the bill's sponsor, Virginia senator Carter Glass. "I
couldn't hit you," Huey told the seventy-year-old Democrat who had
challenged him to fisticuffs. "You are too old a man."[21]

Next came the Government Economy Act, a budget cutting-measure in
which Roosevelt proposed deep reductions in veterans' benefits and government payrolls. Huey bitterly fought that legislation, as well as the
Agriculture Adjustment Act, which he believed represented Roosevelt's
abandonment of his promise to expand the nation's money supply. When
Roosevelt proposed the National Industrial Recovery Act, with a system
of wage and price controls, Huey claimed that the bill would become the
tool of the nation's industrial leaders to fix prices and drive their smaller
competition out of business. "Every fault of socialism is found in this bill,
without one of its virtues," Huey charged. "Every crime of a monarchy
is in here, without one of the things that would give it credit." He claimed
the legislation was "a combination of every evil that can possibly be
imagined."[22]

In spite of his fierce opposition to these and other Roosevelt proposals—most of which were quickly passed into law during the new
administration's first one hundred days—Huey continued believing that he
and Roosevelt would eventually reach an accord. When Roosevelt summoned Huey to the White House to inform him that he would no longer
consider Huey's recommendations for federal appointees in Louisiana,
Huey remained hopeful. Even after the denial of a senator's most cherished political privilege, Huey refused to attack Roosevelt personally.
"The trouble is Roosevelt hasn't taken all of my ideas; just part of them,"
Huey explained. "I'm about one hundred yards ahead of him. We're on the
same road, but I'm here and he's there." Huey believed his break with the
new chief executive was only brief, that their common beliefs would soon
restore the ailing relationship.[23]

As Huey watched Roosevelt consult his political enemies in Louisiana
about federal patronage, he gradually became incensed. His anger with
Roosevelt finally boiled over when Interior Secretary Harold Ickes criticized Louisiana for its reluctance in not spending half of its federal
appropriation for highway funds. Huey had prevented the state from
accepting the money to keep it from his political enemies, and when Ickes
suggested a sinister motive, Huey snapped. In an emotional press conference in New Orleans, he said he did not trust the men Roosevelt had
appointed in Louisiana. "Pay them my further respects up there in Wash-

ington," Huey instructed the gathered reporters. "Tell them they can all go to Hell."[24]

Huey felt most betrayed by Roosevelt's subsequent refusal to support his legislation limiting personal incomes to one million dollars a year. The president, however, had never given Huey his implicit promise of support for his bill. More than likely, Roosevelt seduced Huey with bland assurances that he agreed with him in theory, which Huey eagerly accepted as a blanket endorsement. Finally convinced that he had been duped, Huey declared there was little difference between the timidity of Roosevelt and that of the recently vanquished Herbert Hoover.

The latter months of 1933 were not tranquil for Huey. His declaration of war with Roosevelt coincided with a full-scale attack on his leadership in Louisiana. Earlier in the year, a newspaper report surfaced about an Internal Revenue Service tax investigation of Huey on charges of "evasion of tax payments on a substantial income derived from undisclosed sources." The investigation was instigated during the Hoover administration, but shelved when the more conciliatory Roosevelt came into office. Once Roosevelt's hopes of cooperation with Huey vanished, he ordered the inquiry reopened. Huey faced other embarrassing questions when a special Senate committee conducted an investigation of the circumstances surrounding the 1932 Democratic Senate primary in which John Overton, with the backing of Huey's organization, handily defeated Senator Edwin Broussard. While no damaging facts were revealed, and Overton got his Senate seat, the inquiry proved another unneeded embarrassment.

Further complicating matters was a humiliating incident that focused unwanted national attention on Huey's flamboyant and reckless life-style. While visiting New York in August 1933, Huey attended a charity event with friends at a bath club in Sands Point, Long Island. Huey had a grand time, flirting with various women and drinking himself into an extremely pleasant state of mind. On one trip to the men's room, Huey ran into trouble. He emerged bleeding profusely above a very swollen left eye, the recipient of some sort of beating. Although the exact facts of the incident have never been clear, there are two plausible theories: One is that Huey relieved himself at a urinal that was in use and was reportedly unsuccessful in trying to negotiate between the legs of the occupant. Others reported that Huey had insulted a woman, whose date defended her honor by punching Huey. Whatever the facts, Huey only made matters worse by his incredible explanation of the events when he maintained he had simply been washing his hands when he was accosted by a group of thugs. "A member of the house of Morgan sneaked up on me with a blackjack," he explained. The national press had a field day with the incident, and Huey was suddenly beset with the buffoonish image he had so skillfully shed since arriving in Washington.[25]

The Sands Point affair hurt Huey's popularity in Louisiana. While he had never taken a strong stand in favor of the now-repealed Prohibition, reports of Huey's cavorting did not please straitlaced north Louisiana constituents who assumed he shared their strict beliefs about abstinence. He was greeted by hostile, jeering audiences in several Louisiana towns upon his return. He was pelted with eggs during a speech in Alexandria. "The Kingfish had become a crawfish," observed one journalist. What many observers believed was the coup de grace came in January 1934, when Huey's enthusiastic backing of a candidate for New Orleans mayor fell far short and his man was buried in a landslide. Huey, however, was undeterred. He proudly pronounced that he had "more enemies in the United States than any little man I know of. I am proud of my enemies." He vowed to fight on and conquer his growing array of detractors.[26]

"The Kingfish," wrote biographer Forrest Davis, "came back by means of brass, guns, a moral issue and a revolutionary, class-taxing program." Huey, in fact, fired back in early 1934, beginning his counterassault when the legislature met in regular session. Pushing through several popular proposals—a homestead exemption on property taxes, an exemption of automobiles from property tax assessment, and a significant reduction in state license plate fees—Huey began wooing back the lower-class white voters who had always been his base of support. As icing on the cake, and to maximize his electoral support in the future, Huey also pushed through the abolishment of the one-dollar poll tax as a qualification for voting.[27]

Huey's program for regaining the political upper hand was not altogether based on a program of continued populist reform. His carrot-and-stick approach leaned heavily on the stick as means of prodding Louisiana back into his corner. To solidify his hold on New Orleans, he dispatched the National Guard, ostensibly to quash rampant gambling activity. His real motive was to gain control of the city's voter registration rolls, which had been used to effectively shut out his organization in New Orleans. More significantly, Huey railroaded legislation through the legislature that vested enormous, unprecedented powers in his organization during seven special legislative sessions from August 1934 to September 1935. Among a host of bills quickly passed at Huey's urging, a subservient legislature gave the governor the authority to fill vacancies on governmental bodies at every level, as well as the power to fill almost every appointive municipal and parish position in the state. State government, dominated by Huey, controlled virtually every governmental office in the state. Naturally, Huey's enemies were ousted from most of those posts and his allies appointed to fill their places. "Everywhere that a Long enemy remained," historian Alan Brinkley wrote, "it seemed, a new state regulation appeared to make the enemy powerless or, if he was already powerless, to inflect humiliation and exact revenge."[28]

The effect of all this legislative activity, one historian noted, "reduced the citizenry of Louisiana to political vassalage to the Kingfish and his faction." Harnett Kane observed that Huey "took over Louisiana in an iron fist, extending his control to an extent that the most pessimistic oppositionist had not thought possible under the Constitution." Said one Old Regular: "If you were for him, you could have anything you wanted. If you were against him, God help you unless you were an extraordinary man." The heavy-handed tactics worked. Huey had quickly reversed his political fortunes. "He had been able," Williams added, "to save himself because the people still supported his program. But he was no longer willing to rely solely on their support."[29]

Against this backdrop of the exercise of raw, brutal power, Huey had moved decisively to reform his public image, still suffering badly from the aftermath of Sands Point. He had stopped the heavy drinking, quit smoking cigars, given up his ribald public behavior and adopted a more sober public demeanor. He even went on a diet and lost thirty pounds. Late in 1933, Huey also published his autobiography, *Every Man a King*, an amusing and self-congratulatory account of his life as protector and guardian of the little man. He revived publication of his newspaper, the *Louisiana Progress*, renaming it the *American Progress*, with a new emphasis on a broader, national readership. With a circulation that eventually grew to 1.5 million, Huey began pushing the program with which he would become synonymous: the Share-Our-Wealth plan.

Huey delivered a national radio speech in February 1934 to announce the creation of a Share-Our-Wealth Society, which would hold as its basic tenet the redistribution of wealth in America. Under Huey's plan, the federal government would tax away vast fortunes, preventing heirs from inheriting a fortune worth more than five million dollars. A progressive income tax would put a 100 percent tax on earnings over one million dollars a year. The revenue collected from this plan would fund Huey's redistribution program: Every family in the country would get five thousand dollars, or "enough for a home, an automobile, a radio, and the ordinary conveniences." Furthermore, every family would be guaranteed a yearly income of between two thousand and three thousand dollars. The elderly would be properly cared for, the young would have their college educations subsidized, and veterans would be justly recognized for their contribution to the nation. Under Huey's plan, the government would abandon its hands-off approach to the economy, limiting work to thirty hours a week and eleven months a year.

The underlying rationale for this plan was that too much of the nation's wealth was in too few hands, Huey said, explaining in one speech "about eighty-five percent of the wealth is owned by five percent of the people." Politically, offered in the midst of the Great Depression, it was a brilliant plan. Realistically, however, Huey had a difficult time explaining exactly how he could generate enough revenue from the wealthy to finance the plan adequately and fairly. "I am going to have to call in some great minds to help me," he admitted.[30]

Huey first organized Share-Our-Wealth clubs in Louisiana, but the fever soon spread to other states. Huey's office was flooded with mail, forcing him to hire sixty typists to handle the deluge of mail from Huey's fans, which averaged sixty thousand letters a week. In one week, Huey received 140,000 letters. By 1935, Huey announced more than twenty-four thousand Share-Our-Wealth clubs existed in every state, with a total membership of 4.6 million.

Huey's enemies had reason to believe he had another more frightening motive in mind when he announced the Share-Our-Wealth Society. They believed, with good reason, that Huey was preparing to run for president in 1936. Although he said he "would rather see my laws passed than be president," Huey delighted in speculating about a possible challenge to Roosevelt in 1936. "I'll tell you here and now," he said to reporters, "that Franklin Roosevelt will not be the next President of the United States. If the Democrats nominate Roosevelt and the Republicans nominate Hoover, Huey Long will be your next President." While Roosevelt did not speculate publicly about a Huey Long threat, there are indications Huey gave the administration reasons to worry.[31]

Time reported in 1935 that Huey was among the top five contenders in its competition for 1934's "Man of the Year." Roosevelt and his aides must have seen the stream of nervous reports in early 1935 from friends of the president, as well as newspapers, all alarmed at the meteoric rise of Louisiana's senator. A St. Louis man reported to one of Roosevelt's advisers that Long was "a factor to reckon with and he's gaining ground every day." The publisher of a midwestern newspaper observed, "Long is developing a more dangerously large following than most people realize."[32]

Most alarming was a poll that the Democratic National Committee commissioned in the spring of 1935 to assess Long's potential strength in a presidential contest. In spite of the president's decisive support—54 percent of the total—Huey polled a surprising 11 percent. "It was easy," a Roosevelt aide wrote years later, "to conceive a situation whereby . . . Long might have the balance of power in the 1936 election." To friends, Huey confessed his plan: He would attend the 1936 Democratic convention as a candidate for the party's presidential nomination. Following an almost-certain defeat, he would announce his plans to form a third party. He knew he could never win, but his presence in the race would lure enough Democratic voters away from Roosevelt to throw the election to the Republican candidate. The Republicans, Huey believed, would handle the economy even more ineptly than Roosevelt. Thus, the country would soon be crying out for a strong leader, like Huey, by 1940. "It was a bold plan and also a coldly calculated one," wrote T. Harry Williams. "He was willing to let the country suffer for four years so that he could then save it."[33]

By the time Huey had returned home in September of 1935, Louisiana was firmly under his control. His enemies, muzzled by the repressive legislation he had railroaded through the legislature during the past year, could only dream of his overthrow, knowing he continued to have the support of the people. The poll tax had been abolished, meaning Huey and his organization stood to gain even greater majorities in the next election. Despite the intensity of his determined opposition, Louisiana was his undisputed domain. His enemies knew the only way he would ever be deposed was at the hands of an assassin, an option that grew more attractive every day.

Huey announced on September 7, 1935, that Governor Oscar Allen— his handpicked, subservient successor—had called the state legislature into special session to consider a host of legislative business that would give Huey's organization even greater control over every aspect of state and local government. Among the forty-two bills was one that caught the attention of many flabbergasted political observers in Baton Rouge. It was designed to terminate the political career of one of Huey's most enduring enemies: State Judge Benjamin Pavy, a twenty-eight-year veteran of the bench from St. Landry and Evangeline parishes. Knowing they could never defeat Pavy in the fierce anti-Long stronghold that made up his judicial district, Huey's men devised a clever plan to rid the district of a bitter enemy. The bill simply gerrymandered Pavy into a different district, one in which Huey had much greater political strength and the ability to defeat Pavy in the next election.

Typically, Huey, not Governor Allen, orchestrated the session. As lawmakers began their work on the bills, all destined to pass easily after perfunctory debate, Huey seemed to be in every corner of the house and senate at once, slapping backs and barking orders to his legislative leaders. On the second night of the session, shortly after nine o'clock, Huey abruptly left the house chamber to visit with a newspaper reporter waiting for him in the governor's first-floor office. Walking briskly down the marbled hallway, Huey's troup of bodyguards raced frantically to keep pace. As Huey neared the governor's office, he walked directly into the path of a young, bespeckled man in a white suit, who had appeared from behind a marble column. Before Huey noticed anything amiss, the owlish man produced a small pistol and fired one shot into Huey's abdomen. As Huey staggered alone down a nearby stairwell, his bodyguards riddled the assailant with bullets.

Downstairs, Huey encountered a friend, Jimmie O'Connor. "Kingfish!" he cried as he saw Huey stumble from the base of the stairs, blood dripping from his mouth. "What's the matter?" "Jimmie, my boy, I've been shot," Huey groaned. O'Connor helped Huey out to the parking lot, where he commandeered the first passing car and sped to a nearby hospital, Our Lady of the Lake. As the car rushed through the night, Huey spoke only once. "I wonder why he shot me?" he asked.[34]

Later, as doctors prepared for surgery on his wound, a state policeman entered the room to tell him the name of the man who had shot him. Huey did not recognize the name. "Weiss, Dr. Weiss," Huey grumbled. "What did he want to shoot me for?" Later, when told by one of his doctor's that his assailant was the son-in-law of Judge Benjamin Pavy, Huey was dumbfounded, saying only, "I don't know him."[35]

Efforts to save Huey, including a bungled operation and several blood transfusions, proved futile. Two days later, on September 10, Huey Long died. Recollections about his last words vary. Most, however, remembered that he said: "God, don't let me die. I have so much to do."[36]

3

LITTLE HUEY

$\mathcal{R}$USSELL LONG BURST INTO HIS PARENTS' WORLD amid the greatest upheaval of their young lives. Unfortunately, his birth on November 3, 1918, had little to do with the coinciding celebration. Russell was the victim of poor timing. He arrived two days before his father's stunning upset election to the Louisiana Railroad Commission. "Because of the excitement and commotion," Russell once joked, "nobody paid any attention to me. I was five days old before anybody got around to buying diapers for me." Although he was exaggerating, it is no overstatement to observe that his father's first election eclipsed Russell's birth. Politics, as the newborn child would grow to understand too well, overshadowed everything in the Long household.[1]

Despite the distractions of the impending election, Russell's arrival elated Huey. He halted his campaigning to rush to Shreveport as soon as he learned the news. Reaching the hospital after the birth, Huey learned that Rose had named their son after him, Huey Pierce Long III. Huey, curiously, was displeased. He demanded a different name. "When a man is in politics, he almost always winds up being repudiated," he told Rose. "It's better for the boy to have his own name so if things go badly for me, he can have his own name to make it on." Whether or not Huey had the amazing foresight to predict his political fortunes and the degree to which he would become a polarizing political force, Huey III was given a new name, Russell Billiu. Friends and family, however, quickly gave him the nickname "Bucky," which stuck into his teenage years. Unfortunately for

Russell, in the delirium over Huey's election no one took the time to change his name officially. Twenty-five years later, when he enlisted in the Navy during World War II, he learned his name was still legally Huey P. Long III. "Nothing hurt me more than to change my name to what it had been all my life," Russell wrote years later. "But if I had not, people would have assumed I was trying to capitalize on my father's name." Being named Russell, not Huey, probably had been a blessing. Even so, the last name, a heavy burden on its own, would in time become an extraordinary asset.[2]

By the time Russell was born, the lean years gave way to more prosperous times for Huey and his family. Although they were not rich, Huey had become a renowned attorney, having successfully represented plaintiffs in several celebrated cases. His election to the Railroad Commission further enhanced his standing in the legal community and, not coincidentally, his income. By any standard, their life-style was modest. Huey and Rose bought an unpretentious wood-frame house on Laurel Street on Shreveport's west side, where they had moved from Winnfield just several months before Russell's birth. "You would call that area a slum nowadays or a ghetto," Russell recalled, "but back in our day you might say there were a lot of poor people living in that area, but we didn't know we were poor." Russell's older sister, Rose, had the same recollection. "The people who lived out there didn't have any money," she said, "but there were a lot of very good, very fine respectable people all around us."[3]

Little Rose, Bucky, and Palmer, three years younger than his older brother, enjoyed a carefree and optimistic childhood. Down the street lived their maternal grandparents, and the children spent many hours helping their grandmother as she tended her vegetable garden. Often, they watched their grandfather, a carpenter, tinker in his workshop behind the house. At home, the children had light chores that included gathering eggs from the henhouse or picking fruit from the backyard fig tree. "We were brought up where we ought to be useful," said Russell.[4] Their maid, a black woman named Ella, performed most of the important household duties. It was Ella who evoked one of Russell's earliest and most endearing memories:

> If you had told me when I was five years old that Ella was my real mother, I would have probably believed you, because she did our housework and carried me around in one arm while she worked with the other arm. . . . And I loved Ella. At one point, I detected that she wasn't respected as much because she was black and I thought I was going to make her white. I got a bar of soap. She

seemed to be amused. And I wanted to scrub that black off, so she could enjoy the same advantages that the white people had. I didn't succeed. That was when I first began recognizing the fact a black person was subject to discrimination.[5]

As Huey's law practice flourished from the publicity of his legal and political exploits, Bucky slowly became aware of his father's growing status. "I began to sense that my father was just more than an ordinary guy." When Huey first ran for governor in 1924, Russell recalled, "Hell, I didn't even know what governor was." He did remember working in the campaign. At age five, he enthusiastically stamped and licked envelopes that his mother and other relatives had stuffed with Huey's campaign literature. "I would stamp and seal those envelopes all day long," Russell said, adding at day's end the family would pile into the family car for the drive to the post office. "That was always the high point of the day."[6]

Bucky was eight years old when his father won his most celebrated case, *Bernstein v. Commercial National Bank,* in which Huey represented a former bank officer, Ernest Bernstein. The bank's board had driven Bernstein from his position by forcing him to assume the debt for a bad loan, which he had urged the bank to make to a local oil company. As if this had not been grounds enough for the suit, the bank then circulated a pamphlet throughout the state detailing Bernstein's alleged misconduct. Failing to find an established Shreveport attorney to represent him against the city's most powerful financial institution, Bernstein turned to Huey, who gleefully accepted the case.

Huey filed three separate suits against the bank, pursuing the case with unusual determination, laboring over his briefs at home to escape the distractions of the office. Finally, when the children became an annoyance, Huey told Rose, "I've got to win this case," and left for a hotel downtown, where he lived for two months. All his hard work, four years' worth, had not been in vain. Huey won the first suit on appeal. He settled the other two cases out of court for a substantial sum. Huey received forty thousand dollars, a fantastic amount in 1926.[7]

At first, Huey had no idea what to do with so much money. Rose did, as Russell recalled: "My mother saw that was her chance to have a nice home for her children and grow up in a better neighborhood and all. So, that was when we moved across the tracks, you might say." Huey readily agreed to Rose's wish, locating and buying a lot at 305 Forrest Avenue, in Shreveport's finest residential section. On the lot, he ordered a large, Spanish-style white brick house and watched over its construction with typical impatience. The night before the family was to move, Huey was unable to contain his enthusiasm for his new home. He slept by himself on the floor of the empty house. "And from that point forward, I could detect a difference in the attitude of the people," maintained Russell, who soon realized, as did his sister, that their radical, upstart father was much more popular in their old neighborhood. "People were not mean to you. They were just cool. They just weren't as nice."[8]

Nowhere was this more apparent than at Creswell Elementary School, which Rose and Russell attended. As Huey mounted his successful 1928 gubernatorial campaign, the children began, for the first time, to suffer the scorn associated with a political life. "Children can be cruel," said Russell of the taunting he received from classmates because "their parents were all against Huey Long." Early returns showed Huey losing, meaning Rose and Russell could expect added abuse at school. Within a matter of days, Huey had taken the lead permanently. Rose, sensing her children's suffering from the indignity of their father's brush with defeat, cut the headline— "LONG TAKES LEAD"—from the local newspaper and pinned it on them to wear to school.[9]

The excitement of moving into the governor's mansion was enough to overcome any homesickness the children might have had for Shreveport. Soon, however, the Longs found that the luxurious palace they had imagined was actually a dilapidated old fire hazard, which Huey ordered destroyed during his first year in office. "The floors were falling in," said Russell's sister, Rose Long McFarland. "You could walk on the floors upstairs and you'd start to fall through a hole. The whole thing was in bad shape." Despite the mansion's condition, the new surroundings delighted the children. "It was a wonderful period for us," Rose said of the summer in Baton Rouge. "We were very, very happy with it, but the old mansion was just dangerous." While the new mansion was built, Huey sent Rose and the children back to Shreveport, where they remained until the summer of 1930.[10]

Another more personal reason drove Rose back to the sanctuary of Shreveport. Huey had audaciously furnished his twenty-two-year-old personal secretary, Alice Lee Grosjean, with a bedroom in the mansion. For years, Rose and many of Huey's friends had suspected that Huey and the pretty, dark-haired, hazel-eyed Grosjean were lovers. Grosjean's presence in the mansion confirmed their worst fears. From Shreveport, Rose angrily relayed word to Huey that she would file for divorce if Grosjean remained in the mansion. When Grosjean moved to more discreet quarters at the Heidelberg Hotel, Rose returned with the children.[11]

Although Rose and her children were apart from Huey for long periods, the separation may have been a blessing. Rose, Russell, and Palmer—all young and impressionable—did not witness the first crisis of the young governor's term—the impeachment trial. "I heard my mother saying a little about it," said Russell, who admits in spite of snippets of information, "I didn't know a damn thing at all about it." That is not to suggest Russell was ignorant of his father's exploits. "I think I understood a great deal more about politics than the average young person my age, because that was what my father was doing." In fact, when Huey wanted to bolster cotton prices by proposing a one-year moratorium on planting, he sent twelve-year-old Russell to Austin, Texas, along with his associates, O. K. Allen and Seymour Weiss, to sell the plan to Texas lawmakers. "Papa couldn't leave because he was afraid Lieutenant Governor Cyr might make a mess," Russell candidly told reporters. Despite the constant controversy and turmoil engulfing their father, none of the children believes Rose or Huey shielded them from the news, much of it negative, about their father's activities. "There wasn't any way to shield you," Rose McFarland maintained. Nevertheless, the burden of having a famous, controversial father took its toll on Russell: "Back at that time people would say, 'Well, if you are half as smart as your dad, you will be a big success.' And I heard enough of that until I finally got to where I said, 'I guess I am not going to be a success, because I am not going to be as smart as my father.' "[12]

This pressure applied by adults—unreasonably high expectations for a boy—coupled with the persecution and indifference from classmates undoubtedly had a profound affect. Most often, it manifested itself in one outward sign: stuttering. By his early teens, those who knew Russell remember him as a quiet, studious, introspective child who could barely utter a sentence without stumbling over his words. He could not have been more than twelve when he scribbled a joke in a scholastic notebook: "I feel sort of like old man Hibbs. You see, old man Hibbs used to stutter something awful. Some friends got him to go to a specialist in curing folks of stuttering. After ten tedious lessons, old man Hibbs learned to say 'Peter Piper picked a peck of pickled peppers.' When his friends congratulated him he said, 'Y-y-y-yes, b-b-b-b-but it is s-s-s-s-s-so h-h-h-hard to work it into the c-c-c-c-c-conversation.' "[13]

Childhood friend Bill Dugan vividly remembered how Russell's stuttering became annoying to his sister Rose. Stomping her feet impatiently, Rose demanded, "Stop that stuttering. You don't have to stutter. Stop stuttering!" Russell's problem became so serious—"His stuttering was awful," Dugan said—that his mother persuaded one of the debate teachers at Russell's school, Alcee Fortier High School in New Orleans, to enroll him in a debating course. "The amazing thing about it," said Russell, "was when I got up to speak to the class, I didn't seem to stutter. I stuttered in personal conversations, but when I had to get up to speak to the audience, seeing a whole different situation and different atmosphere . . . I wouldn't seem to stutter speaking to a crowd in front of the class." Dugan observed, and Russell agreed, debating "damn near was a miracle cure."[14]

With Huey Long for a father, life was an exceptional experience. The children rarely saw their father after he was elected governor. Each year would find his political activities more frantic than the last. As north Louisiana's railroad commissioner, Huey had spent much of his time in Baton Rouge on commission business. While not attending to official duties, he was likely campaigning for a political ally or stoking his own political fires. By the time Russell was five, Huey had lost his first race for governor. He was nine when his father finally captured the governor's office. Two years later, Huey was elected to the U.S. Senate. By then he was a national figure, allowing even less time to spend with his family.

It was simply a rare occasion when Huey was at home like a normal father, especially after he and the family moved to New Orleans when Huey took his U.S. Senate seat. Even his homecomings were extraordinary. With sirens from his caravan screaming the news of his arrival, Huey and his entourage of aides and bodyguards rolled down Audubon Avenue, screeching to a boisterous halt in front of the Long residence. "It was," remembered Palmer Long, "an event like the Fourth of July." Bill Dugan was witness to more than one of Huey's spectacular appearances: "When Huey would walk in the house, he completely electrified the whole household."[15]

Huey undoubtedly loved his family, but possibly not as much as he loved politics. Like many men of his time, Huey considered it his wife's duty to care for the children. His responsibility was providing a good living. Unfortunately for his family, providing the living became a consuming obsession. Perhaps Long biographer T. Harry Williams offered the most perceptive analysis of Huey's relationship with his family when he observed:

> Huey was oppressed by time. He often remarked to Rose that time frightened him; he feared he would not have enough of it to accomplish all his goals. He begrudged giving much of it even to his family. "I can't live a normal family life," he once confessed to Rose. . . . On those rare occasions when he spared some time to his family he could be a solicitous husband and a devoted father.

. . . He enjoyed being with the children, but because he was tense and nervous, he sometimes found the noise of their play intolerable. Then he would
"blow up," and storm at them in sudden, frightening fury.[16]

Because of Huey's sometimes choleric nature, the children were always
careful to be on their best behavior in his presence. "When he was home,
we were good and quiet and tried to be nice and not bother him," Rose
McFarland said. "He was always obsessed, usually—not all the time—but
lots of the time, with whatever was going on in political circles."[17]

When he did give the children attention, it was only for brief interludes.
One weekend afternoon Russell, by then a teenager, persuaded Huey to
take him to a movie. As they sat in the Orpheum Theater in New Orleans,
Russell became engrossed in the film. He failed to notice his father had
remembered some urgent business and left for his hotel suite, across the
street at the Roosevelt Hotel. When he realized that he had been abandoned, Russell finished watching the movie and joined his father at the
hotel. What is most telling about the episode is not Huey's very typical
behavior, but Russell's nonchalant reaction. "That problem may have
created a problem with some of the other children," Russell explained,
"but it didn't with me. I loved him very much and I understood. I knew he
was under a huge amount of pressure. He had a huge number of people
counting on him, depending on him, and his time really wasn't his own."[18]

While he did not begrudge his father's absences, as he grew older
Russell avidly followed his political career. Happily, Huey sometimes
invited his son to join him on brief campaign swings. On several occasions,
he accompanied Huey to Washington, where he watched, enthralled, from
the gallery as Huey espoused his populist program. When at home,
Russell listened intently to every speech Huey delivered over the radio.[19]

With little time to spend with his father, Russell retreated into his own
private world. While his friends played games in the front yard after
school, Russell could usually be found in his room, alone, reading. "He sort
of liked to be by himself more," said Palmer Long, who remembers several occasions when Huey would ask, "Where's your brother?" Palmer
would reply, "Where else?" "He was a thinker, for sure," said his sister,
Rose, adding that Palmer, unlike his older brother, "was more active in
things. Palmer just didn't sit around and read and try to invent things [like
Russell]." When he did put down his books to play, the game was usually baseball, Rose recalled: "He and two or three of the neighbors played
baseball in our side yard [in Shreveport] a whole lot. Russell always liked
baseball."[20]

By the summer of 1930, Rose and the children had returned to Baton Rouge after completion of the new governor's mansion. While the move afforded Russell more time with his father, the reunion of the family lasted less than a year and a half. In January 1932, Huey occupied the U.S. Senate seat to which he was elected in 1930. This meant he would spend even more time from home, now more than a thousand miles away in Washington. It also meant vacating the spacious, new governor's mansion. In early 1932, Huey moved Rose and the children into the large, two-story Mediterranean-style mansion he bought on Audubon Boulevard in one of New Orleans' most fashionable neighborhoods. Russell, having only recently made new friends at University High School, begged his parents to let him finish the school year in Baton Rouge. Rose sided with her son, permitting Russell to stay.[21]

It was anything but a normal experience for a high school student. Russell took up residence in a suite of rooms that his father held at the downtown Heidelberg Hotel, on the banks of the Mississippi River. For guardians, Huey assigned two state policemen to keep a constant eye on Russell. "One of them would pick me up in the morning and one of them would pick me up in the afternoon and bring me home," Russell said fondly of those days. "They would see that I had something to eat in the morning and had something to eat in the evening. I was living the life of Riley." This cozy arrangement did not last for long. LSU president James Monroe Smith, a family friend who looked disparagingly on the living condition, offered to take Russell into his home, where he lived until the semester ended.[22]

While living in the Smith home, at age thirteen, Russell granted his first newspaper interview. "I miss my father a lot since he went to Washington," he confessed to the visiting reporter. "Of course, I miss my mother and my sister and my brother who are in New Orleans, but I miss Dad the most because I do not get to see him often. . . . I would rather hear him speak than do most anything else I know." When the interview ended, Russell politely escorted the reporter to the door. "When I get big and run for office," he said, "I want you to remember the promise you made to vote for me." Even at this early age, Russell dreamed of following his father into politics.[23]

Family and friends are generous in their assessment of Russell's academic career, and the record supports that appraisal. His elementary school report cards revealed high grades in every subject, save Latin, at Alcee Fortier High School, a New Orleans public school. Early in their friendship, Bill Dugan was impressed with Russell's extraordinarily retentive mind: "We were studying together and we only had ten Spanish words to memorize. He could do it in one-tenth the time I did, or any of my buddies around there."[24]

Nonetheless, Russell did not regard himself as an exceptional student. "I never was all that great a student," he confessed, explaining that although he was a voracious reader—"I would read, but read for the fun of it"—he did little homework. Nevertheless, at University High School in Baton Rouge, Russell began to study and learn his most important subject—politics—by defeating President Smith's son, Jimmy, and another classmate, for class president.[25]

By semester's end, Russell was ready to join his family in New Orleans, where he enrolled at Alcee Fortier High School. Like Shreveport, New Orleans was not his father's political base. Hostile detractors opposed to Huey's aggressive, authoritarian style of governing pervaded the city. While he made friends, many to whom he remained close for more than fifty years after graduation, he constantly encountered the open malevolence his father engendered. One afternoon, Russell and a group of friends were lounging on the front porch of a classmate's house when the classmate's father opened the afternoon paper to a story about Huey Long. "This guy started tearing into Huey, to his wife and a friend of his," said boyhood friend Bill Dugan. "These adults were talking and it was terribly embarrassing to all the kids."Aware that the man did not know he was Huey's son, Russell gathered his courage and spoke up. "Pardon me, sir, that is not the way it happened," Russell forcefully declared. "What the papers said is not what my father did." Dugan was stunned by Russell's emphatic defense of his father. "But the way he handled it was very smooth, very quiet," Dugan said.[26]

Like this adult, most of Huey's detractors expressed their displeasure verbally. Some even resorted to violence in the highly charged summer of 1935, when Huey's methods increasingly became more severe and heavy handed. Talk of plots to assassinate Huey were rife. Nowhere was the atmosphere more tense than in New Orleans. Huey had recently imposed several oppressive laws enlarging his control over the city's government, aimed at driving Mayor Semmes Walmsley from power. Early one evening, the Long family got its first taste of violence as the crack of gunfire shattered the nighttime calm. "They had revolvers and they emptied those pistols right into that house," Russell said, remembering that one of the bullets lodged in the autobiography of Italian artist Benvenuto Cellini. No one was hurt, but the Longs' unproven assumption was that disgruntled police officers had carried out the attack. Whether it was an assassination attempt on Huey, not home at the time, or simply intimidation tactics, no one knew for sure. Even so, the incident, no matter how serious, did little to prepare Russell for the devastating events of the coming September when his father was assassinated.[27]

"The question in my mind back then [was] whether it affected him or Rose more, but Russell was [more affected], really," high school friend Bob Chinn observed. For months, the entire family was in "a state of bewilderment," said Bill Dugan, observing the only sign of Russell's grief was that he "just got very, very quiet." Katherine Hattic, whom Russell later married, met him shortly after his father's assassination. Struck by the profound impact that Huey's death had on Russell, she said, "After his father died, his father became an obsession with him. Huey could do no wrong in Russell's eyes at that time. He was very, very affected by his father's death, more so than the other children."[28]

To lose a father, senselessly, at the hand of an assassin, would have embittered many young men. Years later, Russell would gratefully recall his good fortune to have just completed a book by a well-known inspirational writer, Lloyd C. Douglas. *Forgive Us Our Trespasses* is the story of a bitter young man whose life was changed when he discovered an old letter left by his mother before her death. "I didn't want to get even with anybody or anything like that. I had taken the lesson of that book to heart: People do unkind things, not because they want to hurt you . . . but for all sorts of reasons. . . . And you must learn to forgive people for that, rather than hate them or want to get even or revenge, because it is only by forgiving others that you can someday be forgiven."[29]

Russell was not the only family member drastically affected by Huey's death. After the family resumed its usual routine in New Orleans following the funeral, Russell's mother remained in shock: "It was like she went into a coma or something like that," said young Rose of her mother, "just like she passed out." Palmer Long believes what his sister interpreted as shock may simply have been the manifestation of his mother's strong desire to maintain her composure for the children's sake. "I don't guess she allowed herself to be uncontrollable, as I remember going back on it, in any instance."[30]

Rose Long's stoicism also extended to rarely betraying her concern over the family's perilous financial circumstances following Huey's death, even though the children were mature enough, in at least some cases, to perceive the situation. Despite the belief that Huey Long had amassed great personal wealth during his brief career, the truth is that Huey left his family a relatively small sum of money, and some rather large debts. The final accounting of Huey's estate revealed that he left his family about ninety-seven thousand dollars in assets and debts totaling twenty-seven thousand dollars. His assets included thirty-one shares of Win or Lose Oil Company stock, eventually worth millions, but then valued at only thirty-one hundred dollars. He also owned land in Shreveport, New Orleans, and Winn Parish, in addition to his law books, valued at twenty thousand dollars.[31]

Unfortunately, cash was not one of Huey's major assets. Rose spent many sleepless nights wondering how she would support three children, a role she had never anticipated. "My mother really didn't know much about my father's business," Russell explained. In the ensuing years, Rose Long would prove she was much more than the shy, reticent wife she had often been when Huey was alive. Through sheer determination, and the benevolence of friends, Rose kept the family out of bankruptcy. New Orleans mayor Bob Maestri, who held a mortgage on their Shreveport home, saw Rose's plight and forgave the note. "He saw that our situation was precarious and he said he was just going to tear that mortgage up and forget about it," Russell said. Governor Richard Leche arranged for the state to purchase Huey's law books. Leche later persuaded the legislature to buy the Audubon Boulevard home. Others, Russell recalled, were not so generous: "I hate to tell you how poorly some of the rest of them performed. As far as putting up anything, they had a chance to grab stuff that rightly belonged to Huey and proceeded to do so." For example, Huey had contracted with the state of Louisiana to collect delinquent property taxes, thus entitling him to a percentage of the amount he collected. Although the family maintained that the state and Huey's partners in the enterprise owed him thousands of dollars, "we got practically nothing out of it, hardly anything," Russell said.[32]

Perhaps the greatest element in the family's financial recovery is attributable to Rose and her newfound entrepreneurial savvy. Rose's brother, Dave McConnell, was an experienced oilman who advised his sister investing in a gas well near Shreveport might yield all the income needed to support her family. The venture was a colossal risk. To realize such a return, she was required to make a sizable investment in the well. With no real business experience and even less knowledge about the oil and gas business, Rose gambled. "She put every nickel she could lay her hands on into it, even including a lot of money that was there for the children from the insurance," said Russell, who knew little of the matter then, but who observed that many widows were lured into similar investments only to lose everything. To Rose's relief and elation, the well proved to be one of the most productive in north Louisiana. Along with her subsequent investments in other area wells, Rose never worried about financial support for her children. According to Palmer Long: "If it hadn't been for the little money coming off that at the time, and that thousand dollars a month that thing made for her many a day, I don't know what we would have done, 'cause we needed every dime of it at that time."[33]

As Rose successfully maneuvered her family around the financial pitfalls resulting from Huey's death, she could not have anticipated the greater challenge that presented itself in early 1936. While House speaker Allen Ellender, Huey's closest political ally, had won the Democratic nomination to a full, six-year term to succeed Huey in the Senate, Governor O. K. Allen had been elected to the remaining year of Huey's unexpired term. Tragically, Allen did not live to fill out the term of his boyhood friend, his life claimed by a brain hemorrhage before he left for Washington. Lieutenant Governor James Noe, who assumed the governorship when Allen died, quickly concluded that appointing Rose to the Senate would be an immensely popular move.[34]

Rose initially declined Noe's offer. Only when her daughter Rose agreed to leave LSU for a semester and accompany her mother to Washington did she agree. "She would not have gone if I had not agreed to go," McFarland explained. Palmer Long agreed: "I think my sister may have helped a little bit there. . . . Don't forget the difference. I mean, mama didn't have any great education. Hell, my sister was a smart tomato."[35]

On February 10, 1936, Rose and the children arrived in Washington by train. They went directly to the Capitol, where she walked down the center aisle of the Senate on the arm of Louisiana senator John Overton. Immediately, Rose encountered the briefly quiescent hostility toward her dead husband. As she and Overton passed, one Democratic senator began whistling "Here Comes the Bride." After she was sworn in, Rose forsook her assigned desk to sit next to the Senate's only other woman member, Arkansas senator Hattie Caraway, who owed her Senate seat to Huey Long and his campaigning on her behalf.[36]

Later in the morning, Rose and her daughter received reporters in her office. Behind a desk piled high with flowers, Rose read a statement: "I shall complete the work of Senator Long as far as I can. I have asked that all the Share-Our-Wealth correspondence that comes to me in Louisiana be forwarded to me here in Washington. I am one hundred percent for labor and for the farmers. They will be my first interest." When a reporter asked her which of Huey's goals she would give priority, daughter Rose quickly interjected, "No one can state his aims better than he did. As time goes on, people will better realize and appreciate his work." When another reporter asked about the future of the Share-Our-Wealth program, Rose hesitated, only to be rescued again by her daughter, who spoke up to say, "The movement will go on."[37]

While Rose spent much of the year in Washington, Russell returned to Louisiana, where he enrolled at Louisiana State University shortly after his father's death. That Russell would attend LSU was not always certain. His academic future had been the subject of at least one heated discussion between Russell and his father, who took more than a casual interest in the university's progress. The fuss started with Palmer. More than three years younger than Russell, Palmer had inherited the gregarious and adventurous spirit Russell lacked. He regularly became embroiled in school yard fistfights from which he was often rescued by his older brother. By the time Palmer was about thirteen, Huey and Rose decided he needed the rigors of a quasi-military school to instill discipline. They agreed to send him to Chimney Rock Camp in North Carolina. Next, they persuaded Russell to accompany his younger brother, believing it was the only way Palmer would agree to stay. To Russell's chagrin, Palmer refused to go. "She should have made him go, spanked his rear and said this is one time you're going to do what I tell you," Russell said of his mother. "No, she didn't do it. So, he didn't go and I went."[38]

To his surprise, Russell loved Chimney Rock and its students. There, he met his lifelong friend, George Smathers, with whom he later served in the United States Senate. He was especially fond of the camp counselors, many of them instructors at Lawrenceville Academy, a preparatory school for Princeton University. "I came back from Chimney Rock wanting to go to Princeton." According to Russell, "the roof blew off the house" when he informed his father of his desire to attend the Ivy League school. "My God," Huey shouted, "here I have worked and strived and risked impeachment to build a university here that a state can be proud of, that people can send their sons and daughters to and it's not good enough for my own son!" Huey, said Russell, "was utterly disgusted about the matter, that I'd even suggested it." Later, Rose pulled Russell aside to assure him that she would try to change Huey's mind—"Now, don't you take that for an answer, Russell," she told him—but Russell considered the matter closed. "As far as I'm concerned, it had been decided," he said. "But when my father was assassinated, as far as I was concerned, he wanted me to go to LSU, that was what I was going to do. I respected his wish."[39]

Within a few weeks of his father's death, Russell enrolled at LSU. The decision to abide by his father's wishes was a turning point. It would render rich political dividends for decades to come.

4

I GOT AN "A" IN POLITICS

$\mathcal{L}$OUISIANA STATE UNIVERSITY HAD TWO MAJOR SPORTS in 1935—football and campus politics. The gridiron was not Russell's forte. Politics was. True to family form, he attacked LSU student government with the intensity of an enraged linebacker and the finesse of a graceful running back. During four years of undergraduate studies, political activities almost always subjugated scholarly endeavors. Politics became Russell's realm of acclaim, the arena in which he finally emerged as his own person and left a significant, lasting imprint on campus life. In time, LSU was his political domain.

In the 1930s, two student organizations dominated LSU politics: The New Era, or the TNEs, and the Cavaliers. Controlled by members of social fraternities, both groups were aggressively competitive for student government's reins. Support from one of these organizations was the only route to success in campus elections. Those not invited to join were, with rare exception, excluded from any significant role in campus politics. This intense rivalry was more than a diversion. Political success at LSU, especially for those who attained the office of student body president, was an essential preliminary to elective office after graduation. "It is sort of considered a crucible of Louisiana politics," Russell's classmate Bob Chinn maintained. A student with ambitions for statewide office might someday find the friends and associations made during four years at LSU—and possibly three more years of law school—an invaluable resource. LSU was minor league politics, with the promise of a trip to the majors for those who mastered the game.[1]

To comprehend the exclusive nature of campus politics in that era is to be astounded by Russell's remarkable success. Already, his controversial name was a hindrance. Although neither campus political organization offered him a membership, Russell was undaunted. Much like his audacious, outsider father, who first ran for public office by attacking the status quo, Russell arrived on campus running for freshman class president. While his opponents largely rested on endorsements proffered by the TNEs and Cavaliers, Russell overcame his basic shyness and stuttering to take his campaign directly to the students. "I just went from room to room all through the barracks and just shook hands with every freshman. Every night, I would just start right out. As long as you could until they said, 'Lights out,' I would just go from room to room talking to those freshman."[2]

His hard work paid off. He won the election by a large margin, partly because of his famous last name. As important, many freshmen had not joined a social or political fraternity and, therefore, had not established loyalties to either of the organizations. Perhaps most important, Russell was simply a likable young man, sincere, amiable, and polite to a fault. Basking in the glow of what the Associated Press called "his initial political test," Russell took to the stump during the 1935 Christmas break in support of the Long organization's statewide ticket. The Long slate was headed by its gubernatorial candidate, state judge Richard Leche, and Huey's younger brother, Earl Long, a candidate for lieutenant governor. While he made a few brief speeches, his simple presence alongside the other candidates was more important than anything he could say. "I have come here because I know all of you were my father's friends and I want to thank you for the appreciation and support you have given him," Russell told more than one campaign rally. Uncle Earl, who once engaged in a public feud with brother Huey, needed Russell to lend credibility to the Long candidates. "He has a fine speaking voice," one of the candidates told the Associated Press, "and makes a splendid appearance." Russell judged his performance more critically. "God, I had no idea how lousy I was on the stump 'till I heard myself over a wire recorder played back," Russell recalled. Several weeks after Russell's campaign debut, Leche and Uncle Earl won the election.[3]

Despite his early rejection by the political organizations, Russell yearned to join a social fraternity. Although courted by members of several fraternities, none offered him a bid. "I think that was because in every last one of them there was somebody that didn't like Huey Long [who] would blackball me," Russell speculated, "even though my father had been assassinated." Fraternity members expressed opinions of prospective pledges in secret elections, dropping a black or white ball into a cigar box. One black ball was needed for rejection. This happened when Russell sought a bid from the school's most prestigious fraternity, Delta Kappa Epsilon. His acceptance came only after Oscar Allen, Jr., son of late governor O. K. Allen, intervened on Russell's behalf. Russell's friend Bill Dugan recalled that Allen resolved, "if Russell doesn't get in, nobody gets in." He kept his word, blackballing candidate after candidate until his brothers relented and offered Russell a bid. While he gladly accepted, Russell did not learn of Allen's intervention until many years later. "If I had known that," Russell said, "I probably wouldn't have accepted the bid."[4]

Fresh from his LSU victory, his successful debut on the stump and his membership in one of LSU's most prestigious fraternities, Russell began laying the foundation for his next campaign later that year—a run for sophomore Arts and Sciences class president. Indeed, from his first day at LSU, politics almost totally dominated his time and energy. When he was not in class or working as a minutes clerk at the state senate—a job Uncle Earl secured for him—Russell was politicking. "I learned pretty near nothing that first year at LSU," Russell admitted. Instead, he invested his greatest effort in building his own political organization, a group of friends—disenfranchised by the other political groups—who met regularly to discuss campus politics. At each meeting, the freshman society grew larger, as he pressed members to bring friends to their weekly organizational gatherings. By year's end, Russell was ready to test his growing political strength.[5]

Early in his sophomore year, Russell saw such an opening, a chance to secure his undisputed dominance over the campus political landscape. He joined forces with an upperclassman, a popular student who was defeated for student body president because neither political fraternity had endorsed him. The young man approached Russell, suggesting they join forces to challenge the two political organizations. Russell readily agreed. "On that election," Russell said, "we just swept that lower division by a huge majority and that just wiped the opposition out." Russell was elected sophomore president by a wide margin. His allies who ran for other offices also won, including his sister, Rose, elected junior class secretary.[6]

Emboldened by his success, Russell and his friends formalized the alliance, creating a hybrid political organization, the Independent Party. The only condition of membership, Russell said, was "you can't be one of theirs." The result of his new political alliance was the ultimate demise of the other two political fraternities. "We just put them out of business," Russell said.[7]

The leaders of the suddenly defunct organizations did not understand Russell never would have labored so arduously for their extinction had they not spurned him during his freshman year. While the stigma of his family name may have been an encumbrance at the time, it forced him to blaze his own course in campus politics. Like his father's first campaign for the Louisiana Railroad Commission, if Russell had relied on the existing political structure for success, he might have failed. He certainly would not have overcome his bashfulness as quickly and would never have formed his own political coalition. With no organization upon which to rely, Russell developed social skills he never knew he had. He certainly had the mind for politics. As an independent candidate, he mastered the mechanics, as well.

As sophomore Arts and Sciences president, Russell continued expanding his political organization through his election as chairman of the sophomore presidents. He increased his campus renown, and his rhetorical skills, by successfully competing on the school's debate team. By year's end, however, he surprised his friends by not running for junior class president. "I felt like I was losing the esteem from the students," he said, "because they had seen how I was just always out there running for something." His one-year hiatus was a clever calculation. It did not mean he lost his political ardor. To the contrary, by the end of his junior year, Russell was well prepared for the student body president campaign. "Russell knew more about politics than other people on the campus," observed classmate Alvin Rubin, who attributed Russell's political success to "more sophistication, more finesse and more access to outside people." Russell understood the political, postgraduate benefits of the student body presidency. He was willing to sacrifice his studies to achieve his goal. "You might say I wound up with an A average in campus politics, which is something that was very important to me," Russell said. "My thought was if I could be elected president of the student body someday, I could become governor of the state someday."[8]

It is difficult to imagine more audacity and ambition in a nineteen-year-old—other than Huey Long. Russell's aspirations were matched only by his aggressive and innovative campaigning, based on a series of promises directly addressing several of the most pressing concerns for LSU's students. He promised a cooperative textbook exchange and to arrange crosstown bus service to the campus. He vowed to provide ice water for the students who lived in the football stadium barracks. Most important, Russell pledged to create a campus laundry, a promise which hit one of his opponents, "Blondie" Bennett, square in the pocketbook. Bennett was a muscular, handsome youth, one of LSU's most popular students, who, among other activities, announced the campus boxing matches. "Back in those days," recalled Bob Chinn, "we didn't have P.A. systems and it was customary for somebody to get in the middle of the ring and shout, and Blondie had this loud, piercing voice." Bennett's other claim to fame was his financial interest in an off-campus laundry. The business did a significant amount of business with LSU students, a practice strictly forbidden by school regulations if Bennett did not pay the school a concession on his profits.[9]

The previous year, Russell and Bennett had struck a deal. Russell agreed to support Bennett for student body president if Bennett would support Russell's campaign the following year. "But he made a mistake his junior year," Russell said. "He let other fellows move in on him and get a head start on him. And so, by the time it came for him to make his move, he had been preempted by some of the other fellows." Blondie did not run and Russell blithely assumed that Bennett would honor their agreement. He did not know Bennett had simply postponed his campaign for a year. He now planned to challenge Russell.[10]

Bennett's betrayal may have been the motivation behind Russell's promise for the on-campus laundry. Regardless, it made Bennett nervous enough to devise a scheme he hoped would knock Russell completely out of contention. As Russell and a friend, Alva Jones, strolled through the crowded LSU Field House one afternoon, Bennett sprung his surprise. When Russell passed, Bennett snatched him by the arm and announced that Russell had tried to bribe him out of the race: "I accuse Russell Long of coming to my barracks on a number of nights this spring and attempting to bribe me to remain out of the race against him. I was offered $1,200 in cash, a job as an assistant to the secretary of the Senate [and] a gross income of about $720."[11]

Knowing better than to refute Bennett's charges in the midst of a hostile crowd, Russell said only, "That's a lie," and marched toward the door. "Dammit, my dear old friend Alva Jones did something he shouldn't have done," Russell remembered. "He stayed with that gang and got up on top of a table to make a speech to that gang on my behalf." Russell was almost out the door when he glanced back to see Jones standing on the table. He knew he could not abandon his friend. "I felt like I had no choice but to get in the thick of the damn thing," lamented Russell, who charged into the fray and announced to the laughter of Blondie's friends: "Now, Blondie, if you wanted to lie about me, you made one great big mistake. You told such a big lie that nobody is going to believe you. Anybody in his right mind, who knows who Blondie Bennett is and knows your record, knows that if I'd offered you all that, you'd have taken it." In fact, Russell had offered financial enducements to lure Bennett from the race. He proposed financial help with his laundry business and a good word on his behalf with Uncle Earl about a state job. "As far as I was concerned, that was a political deal," Russell maintained. "He exaggerated something awful about what the deal was."[12]

After the incident, Russell only intensified his campaign and his campus laundry promise. A Long handbill extolling Russell's pledge, "Airing Dirty Linen," charged LSU students paid an average of $1.92 a week for laundry, while Louisiana Tech students were charged 51 cents for the same amount of cleaning. In the handbill, Russell vowed: "I will either get a student laundry or resign as president." Meanwhile, he accused Bennett of entering the race only to save his bootleg laundry business. "Blondie Bennett and his crew," Russell charged, "are battling desperately to keep from losing the laundry racket—the juiciest pickings that's come down the pike in many a day."[13]

Russell's campaign was more than prosaic promises. Like any Long campaign, Russell added dashes of flamboyance. He enlisted coeds to parade around campus in scanty bathing suits with the letters L-O-N-G painted on their backs. Speaker trucks traversed the campus blaring the Long message. Classmate Bill Dugan—to whom Russell loaned the money for a small airplane—buzzed the campus, unleashing a hail of Russell's handbills. On the first swoop, Dugan said, the handbills "all ended up in Baton Rouge, instead of on campus." Determined to hit his mark, Dugan made another pass. "He flew that thing so low he could almost shake the students' hands as he zoomed through," Russell recalled. "He just put those circulars all over the place." Such hair-raising stunts helped draw the highest turnout of any previous LSU campus race. Russell almost won outright, polling 48 percent of the votes, placing him in a runoff with the third candidate, Claiborne Dameron. Blondie Bennett, whose bribery charges against Russell backfired, finished a poor third.[14]

On election eve, Russell unveiled his most sensational campaign weapon, an appearance by one of the nation's most popular band leaders and his orchestra, Ted Lewis, whose song "Me and My Shadow" was a national hit. Russell had called on Seymour Weiss—former manager of New Orleans' Roosevelt Hotel and one of Huey Long's closest friends and advisers—for help in persuading Lewis to perform at an election-eve rally. It was a stunning coup, sure to win him the gratitude of every student who attended. But as Russell littered the campus with circulars announcing the event, Dameron and his supporters counterattacked. They sent word to Lewis they would disrupt the performance with stink bombs and rotten eggs. "They were going to do whatever they could because they didn't think that was fair," Russell said. The scare tactics succeeded. "They had [Lewis] intimidated," Russell said. "Look, I've never been stink bombed and rotten egged in my life," Lewis told Russell. "I'm not going to do it now."[15]

Only when Russell agreed to invite Dameron to cohost the rally did Lewis agree to play. But now, Russell feared the credit he would have received for Lewis's performance was lost. Russell was relieved when Lewis announced to a jubilant crowd of about five thousand—including a large group of state legislators and townspeople who gathered in the campus gymnasium—he was in Baton Rouge to pay a debt he owed to a "dear friend." "I suspect," Russell said, "he was talking about a debt he owed to Seymour Weiss. But it sounded to people like he was talking about Huey Long." Although they had been forced to invite Dameron to host the rally, Russell's supporters—not about to give Dameron any credit—paraded through the gym, hoisting banners which read, "Let's swing A-Long with Ted Lewis." Whether the rally was a significant factor in Russell's victory the next day, it certainly received much of the credit. Russell soundly defeated Dameron with 57 percent of the vote. He carried six of the eight colleges. His strongest showing came from his old citadel, the freshman class.[16]

Russell quickly fulfilled his campaign promises. By summer's end, he had accomplished the three major planks of his platform: the laundry, the express bus service, and ice water for the stadium barracks. After persuading the state's Board of Supervisors to finance the laundry, Russell negotiated with city officials for the express bus line. The ice water was the easiest promise, fulfilled shortly after the election. "They had the equipment over there," he acknowledged. "All they had to do was turn the damn stuff on. Throw the switch and we had it." In time, Russell also delivered on his promise for a book exchange. LSU never had such an active student body president. "Nobody had ever thought of offering all that, especially doing it," Russell explained. "But you see, at that time, I had a job down there at the state legislature and I was close to [Governor] Dick Leche. Folks figured I might be able to do it."[17]

In three years, Russell Long underwent a metamorphosis. When he began college, he was a quiet, brainy young man whose shyness was only exacerbated by his stuttering. LSU gave Russell his first taste of independence. Although he deeply mourned his father's death, his college years marked his emergence as a man, free from the burdens of his father's direct influence and domination. Bob Chinn was one witness to Russell's transformation: "He moved from complete shyness—kind of a shrinking shyness—to a point where he could face any situation." Not only was Russell now a man in his own right, he was becoming a first-class politician.[18]

Another source of Russell's maturation was his romance with a beautiful brunette freshman from Mississippi, Katherine Mae Hattic. They met during his sophomore year when Russell's sister helped arrange their date to an LSU football game. Before he met Katherine, Russell rarely had the time, or motivation, for dating. To Katherine, "Russell was what I would call introverted at that time. He was very, very idealistic. Not a typical college student." Russell revealed the reason behind his subdued behavior. "During my freshman year," he explained, "feeling as I did about my father, I just didn't think I ought to go out. I wouldn't dance at the dances and I just felt I ought to respect my father." That attitude changed when he met Katherine. In a matter of weeks, by his own admission, Russell was enchanted. They were engaged by the time he finished his undergraduate studies and began law school. In June 1939, at the end of Katherine's junior year, they were married.[19]

Scandal erupted in Baton Rouge as Russell and Katherine drove north to Canada on their honeymoon. *The New Orleans States* uncovered a pervasive pattern of corruption within Governor Leche's administration. Leche, LSU president James Monroe Smith, and Seymour Weiss, all close associates of Huey Long and friends of Russell, were indicted along with various other state officials. Leche—who reportedly asserted, "When I took the oath of office, I didn't take any vows of poverty"—was caught making more than ninety thousand dollars a year by smuggling oil out of state while avoiding severance taxes. Smith was charged with stealing a half-million dollars in university money and squandering another half-million by investing in high-risk stocks and bonds. Weiss and Leche sold a New Orleans hotel to LSU for use as a dormitory and then sold its furnishings to the school for a handsome profit. In all, 250 indictments were lodged against various members of Leche's organization. By June, Leche resigned, citing poor health. Leche, Smith, Weiss, and others were later convicted and imprisoned, and Lieutenant Governor Earl Long assumed the governorship upon Leche's resignation.[20]

Although Huey Long had been dead for four years, the anti-Longs were quick to lay the blame for the scandals at his feet. Huey was said to have remarked once that without his calming presence his cronies might all wind up in jail. What he failed to predict was, even in death, his enemies would find a way to finger him for the crimes of his associates. That his father was blamed for the crimes of others pained Russell deeply, more so than any other aspect of the scandal. "Russell did not have an easy time," said Katherine. "He had hardly gotten over his father's assassination and then right on the heels of that came the Louisiana scandals." The scandals had a profound effect on Russell, sparking in him a strengthened resolve to clear his father's reputation.[21]

Even in his late teens, Russell began to emerge as the standard-bearer for his family name. He was the one sibling who strived to repair and enhance his father's memory. At age nineteen, he attended a dinner in Baton Rouge for the surviving members of the group of fifteen state senators who had signed the famous Round Robin that stopped his father's impeachment in 1928. "I only hope that someday I can do a service for someone as great as that which you performed for my father," Russell told the gathering, which included Governor Leche, a friend of Huey's, but not a Round Robin signatory. The next year, Russell actively lobbied the state legislature to approve a bill authorizing a statue of his father in the U.S. Capitol's Statuary Hall, where each state honored two of its most prominent and noteworthy citizens. "You will never know what a professional politician your beau is," he bragged to Katherine in a letter, "unless you get the dope on how he arranged to get the bill introduced." Several years later, Russell even briefly entertained the idea of writing his own biography of Huey, but was thwarted when he discovered that his mother had burned much of Huey's correspondence. "That made me sick," he wrote in his diary. Law school was Russell's immediate priority and may have been the best salve for his despair over the scandals. "I think Russell buried his head in the books a little more and got intensely interested in law school," said Bill Dugan, who said he never saw any visible sign that the scandals deeply pained Russell. "I think it did, but it didn't show."[22]

As Russell began law school, he knew he must finally apply himself to studying, not campus politics. At the time, LSU's high attrition rate was enough to intimidate even the most brilliant freshman. As classmate Alvin Rubin remembered: "In those days, the notion in most law schools, including some of the prestige law schools like Harvard, was admit a lot of people, flunk them out if they don't make it. . . . I vividly remember at LSU and many other schools, there was a hackneyed expression: Look to your left and look to your right and of the three of you, only one of you is going to graduate."[23]

This pressure forced Russell to apply himself as never before. "I felt, at that point, having been president of the student body and about everything campus could do, that I needed to really settle down and make good grades and work hard," Russell said. Yet, he admitted, "I didn't work as hard during that first semester as I probably should have. I mean I didn't study as hard, as consistently and as religiously as I should have." By the semester's end, Russell grew uneasy about his prospects for passing the all-important final examination. "And so I was just grabbing anything I could find to study and read and burn the midnight oil over. I went to those examinations fearful I was going to flunk out." Russell was surprised when the examination scores placed him first in his freshman class.[24]

Classmate Alvin Rubin, who eventually edged out Russell for class valedictorian, assessed the elements of Russell's early law school success: "Russell gave less time to study, I think, than many people in the class, although certainly not at the bottom. He was better prepared, perhaps in memory, than he thinks he was. But he was not a grind or a drone. I think he was helped by the fact that he does have a good memory." While he may not have been a drone, Katherine must have thought he was. Her memories of the law school days are of endless days and nights waiting for Russell to finish class, and often his late-night studies.[25]

Law school classmates of Russell do not have many vivid memories of him during this period. As one of the few married students, Russell rarely socialized with his classmates, choosing instead to spend his free time studying or with Katherine. "There were not many married students at the law school at that time," said Alvin Rubin, who said only a handful of students, including Russell, lived off campus. "I think being married, if anything, helped," Russell maintained. "I had very little to do, other than my work, other than my studying."[26]

By the end of his senior year, three students contended for class valedictorian: Russell, Alvin Rubin, and Dupre Litton. Although Rubin had the highest grade-point average, law school tradition mandated the class elect its valedictorian from the top three students. Russell gave no thought to challenging Rubin's right to the honor. But when Litton, second in the class, announced he was running, Russell went to Rubin to offer assistance. Rubin was Jewish, and Russell believed Litton would play on student prejudices to win. "I thought that was totally out of place," Russell said of Litton's candidacy. "I thought the only chance he had to win that race would be anti-semitism. . . . And so, when I saw that Litton was going to run for it, I went to Alvin and said, 'There's no way you can lose this thing if you've got a good campaign manager.' " Rubin accepted the offer and Russell personally urged every classmate to support Rubin. "Why in the hell would you want to do something like that and have it disgrace your whole class, which reflects on you?" he told more than one classmate. "Here's a guy that clearly won it, won it fair and square, and because he's a Jew, you elect someone else valedictorian? You ought to be ashamed of yourself to do that." Confronted with Russell's forceful appeal, Litton lost badly. For his part, Rubin—who eventually became a federal judge with Russell's assistance—never forgot the selfless gesture. "He spurned both the personal ambition and the appeal to anti-semitism," said Rubin. Although not valedictorian, Russell did win another of the school's highest honors. He and classmate Gordon West, also appointed to the federal bench with Russell's help, won the school's moot court trials.[27]

The serene path toward graduation was abruptly shattered on December 7, 1941 when Russell received word of the Japanese attack on Pearl Harbor, which he recorded in his diary: "Alvin Rubin and Phil Goode called to tell me that the Japs were bombing Pearl Harbor. They pulled quite a joke on me by saying that the senior class was going to volunteer in mass and I would be expected to go immediately." The next day, Russell and his classmates huddled nervously around the radio as President Franklin Roosevelt asked Congress to declare war against the Japanese, signaling American involvement in the world war. "At present," Russell confided in his diary that day, "none of us know just what to do. The war is going bad for us just now."[28]

5

OFF TO THE WAR

$\mathcal{L}$IKE HIS FATHER, RUSSELL WAS WARY of U.S. intervention in a foreign conflict. The attack on Pearl Harbor on December 7, 1941, changed that. He now understood, along with most of his classmates, that he must enlist following graduation. In August 1942, Russell boarded the train in Baton Rouge, bound for his Navy midshipman's training at Columbia University in New York. "You really stood up fine," he wrote to Katherine on the train. Several days later, another letter brought her the assurance "your love will be my greatest asset in this new life."[1]

Russell's abundant idealism was evident in his letters home. Shortly after arriving in New York, he wrote Katherine about a sermon he heard his first Sunday in town. The chaplain told the story of a young American trainee who concentrated on his work by imagining his young Japanese counterpart. When the young American was not studying, he would wonder if "his Jap" was becoming better prepared for their battlefield encounter. "I am going to adopt something of that 'my Jap' philosophy in an effort to make a very good record here," Russell assured her, adding "one thing you can be sure. I will be a properly behaved husband. You may lose me to the navy, God forbid, sweetheart, but you will never lose so much as a puff of my breath to the foul temptations that some soldiers and sailors may crave when they find the time."[2]

Shortly after arriving in New York, Russell wrote to ask, in a code he and Katherine devised, "Am I going to be a father?" Katherine responded she believed she was pregnant, a suspicion confirmed within days. Less than a month later, she suffered a miscarriage. Russell consoled her, writing, "[W]e will still have our little family yet, Darling, and after all, we have been blessed so much in having one another that it would be unreasonable for us to have all the sweet without a little of the bitter from time to time."[3]

By September, Russell was a full-fledged midshipman, a joyous event overshadowed by his difficulties in maintaining good grades in his navigation course. "I am almost doomed to finish somewhere in the lower thirty percent of the class," he groused to Katherine, who tried to cheer him by responding, "[Y]ou can't always expect to be the best in everything." By Christmas, Ensign Long completed his training, received his naval commission and was ordered to Camp Bradford, near Little Creek, Virginia. At Little Creek, where Katherine joined him, the navy assigned him to amphibious training on a landing craft tank (LCT) vessel, a small, odd-looking, flat-bottomed boat, designed primarily to ferry cargo from Liberty ships to shore. After what he described as a brief, inadequate amount of naval schooling, Russell shipped out to Oran, a coastal city in northern Algiers, to join a flotilla of LCTs already in the Mediterranean Sea. From there, Russell would be part of the Allied invasion known as Operation Torch, America's first venture in the European war. The plan of attack started from the Allied-controlled positions in North Africa to Tunisia. Next, Sicily was a stepping-stone for the Allied march into Italy and the rest of German-occupied Europe.[4]

Under normal conditions, the LCTs of the Mediterranean could accommodate no more than a dozen men, but until the navy built more boats, each craft sustained manpower twice its designed capacity. Members of the enlarged crews were crowed together. The short supply of LCTs—more men and officers than boats to accommodate them—gave Russell his first opportunity for wartime leadership. The Navy appointed him assistant officer in charge of an overflowing LCT. "They packed us in there like sardines," he remembered.[5]

From Arzew, the navy advanced eastward along the North African coast, across Algeria toward Tunisia and then to Sicily. In one letter, Russell told Katherine of his tedious routine: "After the invasion becomes an assured success, we still stick around to continue the unloading. The small boats and transports, as well as much of the fleet or all of it, departs and leaves the situation in the capable hands of the LCTs and the Army port battalion. . . . Eventually, we get control of the ports and work them until they are made navigable or usable by the larger ships, then we go home." During the invasion's early hours, he wrote, the Germans "bother the hell out of us, coming in from everywhere. An average loss at a beach would be one and a half Liberty ships, one LST, and some damage to a cruiser or a destroyer. . . . Sometimes their planes come in from all sides at once, like mosquitoes, but they are damned inaccurate and the low level ones dare not try to fly all the way thru [sic] a formation. They would never get through and they know it."[6]

For months, Russell's LCT flotilla hopscotched the Mediterranean as the Allies invaded the beaches of northern Africa and Sicily, finally reaching Palermo on the northwestern coast of Sicily. Unlike the soldier storming ashore, gun blazing, an LCT crewman's life was drudgery. "I have been merely a freight barge operator with nothing to do but run back and forth endlessly loading and unloading ships," he complained to Katherine. "Little Creek was much harder work than this." Such was Russell's idleness that later in the month he wrote to Katherine, "I really feel at times that I am getting the vacation that I needed after three years intensive work in law school." Russell again vented his frustration several months later, lamenting to Katherine, he felt "cheated that I am not getting more action at the moment, but as I always said, the guys planning things probably know where I am and figure that they would prefer me to be doing exactly what I am. Anyway, I'll be there whenever they want me."[7]

Ordered back to Bizerte, Tunisia, after the Palermo invasion, Russell finally received good news. In October 1943 he was given command of an LCT. His elation over commanding his own craft was soon deflated. "I hadn't seen what I was going to get," he said, explaining that each LCT in the flotilla released to Russell one man. This meant, Russell suspected, that each officer would relinquish his most undesirable crewman. "Oh, shit, that's what you call a Hobson's Choice crew," Russell muttered. The suspicions were accurate. His crew, he complained to Katherine, was a group of "loud, ornery characters who often turned the boat into a resounding din of blasphemy and filthy speech."[8]

Delighted to have his own command, despite the crew, and eager to plunge into battle, Russell waited for orders. Unfortunately, an invasion was not in the navy's plans. His flotilla was ordered back to Arzew. Even then, this simple order was impossible to fulfill. Russell never made it, nearly losing his LCT in rough seas after its engines flooded. The wait for repairs in Sicily was interminable. "The war goes on and Harbor Harry still sits where he had since time immorial [sic]," he wrote Katherine. Finally, after months in Palermo, the repairs were complete. Russell's LCT headed to Anzio, but arrived after the main invasion forces had stormed ashore. For three months, he simply resumed his usual drudgery, unloading ships following beach invasions at Anzio, Civitavecchia, and Piombino.[9]

Breaking the dull routine in March of 1944 was Russell's promotion to lieutenant junior grade and news later in the month of the birth of his first child, a daughter whom Katherine named Rita Katherine. "I am the proud father of a big baby girl and the proudest man in the world," he wrote to Katherine upon receiving the news. "I am so proud that I have been passing out cigars all day." The next day, he wrote Katherine again, offering his advice on child raising: "It is a good idea not to spoil her. You know that children do spoil easily." Although he never revealed any disappointment that his first child had been a girl, Russell had devoted considerable thought to what he would have named the child had it been a boy, writing to Katherine before the birth:

> I have always been crazy about my father and desired to honor his name. I know that you do not think that Huey is a very refined sounding name— possibly a deviation from Hugh. Yet, I do not so much like the name of Russell for the child because that would make a junior of him. . . . Naturally, I would not want to give the child a persecution complex by having him run into a lot of controversy over his grandfather's politics, but the name Long is enough to assure him of just about as much of it anyway. . . . In the end, the child, if a boy, will have to stand on his own personality. He should always be proud of his grandfather and so I think he would like the name.[10]

By the spring of 1944, Russell sensed his lust for battle would soon be satisfied. "I expect to be 'in there' sometime after you receive this letter," he predicted to Katherine. In another letter, he diminished his role in the war after Katherine wrote to say she had met one of his navy buddies who praised his heroics in Sicily. "My action was not so outstanding," he replied. "My boat was never been directly hit. I can't tell all the details of it, but it was more of a case of getting a burning smoke screen pot overboard and getting a badly burned hand in the process, but not serious enough to leave a scar." Assuring Katherine he was not longing to win any medals, he wrote he would "be quite content to come back with a whole body and mind."[11]

Despite reassuring Katherine, Russell was ebullient when he received instructions to join the invasion forces ordered ashore on the south of France in August 1944. But when he discovered his LCT would hit the beach on the eighth wave, he complained vociferously to his flotilla commander, as he recalled:

> I said, 'You've got guys here who were in the first wave in Sicily and the first at Salerno and whatever . . . but it's not fair for whoever the guys were in the first wave in these other invasions to be in the first wave in this one, because frankly I think I'm just as good a man as they are and it's only fair that someone else be in the first wave, specifically me. I think I ought to be in the first wave.' [He said,] 'Do you really mean that?' I said, 'Yeah.' So the next damn thing you know, he gave me some orders that I'm going to be in front of the first wave. . . . I never did tell the guys that I'd volunteered. That's a good way to find yourself dead in your bed.[12]

On the day of the invasion, as his LCT headed for the shores of Cavalier sur-Mer on the French Riviera, Russell and his navigation officer began feuding. They were unable to agree on whether they were on a course for the right or the left flank marker, a vitally important distinction considering the Germans had heavily mined the right flank of the invasion area. "Now, you are headed right for the right flank marker," the navigation officer reported. When Russell disagreed with the assessment, the officer responded, "I'm a specialist. That's what I'm doing here. That's why I'm with you." "Well," Russell shot back, "you may be a specialist, but I've lived for a couple of years on these damn beaches. I know a right flank marker from a left flank marker and that's a left flank marker."[13]

Eventually, Russell relented, deferring to the navigator's judgment. "We swing out and it turns out I was right all the time," Russell recalled. "So, we just went right through the mine field onto shore. We went through water that hadn't been swept at all, not even a pretense of sweeping." As the boat crept through the treacherous waters, Russell's eyes caught the shattered remains of a small American boat. "That thing had been blown to smithereens. It had been blown to a thousand pieces. And so, obviously, everybody on it had died. That guy took what would have been my mine."[14]

Scattered, ineffective gunfire pelted the water around Russell's LCT as it approached the beach. Battleships offshore had destroyed German artillery guns in the inland hills, leaving only one machine-gun nest several hundred yards from where Russell's boat landed. "That damn guy was hitting everybody there," said Russell, who sent one of his men ashore to place a smoke pot to obliterate the German's view. As the battle raged around him, Russell quickly realized his boat could go no farther. It had lodged against a sand bar, still several hundred feet from the beach. While his men could reach the shore on foot, he knew it would be impossible for them to drive the jeeps and most of the other equipment through the water. Russell quickly concluded the only way to unload his cargo was to send a bulldozer, the sole piece of equipment which could possibly make it through the water, to shore. From the beach, the bulldozer would tow in the jeeps and other equipment, as Russell recalled:

> At that point, I was standing in the pilot house that sort of sticks up atop that thing. And there's a little trap door. You can lift it up and you can have a helmet on and stick your head out there. I told them to get out there in that water with those mooring lines, through a megaphone. They didn't move. And I realized why they didn't move. Here I was, standing inside a pilot house that was made of steel, that had some armor plating around it, and telling them to get out in that water.
>
> I climbed up on top of the pilot house and stood all by myself, like a sore thumb on top of the pilot house, and took that thing and said, 'You sons of bitches, take those ropes and get out there! Hook those things up to those trucks and tow them in. Get the ropes. We're going to tow them all in.' And I said, 'We're not going to leave this beach until we get them in here.'
>
> Those guys could look at me standing up on top of that pilot house and say, 'Well, damn it, that must be pretty safe, because he's still there and you'd think that any guy doing that, standing all by himself on top of that damn pilot house, all alone up there, just on top of the whole thing, right alongside the flag, you'd think a damn fool doing that must be pretty safe, because it wouldn't take but one man with a rifle to knock him down.' They got out in the water and did that, and I got my ass back inside the pilot house were I came from.[15]

When his men finished unloading the boat, they dropped the mooring lines and returned to the boat, ready to abandon the beach. Once again, Russell astounded his crew, ordering them back to retrieve the lines they would need to unload more ships. "So they went back and got the mooring lines," Russell said. "Mind you, that's where I really took a chance I shouldn't have taken. They went out and got the mooring lines, pulled them back and we backed off. And just as we backed off—bloom! bloom! bloom! That damn gun hit just exactly where we had been. I swear, we backed out just in the nick of time." While the landing was not the last Russell would execute—the navy awarded him four battle stars for bravery—it was the most memorable. Almost fifty years afterward, his memories of that day remained vivid and intense. Later, Russell's flotilla was dispatched briefly to Corsica and then to Tunisia. In September 1944 came welcome orders for Russell to return to Camp Bradford at Little Creek, Virginia, where he served until discharged in November 1945.[16]

The mere boys who the United States sent across the world to fight for their country returned as men, their experiences having matured many of them beyond their years. The most fortunate, like Russell, arrived home intact, without physical scars or crippling injuries. Nonetheless, the war, and its horrors, had not left him unchanged. "I think I have learned a lot about people," he confessed in a letter to Katherine in 1944. "I have lost some of my respect for women in general and men, too, after some of the widespread infidelity and debauchery I have seen, but I have come to respect good women and men more than before."[17]

Katherine immediately detected one sign of war's impact. "Russell came back with a distinctly better appetite for liquor." Russell confessed this to Katherine before he returned, writing, "[A]nyone who advocates prohibition during a time of war must be stupid from all I can see. I know that for the past few days what liquor I have had has done wonders for me in relieving the tension in the work I am now doing." At the time, neither Katherine nor Russell could have known the ultimate repercussions of Russell's newfound wartime reliance on the bottle.[18]

6

HUEY P. LONG HAD COME ALIVE

$\mathcal{A}$LTHOUGH HE WOULD NOT ADMIT IT THEN, Russell's feet hit American soil running for public office. Shortly before his discharge, he returned to Louisiana for several weeks. One day, he called on New Orleans mayor Robert Maestri, a staunch ally of his father and a close family friend. It was a routine meeting. Nonetheless, it attracted considerable attention from local reporters who correctly deduced Russell had politics in mind. An Associated Press account reported city hall "chorused that Russell was 'just like his dad.' " Emerging from Maestri's office, Russell dismissed the significance of his euphoric reception. "Don't run me for office yet. This is just a friendly visit. No politics. I'm still in the war, you know."[1]

While eschewing any interest in politics, the fires of political ambition burned brightly inside, stoked by a lifetime in the maelstrom of Louisiana politics. Despite what he told the reporters, Russell knew it was not long before his name appeared on a Louisiana ballot. For years, Russell knew his fate was politics. If he succeeded and served well, public service was the surest way to disprove the critics' harsh assessment of Huey Long. Russell resolved his political career would be proof that, as the maxim affirmed, the fruit never falls far from the tree.

Twenty-eight when released from the navy, Russell returned home for good in November 1945. Immediately, he devoted himself to winning social and political acceptance in Baton Rouge. In the state capital, his notoriety alone did him little good. Much of the city had despised his father, particularly its business community. "Nobody liked the Longs in Baton Rouge," observed one of Russell's childhood friends. At one time, Huey Long biographer William Ivy Hair noted, Baton Rouge was populated by "hundreds of mostly upper-class men and women who talked, sometimes openly, of armed revolt and assassination." Understanding the hostility that his family name engendered, Russell resolved to certify his independence. Resting on his family notoriety, an asset in many parts of the state, would do little for him in Baton Rouge.[2]

Russell's sensitivity about his family's reputation was apparent in how he established his law practice. On his first furlough to Louisiana, Russell also called on a law school classmate, Gordon West, an attorney for the state Revenue Department. Although the two graduated together and shared moot court honors, they were only casual acquaintances. Their friendship blossomed in Sicily, when they encountered one another during a movie aboard a ship docked in Licata. Homesickness and common ties to Louisiana and LSU sparked a fast friendship.

In uniform when he saw West in Baton Rouge, Russell was en route to an assignment in San Francisco, eventually cut short by the war's end. After reminiscing briefly about school and the war, Russell asked West why he was not practicing law. "I can't find an office," West replied, explaining that office space for young attorneys was scarce in Baton Rouge. Russell immediately offered a solution to West's problem. He proposed they share the office space he had secured in a downtown building. As they discussed the proposition, West had a better idea. "Why don't we really practice law together?" he proposed. "Why don't we form a partnership?" West startled Russell with the suggestion. "That's the nicest thing I've had said to me," he answered, explaining to West he would never have asked a friend to form a partnership. Incredulous, West asked why. "Because I just would have felt that maybe I would be a millstone around their neck," Russell replied.[3]

Out of their one-room office, partitioned down the middle, Russell and West soon opened for business. It was a spartan operation. They performed every menial task any larger firm would have assigned to secretaries and law clerks. The greatest hardship was the size of the tiny office, which barely afforded enough room for one attorney. "To get from the front of the desk around to your seat at the back of the desk," West recalled, "you had to kind of turn sideways and slip down the side of the desk."[4]

While Russell cultivated credentials as a plaintiff's attorney, representing indigent clients to obtain trial experience, West focused on enhancing his skills in business law. The fledgling enterprise was scarcely profitable. Bar association rules prevented the new firm from advertising its creation. "You were just supposed to just open your office and sit and hope that somebody knew you were there and might drop by," said West. Russell's income by 1947, after more than a year and a half, was about $250 a month. Fortunately, his inheritance, the Win or Lose Company—now called Independent Oil and Gas—was producing revenues; his monthly dividend averaged about six hundred dollars.[5]

Like any aspiring politician, Russell devoted considerable time to civic interests. He was an active member of the Amvets, a veterans' organization. He enlisted in the Jaycees and the Boys Clubs of America and was chairman of the Junior Chamber of Commerce. He joined the Baton Rouge Country Club and began fraternizing with many who, if not his father's bitter enemies, were certainly not among his greatest admirers.

While struggling to build the law practice, Russell devoted abundant energy to defending his father against what he considered unfair and vicious attacks by a hostile national media. In August 1946, he corresponded with a local writer, expressing willingness to help with a biography of Huey Long "to correct many of the misimpressions in the minds of the general public." In December, *Life* magazine published a lengthy article that cast Huey Long in a most unfavorable light. Author of the 1942 novel *Sun in Capricorn*, Hamilton Basso reviewed four novels based on Huey's life. The nine-page essay reviewed Long's stormy career and examined the treatment of the Long character in each book. While somewhat impartial, Basso's conclusions were surely offensive to Long admirers in general and Russell in particular. Describing his own literary approach to Long, Basso saw him as "a stripped-down example of the dictatorial idea whose only equipment other than an animal-like cunning was a brutal energy and the ability to sway thousands of people by the sound that rhetoric makes." Basso's conclusion was most unkind, depicting Long as a malevolent character. "He would always serve to remind us," he wrote, "that heaven itself was once threatened and that our democracy, which is a long way from being heaven, is threatened as never before—even though he, like Lucifer, has been hurled down."[6]

"It hurt Russell terribly when he read that," said Gordon West. Furious over his father's denigration in a widely read publication, Russell fired off several letters to *Life*'s editors, demanding equal space for a rebuttal. "I venture that no man of our times has been more abused, vilified and misrepresented by the American press to its reading public than my father," he wrote. "Murder is not enough. . . . His praiseworthy deeds must be obscured or made to appear as the means of fostering fiendish purpose. He must live in history as a legendary character of the underworld."[7]

When *Life* refused to print his lengthy defense, unedited as he demanded, Russell offered five thousand dollars, "which is more than I can afford, for adequate space to print an answer to your malicious misrepresentation." *Life* refused, but offered to publish a shorter, edited version. Russell balked at this proposition and continued his attacks on *Life*. He even appealed to *Reader's Digest* to print his rejoinder to the article, explaining, "I feel I am entitled to at least being heard in defense of my father, since he is not here to defend himself," adding he "would prefer that you print nothing unless you print it all." *Reader's Digest* rejected the letter. Although several Louisiana newspapers published his defense, he remained disgruntled. Finally, Russell enlisted the aid of Louisiana senator John Overton, who placed the letter in the *Congressional Record.*[8]

Occupied with the occasional defense of his father, his civic affairs and the law practice, Russell kept a constant eye on the state's political scene. He waited for the right moment to make his move. His opportunity came sooner than he had expected. After several years in political exile, Russell's uncle, Earl K. Long, was back, running for governor in the Democratic party primary. Huey's younger brother, Earl was elected lieutenant governor in 1936, the year following Huey's assassination. The next year, Earl ascended to the governorship when Governor Richard Leche was imprisoned on corruption charges. Seeking the office on his own in 1940, Earl lost to Sam Jones, a reformer who vowed to stamp out all vestiges of Longism. "I'm not running against a dead man," Jones said of the Long regime, which enjoyed substantial power in the state. "I am running against a gang of rascals as live as any gang that ever lived, and I'm running to clean out every one of them." Jones charged Earl was "captain of the ship of state" during the scandals. Although Earl led the pack of five candidates in the Democratic primary by a wide margin, Jones narrowly captured the nomination in the runoff and easily won the election. Having endured another loss for lieutenant governor in the meantime, Earl had wandered the political wilderness for too long. He thirsted for the governor's office in his own right. It was a proposition with interesting and troubling possibilities for Russell.[9]

Other than their populist appeal and their physical similarities, Earl and Huey Long could not have been more different. Earl was a simple, plainspoken man of raspy voice and down-home charm. Huey preferred one-hundred-dollar tailored suits. Earl's wardrobe was store-bought. Although both were born in rural Winnfield, Huey was more at home in the city—Washington, Baton Rouge, or New Orleans. Earl loved his "pea-patch" farm in Winnfield. He escaped there whenever possible, tending his garden, visiting with neighbors, and hunting wild hogs in the nearby woods.

Members of a family renowned for its spiteful squabbles, Russell and Earl, like Huey and Earl, had not always enjoyed warm relations. In 1943, as Earl stumped the state in his ill-fated lieutenant governor's campaign, he received a letter from Russell, in Sicily, describing his war experiences and wishing Earl "the very best of luck" in the election. Earl released the letter to the press and printed it on thousands of campaign fliers, which he distributed throughout the state. When he learned how Earl had used the letter without permission, Russell wrote Katherine complaining that Earl "does not give a damn for me aside from what little political value I may have." Furthermore, Russell said, "[H]e never answered my letter. Pretty small way to be, isn't it?"[10]

Three years later, Earl still needed Russell. He was not above pressuring him for his help. This time, Earl knew he needed more than a letter. His name was Long, but Earl was rarely in favor with a sizable portion of his brother's supporters who still had vivid memories of his belligerent break with Huey. In 1931, Earl had insisted on running for lieutenant governor. Huey had already selected the Long ballot and had placed another man in the spot Earl wanted. Huey pleaded with Earl to withdraw. Headstrong and defiant, he ran anyway and was badly beaten. In the process, Earl opened deep wounds with his vicious attacks on his older brother, whom he called "a yellow coward." The incident sparked a protracted public feud between the two brothers, which culminated when Earl told a congressional committee that Huey had accepted a ten-thousand-dollar bribe from a Louisiana utility.

The brothers had reportedly made peace before Huey's death, but their reconciliation could not erase the headlines created by years of hard feelings and public animosities. This rift had troubled Earl in the 1940 governor's race, leading him to sputter in exasperation at one point, "God knows I'm sorry Huey and I fell out. What more can I say?" Nonetheless, the breech lingered in many voters' minds. Russell's longtime friend and aide, Buddy Gill, summed it up best: "We were Huey Long people and Huey Long people didn't like Earl Long people." To many voters, especially the Long forces, Earl had been a traitor. He desperately needed

Russell's support to recapture the credibility he lacked with Huey's still-loyal and massive constituency. [11]

Russell resisted joining Earl's campaign. He was comfortable in his law practice, content to wait for the right moment to enter politics, on his terms, not Earl's. As Russell recalled:

> I had thought dating back to the days when I was a freshman in college that I would try and follow in my father's footsteps, that I would run for governor of the state and then if successful at that, having served for four years, I would run for the United States Senate as my father did and proceed to carry on his tradition. . . . Now, the one thing that was difficult about that problem was that the dates did not fit. . . . At the time of the governor's race, I would have been twenty-nine years old and I would have been twenty-nine years old at the time of the inauguration. In other words, assuming I had run and been elected, I'd be about ten months shy of being the constitutional age for the job. . . . I'd have to wait until I was thirty-three to run for governor. [12]

A four-year wait to seek public office was not an attractive prospect. Therefore, Russell turned his sights to Washington and the Senate seats occupied by Allen Ellender and John Overton, two offices that presented perplexing choices. Ellender, one of Huey Long's closest allies in the Louisiana legislature, faced reelection in 1948. Overton, too, was Huey's friend and served with him in the Senate. In poor health and known to be a heavy drinker, Overton shocked Louisiana's political community when he sought reelection in 1944. Despite the absence of any enthusiastic support, most political observers thought he would run again in 1950.

These scenarios left Russell only three options: run against Ellender, wait two years to challenge Overton, or seek his open seat should he retire. In the summer of 1947, Russell was impatient. He favored the first option, an audacious decision considering his family's long relationship with Ellender. As Russell remembered: "At the time when I started out, before I decided what I was going to do, I had thought that I might run for Ellender's seat, because that's the one that came open. . . . I thought, hell, I can't wait forever for those guys to die. Hell, at some point, if I'm going to be something, I've got to go ahead and run. So, I looked upon either one of those seats, [as] seats that I had a right to run for if I wanted to." Realistically, and with more than forty years' perspective, Russell admitted, "I could not have run against Ellender. Earl Long would have told me, 'You just can't do that.' And I would have bowed to his wishes." [13]

While Russell quietly plotted his political future, Uncle Earl did the same, with a most distinctive and devious strategy. Earl reasoned the key to winning the governor's race was ensuring his chief opponent was a candidate dynamic enough to reach the runoff with him, but too weak to win. He did not search far to find his old nemesis, former governor Sam Jones, the reformer who vanquished Earl almost ten years earlier. Jones narrowly denied Earl the nomination, but had not celebrated the victory unscathed. In usual style, Earl went down swinging. Painting Jones as a patrician and charging, among other offenses, that his opponent smelled sweet and wore pajamas. "He's high hat Sam . . . the guy that pumps perfume under his arms," Earl sneered in one of his famous verbal muggings. During his term, Jones had enacted scores of reforms, creating a civil service and decentralizing state power away from the governor's office. To some—especially the Long faction, which he zealously persecuted—Jones's performance was more accurately described as vengeful reform. His crime commissions badgered the Long faction, with little result, and left him many enemies who maintained Jones used the spoils system as extensively as his predecessors. Earl Long biographers Michael Kurtz and Morgan Peoples maintained that Jones had "fired more state employees than did Huey Long, and he appointed more of his followers to state positions than did the Kingfish."[14]

Generally considered honest and circumspect, Jones was not a charming person, nor was he known for keen political instincts. A man of few words, he bluntly spoke his mind, regardless of injured feelings. Earl understood Jones had a significant following, but not nearly enough to win a runoff. With three attractive reform candidates already running for governor—south Louisiana congressman James Morrison, New Orleans mayor DeLesseps Morrison, and north Louisiana state judge Robert Kennon—Earl badly wanted "high-hat Sam" to run. The thought of facing Morrison or Kennon in a runoff was disconcerting. Earl believed both had potential as formidable obstacles in his acquisition of the governorship. But, he correctly reasoned, none could edge Jones for a runoff spot. "Earl did all he could to get Jones into the race rather than have a head-to-head race with Bob Kennon," said one of Earl's allies. "Earl realized that Kennon was a fresh face and he was a war hero."[15]

This was not the only time Earl had employed this Machiavellian political strategy. Near the close of the 1939 campaign, Earl urged voters who planned to vote against him to "vote for Sam Jones, because you'll be throwing away your votes if you give them to [Jimmy] Noe and [Jimmy] Morrison." This time, the missing link in Earl's clever strategy was Jones, who had no plans to run. Ever the resourceful conniver, Earl despatched several surrogates to Jones who urged him to make the race. State representative Ragan Madden of Ruston was one of Earl's co-conspirators, sent to lure Jones into the race. Jones "was very egotistical, he was gullible," Madden recalled. "He liked that job being governor. So, it wasn't too hard to talk him into it." In almost no time, Jones sensed a groundswell of support. He was itching to be governor again. Once, during the campaign, Earl asked Buddy Gill for his prediction of the Baton Rouge vote. "Well, governor, you're not going to get anything, not enough to wad a shotgun," Gill responded. "That's great," Earl shot back. "Be sure you get 'em to Sam Jones." Madden said he encountered Earl the day after Jones announced his candidacy. Earl, he said, "was the happiest fellow you ever saw in your life." Years later, even Jones conceded Earl tricked him, but by the time he discovered the skulduggery it was too late to with-draw.[16]

Having lured Jones into the race, Earl turned to the next phase of his campaign—enlisting Russell's help. Earl made regular visits to Russell's law office throughout the spring and early summer of 1947, cajoling his nephew to join the race. From the beginning, Russell had serious doubts. To run successfully for governor or senator, his best chance rested in selling himself as an energetic, new breed of Long—a breath of fresh political air. This could happen only when he was the sole Long on the political landscape. Earl's presence complicated matters. Of one north Louisiana politician, Earl once said, "He's dead, but he just won't lay down." At the time, Russell believed that applied to Earl.

Earl did not rely on his persuasion alone to prod Russell into the race. One high-ranking surrogate, sent by Earl, told Russell, "If you help Earl and he loses, that will be the end of Earl with the Long people. People will rally around you someday if you are interested in politics. You'll win even if Earl loses, but if Earl gets elected, you'll get the credit for electing him."[17] Earl even applied pressure on Russell through law partner Gordon West, who feared Russell would abandon the law practice. West remembered:

One time Earl came to the office. Russell wasn't there. He asked me to go across the street with him to the Elks Club, which was located right across the street from the Roumain Building, and have a cup of coffee. I went across there with Earl and Earl told me then that he wanted Russell to come out and help him. He said, 'He won't listen to me. I asked him and he won't listen to me.' And he said, 'I know he thinks the world of you and he will listen to what you say and I would consider it a favor if you would urge him to come out and help me in the campaign.' And then he kind of made the mistake of saying that, 'All he has got to do is name what he wants and he can have it if he will come out and help me.' Well, I told Russell about the conversation and Russell blew his stack. And he said, 'I can have what I want? I'm not for sale!'[18]

Despite those clumsy tactics, Russell gave Earl a proper hearing. He even prepared two lists, on one listing all the reasons in favor of his involvement and, on the other, the reasons for refusing Earl's entreaties. One of the affirmative reasons, which eventually proved to be the most persuasive, was Russell's belief that if Earl lost, traditional Long supporters might look elsewhere for a new leader. Most likely, they would gravitate toward Democratic congressman James Morrison, the rising political star from Hammond and one of Earl's detractors. Russell reasoned that if Morrison were governor, many of the Long disciples might shift their allegiance. Were this the case, Morrison, not Uncle Earl, would hold the key to Russell's political future.

Russell essentially reached his decision the day Earl paid one of his regular visits. As he watched Earl settle into his chair, he was prepared to resist another series of increasingly persuasive arguments. Earl, Russell said, "made a very good, logical argument that I ought to get into it and help him. And after he left, I pulled out that list, and I'll be darned if he hadn't hit all five of the reasons I had listed that I should consider supporting him. . . . Just exactly in that order. So he was really reading my mind in terms of the reasons I ought to support him." From that point, the question was not whether Russell would campaign, but how much. Earl demanded complete commitment, while Russell promised only one month, not wanting to abandon the law practice. They compromised. Russell gave Earl his choice of the one month he needed Russell most. Earl chose the first, no doubt knowing he would not let Russell quit the campaign until after the election.[19]

To a newcomer, Louisiana politics in 1948, as always, was bewildering. Almost completely Democratic, it was nonetheless a two-party state, bitterly divided among so-called Longs and anti-Longs. Long candidates could count on a solid 25 to 30 percent base of support at the beginning of any statewide race. Point by point, they methodically acquired the percentages needed for victory. They did not always win by overwhelming majorities. They usually just won. This traditional 25 percent Long base was a crucial element in Earl's quest for the governor's mansion. Without it, there was no sense in running at all. Possibly Russell's presence on the stump, and Rose Long's endorsement, would be enough to make voters forget the brotherly feud. To be sure, Russell did not miss an opportunity to set the record straight whenever someone challenged Earl's loyalty to Huey.

Writing to a north Louisiana supporter of his father, who still had vivid memories of the two brothers' fight, Russell said: "I cannot go along with you in endlessly blaming Earl Long for his differences with my father. There is a lot more to the story than a lot of people know." Earl, he said, "has learned his lesson about discussing his differences with my father openly, and he has said the last unkind thing he will ever say against his brother Huey Long." While forceful, it was not a ringing endorsement of Earl's allegiance to his father's cause. Russell could not deny the existence of the rift. He could only claim the wounds had healed. Russell's brother, Palmer, maintained Russell's effort required substantial alteration of the truth. Another campaign associate, who knew Huey and Earl well, agreed. "He was lying. [Huey and Earl] hadn't made up," he maintained.[20]

Perhaps as effective in the amelioration was Russell's stunning resemblance to his father. Large crowds turned out for their half-dozen rallies each day. While many came to hear Earl's fiery and entertaining speeches, equal numbers were drawn in curiosity of this young son of Huey Long, who looked and talked so much like his father. "It was like Huey coming back to life," noted one of Russell's campaign aides. Like Huey when he spoke, Russell's arms waved wildly, frantically, reminding some of a windmill out of control. Quieter and less intense than his father, to many people Russell was, nonetheless, Huey Long incarnate. "The old Huey Long worshippers saw such a physical resemblance to his father," said Earl's lieutenant governor, Bill Dodd, "that for a short time they transferred their love for the father to the son." The sight of elderly men and women, sobbing as they emerged from the crowd to kiss Russell's hand was not uncommon. Writing of Russell's likeness to Huey, a New Orleans columnist wrote, "[T]he resemblance is literally startling." The first time he saw Russell, the writer recalled, he "gasped in momentary astonishment because the figure looked so much like Huey's."[21]

One man who accompanied Russell as he campaigned recalled his initial speeches from the stump were not always received warmly: "Russell got better as the campaign went along. He would get up and say families have fights, but they get back together. And his daddy and Uncle Earl had made up—things like that, which were real effective." Hoping they had dispensed with the estrangement question, Earl and Russell gradually devoted more time to touting Earl's populist, liberal platform, designed to appeal to the traditional Huey Long constituency—working-class whites.[22]

Earl believed he lost the 1940 governor's race because Sam Jones outpromised him. This time, he would not be outdone in the promising department. He dubbed his program "do-everythingism," a platform on which Earl promised a monthly fifty-dollar pension for the elderly, a $2,400 minimum annual teacher salary, more and better highways, a trade school for each of the state's sixty-four parishes, a homestead property tax exemption of five thousand dollars, bonuses for war veterans, better hospitals, and hot lunches for all public school students. Earl bragged that the state under a Long administration would be "the like of which has never been seen before in the history of this state." Jones, meanwhile, saw the race as a repeat of the 1940 contest, believing he could win by dwelling on Earl's association with the 1939 scandals. He did not realize that, in political time, the eight-year-old scandals and the outrage that accompanied them, were ancient history.[23]

Earl's was an ambitious program, requiring millions of additional dollars. While he refused to discuss this aspect of his platform, publicly or privately, Russell was troubled by the consequences of making grandiose commitments, without contemplating the methods to finance them. Finally, one day early in the campaign, he voiced his worries to Earl. "That's all fine, if we have the money for it," Russell argued. "But how are we going to pay for all of this?" Earl ignored Russell, refusing to acknowledge the question. Several weeks later, Russell renewed his inquiry. Exasperated, Earl finally barked: "Let's wait and see if we get elected. If we don't get elected, we ain't got to worry about none of that. If we're elected, we'll figure out a way." He forbade Russell or anyone associated with the campaign to mention the possibility of taxes.[24]

Earl may have needed Russell to ingratiate himself with Huey's flock. He did not require help in attracting an audience. Earl's bizarre personality was enough to draw a good-sized crowd in any Louisiana town. An Earl Long rally was a sideshow, medicine show, and vaudeville act rolled up into one countrified extravaganza. As sound trucks blared the news of Earl's arrival, the candidate and his entourage rumbled into town, their automobiles kicking up dust. Eager fans flocked toward him as he emerged from the car's backseat. Earl immediately set about distributing turkeys, hams, watermelons, beer, and anything else he might have bought along the way. He threw coins to the children and said, "a quarter to the white kids and a nickel to the niggers." In his unique, raspy tones, he attacked enemies with such vigor and outrageous humor few bothered to ask the question foremost on Russell's mind: how to pay for the promises he made. Governor Jimmie Davis was "a liar and a thief, and he's got diabetes!" Of Bob Kennon's prominent ears, he observed: "Judge Kennon has perfectly good ears. He can stand in a courthouse in Opelousas and hear a dollar bill drop in Ville Platte." He mocked New Orleans mayor DeLesseps Morrison, a Jones supporter, as "Dela-soups," and scoffed he was "smoother than a peeled onion." Earl was a common man, evidenced by shoes with worn soles which he proudly displayed to delighted audiences. He wore droppy white cotton socks and his baggy old pants were held high over his belly by suspenders. A loosened, flowered tie usually dangled over his white, cotton short-sleeved shirt. As he shouted from the stage or the back of a pickup truck, Earl constantly mopped his brow with a handkerchief soaked in Coca Cola. One southern historian who observed Earl's antics with amusement called him "a wheezy, Dixified Mad King Ludwig of Bavaria." He looked like a one-man disaster. In his prime, however, Earl Long related to voters like few politicians in history. [25]

Typical was Earl's down-home explanation of his desire to be governor: "You live in the best house I ever lived in. You have servants and you don't have to buy even your food. Every time you open the door someone hands you a turkey or a blanket or all that free stuff. Well, I like that free stuff." Those in the crowd no doubt nodded knowingly, sharing Earl's fascination with the trappings of power, as he finished the thought. "Sure, I want to be governor. Only one person in more'n two million people can be governor of this state. Think about that. Ain't that an honor?" [26]

While Earl touted his program on the stump, Russell temporarily set aside his concerns about the financing of the plan and went to work trying to sell it. His efforts included several statewide radio speeches. In one speech, he noted charges the old-age pension would take money "out of the channels of commerce and business." Far from it, Russell asserted. "This program will put a great amount of additional money into circulation," he said, ignoring his own worries about the taxes required to pay the pensions. In another radio speech, Russell painted his utopian portrait of Louisiana under Earl Long: "When Earl is governor, the old folks will be properly cared for, the children will have a first-class free hot-lunch program (and) the charity hospitals of the state will be open to all people in need of help." [27]

Despite Earl's activity and his auspicious program, the campaign had not caught fire. The state's newspapers and most public officials, in Earl's words, "gave me the cold shoulder." The month to which Russell and Earl agreed expired and Russell prepared to return to his law practice. "You can't do that," Earl said. "What you're doing here is a lot more important than what you'd be doing back in your law office. Besides the people like you. You've got to stay." Russell was actually enjoying the campaign and the favorable way the crowds reacted to him. It did not require much persuasion from Earl for Russell to postpone his return to the law practice.[28]

Earl's fledgling campaign suffered a minor setback early on, when Senator John Overton endorsed Jones. Russell was stunned that his father's former ally would side with a man who so thoroughly vilified Huey Long. "How could you bring yourself to support Sam Jones?" he implored in a letter to Overton. "He represents the group that sought Huey Long's assassination." Although he never mailed the letter, his anger with Overton gushed forth in a radio speech several days later. "We are informed that many of the same men who said [Overton] was unfit to serve in the United States Senate are laughing up their sleeves at statements they are getting the old boy to make against Earl Long." Overton was not the only major public figure supporting Jones against Earl. Incumbent governor Jimmie Davis threw his weight behind Jones in the late innings, as did New Orleans mayor DeLesseps Morrison.[29]

Jones, meanwhile, continued tying Earl to the Leche administration scandals. "We saw men commit suicide," said Jones, attempting to summon the outrage of eight years earlier, "saw officials resigning wholesale and heard newsboys crying on the corners, 'Buy a newspaper and see if you've been indicted.' " They may have been political enemies, but Russell and Jones shared a common perception: They believed the election was a referendum on Huey Long's legacy. In a statewide radio address just days before the election, Russell made headlines throughout the state with a dramatic defense, not of Earl, but of his father. Ignoring Jones, he attacked the New Orleans news media and unnamed "northern magazines" who he charged were waging "a slanderous campaign against my father." Addressing once again the feud between Earl and Huey, Russell said it was unfortunate "that brothers sometimes have a quarrel or a spat. When it happens, all they can do is shake hands and forget it. That is what Huey Long and Earl Long did sixteen years ago and my family doesn't care to hear any more about these differences." Given an opportunity to defend his father or Earl, Russell opted for his father. Rehashing a thirteen-year-old unsubstantiated charge of tax evasion lodged against Huey after his death, Russell said Huey's accusers were "blackmailing sharpshooters." He attacked the New Orleans' papers, charging that they opposed Huey because he "dared to fight their selfish and bigoted little clique." The newspapers "may print a quarter of a million copies of their prejudiced editorials every day," Russell added, "but they can't hurt my

father now. The great judge who heard Huey Long's case does not heed
half-truths and unfounded accusations."[30]

On election day in January, Earl led the field with 41 percent of the vote
to Jones's 23 percent. He made the runoff with the opponent he wanted
most. Kennon was a close third, with 23 percent, four points ahead of
Morrison, once considered a formidable candidate. A month later—almost
twenty years to the day after Huey was elected governor—Earl Long's
assumptions about Jones's vulnerability proved correct. Earl captured the
Democratic nomination, tantamount to victory, in a landslide.[31]

While Earl basked in the glory of his victory, some observers recognized one of the basic components of the Long triumph. Syndicated
columnist Robert Ruark wrote of Russell:

> He is the stone on which the resurgence of the Long party was based.
> Friends and enemies alike will tell you that Russell was greatly responsible for
> the top-heavy election of his uncle, Earl, as governor, in the recent victory
> over Sam Jones. What happened was that Russell, looking like Huey and talking
> like Huey, healed an ancient breach between the brothers to the voters'
> satisfaction. When he took the stump in the last elections, it was as much as if
> Huey P. Long had come alive again.[32]

Palmer Long, noting his brother's role in fabricating the reconciliation,
phrased it more directly. "That was important as winning or losing. If we
hadn't supported him, he wouldn't have won—no way." Sensitive to Earl's
feelings, Russell claimed his credit for the victory in private, content that
the positive depiction of his role would increase his political capital. Shortly
after the election he bragged in a letter to a navy buddy "[A] lot of people
in Louisiana feel I deserve a great amount of the credit." As Russell soon
learned, he would receive much more credit for Uncle Earl's success than
he ever wanted.[33]

7

UNCLE EARL'S BAGGAGE: THE FIRST CAMPAIGN

*T*HE CAMPAIGN WAS OVER. Russell completed his job. Now, he planned to return to his law practice. "At present," he wrote to himself, "I do not know what my next move may be as far as politics. I am engaged in the practice of law and intend to stay in it for the next few years." Even so, he admitted that the race had whetted his political yearnings. "I came to feel a deep debt of gratitude to the people who stood loyally by my father," he wrote. Seeing the affection and emotion his father's memory continued to evoke, "I came to feel it more and more my duty to them I should pick up my father's end of the load."[1]

Despite the obligations he felt to Huey's followers, Russell told Uncle Earl that he would return to his law practice. Earl would not hear of it. He wanted Russell as his executive counsel. As he leaned on him through the campaign, Earl now needed Russell more than ever. Russell could help enact Earl's programs and, more important, pass the taxes to finance them. Russell politely, but firmly, declined the job. He told Earl that other men were much better qualified. Confident that he settled the matter, Russell soon learned that Earl planned to bypass more qualified candidates to appoint someone only a few years Russell's senior. The news raised Russell's ire. "I've changed my mind," he told Uncle Earl. He accepted the job.

On inauguration day, Earl took the oath of office on the steps of Louisiana's majestic capitol. In his speech, he outlined his program to thousands of enthusiastic supporters who flocked to town to witness the state's return to Longism. Earl did not disappoint them. In populist tones, he pledged the sick and the needy "will be welcomed in a place provided by a grateful state which recognizes the fact that we are our brother's keeper." The event was one of down-home extravagance. Following the ceremonies, the crowd retreated to LSU's football stadium, where Earl treated them to a feast of free buttermilk, soda pop, hot dogs, and cornbread.[2]

One of the inaugural's most poignant events took place the night before in the sunken gardens at Huey Long's grave on the capitol grounds. There, Russell and Earl presided over a brief ceremony to rekindle the spotlight atop the capitol that illuminated Huey's bronze likeness, dimmed since the beginning of World War II. Standing before the majestic statue, Russell proclaimed: "Let this be a symbol that none shall be too rich and none too poor, that the best able shall help the least fortunate—the needy and the underprivileged." The next day, Russell signed the decree ordering the light to shine continuously—his first act as executive counsel.[3]

The inaugural celebration had barely ended three days later when news came that Huey Long's old ally, Senator John Overton, had died in Washington after a lengthy illness. The moment he received the news, Russell knew he would run for Overton's seat. Perhaps he should have been more diffident. When Earl asked if he would consider running for the office, Russell responded, "Hell, I *am* running." Russell's cocksure response offended Earl, who expected his nephew to solicit his support as a supplicant. His injured feelings aside, Earl was eager to help Russell. Questioned by reporters, he said, "If Russell wants it, I'll support him."[4]

Earl's first order of business was who would fill Overton's seat until his successor was elected. Earl wanted to appoint Russell. At twenty-nine, however, he did not meet the constitutional thirty-year age requirement. Even so, there were precedents for such an appointment. Unsure about how they should proceed, Earl and Russell consulted Senator Ellender, who never knew of Russell's now-abandoned plan to challenge him. Ellender argued strongly against appointing Russell, warning that the age question might take months to resolve. Ellender counseled that a delay over his age would be an embarrassment to Russell and a political liability in the fall election to fill Overton's unexpired term. Instead, Ellender suggested that Earl appoint a trusted ally to keep the seat warm for Russell. Earl found his man in William C. Feazel, a fifty-four-year-old millionaire oilman from Monroe who had reportedly given more than three-hundred-thousand dollars to Earl's gubernatorial campaign. The Senate appointment was ample reward for Feazel's financial generosity. He readily agreed to step aside after the seven-and-a-half–month term.

The Senate election still months off, Russell focused on helping Earl enact his legislative program. His first assignment took him to Washington to lobby for additional federal funding for Louisiana's old-age pension program. After discussions with federal officials, Russell persuaded them to match the amount by which Louisiana planned to increase its pension. To Earl, Russell performed a fiscal miracle. To keep his promise to the elderly, the governor now needed half as much revenue as originally anticipated.

Although Earl inherited a state budget surplus of forty-five million dollars, the sum was not nearly enough to support his expansive, and expensive, campaign promises. His "do-everythingism" program would require extra revenue—eighty million dollars a year in additional taxes. To pay for the increased pensions, Earl proposed doubling the state sales tax and broadening its application. He asked lawmakers to hike the tax on beer 500 percent to finance his veterans' bonuses. For road improvements, he proposed increasing the gasoline tax by two cents a gallon. He wanted three-cent-a-pack tax on cigarettes to pay for his school lunch program. To give teachers a salary increase, he proposed tripling the severance tax on oil.

While some urban legislators and many of the state's newspapers opposed the plan, the general attitude toward Earl's proposal may have been best captured by the pro-Long *New Orleans Item*, which accepted the inevitable. In an editorial entitled, "It's What They Voted For," the *Item* said that because Earl's promises "were so overwhelmingly endorsed by Louisiana's voters last February, it is up to him to obey the mandate then given him." Said Earl in a statewide radio address: "If you look these taxes over carefully, you'll find that they won't hurt anybody."[5]

For help in persuading pliant legislators to approve the taxes, Earl leaned on Russell. Appearing before house and senate committees, Russell dutifully defended Earl's programs, even the ones he had opposed privately. To his chagrin, Russell became inextricably tied to the tax plan. One news story called him "the top administration spokesman before legislative committees which have the power to kill or advance bills." In the end, Russell's help was barely needed. The legislature dutifully passed every administration proposal by a combined total of 1,620 votes for and only eight against. Earl's election, observed then-representative Ragan Madden, had been a revolution, "a return of the Longs to power. And, of course, it swept in the legislature with him. He had a strong legislature back of him there. So, whatever he wanted, he got." Although the legislature approved each of the measures with little debate, the public soon realized the punch of the massive tax increases had never been mentioned during campaign.[6]

While he supported most of Earl's program, Russell thought one package of tax measures was particularly unwise. Earl used the legislature to punish New Orleans mayor DeLesseps Morrison. One of the state's most prominent anti-Longs, Morrison had supported Sam Jones in the governor's race and lustily attacked Earl. Now, Earl wanted revenge. While proposing to double the state's sales tax, Earl asked the legislature to allow New Orleans' to raise its sales tax rate by a meager one cent. Such a limitation would devastate the city's tax base, requiring Morrison to cancel many basic services. Earl arbitrarily fixed the city's portion of tobacco tax revenues at a meager $650,000, more than $1.3 million less than city residents paid in those taxes. When totaled, the tax measures would cost New Orleans more than $4.5 million a year.

By the time Earl finished bludgeoning the city, New Orleans bore 25 percent of the state's total tax burden, yet received less than 10 percent of the revenues. Another bill Earl rammed through the legislature gave the governor total control over the appointment of all New Orleans Dock Board commissions, robbing Morrison of important patronage. Earl also persuaded legislators to modify the composition of city government, further weakening the mayor's appointive powers.

Earl's vendetta, commonly known as "the rape of New Orleans," virtually destroyed his popularity overnight among the city's voters. Morrison, meanwhile, was elevated to hero status by local newspapers and the city's business community for bravely resisting Earl's reprisals. Russell and Lieutenant Governor Bill Dodd pleaded with Earl to abandon the plan, to no avail. His assault on New Orleans was inflicting serious political damage on Earl, not Morrison. Furthermore, the vendetta was hurting Russell, who was closely identified with all of Earl's programs. Finally, in a fit of desperation, Morrison went to Baton Rouge, where he implored Russell to dissuade Earl. Russell could do little more than assure the mayor he did not agree with all his uncle's proposals. Russell was power-less to save New Orleans. The legislature slavishly enacted Earl's pro-posals.

Not long afterward, Russell got a firsthand look at the political damage Earl's program caused as he stood in a checkout line in a Walgreen's Department Store on Canal Street in New Orleans. As he waited, he listened to the sales clerk adding customers' purchases. "That's one dollar. And one cent for Earl Long," she said. To the next customer, Russell noticed, she said virtually the same thing. "That's two dollars. And two cents for Earl Long," the woman said dryly. By the time he reached the counter, Russell was demoralized. The young woman easily encoun-tered at least as many voters as he did each day. The disgruntled sales-clerk represented a growing attitude of resentment toward Earl that spread throughout the state as people felt the impact of the tax assault.[7]

The taxes were not the only aspect of Earl's program to draw fire. Earl also forced various forms of spoils legislation through the legislature, repealing many of the reforms enacted under the Jones administration. He created new boards and commissions, to which he appointed political supporters, a return to the practices of the pre-Jones era. Most offensive to the anti-Longs were Earl's first steps toward demolition of the state's civil service system, the hallmark of Jones's tenure. Earl had promised to leave the system intact, a pledge promptly cast aside.

By the time the 1948 regular legislative session adjourned, the legisla-ture had increased state taxes 50 percent. It hiked the state's debt burden 33 percent. As hostility fermented in every corner of Louisiana, Earl was characteristically unflappable. He was certain the taxes would be forgot-ten, his tactics forgiven, and his popularity restored once the public received the benefits he had promised. Russell, however, viewed the situation differently. He feared that his election hopes would be dashed when the impacts of Earl's taxes were felt in the pocketbooks of most Louisianians.

In mid-June, Earl offered Russell the opportunity for greater notoriety, asking him to deliver a series of statewide radio speeches in defense of the tax plan. Russell dutifully complied, telling his radio listeners that his uncle did nothing more than faithfully keep the promises he made during the campaign. "In my opinion, there are two schools of politics," Russell told his listeners. "One group of politicians seems to feel that the thing to do is to go around the state for six months making promises and then spend four years searching for ways to get out of them." While a forceful defense of Earl, Russell's speeches were not particularly shrewd. Nonetheless,

Russell had few political options. He could not deny his role in passing the taxes, yet defending them only solidified his ties to an immensely unpopular program. Accentuating the positive was difficult; the attributes of Earl's program were, for now, elusive.[8]

Although tarnished by Earl's nose-diving popularity and still unsure about his chances in the coming election, Russell grew more confident about his abilities as a campaigner. At least one childhood friend warned him about his growing certitude. "In growing up, you made a lot of friends on your merits," wrote Ronnie Caire of New Orleans, explaining that even Huey and Earl's enemies "liked you because of yourself." Caire added, "[A]ll I can say is—don't chuck this out the window! Stay the same approachable, idealistic but realistic guy that sold you to a lot of people." From his reply, it appears Russell took the unsolicited advice to heart. "What you say was one thousand percent correct and I hope that you will help me to follow your advice,' he replied, adding, "I have always been a fellow who is inclined to get so close to the forest that I cannot see the trees."[9]

What Russell could see was the political damage of Earl's taxes, a view that eluded several out-of-state reporters who all but awarded the Senate seat to Russell. "His election is as certain as anything ever was in politics," said a United Press reporter. The *Washington Times-Herald* said, "[I]f there is anyone in Louisiana who can take the place of the late Kingfish in the hearts of the Bayou folk, it is Russell. . . . Now he appears almost certain to win." Like Earl, the national media seemed oblivious to widespread voter resentment over the tax increases.[10]

Meanwhile, Judge Robert Kennon, who finished a strong third in the governor's race, was poised to challenge Russell, as was popular north Louisiana congressman Overton Brooks. Both were itching to assail Earl and Russell for the tax hikes. Although Brooks would eventually withdraw, Kennon proved a formidable opponent. Like Russell, the judge had an early start in politics. At twenty-eight, he became one of the nation's youngest district attorneys. Not long afterward, he won a state appeals court seat and later served briefly on the state's Supreme Court. A popular but humorless politician, his most prominent physical features were large ears. In the governor's race, Earl derisively called Kennon, a staunch anti-Long, "that pitcher-eared big goof."[11]

Russell girded for the race, dispelling any remaining doubt about his intentions on July 2, when he resigned as executive assistant and formally announced his candidacy. His written statement spelled out a program strikingly similar to Earl's: greater federal aid for education, highways, social security increases and free school lunches. To the chagrin of some friends and advisers, Russell made no effort to downplay his role in helping Earl raise taxes, believing he could characterize Earl's program as a continuation of Huey Long's legacy. "I am glad I have been of some assistance in helping raise money to pay for old-age pensions, charity hospitals, free school lunches for hungry little children, good roads, to guarantee to the school teachers of Louisiana adequate salaries and to help all our educational institutions," he said in his announcement. Paying tribute to his father, he promised to "always strive to be loyal to the cause for which my father gave his life—that none shall be too rich and none too poor, and that everyone should have the opportunity to lead a prosperous, happy life in this land of plenty."[12]

The next day, Russell was on the stump in west central Louisiana, whipping up supporters at a campaign rally in Leesville with attacks on U.S. foreign aid. "We are feeding every Jap, every Chinaman, every Hindu and every Arab that we can find to feed," he said. "I intend to see that we get our share of that money to feed our people here at home." In Ville Platte the following day, he took aim at the state's newspapers, playing off their opposition to his father. "I'm not supported by no newspaper," he reminded his audience. "And like my father, I'm not seeking the support of any." If elected, he said, he "would appreciate a penny postcard from any one of my supporters as much as an editorial in the (New Orleans) *Times-Picayune* or the *Shreveport Times*."[13]

To those who campaigned with him, Russell was unsophisticated on the stump, a young city politician in need of the common touch his father and uncle possessed. "He was kind of green at a lot of things," remembered one of Russell's campaign aides. Adding to his alarm, the aide noticed, unlike most rural Louisianians, Russell properly pronounced "Arab." "Look, boy," the aide reportedly instructed, "don't you say Arab. Say, A-Rab." In the campaign's early days, Russell was not among Louisiana's more polished orators. "He wasn't a good speaker," one of Russell's campaign cohorts flatly declared. "He gestured below his belt and stuck his left hand out like he was pushing air out in front of him, and he stuttered." Even so, Russell was no political neophyte. He had been raised at the feet of Huey and Earl Long. With such splendid tutelage, Russell had learned more than a little about Louisiana politics. Furthermore, his intellect was razor sharp. His political instincts were sound. In time, he would acquire the rhetorical skills he now lacked.[14]

Unlike modern-day, high-tech, highly organized political events, in which audience members are bit players in a production tailored to appeal to television cameras, Russell's campaign was basic retail politics. Typically, each of the day's half-dozen rallies were held at the courthouse square or, in smaller communities, at a central location. While Russell spoke from the back of a pickup, two or three sound trucks headed to the next town on the campaign's schedule. They plied the streets, playing music and announcing Russell's visit. In most small Louisiana communities, the arrival of any politician, especially the son of Huey Long, was cause for excitement. "In those little towns, that's sort of like a holiday, all that music playing, they're running out to see what the sound truck's doing," recalled then-aide Buddy Gill. Even before Russell arrived, the rally began. Lieutenant Governor Bill Dodd or Cajun humorist Justin Wilson warmed up the gathering with jokes and, usually, a flurry of broadsides against Kennon. Dodd was the hatchet man, the surrogate who attacked Russell's opponents, leaving him to deliver a positive message. Those offended by the negative rhetoric would, they hoped, direct their anger at Dodd.[15]

After only a week on the stump, Russell was dejected. He concluded that his prospects for victory were bleak. He had surveyed the political landscape and concluded any chance of victory was lost when he and Earl herded the tax increases through the legislature. He returned to Baton Rouge for an emotional meeting in which he told Earl of his decision to withdraw from the race. According to one participant, Russell bluntly announced to Earl, "I want to get out of the race." Forbidding Russell to discuss his decision with anyone, Earl advised, "[Y]ou'd be a lot better off, after you said you were going to run, to run and get beat than have people say that you showed the white feather." Russell obeyed Earl's instruction to keep silent about his decision. Nonetheless, he remained committed to returning to his law practice. He would run again when the public recovered from the shock of the tax increases and his own role in aiding their passage. In the meantime, Earl dispatched several political friends to dissuade Russell from his retreat. Gradually, the lobbying had its effect. Within days, Russell was back on the stump.[16]

While Russell could say little in defense of the tax increases, he effectively accentuated the programs the increased revenues had financed. At one early rally, he reminded his audience that fifty thousand old-age pension checks would be mailed throughout the state in the coming week. "Every cent of the newly increased sales tax will be poured into the pension fund. You people will reap more money from the funds than the taxes paid in," he explained. Several days later, before a large crowd in Bossier Parish, Russell went a step further in exploiting the pension increase. He summoned several elderly supporters on stage to brandish pension checks they had just received.[17]

Kennon, meanwhile, took every opportunity to assail the tax increases, charging that Earl and Russell had sabotaged the state's economy. In a radio speech to New Orleans voters, he attacked Earl for erecting a "high anti-industrial fence" around the state's borders which new industries would not try to climb. "And industries already here must, in self defense, plan to route goods to out-of-state ports for delivery to out-of-state customers," he added. Kennon laid much of the blame on Russell, whom he called "Earl Long's tax executive." Russell and Earl, Kennon charged, ignored public opposition to the taxes and "steamrolled committee hearings in such a manner as to deny protesting citizens the right to be heard." At first, Russell merely ignored Kennon's attacks, once comparing him to "a mosquito dodging through a barrage of Flit."[18]

Lieutenant Governor Dodd, who did not have Russell's initial compunctions about returning Kennon's fire, responded by questioning Kennon's patriotism. Dodd noted that Russell had distinguished himself in battle, while Kennon held an army judicial position in Paris. Kennon, Dodd said, was "the Olympic judge who starts running every time he hears a gun shoot. The only powder Kennon every smelled was the powder he used on his face after shaving." In his conciliatory role, Russell was slow to raise questions about Kennon's war record. More than a month later, when urging a crowd in Norco to vote for the constitutional amendment approving the state soldiers' bonus, Russell finally fired back. He remarked that he and Kennon would receive the bonus, but suggested that Kennon did not deserve his. "I'm going to get $250 for the fighting I did overseas," Russell said. "I could get along without it, but I'd like to see my buddies who fought with me get it. We're even going to give the judge $250 for the sitting he did over there in Paris during the war, and you don't hear the judge complaining about that."[19]

Kennon countered with harsher attacks on Russell, charging that he was too young for the job, evidenced by his criticism of foreign aid. "That means a lack of maturity," Kennon explained. "Of course, the young man can always phone here and find out how to vote. But I, for one, am not willing to see Louisiana's vote in the U.S. Senate go for mere political expediency." A few days later, Kennon turned up the heat further, attacking the "one-man's family government" being offered Louisiana by its "royal family." At a Shreveport glass plant, Kennon told workers that Earl Long's administration "has played into your hands. First, they gave the senatorial appointment to their financial godfather [William Feazel] and now they're trying to knight the royal nephew."[20]

In a statewide radio address several days later, Russell suggested Kennon's real aspiration was the governorship in 1952. With that ambition, Russell noted, he "will not be able to accomplish anything that will benefit Louisiana." Furthermore, Russell said, Kennon would be reluctant to seek federal funds for Louisiana. "It stands to reason that he would not wish to see additional benefits passed to the people of Louisiana through [Earl Long's] state administration." Answering Kennon's questions about his youth and inexperience, Russell reminded his listeners that Huey Long was twenty-four when elected to the state's Railroad Commission. "The fact that my opponent has not given any indication of great accomplishment at the age of forty-six may be taken as an indication that he would not set the world on fire as a United States senator."[21]

While Russell and Kennon crisscrossed the state during the summer, they were not the only candidates vying for the public's attention. South Louisiana congressman James Domengeaux was challenging incumbent senator Allen Ellender for the Democratic nomination for Louisiana's other Senate seat. Meanwhile, President Harry Truman easily won the Democratic nomination for president, but was the underdog against Republican nominee Thomas Dewey. It was the Dixiecrat party candidate, Governor Strom Thurmond of South Carolina, who particularly beguiled Louisiana's voters. Thurmond skillfully exploited white Louisiana's fear and outrage over Truman's liberal civil rights programs, particularly his Fair Employment Practices Commission.

Louisiana's segregationist white wrath culminated when the Democratic party adopted an aggressive civil rights platform plank at its 1948 national convention. In disgust, many southern delegates stormed out of the convention hall, returning home to organize the State's Rights, or Dixiecrat, party. In Louisiana, the Dixiecrats seized control of the state Democratic party. Led by Plaquemines Parish boss Leander Perez, the Dixiecrat-controlled Democratic State Central Committee awarded the state's Democratic ballot symbol, the rooster, to Thurmond. The move proved an enormous advantage for Thurmond. Many Democratic voters habitually voted the entire ticket under their party's ballot emblem. By any measure, the central committee's decision was astounding. The president of the United States had been denied a place on Louisiana's ballot! The only prominent Louisiana politician besides Senator Feazel who supported Truman, Earl hastily convened a special legislative session to create a special Truman column on the ballot. To assure that Democratic candidates—chiefly Russell—would not be imperiled by the Dixiecrat ruse, Earl persuaded lawmakers to place the names of all Democratic candidates under the Truman *and* Thurmond columns.

Cowed by Louisiana's segregationist fervor, Kennon and Russell both made obligatory tributes to segregation and states' rights. Quietly, Russell supported Thurmond. At a Lake Charles gathering in late July, he promised to "oppose any attempts of the federal government to interfere with states' rights." Truman, he said, "has been giving us a pretty raw deal." But, he added, "I can't see where Thomas Dewey would do any better." Throughout the campaign, he said little about Thurmond's candidacy.[22]

Despite Russell's pledge to segregation, Kennon raised questions about his segregationist mettle. "My opponent is quoted as saying he is an advocate of states' rights, and yet he is an integral part of the despotic regime which has trampled the rights of citizens of our state under their feet," Kennon said. "Does he intend to pursue this course if elected to the United States Senate?" In even harsher words, Kennon offered his assessment of the choice facing voters, no doubt hoping to evoke memories of Huey Long's regime. "We will either have a democracy or we will have a dictatorship." Kennon honed on Earl's silence on civil rights, observing, "[I]t is about time that he publicly declares himself."[23]

In fact, throughout their careers, Earl and Huey Long rarely used racial fears to win votes. "On occasion," observed journalist A. J. Liebling, "they might talk like typical segregationists, but they did not really exploit race in their campaigns and they did not ask for repressive racial laws from their legislatures." In fact, Earl was responsible for legislation that equalized the salaries of black and white schoolteachers. Kennon knew that Earl had vulnerabilities with white segregationists. He hoped to draw Earl into the debate. "The governor remained silent on the question of civil rights," Kennon said, alleging Russell, too, was "in league with President Truman."[24]

Again, Earl did not respond. He was too occupied with helping Russell in more furtive ways. Three weeks before the election, in letters to hundreds of key supporters around the state, Earl tried to rouse his troops for Russell. "I would appreciate anything that you can do for Russell by way of expressing your support of him to our people in your section," he wrote. In spite of his good intentions, Russell found Earl more effective when his aid was covert. At times, however, Earl could not resist going public. His misguided attempt to extract retribution from Congressman

Jimmy Morrison, a former opponent running for reelection on the September ballot, was particularly frustrating for Russell.[25]

Earl had thrust state senator Speed Richardson into the race against Morrison. No one gave Richardson a chance of winning, but Earl thought forcing an opponent on Morrison might help settle the score. To Russell's consternation, Richardson behaved as though he were the Long candidate. In time, he latched onto Russell's Senate campaign. For weeks, Richardson followed Russell throughout the Sixth Congressional District, elbowing his way on stage, while Russell worried his reluctant association with the pesky politician was costing him the votes of Morrison supporters.

One afternoon, as Russell pulled into the small town of Gonzales, he was delighted to find a large crowd. His pleasure turned to alarm when he saw Uncle Earl waiting onstage, eager to speak for Richardson. Russell implored Earl to reconsider. "I wish you wouldn't do what you've got in mind," Russell said. "If you want to say something for me, all right. But if you're going to say something about Speed Richardson, I wish to hell you'd just forget about it." Russell could not dissuade Earl. "Russell," he said, "I've waited as long as I could. I waited until I knew you had your race won before I came out here and got into this thing. But I've got to say something for that man because I pushed him into the race. I just can't sit here and do nothing while he goes down." Disgusted, Russell watched helplessly as Earl attacked the popular Morrison, who handily beat Richardson on election day.[26]

Despite his bleak prospects in New Orleans, Russell's campaign picked up momentum elsewhere in the state, attracting larger, more enthusiastic crowds. While his election was far from assured, he nonetheless allowed himself to speculate on a large margin of victory. In a speech in Leesville in late August, Russell attacked Kennon for "going around the state telling a lot of things that nobody with any sense would believe." He predicted when Kennon "wakes up on the morning after the votes are counted, he's liable to change his mind about who's got that one-hundred-thousand vote majority." In an August 16 radio speech, Russell confidently predicted he would carry at least fifty of the state's sixty-four parishes. He would win at least thirty by two-to-one margins, he said. "If we have a fairly heavy vote, I will win this election by more than one hundred thousand votes." A light vote, he speculated, would produce "a winning margin of at least sixty thousand." In a note to himself, Russell wrote, "Will carry Webster Parish." Webster was Kennon's home.[27]

In the campaign's final weeks, Russell stepped up his attacks on Kennon. At a rally in Norco, he said Kennon "has been given twenty-six years on the payroll on his plea to give a young man a chance. That's one time I think he is right. You should give a young man a chance and I am sixteen years younger than the judge." Kennon had not accomplished "a solitary thing for the people that shows up in his record," Russell told the crowd. He promised "if in the next two years I can't show you where I have done ten times as much as the judge has in his twenty-six years at the trough, I'll gladly step aside for somebody else."[28]

In the same speech, Russell responded to the previous day's editorial in the anti-Long *New Orleans Times-Picayune*, which attacked Russell while endorsing Kennon. The paper's editors drew a severe, and unfair, portrait of Russell, alleging his "youth, inexperience, boundless ambition and manifest determination to perpetrate dictatorship and profit by it politically, would destroy his usefulness" in the Senate. "That's fine," Russell replied. "Let them keep it up. When I have the *Times-Picayune* against me, I know I'm doing right for the poor people of this state." More than a dozen years earlier, Huey Long made Louisiana's conservative newspapers his favorite foil after Standard Oil. To Russell, the harsh, antimedia rhetoric came easily. The *Times-Picayune*, Russell said, "has never done anything in the last one hundred years that was for the good of the people. When my father wanted to give you free textbooks, they fought it. Everything he tried to do for the people, they fought."[29]

Less than a week before the election, Russell took to the radio waves in a statewide broadcast, responding to Kennon's absurd allegation that his role in enacting Earl's tax increase program was a betrayal of his father. "Now, Judge, I believe I'm a little better authority on that than you are," Russell said sarcastically. "But even at that, you must know how much my father wanted to pay the kind of old-age pension we're actually paying now. He didn't because he couldn't. Didn't have the money. The increase we made in the sales tax will fulfill that dream. Did I betray my father by making that dream of his come true? Of course not."[30]

By the campaign's end, Russell had grown adept at exploiting his political birthright while maintaining an almost charming degree of humility. "Don't think you owe Russell Long anything for whatever he has been able to do for you," he said in one speech. "It's just the other way around. You folks have been good to my family, and I owe you far more than you could ever owe me." But for those who loved his father, Russell promised,

"I'll try to achieve all the things for which he stood—such things as old-age pensions, federal aid to education, and state welfare programs."[31]

Observing Kennon endlessly bragged about his war record, Russell took one last opportunity for comparison. He noted the judge would "make out better if you never brought up" the subject. "But, since you did, let's look at the record. It shows that Russell Long had eighteen months of actual combat duty, that in those months I took ashore more ammunition and men than you, thumbing through your law books to send men to the brig, probably ever saw."[32]

On election eve, the Long forces fired up their massive machine. Earl dispatched sheriffs' deputies and school bus drivers throughout their parishes to deliver sample ballots, campaign materials and voters. On election day, turnout was heavy. That night, however, a cloud of gloom hung over the Long headquarters as returns from the state's major cities were announced. Kennon was ahead in every one, except Alexandria. He commanded a two-to-one lead in New Orleans. Russell, when he and Katherine finally appeared at his New Orleans headquarters, paced nervously, bravely talking about victory, but not convincing anyone. Telling reporters that he "didn't look for much help in some of the big cities," he predicted, "I'll do alright [sic] in the rural areas. Can't see how I can lose this one." Later that evening, after he examined parish returns, Russell's confidence was more credible. "We'll carry the boxes at the frog of the creek five to one," he told reporters. "Drink your coffee and stay on hand to count the votes."[33]

As the returns trickled in through the next day, the lead changed hands half a dozen times. At one point, the *Times-Picayune* told its readers that Long was leading by 1,500 votes. The city's other newspaper, the same day, declared Kennon held a 16,488-vote lead. A Baton Rouge newspaper reported that Long was in the lead by 4,575 votes. Finally, after a long day of nervous vote counting and recounting, state election officials declared Russell the winner with 264,143 votes to Kennon's 253,668—a difference of less than eleven thousand votes. Russell had carried forty-four of the state's sixty-four parishes. He even won Kennon's home parish, as he had predicted, by more than 1,700 votes.[34]

Like his father before him, Russell knew he owed his majority to the state's rural voters. Although he carried a majority of the state's parishes, he had fared miserably in the urban areas of New Orleans—which Kennon won with 60 percent—Shreveport, Baton Rouge, Monroe, and Lake Charles. On a New Orleans radio station the night after the election, Russell acknowledged the importance of his rural support. "I never would

have made it without a heavy country vote," he said, paying tribute to
"those good old boys who laid down their cotton sacks, plows and hoes and
went to the polls to elect Russell Long U.S. senator."[35]

From the minute that election returns began turning against him, Kennon cried foul. "They're phoney and baloney!" he cried angrily in a radio
interview, singling out St. Bernard Parish, a New Orleans suburb, as a
prime example of voter fraud. In that parish, Kennon received 121 votes
to Russell's 3,039. "Why, I have more personal friends than that in the
parish who told me today they voted for me," he protested.[36]

St. Bernard was not the only parish where Russell received a lopsided
majority in the tight race. In Plaquemines Parish, ruled by the iron fist of
segregationist district attorney Leander Perez, Russell received 2,150
votes to Kennon's 396. Several years later, Russell admitted that Perez,
who broke with the Longs before the next election, delivered votes for
him in Plaquemines. Perez was well known for his ability to carry his
parish for candidates he supported. "We knew he could deliver
Plaquemines Parish," said Russell's friend and aide, Buddy Gill. "He had
control of it. We knew he'd get all those votes for somebody. We wanted
them if anybody was going to get them." Early in the campaign, at Earl's
behest, Russell went to the all-powerful Perez to plead for the support of
his parish machine. "You go there and do what you gotta do," Earl
instructed a reluctant Russell. The stolen votes, Russell later insisted,
would not have made a difference in the election's outcome. Even before
the election, congressional investigators inquired about allegations that
Earl had summoned a group of Louisiana sheriffs to Baton Rouge and
ordered them to carry their parishes for Russell. No one doubted that Earl
pulled every lever at his disposal for Russell. Several of Earl's deputies
later claimed that Earl stole the election outright. Earl, they alleged,
stalled the reporting of returns from several rural parishes until he could
determine the votes needed to win. In Louisiana, vote stealing was as
common as sugarcane. But other than suspicious returns in Plaquemines
and St. Bernard parishes, no solid evidence ever directly implicated
Russell or Earl in vote stealing.[37]

The Democratic nomination in hand, Russell coasted to victory against
his token Republican opponent, Clem S. Clarke, in the November general
election, merely a formality in heavily Democratic Louisiana. Elected with
a 75 percent majority, Russell turned thirty the day after the November 2
election. In an interview aired on most of the state's major radio stations,
Russell thanked his supporters and paid the campaign's final laurel to his

father: "To the thousands of you who have made this tribute to my father possible, believe me, you have and will always have the heartfelt thanks of the family and friends of Huey P. Long."[38]

Pleased that his nephew had won, Uncle Earl nonetheless could find little in the returns to give him hope that the hemorrhaging of his own popularity had abated. Russell's margin of victory in the Democratic primary, in spite of Earl's efforts to increase it, had represented a 95 percent decrease in the Long power base within eight months. Furthermore, while Russell buried his general election opponent in a landslide, Clarke—aided by a heavy Republican turnout in the presidential election—received the highest Republican vote in Louisiana since Reconstruction. Possibly just as discouraging to Earl was the knowledge that the Long family baton had been passed to the younger generation.

The U.S. Senate, meanwhile, prepared to induct several new members in addition to Russell: Lyndon Johnson of Texas, Hubert Humphrey of Minnesota, Paul Douglas of Illinois, Robert Kerr of Oklahoma, and Estes Kefauver of Tennessee. "Seldom has so colorful, so varied and so exceptional a band of new Democratic senators come at once into the Senate," wrote Roland Evans and Robert Novak in their biography of Lyndon Johnson. All of these men would eventually leave their mark on the Senate in differing ways and to various degrees. None, however, could match the commotion created by the news of Russell's election. Word that the son of Huey Long was coming to town alarmed Democrats and Republicans who worried that Louisiana might be exporting, as one reporter wrote, another "hillbilly Marxist." As Washington waited for his advent, one Louisiana editorial writer summed up the capital's nervous speculation about Russell's arrival. "We'll see just how far history and/or heredity will repeat."[39]

8

RUSSELL'S DEBUT

$\mathcal{R}$USSELL'S SENATE CAMPAIGN was a parochial exercise, driven almost entirely by state issues. He and Kennon rarely debated broad national questions. As he prepared to leave for Washington, it was time to surrender the state's internal affairs to Uncle Earl. For now, Russell knew he must look beyond Louisiana to matters of national scope. In this realm, there was no issue more controversial and divisive than civil rights. Repudiation of northern liberal attempts to reorder southern traditions and customs—white supremacy and segregation—was the single most important concern for southern members of Congress. At least, southern congressmen and senators *believed* that there was no issue more important to their constituencies.

Shortly before he left Louisiana, Russell set about drafting a speech on the issues facing the upcoming session of Congress. He scribbled ten pages of random thoughts on the growing unrest over southern race relations. There is no record the speech was delivered as Russell penned it or, if delivered, that it drew any press attention. Had his thoughts—moderate by 1948 standards—been widely reported, they might have ignited some doubt about the new senator's devotion to the South's absolute adherence to racial segregation. With his reelection to a full term less than two years away, such radical remarks could have opened the door for a more dogmatic segregationist challenge. The trouble with campaigns based on racial issues, Russell wrote, is that all logic and understanding goes out the window and the scum of politicians on both sides come to the front. For example, when [Mississippi's late senator and racial agitator, Theodore] Bilbo, was on his last legs politically, he won his last race on the Negro issue. Maybe a majority of the whites would not vote for Bilbo but they would vote against the Negroes.

The racial issue immediately obscures all other important issues and it distracts interest from the business that should be foremost before the American Congress. Everything else gets lost in the scramble. True progress waits. Furthermore, it keeps the South on the defensive. Being in the minority on this issue we never get the chance to take our proper place at the head of the parade of progress. We are always battling to defend ourselves in the rear.

What is the answer? In my opinion it is to work it out. Let's start out by agreeing that the Negro as a class is underprivileged and that he is denied opportunity that should be his. Then let's work it out. Let us strive to make the North agree that the problem cannot be solved in a day or a year. Let's see that the colored race is properly educated, let's see that they are properly qualified to cast their ballots and then as they learn to understand the issues, let's give them the opportunity to vote.[1]

In 1948, this was a treacherous position, about as far as a southern politician dared to stray from the segregationist mainstream. Hastening to dispel any notions he might not embrace racial separation and white superiority, Russell quickly added:

> For our time, certainly for the present, white people will not stand for the abolition of segregation in schools and in public transportation or places of public accommodation. But let's work to offer the colored man equal facilities. Let's convince the federal government that it should recognize the problem as a national one and that the entire nation should pay to bear the expense of providing equal educational facilities for the Negro.[2]

Considering the time and the atmosphere, the speech is remarkable, even if undelivered. Almost as important in revealing Russell's moderation on racial issues, it illustrates the attitude of many southern politicians in the 1940s and 1950s: Open-minded enough to acknowledge privately that blacks were being denied basic rights and opportunities as citizens, but politically astute—or hypocritical—enough to know that voicing those opinions would mean sure and swift retribution by the voters. Russell went so far as to publicly admit the reality facing many southern members of Congress who worked to keep federal education money free of integrationist stipulations. "I don't believe any Southerner could vote for the federal aid bill without this, whether he wants to or not," he said in his first press conference as senator-elect. "His folks back home will not let him because they're not going to submit to that." He was for federal aid to education, he affirmed, but only "if you provide it with segregation."[3]

Russell knew Louisiana, like the entire South, was in many ways still the Confederacy, a region desperately clinging to a way of life that was being laid to rest in other regions. In the South, blacks were regarded as a lower form of human life, different and inferior, by law a sad and pitiful permanent underclass, denied basic rights as citizens. In Louisiana, the visible signs of racial separation abounded. Black citizens were constantly reminded of their proper place in society by "White" and "Colored" signs that directed them to separate lunch counters, rest rooms, and water fountains. On streetcars and buses, blacks sat in the rear. At movie theaters, they were relegated to the balconies. "These citizens of Louisiana," wrote a group of historians in a 1984 history of Louisiana, "had no choice but to be born in an all-black hospital, to be wed in an all-black church, and even to be buried in an all-black cemetery. Denied the right to attend the public school of their choice, they had to attend one with decidedly inferior facilities and with inadequately trained instructors." Segregation not only conformed to the legal and social mores of the time, it was hailed as God's will. Even though Louisiana had not been cursed with an overabundance of governors and prominent leaders skilled in the art of racial agitation, segregation—or the defeat of forced integration—was truly a religion. For a public official to reveal any sign that he was anything less than fervent in his devotion to preserving white supremacy was heresy. Such public tolerance invited defeat in the next election. Said Russell's aide Buddy Gill: "Politics was one thing, and the way you thought was something else in those days."[4]

Leaving Baton Rouge for Washington in late December 1948, Russell realized that his first test as the nation's youngest senator would be acted out in the civil rights arena. With less than two years remaining in Overton's unexpired term, he well understood the political importance of surrendering personal moderation on the issue to overwhelming public opinion.

The untested, unknown freshman senator has as much to prove to the Washington power structure as he does to his new constituents. Like a new student in a strange school, a rookie senator wins respect among his colleagues by conforming to and playing by the rules of "the Club." Making waves, drawing attention to oneself, or not demonstrating proper respect for the Senate's gray eminences was, in that era, the surest way for a new senator to close important doors of opportunity.

The Senate of 1949 was in transition. Prior to the war, Senator Clinton Anderson of New Mexico recalled, "[A] man considered it a fine time to become a senator when he was sixty years old." The difference between the old and new Senate, Anderson suggested, was most evident in the way the older senators dressed. "Before the war, no senator would have thought of attending the opening session of the Senate attired in anything but the proper spiked coat and afternoon clothes." "Occasionally," Anderson remembered, "a senator would even appear in a frock coat."[5]

The dress, and the stiff formality conveyed by the senior members, was a symbol of the unwritten rules to which most younger senators were expected to conform: no speeches during the first two years and no legislation until the second term. "Like children," a freshman senator once remarked, "we should be seen and not heard." J. William Fulbright of Arkansas, who preceded Russell in the Senate by three years, also found a Senate governed not so much by written rules, but by unwritten customs. "To get up and make a speech about some issue, not particularly relevant to your state," Fulbright recalled, "just an issue of normal governmental policy, or particularly foreign relations or something like that—you didn't do that. There was no law against it, but you just didn't do it."[6]

The making of a good senator, wrote William S. White in his classic book on the Senate, *Citadel*, "involves several intangibles." First, White observed, the good senators have demonstrated "the absence of petty exhibitionism," in addition to "an understanding acceptance of the requirement of compromise, and therefore a willingness to abide dissent." In other words, White said, the good senator has "a deep skill in sensing what may and may not be done." The newcomer suspected of not possessing these important qualities must work even more diligently than the unknown newcomer. Better to arrive in Washington a complete unknown than step from the train at Union Station laden with the preconceived notions and suspicions of colleagues.[7]

If Huey Long had been a newcomer who announced his arrival at the party by belly-flopping into the pool, Russell's appearance in Washington alarmed senators enough to take a few cautious steps away from the water. Despite a striking physical similarity to his father, Russell was a different breed. He was soft-spoken where Huey was boisterous, meek where Huey was boastful, patient where Huey was restless. But Russell was well known only in Louisiana. More than a few senators viewed the newcomer with suspicion.

It was not his manner but his rhetoric that may have worried some of the Senate's veterans. "The only way to overcome what has been said about my father," he told one reporter in the fall of 1948, "is to climb to the top and get my chance to answer." In another interview, he talked openly about Huey's wealth redistribution ideals. "The man with a billion dollars is a danger to the country," he declared, adding that such people are "greedy." His call for an expanded social security program was tinged with a stern warning. "If we have another depression we are going to have to compete with communism," he said. "We will have little chance against it when we have hungry children."[8]

To another newspaper, he acknowledged a "burning desire to get a fair hearing for my father," arguing Huey's enemies never understood him. "He was ruthless against his opponents, but if you could know the things they did, you would say he was justified." He promised to carry out some of Huey's ideals, "and if I can't do it, I shall help someone else who can." When he told reporters that he "might be susceptible to a draft for governor" in 1952, he did little to allay the fears of the anti-Longs, who suspected another attempt at Long domination of Louisiana. Senators, meanwhile, were hardly predisposed to appraise seriously a new senator who transmitted signals that his career goals did not include lengthy Senate service. "I think they thought he would be a flash in the pan," said Katherine Long, frustrated his colleagues greeted Russell with such skepticism. "They didn't think he would last."[9]

To his credit, Russell took pains to demonstrate that he was unlike his father in the most important ways, revealing a degree of temperate rhetoric rarely heard from Huey. Of his wealth distribution goals, he said he could "wait for a gradual reduction in the big fortunes. The trend is that way." To the same reporter, he said that he was motivated by the desire to prove himself an exemplary senator, "so people will have to say Huey couldn't have been so bad." Shortly after his election, Russell predicted, "[N]o doubt I will disappoint some people" by being less spectacular than Huey and added, "I don't think I'll get myself into as many fights as my father did, but I think I'll get out of them just as well."[10]

In Louisiana, Russell displayed what one Long family biographer termed "his most significant characteristic, his earnest willingness to make friends out of his enemies." Shortly after his election, a conference of industrial leaders applauded Russell when he humbly told them, "I doubt whether a man in this room voted for me. But I'm going to try to do such a good job that you'll vote for me next time."[11]

As the nation's press and the Senate strained for a clear picture of what they could expect from Russell, it is fair to conclude that he sometimes sent mixed signals, uncertain of the correct image to put forth. "When you reach behind these things for a picture of Russell Long," a *Kansas City Star* reporter wrote, "it emerges with its own areas of light and shade."[12]

* * *

Katherine, five-year-old Kay, one-year-old Pamela, and former law partner Gordon West peered proudly from the Senate gallery as Russell strode down the center aisle of the chamber on December 31, 1948, to take his oath of office from outgoing Senate president pro tempore Arthur Vandenberg. Escorted by newly elected president pro tempore Kenneth McKeller of Tennessee, Russell entered a chamber inhabited by at least sixteen of his father's former colleagues. McKeller himself once lectured Huey Long that "many things have happened to the United States since our government was established, but nothing that would be so unspeakable as to have at the head of this nation a man who has the venom and the hatred and the malice toward everyone who disagrees with him that the senator from Louisiana has." Like McKeller, many of Russell's new colleagues had been Huey's bitter enemies. Vice President Alben Barkley, who had served as senator from Kentucky, and the cantankerous Tom Connolly of Texas, often clashed bitterly with Huey. Harry Byrd of Virginia, who sat next to Huey on the Senate floor, detested him so much that he finally asked for a new seat, "even if I have to sit on the Republican side." Russell was aware that his arrival in the Senate had been greeted with overwhelming nonchalance. "Most of them were in no hurry to get acquainted, it seemed like," Russell recalled, adding he was not concerned by the cool reception. "They weren't judging me. They'd find out what kind of guy I was soon enough, without pushing it."[13]

This detached welcome did not manifest itself in the gracious gesture of at least one of Russell's Republican colleagues, Henry Cabot Lodge of Massachusetts. When Russell requested the desk that his father had used on the Senate floor, the records revealed that it was in Lodge's possession. "Now, he was always a stickler for tradition, anyway," Russell said of Lodge. "And so, from his point of view, that was a reasonable request and he was quite willing to let me have it." The desk was no ordinary piece of furniture even when Huey Long fulminated during filibusters, pounding on its mahogany top as he espoused a radical vision for America. It once belonged to another Senate legend, John C. Calhoun of South Carolina. In years to come, it would become a prized possession, passionately coveted by more than one South Carolina senator.[14]

On his first day in the Senate, Russell received an amusing reminder of his youthful and unsenatorial mien. After riding the elevator from his office in the Senate Office Building, just across Constitution Avenue from the Capitol, Russell walked toward the subway car that shuttled senators, their staffs, and tourists back and forth between the two buildings. Normally, the car was available to anyone. During votes, however, guards kept it free of tourists so that senators could dash to the Senate floor when the bells signaled a vote. This day as Russell climbed aboard one of the cars, a guard stopped him. "Sorry son," he said, "We're reserving this car for the senators." Russell, polite as always, informed the embarrassed guard of his new status and was quickly on his way.[15]

Junior senators traditionally did not garner the most prestigious committee assignments until they paid their dues on the lowly administrative committees. To his chagrin, Russell was no exception, despite his seniority to the seventeen freshman who took office several days after him. "That didn't do me any good at all," he said, complaining that "by the time they got through, they gave all those other guys what they wanted, in the order which they liked them and then, since Louisiana had gone for Strom Thurmond, the State's Rights candidate, and Uncle Earl hadn't done much to head it off, well, they just figured they didn't owe me anything." As the eighty-first Congress began, Senate leaders appointed Russell to three tedious committees: Post Office and Civil Service, Rules and Administration, and Expenditures in the Executive Department.[16]

One early indication that Russell, unlike his father, held the Senate in high regard was the delight he took in his most mundane committee assignment. One task on the Rules Committee involved the loathsome duty of overseeing the Senate's dining facilities. The early days of 1949 found many Senate staffers startled by the sight of the nation's youngest senator, tray in hand, waiting in a Senate cafeteria line, foregoing the more prestigious Senators' Dining Room in the Capitol. For weeks, Russell reviewed the service, the food quality, and the prices, and suggested improvements. No one could remember a senator who had taken this routine job so seriously.[17]

Despite their lack of luster, Russell's other committees were not entirely without prestige or possibility. The Rules and Administration Committee, for example, would be the committee battleground for moderate Republicans and liberal Democrats who wanted to liberalize the cloture rule, the Senate's procedure for ending filibusters. As Russell soon discovered, the Rules Committee "was just what the doctor ordered."[18]

For more than one hundred years, the Senate had functioned with no limitation on debate, until 1917, when senators capitulated under pressure from President Woodrow Wilson. The new rule stipulated that debate on a measure could be choked off if two-thirds of senators present voted for cloture. Realistically, the rule had little effect, as it applied only to measures, not motions. Since motions are the vehicles by which the Senate decides whether to consider legislation, the Senate remained married to its tradition of unlimited debate. By 1948, with President Truman pushing for his civil rights program—including elimination of the poll tax, establishment of a permanent Fair Employment Practices Commission (FEPC), an antilynching law, and an end to racial discrimination in public housing—the cloture rule was destined to become a centerpiece in the debate over civil rights.

"Here at issue," historian William S. White wrote of cloture, "was a great deal more than proper treatment for a minority, in this case primarily the Negro minority. Involved was the whole long concept, so closely held by the Senate generally since the outcome of the Federal Convention, of the ultimate supremacy of the individual state." Cloture was an emotional issue for small-state senators whose congressional delegations were vastly outnumbered in the House of Representatives by the populous states. Those opposed to relaxing cloture believed their meager influence and power was in danger of disappearing completely.[19]

More significantly, cloture was a magnificent curtain behind which southern senators could conceal their opposition to Truman's civil rights program. Without cloture, the pro-civil rights majority was powerless in the face of the resolute minority which always recruited enough votes to sustain a filibuster. The southern senators who opposed civil rights could argue, somewhat disingenuously, that they were only preserving one of the oldest, most venerable Senate traditions. In fact, Russell made that argument during his first Rules Committee hearing in late January.

At the hearing, Russell promptly picked a fight with liberal Republican senator Wayne Morse of Oregon. Morse favored a proposal championed by Senate liberals and President Truman to modify the cloture rule to permit a simple majority to impose cloture. Did not the majority, Russell quizzed Morse, have the ability to break a filibuster without changing the rules if it had "the same determination to break it that the minority has to make it?" The only way to stop debate, Morse shot back, was by "physical endurance," and the Senate should be "beyond settling things by combat." If legislation would harm the interests of "one section" of the country, Russell retorted, its senators should "have the right to fight it out to the limit of their endurance." Russell ominously bowed out of the debate, hinting that southern senators were prepared to tie up the Senate for the entire year to save the filibuster.[20]

Russell was not motivated entirely by a desire to preserve unlimited debate. Despite the moderate views he held in private, he left little room for interpretation of his public views on Truman's proposal to give more rights to blacks. To a suburban Washington civic club in February he charged that "the do-gooders don't ask what progress is being made in raising the status of the colored race, but want to ram through Congress laws to let a colored school child sit next to the white child." Several days later on NBC's radio program, "Meet the Press," Russell argued against Truman's proposals to make lynching a federal offense. "It is the duty of the states to enforce their own criminal law," he declared, adding that it was "unconstitutional for the federal government to take over that responsibility." He also spoke against curbs on debate, maintaining that "the whole idea of the Senate is to place control on the majority."[21]

Several days later, however, the Senate took its first historic steps toward breaking the back of the southern Senate bloc when the Rules Committee sent to the Senate a relaxed cloture rule, permitting an end to debate on motions as well as measures. For the southerners, the proposal was not a total defeat. The committee had compromised. It expanded cloture's application, but also tightened it in another important area—a two-thirds vote of the entire Senate, not just those voting, was required to end debate. This concession did little to mollify Russell, one of four committee members opposing the rule change, who promised to talk "at great length" on the Senate floor. A filibuster was imminent. "We of the South," Russell said, "have been backed up against the wall so long in Congress that the South really knows how to fight."[22]

The filibuster was the tool Huey Long had employed so often in his three years in the Senate to drive his opponents into a mad, frustrated frenzy. It was appropriate, therefore, that the son of the man who still held the Senate's record for the longest filibuster would make his maiden Senate speech in defense of that very device.

In 1949, a freshman senator's first speech was an event. Because the Senate had not yet waned as the nation's premier arena for electrifying public debate and the Senate chamber was much more the hub of activity than today, a freshman's first speech was the Senate's way of assessing a new member. Russell delivered his first floor speech on March 2, more than two months into his term, as twenty-two southern senators filibusted the Rules Committee's cloture proposal. It was not the first time he had spoken to the Senate. He had briefly joined the filibuster a few days earlier. The speech, however, marked Russell's first formal remarks as a senator. Aware that he would violate the Senate tradition concerning orations by freshman, Russell reluctantly yielded to the cajoling of his good friend, Democrat John Stennis of Mississippi. "We need you to help with this filibuster," Stennis told Russell, arguing that "it don't make much difference what you say, just as long as it's something you believe in."[23]

Entering the Senate chamber, Russell was jittery, intimidated by the curiosity his debut aroused. The galleries were filled with the largest crowd since the filibuster began. In all, eighty-three senators were in their seats, eager to learn if Huey Long's son was cut from the same cloth as his father. Standing nervously at his desk, Russell began slowly reading his prepared remarks:[24]

Mr. President, it is with very mixed emotions that I arise to address the Senate this afternoon. In these first formal words I have to utter before this body, I say in all earnestness that I would very much prefer to speak to my colleagues initially on some substantive legislation; I would prefer to be advocating some measure designed to help all our people, or certainly large portions of them, some legislation calculated to unify and benefit the great masses who look to us for guidance and for relief from their oppressions. . . .

While my desk is burdened with letters from the poor, the disabled and the sick importuning for broadened social security benefits and for welfare laws, I must come here in an effort to protect those unfortunate people from a change in our own rules which might well serve hereafter as the vehicle which some future oppressive group could use to grind them to dust. . . .

The United States Senate stands as the last great protector of the rights of the minority. Why is that true? It is because of the right of unlimited debate in these halls. A mere handful of men, armed with sincere conviction, can hold off the majority days on end. The minority, through its right of unlimited debate, may test the determination and the conscience as well as the endurance of the majority. . . .

Today we of the South are in the minority, Mr. President. We insist that the rules designed to protect the minority remain unchanged. Would not any minority do the same thing? . . .

But Mr. President, we of the South are not the only minority in the great country. It merely happens that we are the whipping boy today. Actually, every American is both a member of the majority on some issues and the minority on others. . . .

If there were not pending certain proposals dealing with the so-called civil rights program, the Senate would now be proceeding to the consideration of other legislation in an orderly, systematic way. I do not care to dwell on the proposed measures at the present time, but I am constrained to say that this great land of ours has indeed reached a sorry day when, in an effort to satisfy the clamorings of paid propagandists and professional purveyors of hate, we must put aside all else, change the rules and ram through legislation which a large segment of our country does not want and will never tolerate."[25]

Russell spoke for almost an hour. When he finished, his new colleagues responded warmly. Senator Arthur Vandenberg, who served with Huey, rushed up to Russell with gushing praise. "I wish your father could have been here and heard you," the Michigan Democrat told Russell. "I would have liked to said to him, 'Is that really your boy?' " The next day, the *New Orleans States* applauded Russell more for what he did not say, observing the "most startling difference between the speeches of father and son were their context." Huey, the paper said erroneously, "talked about every subject under the sun except the business actually before the Senate. Today, Russell carefully confined his entire speech, with only one exception, to the proposed change in the Senate rules." The paper congratulated him on his "vigorous attack upon the civil rights program of President Truman." The *Memphis Commercial Appeal,* in an editorial, applauded Russell for making "it very plain that he intends to be a senator in his own right—that he is not trading on his father's name or characteristics."[26]

The speech prompted at least one note of discord. A New Orleans reporter, Tom Sacton, covered maiden speeches by two new senators that day: Russell Long's and Minnesota senator Hubert H. Humphrey's. Humphrey was Russell's good friend, neighbor, and former LSU schoolmate. Later, in *The Nation,* Sacton drew a gloomy comparison of the two speeches: "Humphrey's concern was the future of the West. . . . Long's concern was the past of the South." Long's future, Sacton concluded, was tied up "with interminable and bitter conflict of the Southern race question."[27]

Russell, nonetheless, continued to impress his Senate colleagues and constituents with his quiet, polite manner, his poise and command of the issues. Perhaps nothing did more to demonstrate he was not to be taken lightly than his February 4 appearance on the NBC Radio Network's "Meet the Press." A senator for barely a month, Russell fielded questions from five skeptical reporters. Russell fielded their queries with the aplomb of a veteran, evidenced by an exchange with Lawrence Spivak of the *American Mercury,* who tried to stump him on civil rights: "Senator, when you ran for the Senate you said, and I quote: 'I'm in favor of State's Rights without dictation from Washington and federal interference with our local activities.' And yet you've asked the federal government to give you funds for highways, flood control, recreation, for schools, for hospitals and almost everything. Don't you think the price you're going to have to pay for federal money is some federal control?"

"Well," Russell responded, "if they're going to run us as though we're a territorial government anyway, whether we like it or not, we might as well get some economic benefit out of it."

Warren Moscow of the *New York Times* interrupted. "Why do you keep referring to Louisiana as a territory?" he demanded. "Why is it any more of a territory than any one of the other forty-eight states which has two United States senators?"

"Well," Russell answered, "right now it's—I'd say so because you're trying to get the rules fixed up so you'll run roughshod over us with your northern majority."

"Any more than the free silver senators had their chance in the United States Senate, any more than the cotton states have been able to dictate the price of cotton?" Moscow replied. "I mean aren't you being a little sensitive about this territorial business?"

"Well, you know," Russell said, "it's all according to whose ox is getting gored. If you were getting gored here in New York you'd be a little sensitive, too."[28]

Russell's appearance generated more than one hundred letters of congratulations from friends and constituents impressed with his conduct under fire. "I accepted the invitation to appear with some misgiving," he confessed to a friend, "but am inclined to believe now that it was a very wise selection on my part." The *Shreveport Journal* agreed, praising him and noting that, "although the youngest member of the United States Senate, Mr. Long acquitted himself in a way that would have done credit to one of much longer experience in Congress. He was self-possessed, and never disturbed."[29]

As the pundits in Washington and Louisiana expressed more confidence in his abilities, Russell himself possessed something less than supreme certainty about his aptitude for the new responsibilities. "This job in the United States Senate is still a big adventure for me," he confided in a letter to his predecessor, Bill Feazel, "but I must confess that I like it." The upcoming filibuster over civil rights by southern senators had Russell worried. "I don't think I have ever made a speech lasting more than one hour," he told Feazel, "but, when it gets down to the in-fighting, I guess I can talk considerably longer."[30]

As the civil rights showdown neared, passions over President Truman's program to expand minority rights ran high. In Louisiana, these emotions were eagerly fanned by one of the most powerful, ruthless, and racist

political bosses in the South—Plaquemines Parish district attorney Leander Perez, who doubled as head of the States Rights party. An excellent
example of the malice Perez aroused, and to which Russell was forced to
pander, was the district attorney's testimony in July 1949 before a Senate
committee, reported by an adulatory reporter for the *Shreveport Journal*:

> Seldom in congressional history have senators been more amazed and
> shocked than they were by the well-documented evidence presented to a
> Senate judiciary subcommittee by Leander Perez . . . showing that the
> McGrath so-called civil rights bill was the "brain-child" of Communist Russia's
> dictator Joseph Stalin. In a masterly presentation, the staunch champion of
> states rights traced the origin of the bill sponsored by Rhode Island's Senator J.
> Howard McGrath, the Democratic national chairman, back to Stalin's "all races
> law," which he used as a spring-board to power and the enslavement of the
> Russian people. [31]

While Russell waited to offer his own testimony in opposition to the bill,
he could not resist praising Perez and his ridiculous theory. "Judge Perez," Russell declared, "made a powerful and stirring statement. He
brought out a multitude of hidden implications involved in this so-called
civil rights bill." He later told the subcommittee that abolishing segregation
"would not only bring great violence," but might also destroy any chance
of blacks and whites living in harmony. [32]

Perez and other states righters had been urging southern whites to
abandon the Democratic party for the States Rights party. Perez's departure from the party, however, had as much to do with greed as racial
politics. An erstwhile New Dealer, Perez had made millions from oil and
gas drilled on vast tracts of land he owned. When President Truman
asserted federal control over much of Louisiana's offshore tidelands,
Perez became a states' rights disciple and Governor Earl Long made him
an unpaid assistant attorney general in charge of Louisiana's claim to the
disputed tidelands' revenue. While he was careful to accord Perez proper
deference, Russell was no disciple. At a convention of parish officials,
Russell told white Democratic police jurors the "worst thing we could do is
leave the Democratic party, because of the enormous power southern
Democrats have within that party." Russell, like most southern Democratic senators and congressmen, knew a large defection would jeopardize
their political careers. If he left the party, he would lose valuable influence
and any chance at a powerful committee post. But, if large numbers of
Louisiana voters did forsake the Democrats, his reelection as a Democrat

might be more difficult. The key to the southern Democrats' survival rested in their continued effectiveness in thwarting the Truman civil rights program and the extreme rhetoric they employed to make their case.[33]

Russell's first year in the Senate ended as Southern Democrats stopped Truman's civil rights legislation cold. The only crack in the dike appeared when the Senate modified cloture. The Senate finally gave the rule real meaning, approving the Rules Committee's proposal to allow cloture on motions as well as measures while increasing the necessary number of votes to two-thirds of the Senate membership.

For Russell, his first year as senator was an unqualified success. In a year's time, he had stepped from his father's shadow into the favorable glow of public attention. His assiduous performance drew praise from virtually every quarter. "Those fellows took me in very well, and I appreciated it," Russell said, noting "most of those men had not been close to my father." Russell's acceptance was no accident. His early achievements were worthy of the praise he received. He fervently fought for increased social security and government assistance for the handicapped and aged. He was articulate and forceful in opposition to foreign aid. When a vacancy occurred on the Senate's Banking Committee, Russell was named to the important panel, a rare appointment for senators serving unexpired terms. He won high marks for his strong and intelligent rhetoric in opposing the Basing Point Pricing Bill, legislation to permit a monopolistic pricing scheme that was designed to end price fixing for steel and other bulk commodities. His role in reorganizing the civil service system also earned him applause. "He turned (those bills) inside out and understood every comma," said columnist Drew Pearson.[34]

Pathfinder named Russell one of the three outstanding new senators, describing him as "Louisiana's mild and well-mannered Russell B. Long," who "buckled down to work with a quiet diligence which surprised many who had vivid memories of his rambunctious father." Pearson declared, "whereas Huey was a one-man tornado who believed in the political doctrine of an eye for an eye, Russell Long is a gently breeze who prefers to turn the other cheek." *Redbook* featured Russell in its December 1951 edition, predicting effusively he was "potentially the most powerful member of the United States Senate."[35]

Russell himself delightedly pointed to his differences from Huey and bragged that many of his father's enemies were among his admirers. "Many men who were consistently at sword points with my father," he said in an Associated Press interview, "have been most friendly and helpful to me." In an earlier interview, he suggested his success in making friends was because "maybe I'm not as far to the left as he was and I may be willing to take a little more time to reach the goals I am after than he was."[36]

Russell's strategy for his first year in Washington was rather simple, but shrewd, as he recalled:

I figured out early in the game that it was not to my advantage to be Huey Long reincarnated. There were a lot of people, who for one reason or another, didn't get along with my father. A lot of them, because of their difference in views, and a lot of them, because he was the guy who seemed to feel, and I guess correctly, that time was not on his side—that time would run out on him. So, I guess that he felt that he had to keep moving. He couldn't put up with delay. Well, I felt that I could. I had time on my side, I felt. Furthermore, I felt that he was an enormously talented person and if I tried to be another Huey Long, to out-Huey Huey, that I'd look like a faker, an imitation. . . . I was going to have to start out on my own, who I was, what I was, and not expect any special consideration from these guys. I wasn't likely to have it. It would be a mistake to expect it.[37]

By all accounts, Russell's unpretentious strategy worked. "They thought he was just going to come up there and raise all that hell," said Buddy Gill, one of Russell's first Senate aides. "They were just waiting for him to, and he did just the opposite. And they all fell right in his lap."[38]

9

WHEN YOU'RE GETTING CORNS ON YOUR HANDS

IN WASHINGTON AND IN LOUISIANA, Russell often worked at a frenetic pace. When a legislative issue captured his interest or imagination, he was oblivious to time. Like his father before him, Russell often rose at 3:00 or 4:00 A.M. when some profound idea hit him. Over the years, Russell's friends and staff members grew accustomed to early morning phone calls from their boss, exuberant over some initiative hatched during bedtime musings. Likewise, when obsessed with his work, Russell toiled late into the night, never glancing at the clock. Often during these fervant periods, he routinely worked eighteen-hour days and split his staff into day and night shifts. Many nights, after dinner at home, Russell returned to the office. Kicking off his shoes, he would fall into his favorite rocking chair and instruct an aide on how to answer his correspondence. "Our life was sort of the kind of thing his father's had been," said Katherine. "Russell was gone all the time."[1]

Innovative thoughts and brainstorms often burst in Russell's mind like fireworks. To bewildered staff members, his complicated notions some-times made little sense as he sputtered them forth in rapid-fire velocity.

Almost always, Russell found a unique angle from which to view an issue or question. To those who knew him best, it seemed as if his complex mind never stopped churning. Staffers were sounding boards for his unconventional thoughts, which he usually repeated to them several times as he honed his idea into a logical concept. Even at thirty-two, his mind was as keen as any in the Senate. A reporter who profiled Russell in the December 1951 issue of *Redbook* marveled at Russell's "remarkable powers of concentration." Noting that Russell recently had heard a speech by the chief of army engineers, the reporter was astounded at his near photographic memory and his ability to recite the speech almost word for word. After a few years of observing Russell at work, one of his mentors, Georgia senator Richard Russell, remarked Russell was one of the two smartest men he had served with in his Senate career. The other, he said, was Huey Long.[2]

Unlike Huey Long, Russell adopted a quiet, orthodox manner in the Senate. He dressed conservatively, favoring brown or blue suits. His shoes were plain, never the two-tone bucks so common in the South during the period. Only his expensive, loud ties expressed the slightest trace of flamboyance. His only vices were after-work cocktails and his ever-present cigars and cigarettes.[3]

Despite impressing his colleagues with his intellect and his work ethic, Russell took nothing for granted as he looked to his 1950 reelection campaign. While he may have converted his Senate adversaries, he was certain the anti-Longs would unearth someone to challenge him in the election to a full, six-year term. Nonetheless, by all indications he had successfully negotiated his first year. He had steered clear of controversy and was poised to win the Democratic party primary in July 1950.

Uncle Earl's slightly improved political circumstances—rebounding from their subterranean lows of 1948—did not hurt Russell. (Those who reaped the benefits of Governor Long's social programs far outnumbered those who felt the bite of the increased taxes. Furthermore, Earl sought to prevent arousing anti-Long sentiment by adopting a more subdued manner in the 1950 legislative session.) Although his reelection seemed a formality, Russell did draw opposition for the Democratic nomination. His challenger was an unknown U.S. attorney from Louisiana's Western District, Malcolm Lafargue, a dogmatic conservative alarmed by the loathsome and creeping effects of socialism he saw at every level of government.[4]

Supported by Uncle Earl's ardent detractor, New Orleans mayor DeLesseps Morrison, Lafargue trumpeted a simple message: "Whether he admits it to you or to himself, Russell B. Long is a socialist at heart." Despite Russell's mellow brand of liberalism, this charge proved simply too outlandish for most voters. It prompted a skillful response from Russell, long accustomed to defending his father's liberalism, and now his own. "The big fellows ought to help the little fellows," he replied, noting "Jesus Christ was no socialist and he said that almost twenty centuries ago."[5]

In its endorsement of Lafargue, the *New Orleans States* framed the campaign in equally simple and blunt terms. "A vote for Russell Long," the paper said, "is a vote for taxes and more taxes and still more taxes and waste and still more waste. Where is the money coming from to support Uncle Sam after the Longs get their share?" Another detractor was Leander Perez, the States Rights party leader and Plaquemines Parish district attorney. Perez delivered his parish's votes for Russell in 1948 and was now disenchanted with Russell's refusal to bolt the Democratic party. Ignoring Russell's fierce opposition to President Truman's civil rights programs, Perez defined Russell's ilk as "Trumancrats," a cross between "communists and homos" which could only produce a "bastocrat." None of these attacks was cause for real concern. Uncle Earl offered the best analysis of the opposition's antipathy toward Russell when he observed "the only thing they've got against that boy is that his name is Long."[6]

Russell derived his own confidence from at least one unusual source, as he remembered: "I found that coming down the home stretch, something seemed the matter with my hands, at least my right hand. I couldn't figure out what the trouble was at first. And then I realized I was developing corns from shaking hands. . . . But the reason was people didn't want to turn my hand loose. I've told people ever since that time, frankly, when you're getting corns on your hands, on your handshaking hand, because people don't want to turn your hand loose, you're going to win that race." Russell's corns did not betray him. On election day, he breezed to victory, defeating Lafargue and another minor opponent with almost 68 percent of the Democratic vote. The November general election was a formality.[7]

Heady from his easy reelection—his father's best percentage in a statewide race had been only 57 percent—Russell sparked a minor international controversy when he suggested in a network radio interview that "war with Russia within one or two years is entirely possible." Furthermore, he added, "we would be foolish, realizing that, if we didn't prepare as if it were coming within one or two years." When pressed by the interviewer to explain, Russell only made matters worse. He predicted in the event of war, "fifteen to thirty of our larger cities will have atomic bombs dropped on them within the first week or two."[8]

Attempting to dramatize the necessity for military preparedness, Russell had technically said nothing wrong. It was the press interpretation of his remarks that caused him extreme embarrassment, evidenced by Louisiana newspaper headlines: "ATOMIC WAR SEEN BY RUSSELL LONG," "LONG PREDICTS ATOMIC WAR IN NEXT TWO YEARS," and "SEN. LONG SEES ATOMIC WAR IN NEXT TWO YEARS." The Soviet newspaper *Trud* even weighed in, labeling Russell a "psychopathic case."[9]

Considering the prevailing world anxieties, Russell's remarks were not overly radical. They came in the midst of unstable world affairs, barely less five years after the end of World War II and less than three months after the invasion of South Korea by communist North Korea. American distrust of the Soviets—many thought them behind the Korean invasion—was also widespread and intense. Nonetheless, Russell quickly realized that, while he may have reflected the nation's distrustful mood toward the Soviets, he should never have speculated on the inevitable destruction of American cities. It was a statement too inflammatory to be ignored by the media. Within several days, he took to the Senate floor to insert into the *Congressional Record* the full transcript of the interview, claiming press reports left the incorrect impression he was predicting an atomic war within a year. "I do not believe war is inevitable," he assured his colleagues. The flap, soon forgotten, undoubtedly taught Russell a valuable lesson about the pitfalls associated with outspokenness on such volatile issues. Even so, the remarks were not totally without profit. He was now known as a bona fide hardliner on foreign policy.[10]

Not allowing the brief furor over his unfortunate remarks to send him retreating for the sanctuary of domestic issues, Russell soon reveled in the opportunities afforded senators in the world arena. In January 1951, President Truman sent him to represent the United States at the inauguration of Brazil's new president, Getulio Vargas. The following month, he spoke to the Tennessee legislature and declared his support for Truman's policy of U.S. support for Turkey and Greece. He told lawmakers he supported the president's general doctrine of assistance to countries threatened by, as Truman said, "subjugation by armed minorities or by outside pressures." In Nashville, he also offered general support for Truman's decision earlier that year to commit U.S. troops to the conflict in Korea. He told a group of Tennessee Democrats, "the masters of the Kremlin made the greatest mistake ever in Korea. Because of Korea, the day the Soviet Union could look forward to easy conquest of the world is past."[11]

Further confirmation of Russell's interest in foreign affairs was his announcement in March that he wanted the seat on the powerful Senate Armed Services Committee left vacant by the death of Kentucky senator Virgil Chapman. Two other senators expressed interest in the position—William Benton of Connecticut and newly elected George Smathers of Florida, Russell's boyhood friend from summer camp. It was soon apparent that Russell had the upper hand. His quiet, deliberative style paid off. His deference to committee chairman Richard Russell of Georgia, his own military record, and his seniority over Smathers and Benton provided the edge he needed to win Chapman's seat.[12]

Russell's induction on Armed Services came at an opportune time. The Korean conflict divided Congress, pitting the Republican Senate leadership against Truman in a bitter disagreement about U.S. objectives in Truman's so-called "police action." To them, Truman's containment policy was not enough. So strongly did many Republicans want to pummel the communists in North Korea that they suggested abandoning efforts to rebuild war-torn Europe to provide more resources for the fight to save Asia.

Two men stood at the center of the debate: Secretary of State Dean Acheson and Supreme Allied Commander General Douglas MacArthur. Acheson was one of the most controversial figures in Washington, a lightning rod for Truman's foreign and defense policies. Senate Republican Leader Robert Taft considered him an "appeaser." "I look at that fellow," moaned another critic, Senator Hugh Butler of Nebraska. "I watch his smart-aleck manner and his British clothes and that New Dealism and I want to shout, 'Get out, Get out. You stand for everything that has been wrong with the United States for years.' " This view was held by many conservatives who believed Truman's urbane chief diplomat had invited the North Koreans to invade South Korea when he suggested in a speech that it was not among areas of the Pacific which the U.S. would defend. ("It all started when Dean Acheson made that dumb-ass speech," Russell said years later.) Whether an accurate interpretation of his remarks—no one had publicly attacked Acheson for his comments at the time—Acheson certainly drew most of the fire from hard-line and militarily aggressive Republicans and conservative Democrats. Like Russell, these men viewed the controversial and polarizing secretary of state an impediment to a foreign policy consensus.[13]

In a speech to the New Orleans Chamber of Commerce in June, Russell joined the chorus of senators calling for Acheson's resignation. "So long as Dean Acheson is secretary of state, the Republicans won't agree to any program he advocates," said Russell, explaining that Acheson "should realize, in the interests of national unity and for the benefit of our country he must leave office." He also attacked Truman for not consulting enough with the Republicans in Congress on foreign affairs.[14]

If the beleaguered Acheson was a stumbling block to greater harmony over foreign policy, his problems were trifling compared to those of MacArthur. A national hero and commander of U.S. forces in Korea, MacArthur strongly disputed Truman's objectives in Korea. While the president considered it a temporary police action, MacArthur's goals were loftier. The general had already enraged Truman by publicly suggesting that escalation of the war—which amounted to invading and vanquishing China and Russian Siberia—would turn the Pacific Ocean into a "peaceful lake." Truman ordered MacArthur to cease airing his views publicly on the subject. In March 1951, MacArthur sealed his fate when he released to the press his plans to end the war: Given the choice of invasion by superior U.S. forces or capitulation to U.S. demands to end the conflict, MacArthur said he was certain the Chinese would choose the latter. Furthermore, he said, he stood ready to present this option to Chinese leaders. Enraged, Truman relieved MacArthur of his command on April 11.[15]

"The recall of MacArthur by President Truman set off one of the great emotional binges of American history," remembered George Reedy, then a top aide to Democratic leader Lyndon Johnson. Republicans and Democrats exploded in outrage. "That was about as much hysteria across the land as I've seen," said Russell. Senator Richard Nixon demanded Truman reinstate the conquering hero of the Pacific war. Impeachment threats were shouted on Capitol Hill. Senator Joseph McCarthy condemned Truman as an "s.o.b. who decided to remove MacArthur when drunk." Public opinion was heavily on MacArthur's side, almost two to one. Western Union reported that 125,000 telegrams, most of them supporting MacArthur, were wired to the White House and Congress within a two-day period. When he returned to Washington, the general was given a hero's welcome. He majestically addressed a joint session of Congress, where he made his famous and emotional speech concluding, "Old soldiers never die, they just fade away." Maintaining that MacArthur's scheme might have provoked another world war, Truman stood fast. Meanwhile, the chairmen of the Senate Armed Services and Foreign Affairs committees announced they would begin hearings into the circumstances surrounding MacArthur's firing.[16]

Russell was quick to add his thoughts to the dispute, but succeeded only in confusing observers about where he stood. Truman, he said, had only prevented MacArthur from "taking the final gamble that Russia would not come in if we bomb China." He added that even if MacArthur's plan was militarily feasible, foreign policy considerations must be considered. "Militarily, it's always good strategy to bomb the [enemy's] supply lines and even his cities," Russell explained to a reporter. "It might be good strategy to send our Navy to bombard Shanghai. But politically it probably would not be the thing to do."[17]

While his statement left the impression that he stood with Truman, Russell was uncertain exactly who was right. In a letter to a Louisiana newspaper, he tried to clear up any confusion left by his previous, pro-Truman remarks. He wrote that he remained neutral and favored a full investigation of events. Truman was to blame, he said, for not taking Congress "into its confidence in our Far Eastern policy," which he termed "a serious and inexcusable mistake." Furthermore, Russell said that earlier press reports had "given the false impression that I agree with the policy that President Truman has followed in the dismissal of Gen. MacArthur."[18]

In the face of public opinion, Russell must have known his impartial position was risky. A readers' survey conducted by the *Shreveport Times* showed that MacArthur was supported by an overwhelming 97 percent of those who responded. More troubling for Russell was the paper's report that many who scribbled comments about the issue on their ballots bore down heavily on Russell's indecision and Senator Allen Ellender's open support of Truman. The paper leveled indirect criticism at Russell, suggesting its poll "should be a warning to Southern senators and representatives who have been straddling the fence or backing the Truman-Acheson course in Washington. It is time for these gentlemen to dismount from the spavined party line chargers they have been riding up and down Pennsylvania Avenue."[19]

In the meantime, nationwide public furor over the episode reached a fever pitch. More than seven million people turned out to cheer MacArthur as he paraded through central and lower Manhattan in New York. That same day in Washington, spectators booed and heckled Truman when he threw out the first ball at the Washington Senators season-opening game.

For forty-two days, the nation's attention was riveted on the dramatic closed-door joint hearings of the Armed Services and Foreign Relations committees. Ostensibly, the hearings were convened to determine why MacArthur had been fired and to assess the "military situation in the Far East." Senators heard testimony from thirteen witnesses, including MacArthur, Defense secretary George C. Marshall, Joint Chiefs of Staff chairman General Omar Bradley, and Secretary of State Dean Acheson. To guard against any disclosure of vital national security information, Defense and State Department officials transcribed the proceedings and deleted any sensitive testimony before releasing it to the press. The decision to bar television cameras—proposed by Armed Services chairman Richard Russell and opposed by committee Republicans—had been a wise one for Democratic senators. As *Time* magazine correctly observed, the Democrats wanted "to keep General MacArthur's thundering rhetoric out of earshot of the microphones and his dramatic profile off the screens of twelve million television sets."[20]

From his seat as the most junior Democrat on the Armed Services Committee, Russell played only a minor role in the unfolding national drama. For Russell, his cautious approach to the hearings was simple: "I am not going to ask any questions, say anything in the course of this hearing that would give someone the basis for saying that I thought the president was wrong to dismiss General MacArthur."[21]

On the second day of hearings, Russell began his questioning with high praise for the general, whom he deferentially complimented for being "a magnificent witness and extremely helpful to us."

"Thank you, senator," MacArthur responded. "I remember a day in this very room when I saw your brother. I was the chief of staff. That is the last time I saw him."

Russell corrected the general. "I believe that was my father, sir."

"Your father?" MacArthur replied. "I didn't realize you were quite that young."

True to his strategy, Russell's questions for MacArthur were courteous. He was probing, yet never aggressive or challenging. "You have indicated that in your opinion it is a good idea to stop communist aggression wherever it breaks out or at least to resist it, not to simply let it go without resistance," Russell said, to which MacArthur simply replied, "Correct."

Later, Russell asked, "Do you believe that we could have possibly armed this nation to the degree that we have, and are arming it, if the communist aggression had not broken out a year ago?"

"That, I would not be able to answer," MacArthur said, "except on the general concept that as the danger to your security increased, the vividness of the public response to preparedness increases."[22]

Several days later, when he questioned MacArthur again, Russell posed no questions about Korea at all, focusing instead on MacArthur's role in the American occupation of Japan after the war. He generously observed

"[Y]our occupation command has been pointed out as the most successful of any occupation force in history."[23] Russell left it to others to pose the tough questions to MacArthur, as he explained:

> I did not put myself out front of the parade on that. My thought was that would pass. I had mixed feelings on it. Looking back on it, one thing I was sure about, though, was that we had no business putting that thing on television, which I voted against and supported Dick Russell on. The thing that impressed me was that Dick Russell managed to handle it so that he took the steam out of it . . . like taking a great big balloon of hot air and just gradually let the steam out of it until it collapsed. Because basically, looking back on it, the president was right about dismissing General MacArthur, for just one reason. The president of the United States must have a [field] commander in whom he has confidence. Frankly, Truman couldn't have confidence in MacArthur for one main reason—MacArthur had no confidence in Truman.[24]

While striking a low profile during the hearings, Russell demonstrated an impressive depth of knowledge and maturity for a thirty-two-year old, as evidenced in one exchange with Secretary of State George C. Marshall: "Do you believe that we could win a war against Russia, if the war was started now?" Russell asked.

"I don't want to talk about it on the record, and I would rather hesitate to talk about it off the record," Marshall answered.

"The point I had in mind," Russell replied, "is that it has been my feeling that if a war against Soviet Russia occurred in another two years or another year, say, we might have a greater certainty to winning the war, but that to win it would mean a greater cost. For example, if the war occurred later on, even though we might have our nation better prepared, you would have to recognize the fact that the progress our enemies would make, in terms of atomic preparedness, would enable them to inflict much greater damage upon us, even though we correspondingly would be able to increase—inflict much greater damage upon them."[25]

Those who had hoped Chairman Russell would conduct a hasty whitewash of the matter were disappointed. The committee recorded more than 3,500 pages of testimony. Said *Time* of the proceedings: "Never before in the history of Western parliaments has there been an examination of fundamentals so painstaking in detail, so sweeping in scale." While the public's angry reaction to MacArthur's firing threatened to stampede Congress into forcing Truman to escalate the war, the hearings had the opposite effect. "It was certainly a time for caution," Russell observed, "if you did just what you did do: Drag this thing out while you put a new man in there. And our situation [in Korea] was not as desperate as it was made to appear." Said Lyndon Johnson aide George Reedy: "The Russell hearings defanged MacArthur. Upon examination, his plan for winning meant a major risk of a war with China and possibly the Soviet Union. No one was ready for that."[26]

Despite Senator Russell's skill in defusing a potential disaster, bickering over the war soon began to poison American politics. "Perhaps the Korean War's major effect in the United States was on the mass public's fears and hostility," said historian James MacGregor Burns. "Anticommunists now cried out that their warnings had been justified, that the North Korean attack proved Russia to be bent on world conquest, that the Chinese attack across the Yalu confirmed that Peking was bent on Asian conquest. It was in this context that anticomunist feeling was reaching a new pitch among Americans."[27]

10

THE SULTAN OF SMEAR

$\mathcal{R}$USSELL NEVER TRUSTED SENATOR JOSEPH MCCARTHY after the Wisconsin Republican lied to him during his first year in the Senate. In October 1949—based on solemn assurances of White House support—Russell supported McCarthy's obscure fur amendment to the Foreign Trade Zone Bill. When he later learned that President Truman not only opposed McCarthy's amendment, but that it might be the basis for a veto, Russell was furious. McCarthy had blatantly violated a sacred trust among senators. Once lied to by a colleague, confidence and goodwill were nearly impossible to restore. Summoning McCarthy off the Senate floor, Russell forcefully confronted his colleague about the breach of faith. After the incident, McCarthy was always suspect.[1]

Russell was immediately skeptical in February 1950 when he first heard McCarthy's wild allegations of a U.S. State Department replete with communists who were helping guide the nation's foreign policy. A cold warrior, Russell was no fan of Secretary of State Dean Acheson and the Truman foreign policy. However, to suggest that Acheson harbored communists was absurd. While he voted for creation of a special Senate panel to investigate McCarthy's charges—because "I feel that any senator is entitled to have such serious charges investigated"—Russell said in April, "[W]e can only judge his accusations and know the justifications of charges

119

that amount to treason against thousands of our citizens by the results."
If McCarthy were correct, Russell said, "then he has done us all a
service. But if the charges are not true, he has done us a grave national
injury."[2]

When the special committee ended its exhaustive investigation having
found not one communist, Russell and other Senate Democrats hoped
McCarthy's powerful anticommunist rhetoric would lose its luster. Instead, McCarthy continued to fulminate on the Senate floor, immune from
prosecution for slander, knowing that the American people—gripped by
Cold War fever worsening after the advent of the Korean conflict—were
deadly afraid of the communist threat.

Meanwhile, while many of Russell's Democratic colleagues were eager
to crush McCarthy with censure or expulsion proceedings, Senate Minority leader Lyndon Johnson was cautious. "He'd say, 'If you're going to kill
a snake with a hoe,' " former Vice President Hubert Humphrey once recalled, " 'you have to get it with one blow at the head.' " Johnson would
wait, slowly feeding McCarthy all the rope he needed with which to hang
himself. To their discredit, Senate Republicans regarded McCarthy as a
potent weapon against the Democrats, especially if he could document his
allegations. Many remained silent in the wake of McCarthy's unscrupulous
attacks on various government officials, including Defense Secretary
George C. Marshall, who, he said, was tolerating a communist conspiracy
in the United States. Campaigning in Alabama for Democratic presidential
nominee Adlai Stevenson, Russell attacked McCarthy again in November
1952, dubbing him "the sultan of smear," observing that Republican
quietude on the matter had allowed McCarthy to "drag them from the
gutter to the sewer."[3]

With his reelection in November 1952 and the simultaneous shift in
Senate control to the new Republican majority, the new leadership gave
McCarthy chairmanship of the Permanent Subcommittee on Investigations
of the Senate Government Operations Committee. From this perch, the
demagogic Republican began investigating suspected communist activity in
the army. This time, Lyndon Johnson concluded that the Democrats finally
had a simple opportunity to crush their adversary—they would support
televising the hearings. It worked. From April to June, a nationwide
television audience watched as McCarthy browbeat and blustered his way
through the inquest. He rudely interrupted witnesses. He preached. He
frustrated fellow senators, often ignoring them to play to the ever-present
cameras. By May, Republican senators—suspecting that the public's exposure to McCarthy and his heavy-handed theatrics had been a serious

mistake—backed off. They wanted the hearings ended. Johnson, his Democrats, and the army would hear nothing of it.

"They know what these hearings are liable to uncover," Russell groused to reporters. "If these charges are untrue, they should be exposed as not being true. But this idea of these Republicans meeting before television by day and meeting in closed rooms by night to try to agree that they will not further expose one another is the kind of thing the American people will not approve."[4]

Generally critical of McCarthy, Russell was sometimes hesitant. As his 1956 reelection campaign drew near, he questioned the wisdom of harsh public attacks on McCarthy, as he confessed in a 1954 letter to his Senate predecessor and confidant, William Feazel:

> I rather doubt that McCarthy will be very much of an issue in the next campaign, because most Republican voters do not approve of him and yet he has many rabid supporters. The problem is: How do you have your cake and eat it too? It is my guess that a man who attacks McCarthy may chase off more votes than he picks up in the process. Meanwhile, I hear from some Republicans that they feel it is suicide for a Republican candidate to take a position either for or against McCarthy, inasmuch as over half of the Republican voters are against him.[5]

Russell's fears were unfounded. In the end, McCarthy had little impact on the 1956 Senate elections. He and his elaborate case began to unravel—in full view of millions of television viewers—when McCarthy bullied the wrong man. In June, he and chief committee counsel, Roy Cohn, began intense questioning of army counsel Joseph H. Welch about whether he had pressured the committee to hire an associate in his Boston law firm. This man, McCarthy bellowed, has leftist connections. Another senator disputed McCarthy's charge, insisting that he had no recollection of Welch trying to force his associate on the committee. McCarthy cavalierly ignored his colleague. He instructed his press assistant to release the allegation anyway. Welch passionately defended his associate, but scored his most stinging rebuke of McCarthy when he calmly turned to him in quiet anger and declared, "Little did I dream that you could be so reckless and so cruel. I like to think I'm a gentle man, but your forgiveness will have to come from someone other than me. . . . Have you no sense of decency, sir? At long last, have you left no sense of decency?" The audience, which had gaped in stunned silence, erupted in applause at the end of Welch's testimony. Welch had done what others could not. He exposed the moral destitution of McCarthy's reckless conduct. Many agreed it was the beginning of McCarthy's downfall.

In August, the Senate finally appointed a special committee to consider disciplinary proceedings against McCarthy. Members did not investigate his witch-hunting tactics or his veracity. Only considered were violations of Senate decorum, that is, rules against questioning the integrity or motives of another senator. McCarthy had done this with reckless abandon, calling the committee's chairman, Republican Arthur Watkins of Utah, "stupid," and labeling the entire committee "handmaidens of the Communist party."

While he did not serve on the committee, Russell nonetheless paid special attention to its hearings, knowing he would vote on a resolution of censure when the committee made its report to the full Senate. Although he detested McCarthy and his underhanded ways, Russell could never quite escape the painful memories of how his father's assaults on the status quo had engendered such intense hatred and scorn. As the son of one of the Senate's most renowned mavericks, Russell had more patience and understanding for unusual and outrageous behavior than most of his colleagues. Many senators, he knew, would not have required much evidence before voting to condemn his father's outrageous and sometimes flamboyant behavior. Furthermore, Russell remembered how Huey's Louisiana enemies viciously attacked him in 1929 and nearly turned him from office during the bitter impeachment proceedings. Huey was always the underdog and, in a sense, so was McCarthy to Russell. Besides, McCarthy had his avid supporters in Louisiana, a fact not lightly dismissed. "If Sen. Joe McCarthy's voice is silenced," one north Louisiana newspaper proclaimed, "it will pave the way for government leaders with Red-tinged sympathies and Soviet-dominated loyalties to re-echo Harry Truman's famous 'red herring' defense of the sinister threat of the hammer and sickle to America's strength."[6]

In November, the special committee recommended McCarthy's censure. McCarthy continued to rage against his accusers. Russell, meanwhile, agonized over his vote and began preparing a speech opposing McCarthy's censure. Like Russell, several other senators found it troublesome to condemn McCarthy. Some even feared a censure vote might set a dangerous precedent, jeopardizing the autonomy of other committee chairmen whose investigations were offensive to politically powerful groups. To Russell, a censure vote was rather meaningless, "a slap on the wrist by which we say 'You've been a bad boy—go and sin no more,' " as he then described it. For these and other reasons, the Senate eventually dropped the committee's charges, limiting its censure resolution to McCarthy's attacks on the special committee's integrity.[7]

On the day of the vote, McCarthy was surly. He demanded a quorum call. "I think the most disgraceful spectacle I have ever seen is the one before my eyes when I look at the Democrat side of the aisle," McCarthy complained, noting the presence of only three Democrats, including Russell, on the Senate floor. "Perhaps we should consider preserving the dignity of the Senate by having senators present, because senators are the jury in this case, which involves the rules."

As the Senate's leaders discussed McCarthy's quorum request, Russell shot from his seat. For most of the day, he forcefully informed McCarthy, "more than fifty percent of the Democratic senators" had been on the floor. "I am sure that if the junior senator from Wisconsin had been present during the entire day he would have noticed that."[8]

By then, Russell had decided how he would vote. He waited, however, until moments before the roll call to announce his decision:

> Mr. President, so much do I dislike the idea of censuring one's colleagues that I cannot conceive of myself ever bringing before the Senate a censure resolution. Nevertheless, this unpleasant task has been brought before us and I have been compelled to reach an unhappy decision. . . . It is not enough, in my opinion, to disapprove generally of the personal conduct of a senator or the manner in which he carries out his duties as a senator. Specific misconduct is essential as a basis for censure. I disagree with the statement in the select committee's report to the effect that a senator does not have the right to impugn the motives of a fellow senator or a senatorial committee. I believe that all of us have that right, and I would certainly regret to see it otherwise. . . .
>
> In most violent form we have witnessed his attitude and attack on the chairman, and indeed all the members of a select committee of the Senate appointed with the greatest care. . . . He has said that this committee as a whole was serving the cause of communism, but he has produced no evidence supporting this charge, and I emphatically state that I do not believe that any member of this committee knowingly or unknowingly is serving the cause of communism. . . .
>
> Except for repeated assaults by the junior senator from Wisconsin on individual senators and duly constituted committees, which have not been mitigated by any generous expression on his part and which have not been supported by evidence to prove his charges of wrongful motives and harmful actions, I should never have decided to vote for censure in this case. . . . The right to challenge must be undisputed and, equally so, the burden of proof must rest with the challenger when his challenge is accepted.[9]

The Senate voted overwhelmingly—forty-six Democrats and twenty-two Republicans—to censure McCarthy, who, former Johnson aide Harry McPherson recalled, "never recovered." Like the fabled emperor, the nation began to see the moral nakedness of McCarthy's platform.[10]

* * *

For weeks after his censure, McCarthy was quiet. On the afternoon of January 14, 1955, he broke his silence. He entered the Senate chamber for the first time since the Senate censured him. He was there to denounce Democrats who had introduced and supported a resolution that branded the U.S. Communist party "part of the international Communist conspiracy against the United States and all democratic forms of government." Only a handful of senators were on the floor at the time, but Russell, serving as the Senate's presiding officer, listened to McCarthy attack the resolution as hypocritical. As word of McCarthy's tirade spread, senators scurried to the Senate floor. Within minutes, the chamber was full. Texas Democrat Price Daniel was the first to challenge McCarthy's allegations that the Democrats only voted for the resolution to absolve themselves of guilt for not supporting vigorous efforts rid the government of communists. Facing Daniel, McCarthy ridiculed the resolution as "meaningless except as a political gesture," adding, "I think some of those who sponsored the resolution were trying to get some dirt off their hands. I am not referring to the junior senator from Texas."[11]

Daniel angrily retorted, "I regret that the senator from Wisconsin would make such a statement about other sponsors of the resolution. Let us assume that all other senators had the same good intention in the wording of the resolution as the junior senator from Wisconsin and I have." McCarthy answered, "I cannot assume that, when I look at the names of senators who have voted to put up the fight they did against anyone who has dug out Communists. When I find a senator who has voted for this pious resolution and I then check his record and find that he is against anyone who tries to implement this type of resolution, I cannot give him credit for being sincere."

Intently following the spirited debate from the presiding officer's chair, Russell found himself growing angrier by the minute. Finally, he erupted. "The chair is compelled to call the junior senator from Wisconsin to order," Russell commanded. "His remarks are contrary to the Senate rules, and he must take his seat."

Stunned by this instruction, McCarthy sputtered, "I did not understand the statement of the chair."

Russell explained. "The statement of the junior senator from Wisconsin was that other senators were insincere. In making that statement, the senator from Wisconsin spoke contrary to the rules of the Senate."

Senator Herman Welker of Idaho rushed to McCarthy's support. "Mr. President," he addressed Russell, "I ask that the junior senator from Wisconsin be allowed to proceed in order."

Russell was unwavering. "The senator from Wisconsin may not speak."

McCarthy regained the floor only when Daniel yielded to him moments later, whereupon he turned his wrath on Russell. "I certainly appreciate having the chair follow the rules so closely," McCarthy said sarcastically. "I observed the present presiding officer, when he was seated on his side of the aisle within the last two or three months while every rule of the Senate was violated, and he never once opened his mouth. I was being criticized and accused of everything but murdering my great-grandmother, but the junior senator from Louisiana, who now occupies the chair, sat in his seat like a bump on a log. He was not worried then about the Senate rules."

Russell remained silent, but kept his eyes trained on McCarthy until more than thirty minutes later when the Wisconsin senator again violated the Senate rule, this time while he debated Senator Thomas Kutchel of California: "I now say to the senator from California that he or any other senator can have me compelled to take my seat, if he wishes to do so; that can be done under Rule 21. But after looking at this list and after listening to the vote, I am utterly convinced that there are those who signed that pious resolution who are opposed to digging out Communists and will oppose anyone who digs out Communists, and who are attempting, as I said, to remove the stench from their hands and the mud from their skirts." Again, Russell ordered him to sit. But this time Russell left the chair so he could directly engage McCarthy, who asked him, "Can a senator criticize another senator on the floor, or any other place; in the future, can the senator from Louisiana expose wrongdoing on the part of a senator, if that rule is followed?"

"It is my understanding and feeling," Russell answered, "that if a senator makes charges against another senator as being guilty of dishonest, unpatriotic, or traitorous conduct, and if the question is brought before the Senate by way of a resolution to censure the senator making the charge, if the senator making the charge does not proceed to support it or prove it, then it seems to me he is liable in a court of law if a slander suit were filed against him."[12]

Russell later discussed the brush-up with reporters, dismissing McCarthy's charges of hypocrisy against the Democrats. "The Democratic record will speak for itself on efforts to investigate and ferret out subversive activities. There is a determination among the Democratic leaders to expose communism wherever it might be." Honoring Senate tradition, Russell declined to carry his dispute with McCarthy out of the Senate chamber. For the benefit of Louisiana's voters, the next day's *Shreveport Times* and *Baton Rouge Morning Advocate* featured photos of Russell and McCarthy shaking hands and smiling as they stood in the Senate Reception Room.[13]

This was not the last encounter Russell would have with McCarthy. Later in the summer, in a newsletter to Louisiana constituents, Russell criticized McCarthy for exerting undue influence over President Eisenhower's conference with U.S. allies at Geneva by offering a resolution demanding Eisenhower give priority to demands for the liberation of all enslaved people behind the Iron Curtain. "This may well be President Eisenhower's intention," Russell wrote, "but most of us felt we should not tie the President's hand or attempt to make him an agent of the Senate. Senator McCarthy argued anyone who failed to vote for his resolution would be an appeaser or something worse. Few Senators agreed: The McCarthy resolution was defeated, 77 to 4." This was rather mild criticism and would have probably gone unnoticed by McCarthy had it not been for a blunder in the Senate's mailing room, which sent out Russell's attack on McCarthy in the envelopes of McCarthy's senior Wisconsin Republican colleague, Senator Alexander Wiley.[14]

McCarthy never recovered from the unmasking at the hands of his Senate colleagues. New Mexico's senator Clinton Anderson accompanied a group of southwestern oilmen to McCarthy's office one afternoon several months later. "During the discussion," Anderson remembered, "McCarthy, sallow-faced and haggard, swigged from a bottle of whisky at his side."[15]

For all the damage the ordeal inflicted on its instigator, the damage to the nation was as severe. Paranoia helped to set the nation's hard-line Far Eastern policy in concrete for decades, meaning President Truman, under siege as a harborer of communists, continued to fight the Korean conflict for fear his detractors would label him an appeaser. As historian William L. O'Neill observed: "Many Americans, and many more Asians, died as a result. It meant Eisenhower, though he ended the Korean War, could not exploit the Sino-Soviet rift, nor could Kennedy and Johnson. They could

not avoid war in Indochina either for fear of being accused of 'losing' South
Vietnam." McCarthyism indeed took its toll on the American psyche
through the Vietnam War, though McCarthy himself never lived to witness the damage he caused. He died of hepatitis on May 2, 1957, a broken
and, aptly, discredited man.[16]

11

I'd Rather Be Dead!

Russell, Katherine, and the girls had settled into a quiet, comfortable life in suburban Chevy Chase, Maryland, northwest of Washington. On weekends not spent in Louisiana, Russell sometimes took the girls—Katherine was now seven, Pamela three—to the Washington zoo. Other times, he played golf with friends at the Army and Navy Country Club. Left-handed and somewhat reckless off the tee, Russell enjoyed the sport into his seventies. At 160 pounds, Russell now weighed ten pounds less than after his first year in the Senate when his new active social life added almost a pound a month to his five-foot-nine frame. A diet and a swimming regimen took most of the weight off.

Russell and Katherine's circle of friends grew quickly. Bruce Tucker, a veteran aide to senators Overton and Feazel, was now Russell's top assistant. The two men—Tucker was several years older than Russell—became fast friends. When the workday stretched into the evening, they often ate dinner together or shared a drink at a Capitol Hill pub. Many nights, they spent late hours at the office, where Tucker tutored his younger boss in the ways of the Senate.

Another new friend was Thomas Hale Boggs, the young, energetic congressman from New Orleans. Boggs was one of the first friends Russell and Katherine made in Washington. At first glance, Russell and

Hale had much in common. They were attorneys and navy men, and Boggs was only four years older. Like Katherine, Boggs's wife, Lindy, had small children and shared the wonderment of starting a family in the nation's capital. Both men loved Louisiana and its rambunctious politics with equal appetite. Just below the surface, however, Russell and Hale were actually a very unlikely match. Boggs's scorn for Huey Long had helped kindle his early political pursuits in the 1930s, when he and his law partner, DeLesseps Morrison, formed the People's League of New Orleans. A group of anti-Long activists, the league tried to exploit the legal troubles of the Long faction by fielding candidates for various offices and championing indulgent voter registration laws.

Russell's arrival in Washington was the first time the two men were exposed to each other on a personal level. And so, Boggs, the reformer, and Russell, heir to the dynasty Boggs once struggled to topple, soon discovered the common political ground they shared. As they increasingly got acquainted, socially and professionally, they discovered that despite diverse political backgrounds they were actually more alike than different. Indeed, the ideology they shared most intensely was political—their belief that Louisiana could prosper in the late 1950s only if the political feuds and the regional and ethnic divisiveness of the previous twenty years were laid to rest.

Equally appealing to both men were the political advantages inherent in a Long-Boggs coalition. If they could assemble the Longs and anti-Longs under one political umbrella, the possibilities for the leaders of such a confederation were staggering to anyone who could count a vote. Russell clearly wanted to form such an alliance with a young, fresh leader—namely Boggs—in the 1952 gubernatorial election. He hoped he could do so without a confrontation with his Uncle Earl. As he soon learned, it was unavoidable.

Russell wanted his uncle to retire from politics, for several reasons. Earl was in poor health, having suffered a serious heart attack in February 1950 during one of his renowned hog hunts in the hills near his pea patch farm in Winnfield. To compound his problems, Earl's political health, although much improved from the previous two years, could only be classified as satisfactory. Although much of the hard feelings from the massive taxes of 1948 had abated, Earl nonetheless was rebuffed by voters in 1950 when he sought approval for a $140 million road bond issue. Furthermore, Earl fell out with one-time ally lieutenant governor Bill Dodd. What frightened Russell was that none of Earl's physical or political difficulties dampened his lust for the political fray. While the state's constitution prevented him from succeeding himself as governor, Earl dropped hints he might run for lieutenant governor on a ticket with a handpicked candidate for governor.

Sometime in early 1951, Russell went to Winnfield to see his uncle Earl. It was a mission to persuade him to place the state's interests first and step aside for the younger generation. The meeting, as recalled by Russell, was not fruitful:

> I said, "Well now, Uncle Earl, you've told the people that you weren't going to run again."
> He said, "Roosevelt said that twenty times."
> "Well, even so, you said you weren't going to run again and people will say that you're not keeping the commitments you made and I don't know why you want to run for office. It seems you'd be best advised to be a senior statesman. You're not hard up for money. You've worked hard to get where you are. You could retire a winner and go out as a very effective governor. People who might be down on you now would feel more kindly toward you when you're no longer running for office, no longer in office. Why don't you just consider being a senior statesman?"
> He said, "I'd rather be dead."[1]

The discussion persuaded Russell that Earl's time had passed. Now, he was certain his support of Boggs was correct, even if it meant a confrontation with Uncle Earl. Not long thereafter, the first evidence of a spat with Earl appeared in the *New Orleans Times-Picayune*. Washington correspondent Edgar Poe reported that all official communication between the governor's office and Russell was being conveyed by Congressman Edwin Willis of St. Martinville.[2]

Meanwhile, Boggs had been traveling the state, sizing up his prospects. He and Lindy scouted for signs that Louisiana had changed to the point where voters would consider voting for a New Orleans Roman Catholic. Day after day, Hale and Lindy traversed Louisiana, meeting with groups of prospective supporters in every major city. The week was an unqualified success. "There was this wonderful enthusiasm," Lindy Boggs remembered, adding that as they returned home, Hale pulled the car to the roadside as they approached New Orleans.

"Well," he said turning to Lindy, who had initially opposed Hale's candidacy, "what do you think?" "I hate to say it, but I don't think you have any choice," she answered. "All those people with those bright prospects think you're the person who can do it." Hale shook his head in agreement, and wept.[3]

In June, Hale announced that he would seek the Democratic nomination for governor of Louisiana. Boggs's candidacy would attract an impressive and unlikely list of supporters, including former governor Sam Jones, former law partner and now New Orleans mayor DeLesseps Morrison, former senator Bill Feazel—Earl Long's major financial backer—and Congressman Jimmie Morrison. Less than twenty-four hours after Boggs made his candidacy official, Russell issued his own statement of support: "I have long felt that Louisiana suffered from the bitter fight of issues of the past. It is time the progressive, sincere people of our state stop fussing and feuding over the issues of the dead past and join together in leading our state into the bright sunshine of the future."[4]

Russell's endorsement of Boggs, Long family biographer Thomas Martin speculated, was not prompted only by altruism. "It was a bold and calculated move," Martin said. "With Earl a lame duck, his popularity at an ebb . . . a Boggs victory would establish Russell as the most politically powerful Long in Louisiana. Moreover, Russell's Senate term expired in 1956. If he chose to run then, Boggs—unable to succeed himself—would be showing only elemental political courtesy in supporting him."[5]

Russell's support for Boggs immediately drew fire from at least one Long. Another of Russell's uncles, Dr. George S. Long, charged his nephew with "treason" for supporting a man who had opposed his father. "It is a peculiar thing and an astonishing thing to see the son of Huey Long politically in bed with such people—people who plotted day after day to get his father out of office," Dr. Long said. The doctor conveniently neglected to mention that he and Earl had often fought bitterly with their brother Huey, to such an extent that Dr. Long had once left Louisiana for Oklahoma.[6]

Earl, however, was not as quick to attack his nephew. His silence lent credibility to speculation that he was having difficultly locating someone to run on the Long gubernatorial ticket. His hesitancy to challenge Russell, the *New Orleans Item* speculated, "may mean he hasn't decided yet on an all-out fight. If it is too powerful to fight, if he can't get a strong enough ticket to fight it with, he may have to sit the race out." Of course, Earl had no plans to watch a Louisiana a governor's race from the sidelines and Russell knew it, remembering that his feisty uncle had said he would rather be dead. Soon, the Long organization announced that it found its candidate: Baton Rouge district judge Carlos Spaht, a World War II veteran and former president of the LSU Alumni Association. Spaht was not a household name. He was promptly dubbed "Earl's boy" by detractors. But with the backing of Earl's organization, he was destined to have

an impact on the race. Later, when someone asked Earl why he had picked
such an obscure candidate, he replied, "Why not? Hell, (former Governor)
Dick Leche was a judge, wasn't he? If Dick Leche could get elected, so can
Spaht." It was just this obscurity Earl wanted in a candidate. Spaht had no
following and could never challenge Earl. As Earl Long biographers Kurtz
and Peoples observed, "Earl Long picked Spaht because he knew that
Spaht would lose." Even in defeat, Earl would remain head of the Long
organization, poised to run again for governor four years later. Former
lieutenant governor Bill Dodd put it more bluntly. "He wanted the opposition to elect someone who could screw up so badly that the voters would
be crying for Uncle Earl's return in 1956."[7]

As Spaht's running mate for lieutenant governor, Earl chose north
Louisiana state representative John McKeithen, a law school classmate of
Russell's. A handsome, eloquent legislator, McKeithen was also Earl's
protégé and house floor leader. In all, the governor's race would not suffer
for lack of big names: Lieutenant Governor Dodd was running, as was
Russell's old nemesis, Judge Robert Kennon. Huey Long's former secretary and now registrar of the state Land Office, Lucille May Grace,
announced her candidacy. And Dudley J. LeBlanc, the wily, smooth-
tongued inventor of the elixir Hadacol—who ran for governor in 1932 and
1944—threw in his hat, as well. There were also several minor candidates
who would influence the race, including an Alexandria cattleman, James M.
McLemore; the legislature's sergeant at arms, Cliff Liles; and, the first
black man to run for statewide office in Louisiana since Reconstruction,
Kermit Parker, a New Orleans druggist.

The issues were neither exotic nor diverse. To boost Spaht, Earl
promised to convene a special legislative session to distribute the state's
twelve-million-dollar welfare surplus, in one-hundred-dollar payments, to
each of the 120,000 elderly on the state's rolls. LeBlanc was more
expansive. He wanted a seventy-five-dollar old-age pension, free college
educations for everyone, and bonuses to veterans. Dodd's platform was
similar. He promised a sixty-dollar old-age pension and free college tuition.
Kennon pledged sweeping government reforms, while McLemore tried to
capitalize on the sentiment against civil rights. Earl Long, McLemore
charged, was a "nigger lover."[8]

From the campaign's first day, Russell's top priority was Boggs's election.
He abandoned Washington to spend virtually the entire summer in Louisiana
helping his friend. So enthusiastic about Boggs's chances, Russell brought
half his Washington staff to New Orleans, with most of the office files, so he
could conduct official duties in Louisiana while campaigning for Boggs.

As they moved about the state, Russell and Hale found that the enthusiasm that had lured Boggs into the race was still strong, even in north Louisiana. After a swing through Shreveport, Monroe and other northern towns in July, Russell bubbled with optimism. He told one newspaper that he had never seen "a campaign that looked so good in the beginning." To a constituent in Ferriday, Russell wrote he could "see no way that Hale Boggs can be prevented from going into a run-off."[9]

In many ways, Russell was heartened by the new relationships afforded by the campaign. Most impressive was his newfound friendship with an old Long nemesis, DeLesseps Morrison, the mayor of New Orleans. In an extremely cordial letter to Morrison, Russell touted Boggs's prospects, using one of his father's stories to make his point:

> You might recall the story my father used to tell about the baptizing of his uncle when the royal flush floated out of his pocket. As the story goes, the wife screamed, "Stop it, he's lost," and the son said, "Wait a minute Maw, if Paw can't win with that hand, ain't nobody ever gonna win." I am sincere in saying that if we can't elect Hale, it will be either that we didn't try hard enough or that we fumbled the ball all over the backfield.[10]

Russell found his new alliance with many of his father's old enemies was winning him plaudits in Washington, as well. When Morrison called on Russell that summer to discuss the governor's race over lunch in the Senate Dining Room, Illinois senator Paul Douglas and Tennessee's Estes Kefauver—both friends of Morrison—dropped by the table. As Russell later told a friend, the two men "were tickled pink to see us together for a change." Douglas was so delighted to see Russell with Morrison he later found him outside the building and bear-hugged his younger colleague.[11]

The enthusiasm that propelled Boggs and Russell headlong into the race was soon dampened by several events that eventually taught them that Louisiana had not progressed as far and as fast as they originally believed. The first sign of trouble came in the form of a sensational charge by one of Boggs's opponents, Lucille May Grace, who was conspicuously prompted by her benefactor, Plaquemines Parish district attorney Leander Perez. Grace dropped a bomb, charging that Boggs had belonged to a communist organization while at Tulane University. In truth, Boggs had once helped raise money for a student union building on campus when he was in law school. On one occasion, he spoke to a leftist group, the campus chapter of the American Student Union, about the benefits of a student activities facility. Thus, the charge: Grace brazenly claimed that Boggs had belonged to the American Student Union, which she labeled a communist-front organization. Boggs, of course, denied the charge. "Throughout my life, I have fought the dictators Hitler and Stalin," Boggs replied, aiming his remarks at Perez. "The tin-pot imitation from Palquemines has my contempt and that of every fair-minded man and woman in Louisiana." Both New Orleans newspapers were sympathetic to Boggs. They dismissed the allegation as smear tactics by Perez. "Among fair-minded Americans," the *Item* said in a front-page editorial, "it can only arouse disgust for the demagogue who manufactured it." Seven congressmen rushed to Boggs's defense. One of them, Frank Chelf of Kentucky, said "to say that Hale Boggs is a communist is to say that the American flag carries a hammer and sickle, Boston has no beans and that Louisiana has no politics."[12]

The charge was more serious than simply the damage it might inflict among Boggs's supporters. Under the rules of the Louisiana Democratic party, such allegations, if proven, were cause for disqualification. As if this charge alone were not enough to derail the campaign, Grace also challenged the legitimacy of Boggs's campaign under a provision of the state's constitution that seemed to prohibit a federal official from seeking a state position without first resigning his office. Governor Long quickly convened a raucous special meeting of the Democratic party's State Central Committee in Baton Rouge to hear the charges. Committee members dismissed the communist sympathy charge, finding Grace had improperly filed it. Perez objected loudly, but, strangely, so did Boggs, who wanted the charge dismissed on the merits of a full hearing, not a technicality. Ignoring Boggs's appeal, the committee dismissed the charge, sixty-eight to twenty-four. Disgruntled, Perez and Grace unsuccessfully pursued their case against Boggs in three different state courts.

The entire episode, said Lindy Boggs, "almost brought the campaign to a screeching halt" and forced Boggs to waste several weeks of valuable time that should have been spent on the campaign. The charge also created problems for Russell. "Not only was he for this guy who had been associated with anti-Long activities," said Boggs, "but was [labelled] a communist."[13]

Perhaps the misgiving most difficult to dispel, especially in the northern parishes, was the question of Boggs's Catholicism. In 1951, this fact gave Earl Long a compelling weapon against Boggs. North Louisiana was heavily Protestant and its citizens were wary of Catholic politicians and the suspected influence of the Pope on political affairs. Earl masterfully exploited Boggs's religion. As he campaigned for Spaht before Protestant crowds, he rarely missed an opportunity to remind his audiences of Boggs's Catholicism. At a rally in Alexandria, Lindy recalled she and Hale arrived early, simply to listen and assess the opposition:

> And then Earl got up and I thought, "Oh, dear." . . . And so the classic speech was: "Now they say my good friend, my close friend, Hale Boggs is a communist. Now you know that fellow can't be a communist. He's a good Roman Catholic. And they say that if Hale Boggs is elected governor, the Pope of Rome is going to come over here. Now, you know that's silly. The Pope of Rome is a busy man and he's got that archbishop right down in that big city of New Orleans that Hale Boggs comes from. And Hale Boggs and that Roman Catholic archbishop are just like that."[14]

On the last word, Earl crossed his fingers, letting the crowd ponder the information just disclosed. Frightened he might explode in anger, Lindy glanced nervously at her husband. "Hale couldn't help laughing. I was so relieved, I didn't know what to do."[15]

It was a brilliant device, a classic illustration of Earl's unique rhetorical skills, especially when on the attack. In just a few brief lines, he had devastated Boggs, reminding the crowd that he was from the Big City, that he was Catholic, and that he could possibly be influenced by the Vatican. Furthermore, he reminded the audience that Boggs had been accused of communism! "He put a double whammy on Boggs," said Bill Dodd, "and it not only killed him, it buried him." Lindy Boggs agreed. The negative impact of Boggs's Catholicism in north Louisiana was profound. "All the old feelings got whipped up. And then, all this communist stuff under the attitude of the time—people saw communists under every bed—it was very, very difficult. Especially with fundamentalist preachers, which was [sic] a big political force."[16]

For his part, Russell did his best to dispel any notion the attacks on Boggs's religion and patriotism would have any effect on the election. In an interview, he argued that south Louisiana voters would not pay attention to charges by "peanut politicians" and that voters in north Louisiana were too open-minded to vote against someone "because he worships according to his convictions."[17]

Although he refrained from attacks on Russell in the early stages, Earl soon found his stride. By the fall, Earl had taken to the stump and unloaded a fusillade of insults. "Russell and Boggs aren't bad boys," Earl said in more than one campaign speech. "They were just pulled too green." To another crowd, he offered a comparison with former governor Sam Jones:

"Why [Boggs] is as much like Sam Jones as two peas in a pod. He's even so much like Sam Jones that he struts when he walks." Russell's and Boggs's ages were also fodder for ridicule. "Hale is thirty-six," Earl said in the small southeast Louisiana town of Albany. "Russell is thirty-two. Both added together, they are hardly my age. And yet those two young squirts want to come back from Washington and rescue this state?"As the campaign progressed, Earl got meaner. His nephew, on whom he had heaped generous praise only the year before, was now "Louisiana's leading deadhead." In mock sadness, Earl made certain his listeners understood his grief at being forced to attack his nephew. "I hate to say these things about poor little Russell," he moaned, "but he started this."[18]

Russell's rhetoric was not as bitter and pointed as Earl's, yet he did respond on occasion to his uncle's verbal assaults. Reacting to Earl's assertion that Russell and Boggs had been "picked too green," Russell replied, "If I was picked too green on the vine, then Uncle Earl is too ripe on the vine and should be picked at once." Of Earl's characterization of Russell as a "deadhead," Russell said, "Earl Long is getting as bitter toward me as he was toward my father. Anytime he begins saying that kind of thing against me, it shows he thinks he's getting beat." Earl, Russell speculated, had contracted "mansionitis, an ailment that comes from sitting in that big mansion with all those servants and all those limousines and chauffeurs."[19]

The truth was that Boggs, whose prospects appeared so bright only months before, was sinking from the weight of Grace's charges and Earl's attacks on his religion. As an added insult, the *New Orleans Times-Picayune*, for which Boggs had once worked, endorsed McLemore. It was "a real blow," Lindy Boggs recalled. "It lent credence to the fact that there must be something about [Hale] that makes people hesitate."[20]

To make matters worse, Boggs frustrated Russell and others by refusing to consider paying Senator Dudley J. LeBlanc to drop from the race. Besides drawing away large numbers of south Louisiana Catholic votes, LeBlanc told crowds of unknowing Cajuns that Boggs had violated church principles by marrying outside the Catholic church. The charge was simply not true, but given LeBlanc's credibility, the perception was almost impossible to reverse. Russell was exasperated. Had Boggs been willing to strike a deal with LeBlanc, Russell believed he might have won:

> If we'd been willing to play that game of cards, the Earl Long handbook you might say, we'd have won it. Because we'd have done things we had to do in order to win that race. Hale was above making deals with anybody. . . . And

(former Senator) Bill Feazel told me subsequently, when just the two of us were together, when it was all over, he said, "I should have just gone on the side and paid Dudley LeBlanc off and we'd have won that race." The idea being—make a deal, that Dudley would go back and run for state senator, perhaps make him president pro tempore, as he had been before. . . . And so, it could have been handled in such a way that they would get the man out of the race and those votes would have gone almost solid to Hale.[21]

By election day, the die was cast. Spaht led the field with almost 23 percent of the vote to Kennon's 21 percent, sending the race into a runoff. Boggs finished third with 19 percent, missing the runoff by about twenty thousand votes. All the defeated candidates, including Boggs, threw their support to Kennon, who won an overwhelming 61 percent in the runoff to capture the Democratic nomination, tantamount to victory. Russell, the *New York Times* reported, "out of distaste for Kennon, rather than love of his uncle, kept hands off" the race. He declined to endorse either man.[22]

If the outcome was disheartening to Russell, it was downright depressing to the Long forces. "Longism thus had been rebuffed by a large majority of voters for the first time since 1928," observed a Louisiana historian. "Upon the actions of the Kennon administration rested the fate of the formerly dominant faction in state politics." Voters had not rebuffed every Long. Russell's uncle George, who attacked his nephew for supporting Boggs, was elected to Congress from Louisiana's Eighth District in central Louisiana. "There is no question," George Long asserted, "that my election represents a comeback for the Longs in Louisiana."[23]

Despite that one glimmer of hope, Russell briefly worried about another challenge from a politically energized Kennon in the next Senate election. His old friend, Bill Feazel, told him not to fret. "Uncle Earl is still shaking down the gamblers and everyone else that he can," Feazel wrote to Russell shortly after the election. "Earl is trying to convince your friends that Kennon will run against you, but don't let that bother you because Kennon will be a dead duck long before you come up again."[24]

While Russell may have arguably lost some political luster by investing so heavily in an unsuccessful candidate, the experience was not a total loss. In fact, one could argue that Russell's decision to forge new alliances and bury old enmities was a turning point in his political career. "If the last campaign accomplished no other purpose," he wrote in a conciliatory letter to Bill Dodd, "I believe that it will tend to cause a realignment of public officials more in line with the true issues and circumstances of our time. Those of us who are striving to work as a team for the greatest good of our state will now have an opportunity to associate with one another based upon our mutual desire to get a good job done."[25]

Indeed, the governor's race had decisively shown Russell was unlike his father in one very significant way—his political success would be fueled on friendships and coalitions, not enemies and dissention. Supporting Hale Boggs introduced Russell to the other side of Louisiana politics—the traditional anti-Longs. Many of those men, like New Orleans mayor DeLesseps Morrison, found in Russell a refreshing and honest public servant whom they liked and would support in years to come. Had Russell not supported Boggs, many of the anti-Longs might never have seen this side of their junior senator. While some declared the campaign a setback, Russell knew better. He had sown the seeds that would sustain his Senate career for another thirty-four years.

12

THOSE TWENTY VOTES

$\mathcal{T}$HOSE WHO REMEMBER PRESIDENT HARRY TRUMAN only through the forgiving lens of historical revision cannot fully understand the scorn he engendered, particularly in the South, during his second term. Political and legislative stalemate on virtually every front, charges of corruption and communism in his administration, the strife of the Korean conflict, and his civil rights program had alienated all but the most steadfast Democrats. In 1952, public opinion weighed heavily against another term for Truman. The debate over his future generated such spirited discussion at a Washington reception that one southern senator reportedly doused a colleague with wine as they argued whether Truman should retire.

Truman had few friends in the capital compared to the resplendent war heroes—Douglas MacArthur and Dwight Eisenhower—who seemed willing to avail themselves to either of the major political parties. As early as the previous summer, Russell derided Truman's political future while extolling the two generals. "General MacArthur is the only man who can keep MacArthur from getting the Republican nomination for 1952. I don't think President Truman will run for a third term. General Eisenhower would [also] be a good candidate for either the Democrats or the Republicans. He's a great American."[1]

Early in 1952, Russell joined a group of southerners endorsing the candidacy of Georgia's Richard Russell, the Senate Armed Services Committee chairman and leader of the southern bloc. None of the group were ever Truman stalwarts, yet *U.S. News and World Report* concluded that senator Russell's campaign might "spell defeat for Truman" if he ran. One southerner not supporting Senator Russell was Tennessee Senator Estes Kefauver, a liberal hero whose recent victory in the New Hampshire primary was diminished only by Truman's nonparticipation. In late March, the president finally dispelled any suspense. He would not seek another term. Truman's decision sparked a mad scurry for the Democratic nomination. Kefauver—whose candidacy may have hastened Truman's announcement—was the most ambitious. There were other aspirants, including Vice President Alben Barkley, Senator Robert Kerr of Oklahoma, Illinois governor Adlai Stevenson, and House Speaker Sam Rayburn.[2]

Russell quickly applauded Truman's decision, announcing that the president's withdrawal meant a "more unified Democratic Party. Had he decided to seek another nomination, he would have struck a serious blow at the party. I think he's a bigger man for deciding not to run." Meanwhile, Russell continued extolling Senator Russell, this time before the state's Democratic Central Committee in Baton Rouge: "He's a regular Robert E. Lee when it comes to leading an army in the field."[3]

At that meeting, Louisiana Democrats sowed the seeds of dissension that would thrust their delegation onto center stage at the upcoming national convention. Incited by the party's radical segregationists, they fell into a bitter dispute over party unity and civil rights. At this meeting, Louisiana's twenty delegates to the July convention in Chicago—including Russell and Plaquemines Parish district attorney Leander Perez—received no instructions for whom to cast their ballots. The state central committee only required them to vote as a unit.

Meanwhile, Perez correctly suspected that the Democrats would reject the southern candidacy of Senator Richard Russell and nominate a liberal candidate with a progressive civil rights agenda. Earnest in his belief that Eisenhower was the party's only hope for retaining the White House, the Plaquemines Parish boss concocted a treacherous scheme. He hoped to award the rooster—the Louisiana Democratic party's ballot symbol—to Eisenhower, even though the general was the Republican party's nominee. If Perez succeeded, he would deny the Democratic party's presidential standard-bearer a meaningful spot on Louisiana's ballot. Although the central committee had rejected Perez's plan during its Baton Rouge meeting, Russell suspected that his crafty detractor would try again at the convention. His suspicions were well-founded.

Russell at about age four. (*Louisiana State University Libraries*)

Huey Long and family. An early family portrait at the Long home on Forrest Avenue in Shreveport. Left to right, Palmer, Rose, Huey, Russell, and little Rose. (*Louisiana State University Libraries*)

Russell, about age fifteen, delivers a basket of Thanksgiving food for the poor in New Orleans. (*Louisiana State University Libraries*)

The Kingfish in a typical pose. Senator Huey Long gestures forcefully during a 1935 speech to the Little Congress, an association of Washington, D.C., congressional aides, then headed by Lyndon Johnson. (*Wide World Photos*)

Vice President John Nance Garner administers the oath of office to Russell's mother, Rose McConnell Long, appointed to the U.S. Senate after Huey's death. (*Wide World Photos*)

Russell campaigns for student body president at Louisiana State University, a race that changed the nature of campus politics. (*Louisiana State University Libraries*)

Senator Huey Long and his wife, Rose, in New Orleans in the early 1930s. (*Louisiana State University Libraries*)

Russell, around age fourteen, with his father in New Orleans. (*Louisiana State University Libraries*)

Russell aboard his LCT boat during World War II, somewhere in the Mediterranean. (*Louisiana State University Libraries*)

Uncle Earl and Russell, now the governor's executive counsel, in the state capitol in 1948. (*Louisiana State University Libraries*)

Russell shares a Coca Cola with a group of farmers at the Governor's Mansion in 1949. (*Louisiana State University Libraries*)

The nation's youngest and oldest senators, Russell and Senate president pro tempore Kenneth McKellar, pose for photographers after Russell's swearing in on December 31, 1948. (*Louisiana State University Libraries*)

The new senator at his suburban Maryland home plays with daughter Kay while Katherine holds Pamela. (*Louisiana State University Libraries*)

Running for reelection in 1950, Russell addresses a New Orleans crowd from a produce truck. (*New Orleans Times-Picayune*)

As it arrived in Chicago, Louisiana's delegation was a mare's nest of internal feuds and conflicting egos. The delegates immediately elected Governor Robert Kennon, a Perez crony, as delegation chairman. Like Perez, Kennon promptly announced that he supported Eisenhower. Former governor Sam Jones, a bitter enemy of both Perez and Kennon, was also a delegate. Russell was a virtual outcast among such insurgents. He was no political friend of Perez, Kennon, or Jones. This diverse collection of personalities and political agendas was a recipe for discord. From the moment he arrived in Chicago, Russell knew that Kennon and Perez would miss no opportunity to sow conflict among the delegation. "That was their purpose to begin with: to be as quarrelsome and argumentative and contentious as they could be." As if on cue, Kennon commenced the drama when, as a member of the convention's platform committee, he attacked the party's liberal positions on civil rights, fair employment, and tidelands. The next day, the full convention further enraged Kennon and his cohorts by adopting a resolution to exclude any delegation unless its members pledged to help place the party's nominee in the Democratic column on their state's ballot. Perez now saw an opening to push his scheme to award the Democratic rooster to Eisenhower.[4]

With Perez's goading, Kennon persuaded the delegates not to sign the loyalty oath on grounds the Louisiana Democratic Central Committee had granted its permission to oppose any objectionable platform. Informed that delegations from Louisiana, Virginia, and South Carolina had refused to sign the oath, the credentials committee went to great lengths to accommodate the renegade delegations. It amended the resolution to say the oath should simply not be contrary to state law or state party rules. Kennon and Perez were not seduced by such transparent accommodation. Unfazed, the delegation stuck with Kennon's and Perez's unwavering position.

Russell correctly observed that the so-called loyalty oath merely said that "they would use their best efforts to see that that ticket was on the ballot under the proper label. Now, applied to Louisiana, that amounted to say that your guys will not do what you did the time before when you came to this convention, participated in the convention, then proceeded to stomp out of there and went back home and took Harry Truman's name off the ballot."[5]

At an acrimonious delegation caucus, Russell implored the delegates to sign the watered-down oath. "I know all about ballots that don't carry the nominee under the party seal," Russell declared. "President Truman [in 1948] was at first ruled off and subsequently put back on—but not under the party's symbol." As reported by the *New Orleans States,* the emotion of the moment carried Russell away, as he shouted:

> Perez was responsible for that. I don't like his tactics. Yes, it's true that he gave me stolen votes in that election and kept President Truman's name from going under the symbol on the ballot. I accepted all of that—the votes and the ballot—because I had my name so arranged on the ballot that I benefitted by it. I accepted all Perez did, the stolen votes and the ruse to confuse the voters by the marking of the ballot. I'm sorry that I did. I was wrong and I regret it. In 1948, he gave me the votes but in 1950 he did not. So the way I look at it now is like this—once for me and once against me and now it's even.[6]

Russell's remarks created an instant furor. The next day's *States* front-page headline screamed: "SENATOR LONG ADMITS TAKING STOLEN VOTES." Perez indignantly scoffed at Russell's charge and demanded a congressional investigation. "This is a very serious proposition," Perez replied. Quickly realizing the implications of his statement, Russell retreated. "I don't believe now that I needed the stolen votes in the first election because I am sure I would have beaten Kennon anyway. I will never again approve anything like rigged ballots and stolen votes. And that is why I am against the stand the delegation took in opposing the oath. The oath will guard against another ballot ruse." To a New Orleans reporter he maintained, "I have never to my knowledge received a single stolen vote and could not prove that I have or have not received such votes at all. To be perfectly truthful, however, I have always heard it said that you either get all the votes in Plaquemines Parish or you get practically none."[7]

The decision not to sign the oath was an important one for Louisiana's delegation. Unless they signed it, they could not participate in the convention's proceedings. Even so, Kennon and Perez vowed not to leave. They wanted to be ejected. "Personally," Perez scoffed, "I would consider it an honor to be thrown out of this convention." Virginia senator Harry Byrd revealed the scheme of the Louisiana, Virginia, and South Carolina delegations: "Our strategy is not to communicate with the credentials committee, just remain in our seats and let them be the aggressors and let them read us out of the convention or throw us out bodily if they will." Their disruptive strategy might have worked had it not been for the convention's chairman, taciturn house speaker Sam Rayburn, and a little help from Russell. Rayburn vowed he would foil attempts by the three renegade southern delegations to destroy Democratic unity and, with it, any chance the party had of winning the November election.[8]

On Friday afternoon, supporters began their nominating speeches, placing the names of front-runner Adlai Stevenson and senators Richard Russell, Estes Kefauver, and Robert Kerr into nomination. The clerk routinely called on each state delegation for candidates it might wish to nominate, finally arriving at Louisiana, the first of the rebellious delegations. For the moment, all eyes fixed on Governor Kennon. Would he bow to the will of the convention or remain defiant? He did neither. Instead, Kennon promptly yielded to Virginia. Minnesota's Hubert Humphrey was outraged. How could a state that had not been officially seated, he asked, yield to another state? "Follow the rules," he shouted as he and other delegates, waving their states' standards, came surging toward the platform.[9]

Rayburn angrily demanded, "Get those things away. There'll be no recognition of anyone until there is order. The Chair treats everyone with respect and expects to be so treated." When the commotion died, Rayburn recognized Virginia governor John S. Battle, who asked for Rayburn's "specific ruling as to whether we are, or are not, members of the convention, entitled to full participation in its deliberations and votes." Rayburn halted the nominations. He turned to the Credentials Committee for a ruling. As he awaited the committee's decision, Rayburn fired a shot through the heart of the rebellious delegations. Any dissenting delegate who signed the oath, he announced, was now welcome to participate in the convention. Russell, fuming over Kennon's belligerent behavior, eagerly accepted Rayburn's offer. He leapt to this feet, shouting for recognition. Rayburn invited him to the podium, where he announced to the convention,[10]

Mr. Chairman, the junior senator from Louisiana does not propose to leave. If I am the only man who stays, I propose to stay here. Now, Mr. Chairman, what has the Louisiana delegation been asked to commit themselves to do? They have been asked to say that they will let the people of Louisiana have the opportunity to vote for the Democratic nominee for the President of the United States. That is all they have been asked. . . . I am willing to say right here and now that as the junior senator from Louisiana, I am willing to stake my entire political fortunes on this principle, that the people of my state should have that God-given right under the American Constitution to vote. . . . That is their right. I am willing to fight to give them that right, no matter who the candidate of this convention may be.[11]

When he finished, Rayburn declared that Russell and another Louisiana delegate who signed the oath were recognized as members of the convention. Governors Battle and Kennon were furious. They rushed to the podium with impassioned attacks on the oath, arguing that they were only upholding the law and abiding by wishes of their state. Kennon vowed to stomp from the convention hall in protest. But Rayburn was not bullied. He resolutely announced the decision of his Credentials Committee. The renegade delegates, he said, "have not compiled with the rules adopted in this convention" and could not, therefore, participate. The hall buzzed with excitement as attention turned to the three state delegations who remained in their seats waiting to learn if they would be forcibly removed from the convention hall. Contrary to the wishes of most delegates, Rayburn would not dream of throwing out Kennon, Perez, and their cohorts into the political brier patch. He would thwart their scheme by forcing them to stay.

Hoping to salvage whatever was left of party unity, Rayburn's men quickly persuaded a Maryland delegate to offer a motion seating Virginia's delegates on the flimsy logic the state was "in substantial compliance with the spirit of the rule." The vote went heavily against the motion. The hall, however, was merely half full. Many delegates were only now returning from dinner. As Rayburn stalled for time, Stevenson's forces came to his aid. In a frenzy, they dashed around the room, pleading and cajoling delegates to maintain party unity by seating the three delegations. Despite their efforts, the second vote was also a disappointment. Another large majority opposed Virginia's seating. Then, Rayburn got the break he needed. Three of Illinois's most skilled politicians, Joseph Gill, Jacob Arvey, and former senate majority leader Scott Lucas, returned from dinner to discover Rayburn's and Stevenson's frantic lobbying. Immediately, the three men flew into action. For at least an hour, they swept through the hall, coaxing numerous delegations to reverse their votes.

As Gill, Arvey, and Lucas worked the convention hall, Russell received an urgent message from Texas senator Lyndon Johnson, the new Senate Democratic leader: "He was in Dick Russell's room with Dick Russell, [and] said, 'Tell Russell [Long], for Pete's sake, vote the whole twenty votes.' " Minutes later, New Mexico Senator Clinton Anderson approached Russell with the same message. "Russell, vote that twenty votes." But before he would agree to casting the entire delegation's vote, Russell needed assurances from Rayburn that such a stunt would be upheld by the chair, as he recalled:

And so I said, "I'll vote the twenty votes if Sam Rayburn will tell me he'll stay with me." I had already spoken to Sam. I managed to speak to him about that matter. He said, "Son, what you did [Russell's speech and signing the oath] was a brave thing." But he said, "If you vote the twenty votes in this convention, the same crowd that applauded you when you made that speech are liable to throw you out in that Lake Michigan. So, I'd advise you not to do that." So, I told Clinton Anderson, "If you can get through that crowd up to Sam Rayburn and you can get some kind of assurance that he will uphold me if I vote the twenty votes, I'll do it." He said, "How can I get the word back to you?" I said, "Just give me an old railroad high ball and I'll know what you mean." So, he got to Sam Rayburn and . . . he gave me that signal.[12]

When he received the sign of Rayburn's assent, Russell looked around him. Most of Louisiana's delegates had not returned from dinner. Quickly, he looked for the nearest microphone. It belonged to the Indiana delegation. Russell grabbed the microphone and shouted for recognition. He was ready to make his audacious move. Rayburn called on Russell, who announced he was casting Louisiana's twenty votes in favor of seating Virginia. Rayburn swiftly rejected a point of order protesting Russell's maneuver, declaring that the convention's rules provided that if part of a delegation was absent, the remaining members could vote on their behalf. Finally, with Russell's help, Rayburn had won his battle to hold the convention together. Virginia was narrowly seated. By voice vote, the convention admitted the other two states. Later, Stevenson was nominated on the third ballot. The Louisiana delegation never wavered in its support of Senator Russell, casting its votes for the Georgia senator on all three ballots.[13]

With the help from Rayburn, Russell had won, although his victory was not without consequences. Some critics thought Russell, as one south Louisiana newspaper maintained, "pulled a fast one when he voted the entire Louisiana delegation without authority." Another newspaper praised Kennon for refusing to sign the oath, but attacked Russell for not being properly alarmed that "if and when the 'liberals' do gain control, then our system of freedom in this country will be passe and we will have a dictatorial system of socialism thrust upon us." An editorial in a New Orleans paper observed that Russell's actions in Chicago "certainly give weight to the rumors that he was carrying the ball for the New Deal and Truman interests in the gubernatorial election" when he supported Hale Boggs. Despite the criticism in Louisiana, Russell's performance drew praise in at least one national newspaper. In the *Washington Evening Star*, columnist Doris Fleeson lauded Russell for not succumbing to segregationist pressure and said, "The voice of the new South was the son of Huey Long."[14]

"Basically, what it amounted to," Russell said years later, "I'd put those guys in a position where it looked like if they walked out of there, that all they were really reserving was the right to go home and steal the election, which is what they had in mind." At the time, Russell worried enough about the backlash from the convention he felt the need to interpret the episode in a statewide radio broadcast. In a lengthy and technical speech, he explained his reasons for supporting the loyalty oath and why he had cast the delegation's votes. He closed with an attack on Perez:

> He has been for and against Russell Long. He has been for and against Earl Long. He has been for and against Bob Kennon. He has been for several unsuccessful candidates, some of whom were ignominiously defeated because they were associated with Mr. Perez and had to bear the stigma that his support carries in the minds of some people. For example, Mr. Perez has given his support to Mr. James McLemore, Mr. Malcolm Lafargue, Miss Lucille May Grace. You can see that there is no assurance that Mr. Perez's support means victory. I have no intention of leading a crusade into Plaquemines Parish. However, I expect to do what I can to prevent the police state methods of that area from being extended throughout Louisiana.[15]

Meanwhile, Adlai Stevenson's supporters in Louisiana and the rest of the South had little reason for optimism about their candidate's chances in the weeks following the convention. Governor Kennon and former governor Sam Jones endorsed the Republican nominee, General Dwight Eisenhower. Kennon explained that he was obligated to Eisenhower as he had openly campaigned for governor on an anti-Truman platform. Despite Perez's efforts to deny the rooster emblem to Stevenson and his running mate, Senator John Sparkman of Alabama, the Democratic State Central Committee placed all Democratic nominees on the ballot under the rooster. Bitter and disgusted with the Democratic party, Perez continued supporting Eisenhower, heralding the Republican nominee's support of Louisiana's claim to the tidelands. Stevenson, meanwhile, did nothing to enhance his chances in Louisiana by declaring that he supported federal ownership of the tidelands, leaving many loyal Louisiana Democrats little reason to support their party's nominee.

Russell, who had not yet formally endorsed Stevenson, nonetheless was criticized for his tacit support of the ticket. "Senator Russell Long," the *Shreveport Times* said in an editorial, "has been forthright, but on the side of the fence that hardly is beneficial to Louisiana." Finally, Russell declared his support of Stevenson, a subdued statement more supportive of the party than its nominee: "I'm content to stay with the Democratic Party. It's the largest party in the world because it's the party of the people." Several days later, at a Democratic rally in New Orleans, he grew more enthusiastic about the ticket and took a backhanded swipe at Kennon's and Perez's support of Eisenhower: "The day I want to support a Republican, sit on the Republican side of Congress or become a member of a Republican committee, that's the day I resign the Democratic party and join the Republican party. But until I do, I am a Democrat and will support all Democrats."[16]

Russell found even more enthusiasm when Stevenson's running mate, Alabama senator John Sparkman, became ill. For several days, Russell assumed Sparkman's campaign schedule, stumping for his colleague in Monroe and New Orleans in Louisiana, Texarkana, Texas, and Anderson, South Carolina. In Anderson, Russell addressed an estimated two million listeners over a network of South Carolina and Georgia radio stations. Southerners who voted for Eisenhower, he told the radio audience, were inviting a return "to the Republican days of the 1920s when one hundred thousand persons elsewhere were making more money than all the millions of the people of the South put together. The little handful that wants to go with the Republicans can go, but the large majority of reasoning people in the South are going to stand by the Democratic party."[17]

On the stump, Russell displayed the rhetorical bravery and gumption that often marked his Senate career. A lesser politician might have hesitated attacking a war hero like Eisenhower. Not Russell. He excoriated the immensely popular general. He assailed Republican senator Joseph McCarthy at a time when many politicians were intimidated by the Wisconsin Republican's charges of communism in the State Department. In late October while in Montgomery, Alabama, Russell accused Eisenhower of duplicity on civil rights. The general, he said, "is speaking out of both sides of his mouth" on the issue, adding that Eisenhower made no mention of his moderate views when he campaigned in Louisiana. "But he promised to fight all segregation—wipe it out—when he spoke in California."[18]

Russell's disgust with Eisenhower seemed to be more than political rhetoric. "I must confess my disappointment in General Eisenhower," he wrote in notes for a speech during the campaign. "I find that the general is backtracking, he is now blaming others for unfortunate decisions which were largely of his own making. For a whole year in the Senate I helped support the general as the chief of the North Atlantic Treaty Command against the ruinous attack of Senator Taft['s isolationist rhetoric]. Now I find the general adopting the Taft foreign policy. When I witness such flip flopping and double talk in quest of votes I cannot feel that the general is demonstrating the kind of leadership that our nation so desperately needs."[19]

As the campaign closed, no Democrat could say Russell had not been a loyal foot soldier for his party's nominee. He had risked the wrath of his constituents by his high-profile support of party unity in Chicago and had campaigned extensively for Stevenson and Sparkman throughout the South. With the sting of Hale Boggs's rejection still fresh, Russell had enthusiastically plunged into an all-out effort to persuade Louisiana to support his candidate for president.

On election day, Eisenhower won with a comfortable margin. To his credit, Stevenson carried every state in the Deep South, including Louisiana, which he won with 53 percent. Although Senator Allen Ellender and Governor Earl Long supported Stevenson, Russell clearly deserved much of the credit for mobilizing the state's Long forces for the Democratic ticket. Even so, Eisenhower had made the largest Republican showing in Louisiana since Reconstruction. Louisiana was still a solidly Democratic state on every level. But as Stevenson's narrow margin proved, the Democrats—with a civil rights platform loathsome to most southern whites—could no longer take the state for granted in national elections.[20]

13

JOINING THE CLUB

$\mathcal{L}$IKE A SMALL TOWN, the Senate of the 1950s had its cliques. The most eminent was a nebulous group, known only as "The Club," the Senate's powerful, but informal nucleus. No listing of members and no written rules for admission existed. The group never met in any formal session. Nonetheless, those who followed the Senate knew who was in and who was out. A Club member might have twenty fewer years of seniority than a nonmember and was as likely to be a Republican as a Democrat. Political ideology had little or no influence. Election from a Southern state was one credential that hastened membership. Almost as important was a senator's attitude toward the Senate and his regard for its traditions. New members who often orated on matters unrelated to their committee assignments or appeared to use the Senate as a springboard for presidential aspirations (demonstrating a lack of commitment to the Senate), were denied admission. Patience, respect for Senate folkways and hard work were dependable paths to Club membership. This, in turn, led to influence, effectiveness, and power.

"What really holds the members of 'the Club' together," said former Lyndon Johnson aide George Reedy, "is a mutual recognition that *all* members have constituency pressures that are overriding. This makes for a great deal of back scratching and horse trading. But it also gives a degree of cohesion without which the affairs of the Senate would be very chaotic indeed." Non-Club members, Reedy added, are those "ultraliberals or the ultraconservatives" who "entertain the curious delusion that they have a monopoly on political morality."[1]

By the beginning of his first full term, as Russell continued to prove he was serious and hardworking, his influence and effectiveness grew. Eventually, he was welcomed into the fellowship of men his father had despised and spurned. Only his age, thirty-two in 1950, kept him from the center of the Senate's inner sanctum. While his skill, intellect, and vigor surpassed that of many senior senators, reporters invariably noted his distinction as the Senate's youngest member, even though he outranked more than one-third of the body after only three years of service.

Thus, these early years were crucial for Russell as he struggled to distinguish himself in an institution largely dominated by men old enough to be his father. Equal to this task, his able and often controversial battles against foreign aid won him respect, if not real reductions in the program's budget. No one questioned his anticommunist credentials. Despite his relative moderation, other southern senators accepted him as a steadfast defender of segregation. Furthermore, his efforts to increase federal support for the sick, disabled, and aged won friends among the Senate's liberals. Possibly most important, but unnoticed at the time, was his appointment in 1953 to the Senate Finance Committee, beginning a thirteen-year trek toward the most powerful committee chairmanship in Congress. Russell's influence during his first decade was trifling compared to the vast power he would wield in the mid-1960s through the 1970s. Even so, he carved his niche in several areas of lasting significance. He played important, and sometimes leading, roles in several national dramas. In his own unspectacular way, Russell had become, in a brief amount of time, a bona fide member of the Club.

* * *

By the early 1950s, a handful of senators and congressmen had decided much of the U.S. foreign aid budget was a waste. It was a sentiment largely born of disillusionment over the growing costs of America's troublesome foreign entanglement, the Korean conflict. As for Russell, he had argued since his first Senate campaign that Congress should insist on diverting a large portion of U.S. foreign assistance into domestic needs. Decrying the feeding of "every Jap, every Chinaman, every Hindu and every Arab that we can find to feed," Russell told an early campaign audience in 1948 that he would "see that we get our share of that money to feed our people here at home." Indeed, no domestic program was more important to Russell than social security. Helping the aged and disabled was his father's unfinished legacy. Russell was outraged that taxpayer dollars were shipped overseas to help foreigners at the expense of needy elderly Americans.[2]

While he had supported the Marshall Plan to rebuild war-torn Europe, he did so "with the understanding that it was a program with a definite limitation of time." After the program's completion, Russell observed in 1955, "up came the military-aid program; and the funds left from the Marshall Plan were shifted, without any great amount of restudy." Russell believed that the government was wasting great amounts of this aid, bestowing it on foreign nations with no incentive for them to assume a greater burden for their defense. Russell finally concluded that the United States government had created a budgetary dragon that devoured huge amounts of taxpayer money. As President Truman's ambitious foreign aid proposal arrived on Capitol Hill in 1952, Russell girded for a decade-long, sometimes maverick role as the Senate's top dragon slayer.[3]

His first chance to test these views came in May, when Truman sent his $7.9 billion foreign aid authorization proposal, the Mutual Security Bill, to Congress. Conservative lawmakers, including Russell, immediately attacked it as wasteful. Truman responded that he needed the money to counter threats against the "survival of civilization." Furthermore, he suggested that the only question about his request should be whether it was too frugal. The Senate Foreign Relations Committee held extensive hearings on the bill before it cut one billion dollars and sent it to the full Senate. The Senate, in turn, bounced the bill to the Armed Services Committee for even more study.

Here, Russell made his first move. He asked the committee to slash the bill by an additional $400 million. The amendment failed narrowly, six to seven. Russell might have won had committee chairman Richard Russell not cabled General Dwight D. Eisenhower, then commander of North Atlantic Treaty Organization forces, for advice. From Europe, Eisenhower said the one-billion-dollar Foreign Relations Committee cut "would be heavily and seriously felt." Any further reduction in the program, he asserted, would require "drastic revision of the whole program."[4]

When the bill reached the Senate floor, Russell was undaunted. Armed with a handful of amendments, he began chipping away. He first proposed cutting the bill by the $400 million he wanted in committee. "This country has already appropriated and spent more than thirty billion dollars in aiding Western Europe to rebuild and to encourage their resistance to communism," Russell told the Senate. "Somewhere the point should be reached where we could expect those who want our assistance to be willing to contribute to their own defense. It is completely unprecedented that one nation should do as much as we have done to help other nations to help themselves." Russell lost, but barely. His amendment failed, thirty-seven to forty.[5]

Heartened by his near victory, Russell returned to the Senate floor later in the day. This time, he demanded a $200 million reduction. "It seems to me that this small amount of reduction would not greatly hamper the program, but the savings of $200 million would be a substantial saving to our taxpayers." Russell's persistence maddened Senator Tom Connally of Texas, chairman of the Senate Foreign Relations Committee. A blunt, abrasive man, Connally was ferocious when fighting reductions in his foreign aid budget. He cared little about whom he offended. During debate over one of Russell's amendments, Republican senator Bourke Hickenlooper of Iowa asked Connally to yield for a question. "I know the senator is as full of questions as a dog is full of fleas," Connally sarcastically responded. "But go ahead."[6] When Russell returned to the Senate with his latest amendment, Connally was exasperated. He launched into an angry tirade:

> The Foreign Relations Committee reported a bill, but the Senator from Louisiana was not satisfied with it. He said, "Oh, Mr. President, for God's sake send the bill to the Armed Services Committee, because I am a member of that committee and I want to cut its throat when it gets there." It was sent to that committee and what happened? His own committee, which he is supposed to have in the palm of his hand, held hearings and looked over the bill (and) voted to approve the bill without amendment. . . . I must pay my respects to the senator from Louisiana for his persistence, for he is a persistent man. If the pending amendment should be defeated, he probably will come back with an amendment to cut off one hundred million dollars. If that fails, he will return with a proposal to cut fifty million dollars. He will finally get down in the basement.[7]

Connally was correct about Russell's persistence. But this time, despite the outburst, Russell's amendment carried, thirty-seven to thirty-four, largely on the support of Republicans. "After he got through making that demagogic speech, I had more votes than I did before he got up," said Russell. "He changed [Vermont Republican] George Aiken's vote, for example. George Aiken would have voted with him, but after that speech, George decided he was going to vote against him." The Senate and House finally agreed to a $6.1 billion authorization, $1.4 billion below Truman's original request. The amount was precisely the level Russell had proposed in committee.[8]

Russell's attack on the Mutual Security Bill was the first of many efforts throughout the early years of his career—some successful, many not—to trim the size of U.S. foreign aid while fighting for equivalent increases in social security. By the end of his first term, he would become the Senate's most vociferous and persistent opponent of foreign assistance and the most dogged proponent of social security.

An early experience solidified Russell's tightfisted view of foreign aid. In August 1952, he and Oregon senator Wayne Morse, both members of the Armed Services Committee's Subcommittee on Military Public Works, spent more than a month hopscotching Europe and North Africa. In all, they explored more than sixty U.S. military installations in Greenland, England, France, Germany, French Morocco, Libya, Greece, and Italy. (In Turkey, Russell even took time from his travel rigors to swim from Europe to Asia—over the half-mile expanse of the Bosporus—with the U.S. ambassador to Turkey, George McGhee.) The trip's result was a fourteen-page report, released in January 1953, highly critical of preparedness, manpower, and wasteful spending at these installations. "We cannot say with the slightest assurance that it would be beyond an enemy's capabilities to break the backbone of our armed services by surprise attack," Russell and Morse reported. "Nor can we rely upon our present planning, if pursued, to assure us of the ability to carry on sustained offensive operations against a powerful adversary."[9]

Russell and Morse reserved their strongest criticism for what they regarded as a misguided U.S. policy of spending billions each year to defend dozens of far-flung countries—the U.S. foreign aid program.

> We feel that this Nation should concentrate on building airfields, supply depots and naval installations in friendly and Allied countries rather than keeping our youngsters overseas for a lifetime. We consider it far preferable to rely upon our allies to guard and maintain airfields and other defense installations until American reinforcements could arrive in the event of a great global conflict. . . . We cannot understand a program which has 100 or even 200 groups of men in units of 2,000 to 5,000 sitting idly in the muck and mire of Europe, Africa, Asia, and the Arctic Circle, waiting for a war which we hope to avoid.[10]

Most stinging was this conclusion: "It is our feeling that the United States has made a fundamental mistake in departing from the sound principle that the only people who deserve freedom are those who are willing to fight for it. In many of the agreements consummated up to this time, our Government has been asked to contribute altogether too much and our allies too little."[11]

While the Armed Services Committee did not immediately release the report, news of its brutal assessment of U.S. military spending spread quickly through Washington, sending tremors through the military community. The Armed Services Committee stalled funding for $146 million in overseas military construction, mostly new air bases. Committee members summoned General Omar Bradley, chairman of the Joint Chiefs of Staff, and other top military brass for a closed-door session to discuss the report. The new secretary of defense, Charles Wilson, announced that he had ordered no new military projects started until "studied and justified." To Virginia's senator Harry Byrd, renowned for his frugality, the report was "pretty startling in showing excessive extravagance."[12]

Some newspapers chimed in, demanding the report's immediate public release. "Any conditions which Sen. Long regards as wasteful should be publicized and corrected," the *Memphis Commercial Appeal* said. "There has been altogether too much covering up and too many alibis offered whenever governmental extravagance has been suspected or hinted." The *Shreveport Times* agreed, arguing "pitiless publicity, so far as is possible, should be the order of the day." Russell's trip, the *New Orleans States* said, was "one of the few Congressional tours, we would say, that brought a high return for the cost to taxpayers."[13]

On February 14, the committee released the report, but first expunged a section on military installations in France. Russell and Morse reported they made the deletion "with great reluctance and only because of the security argument advanced, because [the subcommittee] believes that some of the facts under this heading should be made known to the American people." Later on the Senate floor, they claimed the Pentagon tried to suppress the embarrassing report. "The use of unnecessary secrecy," Russell complained, "is a vicious offense to the taxpayers of this country."[14]

While several of Russell's colleagues lauded the report, not everyone in Washington viewed it as a sound criticism of military spending and priorities. Democratic senator Albert Gore of Tennessee said that the report "challenges our concept of retaliatory readiness and with this I strongly disagree." Gore believed that the abundance of bases "surrounding the industrial heart of Russia, from which devastating atomic retaliation could be launched within a few hours, is in my opinion the greatest deterrent against World War III." The *Washington Post* had perhaps the harshest criticism. An editorial said Russell and Morse's work was "filled with slapdash thinking and it is unworthy of the usual high standards of the Senate Armed Services Committee."[15]

These and other critics found fault not with the report's facts, but with the conclusions based on its evidence. They may have feared Russell and other foreign aid opponents would use it to force deep cuts in foreign assistance. Some, such as Gore and the Truman administration, viewed the far-flung U.S. military as essential deterrence to prevent another war. Russell and Morse never rejected the principle of a strong military deterrence. They merely maintained that America's allies should bear a much greater share of the defense burden. In this respect, the U.S. military collage was like abstract art: Its beauty, necessity, and utility were in the eye of the beholder.

Those who feared Russell would use his report to sustain his crusade for foreign aid cuts were correct. In July, he made three separate, but unsuccessful, efforts to scale back the $4.5 billion Mutual Security Assistance Bill passed by the Senate Foreign Relations Committee. His third amendment lost by only four votes. "Why can we not go along with economy for a change?" he complained to the Senate after the vote. Later, he was back, this time with a two-point plan for balancing the federal budget using sharp reductions in American troops overseas, except Korea, and deep cuts in foreign aid. The U.S. could "justify about one-fourth of our troops in Europe," he said. Instead of supporting such a large, full-time military, Russell proposed greater reliance on reserves. "We wouldn't reduce the arms we're buying. We could still strike with devastating force. We could rely more on reserves and have arms and equipment for these."[16]

Later that month, the Senate rebuffed Russell when he tried to cut the Eisenhower administration's first foreign aid proposal. By fifty-three to thirty-five, the Senate rejected his amendment reducing the program's appropriation to the level approved by the House. Senators then approved the president's $4.5 billion proposal, in addition to $2.2 billion in unspent foreign aid from the previous year. Both houses delivered a $6.7 billion appropriation for Eisenhower's signature.[17]

In August 1954, Russell returned to take another swipe at Eisenhower's $3.2 billion foreign aid authorization bill. "Anyone who wishes to go overseas and see what happens to this money," Russell said during the Senate debate, "will find that this is the most loosely handled of any of the taxpayers' money, under any program in our government." This time, he shocked the White House. His amendment to slash the bill by $500 million, down to $2.7 billion, carried by a four-vote margin. (A previous try at cutting more than one billion dollars had failed.) Russell's amendment represented the largest single cut in foreign aid ever approved by the Senate. Savoring his victory, Russell declared, "[T]he tide is running against these large appropriations when it is clear that the money is being wasted." Later, the House restored most of Russell's hard-fought cut, although the final House-Senate conference bill was $500,000 less than the president's request.[18]

Heartened that his campaign to reduce foreign aid was gradually winning support, Russell charged again into the fray in 1955. He opened debate on the $3.4 billion Mutual Security Act authorization, approved by the Foreign Relations Committee, by demanding a one billion–dollar reduction. "There is no war going on. World tension is somewhat reduced. . . . The policy of Congress should be one of gradual reduction of foreign aid." When his argument for this amendment failed to muster more than sixteen votes, Russell offered another amendment, this one to cut $318 million. Again, senators turned him down. Reluctantly, Russell voted for the bill's final passage. It was the first time since 1950 that the Senate had not reduced funds from foreign aid. All the progress that Russell thought he had achieved the previous year had evaporated.[19]

In July, however, Russell voted against the Foreign Aid Appropriations Bill, explaining that "there is an obvious need for a restudy of the entire program" because of a $9.9 billion in surplus foreign aid funds. "Year by year, those vast sums have been piling up," Russell complained moments before the Senate voted on the House-Senate foreign aid compromise bill, which was $100 million less than the year before. "Some of us feel the government has lost control of these funds."[20]

In May 1956, Russell took another step to trim the government's foreign largesse: He resigned his seat on the Interior Committee to fill a vacancy on the Foreign Relations Committee, created by the death of Kentucky's Alben Barkley. Quickly dispelling any doubts about his intentions, he said of his appointment, "I have long had the belief . . . that our expenditures for military aid are excessive and that we are not likely to get our money's worth. My feeling is that a great amount of the aid has been futile—that few of the nations armed could be depended upon to fight the Soviet Union if we found ourselves at war."[21]

Russell soon found he had few allies on his new committee: Foreign Relations members overwhelmingly approved a $4.5 billion foreign aid authorization bill in July, only $400 million less than Eisenhower's request.

Russell and Republican William Langer of North Dakota were the only senators to oppose the bill. Later, on the Senate floor, Russell suggested freezing foreign aid appropriations at the 1955 level by slashing the committee bill $1.5 billion. "I am willing to assist nations to provide for their own defense against Communist aggression when they are unable to provide it for themselves," he said during debate, adding he was "unwilling to vote American funds to assist foreign powers to do that which they could do for themselves, but refuse to do, even for their own defense." Only twenty-six colleagues supported his amendment.[22]

The next day, he was back on the Senate floor shortly before the bill's final passage to explain why he would vote against it. "The American people feel that we are spending far too much on this program, and I think they are right in that feeling. So long as additional funds are to be appropriated, and so much money is to be carried forward, I feel that I must vote against the bill." Shortly thereafter, senators approved the bill, fifty-four to twenty-five.[23]

On foreign aid, Russell was the Senate's Don Quixote, vainly tilting at the windmills of military largesse. As dependable as the advent of spring, Russell once more charged into the Senate foreign aid authorization debate in 1957. He hoped to reduce President Eisenhower's foreign aid request after his futile vote against the $3.6 billion bill in the Foreign Relations Committee. When the committee authorized defense support aid for two years, Russell proposed cutting the second year's funding. The Senate rejected this amendment, thirty-four to fifty-five. Russell immediately filed another amendment. This one placed a ceiling of $710 million on the second year's defense support spending. The amendment failed, but this time by a narrower margin, forty to forty-nine. Russell offered one more amendment, seeking a $100 million dollar reduction in the total bill. "I offer this amendment in an effort to see if there is any disposition on the part of a majority to make any reduction within the bill," Russell said dejectedly. As expected, there was no such sentiment. Once again, Russell lost, thirty-three to fifty-two.[24]

While Russell and other opponents of foreign aid—including his senior Louisiana colleague, Allen Ellender—occasionally achieved small victories throughout the 1950s, they were never able to make the deep cuts necessary to end the waste and abuse they charged was rife in the program. Strong congressional support for foreign aid had little association with the program's importance. More important was the bipartisan attitude which pervaded Congress during the Eisenhower administration. "Democrats and Republicans alike agreed that politics stopped at the water's edge," West Virginia senator Robert Byrd explained in his history of the Senate. "While there was still much criticism of individual policies and policy makers, a broad-based consensus in the government and in the country supported the fundamental objectives of the United States in those difficult early years of the Cold War."[25]

Although he opposed extravagant foreign aid, Russell never maintained that the entire program was a waste. He faulted what he perceived as often sloppy, inattentive planning and management of a worthwhile and necessary program. More so, Russell believed the government had confused its priorities. He wanted to divert much of the foreign aid budget to important domestic needs. For all his efforts to accomplish this, throughout the 1950s foreign aid remained largely sacrosanct.

* * *

While Russell strenuously opposed presidents Truman and Eisenhower on foreign aid, he gave wide latitude to presidents in matters of foreign or military affairs. There were notable exceptions. All involved Eisenhower.

President Eisenhower faced two international crises in October 1956. In Europe, Hungarians revolted against their Russian overlords and briefly established an independent government. While the United Nations and Eisenhower paid lip service to the freedom movement, the Russian army rolled back into Hungary and crushed the revolt. Meanwhile, in the Middle East, Israel—supported by Great Britain and France—seized Egypt's Suez Canal. This time, unlike in Hungary, Eisenhower was bolder. He requested congressional authority to send American armed forces to the region to "protect the territorial integrity and political independence" of those nations from foreign aggression. While the United States had persuaded Great Britain to withdraw its troops, Eisenhower and Secretary of State John Foster Dulles feared that Britain's absence and loss of prestige in the Middle East might create a dangerous vacuum which would invite Soviet intervention.[26]

Congress had authorized Eisenhower to use American troops to protect Formosa and the Pescadores from Chinese communist attack in 1954. This time, senators and congressmen were less eager to hand the president a military blank check in a region where the United States had little formal presence. Arkansas senator J. William Fulbright, who would later chair the Foreign Relations Committee, was among the most skeptical. He argued there had been

no real prior consultation with Congress, nor will there be any sharing of power. The whole manner of presentation of this resolution—leaks to the press, speeches to specially summoned Saturday joint sessions, and dramatic secret meetings of the Committee on Foreign Relations after dark one evening before the Congress was even organized in an atmosphere of suspense and urgency—does not constitute consultation in the true sense. All this was designed to manage Congress, to coerce it into signing this blank check.[27]

Transcripts of that closed-door session of the Foreign Relations Committee in early 1957 offer revealing insights into why Eisenhower's request generated such stiff opposition. In one exchange with Russell, Secretary Dulles only hurt the administration's cause:

LONG: Mr. Secretary, all I am going to ask you at this moment does not have anything to do with the wisdom of sending troops or the wisdom or unwisdom of President Truman in sending troops to Korea, anything of that sort. All I am asking you to enlighten me on is just the question of the attitude of the executive department of this Government whether the President does have the power to send the troops without a congressional authorization.

Here is a State Department document which says it is the position of the executive department that he does have the power. That is all I am asking you about, and I am asking you, does he have the power to send troops without an authorization?

DULLES: I would not be prepared to answer that question in the abstract, because—

LONG: Let me ask you this question: Did President Roosevelt have the right to put troops on Iceland during World War II?

DULLES: I don't know.

LONG: I am sure you have given some thought to the matter.

DULLES: No, I have never given thought to that one.

LONG: In your judgment, did President Jefferson have the right to send American forces against the Barbary pirates?

DULLES: I don't know, sir.

LONG: In your judgement, did President Truman have any right to send American forces or any power to send American forces into Korea?

DULLES: I never studied that as a lawyer.

LONG: Never considered it?.

DULLES: No, sir.[28]

Russell was incredulous, later telling the Senate that Dulles was "one of the least candid and most evasive witnesses we have ever examined. In my brief experience as a lawyer, and in my experience of eight years in the Senate, I have never examined a more evasive or less satisfactory witness." He inserted the exchange into the *Congressional Record,* offering a withering condemnation. Of Dulles's answer about Truman's power to send troops to Korea, Russell commented:

> Mr. President, if I recall correctly, John Foster Dulles was in the State Department at that very time, perhaps working on the Japanese Peace Treaty. He said he never thought about a matter on which he is regarded as an expert. That is the kind of answers we got, day after day, until we finally gave up trying to find out what this is all about. The press keeps saying that the Democrats are not willing to cooperate. Mr. President, I am one who wants to cooperate. However, how can I cooperate if I do not know with what I am supposed to cooperate?[29]

A month later, as Congress continued grappling with the issue, Russell's opposition sharpened. He angrily took the Senate floor on March 15, rebuking reporters who characterized the resolution "as a mere vote to express confidence in the president." "Nothing," he said, "could be further from the real truth." Should Eisenhower choose war as did Truman, Russell asserted, "his decision is subject to review by the Congress. If his decision cannot be justified, he is subject to impeachment. It violates the basic fundamentals of our Constitution and it involves an abject surrender of the responsibilities entrusted to the Congress."[30]

Congress finally amended the resolution, omitting references to Congressional authorization, reducing it to a statement of U.S. policy. Thereafter known as the Eisenhower Doctrine, the U.S. pledged to protect the "territorial integrity" of any nation requesting help in its fight against armed aggression from a communist power. Eisenhower never sent troops to the Middle East. The experience persuaded him and Dulles to forego a request for congressional authorization when the president sent troops to Lebanon the next year.

Russell's most passionate challenge to Eisenhower's foreign policy was in 1959, when he was the only member of the Foreign Affairs Committee to oppose the nomination of C. Douglas Dillon for Under Secretary of State. As Under Secretary of State for Economic Affairs, Dillon controlled the U.S. foreign aid budget. Russell surprised no one when he seized the opportunity to underscore the "graft, waste and extravagance" that he believed pervaded the foreign aid program. Rekindling memories of his father's dramatic battles against the upper-class captains of industry and wealth, Russell declared his opposition to Dillon, warning he would "engage in deliberate, dilatory tactics to slow down this steamroller." To most senators, Dillon was nothing like the dangerous, insensitive patrician Russell portrayed. The Harvard-educated son of a wealthy international banker, Dillon was elected to the board of the New York Stock Exchange at twenty-two. He was later chairman of one of the largest Wall Street investment banking firms and served as U.S. ambassador to France from 1953 to 1957. With such impeccable and impressive credentials, Dillon's confirmation was a certainty, despite Russell's one-man battle.

Attacking Dillon's stewardship of foreign aid, Russell told the Senate that the nominee's privileged background alone disqualified him. "Is it any wonder that we find ourselves confronted with deals to permit this nation to be short-changed in the international handling of our foreign aid money? What else would one expect when he places a Wall Street tycoon in charge of handling the program?" Coming from a privileged background, Russell said Dillon "can understand the point of view of the rank and file of the masses only with great difficulty. He has had little or no contact with their problems and has little understanding of the way they feel, think and react."[31]

Perhaps most galling to Russell was Dillon's role in allowing the Greek government to use U.S. foreign aid to reduce its national debt. Russell was also offended by Dillon's reported admission "that it was unlikely that any more than a handful of people in Greece would know that this ever happened." Russell said Dillon had acknowledged that "there is little prospect that this nation would receive any benefit in terms of good will or gratitude from the people of Greece as a result of this transaction." Russell believed the refusal of the State Department to publicize the benefits of foreign aid "is at the heart of the failure of our giveaway program. Most people in other countries do not know that we are sacrificing to help them."[32]

Russell's condemnation of "graft, waste and extravagance" offended Connecticut senator Prescott Bush (father of future president George Bush). "I consider that an innuendo which is highly inappropriate, to say the least. I consider it quite offensive." Before Bush could continue, Russell leapt to his feet. He demanded the presiding officer invoke the rule prohibiting senators from questioning the motives of another senator. When the chair overruled him, Russell invoked the rule again. Bush protested: "Mr. President, in my opinion I have not violated the rule. I do not think it is a fair conclusion that I have been guilty of the rule. I have not questioned the senator's motives. I have questioned what he said." In the end, Russell's crusade against Dillon had little effect. The Senate overwhelmingly confirmed his nomination.[33]

The challenge to Dillon, and his larger battle against foreign aid, was typical of Russell throughout his thirty-eight years in the Senate. Rarely, if ever, did he allow popular Senate opinion to deter him when he believed strongly about an issue or principle. Sometimes, it seemed, the more unpopular the cause, the more fervor he would summon to bear. As the stakes grew higher and the odds longer, Russell worked harder and with more passion. While he was a creature of the Senate and a secure member of its inner Club, the profound influence of his maverick father's legacy was often overpowering. During these periods, an issue or an event would propel him to the Senate floor to wage a lonely, spirited battle. Casual observers or detractors invariably saw him as the Senate's Don Quixote, viewing the episodes as evidence he often lacked wisdom and judgment. Those who understood his nature and his background, however, realized the true depth and source of his passion to fulfill his father's legacy.

In 1959, just as in 1949, Russell continued to complain that wasted foreign aid could better be used for domestic needs. To a radio audience in March, he lamented Eisenhower's attempts to cut domestic programs in the name of fiscal responsibility. "But, brother," he cried, "when it comes down to the foreign aid bill . . . this administration works overtime to just spend everything they can get rid of somehow."[34]

At the decade's close, Russell's lust for fighting foreign aid had not diminished, even though success was limited to only a handful of marginal victories. Years of defeats and scattered successes had left him undeterred, as he explained: "As long as the position I was taking was right, I didn't mind fighting a losing battle, going down in a righteous cause. My view was, well, we'll come back and fight it again later on."[35]

14

THE GRANDMA AMENDMENTS

$\mathscr{I}$N A POIGNANT MOMENT of his first Senate campaign in 1948, Russell told a radio audience of the day an elderly couple from Hammond, Louisiana, had handed him a letter, handwritten in pencil. They thanked him for helping obtain the federal money used to increase Louisiana's monthly old-age pension check from thirty to fifty dollars. Russell read the letter to his listeners:

> Just a few months ago I had a light stroke—I knew I wouldn't be able to work again. It sure looked hopeless for me for I didn't have any children able to take care of me and my wife, but a few days ago I received my old age check for ninety dollars and today everything looks bright and hopeful. . . . We sure thank you for your great effort in our behalf and many thousands of others in getting these old age pension checks. We know you will be our next senator. May God bless you forever.

Russell paused. "Now, if I had to be defeated for United States senator because I helped pay that dear old lady and her husband the old-age pension, I would still have done it."[1]

Throughout his first campaign, no theme was more common and recurring than Russell's promise to secure more federal dollars for Louisiana's

163

old-age pension program. During his first decade in the Senate, he devoted himself to keeping his promise. Indeed, Russell's early years in Congress were marked by his passion in two legislative areas: cutting foreign aid and increasing social security benefits. The two issues were not mutually exclusive. His battles to slash foreign aid often were predicated on the argument that domestic programs, primarily social security, were more worthy of the government's largesse.

His interest in Social Security was greatly motivated by his father's role in the program's inception more than a decade earlier. President Franklin Roosevelt had always received credit for Social Security. Nevertheless, Russell believed that his father's damning criticism of Roosevelt's early conservative policies and tentative approach to ending the Great Depression had forced the administration to propose more liberal measures. President Lyndon Johnson, among others, shared this view, believing that Huey Long and his Share-Our-Wealth plan had been the impetus for Roosevelt's eventual social liberalism. "He thought that the old folks ought to have Social Security and old age pensions," Johnson said in 1964, "and I remember when he just scared the dickens out of Mr. Roosevelt and went on a nationwide radio hookup talking for old folks' pensions. And out of this probably came our Social Security system." Huey Long's biographer William Ivy Hair agreed, writing, "In part, the leftward shift of Roosevelt was a political maneuver to blunt the attacks of Huey Long and others who said the New Deal was not doing enough to help the poor." Joked cowboy humorist Will Rogers of Roosevelt's ideological tilt toward Huey: "I would sure like to have seen Huey's face when he was woke up in the middle of the night by the President, who said, 'Lay over, Huey, I want to get in bed with you.'" So, it was with no small amount of emotion that Russell arrived in the Senate on a crusade to help those poor, elderly, and disabled constituents whose voices were quelled by Huey Long's murder. Perhaps more significant to Russell, he believed the successful fulfillment of his mission would perpetuate and enhance his father's legacy. A steadfast and reliable conservative in areas like civil rights and foreign affairs, social security revealed one of Russell's true streaks of old-fashioned liberalism and populism. Recalled Julius Edelstein, then the secretary for the Senate's liberal caucus: "When [Russell] came up, he brought the breath of his father with him. In everything except civil rights, he was a populist and a liberal."[2]

Social security was not the only arena in which Russell battled for the nation's middle-class and downtrodden. For years, he vigorously assailed the agriculture and high-interest rate policies of several presidents and fought for greater tax cuts for the common man. It was social security, however, where Russell fought most passionately. Soon after his arrival in Washington, Russell's amendments to increase monthly pensions or to expand benefits for the elderly and the disabled became perennial events. More often than not, he cast the issue in such heartrending terms that many senators could not bear to oppose him. Before long, some colleagues affectionately called his legislation, "Russell's grandma amendments."

Russell's first attempt to expand social security benefits came in 1950 as Congress considered the first major revision of the program since its inception fifteen years earlier. The legislation enacted more than thirty revisions to social security, extending new benefits to an additional ten million Americans. Nearly three million beneficiaries would have monthly checks increased by up to 90 percent. Russell could find little fault with such a bountiful bill. Nonetheless, when he examined the Senate Finance Committee's version of the House-passed bill, one omission was glaring. Generous as they were, Finance Committee members had removed a provision from the bill establishing a benefits program for permanently disabled workers. On the evening of June 19, after the bill reached the Senate, Russell implored his colleagues to restore the disability program. He painted a vivid picture of the pitifully disabled, left helpless by the federal government:

> There are persons who have lost their arms, there are persons who have lost their legs, persons who have TB, cancer or have heart disease, who will never be able to work again in their lives. I see some of them in my home state of Louisiana in wheel chairs. I have occasion to visit some of them now and then at their homes, some who may live for six months, some who may live for two or three years, some who may live for five or six years. Those are certainly cases of more crying need than is the case of the ordinary aged person . . . Mr. President, I should think that anyone who would ponder on his Bible teaching would realize that we should not deny such people a little charitable help from the Federal Government. Yet, we see the Federal Government ignoring them but ready to match the States under very liberal programs for aid in the case of aged people. . . . In this great nation, we should eliminate this thing of having beggars on the streets trying to sell pencils, or the kind of cases I see in my home town occasionally—and I know every Senator sees such cases in their own states—of a man who has lost both legs, pushing himself along with two weights along the street, playing on some sort of instrument, or inciting sympathy in some fashion to encourage people to buy pencils for two-bits, trying to get them to help him to exist, because no provision is made by our welfare program to help such people.[3]

Despite Russell's emotional appeal, his amendment failed by only one vote, forty-one to forty-two. Hoping he could round up the additional two votes he needed to win, Russell would not concede defeat. Immediately, he asked the Senate to reconsider his amendment. "I am sure many senators did not have a chance to understand the amendment fully," he argued. "We had only five minutes to debate the amendment on our side." Having spent an entire day on the bill and facing several more pending amendments, few senators were eager to reopen this debate. Fewer than a dozen senators supported Russell's motion. A subsequent attempt, led by Democrats Francis Myers of Pennsylvania and Paul Douglas of Illinois, to restore the House provision, also failed. Despite assurances from several opponents that the Senate-House conference committee would reconsider the provision, Congress passed the final bill absent the disability program. In its place, the conference committee inserted a weaker provision providing a small amount for federal grants to states for the permanently and totally disabled needy. Despite this defeat, Russell had his allies. President Truman signed the Social Security Act, but did so reluctantly, citing one of Russell's concerns—the omission of "urgently" needed benefits for the disabled.

Russell lost his first skirmish over social security. Nonetheless, he was patient. He knew he had taken a first step toward a record as the Senate's chief proponent of a greatly expanded social security program. Unlike his frenetic and impatient father, Russell was content to stake out a position and toil for years to achieve his aim. "In some respects, my view was I wanted my position to be known," he later admitted, adding that he also wanted to force Republicans to vote on these issues. "If they didn't want to do anything for the aged, I wanted to make them go on record as voting that way." Indeed, throughout his first decade in the Senate, Russell forced his conservative colleagues to vote against his liberalizing social security amendments on almost a dozen separate occasions. During this time, he doggedly sought to expand every social security bill Congress considered.[4]

In his State of the Union address to Congress in January 1954, President Eisenhower unveiled a comprehensive plan to expand social security. Among many items, Eisenhower's program called for adding millions of people to the benefit rolls and increasing monthly checks to the elderly by an average of five dollars. Believing that Eisenhower's increase was inadequate, in February Russell introduced legislation of his own to raise monthly old-age pensions by ten dollars, from fifty-five to sixty-five dollars. "No one can live adequately on fifty-five dollars a month." His bill also proposed increased payments to the blind, dependent children and the permanently disabled at no additional cost to states.[5]

When debate on the president's proposal commenced that summer, the Senate Finance Committee sided with the White House in approving the monthly five-dollar increase, shoving aside Russell's more generous proposal. Perhaps resigned to the reality of the Senate's frugality in this area, Russell tried again for his benefits increase, this time employing a roundabout tactic. He offered an amendment to prevent the government from penalizing social security recipients by reducing other public assistance by the amount of their social security increase. For too long, Russell argued, the elderly and disabled had been denied any real increase in social security benefits. These people were victims of what he called the "cruel paradox" of allowing six million affluent recipients to earn as much as $1,880 a year with no corresponding reduction in their pension checks. Russell added:

> In other words, we are going to take care of six million, but those who are classified as being needy, those who have been compelled to go to the welfare agencies and apply for welfare assistance, those who have no reserves, those who have no resources, the most needy of them all, receive no benefit. Why? Because without my amendment, federal law requires welfare departments to go down the list and find every one of these 442,000 people, and every time they get a five-dollar increase in income, cut their welfare check by five dollars.[6]

Despite his passionate appeal, Russell's proposal was rejected, first by the Finance Committee and then, later, by voice vote in the Senate. An ineffectual amendment requiring the Secretary of Health, Education, and Welfare to study increases in social security benefits was his meager consolation. His effort to win a larger monthly check for the elderly would wait. Nonetheless, the final product was not a complete loss. Congress had increased overall benefits and added more than ten million new Americans to social security coverage.[7]

Russell next turned to President Eisenhower's proposed $1.25 billion tax cut plan, which featured a cut in dividend income taxes, a boon for the very wealthy. To Russell, the plan was a disaster for the middle class. It would not save "the average family five cents," he scoffed. Only $200 billion of the plan, he complained, would go to working mothers, retired people, and widows. "Six times that would be passed on to corporations and those that own stock," he said in tones reminiscent of an earlier Long era. "I'm not against the corporations or the corporate stockholders getting some relief, but the administration completely ignores the needs of the farmer, the laboring man, white collar workers—the great masses of our people." Russell was also troubled by figures showing "less than five percent of our population owns corporation stock, yet the administration plan would give eighty percent of the tax relief to this minority."[8]

When the bill reached the Senate floor, Russell hoped to kill the dividend cut and substitute it with a twenty-dollar tax credit for all tax-payers. The Senate soundly rejected his amendment, thirty-three to fifty. Later, he unsuccessfully pushed another amendment to increase the individual income tax exemption by one hundred dollars. By his count, this would save the average person eighty dollars in taxes each year. When his proposal failed, Russell reluctantly voted for the bill. "As the bill stands now the average working man will receive no tax relief whatsoever," he said, vowing to continue his fight for tax fairness into the next year. "Never," he told a civic club in Beaumont, Texas shortly afterward, "has so much been done for so few and so little for so many."[9]

Russell again challenged Eisenhower on taxes the following year when the White House made its revenue proposals to Congress, absent any recommendation for an income tax cut. While the House approved the bill with a twenty-dollar income tax credit, Russell and Majority Leader Johnson could not persuade the Senate Finance Committee to follow suit. Committee chairman Harry Byrd of Virginia and Georgia's Walter George, both Democrats, sided with seven committee Republicans in striking the cut from the House bill. They reported a bill almost identical to Eisenhower's original request. Russell and five other Finance Committee Democrats countered by taking their own, more liberal proposal to the Senate floor. The Democratic plan granted a twenty-dollar tax credit for heads of households and a ten-dollar credit for each dependent, offset by scaling back several business deductions.

Arguing for the plan on the first day of the debate, Russell was intent on attacking the Eisenhower administration for having ignored middle-income taxpayers at the expense of big business:

> While stock prices have been soaring, profits of the large corporations have continued to rise, especially those having assets of more than $100 million each. An entirely different picture is found when we look at other elements of the economy. . . . There were 10,300 fewer businesses of all types started in the first six months of 1954 as compared with the same period in 1953. . . . The farmer has certainly not shared in this bonanza. His realized yearly net income has gone down from $13.6 billion in 1952 to $12 billion in 1954. . . .

During the past two years the small wage earner has certainly not been experiencing any such bonanza. Those who have managed to remain steadily employed without having to suffer either part-time or total unemployment have just about managed to stay even with the game. They have had only small wage increases to meet the further increase in their cost of living. . . . What is revealed is the clear and unmistakable need for additional purchasing power to be placed in the hands of the average family.[10]

After five days of debate, the Senate narrowly rejected Russell's plan, forty-four to fifty, and then deleted the House-passed tax cut before approving the bill by voice vote. Once again, the Senate's fiscal conservatism prevailed over Russell's liberalism. As usual, he was unbowed.

By the next year, 1956, White House officials admitted that their strategy was merely to resist any amendments that might destroy social security's actuarial soundness. "The program is sound," Eisenhower told Congress in his State of the Union message. "It must be kept so." Unlike Eisenhower, Russell could not imagine meekly assuming the role as protector of social security's fiscal integrity. To Russell, maintaining the status quo was unthinkable. A Twentieth Century Fund study, he gravely instructed colleagues on February 10, concluded that nearly three-fourths of Americans over age sixty-five had either no income or annual income less than one thousand dollars. "It is rather obvious," he told the Senate, "there are millions of aged people in this nation today whose continued existence depends upon such meager assistance as their children or relatives are able to provide. I feel sure that both great political parties desire to make progress in reducing the wretchedness and penury that are all too prevalent in this, the greatest and wealthiest nation on the face of the earth."[11]

That day, Russell joined Georgia's Walter George in introducing legislation to require the federal government to increase by five dollars its maximum matching share for state old-age pension funds. Russell explained the amendment meant that more than 2.5 million "needy, aged persons over sixty-five years of age, together with 105,000 needy blind persons and 250,000 totally and permanently disabled persons would receive at least five dollars additional in their monthly welfare payments."[12]

"A nation that can afford to spend more than five billion dollars each year in assisting the development of foreign nations and raising living standards throughout the world can certainly afford to care for its own," Russell told the Senate on February 24. This time, Russell attracted wide support for his legislation. Forty-five senators joined as cosponsors. Even so, a fiscally conscious Senate Finance Committee—led by Chairman Harry Byrd of Virginia, who called the amendment "excessive"—rejected Russell's legislation when it considered the entire social security package in June. The committee outcome did not surprise Russell, who told reporters, "[T]he Finance Committee is the most conservative one in the entire Congress and it is the committee that offers the least chance of passage to a public welfare program."[12]

Russell persisted. On July 13, he moved to amend the bill to include his proposal. "I regard this amendment as good government, good economics and good Christian charity. The millions of people who would be benefitted by this amendment have worked hard during their early years to help build this great Nation. At a modest additional cost, we can assist them in a way that will be genuine and meaningful, although the increase is modest. A person attempting to exist on a forty-dollar welfare check will be greatly assisted by an additional five dollars per month." His next thought was the clincher:

> While the amount is small to a United States Senator it is large and important to these individuals. . . . I hardly think that any member of this body who voted to increase his own pay by $7,500 a year on an annual basis could find it in his conscience to vote to deny a mere five-dollar monthly increase in welfare payments to the three million needy persons. As a practical matter, I would like to suggest to my colleagues that those three million needy persons would never understand it.[13]

Russell recalled the words of Finance chairman Harry Byrd in voting against the congressional pay increase. At the time, Byrd accurately warned some senator would eventually use the pay increase to shame the Senate into increasing funds for a government program. As Russell spoke, Byrd shook his head in disgust, knowing that Russell's argument had hit its target. Byrd tried his best to counter Russell, arguing not against the bill's merits, but its cost. "The amendment proposed by the junior Senator from Louisiana would add an additional 208 million dollars a year in cost of the federal government for public assistance." Byrd's parsimonious reasoning could not dilute the strength of Russell's argument. Shortly after Russell's speech, the Senate overwhelmingly adopted his amendment, sixty-two to twenty-one.[14]

Not long afterwards, the Senate turned to the bill's most controversial and significant provision, an amendment by Georgia's Walter George to extend social security benefits to the disabled when they reached fifty.

The issue had been Russell's crusade for several years. Moreover, it was revolutionary, for it signaled a radical departure from social security's initial philosophy of assisting only the elderly. Suddenly, congressional liberals were on the verge of expanding the program's scope to include an entire new class of Americans.

Curiously, Russell was not the amendment's lead sponsor. It was Senator George, who had opposed such benefits in the past. In fact, when labor leaders first approached Russell about his usual support of the provision, he declined. Instead, he sent them to George, the former chairman of the Finance Committee, whom Russell regarded as one of the Senate's most respected elders. "Now you've got a lot better chance to get that amendment agreed to," he told the labor representatives, "if you get Walter George to offer that amendment."[15]

As the Finance Committee debated adding George's provision to the original Senate bill, members of Congress and special interest groups quickly took sides. A spokesman for a group of state medical societies told the committee that the bill "would create millions of malingerers who would falsely claim all types of symptoms which the medical profession unfortunately cannot disprove." The American Medical Association was strenuously opposed. "Virtually every physician in the United States," an AMA representative claimed, opposed the bill. "The plight of the disabled laborer was not, of course, the real problem," journalist Merle Miller noted. "The real issue was whether social security should be used for wider purposes than mere retirement benefits, for if it were once, for the disabled, then would it not be twice, for some other group, and three times, and you know where that would lead. Directly to a social security–financed national health program." President Eisenhower and most of the Senate's fiscal conservatives agreed with the doctors.[16]

For his part, Russell regarded the doctors' opposition with contempt. "Doctors see a red flag when someone mentions social security," he told a labor group in Shreveport. "Every time there are efforts to make the program better, doctors want to come and testify against it." These remarks sparked a prompt protest from the Shreveport Medical Society, which claimed "shock" at Russell's "ridicule and scorn" of their profession. "If this is the attitude of our representatives," the doctors said in a letter released to the *Shreveport Times*, "then it is no wonder we never seem to see any of the proposed tax reductions." The AMA's opposition had its effect on the House, which deleted the disability provision from the bill it sent to the Senate. When the bill reached the Senate floor, George offered his amendment to restore the disability language. Despite mighty opposition, the disability amendment had one important, enthusiastic supporter, majority leader Lyndon Johnson, who for days scurried behind the scenes rounding up votes as the spirited debate raged.[17]

Senate debate on the provision concluded on July 17, shortly after Russell and Republican senator Wallace Bennett of Utah sparred over Bennett's suggestion that the disability provision was unneeded because some experts believed up to 90 percent of all disabled could be rehabilitated and returned to productive work. When Bennett pointed to President Eisenhower, a heart attack survivor, as a prime example, Russell was exasperated. "Does not the senator realize there is a difference between a man who has had successive heart attacks and who is serving in an executive position or as President of the United States, who does paperwork, and a man who has not had that kind of training and who has to do manual labor in the hot sun?"[18]

When the roll was called, the Senate narrowly approved the amendment, forty-seven to forty-five. George's stature, Johnson's behind-the-scenes lobbying and Russell's years of promotion had paid off. Finally approved by both houses of Congress, the bill went to President Eisenhower's desk on July 27. Expressing his earlier opposition to expanding the bill, Eisenhower reluctantly signed it on August 1, telling a press conference the same day "we are loading on the social security system something I don't think should be there."[19]

For Russell, the victory was bittersweet. For more than five years, he had fought for assistance for the disabled, yet he received little or no credit when his dream was fulfilled. "Looking back on it, I feel like that was one of the noblest things I did, when I passed up that opportunity to be the principal sponsor," Russell said. "Frankly, if I had seized that opportunity, I would eventually have prevailed. But we wouldn't have prevailed then. It might have been six or eight years. But you've got a lot of dear old people out there who would have had to wait for such a program. A lot of them would have been in their graves before they ever got any help."[20]

* * *

When Russell campaigned for Democratic presidential nominee Adlai Stevenson in 1952, he appeared motivated more by duty than conviction. Although Eisenhower was a war hero, and courted by both political parties, Russell felt obligated to campaign for his party's leader and was gratified when Louisiana went for Stevenson. By 1956, his attitude was vastly different. Four years of fighting patrician Republican conservatism and frugality in social security and taxes had fueled Russell's partisan fervor.

Throughout 1956, Russell's regard for the president eroded. In February, he told a New Orleans newspaper that he believed Eisenhower would tap Supreme Court Chief Justice Earl Warren to lead the Republican ticket and would run instead for vice president. "In this way," he said, "Eisenhower will sort of be around but will not have the burdens of the presidency." When speculation abounded that Eisenhower would dump Vice President Nixon from the ticket, Russell rushed to Nixon's defense. "I hate to use this word," he said in a radio interview, "but the fact is that in my judgment the president would be an ingrate if he didn't support the Vice President to run with him again."[21]

That fall, in the heat of the campaign, Russell intensified his attacks on the president, charging that Republicans had covered up the facts of Eisenhower's 1955 heart attack and had misled the country about the state of the economy. The conservative Republican economics of President Ronald Reagan—later known to many as "the trickle-down theory"—were more than two decades away. Yet, Russell presciently perceived the philosophy, and the rhetoric, behind the Republican party's fiscal policies. "Republicans believe," he told a Democratic fundraiser in Alexandria, Louisiana, "that prosperity and most good things trickle down from the top." He added Eisenhower had "gone overboard to favor the wealthy few at the expense of the many." In the end, Louisiana did not share Russell's dim view of the president. By a narrow sixty thousand votes, Eisenhower won Louisiana, marking the first time a Republican presidential nominee had carried the state since Reconstruction.[22]

The prospect of another four years of frugal social policy under Eisenhower did little to dampen Russell's enthusiasm for his cause. Throughout Eisenhower's second term, Russell continued his dauntless efforts to expand social security, albeit with limited success. Often guided in these matters by the tight-fisted Finance chairman, Harry Byrd of Virginia, the Senate's moderation was overwhelming. Russell's attempts to increase social security benefits for the elderly, blind, and disabled were not welcomed in 1958. The usual munificence of election-year politics had vanished where social security was involved. Encouraged by the Eisenhower administration's desire to scale back federal public assistance payments to the states, the Senate spurned Russell's efforts to increase the monthly old-age and disability pension by five dollars. To an unemployment benefits bill, Russell offered an amendment to give beneficiaries an extra five dollars by raising the maximum federal-state payment to seventy dollars a person, in the process increasing the federal share of the cost. "Those for whom I am speaking are in greater need than those who benefit from unemployment insurance. Those for whom I am speaking have nothing." A forty-forty tie resulted. Quickly, Russell moved to reconsider the vote, hoping to round up at least one more senator for his amendment. The Senate rejected this motion, forty-one to thirty-eight.[23]

While the Congress later enacted legislation liberalizing the scope of social security, the bill was largely designed to raise payroll taxes to offset a system deficit expected to grow to as much as four billion dollars by 1962. For this reason, President Eisenhower made no social security proposals. Instead, he asked Congress to scale back the federal share of public assistance grants to the states. Largely following the president's budget requests, Congress did make several modifications, the most important of which expanded on Russell's successful efforts in 1956 on behalf of the disabled. The bill enlarged the disability benefits program to include dependents of the disabled, another major and significant social security expansion for which Russell deserved much credit for his leadership in the early 1950s.

The next year, absent a social security bill, Russell cast his sights on the Tax Rate Extension Act of 1959, a noncontroversial bill to extend corporate, liquor, cigarette, and automobile excise tax rates. Conflict soon arose. Succumbing to a natural temptation, senators began to tinker with other provisions. In rapid order, they added provisions to roll back taxes on transportation and on a variety of communication services. Russell entered the fray on June 25, when he offered an amendment to raise the federal share of public assistance paid by the states from 50 percent to as much as 70 percent in most cases. As he had done on earlier occasions, Russell cast the issue in its most vivid terms:

> Some senators may say that their states have small caseloads. . . . All they have to do is make the old people crawl to get that money and they can keep people off the rolls. Make old people swear publicly that their children refuse to help them, for example. Most old folks are very proud. They would rather go hungry than say that their children turned them down. They can be made to sign a lien on their little homesteads. They are so proud they will not take money under such conditions. If states want to follow that kind of policy, they can have a very low caseload.[24]

Despite objections by Republican Carl Curtis of Nebraska that the amendment was irrelevant to the bill, senators accepted it by forty-two to thirty-six. When the legislation reached the other side of the Capitol, House conference committee members sided with Curtis. They struck the

Senate's amendments, including Russell's, which they deemed nongermane. Serving for the first time as a conferee on a revenue bill, Russell was outraged by the House's unyielding vigilance over its constitutional role as the only house that could originate revenue measures. Moreover, he was just as angry at the timidity of Senate conferees who would not defend the Senate's amendments. He refused to sign the conference report, the only member to abstain, explaining capitulation to the House "would set a precedent which would plague the Senate for many years to come." In a letter to Majority Leader Johnson, he complained that it was "a joke" for the Senate to debate amendments for which Senate conferees would not defend. "If the Senate conferees can give the Senate no better representation than existed in this instance," he wrote Johnson, "it might be well for us to inquire of the House in advance whether Senate amendments will be considered . . . and spare ourselves a great amount of trouble and effort."[25]

As the decade ended, tens of millions of older and disabled Americans had, in large part, Russell Long to thank for the government benefits they received. For these people, the new government benevolence had made their lives, especially their retirement years, less terrifying. Others in the Senate and House had surely played a large and significant role—Lyndon Johnson, Walter George of Georgia, Clinton Anderson of New Mexico, Paul Douglas of Illinois, and Hubert Humphrey of Minnesota. But Russell often brought more passion, and personal history to the debate than the others. Had he lived to see the results, Huey Long undoubtedly would have been proud of the role his son had played. For Russell did what Huey never could. He had helped poor elderly people and the disabled finally share in the wealth of a rich nation.

15

OUR SOUTHERN WAY
OF LIFE

$\mathcal{N}$O ISSUE COMMANDED MORE UNANIMITY among southern members of Congress during Russell's early Senate years than opposition to civil rights. "That was the critical and most sensitive political issue during that period and, of course, that affected all of the southerners," former Democratic senator J. William Fulbright of Arkansas remembered. "They might differ very widely on other issues, but on that issue, they felt the same." Russell was no exception. In 1948, he abandoned President Harry Truman to support the States Rights party's presidential candidate, Strom Thurmond of South Carolina. In his first Senate speech, he had denounced Truman's civil rights program. Among the southern bloc, Russell left no doubt that he was foursquare in opposition to civil rights.[1]

Even with such solid credentials, Russell considered himself a moderate. The legacy of Huey Long's populism and the obsession to fulfill the promise of his father's unfinished agenda were mighty influences on Russell when he arrived in Washington. "My father had been good to those people. I wanted to be good to them. I had no desire to hurt them at all. On the other hand, if you pushed that thing too fast, you're going to have some dislocation and resentment. I felt a path of gradualism and moving toward desegregation would be better."[2]

Regardless of a southern senator's personal forbearance on civil rights, political realities were supreme. Intimidated by intense, often emotional public opinion, southern members of Congress were consistent opponents of federal tampering with "our southern way of life," a southern euphemism for segregation. While a constant civil rights foe, Russell was never in the same league with vociferous segregationists like Thurmond or Mississippi's James Eastland and Theodore Bilbo. "Look," Russell explained, "when I ran the first time, there were only ten thousand black voters in the state, but they were for me. I only won by 10,456 votes. Theoretically, you put all the black votes against me, instead of for me, I'd have been beat. But I didn't look at it that way. I felt that, on the whole, if I'd been more strident in opposition to the blacks' position, I'd have probably gotten more votes, but that wasn't where my heart was." Nonetheless, over more than fifteen years, Russell ardently fought the civil rights programs of four presidents. His rhetoric, if not strident in the relative measure of the era, was often harsh.[3]

When the Justice Department delivered its civil rights proposal to Congress early in 1951, Russell quickly declared his opposition. "People are saying that the South is in the saddle in Congress. Well, in the case of the so-called civil rights bill, we'll put a saddle on it and ride it to death."[4]

In 1954, the U.S. Supreme Court abolished segregation in public schools by a landmark decision, *Brown v. Board of Education, Topeka,* shattering the notion of "separate but equal" education facilities. "Separate education facilities are inherently unequal," the Court declared to the immediate outcry of southern members of Congress. While he disputed the ruling, Russell told reporters that "my oath of office requires me to accept it as the law," adding an admonition to "all Southern officials to avoid any sort of rash or hasty action." Despite a nod to civil responsibility, Russell showed little concern that the Supreme Court's ruling might result in southern integration. "When we have better schools for colored children, there will not be as much pressure on school boards to admit colored students into the schools in white neighborhoods."[5]

In Louisiana, reaction to the Supreme Court decision ranged from anger to defiance. Denouncing the decision, Governor Kennon asked President Eisenhower not to enforce it. The state legislature responded by adopting a resolution critical of Chief Justice Earl Warren and by establishing a new Joint Committee on Segregation, chaired by Earl Long's old antagonist, state representative Willie Rainach. Rainach and his committee accepted their new duty with zestful enthusiasm. They searched for, and found, various legal avenues by which the state could circumvent the letter and spirit of the new court order.[6]

The haste and intensity with which Russell and other southern politicians attacked the Court ruling was evidence of the profound passions it evoked throughout the South. "It is difficult to determine whether southern politicians took advantage of the school segregation issue or were entrapped by it," historian James C. Duram observed. "Certainly, some willingly exploited the decision ruthlessly; others only because they had no choice. Both groups were trapped by the long shadow of the South's tragic past."[7]

While *Brown v. Board of Education* was the necessary impetus for the growing civil rights movement, like Russell, almost no southern leader regarded the ruling a serious threat to segregation. Few school systems complied. In Congress, resistance to civil rights among southern members grew even more resolute. In 1956, led by Strom Thurmond and Senator Harry Byrd of Virginia, southern members of Congress formalized their distaste for the growing civil rights movement in a rebellious document known as the Southern Manifesto. Signed by every southern senator but Lyndon Johnson and Tennessee's Estes Kefauver and Albert Gore, the proclamation labeled the ruling "a clear abuse of judicial power." It urged use of "all lawful means to bring about a reversal of this decision which is contrary to the Constitution."[8]

About the time he signed the manifesto, Russell launched another attack on the Supreme Court. In May 1956, he introduced two constitutional amendments—one to limit lifetime Supreme Court appointments to twelve years and another requiring a minimum of six years of judicial experience for at least six justices. "I am confident that the majority of level-headed persons, familiar with our history and our laws will agree that the Supreme Court of recent years has experienced powers far beyond those intended by our founding fathers." Predictably, the proposals were popular in Louisiana. The *Oak Grove-West Carroll Gazette* said that "such action should have been taken many years ago." The *Ouachita Citizen* in West Monroe, agreed: "Bills like these will tell the world that though we may have to put up with the present type of Supreme Court for as long as the justices live, we certainly don't like it."[9]

While few regarded Russell as a serious threat to the Court's future, the amendments at least bolstered his segregationist credentials as his 1956 reelection approached. It was a device employed by more than one southern politician that year. Indeed, vilification of the Court effectively detracted attention from the crucial question raised by the landmark ruling—the inherent injustice of the South's social caste system. Yet, despite consistently joining the chorus of outrage over civil rights and desegregation, the public Russell was often at odds with the private Russell who was sickened by race baiters like Plaquemines Parish boss Leander Perez and radical groups like the Ku Klux Klan and the White Citizens Councils. "There are many racists in America and Perez is one of the worst of them," Russell wrote in a private memorandum in 1954. "Up North, racists seek power by reviling the decent white gentiles of the South. Down South, on the other hand, demagogues and scoundrels have been running for office for a century by stirring racial hatred against the poor Negro, who in most instances cannot even vote."[10]

While defiance of the *Brown v. Board of Education* grew throughout the South—several states even adopted laws requiring closure of integrated schools—1957 was a year of great strides for the civil rights movement. Although the 1957 bill was nearly identical to one rejected the previous year by the Senate, chances for passage improved drastically with the sudden support of Senate majority leader Lyndon Johnson. Along with other Democratic leaders, Johnson was alarmed by the significant numbers of blacks who voted to reelect President Eisenhower in 1956, the same election which had returned Senate control to the Democrats. Furthermore, Johnson easily discerned the obvious reason behind this growing Republican affinity among blacks—southern opposition to civil rights. Passage of civil rights legislation, Johnson believed, was critical for his party to preserve the increasingly important black vote. For months, Johnson nudged the bill through every delicate step in the legislative process. He compromised and cajoled. He twisted arms when needed. He showed sudden interest in moribund legislation of senators whose votes he wanted and signaled his willingness to lose interest in the pet projects of those who opposed him. Sometimes, he took his lobbying directly to the Senate floor. More often than not, he worked his magic behind the scenes. Before long, what was born in the White House had become the adopted child of Lyndon Johnson. He was, as Alabama senator Lister Hill once described him, "the biggest tail twister you ever saw." Even so, one group of tails Johnson never twisted were those of southern senators. An ultimate political pragmatist, Johnson knew his limits. He rarely demanded votes from senators who would suffer politically by supporting legislation he wanted. Above all, Johnson religiously respected his colleagues' constituent pressures. For the southerners, Johnson substituted tail twisting with a finely crafted art of compromise.[11]

As supported by Johnson and the White House, the bill enforced black voting rights by investing broad powers in the Justice Department to seek court injunctions against obstructions to black voting by local and state election officials. Southerners vigorously opposed this provision, arguing that judges could jail anyone in contempt of their rulings without a jury trial. Among other provisions, the bill also created a Commission on Civil Rights and established a Civil Rights Division in the Justice Department headed by an assistant attorney general. In April, asked if he would filibuster the bill, Russell replied simply, "I expect to make a speech or two," but gave little credence to speculation that the bill would pass. "I recall how some people fought to preserve the rights of communists a few years ago. I'm curious to see what their position will be in the fight to preserve some of our fundamental civil rights." Later, Russell's description of the bill was harsher: "It creates a government of contempt and would end only in contempt of government."[12]

Yet, in June, when he wrote a Massachusetts man who had inquired about his views on civil rights, Russell responded more thoughtfully: "Actually, none of the groups have right with them all the way. It serves little purpose to argue about matters long past, however, when persons are more interested in influencing opinions than finding the facts. While I shall continue to represent the prevailing view of the South on segregation, I do not intend to start a revolution. No doubt this nation will continue to be a nice country to live in regardless of the outcome of the integration fight."[13]

In every way, integration was a fight. For months, Chairman James Eastland held the White House bill hostage in his Judiciary Committee, the Senate's traditional burial ground for civil rights legislation. In June, the momentum changed. When the House sent a similar version of the bill to the Senate, minority leader William Knowland and Illinois Democrat Paul Douglas seized the opportunity, employing a clever parliamentary strategy. With surreptitious help from Johnson, the two men persuaded the Senate to bypass the Judiciary Committee. Instead, the bill went directly to the Senate calendar—skirting the Judiciary Committee, the Senate's legislative black hole—and moved one step closer to debate. For eight acrimonious days, senators quarreled over Knowland's motion to begin debate on the measure. "The white men and women of good will in the South," Russell argued in the Senate, "have done and are still doing far more to improve the conditions of the colored man than any act of Congress or any Supreme Court decision has accomplished or ever will be accomplished." The bill would achieve little, he said, "if the majority of the white people of the South are determined to frustrate its terms and conditions." He added:

Mr. President, one of the problems which we southerners have to face constantly is the difficulty in gaining recognition for the fact that the areas which we represent in the Senate are inhabited by honorable and upright American citizens. The South is not a jungle in which the colored races are hunted down by their white fellow citizens. It is not a place in which the colored races have been driven deeper and deeper into poverty and degradation.

Instead, it is an area in which the position of the colored citizen has been improving constantly. It is also a place in which the white citizens desire that the colored races shall continue to advance and improve their position. [14]

Despite passionate arguments by Russell and others, this time the southerners failed. The clever detour around the Judiciary Committee had rendered Chairman Eastland's Judiciary Committee impotent. Knowland's motion to consider the bill passed. The battle began.

While the bill's first section invested the attorney general with expansive powers to seek court injunctions against those depriving anyone of the right to vote, Section Three granted him even more authority. Under its broad provisions, the Justice Department could request injunctions against those who deprived anyone of any civil right. This, in particular, alarmed many white southerners who feared that the Justice Department would use the law to impose wholesale school desegregation throughout the South. They were horrified by images of southern schools integrated at gunpoint by federal troops. Even President Eisenhower seemed not to comprehend the bill's full scope. Asked at a press conference in July if he would support rewriting the bill to apply only to voting rights, the president could not answer in detail. "I was reading part of the bill this morning. There were certain phrases I didn't completely understand." On this provision, the opposition was resolute and formidable. Johnson and Eisenhower retreated in the face of solemn filibuster threats from southern leader Senator Richard Russell of Georgia and his troops. By then, a group of moderate and liberal senators had also abandoned the provision, fearful the controversy might assure the bill's defeat. On July 24, by a vote of fifty-two to thirty-eight, the Senate jettisoned Section Three. [15]

Only Section Four remained unresolved. This, too, was a travesty to white southerners. It permitted judges to impose jail sentences for contempt in civil rights cases without a jury trial. With Senator Richard Russell leading the charge, the Senate's southern troops counterattacked with an amendment to overturn the provision's requirement. Long lustily joined the fray. "Does the Senator know of a single case," Long inquired of Illinois senator Paul Douglas on July 26, "in which trial by jury has been denied under Federal law for the reason that a jury would probably find the

defendant not guilty?" Douglas replied, "That is not the purpose here."
Russell pressed. "Has not the Senator himself made the argument that
southerners should not be permitted trial by jury because juries might find
them innocent?" "No," Douglas answered emphatically.

> What I said was that we could obtain a greater degree of justice in contempt
> proceedings in civil rights cases in the South by having these questions decided
> by judges, who, because of life tenure, are partially insulated from the passions
> and prejudices of the community in which they live, than by juries selected from
> carefully culled lists, from which Negroes are commonly excluded. Such jurors
> at the conclusion of their service, are compelled to return to the communities
> whence they came, and are subjected to the social, economic, and at times
> physical, pressures of the community around them.

"The Senator is saying what he said before, I take it," Russell countered, "which is that juries in the South might find the defendant not guilty,
and the Senator hopes to convict persons whom a jury would find innocent."

Douglas would not let Russell lead him down this path. "No," he
answered for the second time. "What the Senator from Illinois is saying is
that, on the whole, a greater degree of justice can be obtained from
southern judges in such cases than from southern juries."

"Does that not amount," Russell asked, "to saying that the Senator
wants to deny white southerners the right of trial by jury because he fears
juries would turn them loose?"

"Not at all," Douglas said. "The aim is justice."[16]

On August 2, the Senate, with Johnson's tacit support, voted fifty-one
to forty-two to require jury trials in contempt cases. Saying he was
"bitterly disappointed," President Eisenhower complained that the amendment rendered the bill "largely ineffective." Russell hailed the vote "a
great victory for free speech, the free press and free labor." Five days
later, the full Senate passed the bill—Russell in the minority—seventy-
two to eighteen.[17]

The great jury-trial victory was short-lived. In conference committee,
the House refused to accept the Senate's amendment. After long days of
negotiation, Senate and House leaders compromised. The result was a
provision providing that in criminal cases arising out of the legislation, the
defendant could have a new trial by jury when the judge's penalty was
more than three hundred dollars or forty-five days in jail. This did nothing
to endear the bill to Russell, who told the Senate on August 28: "The

worst thing about the bill, as it is now before us, as it has come back from the House of Representatives, is that it seeks to substitute the contempt powers of a Federal court for the ordinary due process of law to which every American citizen should be entitled. . . . If this trend continues, it will not be long until the courts will be able to place people in jail, for any crime, by contempt proceedings, and there will not be any respect left for the courts."[18]

While southern senators were no less opposed to civil rights than in previous years, the 1957 bill had at least signaled a significant change in strategy. In years past, the southern bloc had employed only one weapon. They had successfully attacked every civil rights bill with filibusters or threatened filibusters, an impressive tool under the Senate's conservative cloture rule, which required sixty-four votes to end debate. This time, however, southern leaders had feared a drawn-out filibuster might provoke a fight with liberals over liberalizing cloture. "An unsuccessful filibuster at this point," Russell explained, "would tempt our friends as well as our enemies to change the rules of the Senate and thereby deprive us of our right to free debate which has made it possible for us to defeat such a large number of obnoxious pieces of legislation aimed at the South." Instead, the southern senators, often with the pragmatic help of Lyndon Johnson, focused on diluting the bill with amendments.[19]

This strategy had not been unanimously popular. Senator Strom Thurmond, at least, suspected ulterior motives when Senator Russell and majority leader Johnson persuaded southern senators to forgo the filibuster. "They could have stopped the bill if they had had an organized filibuster," Thurmond maintained many years later. "But the Southerners more or less, or some of them anyway, headed by Dick Russell, wanted to elect Lyndon Johnson president. Johnson had told them that to have a chance, he'd have to have a civil rights program and a civil rights bill." Later, Thurmond asked Senator Russell to reconsider a filibuster. "Anyone can speak as long as they want to," Senator Russell told him. "But I don't feel I can call them back and have it organized."[20]

If the southern bloc would not fight, Thurmond would. From the evening of August 28 through the morning and afternoon of August 29, he swaggered through a marathon tirade of twenty-four hours and eighteen minutes. His diatribe broke the record for a Senate speech, once held by Russell's father, who had raged on the Senate floor for sixteen hours in 1935.

Thurmond's obstinate tactic did more than set a new record. It incurred the animosity of the southern senators who believed they had chosen the

prudent course while Thurmond betrayed them. As southern historian
Robert Sherrill observed, the no-filibuster agreement was only successful
"if it was respected by all southern senators. A maverick would do double
damage, both calling attention to the defeat of the South and making the
nonfilibusterers look like traitors to their region." Other than its seeming
duplicity, Thurmond's impassioned speech had little impact. The Civil
Rights Act of 1957 passed overwhelmingly on August 29 by a vote of sixty
to fifteen. Again, Russell joined the minority in opposing the bill.[21]

"I welcomed it as a step forward at the time it was passed," recalled
Illinois senator Paul Douglas, "and it turned out not to be very acceptable
. . . a pretty weak instrument." Ineffectual compared to subsequent legislation enacted during Lyndon Johnson's presidency, the Civil Rights Act of
1957 did mark an important early step. Furthermore, the bill's passage
accomplished several of Johnson's goals: It helped shore up black Democratic support, which, in turn, opened new doors of opportunity for
Johnson's presidential ambitions. Although most civil rights advocates, like
Douglas, thought the bill was mild, Lyndon Johnson aide George Reedy
noted that "they could not get past the fact that no one else had been able
to pass *anything* for seventy-seven years. They could no longer claim he
was anti-civil rights; merely that he was not 'strong enough' on the issue."
Nevertheless, segregationist critics vilified Johnson in the South for his
prominent role, even though he had tolerated the significant weakening
amendments. "In Louisiana, he was absolutely hated because they considered him a turncoat," the late New Orleans congressman F. Edward
Hebert remembered. "They considered Lyndon the most horrible man
that ever lived."[23]

Several weeks later, President Eisenhower again inflamed white southerners' racial passions by sending federal troops into Arkansas to keep
order after a white Little Rock high school denied admission to two black
students. Russell deplored Eisenhower's decision. "It was a tragic step
and an example of political expediency," he said, adding southern schools
would only be integrated at gunpoint "because the South is not willing to
accept integration."[23]

Despite a consistent segregationist record during his first decade in the
Senate, Russell sided with his liberal colleagues on occasion—but usually
when the civil rights implications were inconspicuous. For example,
Russell had spurned the Senate's southern bloc in 1953 by supporting
statehood for Hawaii—which many segregationists feared would result in
two new pro-civil rights votes in the Senate. After an important Interior
Committee vote—Russell cast the deciding vote for Hawaiian statehood—

columnist Drew Pearson described the angry reaction among southerners: "Democratic senators are treating Russell Long . . . as if he had political B.O. ever since he switched his vote on statehood for Hawaii. When the astute Senator Earl Clements of Kentucky heard of Long's switch, he almost blew his top." Several Democrats later hinted that Russell had crassly traded his vote for Hawaiian statehood in exchange for a political favor from Republican leaders, insinuating, Pearson wrote, another "Louisiana Purchase."[24]

But Russell's support of Hawaiian statehood had been sincere and heartfelt, despite its civil rights implications. "I was particularly impressed by the fact that the people of Hawaii want[ed] full status as American citizens and they want[ed] to share the burdens and responsibilities of the federal government," Russell told the Senate in 1954. "They [did] not want to ride free on the backs of the American taxpayers and expect Americans to make sacrifices and pay the burdens any more than they expected Americans to fight alone to defend their islands [during World War II]." When Mississippi senator James Eastland argued that the Senate should reject Hawaii's statehood because of alleged communist activity on the island, Russell disputed him vigorously on the Senate floor for more than an hour. "I completely disagree with the senator from Mississippi."[25]

Furthermore, while Russell favored school segregation, he detested attempts to deny voting rights to blacks. In October of 1957, for this very offense, he attacked Louisiana's White Citizens Councils—a mainstream white supremacist group of businessmen who sought respectability not conferred on the Ku Klux Klan. In 1956, the White Citizens Council of Grant Parish had tried removing more than 750 black voters from the rolls by challenging the legality of their registration. Only about two hundred were taken off the rolls, but Senator Paul Douglas hauled the episode into the Senate's 1957 civil rights debate as vivid evidence many southern states were still hostile to black voter registration.[26]

Speaking to the Baton Rouge Chamber of Commerce in late October— just months after the bill's enactment—Russell complained that the voter purge had impaired his effectiveness in fighting the legislation. "There's no defense of that sort of thing. I mean, how can you answer the arguments of the other senators, when you yourself believe that every man has a right to vote if he is qualified?" The purge, and its inclusion in the Senate's debate, Russell suggested, "played a major part" in the bill's passage.[27]

That remark sparked angry condemnation from at least two Louisiana White Citizens Councils. The Rapides Parish council claimed that it only opposed "the improper way that many others were put on our registration rolls," although its members presented no evidence they ever challenged the qualification of a white voter. At a White Citizens Council rally in New Orleans, attended by Mississippi senator James Eastland, Claiborne Parish state representative John Garrett attacked Russell to the cheers of the crowd when he declared that "Long is not nearly as embarrassed as the people of Louisiana are at his conduct at not joining all-out in the segregation fight." In Tallulah, in northeastern Louisiana, most of the parish's elected officials signed a resolution condemning Russell's statement as a "blanket indictment against the people of north Louisiana, charging them in effect with committing illegal acts." Russell, the officials said, was "more interested in appeasing the opponents of the South . . . than he is in championing the causes of those whom he has been duly elected to serve."[28]

"The statement is completely untrue," Russell retorted. "I'm strongly in favor of segregation, first because I believe in it, second because every white Southerner wants it and third because the great majority of colored people want it. I'm also in favor of treating the colored man fairly."[29]

This incident was telling. While it again exposed Russell's moderation, it highlighted the severe political consequences reserved for those who strayed from the confining segregationist path. "I didn't want to say anything that was going to alienate the blacks because they had always been for me." As Russell later recalled:

> I'd go back to Louisiana and explain, "Now, look, if I voted the way you wanted me to vote on that particular issue, I wouldn't be around to represent anybody. I couldn't get elected. Now, meanwhile, I can get elected and I'm doing all kind of things to help you everywhere I can. I'm voting for the minimum wage. I'm voting to increase those welfare payments. I'm *leading* the charge to increase those welfare payments. I'm voting for social security to help that. I'm voting to give you better school lunches and even offered the amendments for it. I'm voting for everything I can to help you good folks, but when you ask me to vote for something that gets me at cross purposes with the majority of whites in this state, you don't have enough votes to save me."[30]

For Russell, striking this delicate balance would only grow more difficult and troublesome in years to come as Louisiana's segregationist fervor slowly lost political influence to flourishing black voting strength. Eventually, for many southern politicians, including Russell, civil rights would become a simple matter of mathematics.

16

JUST PLAIN CRAZY

OTHER THAN PERHAPS THE ASSASSINATION of Huey Long, no chapter in Long family lore is more sensational and controversial than the celebrated mental and physical collapse of Governor Earl Long. The events of the summer of 1959 were painful for Russell. In varying degrees of horror and sadness, he watched his uncle, a father figure, slowly destroy his life. Never a paragon of stability and self-restraint, Earl's extraordinary behavior in 1959 set new standards for irrationality. To the rest of the country, Earl staged an immensely entertaining burlesque show. For his family and friends, the episode was an utter disgrace and embarrassment. "Earl Long had just gone plain crazy," *Time* magazine declared. While historians, friends, and his family might debate the exact medical and psychological nuances of Earl's condition, *Time* could not have better characterized the situation.[1]

In the years after his heart attack in 1950, Earl totally neglected his health. His eating habits were irregular and he lost considerable weight. Ignoring the advice of family and friends, primarily his wife Blanche, Earl, sixty-three in 1959, pushed himself to the limits of physical and mental endurance. Instead of relaxing as Blanche had begged him, Earl only accelerated his physical degeneration by falling back into old habits. He drank heavily and slept only sporadically. He began smoking cigarettes again. He gulped generous amounts of Dexedrine to fuel his frantic activities. When his body finally craved rest, Earl needed more pills to induce sleep.

To make matters worse, Earl's marriage to Blanche had fallen apart by the late 1950s. Now, he prowled the streets of New Orleans's French Quarter with increasing regularity, frequenting numerous night spots up and down Bourbon Street. "Earl behaved like a kid brought up by strict Baptist parents who had never seen a cigarette, a bottle of whiskey, or a loose woman in his life," said one disapproving relative. During one of his many visits to the Sho Bar, Earl met the establishment's featured entertainer, a stunning twenty-three-year-old stripper from Baltimore, known as Blaze Starr. Captivated by her conspicuous beauty, Earl fawned over Blaze, who was, in turn, inexplicably enchanted by Earl. Before long, the governor's extraordinary courtship of a Bourbon street stripper was sensational media fodder.[2]

In spite of his confusing downward spiral, Earl's friends and family clung to one hope: Earl's time as governor was running out. He was not likely to stay in politics after his term expired in 1960. Earl himself announced he planned to retire from public life at the end of his term. But sometime in early 1959, the governor abruptly changed his mind. If he found a man "hell-bent on running for governor," Earl declared, he would send him off "to have his head examined." It was a curious statement considering Louisiana's constitution then prohibited the governor from serving consecutive terms. "If I ever run again, I'll run now," Earl announced in April, explaining he would circumvent the constitution by resigning shortly before the election, briefly entrusting the office to the lieutenant governor. In this manner, Earl reasoned, he would not succeed himself. However, the events that began in May destroyed any chance that Earl could retain his beloved governor's office.[3]

Shortly after the legislature convened, Earl went before the House Judiciary Committee to argue for a measure protecting black voting rights. To committee members, Earl seemed drunk and looked appallingly haggard. Worse, Earl eschewed a reasoned appeal to the lawmakers' higher instincts. Instead, he spat an abusive tirade of insults at them. Even championing greater rights for blacks, Earl was insensitive at best, and ignorant at worst. When north Louisiana representative Joe Waggonner upbraided him for his profane language with schoolchildren in the gallery, Earl first apologized, then turned on Waggonner. "I got elected saying 'damn' every now and then," he told Waggonner. "I think it's better to say 'damn' in the open than sleep with a nigger woman at night."[4]

The next day, Louisiana newspapers were replete with graphic accounts of the hearing. Earl's performance had been a disaster. Hoping that they could repair the political damage, Earl and his advisers crafted a conciliatory speech for the upcoming joint legislative session. Days later, before a chamber packed with reporters and television cameras, Earl began a speech, which if delivered as written, might have swayed lawmakers, and the public, back into his corner. "The minute he started to talk," said one of Earl's advisers, "I knew we were in trouble." Drunk and still high on the drugs he had consumed before the speech, Earl swaggered through an incoherent, rambling, and vulgar hour-and-a-half outburst. Few legislators escaped his insults. He called Shreveport representative Frank Fulco a "dago." He labeled one man a "Dillinger in disguise" and branded another lawmaker a "hypocrite." He questioned the racial heritage of several others and nearly became embroiled in a fistfight with Representative Frank Stinson. "I have the experience to be governor," he shouted incoherently. "I know how to play craps. I know how to play poker. I know how to get in and out of the Baptist church and ride horses. I know the oil and gas business. I know both sides of the streets."[5]

Earl reserved his most intense fury for north Louisiana representative Willie Rainach, a staunch segregationist who was the most ardent opponent of the governor's voting rights program. "I think there's such a thing as being overeducated!" he shouted at Rainach. Tapping his forehead, Earl continued, "Scientists tell me there's enough wrinkles up there to take care of all kinds of stuff. Maybe I'm getting old—I'm losing some of mine. I hope that don't happen to Rainach. After all this is over, he'll probably go up there to Summerfield, get up on his front porch, take off his shoes, wash his feet, look at the moon and get close to God." Then, glaring at Rainach, Earl bellowed: "And when you do, you got to recognize that niggers is human beings!"[6]

When Earl finished, friends hauled him out of the chamber and to the governor's mansion. They immediately put him to bed. "I must tell you I was aghast when I saw this played back by film over television," wrote Russell, who arrived in Baton Rouge following a speech in New Orleans earlier that day. "I could not believe my eyes and ears. I believe I have some idea how it came to happen, but I could never have actually believed it had I not seen it."[7]

Later, passing by the kitchen in his Baton Rouge home, Russell overheard his housekeeper, a black woman named Ollie, discussing Earl's situation over the telephone. "What bothers me," Ollie said, "is that he's lost everything you respect about a man." The comment's impact prompted Russell to action. That night, he phoned Earl's cousin, Dr. Dr. Arthur Long, who halfheartedly advised him to avoid the situation.[8]

Next, Russell called his aunt Blanche at the governor's mansion. She was frantic. Russell offered his help. "God, I've been praying somebody would come and help me," Blanche responded. "This thing is awful and I'm at the end of my rope. I don't know what to do." Russell rushed to the mansion. With Earl asleep upstairs, Blanche and Russell convened an informal gathering of Earl's relatives and political advisers—including Earl's sister, Lucille Long Hunt; Earl's cousin, Dr. Arthur Long; and Louisiana labor leader Victor Bussie—to discuss how to save Earl from himself. They quickly agreed on the obvious: Earl desperately needed a long vacation, away from the extreme pressures and demands of the governor's office. That conclusion reached, Russell led a small delegation upstairs to Earl's bedroom. Crouching by his bed, Russell shook Earl awake. "You must get some rest," he told his uncle. "Well, I was getting some rest," Earl angrily shot back, "until you sons of bitches woke me up!"[9]

Upon returning to their conclave, Russell, Blanche, and the others decided to act. Based on the diagnosis of Dr. Long, who believed that Earl suffered from a violent manic-depressive psychosis, the group decided to admit Earl to a mental hospital for treatment. "We went on ahead and planned that if he wasn't going to (get his rest)," Russell said, "then, worse come to worse, then we ought to just grab him. So, we made our plans." Concluding that they could not admit Earl to a Louisiana institution—he would retain the powers of governor while within the state's borders—the family phoned several mental hospitals throughout the South. Finally, the Titus Harris Psychiatric Clinic of the John Sealy Hospital in Galveston, Texas, agreed to accept him.[10]

As the group made its plans, Earl called on Russell to summon his barber for a shave. When he finished, the barber left by the elevator. Several minutes later, Earl summoned the barber again, hoping the diversion would provide the opening for his escape, as Russell recalled:

> So when the barber came up that elevator, Uncle Earl made a beeline for that elevator. I heard somebody say, "Here he comes!" I thought I had these guys all agreed that we weren't going to let him get out of there and we were going to grab him before he could. And, I swear, those men stood there like a bunch of statues. To me, you had to act immediately, or it was going to be too late. So, I just charged forward and tackled him, put my head down. I knew him for the barroom fighter that he was. So, when I charged into him, I had my head down where he couldn't get at me to bite me very well, and I had my knees outside his knees. And I was wise, because, boom, up comes that knee and it would have caught me right in the middle if I just would have gone straight on at him. . . . He had brought with him the only weapon he could find,

that was a big table spoon. And he was trying to stab me in the back with that damn table spoon.[11]

After an exhausting struggle, Russell and the others subdued Earl. They carried him kicking and screaming to his bedroom and locked him inside. Earl was furious and violent. He tossed an ashtray and a bottle of Milk of Magnesia through a window. He shouted "Murder!" to the street below. Only after the doctors threatened to inject him with drugs to induce sleep did Earl reluctantly take a couple of sleeping tablets, which were actually much more potent than he suspected. "They were enough to put four men to sleep," Russell recalled, "yet it took three hours for them to react on him and his rest lasted less than four hours."[12]

That night, Russell urgently called Jesse Bankston, director of Louisiana's state hospitals. Upon returning from a fishing trip in north Louisiana, Bankston was astonished when he learned the reason for Russell's call. Russell directed Bankston to locate a straitjacket in the event it might be needed to restrain Uncle Earl. Bankston balked. Such physical restraints, he told Russell, were a thing of the past. Tranquilizers were now the preferred way to calm hysterical mental patients. Russell persisted. He told Bankston that medication had little effect on Earl. Given Earl's violent nature, Russell demanded a straitjacket. After an exhaustive search, Bankston finally located the desired item at the state's mental hospital at Jackson, north of Baton Rouge. Dutifully, Bankston delivered the jacket to the governor's mansion in a paper bag, where it remained overnight and was never used.[13]

The next day, strapped to a hospital stretcher, the governor of Louisiana was hoisted out of the mansion by plainclothed orderlies from Charity Hospital. Suspecting that his captors were union men, Earl bellowed to labor leader Victor Bussie as the men hauled him out the door, "When this thing's over, I'm going to pass a right to work law that'll make Jefferson B. Davis look like a raving liberal!" The men quickly packed Earl into a state police station wagon and whisked him to the airport. From there, they flew by National Guard airplane to Galveston and admitted him to John Sealy Hospital.[14]

While he resolutely believed his uncle needed mental and physical treatment, the experience was traumatic for Russell. "If we are right," he wrote at the time,

then we are his best friends. . . . If we are wrong, then we are indeed stupid, ignorant and unworthy of the positions in life which the people and our friends

have accorded us. If we prove to be wrong, then we have forcibly seized a
governor from his state, elected by the people to hold the highest and greatest
power which can be entrusted by a free people to a single man. . . . If we are
wrong, then we have made the governor of a sovereign people a prisoner in his
own mansion, flown him against his own will into a neighboring state where his
powers do not exist, imprisoned him in a hospital room against his desires. [15]

For the moment, Russell had more pressing concerns. State govern-
ment was in turmoil. The legislature needed reassurance. For that task,
Russell was the logical choice. But when he announced plans to address a
joint legislative session to explain why he and Blanche had shanghaied
Earl, several lawmakers objected. They preferred to hear from Lieutenant
Governor Lether Frazar, the acting governor in Earl's absence. "In the
opinion of many legislators," a *Monroe News-Star* columnist wrote, "Earl
Long's nephew had come from Washington to attempt a coup." On Sunday
night, before a packed chamber, Russell lashed out at the six house
members who had voted against his appearance. Refusing to speak until
the controversy was resolved, Russell brusquely challenged the men to
state their objections by standing, promising to give his speech in the
senate chamber if anyone persisted in disputing his right to speak. "I will
be glad to decline to proceed with my prepared address," Russell declared. Several lawmakers immediately shot up from their seats, accepting
Russell's dare. True to his word, Russell marched indignantly toward the
door. "Go back," one lawmaker shouted. "I think you have made the
biggest mistake of your life." For several tense minutes, Earl's floor
leaders pleaded with Russell to return to the rostrum. Russell did, but
started out the chamber two more times before Earl's men cajoled him
back to the podium. [16]

"Once again," explained Long family biographer Stan Opotowski, "the
ghost of Huey Long rose up to haunt his son. In any other state, Russell's
appearance under the circumstances would be unusual but understandable, and no one would search for ulterior motives. But this was Louisiana.
In too many minds there still burned the memory of United States Senator
Huey Long coming down from Washington to harangue the legislature
from the podium. Now here was another Senator Long deciding, without
invitation, that he would address the legislature." [17]

"Governor Earl Long," Russell finally began, "has had a breakdown in
his health. The duties of this great office have been more than he could
stand. If he was to be spared the duties of his office while he received the
necessary rest and treatment, it was necessary for him to leave the

state." Russell, however, said nothing of the circumstance by which Earl had left. "With reference to the political situation, Governor Frazar is now your governor." Russell added an admonition: "This state is in a serious and political governmental crisis. There is nothing about it that responsible men with good will cannot handle with ease. The only thing really necessary to provide for the needs of this state is that you lay aside political expediency and refuse to follow those who will not do the same thing."[18]

Reviews of Russell's performance, including the prudence of a U.S. senator addressing the legislature regarding a state matter, were mostly ambivalent. "As it turned out," the *Baton Rouge State-Times* observed, "there wasn't much good in Sen. Long's appearance, nor any harm. What he had to say could just as well been said in a prepared statement to the press. . . ." A New Orleans television station said any political overtones in the speech should not be blamed solely on Russell. "It's simply a fact that it's impossible to separate Russell Long, as a member of the Long family, from Russell Long the political leader. If Senator Russell Long was unnecessarily excitable last night about the objections to his appearance, that is perhaps understandable." Even more supportive was the *New Orleans Times-Picayune,* which concluded that Russell's speech "was reasonable and logical." However, Earl Long biographer Richard McCaughan wrote that some legislators "believe that this incident did Russell Long's career no good," quoting one state representative who maintained Russell "acted small" by initially refusing to speak. Representative George Tessier of New Orleans, who made the original protest, explained that Russell "made the mistake of announcing in the papers the joint session would be held to hear him, before the legislature decided that."[19]

Several weeks later, Russell further muddied Louisiana's political waters when he told reporters that he was "very seriously thinking of running for governor." To those who suspected ulterior motives in Russell's role in Earl's confinement—now presumably confirmed by his expressed interest in the governorship—Russell responded that should he run "it would be just because I thought I might be of greater service as governor than I am at this moment as United States senator." To the *Monroe Morning World,* Russell denied that he was considering the race only to salvage the Long machine. "There is not any Long machine in Louisiana," he asserted. But to the *Shreveport Journal,* he admitted as much. "I've always had an ambition to be governor and follow my father into the mansion," he said, adding he had "serious doubts" about giving up his Senate seniority in order to serve as governor. "However, if it were the only way of keeping the Long faction together, I might consider running."[20]

"Russell's in one hell of a pickle," an anti-Long politician told *Newsweek,* providing an interesting explanation for Russell's flirtations with the governor's race. "Just look at the picture. Ole Earl is done. If he beats the booby hatch, he'll try to convince people that he was kidnapped out of the state, but he plumb tuckered out. So, if Russell wants to hold the machine together, he will have to leave the Senate and run for governor in the Democratic primary. If Russell doesn't run, an anti-Long governor will get in as sure as shooting and that means Russell won't even be sure of being re-elected to the Senate in '62."[21]

Earl, meanwhile, acquiesced to the physical and psychiatric exams at John Sealy. In many ways, the confinement achieved its purpose. Free of the alcohol and drugs, Earl was clearheaded and alert, so much so he now threatened Blanche and Russell with a lawsuit for kidnapping. Russell was certain they were on sound legal footing. He had already consulted Justice Department officials who told him the FBI wanted no role in the episode. Relieved of this threat, Blanche confidently signed the legal papers committing Earl to the Galveston facility, where he remained for seventeen days. Under Texas law, the document required a sanity hearing to determine Earl's mental state. But before the judge could rule, Earl's lawyers counterattacked. They filed a habeas corpus petition asking the Galveston judge to decide if Earl was held against his will, a motion with legal priority over Blanche's sanity petition. If the tactic was aimed at intimidating Blanche, it worked. Fearing that Earl would win his motion, and his unconditional freedom, Blanche dismissed Russell's advice to persist. She capitulated. Instead of insisting on further therapy, she signed papers allowing Earl to receive treatment in Louisiana in exchange for promises that he would not seek damages for the alleged "kidnapping." On June 17, Earl flew from Galveston to New Orleans, where he presented himself to doctors at the Ochsner Foundation Hospital. But by day's end, Earl had reneged on his promise. Within hours of arriving at Ochsner, he left New Orleans for Baton Rouge.[23]

As Earl's caravan raced toward the capital, Blanche ordered a squad of East Baton Rouge Parish sheriff's deputies to intercept the governor's car. When the deputies relieved his state police escort, Earl suspected nothing. Later, when he realized that he had been delivered not to the Governor's Mansion, but to the parish courthouse for an impromptu sanity hearing, Earl was livid. He spewed a tirade of profanity at his new captors. When he refused to leave the car, the parish coroner and a court-appointed psychiatrist examined him from the backseat. For forty-five minutes, Earl shouted and cursed at the two doctors, who finally concluded that the governor suffered from paranoid schizophrenia.

Based on that analysis, a state judge ordered Earl to receive treatment at the Southwest Louisiana Hospital in nearby Mandeville. As he arrived that evening, Dr. Charles Belcher, the hospital's acting director, greeted Earl warmly. "How do you do, governor? I'm Dr. Belcher." In a fury, Earl replied, "The hell you are! You *were* Dr. Belcher!" Later, Earl complained of his torture at the hands of the hospital staff, who he said punctured him "with hypodermics and harpoons."[22]

While his doctors and the public concluded that Earl lost his mind, the governor promptly proved that his insanity was, at worst, only temporary. Within a matter of days, Earl's political faculties were as sharp as ever. He summoned an attorney, Joe Arthur Sims of Hammond, who quickly filed papers of legal separation against Blanche, thereby nullifying her legal status to have him recommitted. Next, Earl directed Sims to seek a petition for habeas corpus to determine the lawfulness of his incarceration. At the June 26 hearing at Covington Junior High School, Earl revealed his brilliant plan: Upon Earl's orders, the state's Hospital Board had fired state Hospital Director Jesse Bankston, an ally of Blanche and Russell. In his place, board members appointed a close associate of Earl's, who, in turn, asked the board to dismiss Dr. Belcher, the Mandeville hospital's acting superintendent. Next, the board replaced Belcher with another Long ally, Dr. Jess McClendon of Amite.

By the hour of the hearing, Earl had executed his elaborate scheme. McClendon, Sims told the court, had certified that Earl was mentally sound. Based on McClendon's decree, the judge was left with no choice but to release Earl. The hearing was over in minutes. Earl was a free man. As he and Sims emerged from the school and fought their way through the throng to his car, someone asked, "What are you going to do now, governor?" As Earl climbed into his car, he replied simply, "Gonna be governor."[24]

Even before Earl's maneuver, Russell confessed that he no longer had the stomach for a protracted struggle with his uncle. "It is neither my right nor my responsibility to do anything more about this situation," he told reporters during Earl's confinement in Mandeville. "I have done my duty as I saw it for the welfare and the interests of the governor, his family and the state of Louisiana." Years later, Russell confessed that he had washed his hands of the matter because Blanche "caved in." Earl was unmoved by Russell's change of heart. In a speech taped from his Mandeville hospital room, Earl told a New Orleans radio audience that he was "undermined by my nephew, by my wife and by my supposed-to-be cousin, Dr. Arthur Long, in Baton Rouge. These people, through Russell Long wanting to be governor, have conspired with my wife, who is one of the most jealous women God ever let live." Several days later, Earl told UPI that Russell "is just burning up to be governor. And so is Blanche." Months after his release, Earl was still furious at Russell, who by then had said he would not run for governor. "It all grew out of his desire to be governor," Earl told a press conference in October. "He tried to take over the legislature while I was in Texas, but a lot of people wouldn't let him. He was trying to prove he was a big man."[25]

* * *

An epilogue on Earl Long: Few who knew him would have expected Earl to live much longer unless, willingly or forcibly, he adopted a saner life-style after his release. That meant a slower pace. To the horror, if not surprise, of his family and friends, Earl did just the opposite. From his pea patch farm in Winnfield, Earl told reporters that he would run for governor. "Last time, I got fifty-one percent of the votes," he said. "But this time, I'm going to get sixty percent."[26]

Still estranged from Blanche, Russell, and other friends and family, Earl continued to defy his doctors' advice for rest. In July, he embarked on much-publicized eighteen-day whirlwind vacation that took him and his entourage through Texas, Mexico, New Mexico, Colorado, Missouri (where he traded dirty jokes with former president Harry Truman), and Arkansas. When he returned, Earl immediately hit the campaign trail in his quest to circumvent the state's constitutional prohibition on consecutive gubernatorial terms. True to his plans, Earl announced that he would resign the governorship before the December 1959 Democratic primary. The Louisiana Democratic State Central Committee, however, foiled him. Committee members adopted a resolution requiring Earl to resign by September 15—seven months before his term expired—if he wanted to qualify as a candidate. Earl simply changed tack. He would, instead, now run for lieutenant governor on a ticket headed by former Governor Jimmy Noe. By then, Earl was back in form. He entertained crowds all over Louisiana with strident, scathing attacks on his opponents. He and Noe finished third, and Earl completed his term of office quietly.

By the summer of 1960, Earl prepared for a dramatic comeback. Now, he said, he would challenge incumbent central Louisiana congressman Harold McSween for the state's Eighth District seat. For weeks, Earl made five to seven speeches a day in ninety-five-degree temperatures, as he swept through nearly every community in the district. On election day, he found himself in second place, in a runoff with McSween. "He knocked on McSween's cage, dragged him out, skinned him from head to toe, salted him down and fed him to the wolves and alligators," Earl's ally, former lieutenant governor Bill Dodd, remembered admiringly. On election day, the day after his sixty-fifth birthday, Earl suffered a heart attack. Stubbornly, he refused to leave his hotel, fearing reports of his illness might cost him the election. Only after he was assured of victory, did Earl check into the hospital. It was too late. At 7:10 A.M. on September 5, Earl Long, the self-styled "Last of the Red Hot Poppas," died.[27]

"Earl thought he could see the end of his political career out there in the distance," Bill Dodd wrote about Earl. "And he was trying to drink enough, dope himself enough, and stay on a hell-raising spree long enough to make the inevitable end just disappear. He literally killed himself with alcohol, dope, borrowed energy, and by overworking his tired and weak old heart."[28]

With Earl's death, Russell lost more than an uncle. For years after his father died, Uncle Earl had been a mentor and surrogate father. Through all his adult years, Earl had been a towering figure in Russell's life. It was Earl who ushered Russell into his first campaign in 1936, asking his eighteen-year-old nephew to accompany the Long ticket on which Earl was running for lieutenant governor. During college, Earl found Russell a job at the state legislature. Russell had returned the favor in 1948, when he gave up his law practice to help Earl win the governor's race. One of the first people Earl hired after his election was Russell. Earl worked tirelessly for Russell's first election to the Senate. While their relationship was sometimes strained, Earl took great pride in Russell's political maturation. "Russell will vote for what he thinks is right," Earl admiringly told *Redbook* in 1951, "regardless of what I say—I have already tried him—or what you say of what any pressure group says. He is an improvement on his uncle, and also on his father. He is better educated and respects other people's opinions more."[29]

While Russell and Earl had distinct, public differences, their quarrels were far less tempestuous than the feuds that Huey had with his brothers, Earl, Julius, and George. "I've never known a Long that likes to play second fiddle," former state representative Ragan Madden maintained. "Russell didn't like to play second fiddle and neither did Earl. I guess that's the characteristic of a Long. Every one of them wants to be the head man." Throughout their years of alienation, Russell rarely made disparaging remarks about Earl. Even at the height of Earl's enmity toward his nephew—over Russell's role in Earl's institutionalization—Russell acted out of concern for Earl's health and sanity. Had Earl lived to serve in Congress, he and Russell would undoubtedly have buried their differences. Now, instead, the torch of the Long name had been passed—for perhaps the last time—to the younger generation. [30]

When he learned of Earl's death, Russell issued only a brief statement: "I am very deeply grieved at the passing of my uncle. He made the state a good governor during his three terms and served with distinction in several other important capacities." In a letter to a constituent, Russell waxed more emotional: "As you know, I loved him very much. When all the partisanship and human selfishness are cleared from the atmosphere, Earl Long stands as a great man who did much for his state. Particularly did he help those unable to help themselves." And in a constituent newsletter, Russell attacked a Shreveport newspaper which reported that only fourteen people visited the Alexandria funeral home where Earl's body was first taken. Noting more than twenty-two thousand people stood in line to pay their respects to Earl at the state capitol, Russell said that the public outpouring of grief "turned my mind back to the telegram which I sent him the night of his last victory. It read, 'Congrats. Your victory proves that little people do not forget their friends.' "[31]

17

A BISCUIT FOR A
BARREL OF FLOUR

ON THE EVENING OF JANUARY 12, 1959, Russell sat quietly at his desk in the Senate chamber as his Oregon colleague, Wayne Morse, discussed his legislation concerning home rule for the District of Columbia. Except for Russell, Morse, and the presiding officer, Senator Frank Lausche of Ohio, the chamber was empty. Not one Republican was present. As Morse introduced his bill and began to explain its provisions, Russell interrupted. "I notice that not one Republican senator is now on the floor of the Senate," he said. "If the Senator from Oregon would yield for that purpose, I would move to abolish the Republican Party."

Startled, Morse shot from his seat. "Mr. President, I rise to defend the absent senators. The Record should also show that there are only three Democratic senators in the chamber—one in the chair and two on the floor." From his perch as presiding officer, Lausche spoke up. "The chair is glad the senator from Oregon has made that observation; otherwise, the chair would have felt compelled to do so himself."

Russell's audacious move was only half-serious. As that night's sentry for the Senate's southern forces—the anti-civil rights bloc was always alert for sneak attacks on civil rights—Russell's motion was a playful way to make a serious point. He believed that it was unfair to keep southern senators on constant alert against stealth attempts to pass civil rights legislation, while Republicans could vacate the floor at will, confident a liberal Democrat would protect their rights. "It seems to me," he told Morse, "we have a wonderful possibility of achieving several worthy objectives tonight. If we could get some understanding from the senator from Oregon for protection on behalf of those of us who come from former Confederate states, as well as his protecting the Republican Party, the Senate could operate with greater facility for the next year or two."[1]

Russell made his point effectively, but the episode also highlighted one of his principal political frailties. As a southern senator, vehemently opposed to most civil rights advances, Russell remained firmly chained to the South's murky segregationist past. As long as he was identified with the anti-civil rights forces, Russell's potential as a national leader was severely limited. Senator Richard Russell's unsuccessful candidacy for president in 1952 proved the folly of southerners reaching for positions of national leadership. The Georgia Democrat, eminently qualified for the White House, was nonetheless saddled by his myopic views on civil rights. Despite his magnificent credentials as a Senate leader of extraordinary world vision, Richard Russell could not overcome the tarnish of his segregationist ideals. Wiser was Lyndon Johnson, who crossed the philosophical Rubicon in 1957, when he broke with the southern forces to push a civil rights bill through to passage. "A civil rights bill credited to Johnson," noted LBJ biographer Robert Dallek, "[helped] transform him from a southern or regional leader into a national spokesman."[2]

Despite this handicap, by 1960, Russell's eleven years in the Senate had brought him to the threshold of genuine power and influence. His jovial manner and easy wit won him many friends throughout Washington. His colleagues admired his intelligence, creativity, and his fidelity to the Senate. He was highly regarded as a skillful, passionate debater. In Louisiana, his popularity soared. Yet, beyond a seemingly inescapable fealty to segregation, Russell had reason to fret over his political future. Republican vice president Richard Nixon was a reasonable bet to win the presidency in the fall election. That meant a continuation of the conservative fiscal and monetary policies Russell deplored. While he could point to several achievements in the social security realm, his influence on foreign policy had been minimal. On the Finance Committee, where he had climbed near the top in seniority, he was mired behind Oklahoma's Robert Kerr, destined to inherit the committee when Chairman Harry Byrd retired. Assuming that Kerr remained in the Senate, Russell might be an old man before he became Finance chairman. The prospect of playing second fiddle to Kerr or anyone else was not particularly appealing. As the

1962 gubernatorial race approached, Russell's lifelong ambition to be governor tugged on him mightily. For the first time since he had arrived in Washington, Russell seriously thought about leaving the Senate.

As the 1960s dawned, Russell was his usual bundle of contradictions on racial issues. He remained strongly opposed to most civil rights measures, believing they would spark strife and division among the races while failing to improve the daily lives of blacks. There were, however, rare exceptions. In 1960 he voted to outlaw the poll tax, an inhibitor of black voting, noting that his father had banned Louisiana's voting levy twenty-five years earlier. The same legislation contained another civil rights advance he supported. It gave the District of Columbia and its large black population the right to vote in presidential elections. Russell further confounded his critics when he hired two black men for his Washington staff. Although they performed only menial duties—mail clerk and messenger—Russell became the first southern senator to hire blacks in the twentieth century. "He's the only Deep South lawmaker to mix his staff," *Jet* magazine reported.[3]

Nonetheless, he remained a reliable soldier of the southern coalition, whose members spewed predictably bellicose language in 1960, when President Eisenhower submitted his administration's last civil rights proposal. In a Senate speech, Russell roared that the bill's name "should be changed to read 'A Bill to Crucify the South.' " As presented to the Senate in February by Republican Leader Everett Dirksen, the legislation included provisions for federal voting referees, criminal penalties against those who obstructed federal school desegregation orders, and federal financial aid for school desegregation programs. Although it would become a cousin of the 1957 Civil Rights Act by beefing up the bill's weaker provisions, southern senators who had tempered their opposition to the 1957 bill dispensed with previous quietude when the White House unveiled the proposal. Southern silence in 1957 had prevented passage of the kind of bill now proposed. This time, a filibuster was the only chance for success. Majority leader Lyndon Johnson and the liberals would never again compromise.[4]

On February 15, shortly after the bill's introduction, Johnson summoned the measure to the Senate floor. He would combat the anticipated southern filibuster, he announced, by holding the Senate in unremitting session until he achieved cloture. It was soon evident that Johnson underestimated the tenacity and craftiness of southern leader Richard Russell. To his surprise, Johnson's old mentor fashioned an extraordinarily organized filibuster. With help from Republican colleagues, he masterfully orchestrated the southern resistance like a symphony conductor. Adroitly, he divided his troops into teams that worked eight-hour shifts on the Senate floor and were afterward relieved by a squad of fresh, well-rested orators. Southern resourcefulness and stamina quickly put Johnson on the defensive. Instead of exhausting the other side, his was the weary brigade, forced on constant alert for quorum calls. The hardball tactics designed to drain the southerners had backfired. Johnson's men were exhausted.

Still one of the youngest members of the southern bloc, Russell pulled more than his share of filibuster duty. "What on earth the South has ever done to justify the kind of discrimination and deliberately intended evil to which it has been subjected, some of us have a great difficulty comprehending," Russell intoned as he began a marathon ten-and-a-half-hour speech on March 2. If the bill's goal was to forcibly integrate Louisiana schools, Russell said the result would be "an end to public education in the state." Then, he warned, "I am here to tell this body that the proud people of the South have been goaded and pushed as far as they expect to go voluntarily. Violence and resistance in every fashion can be expected if they are to be pushed around any more."[5]

Several weeks elapsed. The bill was no closer to passage. Southerners continued to filibuster, but Johnson had mercifully called off the all-night sessions. "We can wear them out just as much as they can wear us out," Russell bragged, adding his earlier loquacious speech was "just a warm-up." By then, Johnson and Dirksen concocted a new strategy. Failing to break the filibuster, they yanked the bill from the floor hoping the House would soon pass something more palatable to the southerners. "The less unreasonable those bills become," Russell admitted to reporters, "the better chance they've got of getting some people who have been voting with the South."[6]

The House did as Johnson hoped, quickly sending the Senate a milder version of the measure, which the Senate passed two weeks later. The vote was lopsided, seventy-one to eighteen, with Russell and seventeen of his southern Democratic colleagues in the minority. Several days later, Russell assured a radio audience that "about eighty percent of the mischief" had been eliminated from the bill, adding that "there is not a great amount in this bill that is not already in the 1957 Civil Rights Act." Russell was essentially correct. Congress deleted the school desegregation and employment provisions. The only real improvement over the 1957 act was court-appointed referees could now register blacks. Once more, the southern bloc prevailed.[7]

Civil rights aside, Russell turned his attention to another of President

Eisenhower's final legislative proposals: the $4.1 billion foreign aid authorization request submitted in April. As usual, Russell left no doubt that he believed "there is a great amount of waste" in the president's bill. "They never do drastically redo it, and I usually wind up voting against the whole thing because of it." This time, he could do little to stop it. As the proposal sailed through the Foreign Relations Committee, Russell demanded the committee record his opposition, although no roll call was taken. By early May, the bill steamrolled through the Senate with minor modifications, including Russell's amendment to reduce the measure's contingency fund authorization by a meager twenty million dollars. Otherwise, senators had no stomach for cutting the bill, which passed sixty to twenty-five. As promised, Russell voted no.[8]

In June, Russell was on familiar ground again. He stood virtually isolated on another foreign policy issue—the Japan Mutual Defense Treaty, a ten-year military pact with Japan, signed by President Eisenhower to remove all traces of the post-war U.S. occupation. In Japan, the treaty was so unpopular that Eisenhower canceled a visit to Tokyo. Riots and domestic rebellion forced Prime Minister Kishi to resign.

To Russell, the treaty was entirely a one-way affair. "We commit ourselves and agree that we are going to defend and save Japan and Japan agrees to do nothing to help us." Russell regarded the treaty as typical American misguided willingness to serve as the world's policeman. "We have made these kinds of commitments all over the world, to defend first one nation and next another who are incapable of fully defending themselves, without those nations agreeing that if we have to go to war to pull somebody else's chestnuts out of the fire—somebody that's just as weak as they are—that they'll assist in the common defense and the over-all undertaking." Russell's impassioned opposition had little effect. Only he and Georgia's Richard Russell voted against the treaty. When asked why ninety other senators perceived the issue differently, Russell explained: "Well, I think that the great majority of them felt that with all these Communist demonstrations going on against this treaty . . . that would mean they were voting the same way the communists would like to have them vote."[9]

Russell swam against the current again in August as the Senate considered the House-Senate conference report of the Medicare bill. While Russell attached a provision to include disability payments for elderly mental patients and tubercular victims, the conference committee scuttled his amendment. He was infuriated the Senate conferees had refused to fight for his provision. For hours he held the floor, frustrating all attempts to set a time limit on debate. "The trouble is that we are too timorous," Russell declared to the Senate. "That includes me, too. We do not fight to do something for the needy, the disabled. We do not vote for what is in our platform. We have surrendered. . . . It is about time that those who favored the great crusade, which has achieved nothing, proceed to tell the public that they are the ones who led the great retreat." As he continued his filibuster, Russell read into the record newspaper and magazine articles about dismal conditions in mental hospitals, stopping to repeat them as senators arrived to the floor. Exasperated, several of Russell's Republican colleagues wired Democratic presidential nominee John F. Kennedy in Massachusetts to plead for his intervention. Russell finally relented several hours later, as the Senate passed the bill without his provisions. As usual in defeat, he was satisfied to have made his point, confident he would win another day.[10]

Meanwhile, the presidential contest unfolded. Kennedy was not Russell's first choice for the Democratic presidential nomination. Not surprisingly, like many southerners, Russell supported Lyndon Johnson, his friend and Senate leader. At the party's July convention in Los Angeles, Russell led the Louisiana delegation in voting for Johnson. When Kennedy prevailed and chose Johnson as his running mate, Russell, the loyal party soldier, supported the ticket, although hinting disappointment. "Now we have the best two men among the candidates, although perhaps in reverse order." He also expressed his hope that the party platform's strong language on civil rights would do little harm in the South. He warned, however, he had "a two-hundred-page speech prepared to fight that platform in case they ever try to put it into effect."[11]

Whatever early reservations he had about Kennedy's candidacy, Russell, as in previous presidential races, put them aside to lead the campaign in Louisiana. In Alexandria, he kicked off the fall contest in a speech to more than one hundred local and state elected officials, accusing the Republican party of "penny pinching" on national defense. He borrowed Kennedy's campaign theme of a "missile gap" between the U.S. and the Soviet Union. "Eight years ago, the nearest Soviet bases were thousands of miles away from our shores, but now they are in a position to develop communist bases in Cuba, just ninety miles away from Florida." Ten days later, after the first debate between Kennedy and Vice President Richard Nixon, Russell confidently said that Kennedy won "by a country mile." Those who watched on television saw a confident, youthful Kennedy challenge a haggard Nixon. While the vice president may have won on debating points, Kennedy triumphed on style. "Nixon's appearance was even worse than his answers," Russell said. "He looked like a man who knew he was taking a bad beating."[12]

By October, the campaign had whipped Russell into a partisan frenzy. When he introduced former president Truman at a campaign rally in Abbeville, Russell referred to Nixon as "Tricky Dicky" and said the vice president "is the only man who has had the experience of being a kept senator of certain special interests." (Years later, when Nixon occupied the White House, Russell and his former colleague developed an extremely warm working relationship. Despite Russell's once-harsh rhetoric, Nixon later placed his Louisiana friend "in the top ranks of Senators in the post-war era.") Selling Kennedy in predominately Catholic south Louisiana was easy compared to his task in Protestant north Louisiana, as Russell remembered: "I was about the first statewide elected official who had the courage to go up there and campaign for Kennedy in north Louisiana. It was rough up there. Those people, they didn't want a Catholic for president and they didn't want any John Kennedy under any circumstances, at least a lot of them didn't." During one campaign stop, Russell reported, an elderly woman brandishing an umbrella angrily approached him, threatening "to hit me over the head" because of his support of Kennedy. When Kennedy won while carrying Louisiana, Russell was pleased, but quick to distance himself from the president-elect's civil rights plan. "As far as civil rights go, I suggest that Senator Kennedy work toward achieving the possible rather than push in some areas where he will meet stonewall resistance," Russell told a New Orleans breakfast in late November.[13]

In New Orleans, a brewing crisis over desegregation of the city's public schools threatened the city's previously tranquil passage into the civil rights era. City business and streetcars, the library system, recreational facilities, and Louisiana State University's New Orleans campus were all desegregated by 1959 with little or no violence or disruption. But in early November, when federal judge J. Skelly Wright ordered two New Orleans schools to enroll four black girls in the first grade, much of city's white population erupted in anger and malevolence. Scores of white mothers, infuriated that their neighborhood schools were targets of Judge Wright's court order, rushed to remove their children from classes. Some remained to jeer, spit, shout obscenities, and throw stones at the black girls. Some sang songs like "Glory, Glory Segregation" to the tune of "The Battle Hymn of the Republic." One particularly angry protester shouted, "Kill the niggers!"[14]

The legislature reacted quickly, seizing control of New Orleans public schools and declaring a statewide school holiday for the scheduled date of Wright's desegregation order. Decisively, Wright restrained Governor Jimmie Davis and the legislature from interference in the city's school system. As the integration proceeded as ordered, white fear and anger turned to violence. On November 15, hostile crowds gathered at the two schools. Police arrested eleven boys as a mob of teenagers marched toward the schools. That evening Russell's old nemesis, Plaquemines Parish district attorney Leander Perez, and state representative Willie Rainach did their best to inflame the passions of five thousand white citizens at the city's Municipal Auditorium. Prodding the gathering to action, Perez shouted, "Don't wait for your daughter to be raped by these Congolese. Don't wait until the burr-heads are forced into your schools. Do something about it now." Perez's call to action was effective. The next day, another mob of about three thousand rowdy teenagers converged on the civic center complex and the board of education. When the firemen dispersed them using high pressure water hoses, the horde spread throughout the business district. They hurled bottles and bricks at buses and cars occupied by blacks. Police arrested dozens of protesters. That night, blacks took to the streets in retaliation. Police arrested more than 250 people after numerous shootings and assaults.[15]

Russell did little to calm the city's rampant fears. In a speech to the Louisiana legislature on November 16, he urged lawmakers to consider abandoning the public school system, in favor of private schools, to preserve segregation. "If this approach is taken, there is no real need of hysteria or undue haste." As for Washington, Russell advised the legislature to expect little from the newly elected president, John F. Kennedy. "The situation in Washington is likely to get worse before it gets better. We simply do not have the votes to reverse the situation and no immediate possibilities of getting them." Ignoring the inciting comments by Perez, Russell blamed the city's problems on "outside agitators" who "are threatening immediate and revolutionary changes to our public school system." To that, Russell added a gratuitous attack on the Supreme Court, declaring his willingness to "impeach the entire U.S. Supreme Court if my vote would do it."[16]

Despite their differences on civil rights, Russell was fond of President Kennedy. Although they were never close friends when they served together in the Senate, Russell quickly developed an amiable working relationship with his former colleague. A telling example was the episode leading up to Russell's eye-opening vote in opposition to a controversial amendment to the 1961 foreign aid bill, and how he used the issue as leverage to reopen a Louisiana military base. Russell had previously supported an amendment by Virginia's Harry Byrd to limit the president's latitude in dispensing loans to developing countries. On the advice of Vice President Lyndon Johnson, however, Russell concluded that the president might need Russell's vote as much as Russell wanted the Pentagon to reopen Fort Polk, Louisiana's only army base. On the last of several visits to the White House that summer, Kennedy assumed that Russell had arrived to discuss the foreign aid bill. Instead, Russell continually turned the conversation to Fort Polk. Frustrated with Russell's inattention to the topic at hand, Kennedy finally snapped, "What's Fort Polk got to do with this?" Nothing, Russell answered, except that he cared much more about the army base than the Byrd amendment's fate. "Oh, I see your point," Kennedy replied. Less than two weeks later, after he had joined Kennedy supporters to defeat the amendment in the Senate, Russell proudly announced the reopening of Fort Polk. Even though the conference committee later restored the Byrd provision, Kennedy kept his word. On a later visit to the White House, Kennedy greeted Russell with an admonition. "Don't tell me you've got another one of those Fort Polk deals. You traded me a biscuit for a barrel of flour, and I didn't even get the biscuit!" Russell replied, "That's why I'd like to trade some more with you, Mr. President. You're a good fellow to do business with."[17]

Meanwhile, southern opposition to the new president's aggressive social agenda was growing. In Louisiana, resentment and criticism of Russell's support for many of those programs flourished, as well. The *Monroe Morning World* said that Russell's "affinity . . . for the welfare state is well known" and observed that he was a "weak carbon copy" of his father "in the matter of seeking to establish socialism." A south Louisiana newspaper, the *Franklin Banner Tribune*, questioned whether the federal government, meaning Russell, should be concerned about housing, banking, farming, communications, wages, and prices. "Those who answer yes are either outright socialists or else give aid to the socialistic trend," the paper concluded, accusing Russell of making "public utterances" which were "socialistic in nature." Indignant at this insult, Russell responded with a blistering letter to the editor. "What makes public service such a challenge for me," he wrote, "is the fact there are so many greedy, prejudiced, misinformed people that must be changed or defeated."[18]

Forced as he was by political considerations to often spurn Kennedy in Louisiana, Russell wanted his new president to succeed, evidenced by a confidential memorandum he sent Kennedy in late November:

> The newspapers in North Louisiana are extremely vicious toward you and your Administration, which will make it tough sledding for you and your friends in that part of the state. In South Louisiana, most of the newspapers are more reasonable and moderate, and you continue to be very strong in that section. . . . The John Birch types are hard at work trying to make "communism in government" an issue. This sounds very much like it is a repeat performance of what the Republicans did under the Truman Administration when they attempted to make it appear that Harry Truman did not know the difference between a communist and a patriot. . . . Undoubtedly the screw-ball right-wingers will confuse enough people to hurt you and your party with . . . demands for a thorough investigation of communists in the State Department . . . unless you beat them at their own game.
>
> It would be my recommendation that you set up your own committee on a nationwide basis to fight communism and subversive activities. . . . In other words, if you will proceed to make yourself the Number One anti-communist in America, and set yourself up as the leader of a world-wide revolution for freedom, you will rid yourself of a troublesome problem.[19]

Kennedy may have spurned Russell's advice, but the president temporarily bolstered his anticommunist credentials in October 1962 during a hair-raising showdown with Soviet leaders over nuclear missiles in Cuba. While the U.S.-supported Bay of Pigs invasion in April 1961—a military fiasco for which Kennedy inherited much of the blame—failed to depose Cuban leader Fidel Castro, Kennedy continued to suggest that military action might be needed to thwart growing Soviet influence in Cuba. He had no more enthusiastic ally than Russell. In September, Russell told the Senate that if Soviet Premier Khrushchev wanted war, he should "acquaint himself with some of our better professional killers, new and old." If the Soviet leader wants a conflict, Russell declared that "we are ready to blow his nation to Kingdom Come."[20]

As the subsequent showdown with Moscow over Cuban-based nuclear warheads terrified the world and brought the two nations to the brink of nuclear war, Russell strongly backed Kennedy. "I know of no American who would have the president back down," he told a business luncheon in New Orleans. After the Soviets withdrew their missiles in exchange for Kennedy's promise not to attack Cuba and to later withdraw U.S. missiles from Turkey, Russell was wary. He told a Shreveport audience that if the

Russians "break their word, then we should invade Cuba." Even so, Kennedy's policies toward Cuba and the Soviet Union only deepened suspicions about him in Louisiana's conservative, anticommunist circles. Anti-Castro Cuban exiles, many of whom now lived in New Orleans, believed that Kennedy had betrayed their cause by denying them crucial military support during the Bay of Pigs invasion. Other hard-line conservatives were critical of Kennedy for his negotiation with Khrushchev over removal of the Cuban-based missiles.[21]

Even in the wake of a world crisis, Russell could not ignore his reelection campaign. He did, however, scorn his Republican opponent, a Shreveport attorney, Taylor O'Hearn, who attacked Russell for neglecting Louisiana. Russell, O'Hearn charged, "not only inherited his money but he thinks he inherited Louisiana, too." Russell rejected O'Hearn's entreaties for a debate. He campaigned lightly and dusted off his opponent by a three-to-one margin. The only blemish on Russell's tally, not surprisingly, was in north Louisiana, where his association with Kennedy cost him the eight parishes O'Hearn won.[22]

Reelection behind him, the 1963 governor's race remained a temptation. For years, Russell had made no secret of his desire to be governor. The pleading of friends in Louisiana, coupled with the likelihood of a long wait before he would be Finance Committee chairman made the race even more attractive. By the fall of 1962, Russell had changed his mind. After two years of pondering the race, he now leaned toward remaining in the Senate. Thirteen years' seniority was a valuable asset for Louisiana and Russell's career. At forty-three, he was still young. The governor's office could wait. Nothing influenced his decision more, however, than the sudden death of Oklahoma senator Bob Kerr.

Kerr was an awesome figure in almost every way. In physical stature, mental agility, personal wealth, and Senate power, he was a giant. His sudden death of a heart attack on New Year's Day 1963 was an enormous loss to Senate Democrats. For Russell, Kerr's death meant he would soon be Finance Committee chairman. "That would be the most powerful position that any United States senator from Louisiana has ever held in the nation's Congress," Russell explained. Had he left the Senate it might have been "another hundred years" before another Louisianian had the chance to chair the Finance Committee. With Kerr's death, he was now the committee's senior Democrat behind ailing chairman Harry Byrd of Virginia. "I'm not planning to run for governor," he announced definitively in early January, adding "that's what I told the people when I was running for the Senate."[23]

Suddenly, real power was within Russell's reach. "If shock was his first reaction," one observer wrote, "sober reflection appears to have been his second." "Now the senator likes a drink," said a reporter who saw Russell on two successive nights following Kerr's death. "But both nights he was drinking ginger ale and talking about the tremendous responsibility—the responsibility entailed in falling heir to a major share of the political estate of one of the most powerful men in the Senate."[24]

Besides the tremendous boost to Russell's career, Kerr's death and Byrd's illness left a power vacuum on the Finance Committee at a time when President Kennedy needed strong leadership in Congress for his effort to stimulate the nation's declining economy. The president hoped that his friendship with Russell would produce such a leader. Judging by the past, he had good reason to believe that Russell would be his ally. Except for Kennedy's attempts at national health insurance, Russell had usually supported his president on finance issues. He had helped Kennedy on trade expansion, public welfare revision, and tax policy. On several occasions, Russell had even opposed southern Democrats in favor of Kennedy's proposals for increasing the minimum wage and aid to depressed regions. Even so, by most other standards Russell was a conservative. However, compared to Byrd, in particular, and the Finance Committee, in general, his positions on social security, public assistance, and veterans' benefits made him a bona fide liberal. Kennedy desperately needed Russell's liberal streak. Without Russell's help, his economic program was dead.

The demand for national economic stimulus grew by the day. While few aspects of the national economy were strong, signs of weakness abounded. Unemployment neared 6 percent, a relatively high figure compared to the full employment of 1950s. The federal budget was unbalanced for the fifth consecutive year. The national debt had surpassed $300 billion for the first time. All this prompted Kennedy to propose an economic shot in the arm, a three-year, $13.5 billion tax reduction. It was a drastic proposal. To spur the economy, Kennedy wanted to cut the upper income tax bracket from ninety-one percent to sixty-five percent and reduce corporate income taxes from fifty-two percent to forty-seven percent.

Not surprisingly, Chairman Byrd and some leading Republicans opposed the plan. They wanted taxes cut, but not until Kennedy produced an equal cut in government spending. Hoping that Russell would use his newly acquired influence to help them in the Senate, Kennedy's advisers soon found their would-be ally was nearly as skeptical as Byrd. What troubled Russell were other portions of the bill, primarily Kennedy's "reform" proposals to require stricter accounting rules for capital gains, dividend credits, and itemized deductions. To Russell, Kennedy's proposal to tighten income tax regulations was designed to squeeze more revenue from rank-and-file taxpayers, while cutting taxes on the wealthy. "It doesn't make much sense to me to put a tax bill out here where some [rich] fellow gets the big tax reduction and the other poor fellow has to pay a lot more," Russell said in February 1963. The president, Russell suggested, should "just send us a bill for a tax cut. My guess is if they want a tax bill, they will be well advised to drop this reform business out of it." In a statewide radio address later that month, Russell again voiced reservations about the president's bill. This time he found an old ax to grind—Kennedy's "tight money and high interest rate policy," which Russell said the president had promised to reverse. "Insofar as this tax bill appears to be a substitute for keeping the pledges of ending the tight-money, high-interest rate program, I don't feel like voting for it." Finally, Chairman Byrd announced a series of lengthy hearings on the bill, which meant no action before 1964. For now, at least, Kennedy's tax plan was dead.[25]

Despite his public disagreement with Kennedy over taxes, Louisiana's conservatives, particularly in Shreveport, were increasingly inflamed by Russell's support of the administration's social programs. Hoping to enlighten his detractors, Russell brought a group of Shreveport business leaders together in April for what he called an "understanding dinner," where he spoke frankly and unapologetically about his alliances with Kennedy. With his mother, Senator Allen Ellender, and Congressman Joe Waggonner present, Russell was blunt. Sometimes, he explained, he voted for legislation he disliked in order to get a favor from the White House. Of Kennedy, he said, "Why can't you work with him to benefit our nation perhaps for three years and six months or three years and nine months and then fight him like heck? I voted for President Kennedy and I know most of you didn't and won't vote for him next time. But if you're going to oppose him, do you have to be so brutal about it?" Several weeks later, Russell elaborated for a Shreveport radio station: "I did the best I could do to work with President Eisenhower when he was president. I didn't vote for him. I had a lot to do with the fact that he didn't carry Louisiana the first time that he was elected president. But, on the other hand, I did all I could to try to get the best deal I could for Louisiana."[26]

Several days later, Russell's attacks on the U.S. Civil Rights Commission did little to placate his conservative detractors. Nonetheless, he warned the president not to accept the commission's recommendation to withhold $650 million in federal payments to Mississippi for that state's

recalcitrance on segregation. Russell said that "southerners would feel
compelled to vote against all federal aid programs" if Kennedy followed the
commission's advice. "There are many programs, such as federal aid to
education, for which the president is attracting very few southern votes
the way it is now."[27]

When Kennedy unveiled his 1963 Civil Rights Bill in June—declaring
that "the fires of frustration and discord are burning in every city, North
and South, where legal remedies are not at hand"—Russell lashed out.
Russell said the bill—aimed at guaranteeing black voting rights, and out-
lawing discrimination in hotels, restaurants, and other businesses in interstate commerce—"could be the end of American freedom as we know it."
Such statements did little to quell anger toward him at the June meeting of
the Democratic Association of Louisiana in Alexandria. There, Democrats
applauded a member who charged Russell had waited "until the South is on
the verge of another civil war" before opposing civil rights legislation.
"Senator Long many years ago put his blinders on and hooked himself to
the New Frontier and to the detriment of the South."[28]

As Judiciary Committee Chairman James Eastland of Mississippi held up
the civil rights bill in his committee, Russell raised the ante with the White
House, disclosing the price Kennedy must pay for progress on his tax
plan. "It depends on what emphasis the Democratic leadership wants to
place on the tax measure. If they want to put civil rights ahead of
everything else, it might prevent us from having action on a tax bill."
Nonetheless, Russell's anti-civil rights fury did little to calm the fears of at
least one of Russell's media critics. The *Monroe Morning World,* a reliable
antagonist, continued to attack his association with Kennedy. "Although
Senator Long speaks out a little more freely against Kennedy's integration
ordeal than might be expected, there are many who believe Kennedy
looks on Russell Long as his No. 2 man in Louisiana."[29]

The constant newspaper attacks enraged Russell. "The manner in
which the two Shreveport newspapers conducted themselves in this regard was a disgrace to journalism," he wrote at the time. "For two solid
years they filled their editorial pages with so-called letters to the editor,
misrepresenting my position, spreading every sort of falsehood and unsup-
ported allegation." He had equal disdain for activists on both sides of the
civil rights issue. "On both sides there are extremists who attempt to
shout down anyone who would discuss the problem sensibly unless he is
saying something with which they are prepared to agree," he wrote.
"Altogether too many of our politicians are inclined to tell their voters what
they want to hear instead of the truth."[30]

Early in July, Russell raised his voice in even stronger opposition to the civil rights bill, threatening to lead the Senate's filibuster. "I'll talk until Hell freezes over, then I'll talk on the ice," he pledged. Asked about reports the Kennedy administration might deny public works projects to Louisiana and other states whose senators opposed the civil rights bill, Russell replied, "I think the Kennedy Administration is too politically astute to put pressure on senators and congressmen which would smack of the worst conceivable type of politics." On a national radio program, Russell speculated that the civil rights program had "tremendously reduced" the president's popularity in the South "to about one half of what it was—perhaps less than that."[31]

Sharpening his already strident rhetoric, Russell took a hard-line view of the historic March on Washington in August. On that day, a multitude of more than two hundred thousand persons, predominately black, converged on the capital in an extraordinary show of unity to hear Dr. Martin Luther King and others speak from the steps of the Lincoln Memorial. "I suppose most Southerners would just as soon they did set out and have a great big riot," Russell told a CBS radio reporter, reflecting popular fears the march would turn to violence. "I would just as soon the whole thing broke into a riot, although I'm not advocating that." At the same time, Russell conceded that the march "if it is conducted in an orderly manner might help them some, but if it gets out of hand it will hurt their cause." On the day of the event, as a safety precaution, Russell gave his female employees the day off.[32]

Despite his ostensible hostility toward the civil rights movement, Russell occasionally revealed signs of a deeper, yet well-concealed, moderation. A story in the December 1963 issue of *The Progressive* reported that when Katherine and their girls had moved to Baton Rouge several years earlier, Russell gave up his home in suburban Maryland and began house hunting in the District of Columbia. "He found some likely places in the District's redeveloping southwest section, he told a fellow senator, but since they were available to rental to everyone, a few Negroes were living in the buildings. They were people of such high caliber, he said, 'that [it] wouldn't bother anyone in his right mind. But where I come from, it would be political dynamite.' So he set up bachelor quarters elsewhere." In Russell, the magazine detected a moderate: "While other southerners rise to fulminate against government intervention in Oxford and Birmingham, he has been quiet. The bitter turmoil and violence that have accompanied the struggle for freedom in the South may change that and force him to align himself more openly with Southern diehards. It will be a pity if it does, for though Long is an avowed segregationist, he would seem to know better, and some of his opposition appears to be a matter of political expediency."[33]

The analysis was an astute one. Indeed, Russell's ostensible opposition to most of Kennedy's civil rights proposals had not prevented him from offering the president some pragmatic advice on enacting his programs. "I felt that a voting rights bill should be passed," he admitted years later, adding,

> One time, I was visiting President Kennedy at the White House and told him, "Mr. President, I don't know that I could vote for it. It might be political suicide. I don't ask anybody to vote for political suicide, without warning him first. . . . If I had gone as far as you've already gone in recommending that civil rights legislation, as far as voting rights for those Negroes, I'd recommend have a federal registrar go out there and register all of them. Put them on the books. Instead of taking four to eight years to get all the people registered, they'd be registered the next election. . . . Not just giving them the right to vote—send somebody out looking for them to sign them up. In my judgment, that'd be the logical way to do it. If you're going to do it, get the job done. Otherwise, you get the blame for it, but you don't get the credit of it."[34]

While sometimes elusive on civil rights, Russell was rarely as complicated in foreign affairs. In August, he was the lone member of the Senate Foreign Relations Committee to oppose the Nuclear Test Ban Treaty with the Soviet Union, which banned all atmospheric nuclear tests. He warned that the treaty would "jeopardize our ability to adequately defend the United States." Furthermore, Russell simply distrusted the Soviets to keep their word. "When we are dealing with the Communists, we must realize that they are seeking to subjugate our country," Russell told the Senate. "They want to take charge; they want to make us bend to their will; and they want to find a way to victimize us. That is their entire purpose. That is why they are willing to sign an agreement of this sort."[35]

The Senate rebuffed Russell and Texas Republican John Tower when the two men proposed amending the treaty to permit nuclear weapons in armed conflicts. Because a formal reservation to the treaty might have meant renegotiation, the Senate agreed to the Long-Tower amendment by terming it an "understanding." Even in its weakened form, the provision was short-lived. Senators later killed it by adopting a tabling motion offered by majority leader Mike Mansfield. On September 24, the Senate ratified the treaty by a vote of eighty to nineteen. On this vote, as usual on foreign affairs and civil rights, Russell had been in a familiar spot—the minority.[36]

By the next year, however, Russell's days as the maverick who operated around the edges of power would end. His influence would flourish in the wake of a breathtaking series of events.

18

I CAUGHT A WHALE

$\mathcal{P}$RESIDENT JOHN F. KENNEDY came to Dallas on November 22, 1963, hoping to calm the intense, partisan bickering within the Texas Democratic Party over his controversial social programs. The atmosphere he countered was only slightly more hostile than in neighboring Louisiana, where great numbers of citizens, goaded by ultraconservative news media, believed that Kennedy advocated socialism and was soft on communism. Reflecting popular fears about the perceived radical social changes inherent in Kennedy's programs, a *New Orleans Times-Picayune* reader wrote on November 16, "I wonder about my country. Has the leadership become infiltrated by communism . . . ?" So unpopular was Kennedy in Louisiana, a major issue in the governor's race was the debate over which candidates had supported Kennedy for president in 1960. Only two days before Kennedy's arrival in Dallas, Plaquemines Parish district attorney Leander Perez derisively branded three gubernatorial hopefuls—former New Orleans mayor DeLesseps Morrison, state Public Service commissioner John McKeithen, and Congressman Gillis Long—"Kennedy candidates." According to Perez, "The Kennedys have demonstrated their position against state and local governments by sponsoring racial uprisings and open defiance of law and order amounting to plain anarchy." None of the candidates would confess to having supported the man Perez so thoroughly vilified. That night, at a Republican rally in New Orleans, Louisiana Republican party chairman Charlton Lyons declared in a statement of chilling, but unwitting prescience: "America stands at the gravest hour of its history. What we do this week, this month and this year is going to determine the course of America for eternity." Less than twenty-four hours later, Kennedy lay dead from an assassin's bullet.[1]

When word of Kennedy's murder reached Louisiana, an official of the White Citizens Council of New Orleans told reporters that his office was flooded with frantic phone calls. They were not messages of grief or shock. Instead, many of the callers, he said, proclaimed that God had finally solved the civil rights problem. Russell was eating lunch at the New Orleans Athletic Club when he heard the news. Later that day, as he hurried to Washington, he issued a brief statement: "None of us is blessed with the wisdom to understand why the Almighty wanted it this way, but we should live in faith that John F. Kennedy did not die in vain." By week's end, he relied on the experience of his father's death to offer comfort to Kennedy's widow, writing her a brief note of sympathy.

> Twenty-eight years ago, I said my last goodbye to my father, who was dying from an assassin's bullet.
>
> The intervening years have accorded me the opportunity to meditate about the sort of tragedy that took your husband's life on Friday. There is no way to explain such a thing unless one has faith in God and believes in the teachings of Jesus Christ.
>
> If it is true that there is everlasting life beyond this place of toil and tears, then we can take solace in the fact that God called a good man to a higher reward. It is hard to believe that God knows about all these things and that He has planned it to be that way. Yet in time we may come to see that all of this is part of a master plan.
>
> In that case, we should find comfort in the fact that He chose you and John Fitzgerald Kennedy to play a significant role.[2]

While Russell paid his respects at the eulogy ceremony for Kennedy in the Capitol Rotunda, he did not attend Kennedy's funeral at St. Matthew's Cathedral in Washington. Although he was entitled by his seniority to join twenty-four other senators at the Pontifical Requiem Mass, Russell graciously relinquished his seat to a junior colleague, Senator Ralph Yarborough. The Texas Democrat had accompanied Kennedy to Dallas and was at Parkland Hospital when the president died.[3]

That night in Washington, the new president, Lyndon Johnson, assembled a small group of advisers to deliberate on one of the nation's most pressing problems—the languid economy. All agreed that the tonic was the slain president's moribund eleven-billion-dollar tax cut bill, which had passed the House of Representatives the previous September. It was held captive by the parsimonious Finance Committee chairman Harry Byrd. "He was probably the most conservative member in either party of the Senate," former Lyndon Johnson aide George Reedy said of Byrd. "He was as far to the right as a man could be and still remain in the bounds of sanity." To Byrd, the matter was obvious: It was ridiculous to slash taxes when anticipated revenues were nine billion dollars short of the proposed $102 billion in spending. The chairman's ransom was well known. He would release the bill only when the administration proved its willingness to cut spending by submitting a budget under $100 billion. Hold your ground, advised Walter Heller, chairman of the President's Council of Economic Advisors. Heller believed that Johnson would win if he insisted on a budget of $101.5 billion. "I can defend $101.5," Johnson retorted. "You take on Senator Byrd."[4]

Johnson's men eventually managed to pare the budget to $97.9 billion. Despite clearing the first hurdle, Byrd remained an obstacle. Although his terms for releasing the tax plan had been met, he remained stubbornly opposed. "Johnson gave Byrd the million-dollar selling job," Russell said. By the time the president finished, Byrd reluctantly agreed to report the bill out of committee, a major victory in itself. Another concession was even more surprising: Johnson persuaded Byrd to appoint Russell the bill's floor manager.

Johnson's and Byrd's compromise was Russell's first big break. His moment at the center of influence had arrived. He would no longer be the lonely renegade lobbing populist potshots at a tax bill he derided as a boon to the wealthy. Now, abruptly, Russell was the president's field general in the most significant fiscal measure in fifteen years, potentially the largest tax cut in the nation's history. For days, he would be scrutinized by Johnson, his colleagues, and the press. His success or failure would create a lasting impression. Russell was unabashedly overwhelmed. "I got my baptism with a whopper," he confessed, "like a kid who has gone fishing for the first time and caught a whale."[5]

In the U.S. Senate, a bill's floor manager is the legislation's chief advocate, its coach and quarterback. Usually he is the chairman of the committee from which the bill was reported. As floor manager, he is confined to the Senate chamber hour upon hour, where he must trumpet the attributes of his bill while fending off myriad amendments. These attempts to amend his bill are often devices to draw a veto by inflicting the bill with provisions objectionable to the president. Other senators do not wish to kill the bill with amendments. They merely want their interests considered. No legislation is more attractive to this kind of amendment than a tax bill. In this way, no bill is more difficult to manage. Russell's years in training, offering amendments to the legislation of others, would serve him well in the coming days. "I think the best training I had was my experience in being 'on the attack,' of trying to amend somebody else's revenue and foreign aid bills in years gone by." Unless Russell could repel hostile amendments, the bill was dead. The stake were indeed high. Johnson vowed to veto any legislation that differed from the original House-passed tax cut.[6]

Debate on the bill opened on February 3 with Tennessee's Albert Gore deriding it as "one of the most important and most ill-advised bills ever to come before Congress." That said, Gore promptly offered an amendment to increase the tax on income earned by Americans living abroad. When the votes were counted, Gore narrowly won, forty-seven to forty-one. Russell and the White House were jolted. "It scared me to lose on the first day like that," he confessed, frightened this first defeat might snowball. If the Senate continued to adopt amendments like Gore's, Russell knew, the bill would collapse under its own weight.[7]

As quickly as he lost, Russell and his allies regained their equilibrium. The next day, three close votes produced three victories for Russell. The Senate narrowly rejected a college tuition plan by Connecticut's Abraham Ribicoff and a similar proposal by Vermont's Winston Prouty. Then, senators rejected an amendment by Republican Leader Everett Dirksen to place a three-hundred-dollar ceiling on the 4 percent credit on dividend income. The next day, another Dirksen proposal—one to repeal the excise tax on jewelry, luggage, furs, and cosmetics—failed by a large margin. Amendment after amendment disintegrated as Russell masterfully steered the bill toward final passage. His tactics were varied and artful. He won over numerous senators by unceremoniously accepting their amendments, even though he made no promises to champion them in conference negotiations. On other occasions, he was simply dazzling. His mastery of the issues was unmistakable as he argued forcefully and intelligently against hostile amendments that threatened the bill. For Russell, it was often a frustrating and daunting exercise, a game of legislative hopscotch. His supporters on one amendment became adversaries on the next. "I never knew who I would have with me."[8]

He defeated Ribicoff's popular tuition tax credit plan by highlighting the amendment's high $1.3 billion price tag and by arguing that an alternative plan of student loans would achieve the same goal at less than half the cost. Addressing Dirksen's excise tax repeal, Russell suggested that it might result in repeal of other excise taxes that could ultimately cost the government five billion to ten billion dollars. Furthermore, he argued, a congressional study on excise taxes was due later in the year.

At other times, Russell showed brilliant and well-timed flashes of humor. He was never more effective than on the last day of debate, as he opposed an amendment offered by Arkansas's John McClellan. A senior Appropriations Committee member and one of the Senate's gray eminences, McClellan presented a seemingly simple and enticing amendment. It required automatic repeal of the tax bill if government spending for the year exceeded $100 billion, the threshold upon which chairman Byrd and the president had agreed. Russell immediately recognized the amendment's peril. Johnson would never sign a bill with such a time bomb. Russell called it his "toughest amendment. I didn't know how the devil I was going to beat that one." Shoving reason aside, he settled instead on ridicule. This amendment, he said, would not be needed "if senators who are members of the Appropriations Committee would quit voting so much money for appropriations." Russell observed that McClellan's proposal would "require me, as a member of the Finance Committee, to show members of the Appropriations how to run their business. I do not feel very well qualified to do that."[9]

To the chortles of a full Senate chamber, Russell ticked off the names of Appropriations Committee members. "Carl Hayden," Russell said, "was a member of Congress before I was born. Am I supposed to tell him how to conduct his business, as I would be required to do under the amendment?" Laughter filtered through the chamber as Russell turned to the next name on his list, Richard Russell, "who came to Congress the same year my father did." Next, was Louisiana colleague Allen Ellender, who Russell said "should have been governor of Louisiana at a time when I was a mere boy."[10]

"Read down the list. Whose name appears next?" Russell asked as the laughter grew louder. "Next, we have the distinguished senator from Arkansas (McClellan). At times I have thought he was well qualified to be President. He is urging me to tell him how to discharge his responsibility." To more spasms of laughter, Russell wryly observed, "I have no doubt that, if I am required to do so, I would have to say, Let your conscience be your guide." Not finished with this rebuttal, Russell continued to spell out possible implications of the amendment, observing that McClellan's amendment might really result in a monstrous tax increase. "How do senators like that as a disappointment?" Russell said gleefully. "The taxpayer would be holding his sack out, waiting for a tax cut. What do senators think he would get? A tax increase."[11]

In only few minutes, Russell turned potential disaster into victory. McClellan's amendment folded under the weight of Russell's logic and derision, sixty-one to thirty-four. Shortly thereafter, the Senate overwhelmingly passed the tax cut bill, seventy-seven to twenty-one. (As for the ultimate impact of the tax cut, a 1980 Congressional Research Service [CRS] study concluded the legislation increased the nation's Gross National Product [GNP] by seventeen billion dollars by the end of 1964 and by thirty billion dollars by the end of 1965.) For his masterful role in the bill's Senate passage, Russell received the credit and, in turn, rave reviews. "Observers, awed by Long's defensive skill in protecting the measure," a *Philadelphia Inquirer* reporter wrote, "likened him to Andy Robustelli of the New York Giants."[12] No tribute to Russell's skill could have been more laudatory than that of Wisconsin's William Proxmire. An ardent opponent of the bill, Proxmire praised Russell moments after the final vote, suggesting the dawn of "a new era in Senate tax leadership," and added:

> Mr. President, if a man murdered a crippled, enfeebled orphan at high noon on the public square in plain view of a thousand people, I am convinced after today's performance that if the senator from Louisiana represented the guilty murderer, the jury would not only find the murderer innocent, they would award the defendant a million dollars on the grounds the victim had provoked him. The senator from Louisiana not only made his monstrous tax bill good enough to win an overwhelming majority of senators. He made those of us who fought it to the bitter end and suffered defeat grudgingly enjoy seeing an obvious legislative artist in action.[13]

Of Russell, another colleague raved to the *Saturday Evening Post*, "He can take an extremely complicated bill and explain it in two-bit language that everybody understands." Even the undemonstrative majority leader, Mike Mansfield, was impressed. "There were all sorts of amendments that could have blown it to hell, but he brought it through in very good shape." All agreed that they witnessed a masterful legislative performance. After fifteen years in the Senate, Russell was finally an overnight success.[14]

19

UNTIL HELL
FREEZES OVER

"*I*N WASHINGTON," Long family biographer Stan Opotowski wrote in 1960, "Russell is like his father in one respect—he lives in an apartment alone." Settled into a comfortable, but sparsely decorated suite in the Potomac Plaza Apartments, for years Russell lived a bachelor's existence. Tired of the bustle of Washington and never suited for the political life, Katherine left for Baton Rouge with Kay and Pamela in 1957. Their marriage would last for another twelve years, but the constant separation did little to strengthen their faltering relationship. Although not a complete phantom parent like his father, Russell's fatherhood life now mirrored Huey Long's in one unfortunate aspect—other than the Senate's recess periods, he rarely saw his wife and children.[1]

In the Senate, Russell's best friends were two staunch liberals with whom he had entered the Senate in 1948—Paul Douglas of Illinois and Hubert Humphrey of Minnesota. Their divergent views on civil rights aside, Douglas and Humphrey found in Russell an ideological soul mate on most other social issues. Humphrey and Russell were especially close. Partners on LSU's debating team in 1940, the two men shared an abiding, almost Quixotic sympathy for lost causes and underdogs. When Humphrey found himself alienated from Lyndon Johnson and the Senate's leadership early in his Senate career, it was Russell who helped usher his older colleague into the inner sanctum of influence. Russell, who once lived three houses from Humphrey in suburban Maryland, advised his neighbor to join the regular group of Democrats who ate lunch each day at a large table in the Senate Dining Room. "You'd like those guys if you get to know them and they'd like you," Russell said he told Humphrey. Heeding Russell's counsel, Humphrey began showing up and quickly developed what LBJ biographer Robert Dallek described as a "spirit of friendship" with Johnson and other Democrats. In time, thanks to Russell's astute counsel, that spirit ripened into a lifelong camaraderie and immensely successful association between Johnson and Humphrey. [2]

Russell's relationship with his senior Louisiana colleague, Allen Ellender—the former Louisiana house speaker and Huey Long's protégé—was not as intimate. Straitlaced and fiercely conservative, Ellender abided Russell's hard-hitting style and his liberal streak with occasional consternation. With twenty-eight years of age between them, the two men settled into a comfortable, correct, but reserved, working relationship. Politically, they made a formidable team for Louisiana. Russell and Ellender were senior members of and, by the mid-1960s, chaired the Finance and Appropriations committees, respectively. With its senators running the Senate's two most important committees, over the years Louisiana profited from an inordinate amount of federal largesse. One philosophical area, in particular, found Russell and Ellender in complete agreement. In their opposition to civil rights legislation, they were resolute and persevering. Nonetheless, their power and influence would count for little in the face of a quickly escalating clamor for stronger civil rights laws. [3]

Demands for comprehensive, meaningful civil rights legislation reached their highest pitch in 1964. The Senate leadership, Republicans and Democrats, wanted it. President Lyndon Johnson demanded it. The House of Representatives had already passed it. Indeed, all eyes were on the Senate in March as it began debating the most far-reaching civil rights bill in history. The landmark bill protected voting rights for blacks and guaranteed them access to all public accommodations—such as hotels and restaurants. It authorized the federal government to file suit to desegregate schools and other public facilities. Furthermore, the bill extended the life of the Civil Rights Commission and gave it expanded powers. The bill also cut off funding for federal programs if those programs were discriminatory.

Predictably, Russell and his southern colleagues were opposed. "This senator happens to believe that there is absolutely nothing wrong or evil about people believing in segregation of the races, in believing that it is the proper order of things that whites should marry whites and negroes marry negroes," Russell told the Senate on March 13 before formal debate on the bill commenced. "If the Lord had intended all of us to be alike, he would have made us that way." Led once again by Senator Richard Russell of Georgia, the southerners prepared their customary, well-organized filibuster. As always, they were confident that they would exhaust their opposition to the point of compromise on the bill's major issues. This dauntless tactic had worked before. The filibuster, when employed, never failed to extract defeat or, at the very least, a face-saving compromise from the civil rights forces. This time, to the southerners' surprise, their tactic would fail miserably. Lyndon Johnson did not plan to lose this fight. When he proposed the bill, the president told Congress that "no memorial or oration or eulogy could more eloquently honor President Kennedy's memory than the earliest possible passage of the civil rights bill for which he fought so long. We have talked long enough about equal rights in this country. It is time to write the next chapter and write it in the books of law." With help from his liberal and moderate allies in Congress, Johnson meant to win this fight.[4]

Full of confidence in his bill's prospects, Johnson knew that the Senate's civil rights forces, led by irrepressible Democratic whip Hubert Humphrey of Minnesota, had a new, winning strategy. In the past, the liberals often lost to the southerners simply because they surrendered the floor during filibusters. Usually, they had appeared only for quorum calls. Only rarely did they engage the southerners in debate. This time, Humphrey and his forces refused to concede the floor to Senator Russell's southern troops. Throughout the debate, the liberals remained in the Senate chamber. Where they had once allowed the southerners to fulminate endlessly, they now aggressively debated them. And when the liberals came to the Senate floor, they were prepared for battle. For every section of the bill, Humphrey appointed floor captains to discuss and debate the provision's finer points. For the first time, the southerners, forced to answer and debate the liberals on the bill's intricacies, were denied the elements of a true filibuster—nonstop talking. Meanwhile, outside the chamber, Humphrey's forces circulated regular newsletters among Democratic and Republican supporters of the bill to keep them involved and informed. At Johnson's behest, Humphrey zealously courted Republican minority leader Everett Dirksen. Eventually, he won Dirksen's support and crucial help in breaking the southern filibuster.

With more vigor than in past years, Russell took a leading role in opposing the bill. He offered almost a dozen amendments to water down various provisions. From the debate's early days—after Senate leaders had bypassed the Judiciary Committee to wrestle the House-passed bill directly onto the Senate calendar—Russell sang a militant tune. In March, he interrupted a speech by John McClellan of Arkansas to direct a hostile remark at Humphrey, his old college friend and debating partner, whom he now called "the generalissimo of the civil rights advocates." Russell advised Humphrey to "yield his position from time to time to senators who have more open minds on this subject." At this, even McClellan felt obliged to defend Humphrey. "I shall never insist that my friend from Minnesota be gagged in this body or anywhere else."[5]

After more than a month of various delaying tactics by southerners, formal debate began on March 30. In a four-hour speech, Humphrey declared, "Until racial justice and freedom is a reality in this land, our union will remain profoundly imperfect. . . . The Negro is going to get justice or this society will be ripped apart." For fifty-seven days, the southerners tried talking the bill to death. While holding to the floor and their fading visions of victory, they allowed votes only on southern amendments to broaden provisions providing jury trials in contempt cases. Throughout the three-month debate, Russell meandered on and off the floor, dutifully fulfilling his filibuster duties. Sometimes, although rarely, he spoke for hours. Other times, he jousted with the bill's proponents over minority living conditions in the South. More often, he engaged in freewheeling question-and-answer sessions—known as colloquies—with like-minded colleagues. As few senators could speak for hours on end without the banter of other senators, these exchanges were the filibuster's backbone. Meanwhile, Humphrey's Senate forces exploited an effective network of religious groups from virtually all denominations to lobby for the bill's passage. From pulpits and in highly public visits to senators in Washington, these clergymen made the bill a moral issue of the highest order. Inch by inch, as Humphrey's side gained ground, the filibuster was fading.[6]

Humphrey had one more reason for hope. The Senate, like the nation, was changing. "Attitudes and political realities had shifted," wrote historian Gilbert C. Fite. "Younger senators had been elected, senators who were not chained so firmly to the old ways by habit, tradition, and custom and who believed in the fight for civil rights. Some of them saw that in time they must also have black votes to stay in office." Time, it seemed, was the southerners' worst enemy.[7]

On April 7, during an exchange with New York's Jacob Javits, Russell cast the debate in his own moral terms, asserting that Louisiana citizens "think it is morally wrong to integrate and that they would be doing an evil thing if they did so." In May, he warned President Johnson of the bill's dire political consequences. "The president and his advisors would be wise to alter their course on this subject . . . otherwise, he is taking a chance of losing a dozen states."[8]

As for his own Louisiana politics, Russell believed that he had no choice but to oppose the bill, while maintaining that the Senate's liberals exerted undue pressure to win southern votes they did not need for passage. "I felt as long as they had the votes to pass that voting rights bill, they ought to leave it up to the judgment of individual members of Congress as to what extent he could afford to vote for that bill without jeopardizing his election," Russell said years later. "They had plenty of votes to pass the bill. Anybody that felt like his election was jeopardized, let him vote against it."[9]

In April, as the filibuster lost its steam, Russell's rhetoric remained fiery. This bill, he declared on April 30, "is about as much a dispenser of civil rights as a cigarette is a dispenser of sex appeal or business success. Each has been grossly oversold to the American public; and at last it seems that each is being branded a bit more accurately for what it really is—one a cancer in our lungs, the other a cancer in our constitutional form of government."[10]

By June 10, weary of arguing the inevitable, the Senate voted seventy-one to twenty-nine to end debate by invoking cloture. The liberals, with help from all but six Republicans, had killed the filibuster. It was an historic vote. Not only did it signal the Senate's readiness to act on strong civil rights legislation, it marked the first time the Senate had shut off debate on a civil rights bill since the cloture rule was created in 1917. Senator Russell's dilatory strategy, employed once too often, failed. Had the southern bloc sought compromise instead of confrontation, they might have achieved some success. As it was, southerners had nothing to show for their efforts. "If Senators Long, Ellender and their colleagues could have shown they were trying to amend a harsh bill in good faith and not simply been obstructive," the *Lake Charles American Press* observed, "the Senate membership might have hesitated to cut off debate. More concessions might have been gained under attempts at compromise than by the filibuster. By yielding something, the Southerners might have gained something in return. Instead, they yielded nothing and gained nothing." Attacking Russell as an originator of the southern approach was unfair. As always, the southern bloc followed Senator Richard Russell's lead. Nonetheless, the paper's assessment of the southern strategy was sound. As their numbers waned, the absolute, united recalcitrance of the anti-civil rights forces was no longer the potent weapon of the 1940s and 1950s.[11]

Once the Senate imposed cloture, southerners could no longer influence the bill. In rapid succession, the Senate spurned more than one hundred southern amendments. "Perhaps we could describe it as a second Appomattox," Russell explained to his constituents in a newsletter in June. "When the Civil Rights bill came to the Senate, I told the people of Louisiana that I would fight against it until Hell froze over and then I would fight on the ice. As I write this letter, we are on the ice, but we are still fighting." By June 19, the ice melted. On that day, the Senate adopted the bill, seventy-three to twenty-seven. Several weeks later, on July 7, the House of Representatives approved the Senate's version. Within hours, President Johnson signed the landmark legislation in a nationally televised White House ceremony, asking Americans "to join in this effort to bring justice and hope to all our people."[12]

Russell reacted bitterly to the bill's passage, calling it "tyranny to the extreme." He urged its repeal. Senator Russell, meanwhile, seemed to better sense the winds of change. He beseeched southerners to obey the new law, to which Russell responded, "While I am strongly opposed to lawlessness in any form, bad laws generate contempt and disrespect for the law. The civil rights act should, in my opinion, be the classic example of a bad law—contrary to public morals—at least as far as the South is concerned."[13]

Throughout the long debate, Russell displayed no rancor or resentment toward blacks, which he recalled in subsequent years to blunt charges of racism. In fact, he claimed he privately urged President Johnson—as he had President Kennedy—to send federal registrars to the South to sign up black voters. Always, he explained, his motives in opposing the bill were twofold: His constituents were overwhelmingly against it, and he feared that the speed with which the reforms were enacted would lead to more racial strife and violence. Furthermore, some of Russell's defensiveness on civil rights grew out of his disgust at attempts of northern liberals to portray Louisiana and other southern states as bastions of hatred and oppression. This sentiment was vividly evident in a question to South Carolina's Strom Thurmond during the filibuster in April: "Would it not be fair to ask what kind of fix the colored folks would be in if they had not been brought to this country, but had been allowed to roam the jungles, with tigers chasing them, or being subjected to the other elements they would have to contend with, compared to the fine conditions they enjoy in America?"[14]

While Russell may have taken a paternalistic attitude toward American blacks, he strenuously disputed suggestions that he harbored anything but goodwill toward them. Even so, his disdain for civil rights activists—whom he often referred to as "outside agitators," "rabble rousers," and "hate mongers"—was evident. In many ways, Russell was once more caught between his populist family heritage and his constituents' fears of legislation that threatened their way of life. It was a dilemma his father had faced more than once during his brief career, as Huey Long biographer William Ivy Hair observed: "Like his aristocratic predecessors, [Huey] understood the depth of racial feelings among the mass of whites; playing to that prejudice was not his favorite tune, but it was a part of his repertoire."[15]

"[Russell] Long was very much one of those who thought we ought to go slow," former aide Charles McBride remembered. "On the other hand, his name is Long, and he is a very caring, compassionate, sentimental man who thinks that, in a profound way, this society exists to take care of what Hubert [Humphrey] used to call: Those who are in the sunrise of their lives and the sunset of their lives." Another aide who worked for Long during the civil rights era, Richard Dashbach, detected Russell's lack of passion for opposing civil rights legislation. "There was never any hate, any concepts of inferiority or anything anti-black. It was just: Protect our southern way of life. Which, obviously, was just some buzz words which he was hoping would pass, and they did."[16]

While senators had debated the bill for months, both sides were often talking not to each other, but past each other, toward outside constituencies. Moreover, southerners, like Russell, often saw the issue as an attack on their region's treatment of blacks. "There has always been Negro help in my home from the day I was born," Russell said as evidence of his affection for blacks. What Russell and other southerners seemed not to understand, nor to admit, was they could no longer bargain for the forbearance of blacks in exchange for humane treatment and adequately funded, but segregated schools, buses, and restaurants. Russell, like the times in which he lived, would have to change.[17]

20

THE CIVIL WAR
IS OVER

$\mathcal{R}$USSELL DID NOT ATTEND the 1964 Democratic National Convention in Atlantic City. He begged off, explaining that he needed time to prepare amendments to the upcoming social security bill "in order that we might provide more amply for the aged, the blind, the widows and dependent children." More than likely, he wanted distance between himself and the party, whose nominees, Lyndon Johnson and Hubert Humphrey, were the two white Americans most closely associated with the civil rights movement. Nonetheless, he expressed pleasure that Johnson had selected his old college friend Humphrey as vice president. Despite "some differences between them over civil rights," Russell applauded Humphrey's "magnificent record" as a champion of farmers, labor, and the underprivileged.[1]

After the convention, Russell shed some of the reluctance that had kept him from Atlantic City. He defended Johnson and Humphrey and lustily attacked the Republican nominee, Arizona senator Barry Goldwater. When he appeared at the October opening of Johnson headquarters in Baton Rouge, Russell charged that Goldwater lacked "the temperament" to be president. "If he was twice hospitalized from the pressures of being a dress salesman in a dry goods store, then how can he face Khrushchev, Mao-Tse-Tung and Castro all at the same time?" A week later, speaking to union leaders in Lake Charles, Russell said that Goldwater was "one hundred percent wrong" on labor and social welfare issues. "He voted against labor thirty-nine times and the only reason he didn't vote against labor more than that was he had only thirty-nine chances to vote." Despite Russell's blessing, Johnson's support of civil rights cost him dearly in the South. The Democratic ticket lost in five southern states, including Louisiana, on its way to an extraordinary landslide victory elsewhere in the country.[2]

Russell was delighted with the election's outcome for several reasons. He liked Johnson and Humphrey. Other than on the issue of civil rights, he believed that his former Senate colleagues were the men best qualified to lead the nation. Furthermore, Russell saw Humphrey's election as an opening for him. As the Senate's Democratic whip, Humphrey had been second in command to Senate majority leader Mike Mansfield. Now, he would resign his Senate seat, creating a vacancy for the whip position. It was a job Russell coveted. As whip, Humphrey had exercised enormous powers. Primarily, he filled the vacuum left by the diffident, introverted Mansfield, who rarely used his influence to coerce legislation through the Senate. "He had permitted the Senate to be what it was," Lyndon Johnson aide Harry McPherson observed, "a hundred disparate adults who ought to have been able to deal efficiently and responsibly with public affairs." Mansfield left the heavy lifting—the vote corraling and counting—to Humphrey. Elected majority leader in 1961 to succeed then-vice president Johnson, Mansfield's passive style was the antithesis of his predecessor's hard-driving, crack-the-whip method of leadership. Mansfield was the Senate's chairman of the board. His whip was chief executive officer.[3]

Even before the presidential election, speculation abounded in Washington over who would inherit Humphrey's powerful position. The early list of possible candidates—Rhode Island's John O. Pastore, Florida's George Smathers, and Connecticut's Thomas Dodd—did not include Russell. "I like John Pastore," Russell told a television interviewer shortly after the Democratic convention, "but Senator Smathers has been a good friend to me and a good friend to Louisiana as far back as I can recall, and, if he wants the job, he'll have my vote." Actually, Smathers had no interest in the job. Feigning disinterest, Russell busily lined up votes.[4]

In August, Russell eagerly tested the waters at the urging of his Mississippi colleague, John Stennis. "It always seemed back in those days that, in the leadership thing, a single request you run was a draft," Russell joked. First, he consulted with southern leader Richard Russell of Georgia. "He's the bell cow," Russell later said, explaining that "you take a cow that the other cows have confidence in, and you put a bell on her and the other cows won't stray far from her. Dick Russell is the bell cow of the southern group." With Senator Russell's approval, he approached other key senators. "I was very pleased with the response I got from those senators." By mid-September, he secretly obtained commitments from virtually every Senate southerner. By November, when Russell announced his interest in the job—along with Pastore, and Oklahoma's Mike Monroney—he was the acknowledged front-runner.[5]

By contrast, Pastore's campaign was a study in indolence and overconfidence. Relaxed and aloof, he waited until November 6, after Congress adjourned, to announce his candidacy. Instead of asking senators for their votes in person, as Russell had, Pastore mailed each of his colleagues a short, formal letter requesting their "consideration." When he followed up with phone calls the next week, Pastore was surprised to learn that many senators were already committed to Russell.

By all accounts, the whip job should have been Pastore's for the asking. A fiery debater with solid liberal credentials, Pastore would have seemed, at first glance, to be the liberal favorite. Johnson had made him keynote speaker to the Democratic National Convention. To some, this was a signal that he was the president's personal choice. Even so, Pastore's aggressiveness and his strident rhetoric in debate bred more than a few enemies. He was the kind of senator, an observer once said, who "makes speeches in intimate discussions just as he does on the floor." Perhaps the trait that most damaged his candidacy was Pastore's abundant self-confidence. A *Wall Street Journal* story in November observed that Pastore "expected to be elected—as most whips in the past have been—without a real contest."[6]

Meanwhile, Monroney—a moderate, former newspaperman—was never a real threat. He was hardworking, had made an admirable legislative record, and was well liked by his colleagues. Few, however, thought he had the qualities needed for Senate leadership. While many factors hindered Pastore and Monroney, none was as crucial as their late entries into the race. "Those were highly regarded, respected senators," Russell observed, "but they made the mistake of giving me too much head start."[7]

With Russell in clear possession of the southern votes, the contest quickly centered around the one group of senators with whom Pastore should have had a natural advantage—northern and western liberals. With this group, Russell had several fundamental problems. He had consistently opposed civil rights. He had voted against the nuclear test ban treaty. He had opposed the Medicare Act and the 1964 Foreign Aid Bill. In other words, Russell's record should have been much too conservative for his liberal colleagues. Undeterred by such ideological disadvantages, Russell had no intentions to concede the liberals to Pastore. Instead, he audaciously courted them. More so than his opponents, Russell thrived on the game and the stimulating quest for votes. He explored every advantage he could find. Any clue to what might influence a senator's vote was exploited. For example, when he learned from Senator Richard Russell that his friend, but frequent legislative foe, liberal Illinois senator Paul Douglas, might be inclined to consider his candidacy, Russell went directly to Douglas's office. In his hand, he carried a copy of his father's autobiography, *Every Man a King.* Keenly aware of Douglas's progressive passions, Russell opened the book to one of its closing passages and recalling his dad's philosophy read aloud the words of his revered father:

> Then no tear-dimmed eyes of a small child will be lifted into the saddened face of a father or mother unable to give it the necessities required by its soul and body for life; then the powerful will be rebuked in the sight of man for holding that which they cannot consume, but which is craved to sustain humanity; the food of the land will feed, the raiment will clothe, and the houses shelter all the people; the powerful will be elated by the well being of all, rather than through greed.[8]

Closing the book, Russell looked up at Douglas and declared, "[T]hat is my political philosophy. That's where it came from." The quotation undoubtedly called to Douglas's mind Russell's lustful fights to strengthen and expand social security and his ardent support of other social programs dear to Douglas. Like most senators, Douglas found it impossible to dislike Russell, even though they sometimes disagreed on legislation. On November 30, Douglas startled Washington by announcing in San Francisco that he would support Russell's candidacy. Douglas, who said that Russell "has a very warm heart," even defended his candidate's civil rights views, explaining that many southern senators were forced by the electorate to be so "obsessed with the race question" they could not become national statesmen. Douglas said passage of the 1964 civil rights bill had "liberated" Russell and several other southerners.[9]

Another leading liberal senator soon tilted toward Russell. New Mexico's Clinton Anderson told reporters that Russell had "asked me to be his campaign manager" and "I've been trying to help him." Liberals like Minnesota's Eugene McCarthy, South Dakota's George McGovern, and Wisconsin's William Proxmire were also known to be leaning in Russell's direction. Russell's affability and effective personal appeals lay at the heart of his success with the liberal bloc. Also important was his own liberal streak, which helped these men to rationalize their votes to the press and civil rights activists. In particular, Douglas and others were said to have remembered Russell's vigorous fight against the 1962 satellite communications bill—which liberals thought gave the telecommunications giant, AT&T, monopoly control over space communications, but which Pastore had supported. They were also swayed by Russell's change of heart on President Johnson's Medicare legislation, which as an influential Finance Committee member he now indicated he might support. Furthermore, his smashing success with the massive tax cut bill proved to colleagues that he had skills necessary for floor leadership. That Russell would soon be chairman of the powerful Finance Committee provided no small additional incentive to undecided senators.[10]

The most telling example of Russell's lust for the whip job was the way he courted South Carolina's Olin Johnston, an unpopular liberal for whom Russell had little, if any, respect. Richard Russell counseled his younger colleague that Johnston would be his most difficult southern vote. Russell, however, had one bit of important information about his prospective supporter: Johnston coveted the Senate desk that South Carolina's immortal John C. Calhoun had once used. Unfortunately, the desk, also used by Huey Long, was in Russell's possession. For a vote of this importance, Russell admitted that he was willing to trade. "Olin," Russell said, "I've heard you're interested. You've never asked, but I've heard you're interested in this John C. Calhoun desk, and I'd like for you to have it." Russell said that he never mentioned exchanging the desk for a vote. It was abundantly understood. Russell got Johnston's vote, confessing that he later uttered a silent prayer. "Please forgive me, Daddy, but this time I'm going for broke." A year later, when Johnston died, Russell reclaimed the desk.[11]

In late December, Russell exuded all the confidence of a sure winner. "I've got the ball on the five-yard line and I'm pretty sure of scoring a touchdown," he said, but he cautioned "I've seen fumbles on the five-yard line, too, and sometimes the other team recovers." By then, the press had noted Russell's improving prospects. "Wouldn't it be strange for a Senate, with a majority of liberal Democrats, to have a whip who is a segregationist, a foe of the nuclear test ban treaty, from a state which gave its electoral votes to Barry Goldwater?" the *Washington Post* asked in an editorial. Curious as it was, the Senate's Democrats were about to elect just such a man.[12]

Nonetheless, civil rights leaders were not prepared to see Russell elected without a fight. Clarence Mitchell, director of the Washington bureau of the National Association for the Advancement of Colored People, sent telegrams to forty-four senators, demanding that they oppose Russell. "It would shock the conscience of the nation if the Democratic Party, which properly attacked Senator Goldwater for his vote against the [1964] civil rights act, would fill a leadership post with a senator who fought against, spoke against and voted against this important legislation."[13]

On the morning of January 4, 1965, the Democratic caucus assembled privately in the walnut-paneled caucus room just off the Senate floor. Russell needed thirty-five of the sixty-eight votes to win. As a page solemnly passed a mahogany box among senators, they dropped their ballots inside. When the votes were counted, Russell was one vote short of outright victory, thirty-four votes to twenty for Pastore and fourteen for Monroney. According to the rules, Monroney, as low man, dropped from the running. On the next vote, Russell won comfortably, with forty-one votes to Pastore's twenty-five. Two liberals, apparently dissatisfied with both candidates, voted for Michigan's Philip Hart.[14]

Russell had won with an unlikely coalition. His winning majority lacked any overriding ideological or geographical commonality. With a solid southern bloc of fifteen to eighteen senators for a base, he had added another dozen western colleagues who were attracted by his engaging personality and his firm commitment to helping them guard their states' natural resources—mining, oil, and agriculture. Russell's populism took root with another group of Democrats—liberals like Douglas, McGovern, and Proxmire. Others, like passionate Medicare proponent Clinton Anderson of New Mexico, remembered that Russell was instrumental in preserving the principle of the fledgling program in a 1960 conference committee, even though he personally opposed the plan.

When the caucus adjourned, Russell emerged from the room, beaming, to meet waiting reporters. "One of my friends said, 'If Russell Long can win an election like this with the support of men like Clinton Anderson and Paul Douglas, it means the Civil War is over.' " Asked how his leadership position might change his attitudes toward civil rights, Russell answered, "[T]he time has come to start looking forward," but acknowledged, "I'd imagine I'd vote the way I did in the past." The previous day, however, Russell had been much more conciliatory in a television interview when he said he had no problem with the Democratic party's civil rights platform "as it stands today." "President Johnson feels that southerners should recognize this is not the same world it was just twenty years ago. As time goes by, the president is going to eliminate this North-South business. I would like to work with the administration to bring that about." He also predicted that increased black voting registration was "something southern politicians will have to learn to live with. Those who are qualified ought to be registered and local officials ought to recognize that."[15]

Russell's victory was national news as newspapers throughout the country interpreted the meaning of the unlikely election results. *The Saturday Evening Post* dismissed Russell's suggestion that his election spelled an end to the Civil War, but maintained that "it does seem to indicate that Huey Long's son is every bit as canny a politician as the old Kingfish himself ever was." Noting that Louisiana's Hale Boggs was House majority whip, the *Birmingham Post-Herald* said "right now, Louisiana seems to be sitting tall in the saddle." Russell "will have his opportunity to disprove some of the things that have been said about senators from his part of the country," the *Kansas City Star* declared, adding, "The whole nation will be watching Russell Long of Louisiana. But this is 1965 and perhaps the election of Senator Long to his important new job may be a sign of change—of healthy change—in the attitude of the nation toward the South and of the South toward the nation." Even the Reverend Martin Luther King, Jr., speculated that Russell's election might be a "blessing in disguise" in that he "may bring an end to the solid Southern bloc."[16]

Despite sending signals of new moderation on civil rights, the next day Russell drew curious stares when he attended a meeting in Richard Russell's office at which southern senators discussed plans to combat liberalization of the cloture rule. He admitted that he might elicit criticism for attending, but stressed his presence was to provide "a moderating influence." Had he been invited, Russell said, he also would have attended the meeting of liberal senators who wanted to change the cloture rule. "I don't think it's a civil rights question anymore," he explained, noting cloture had been invoked on civil rights the previous year. "The South has little to gain by filibustering a civil rights bill."[17]

Those who wondered if and when Russell might challenge Mansfield's leadership did not wait long for an answer. The Senate's Steering Committee—a panel whose primary task is committee assignments—met four days after the whip election. Although Mansfield was the committee's de facto chairman, he had not arrived at the meeting's appointed hour. Russell did not hesitate to take charge. In Manfield's absence, he called the meeting to order. Moments later, Mansfield entered the room, but settled quietly in a seat near the back, allowing Russell to continue. "Neophyte leader Long was winning a challenge against veteran Mansfield seldom equaled on Capitol Hill for breathless audacity," columnists Roland

Evans and Robert Novak reported. "It will happen again—Long's winning over Mansfield," one senator told the columnists, adding, "Unless he overplays his hand, Russell Long is about to become the most powerful man in the Senate." While Russell gave no evidence that he would ever challenge the popular Mansfield for majority leader, he did confess higher ambitions in a television interview in January: "I am frank to tell you that if this was the end of the road, just to be the assistant leader, the so-called whip, I wouldn't have run for the job because it doesn't pay anything extra and there is twice as much work to do."[18]

Russell's first true challenge to Mansfield's authority came early in January when the leader proposed increasing the Democratic ratio on all committees to reflect the overall two-to-one Democratic edge. Preferring not to jettison any Republicans from their committees, Mansfield instead suggested adding new Democrats to each committee, meaning that the Finance Committee's eleven-to-six ratio would increase to thirteen-to-six. "That's where the effervescent Long jumped in—hootin', hollerin' and stompin' in the Kingfish tradition," Evans and Novak reported. Russell was adamant. He would not permit a change in the Finance Committee's ratio, offering even to leave the Foreign Relations Committee if such a sacrifice were necessary. Any Democratic additions to Finance were likely to be liberals who might upset Russell's comfortable bipartisan style of doing business. For three days, Mansfield and Russell faced off. Attempts at mediation by Senator Richard Russell failed. In the end, Mansfield relented. Russell had won. "But it was not cogent argument that won for Long and retained the eleven-to-six ratio," the columnists concluded. "It was an iron will that wilted Mansfield. And, of course, Long did not sacrifice his Foreign Relations seat."[19]

Years later, Russell was nonchalant about his early brazen skirmishes with Mansfield. "I was just very independent. I expressed my opinion, advocated what I thought. Now, if Mike had told me, 'Well, now, look, I want you to vote with me on this, it's important to me,' I think I'd have probably done it. . . . I thought that when we sit down together and talk about what we ought to do about some matter, that I had a right to my opinion just as much as the leader had a right to his."[20]

As assistant leader, Russell was now a tenuous partner of his old friend and former Senate colleague, President Lyndon Johnson. In theory, his maverick days should have ended when he became a spokesman and advocate for his Democratic president. In the beginning, at least, Russell tried to play such a role. To an AFL-CIO gathering in Washington, he said that Congress would enact most of Johnson's Great Society legislative agenda by midsummer and urged the labor leaders to help the president achieve his goal. He joked at first that he had believed four years would be required to get Johnson's program enacted. After talking with the president, "I got the idea we ought to vote on it all this year." Nonetheless, in a subsequent interview, Russell stopped short of completely endorsing Johnson's Great Society. "I think the president has a magnificent program and my guess is that I will be able to vote for him at least eighty percent of the time, and maybe even more."[21]

The first and most controversial test of Russell's fealty to his new job came quickly. In the spring of 1965, President Johnson challenged Congress to enact strong voting rights legislation to "strike down restrictions to voting in all elections—federal, state and local—which have been used to deny Negroes the right to vote." As proposed by Johnson, the bill established a federal voting registration process which suspended all literacy tests and other devices which prevented black registration. In extreme cases, the bill would authorize the appointment of federal voter registrars to assume the functions of local and state officials. Criminal penalties were included for those who intimidated voters or who engaged in voter fraud. The ensuing debate, and Russell's role in it, highlighted the political peril for southern politicians sounding the faintest acquiescent note on civil rights.

Even before Johnson submitted his bill, Russell signaled he would not oppose federal intervention when it was obvious "the state and the local governments will not move on any reasonable basis to permit Negroes to vote." Local officials in some Louisiana parishes, Russell declared, should "reconcile themselves to the fact" of increased black voting strength in their parishes. "They ought to quit obstructing it and actually cooperate with that result occurring," Russell said, adding if blacks voted in greater numbers in the South, many racial problems would disappear. "There are a lot of officials who would be much more considerate to the Negro problem if you have a substantial Negro vote."[22]

When word of the legislation's scope and magnitude reached Louisiana, a mob of White Citizens Council members swarmed the governor's mansion in Baton Rouge. They demanded to meet with Governor John McKeithen, Russell's law school classmate, concerning the proposal to install federal registrars. Informed that Russell supported the provision, McKeithen replied, "then you can put me down we're in complete opposition on that." Soon, White Citizens Councils in Shreveport and New Orleans were reportedly circulating recall petitions against Russell for his position on the bill. Joining the din of protest was the state's Republican

Party chairman, Charlton Lyons, who suggested that Louisiana would soon be a target for mob demonstrations, something he blamed on Russell, "the president's liberal whip," and his general support of the registration provisions. "It is apparent," Lyons said, "that Senator Long hopes to regain the votes he is losing by his support of President Johnson's dictatorial programs, from the new registrations brought on by the president's voter law."[23]

Explaining that he opposed the bill because of problems with other provisions, Russell defended his views on black registration, telling a convention of Louisiana mayors, "[W]e're going to have to do something about it or have somebody else do something about it." He could no longer defend parishes that had registered a minuscule percentage of eligible blacks. "If Congress were required to vote for freedom now or freedom never, they must vote for freedom now. You and I may prefer something not as fast as freedom now, but when the decision has to be made between now and never, don't fool yourself for a minute about what the decision is going to be." While he wanted to temper the bill where possible, Russell told the mayors that he could not do so "if you insist on my sounding like a member of the Ku Klux Klan." When he finished, the mayors responded with a standing ovation.[24]

While he may have charmed the mayors, Russell knew that the voting rights act would be a daring tightrope walk. On one hand, he could not stray too far from Louisiana public opinion. Conversely, to be effective as whip, he must work for the president's legislative agenda. As the *Miami Herald* observed, "If Russell Long can get the Great Society bills passed and still keep his constituents in Louisiana happy, he'll win fame as the Senate's miracle whip."[25]

Russell used bold rhetoric again in April, when he told Louisiana labor leaders that while he often disagreed with the methods of Dr. Martin Luther King, Jr., it is just as bad "for an Alabama sheriff to wear a great big button that says 'Never' to Negroes. No matter what you try to do, you and your children can never hold your heads high." Reaffirming his belief in segregation by choice, he added: "But one of the things I find it hard to speak for as a southerner is to defend situations where a person with no basis whatsoever denies another person a right which is properly his." He could filibuster the voting rights bill, he said, but "do you know how many votes I would change? Not one."[26]

Strangely, Russell drew the ire of the White House when he enthusiastically supported an unsuccessful amendment by Massachusetts senator Edward Kennedy to outlaw the poll tax. This reportedly angered Lyndon

Johnson, who believed that Russell merely wanted to sabotage the bill, knowing a serious constitutional challenge over the amendment was certain. Johnson was wrong. Russell supported the bill out of loyalty to the memory of his father, who had repealed Louisiana's poll tax more than thirty years earlier.

After the Senate once again invoked cloture, for the second time in two successive years, Russell honored his promise to seek a refinement of the bill's federal registration portion. In fact, the Senate agreed to his plan to exempt much of Louisiana from federal voter intervention. Under Russell's plan, the bill did not apply to parishes and counties with more than 50 percent black registration. This meant that twenty-three Louisiana parishes were exempt from federal intervention on voting rights. This was actually no small feat. Precious few amendments were adopted, and only three, including Russell's, were introduced by southern senators.

On May 26, after five weeks of debate, the Senate passed the Voting Rights Act, seventy-seven to nineteen. As he had promised, Russell voted no. After minor changes by a Senate-House conference, Russell again voted against the bill which passed the Senate in final form on August 3, this time seventy-nine to eighteen. Three days later, Johnson signed the legislation.

Not surprisingly, Russell's vote against the bill, and his amendment exempting much of Louisiana, was obscured by his outspokenness on black voting rights. In the racially charged town of Bogalusa, north of New Orleans, members of the Ku Klux Klan circulated fliers demanding that Russell, and a host of other public officials, be tarred and feathered. "The Klan has already sent word down to destroy Senator Long and Hale Boggs politically," a former Klansman told columnist Drew Pearson. "Some of their killers would kill both of these men if they were sure that no jury would convict them." Other than the extreme right, Russell had skillfully negotiated the issue without seriously devaluing his stock with constituents or the White House. In his next confrontation with Lyndon Johnson, he would not be as fortunate.[27]

Instead of lending his influence to support Johnson's Medicare plan for the poor, as he previously said he might do, Russell had his own ideas. When the administration's health care proposal arrived in the Finance Committee, Russell promptly tossed a monkey wrench into the works. He calmly offered an amendment to apply an income test to the amount elderly patients would pay for hospital care before qualifying for government assistance.

Russell's plan would require upper-income patients to share more of the program's cost, while giving a break to the poor. It was more than a slight departure from the administration's proposal. It would drastically transform the entire program. The president's men were shocked when the Finance Committee quickly adopted the amendment. "Senator Russell B. Long has managed, momentarily at least, to gut the medicare bill," a *Washington Post* editorial began. "The Administration's medicare bill has been turned into a monstrosity," the *New York Times* declared. "I did not ask for this fight," Russell said when his liberal opponents howled in protest, "but I do not run from one. I know the White House is doing everything in its power to reverse the decision of the committee on my amendments. In my opinion, I will win." Some hasty arm-twisting by the president and his men was required before Russell was proved wrong. Several days later, the committee reversed itself, and Russell ultimately worked with Johnson for the bill's passage in July.[28]

Medicare was high on President Johnson's priority list. Once again, his Senate Democratic whip made his task more difficult. "As the senator from Louisiana, when you talk about Medicare and Medicaid, you really weren't talking about doing much for [Louisiana] that wasn't being done already," Russell explained. "I was in the position to kind of look at that on the basis of—I guess in time we're going to have to do this, but it's going to cost a world of money and we ought to try to see to it that to the maximum extent possible . . . the people who could afford to pay it, pay."[29]

At about this time, Russell further vexed his president by opposing Johnson's nomination of retired air force general William F. McKee as head of the Federal Aviation Administration. Although the Senate confirmed McKee's nomination, Russell gave the White House a scare when he nearly defeated the appointment. Reported the *Chicago News*, "The Johnson administration has a new problem in the U.S. Senate—its own assistant majority leader. . . . He goes to the weekly leadership breakfasts at the White House, hears the president outline his plans and hopes, and participates in all the closed-door strategy sessions. But no one can be quite sure, after all this, whether he is going to put his shoulder behind a given piece of legislation."[30]

"He was on a tight rope," recalled then-press secretary Charles McBride, who believed Russell was not entirely prepared for the conflicting demands of the whip job. Another aide, Wayne Thevenot, agreed. "He was too much the loner, too much the guy that is not great at taking other people's ideas and coordinating. He had his own ideas, his own way of running things and he was very good at building coalitions around his own positions. The drudgery that goes along with leadership in the Senate, that hanging around on the floor and working out penny-ante problems . . . was just not Russell Long by any stretch of the imagination."[31]

If balancing the job as assistant leader with the demands of representing Louisiana seemed trying, it would pale in comparison with the high-wire act Russell was soon expected to perform. Before year's end, he would inherit the additional duty of chairman of the Senate Finance Committee. As President Johnson escalated the war in Vietnam, Russell's position on the Senate Foreign Relations Committee would take on greater significance. Then, as if Russell needed more burdens, Louisiana's popular governor, John McKeithen, sounded increasingly like a challenger to Russell's reelection in 1968. As McBride observed, "Long was dancing."[32]

21

BLOOD IN MY BOOTS

$\mathcal{F}$OR YEARS, RUSSELL WAS DE FACTO Finance Committee chairman. In November 1965, his ascendancy was official. Chairman Harry Byrd resigned in bad health. Next in seniority, Russell moved into the chairmanship, encountering a growing band of detractors who hoped his new position would compel him to vacate the whip's job. For years, a loosely enforced Senate tradition held senators did not simultaneously hold chairmanships and leadership posts. In this case, tradition mattered little to Russell. He rejected any notion he might relinquish either position. "If they don't want me to do it," he declared, "they'll have to fire me."[1]

While some colleagues were known to grumble privately about Russell's intention to hold two positions of immense power, only one—Senate president pro tempore Carl Hayden—said so publicly. "I assume if he becomes chairman of that committee," the venerable Hayden told a reporter, "we will have to elect another whip." Even the *Washington Star* opined Russell wanted to wear "too many hats," suggesting that "someone should draw his attention to the fact that there are ninety-nine other senators on the Hill, many of them also intelligent and deserving. . . . Senator Long will have his hands full just doing a good job in the tax department." Any senators who looked to majority leader Mike Mansfield for guidance received none. Mansfield said only the Senate's Democrats should decide for themselves if Russell could hold both jobs.[2]

Hopes of any rebellion were dashed when President Johnson—who had once chaired the Senate's Space Committee as majority leader—phoned Russell to say that he saw no reason he should not have both jobs. Russell quickly spread the news of Johnson's call among his colleagues. The message was potent: If Johnson—with more cause than anyone for annoyance with Russell—had confidence in him, how could his colleagues reject him?[3]

Russell's power, impressive before, was now staggering. He was an activist assistant to a very diffident majority leader. He was chairman of Finance, arguably the Senate's most important committee. His seat on the Foreign Relations Committee, at a time when the Vietnam War focused inordinate attention on that panel's activities, afforded him opportunities for even greater notoriety and influence. He was chairman of the Joint Committee on Taxation, an alternating position between chairmen of the House and Senate tax committees. Indeed, to almost everyone, Russell's ascension to Senate preeminence appeared absolute—that is, until mid-January.

Shortly after Congress convened, majority leader Mansfield pruned Russell's power a few notches when he announced the appointments of four liberal senators—Daniel Brewster of Maryland, Philip Hart of Michigan, Daniel Inouye of Hawaii, and Edmund Muskie of Maine—as assistant whips. The move fed Washington's gossip mill. Many Senate watchers concluded that Mansfield made the appointment on advice from President Johnson, reportedly disappointed with Russell's nonconformist ways. Publicly, Mansfield and Russell scoffed at such suggestions. In fact, they claimed, Russell suggested the arrangement to lessen the pressures of his additional duties. The explanation did little to quell suspicions that Mansfield was displeased with Russell. "The Kingfish was gunned down in a corridor of the Louisiana statehouse," the South Bend (Indiana) Tribune remarked, adding that "son Russell's fate may be more gentle. He may be smothered with solicitude."[4]

Mansfield and Russell indignantly appeared on the Senate floor on January 19 to quell the speculation. "A year prior to this," Russell said, "I suggested to the majority leader that we should recruit some senators to serve in the capacity that these four men are now serving and helping us. They are great men, and I appreciate their help." Mansfield followed. "Russell Long has been a great deputy majority leader. He has stepped in at all times when called upon and has carried not only his share of the responsibilities, but also a good deal more." Few accepted Mansfield's affirmation of confidence at face value. Rumors of growing discontent from the White House and some Senate corners persisted. Russell had at least one friend willing to speak in his defense, albeit anonymously. The unnamed colleague told *Time* magazine in January: "We all love Mike, but many of us don't like the way he runs the Senate. With Long, you always know where he stands, because he's not afraid to sound off on issues."[5]

Indeed, Russell and Mansfield were an odd pair. Mansfield's manner was the opposite of Lyndon Johnson's prodding, cajoling, threatening leadership style. Recalled Johnson White House aide Mike Manatos: "Senator Mansfield would never take it upon himself to say to a senator, 'Now look, you have to do it this way,' or, 'This is going to be our party position.' . . . If he were asked for his view, he would give it to them, but he never tried to force anything on them." Russell, meanwhile, reveled in the Senate's internecine warfare. He traded votes, even his Senate desk, to win. Often, he abandoned his party and his president to chart his own course. Nonetheless, when an issue captured his imagination, the Senate offered no equal in ferocity or tenacity. It mattered not to Russell if he exasperated or offended his adversaries, said former aide Wayne Thevenot. "It mattered only to the extent of worrying about how he was going to garner his votes. As far as the idea of carrying on an unpopular fight, I never saw it bother him in the least. Losing didn't crush him. He could carry on a battle for its own intrinsic value, knowing he was going to lose."[6]

While often at odds with his president, Russell was ferociously supportive of Lyndon Johnson's decision to pour American men and resources into winning the Vietnam War. Although he had opposed initial American military involvement in Southeast Asia in the mid-1950s, Russell consistently supported Johnson's escalation of the war. Even as the president misled Congress about the nature of a supposed unprovoked attack on an American destroyer in the Gulf of Tonkin in August 1964, Russell expressed full faith in Johnson's judgment and veracity. Johnson used the Gulf incident to extract overwhelming congressional approval to expand the conflict. Facts of his duplicity were not exposed until Russell and virtually every member of Congress handed Johnson military carte blanche. "Delay would be interpreted by our enemies as a sign of weakness," Russell said prior to the Senate's vote of eighty-eight to two. "The president may find it necessary to act before it is too late." A year later, in July 1965, Johnson deliberated whether to increase American forces in Vietnam from 75,000 to 125,000. At a congressional leadership meeting,

Russell urged Johnson to plunge ahead. In his memoirs, Johnson recalled that Russell advised him that the choices were to "put in more men or take a whipping."[7]

In January 1966, when almost one hundred members of Congress begged Johnson to extend his thirty-seven day moratorium on bombing raids into North Vietnam, Russell was a five-star hawk. "I urge the president to make ever greater efforts to carry the battle to the enemy in every way we can. If these views make me a hawk instead of a dove, I have no argument. There is much fighting ahead if there is to be a dove of peace in Saigon and the fighting will have to be carried out by the hawks. " During televised Foreign Relations Committee hearings on the war in February, Russell's unabashed fervor for the war made him an instant celebrity. "Twenty million Americans have now discovered the moonface and klaxon voice of the Senate Democratic whip," *Washington Evening Star* columnist Mary McGrory wrote. "Long brought all the serenity and reflectiveness of an American Legion convention to the caucus room. He wrapped himself in Old Glory like a beach towel. Spasmodic in attendance, he made his fitful presence felt. . . . Among the doves, the hawks and the soul-searchers on the committee, Long was a screaming eagle."[8]

For more than two years, Russell was Johnson's most reliable defender on the Senate Foreign Relations Committee. Chaired by war critic J. William Fulbright of Arkansas, the panel was dominated by liberal war opponents. Now, after ten years on the committee, weary of fighting for foreign aid cuts, Russell was again isolated on another issue. "And here was the war getting more unpopular all the time," Russell recalled. "I felt it my duty to help the president, because I thought he was right about it. But that's something I didn't need to be in the position of defending—an unpopular war. It was getting more unpopular all the time. So, well, I thought, hell, this thing is an utter liability."[9]

Fed up with the burdens, Russell went to Senator Gale McGee of Wyoming, a war supporter who sat on the Senate Commerce, Science, and Transportation Committee. Russell offered a trade, proposing that he and McGee swap committee assignments. To his surprise, McGee readily agreed. "I think most of those Democrats were delighted to see that," Russell said, "so I just went out and lined up the votes." By the time an angry Lyndon Johnson learned of the deal, it was too late to dissuade Russell. The Democratic Steering Committee had already approved it. While no longer a Foreign Relations member, Russell continued vocally supporting Johnson. In April, he told the Louisiana Press Association that apprehensions of Chinese involvement in the war should not influence

American resolve. "If we are going to let the fear of Red China dominate our policy in Southeast Asia, then we might as well run down the Stars and Stripes and run up the white flag of surrender."[10]

While he backed Johnson in Vietnam, Russell was predictably far from supportive on the conflict's economic consequences. As interest rates and inflation edged up, Russell likewise concluded the rising rates were leading the nation toward recession. In a rare public criticism, he asked Johnson for "the benefit of his leadership" to reverse the trend, which he also blamed on rampant corporate spending. To reverse the trend, Russell proposed a one-year suspension of the investment tax credit, an idea that even Johnson later embraced. In August, Russell assailed the Federal Reserve Board, which set interest rates, charging that its members acted "like the mischievous son of a rich man." Russell later attacked the nation's banks for the unfair profit taking that resulted from the high interest rates. To a group of bankers in New Orleans, Russell boldly proposed voluntary price and profit controls. "This is a bad way to finance a war. The money lenders are enjoying their highest rates in forty-five years. . . . None of us should run up prices beyond what is fair and contribute to inflation."[11]

Despite his public defense of the war, Russell increasingly confined his legislative activism to his most influential domain, the Finance Committee. A potentially powerful and influential panel, under Chairman Harry Byrd the committee was moribund. Conservative and frugal, Byrd used the committee to contain government spending. The committee had only two staff members. The stingy chairman preferred to save money by relying on the Treasury Department and the Joint Committee on Taxation for his information. During his years as chairman, Byrd relinquished much of his committee's influence on tax policy to the White House and the House Ways and Means Committee. When Russell took the reins, he resolved to reestablish the committee as a powerful force. First, he persuaded the Senate to expand the committee's staff from two to fifteen. "If you're going to be an activist committee," he later explained, "you need a staff to help you both draft legislation and help you come up with ideas." Next, Russell used his new platform to generate a flurry of legislative proposals and ideas.[12]

Russell quickly moved to put his own activist imprint on the committee. The Finance Committee chairman was now a man with a philosophy of government radically and diametrically opposed to that of his predecessor. Russell had sought the committee spot in 1953 because of his devotion to expanding social security and other social welfare programs for the elderly and the handicapped. Now, as chairman and assistant Democratic leader, he was poised to wield the kind of influence about which he once could only have dreamed.

Shortly after assuming the chairmanship, Russell flexed his populist muscles, turning his long-standing hostility toward corporate monopolies into an attack on the pharmaceutical industry. Russell lambasted five drug companies who he said formed a "worldwide cartel" to fix prices on broad-spectrum antibiotics at "identical, grossly inflated, and unconscionably high" levels. He filled twenty pages of the *Congressional Record* with documents supporting his allegations. Exhibiting impressive foresight, Russell suggested that drugs sold under Medicare should be purchased under their generic names, rather than the more costly trade designations. Although his idea went nowhere at the time, it was hailed as a momentous reform when it eventually became an accepted practice. Russell next cast his eyes on a bill allowing patents to be awarded to companies who developed inventions using government research money. He called the bill a "billion dollar patent grab" that "does more violence to the rights and interests" of the American public "than any other measure we have considered in my seventeen years in the Senate." Russell vainly fought the bill with his usual gusto, charging "it would put patents worth billions in the hands of a few large corporations."[13]

If Russell's first year as chairman was any indication, the Senate was in for a shock. With a large and professional staff and Russell's unique brand of activism, legislative initiatives would soon pour forth. Sometimes strident and usually obstinate, Russell was turning the Finance Committee upside down. The Senate, too, was in for the same fate. Indeed, his most fractious and controversial Senate session was yet to come. As his colleagues soon learned, Russell had his own ideas about government. They did not involve rubber-stamping the House Ways and Means Committee.

* * *

Tennessee senator Albert Gore was one of the first members of Congress to decry the influence of special interest money in presidential elections. Russell, for one, agreed with Gore. After his Tennessee colleague's 1956 investigation into the influence of special interest money in presidential politics, Russell concluded that presidential campaign finance laws needed rewriting. Like Gore, Russell believed these interests—from whom candidates accepted much of their funding—threatened to eclipse the influence of contributions from average citizens. Under federal laws, there was little to compel candidates to disclose the sources of their money, much less how they spent it. For decades, critics clamored for reform, with no result—until Russell seized the issue.

Although the White House submitted its own campaign reform proposal to Congress in 1966—a program of tax deductions for contributions to encourage greater individual participation—Russell had a different idea. He dreamed of a federally financed presidential campaign fund permitting taxpayers to check a box on their income tax forms directing the government to spend one dollar for presidential campaigns. Money from the fund would be equally distributed to candidates of any major party. In August, Russell held Finance Committee hearings on a version of this idea. By October, he refined his proposal. During the session's closing days, as the Senate debated the Foreign Investors Tax Act, Russell made his move. He offered his plan as an amendment to the bill. It was a nongermane amendment, but as the bill's floor manager, Russell had allowed so many senators to adorn the legislation with pet projects that it became known as the "Christmas Tree Bill." One more irrelevant ornament made little difference.

When the Senate narrowly voted, thirty-nine to thirty-three, to adopt the amendment, even Russell was surprised. He was further astonished when the House Ways and Means Committee agreed to the proposal with one minor alteration. "Long's plan skipped through Congress like a flat stone across a choppy pond—with everyone, including Long himself, expecting it to disappear from sight the next time it touched down," *Business Week* remarked. Despite its easy sailing, not everyone in Congress admired the proposal as much as Russell. Republicans, who historically had no difficulty raising huge sums of money for presidential campaigns, expressed little interest in helping to fund Democratic presidential campaigns. Several senators—chiefly Gore, Robert Kennedy of New York, and Delaware Republican John Williams—favored reform. But they regarded Russell's plan as nothing of the sort. Although he voted for the plan in committee, Gore believed that Russell's program failed to require full disclosure of campaign receipts and expenditures. As senators prepared to leave Washington on the session's final day, Gore threatened to filibuster the Foreign Investors Tax Bill unless Russell agreed to remove his campaign finance proposal.[14]

Russell viewed Gore's opposition as pure jealousy. While he had drawn attention to the problem, Russell said, Gore "didn't even have a bill pending there. He just had this investigation and I guess he just felt that was his turf. And my reaction was, Well, many times people felt that something's their turf because they had been there. But that don't mean they *own* the turf." As for Williams and Kennedy, Russell believed that their opposition stemmed simply from abhorrence of Lyndon Johnson. "John Williams made a pretty good job of playing to Gore's pride of authorship," Russell recalled, adding Williams "had a lot of them thinking that this was a measure to re-elect Lyndon Johnson."[15]

Desperate to pass the tax bill and adjourn the Senate for the year, Mansfield implored Russell to compromise with Gore and end the filibuster threat. Russell stubbornly refused. It was, he said, "the only time [Mansfield] ever told me he was calling on me as a majority leader speaking to the whip to support him on a matter." On this issue, Russell refused to yield. He had come too far to concede defeat on victory's threshold. "I thought it was the most useful thing I'd done in my Senate career." Standing firm, Russell challenged Mansfield to seek advice from President Johnson, who was on a trip to Australia. He would surrender to Gore only if so instructed by Johnson, as Russell recalled:

> So we called up the president and had to wake him up. And Mike said, "Get him up! Get him up! This is important. We got to talk to him." I know the president said, "Well, I guess you know what time it is out here?" I said, "I know, Mr. President, but we have got to have your advice about this matter." So [he said], "Wait a minute while I put some water on my face." So, he comes back to the telephone and he said, "Mike, in the brief time available to me, I've been thinking about this. I really don't think the people of the United States would approve of what Albert Gore is doing." . . . He said, "I think if you'll stand your ground, you'll win. I just don't think you ought to cave in to it." So, Mike said, "O.K., I'll go along with you."[16]

With Mansfield now firmly in Russell's corner, Gore knew that he could not win. He reluctantly dropped his filibuster threat. Johnson later signed the bill. Far from unconditional surrender, however, Gore vowed to attack again in 1967. In April, as promised, he was back. Opening the challenge on the first day of debate over Russell's proposal to repeal the investment tax credit, Gore sounded a hostile note. "We need many things by way of election reform," Gore told the Senate. "But what does the law sponsored by the Senator from Louisiana do? It makes conditions worse. It does not inhibit present practices at all; it merely adds to the slush fund an estimated sixty million dollars from the public purse." Senator Robert Kennedy concurred. "I believe that if you have created a monster that is worse than what existed before, you should destroy the monster." When Kennedy suggested that the national political parties might withhold funds from states whose leaders failed to deliver their delegates at the national convention, Russell scoffed. Anyone using those tactics, he replied, "would end up in the penitentiary." Russell sarcastically suggested that Kennedy's forces were only "interested in preserving the power of great wealth."[17]

During ten days of fierce debate, Russell made several concessions. He agreed to Connecticut senator Abraham Ribicoff's amendment to restrict the fund to certain expenditures and prohibit spending on election-day activities like paying poll watchers and transporting voters. Next, Russell beefed up the bill with an amendment providing fines and possible imprisonment for willful misuse of funds received under the act. When Maryland's Joseph Tydings proposed cutting the fund in half, allowing taxpayers to contribute only fifty cents, instead of a dollar, the Senate went along by a narrow margin of forty-seven to forty-five. None of these reforms satisfied Gore, who would settle for nothing short of total repeal. On April 13, Gore offered a perfecting amendment to abolish Russell's program on July 1. The Senate narrowly went along, forty-eight to forty-two.

As usual, Russell was unruffled. He later told reporters that the defeat was "a small skirmish in a long war." Those who knew him understood the military reference was not hyperbole. While the White House and other senators looked forward to quick action on the investment tax credit repeal, Russell never thought of conceding to Gore, Kennedy, and Williams. "I'm going to win this fight and they had better understand that. I've got a whole warehouse full of tools to use. They haven't won the game. They're just six points ahead at the half."[18]

As the Senate resumed debate over the investment tax credit repeal, Russell counterattacked. He returned a week later with an amendment he called the "Honest Election Act of 1967." While containing different features from his original legislation, it was largely indistinguishable from the 1966 bill. "I am satisfied that the longer this matter is dragged out, the stronger my case will be," Russell told Williams and the Senate on April 19. "I am happy that the word is beginning to get to the American people about the Honest Election Act of 1967, and that we are fighting in the United States Senate to see that every mother's son can run for president, even if he is not a millionaire." This time, Russell had support from two erstwhile opponents—Alabama Democrats Lister Hill and John Sparkman. Drawn to the favorable treatment the bill promised for independent candidate Alabama governor George Wallace, Hill and Sparkman voted with Russell. Several senators who missed the previous vote were also now in

Russell's camp. When the votes were tallied, Russell had won round two. The Senate accepted his amendment, forty-six to forty-two.[19]

This legislative ping-pong game exasperated majority leader Mike Mansfield. Russell's and Gore's obstinacy had tied up the Senate for days. They had delayed action on an important tax bill, while doggedly pursuing the presidential campaign bill. Minutes after the vote, Mansfield addressed the Senate with a reproving eye to Russell and Gore. "We have, in my opinion, been acting like school boys and prima donnas." It was past time, Mansfield said, "that we act like senators of the United States, that we get down to bedrock and apply ourselves to the fundamental question" of the investment tax credit. Mansfield quickly moved to return the tax credit bill to the Finance Committee, asking the Senate to order the committee to report back the bill stripped of all floor amendments. Mansfield's motion also directed the Finance Committee to draft language repealing Russell's campaign fund. Mansfield assured Russell that he supported his reform efforts, and his motion also instructed the Finance Committee to report a new election financing bill within six weeks. Russell balked. Weeks earlier, he agreed to speed consideration of the tax bill by consenting to Mansfield's recommittal motion. But, Russell professed, "I did not know he had this particular motion in mind." Mansfield, he said, never mentioned mandating repeal of the campaign fund. "I cannot agree to repeal what I think is the best thing we did in the whole Congress," Russell said. "Call it pride of authorship; call it anything one wants to; but having fought for it for one week, and then for two more weeks, and won the battle, I cannot agree to this proposal." Setting the stage for a test of wills with his leader, Russell threatened a filibuster. Of Mansfield, he later told reporters, "He's not the only man who can be stubborn."[20]

Days later, however, Russell surrendered. "Our differences of opinion," he explained, had been the result of "a failure of communications for which I freely accept a major share of the blame." If Mansfield insisted on his motion again, Russell said, "I shall vote for it." The issue appeared temporarily resolved on April 25 as the Senate voted sixty-four to twenty-two to return the bill to the Finance Committee. Then, Russell sprang his surprise.[21]

With stunning speed, Russell immediately reported from the Finance Committee the tax credit repeal the Senate had required. But then, he moved to strike Mansfield's language repealing his campaign finance law. "People have asked me about the dark rumors that I will let the investment credit bill die before giving up the campaign fund," Russell ominously told reporters. "These are no rumors. I've promised to do this on the

Senate floor. If I fail to win . . . we'll go at it again. I said I'd kill the whole bill if my amendment fails and I'll ask the help of my friends on the House conference committee. If necessary, I'll urge the president to veto the bill." Acting quickly to head off Russell's scheme, Senator Williams moved to table Russell's amendment. When the Senate rejected Williams' motion, senators mercifully agreed to temporarily set aside the tax bill to consider other legislation. [22]

On May 2, the Senate turned again to Russell's amendment. This time, the seesaw battle leaned in Gore's favor. The Senate rejected Russell's attempt to strike the repeal language from the tax bill, forty-six to fifty-two. Like a punch-drunk fighter, Russell's passion for the fight was not dampened by the blow. "I enjoy a good fight when it starts to draw blood," he declared, "even when it is my own." Asked by reporters if he was persisting at the urging of the president, Russell replied: "Well, that's like the fellow facing the charge of maiming. The judge said, 'You couldn't have done all that violence without some evil presence pushing you on.' The man said, 'Yes, that was true.' He said a voice told him to twist the victim's ear, punch his nose and stomp his head. But the man told the judge, 'When I got to choking him—that was my own idea.' "[23]

Few senators found humor in Russell's antics. To many, he was taxing the Senate's patience. On May 3, the frustrations and anger boiled over. "Three weeks ago I complimented the gentleman from Louisiana for his tenacity," said Ohio's Frank Lausche as he pointed a bony finger at Russell. "I now change tenacity to obstinacy. What I thought was a virtue three weeks ago, I now describe as a vice today." Stuart Symington of Missouri agreed. "Pretty soon he is going to have to worry about his duties. As assistant majority leader of the Senate, it is more than his right, it is his duty to see that the Senate gets back to work." Hugh Scott of Pennsylvania rose to declare that "the proceedings here have humiliated the Senate. They have humiliated the country. I think we have become a laughing stock." Red-faced, Russell leapt to his feet, shouting: "The senator insulted me!" Russell demanded the chair silence Scott, who shouted back, "Don't you threaten me!" Responding to this wave of criticism, Russell was unbowed. He reminded his weary colleagues that the Senate voted three times to repeal his bill and twice in favor. "That's only five innings. Any standard ball game has nine innings."[24]

The extent to which Russell was resolved to force his bill on the Senate was illustrated in an incident reported in the *Detroit News*. At a key moment in the debate, Russell wanted the floor and approached North Dakota's George McGovern, the presiding officer at the time. "Recognize me next," Russell said. "I can't," McGovern replied. "I've promised to recognize (John) Williams." After several minutes of argument, Russell gave up and stalked off to the cloakroom, just off the floor. Spotting freshman Walter Mondale of Minnesota, he said, "Go tell McGovern that he has an important phone call and then you take the chair and recognize me next." Mondale innocently did as Russell instructed. As McGovern arrived in the cloakroom, he spotted Russell, grinning. "Where's my phone call?" McGovern asked. "You didn't have one," Russell replied. "I just had to get you out of the chair."[25]

"What Long forgot in a month of strange and furious antics," the reporter observed, "is something the Senate never forgets. It is its credo that the Senate is a body of gentlemen who are polite in public debate, keep their word even at the pain of personal discomfort and keep their infighting behind the scenes. Long violated every rule." Russell saw the matter differently. "I just felt at that time I was fighting John Williams, who had a way of stopping at nothing to have his way. In fact, I think he sort of made it a point to mislead people to his advantage."[26]

On May 9, the Senate mercifully ended debate on Russell's amendment. Senators first voted forty-nine to forty-eight to reject a Gore-Williams amendment to repeal the 1966 bill on September 15. Then, by ninety-three to four, the Senate adopted majority leader Mansfield's amendment to put the fund in suspended animation. Mansfield's compromise prohibited appropriations and disbursement of the fund until Congress adopted guidelines governing its distribution. Russell, who might have claimed some semblance of victory in the Senate's decision, was bitter. He indignantly suggested he might not support the bill in conference. Then, in a moment of melancholy humor, he offered this graphic description of his battle-scarred condition, telling the Senate, "I'm standing here with blood dripping down into my boots so bad that you can't tell my shirt from my necktie."[27]

In many respects, the Senate was emotionally spent from Russell's five-week war with Gore, Williams, and Kennedy. Criticism from the press and his colleagues was severe. *Washington Star* columnist Mary McGrory said that Russell "has been conveying the impression that he thinks the Senate is not a club but a frontier barroom, where the man with the most chips and the loudest voice can lick any man in the house. The Senate last week put him in his place." Conservative columnist James J. Kilpatrick said that Russell "seemed incapable of accepting defeat with grace."[28]

By the time the dust had cleared, Russell decided that Mansfield's compromise was not the defeat he had first supposed. "Having had a

chance to study it, I find it's not as bad an amendment as I thought it was,"
he said several days later on NBC's "Today Show," adding "everybody
agrees it would be well to nail it down with some specific guidelines."
When a reporter later asked what happened to the man who talked about
blood in his boots, Russell blithely replied: "Well, I just poured the blood
out of my boot and put it back on again. I'm better off than I thought."[29]

Despite all the criticism he received, Russell refused to concede that his
exuberance to pass the campaign bill was excessive. "I've made a few
people mad before," he said on CBS's "Face the Nation," "and if senators
voted for me to be the assistant majority leader not knowing that I am the
sort of never-say-die type fighter when I think I'm right about something,
they'll have to take another look." While Russell undoubtedly made enemies, the Presidential Campaign Fund, later hailed as a major reform,
might have never become reality without his dogged perseverance. As for
critics like Gore, Williams, and Kennedy, aide Charles McBride observed,
"What was important for him politically was to win and he didn't care
whether he pissed off Robert Kennedy. . . . He really didn't care about
these people, and he loved to twit them."[30]

Russell's presidential campaign fund was not revived until after the 1968
presidential election, in which well-financed Republican Richard Nixon
narrowly defeated Democrat Hubert Humphrey and his meager war chest.
"[Humphrey] ran a good race and came close the way it was, but he did it
with little money—very, very little," Russell later said. "If he'd had the
benefit of the money that would have been available to him with that
campaign finance bill, that would have made the difference." Indeed, had
Congress followed Russell's lead earlier, Watergate might be known only
as a Washington, D.C., apartment complex.[31]

* * *

On a warm autumn afternoon, Russell left New Orleans for New York. As
he settled into his seat aboard the airplane, he discovered that his traveling
companion was someone he knew well—Orleans Parish district attorney
Jim Garrison. Garrison was a boisterous, capricious man with a politician's
keen instinct for what made news. As he and Russell eased comfortably
into a wide-ranging conversation, the discussion turned to an area of
intense interest for both men: the assassination of John F. Kennedy.

For years, Russell had harbored deep misgivings about the veracity of
the official government version of Kennedy's murder in Dallas on November 22, 1963. Appointed by President Lyndon Johnson, the Warren Com-

mission—chaired by Chief Justice Earl Warren—quickly "resolved" the case. It concluded that Lee Harvey Oswald—a former marine who once defected to the Soviet Union—fired exactly three shots from a bolt-action rifle from his perch in a sixth-floor window of the Texas School Book Depository building. One shot, the commission said, passed through Kennedy's neck, striking Texas governor John Connally in the chest and wrist. Another shot hit Kennedy in the head. The next shot missed. Despite a maelstrom of evidence and suspicions to the contrary, the commission dismissed the possibility that Kennedy's death was the result of a conspiracy involving persons other than Oswald. Oswald, commissioners concluded, acted alone.

That verdict troubled Russell. He and other skeptics doubted that Oswald, using a clumsy bolt-action rifle with an off-center scope, could have fired three shots—two with deadly accuracy—at a moving target one hundred yards away. Regardless of what a blue-ribbon commission said to the contrary, Russell believed that Oswald was not a lone gunman. Garrison was enraptured by the strength and sound reasoning of Russell's theory. He pushed Russell to speculate about who might have had a motive to kill Kennedy. "I wouldn't worry about a motive," he advised Garrison, "until I find out if there appeared to be more than one gunman." Like Russell, Garrison had harbored suspicions about a conspiracy. In fact, days after Kennedy's death, Garrison had questioned three suspects. Later, he turned the men over to the FBI and the Secret Service, both of which interrogated them before concluding that they played no role in the assassination. As Garrison absorbed Russell's qualms about the Warren Commission Report, his own doubts about the official government story were revived.[32]

While there was yet no conclusive evidence of a conspiracy, even a casual observer was compelled to admit that something very suspicious had happened in New Orleans shortly before Kennedy's death. Dozens of witnesses reported that they had seen Oswald, a New Orleans native, with two other men in Clinton, Louisiana, months before the assassination. Another witness claimed to have overheard Oswald discussing a plot to kill Kennedy with the same two men. With such reports floating about, Garrison needed little encouragement from Russell to launch his own investigation.

Three months later, on February 17, 1967, reports of Garrison's inquest broke. News of his sensational activities sparked headlines around the world. For the first time since the Warren Commission's report, a

U.S. law enforcement officer was investigating evidence that the commission had ignored or failed to uncover. Within days, any of Garrison's reluctance to discuss his case was overwhelmed by his lust for the global media attention suddenly heaped upon him. He brazenly declared to reporters that he had "positively solved the assassination of President John F. Kennedy." Furthermore, he credited Russell as the impetus for the investigation, describing the conversation in which Russell talked of "the incongruity of getting all those shots off in the sequence concluded by the Warren report . . . that made me raise questions of my own."[33]

The Garrison probe raised chilling questions about the confluence of shadowy characters in New Orleans who had ample motive and opportunity to plot and carry out the assassination of President Kennedy. In the early 1960s, New Orleans was a hotbed of opposition to communist Cuban leader Fidel Castro. Furthermore, the city was home to some right-wing elements who hated Kennedy for his refusal to support American military and CIA efforts to oust or assassinate Castro. Carlos Marcello, kingpin of the Gulf coast Mafia, detested the president and his brother, Attorney General Robert Kennedy, for their strident attacks on organized crime. A New Orleans resident, Marcello held particular contempt for the Kennedys after his temporary deportation to Guatemala in 1961. There were other powerful groups and interests in Louisiana for whom Kennedy's death would be an economic and political blessing. Oilmen hated Kennedy for his support of reforms that would repeal the oil depletion allowance, one of the industry's most prized and lucrative tax deductions. Radical segregationists despised Kennedy's efforts towards integration. It should come as no surprise, therefore, that the man later accused of the president's murder spent much of the preceding summer in New Orleans, where he freely associated with several of these nefarious elements.

Garrison's investigation initially focused on one of Oswald's alleged associates, David Ferrie, a former commercial airline pilot fired after his arrest on charges of sodomizing a young boy. Even before his name surfaced in the press, Ferrie had contacted the *New Orleans States-Item* to complain that Garrison had unjustly targeted him as a getaway pilot for Kennedy's assassins. That Ferrie—one of three men Garrison questioned only days after Kennedy's deaths—was in federal court in New Orleans at the time of the assassination did little to quell Garrison's interest in him. Five days after news of the investigation broke, Ferrie's nude body was found in his New Orleans apartment. Two undated letters, which appeared to be suicide notes, were found with Ferrie's effects. Garrison suspected that Ferrie had taken his life. The coroner said that it was neither suicide nor murder, but a brain hemorrhage. Even so, Garrison insisted that Ferrie had killed himself and declared his dead suspect "one of history's most important individuals."

When reporters descended on Russell for comment, he obliged, offering statements of support for Garrison that only fed the media frenzy. "If he turns up evidence of a conspiracy, then it could lead to all sorts of possibilities, including one that Oswald was the fall guy and the real killer is still free." Garrison's problem, Russell astutely observed for reporters, "is that the trail has grown cold since 1963. He may now be looking hard for other witnesses to corroborate the statements. He can either come up with a pretty good case that will make the Warren Commission look pretty bad, or he could end up looking pretty foolish. More than likely it will be a third alternative: He may come up with legitimate evidence that will be hard to prove but that many people will say, 'Yes, that's very possible.' " Russell suggested that the federal government assist Garrison by offering "a reward substantially greater than the FBI has the power to pay, in order to loosen the lips of some people who might, on that basis, be willing to volunteer something that they know about this matter."[34]

Garrison needed no help from the FBI. On the day of Ferrie's funeral, he announced the arrest of his first alleged coconspirator. Garrison fingered Clay L. Shaw, a respected local businessman who had been managing director of the International Trade Mart in New Orleans for nearly twenty years. The evidence against Shaw was flimsy, if nonexistent. Nonetheless, Garrison eagerly fed his suspect to a hysterical horde of worldwide news media who descended on New Orleans. In fact, some concluded that Garrison was much more interested in media attention than in the facts of his feeble case against one of New Orleans's most prominent citizens. Short on hard evidence to implicate Shaw, Garrison revealed some of the unusual items that investigators had discovered in Shaw's home—a chain, whips, a black hood and cape and a black gown. While outraged friends explained that the peculiar regalia was part of his Mardi Gras costume, the motives behind Garrison's disclosure of Shaw's homosexuality were obvious, and odious.

Journalist Henry Hurt, who studied the case, concluded that Garrison had little or no evidence implicating Ferrie. "Most of what Garrison was saying—and he was spewing out thousands of words for public consumption, while coyly refusing to discuss his 'evidence' against Shaw—was indisputably rooted in the gross deficiencies of the Warren Commission. This, of course, was a welcome development for many commission critics who had been unable to attain a national forum for their findings and suspicions."[35]

Russell was among the critics who were delighted that someone—albeit the flamboyant Garrison—was finally scratching beneath the surface of what they considered a whitewash. To charges that Garrison invaded Shaw's privacy by disclosing the kinky discoveries in his home, Russell replied, "I don't think he's violated anybody's civil rights. He's just doing what a district attorney should do if he has reason to think that a very heinous crime has been committed in his jurisdiction." Russell seemed persuaded that Shaw was somehow involved in the assassination. He even accepted Garrison's bizarre theory that a series of numbers found in Oswald's papers were identical to those uncovered in Shaw's effects. The numbers, Garrison said, were a coded version of the telephone number of Jack Ruby, the Dallas nightclub owner who murdered Oswald days after Kennedy's death. "I think that you would say it was somewhat strange that those two men whom Garrison says were in conspiracy had that number listed in their papers," Russell told reporters.[36]

Russell even took his defense of Garrison to CBS's "Face the Nation," where he said he believed Garrison was hot on the trail of Kennedy's killers. Russell's questioners were fascinated by the account of his airplane conversation with Garrison. "I said that it never seemed to me that Oswald was that good a shot from any ninety yards away at a moving target," Russell told the panelists, "and, that I didn't think . . . that he had that good a rifle."[37]

Garrison's case against Shaw was simple: A man named Clay Bertrand was part of a conspiracy to kill Kennedy. Shaw's alias was Clay Bertrand, Garrison said. To bolster this theory, Garrison produced several witnesses. One said that he had attended a party in September 1963 where he overheard Oswald and Shaw discussing their plot to kill the president. The other witness, a heroin addict, testified that he once observed Shaw and Oswald talking at the New Orleans lakefront. Garrison also alleged that Shaw had CIA connections—a charge that was later confirmed by a 1977 CIA document outlining Shaw's intelligence connections. Garrison also produced six residents of Clinton, Louisiana, all of whom testified with remarkable consistency that they had observed three unusual men moving around their town in the summer of 1963. Each witness identified the men as Oswald, David Ferrie, and Clay Shaw. "This fresh evidence, never mentioned by the Warren Commission," journalist Henry Hurt wrote, "was Garrison's most valuable contribution to an understanding of Oswald's activities. It was virtually lost in the circus atmosphere that characterized the rest of the trial."[38]

When Shaw's case finally went to trial—not until January 1969—

Garrison could only prove that Shaw may have known Oswald. Proving that Shaw was part of Oswald's crime was more daunting. During the trial, Garrison rarely appeared in the courtroom. His assistants presented virtually nothing of substance linking Shaw to Kennedy's murder. On March 1, 1969, after only one ballot, the jury acquitted Shaw. Two days later, Garrison filed new charges, accusing Shaw of perjury. Five years later, while he continued to fend off Garrison's legal assaults, Shaw died of cancer.

Viewed by most as an innocent victim caught in Garrison's publicity machine, Shaw was pitied as much as Garrison was vilified. Said the *New Orleans States-Item*: "Mr. Garrison stands revealed for what he is: A man without principle who would pervert the legal process to his own ends." *The New York Times* described the entire trial as "one of the most disgraceful chapters in the history of American jurisprudence." As for Russell—the impetus and enthusiastic supporter of Garrison's probe—the press was virtually silent about his role.[39]

While Garrison raised serious doubts about important aspects of the Warren Commission's investigation and its conclusions, his contributions were overshadowed by his media-hungry persecution of Shaw. His subsequent vilification obscured the one important element of Kennedy's assassination he established—something of consequence to Kennedy's murder had happened in New Orleans just prior to November 22, 1963. To this day, the truth remains a mystery. "The only certainty, really," wrote investigative journalist Henry Hurt, "is the strong feeling that raucous, indomitable New Orleans very likely is the graveyard for the most significant clues to the mystery of the JFK assassination."[40]

For those who knew Russell, the Garrison affair and his strident behavior during the presidential campaign fund debate were troubling symptoms of a deeper, more complex problem. For almost ten years, Katherine and their two daughters had lived in Baton Rouge. Russell lived a bachelor's existence, absent the leavening family influence. More and more, his drinking companions and his staff were a substitute family. As Russell's behavior became less predictable, raised eyebrows turned to disapproving scowls.

22

THE DEFENSE
OF THOMAS DODD

$\mathcal{S}$ENATOR THOMAS DODD WAS A POWERFUL, imposing man. His chiseled countenance and silver mane lent him the air of a person Hollywood might cast for the role of senator. His resume was impeccable. A Yale Law School graduate, the Connecticut Democrat had been an FBI agent and a counsel at the Nuremberg Trials before his election to the House and his promotion to the Senate. He was a confidant and friend of Lyndon Johnson, so much so that the president almost tapped him as his running mate in 1964. He was renowned for his conservative foreign policy views and anticommunist fervor. In 1966, however, this dashing, influential man had one profound problem. He was the target of Washington's most feared investigative columnists, Drew Pearson and Jack Anderson.

For several reasons, Pearson never cared for Dodd. His friendship with FBI director J. Edgar Hoover and his avid support of the Vietnam War displeased the famed columnist. Nonetheless, it was Dodd's personal and financial dealings that attracted an incredible degree of scrutiny from Pearson and Anderson. For seventeen months, beginning in January 1966, the two men published 101 columns about Dodd, alleging a pattern of unethical conduct. In their early reporting, the columnists detailed Dodd's ties to Julius Klein, a Chicago public relations man with extensive West German accounts. Later, they focused on charges that Dodd used

$116,000 from his campaign account for personal expenses and had double billed the Senate and private organizations for travel expenses on numerous occasions. The bulk of their evidence was six thousand letters and documents that three former employees, aided by Dodd's office manager, purloined from his Senate office.

Dodd demanded an inquiry to clear his name. On June 22, 1966, the Senate Select Committee on Standards and Conduct, commonly known as the Ethics Committee, reluctantly began its first investigation since its creation in 1964. Chaired by the Senate's virtuous paragon, John Stennis of Mississippi, the committee concluded Dodd's relationship with Klein did not dictate Senate disciplinary action. Cleared of the first allegations, the cloud of financial misconduct remained. Again, Dodd demanded an Ethics Committee investigation. In March 1967, the ethics panel began its second round of hearings. With Stennis in charge, few doubted that Dodd, guilty or innocent, would receive an impartial hearing. Dodd's defense was simple. He told the Ethics Committee that his constituents knew he was not wealthy. Those who bought tickets to a series of testimonial dinners, Dodd said, did so knowing he might use the money for personal expenses. Despite the testimony of his former office manager to the contrary, Dodd denied having ordered his staff to double bill for his travel expenses. The double billings were simple bookkeeping errors, he said.

"My conscience is clear," Dodd declared. "I do not believe that anybody can look me in the eye and say I did wrong." The Ethics Committee did just that on April 27, when its members recommended that the Senate censure Dodd for "conduct which is contrary to accepted morals, derogates from the public trust expected of a Senator and tends to bring the Senate into dishonor and disrepute." Virtually unnoticed was that while the Senate had established a committee to investigate unethical and illegal conduct of senators, it had not yet adopted a formal code of ethics governing this conduct. In affect, Dodd was charged with violating ethics rules that did not exist.

As the committee released its damning report, and his situation appeared hopeless, Thomas Dodd suddenly felt the warm embrace of a friend who had rushed to his side with assistance and support. "As far as I'm concerned," Russell told the news media, "he has done nothing to deserve censure." Richard Nixon, Russell charged, "had a guy going around picking up his checks. At least Dodd gave them a meal for it. They didn't even get a cup of coffee from Nixon." Then, in an insult to the committee, which included such respected senators as Stennis, Mike Monroney of Oklahoma, Eugene McCarthy of Minnesota, and John Sherman Cooper of Kentucky, Russell wryly observed: "Half of that committee couldn't stand the investigation Senator Dodd went through."[1]

Why Russell rushed to Dodd's defense was certainly a question on the minds of most Senate watchers that day. Dodd had not asked for Russell's help. Whether he wanted it mattered little at the moment. A man in such desperate straits needed every friend he could find. For Russell, there were several reasons he volunteered. "He was loyal to his friends," former president Richard Nixon said, explaining that Dodd's case was "a prime example." While Russell and Dodd were not intimate comrades, Russell gratefully remembered his colleague's unwavering support during debate over his presidential campaign fund in 1966. Dodd had sided with Russell on every vote. Dodd had also voted for Russell for assistant Democratic leader when most New England Democrats favored Rhode Island's John Pastore.[2]

The major reason for Russell's curious behavior, however, seemed to rest partially in his instinctive affection for lost causes. The enormous odds against saving Dodd bothered him little. A friend's reputation was at risk. If no one would stand to defend Dodd, Russell believed he must. "I just felt that if you think a man's right, you think he's done no wrong, you just shouldn't stand idly by if he's your friend and you feel like he's being persecuted."[3]

It was more than simple quixotical lust. Russell always blanched when a colleague was charged with ethics violations, recalling the pain inflicted on his family during his father's 1929 impeachment trial. To Russell, Huey Long's enemies had not been concerned with alleged impeachable offenses. They were searching for ways to thwart the insurgent social and economic reforms that threatened Louisiana's existing power structure. To Charles McBride, then Russell's press secretary, the facts had little to do with Russell's enthusiasm for Dodd's defense. "I think what Long saw in the Dodd thing was . . . the impeachment trial of his father in the (Louisiana) Senate in 1929. And, he saw the thing to do was to be loyal to his friend, and he didn't at that point know beans about the charges." As Russell asserted during the 1954 censure trial of Senator Joseph McCarthy, censure might be improperly employed to silence or neutralize—instead of reprimand—and, therefore, must be carefully exercised. Like Russell, Dodd was a vehement anticommunist. Russell was not about to allow two liberal columnists to bring down a colleague over perceived ideological differences."[4]

Russell's offhand remarks about the Ethics Committee's integrity had been a mistake. Several days later he explained that reporters had quoted him out of context: "I did not then and I do not now say that any member of that committee that investigated Tom Dodd or any member of the United States Senate is guilty of any wrongdoing. I merely tried to point out that any man in public office who was submitted to the sort of thing that Tom Dodd was subjected to would have a tough job defending himself." Dodd, Russell said, was apparently "guilty of two great sins. First of all, he was too poor to run for the United States Senate. . . . In the second place, Tom Dodd was guilty of selecting some disloyal and treacherous employees."[5]

As the Senate prepared to consider the censure resolution in June, Russell exuded confidence. "Unless they have something that I don't know they have, we ought to win this thing going away," he bragged, predicting that sixty to ninety senators would vote against censure. Sometimes, it strangely seemed as if Dodd were an incidental character in the drama while Russell barreled his way through nine days of Senate debate. It was Russell, not Dodd, who circulated memorandums to all senators responding to the Ethics Committee report. When the debate finally commenced on the Senate floor, it was Russell, not Dodd, who did most of the talking.[6]

On June 13, Chairman Stennis opened floor proceedings, explaining that the committee based its charges against Dodd not on sporadic incidents of double billing or on personal use of political funds. Instead, Stennis said, the ethics sanctions were sought because "the practice happened over and over and over again. . . . It amounted to a course of conduct that was wrong on its face and therefore brought the Senate into disrepute." Later that day, as Vice Chairman Wallace Bennett expounded upon the charges, Russell interrupted more than once to question the committee's judgment in distinguishing between personal and political expenditures. Russell argued that country club dues and bills, wedding presents to constituents, and tickets to football games might be considered political expenses. "If you want to, you can excuse every expenditure a senator makes," Bennett replied. "In the end somebody has to make a subjective" judgment.[7]

For days, Russell paced the aisles, waving his arms as he slammed the committee report while a beleaguered Dodd and his lawyer looked on helplessly. At one point, while he questioned Dodd about a double-billed 1961 trip to Philadelphia, Russell tried to administer the oath to his friend. Dodd refused to be sworn in, shoving hands into his pockets. "I took the oath when I came here," he answered. After one morning session, when Dodd left the Senate chamber to pose for photographers with his lawyers, Russell stood by his side. When a reporter asked for his thoughts on Ethics chairman Stennis, Dodd began to answer, but was stopped by

Russell. "Don't answer that," he instructed Dodd, who obediently fell silent.[8]

Essentially, Russell's defense was that the Connecticut senator had actually spent $150,000 of his own money for political activities. He was, therefore, entitled to reimbursement by his campaign committee. "If testimonial dinners are immoral now, they were not so in 1961, 1963 or 1965," Dodd said in a letter to his colleagues in May. "They have been a traditional part of the political life of our nation for at least 100 years." During the debate, Russell recalled that his uncle Earl once counseled a friend to wear old clothes when he campaigned in rural areas. "And Uncle Earl added, 'Furthermore, while you are at it, take that rubber band off that big wad of green bills you got there, and spread some dough around among those country folks. Otherwise, you're going to get beat.' Mr. President," Russell concluded to the laughter of colleagues, "that man had legitimate campaign expenses."[9]

As for the double billing, Russell blamed sloppy bookkeeping and the treason of Dodd's former employees. "It is evidence achieved by corrupt methods," Russell told the Senate. "It was stolen. It is the fruit of the poisonous tree," he said, extending his arms like the branches of a willow tree. "We know that Adam was told not to eat the poisonous fruit. He disdained to do so. But there was a serpent on that poisonous tree. This serpent is Jack Anderson trying to get us to eat the fruit of that poisonous tree. If I might be permitted to use a metaphor, Drew Pearson is the crocodile and Jack Anderson is the serpent on the poisonous tree. He has a poisonous tree acquired at great effort. He wants us to consume the fruit of that tree and destroy a senator as a result of a corrupt plot and theft and burglary and stealing and lying and all of the corruption which constitutes the poisonous tree." Russell was offended with what he considered the Ethics Committee's selective application of Senate ethical standards. For example, when Dodd revealed he had not filed reimbursement vouchers for twenty-one round trips from Washington to Connecticut, this evidence was dismissed as haphazard accounting. Yet, when he double billed on seven other occasions, the committee disregarded Dodd's established pattern of careless bookkeeping and charged him with *purposely* filing for double reimbursement.[10]

On June 23, the drama climaxed. The Senate censured Dodd, ninety-two to five, for using political funds for personal benefit. Three senators sided with Russell and Dodd: John Tower of Texas; Dodd's Connecticut colleague, Abraham Ribicoff; and Strom Thurmond of South Carolina. The outcome was no surprise to Russell or Dodd, as the Senate had already overwhelmingly rejected Russell's substitute resolution that would have simply admonished Dodd to avoid any conduct "which might be construed" as derogatory to the ethics of a senator. Next, Dodd achieved a minor victory. Senators narrowly rejected the committee's double-billing charge, fifty-one to forty-five.

After the vote, Dodd humbly took the Senate floor to thank the senators who helped him, particularly Tower, and Massachusetts senator Edward Brooke, who voted for censure with serious reservations. In a peculiar way, he also acknowledged Russell: "I would be remiss, I think, if I failed to thank the Senator from Louisiana, who volunteered to assist me, and did substantially, I felt, within his way of doing things." Indeed, there was other evidence suggesting that Dodd was less than delighted with Russell's assistance. During the proceedings, when asked by reporters if he was satisfied with Russell's defense, Dodd replied quizzically, "Satisfied?" Then he added, "He's just another senator and he has the same right to speak as anyone else."[11]

Of small consolation to Dodd and Russell was the Senate's adoption the following year of its first formal code of conduct. Included in that code was a curious provision permitting senators to accept contributions from fundraising events for personal use, one of the very deeds for which it had censured Dodd. As for Dodd, Connecticut voters rejected his reelection bid in 1970. Against two challengers, he received a scant 24 percent of the vote.

To many, the episode produced two casualties: Dodd and Russell. "In the cloak rooms and oases around the chamber there is a shaking of heads and general agreement that Long damaged his standing with the establishment to the extent that his future in the job of majority whip is in jeopardy," Associated Press reporter Jack Bell wrote. "If he had presented a quiet, orderly defense of Dodd, there probably would have been a great deal of admiration in the Senate for Long's efforts to help a fellow senator in distress. But the majority verdict of those willing to discuss the matter even privately is that Long has hurt, rather than helped Dodd by his melodramatic tactics." In particular, Russell knew that Senate majority leader Mike Mansfield was particularly displeased over his conduct during the Dodd case. "I think Mike felt that I was doing a disservice to the leadership at that point," Russell confessed.[12]

A *Baton Rouge Morning Advocate* reporter, Jim Talbert, who followed the proceedings, was more generous in his assessment. Although concluding that Russell prolonged the Dodd case, Talbert insisted that he "was out to see that Dodd got as fair a trial as he could get and forced the Senate to hear and re-hear all the facts of the matter, which the body would probably have preferred to push under the rug silently and swiftly."[13]

Russell scoffed at suggestions that his defense of Dodd had injured him politically. "If I voted for a man for the whip's job and I found that he fought like hell for a friend and had the hide of a rhino, then that's the kind of man I'd want there." Years later, as he reviewed his Senate career, Russell acknowledged the political damage inflicted by the Dodd case. "You ask me to name something I did where I'm confident I did what was right and hurt myself doing it, well, I guess that would top the list."[14]

23

IF YOU'RE GOING TO START A FILIBUSTER

$\mathcal{R}$USSELL HAD NOW BEEN in a bewildering vortex of conflict and controversy for nearly three years. Since his ascension to whip, he had usurped and quarreled with his majority leader. To the consternation of Senate liberals, he often abandoned his party on civil rights and various other social issues. His unrelenting determination to enact his presidential campaign fund had maddened more than a few colleagues. Most recently, the brash way he had defended Senator Thomas Dodd exacerbated the growing doubts about Russell's judgment and leadership. Soon, to salvage his position, he must prove that he had not fumbled away his usefulness. He desperately needed a legislative triumph, a smashing victory to inspire new respect and restore his faded esteem. By November, Lyndon Johnson handed him such an opportunity.

The Social Security and Welfare legislation Johnson sent to Congress in 1967 was the most significant expansion of the social security system ever. Its scope was staggering and ambitious, its centerpiece a monthly 15 percent increase in old-age benefits. To finance this, Johnson proposed raising payroll taxes, as well as expanding the tax base to increase the amount of earnings subject to the payroll tax. Moreover, the president wanted Medicare enlarged to cover 1.5 million disabled people under sixty-five. He also asked Congress to require that all state welfare departments boost cash payments to the elderly. Finally, Johnson recommended reducing taxes on three million older people and completely exempting half a million more.

By the time it reached the Senate, the House disassembled the White House bill. House members shaved the social security benefits hike from 15 percent to 12.5 percent. They purged the Medicare expansion for the disabled, canceled tax breaks for the elderly, and removed provisions increasing welfare payments. Even more factious was a provision the House added to the bill, a mandatory work-training program for all recipients of Aid to Families with Dependent Children. The White House and Senate liberals howled in protest, arguing that the program would drive one million mothers with preschoolers from their homes. The mothers, they argued, would be forced to place these children in federally subsidized day care while they worked or received job training. The program, complained New York's senator Robert Kennedy, amounted to "venting our own frustration in a measure punishing the poor because they are there and we have been unable to do anything about them." In fact, Kennedy wanted a bill even more abundant than the munificent White House plan—a 20 percent benefits increase and a larger payroll tax hike than Johnson proposed.[1]

With the bill gutted by the House, the spotlight focused on Russell, who put his own imprint on the legislation. Undoubtedly, from Johnson's perspective, his results were mixed. By now, it was clear the White House proposal had been only a wish list, a negotiable starting point. Even so, Russell was determined to get Johnson the best deal possible in the Senate. Under Russell's guidance, the committee restored the monthly benefits increase to 15 percent, but did not reestablish the Medicare expansion. It liberalized what social security recipients could earn without losing benefits. The committee expanded health care for the blind, but rejected provisions requiring states to boost welfare benefits. Most significant, Russell had no plans to gut the House's unpopular mandatory work-training program. Despite pleas from the White House and much wailing from the Senate's liberals, Russell refused to budge on this one. "People who can work ought to work," Russell declared during the hearings, adding that mothers should not receive welfare for "filling up whole houses with children," yet refuse to work when jobs are offered. Finally, Russell conceded on one point. He agreed to soften the House program by allowing some exemptions for the sick and mothers of preschool children.[2]

The work-training program not only vexed the Senate's liberals, it also angered a group of black and Puerto Rican women who refused to leave the Finance Committee hearing room after testifying against the provision. Irate that only Russell and Senator Fred Harris of Oklahoma were present to hear their arguments, the women squatted at the witness table for nearly three hours. They refused to budge until the full committee heard their objections. Russell was appalled at the women's insolence. He had allowed them to testify for more than thirty minutes, three times as long as the other witness. Annoyed, he left to attend to other business, only to return hours later to find the women still there. Russell angrily adjourned the hearing, slamming his gavel so hard it broke. The next day, Russell barred the women from the hearing room, saying that the mothers—whom he later described as "brood mares"—would wait for other witnesses to finish. Their protest evoked only contempt from Russell. "If they can take the time to march in the streets and sit in the hearing room all day, it seems to me they have enough time to get jobs."[3]

Russell's committee remolded the president's bill. By the time it reached the full Senate in mid-November, it was a far cry from the president's original proposal, but more generous than the House version. Russell estimated that it would cost more than seven billion dollars during its final year of operation, an enormous sum. Even so, liberals still hated its work-training provisions, while to some conservatives its cost was excessive. Democrat Spessard Holland of Florida likened the bill to a overstuffed Thanksgiving turkey, "an extremely swollen bill with numerous provisions in it which cannot be financed." The ranking Finance Committee Republican, John Williams of Delaware, charged that the bill had "gone far beyond what I think our country can afford."[4]

As the Senate began debate, Russell proved that he could still play legislative virtuoso. In a week of intense debate, reminiscent of his skillful management of Johnson's 1964 tax cut, he juggled more than fifty proposed amendments with equal amounts of tenacity and aplomb. On the last day alone, he spent almost twelve hours on his feet, fending off more than a dozen amendments in as many roll-call votes. As the *New Orleans States-Item* reported, "Switching from topic to topic with ease—and some coaching—(Long) argued first the merits of actuarial projections, the $1.2 billion cost of an earnings test, how to streamline Medicare payments, the balancing cost of work incentives, loopholes in the theory of a guaranteed annual wage, a statistical breakdown of child care—talking, shouting, whispering, cajoling, threatening." Plaudits rose from all corners of the Senate. After the vote of seventy-eight to six, dozens of senators stood in line on the Senate floor to offer congratulations, relieved he had comported himself with such intelligence and grace. "I've never seen him as sharp," remarked Russell's close friend, Senator George Smathers of Florida.[5]

For Russell, the battle was far from over. First, a House-Senate conference committee hashed out major differences between the differing versions of the bill, a process that scoured away almost all of the Senate's provisions. By the time the bill emerged from conference on December 11, most of the Senate's costly amendments had been cut. In fact, in almost every respect, the conference committee bill was tailored after the original House-approved measure, which explained why the House swiftly and overwhelmingly approved the conference report on December 13.

For Russell, winning Senate approval of this new, more conservative version would be daunting. While he had helped mold the erstwhile Senate bill, he clearly favored the stringent House measure with its work-training provisions for welfare mothers. Time after time in conference, Russell and his conferees had conceded to the House until much of their handiwork lay scattered on the floor like wood shavings. To the world, Ways and Means chairman Wilbur Mills had tilted with Russell, and won. To the trained eye, however, the story was much different. As usual during Russell's tenure as chairman, the final product was almost exactly the bill he wanted all along. The profusion of amendments and sundry provisions Russell had added to the bill—in committee or on the floor—had been bargaining chips for conference committee.

The conference report prompted more protest from Senator Robert Kennedy and Senate liberals. They warned that a filibuster might be their only hope for delaying the bill's passage until they could muster enough votes to scuttle the work-training program. Russell showed no patience for the filibuster threats. After all, the Senate was mere hours from its scheduled adjournment. Christmas was around the corner. Senators were eager to leave town. A veteran of numerous filibusters, Russell knew that a talking marathon could be devastatingly effective in the session's waning hours. If the bill was not passed before adjournment, it would languish until the next year. Kennedy's forces would then have ample time to build support for their alternative program.

Months of arduous work seemed threatened until the morning of December 14. That day, not long after the Senate convened, Russell surveyed the sparsely populated Senate floor. Except for Maryland's Joseph Tydings, he noticed none of the bill's most strident opponents. Even majority leader Mansfield was nowhere in sight. The situation was obvious: His enemy might be asleep. Naturally, he did what any experienced soldier would do. He attacked. Quickly and audibly, Russell rose and moved for adoption of the conference report, glancing at Tydings, who was deep in conversation in the back of the chamber. To Russell's surprise, his Maryland colleague was oblivious to the maneuver. With not a voice raised to the contrary, the presiding officer rapped his gavel, declaring adoption of the conference report. In a dizzying amount of time, Russell had passed the bill. Kennedy's forces had fumbled, and Russell beat them badly.[6]

Moments later, Mansfield angrily burst into the Senate chamber to protest, explaining that he had intended to give the bill's opponents more time to air their views. Furthermore, he said he had considered filing a cloture petition if the liberals made good on their filibuster threat. "There is such a thing as decorum and dignity in this body. There is such a thing as the right of every single senator, regardless of his views, being protected," Mansfield said to Russell, as he requested the Senate's reconsideration of the vote. Even more outraged was Senator Robert Kennedy. "It is a reflection of those who participated, not only as senators, but their integrity as men."[7]

Russell went along with Mansfield's request, but he had outsmarted the liberals. They had abandoned their post and Russell masterfully, and correctly, seized upon their mistake. "Frankly," he told Mansfield and the Senate, "I have done a lot of filibustering in my day. One thing we know about filibustering—if you do not want the Senate to vote, you had better start talking or engage in some dilatory tactic, otherwise, the Senate is going to vote. . . . There is nothing at all new about someone losing some of his parliamentary rights because of his failure to object or to start speaking when a measure comes before the Senate. It has happened to me." Even one of Russell's usual detractors, John Williams of Delaware, declared that Russell had committed no wrong. "It was obvious," said Williams, an ally on this bill. "There was nothing sneaky. To be kind of funny, we were shouting the votes. We yelled when we passed it and we yelled again when we nailed it down." Embarrassed and stung by Russell's hardball maneuver, Tydings took full responsibility. "I will be a little older and a little wiser because of this error." (Russell later insisted that he did not sneak the bill through to passage, explaining that he offered the motion for unanimous consent only to determine if the liberals would make good on their filibuster threat. At the time, he said, he was unaware that Kennedy and Oklahoma Democrat Fred Harris—two vocal opponents of the bill—were absent from the Senate chamber.)[8]

Russell's gambit was more than parliamentary showmanship. In agreeing to Mansfield's motion to reconsider the vote, Russell cleverly stipulated that the Senate would vote on the conference report the next morning. With that, any chance for a filibuster was dashed. The next day, the Senate passed the bill, sixty-two to fourteen.

Having successfully shepherded such a monumental bill was gratifying to Russell, who especially savored embarrassing Kennedy and the Senate's liberals in the process. "As filibusterers, that group of young turks has a lot to learn," Russell later told a delighted Shreveport audience. "If you want to filibuster, you have to stand up and talk when the bill is called up. I had given no assurances to Bobby Kennedy or any of his group. Those fellows don't seem to understand that if you're going to filibuster, you've got to put someone up there and start him talking." Recalling repeated attempts by some of the same men to crush southern filibusters against civil rights, Russell told the Baton Rouge Rotary Club: "If we Southern boys stop for so much as to draw a deep breath, they'll gavel that bill through on us. We gave that group a whole minute, I'd say, before we voted it through—which is about thirty times what they'd give us."[9]

Finally, the Senate adjourned. Leaving for the holidays, few senators would soon forget Russell's impact on a remarkable session. "Future historians may find another name," *Washington Star* columnist Mary McGrory wrote, "but those senators who barely lived through it will probably think of the session just ended as the Long, as in Russell B. Long, session. The senator from Louisiana has had his way with the world's greatest deliberative body as surely as if he actually were the majority leader, which, of course, he thinks he ought to be. . . . He left ninety-nine other weary men with a distinct impression, after he finally let them go, that they had been working for him."[10]

* * *

Russell always seemed perplexed by the animosity his lightning-fast legislative tricks engendered. He studied the Senate's rules and used them to his advantage whenever he could. Nothing wrong with that, he believed. Every other senator had the same right to employ the rules, he argued, not mentioning that most senators were far less adept, or intrepid, when it concerned the tricks of the legislative trade.

Years later, even Russell admitted, "There was a time or two when somebody had a right to be mad." One episode in which he employed considerable subterfuge came in October 1966. Near the session's end, Russell read a newspaper article about the possible demise of professional football. Before 1966, the sport had consisted of two separate leagues—the American and National football conferences. As they fought over prominent players, the leagues' teams threatened to bid themselves into financial ruin. Soon, the team owners knew they could save themselves, and end the senseless bidding wars, only if the two leagues consolidated. Only one problem stood in their way. Federal antitrust laws protected the very competition that the owners wanted to terminate. The leagues could merge only if Congress granted football the antitrust exemption afforded other professional sports.

The Senate had passed such a bill, but elderly, stern House Judiciary Committee chairman Emanuel Celler of New York kept it bottled up in his committee. The *Washington Star* article about football's imminent demise, "IMPASSE MAY KILL TIE-UP FOR YEARS," gave Russell an idea. That morning, he called to summon NFL commissioner Pete Rozelle to Washington. Over dinner a few nights later, Russell broached the franchise problem. He suggested that he might be of assistance. "Of course," Russell later recalled, "I told him there was a small consideration. The next franchise was to go to New Orleans." Rozelle promised his help. [11]

The next day, Russell went to work. His strategy was simple. He would craft new legislation—designed to bypass the crusty House Judiciary chairman—by concealing the antitrust language in an obscure tax bill. When it reached the House, the tax bill would be referred to the Ways and Means Committee, not Celler's Judiciary panel. "I told Rozelle we'd draw up an amendment that has something to do with clarifying the law on federal admission taxes," Russell remembered, "and that somewhere we'd say, 'Oh, by the way, it's all right to merge those two football leagues.' " To avoid raising suspicions, Russell asked the Johnson administration to "request" legislation to clarify admission and entertainment taxation language. Treasury Secretary Henry Fowler agreed, and requested the legislation. Next, Russell held a perfunctory hearing "so they couldn't say I hadn't had a hearing." [12]

Yet, the bill he passed through committee did not contain the antitrust language. Russell had one more trick up his sleeve. Instead of offering the amendment himself, he instructed Rozelle to persuade Senate Republican leader Everett Dirksen—whose state of Illinois was home to the Chicago Bears—to submit the amendment when the bill reached the Senate floor. Unaware that Russell was behind the whole affair, Dirksen brought the amendment to Russell on the Senate floor. "I'm for your amendment, but don't offer it right now," Russell told the unwitting Dirksen. Dirksen asked why. "Well," Russell replied, "you've got Wayne Morse [of Oregon] sitting over there. If we bring this amendment up, I just see him start asking questions. Next thing you know, he might say that's not orderly legislative process and he might even filibuster."[13]

Later in the day, Dirksen again brought the amendment to Russell, who again surveyed the chamber. "Don't bring it up now,"he whispered to Dirksen, "there are too many people out here. Wait until the cocktail hour." After more delay, Dirksen finally declared, "I can't wait any longer." Dirksen was scheduled for major surgery the next morning. This time, Russell relented. "OK, bring it up now," he told Dirksen. "Please don't explain it too much. You bring it up the way it is now, you and I can shout this thing through without stirring up a hornet's nest about jurisdiction." Dirksen would not hear of such sneaky tactics. "I'm not going to do it that way," he told Russell. "I'm going to explain this in the greatest of detail. Somebody's going to say we sneaked it through, anyhow."[14]

Sitting nearby, Senator Richard Russell of Georgia observed Russell's and Dirksen's conversation. He tugged on Russell's coattail. "Don't tell me," Senator Russell asked, "that you're planning to take an amendment to merge two football leagues on this tax bill." "I'm going to take it if the Senate will let me take it," Russell replied. "I think I've got a good chance to get a football team for New Orleans. Now, you've got a football team over there in Atlanta, but you can't beat anybody. If New Orleans is in the league, at least there'll be somebody you can beat."[15]

Russell's ploy worked. Without a peep of opposition from a sparse Senate chamber, the bill and the amendment passed. In conference, Russell and House Democratic whip Hale Boggs of New Orleans persuaded Ways and Means Committee Chairman Wilbur Mills to accept the amendment. As House leaders prepared to move the bill to final House passage, Rozelle called for Boggs. He wanted to know about the bill's chances for passage. "Well, Pete, it looks great," Boggs answered. There was, however, one clarification. "Just for the record, Pete, I assume we can say the franchise for New Orleans is firm?" Rozelle could make no steadfast commitments. "Well, it looks good, of course, Hale, but I can't make any promises on my own." Boggs was expressionless, but for a tight smile. "Well, Pete, why don't you just go back and check with the owners. I'll hold things up here until you get back." Stunned, Rozelle sheepishly replied, "That's all right. You can count on their approval." With Boggs's consent, the bill sailed through the House and was signed by President Johnson. That night over drinks at Russell's apartment, Rozelle told Russell about Boggs' extortion. "That Boggs," he muttered. "No class."[16]

In November, Rozelle joined Russell and Boggs at a press conference to announce that New Orleans had beaten six other cities competing for an expansion team. The announcement came on All Saints Day. The new team was named, aptly, the New Orleans Saints.

24

A SPECIAL
JOHNSON MAN

$\mathcal{N}$OT LONG AFTER LYNDON JOHNSON became president, Russell and his cousin, Bill Wright, relaxed one afternoon over drinks at Russell's Baton Rouge farm. The state was rife with speculation that the Pentagon planned to close Louisiana's only army base, Fort Polk. Russell had salvaged the base before, trading an important vote in 1961 for President John F. Kennedy's assurance to reopen it. Kennedy had kept his promise and the base was back in business. Russell was determined to keep it that way.

On an impulse, Russell grabbed the phone and dialed the White House. He asked for the president. To Wright's surprise, Johnson quickly came on the line. "Mr. President, I've been concerned about Fort Polk. My constituents are calling. You know, we had an arrangement on Fort Polk." Eventually, as the conversation progressed, Johnson did as any skillful politician would. He passed the buck. He urged Russell to discuss the matter with Defense Secretary Robert McNamara. At this, most men would have politely thanked the president for his valuable time and ended the conversation. Not Russell. Wright was stunned by his response. "Mr. President, you got a hundred senators and four hundred and thirty-five representatives trying to get hold of McNamara to try and find out if a base in their district's going to be closed. Why don't you call him and call me back?" Within thirty minutes, the phone rang. It was Johnson. He had called McNamara, he reported to Russell. Fort Polk would not close. "Thank you, Mr. President," Russell replied, "I didn't think you were going to do that."[1]

The conversation was typical of the easy relationship Russell enjoyed with Johnson. For almost twenty-three years, Russell and Johnson had maintained a loyal, trusting friendship. Of the eight presidents who occupied the White House during his Senate career, Russell always rated his former Texas colleague as the most effective. Only three of the eight— Johnson, John Kennedy, and Richard Nixon—served with Russell in the Senate. While he developed easy rapport with Nixon and Kennedy as presidents, it was Johnson as majority leader who won Russell's respect and lasting affection. Ten years Russell's senior, Johnson was elected to the Senate the same year as Russell, having previously served in the House. Representing neighboring states, the two men had much in common, primarily devotion to protecting their state's oil and gas industries. As Russell took the slow, traditional path to Senate power, Johnson steamed ahead at breakneck speed. Within three years, Johnson was Democratic leader. Never before had the Senate seen a man with such dynamism, ambition, and legislative skill.

Early in his Senate career, however, Russell was not always favorably disposed to Johnson. In particular, Russell's top aide, Bruce Tucker, harbored ill will toward the new Democratic leader. "His point of view sort of reflected itself in some of the attitudes I took toward Lyndon," Russell confessed. "When Lyndon was the leader, I'd find myself either opposing something he wanted to do or at least standing in the way of it or delaying it. It didn't affect Lyndon Johnson as adversely as it affected me because obviously he just made his plans to do business with other senators." In time, Russell concluded he "had made a mistake—that the only way to correct it was just to go to Lyndon Johnson and say, 'I'm sorry. I made a mistake. Hereafter, I'm going to go the extra mile to support your leadership and I'm going to vote with you whenever I can, which is going to be most of the time.' " Russell reminded Johnson of a lesson learned from his father. "My father," he told Johnson, "always taught me, if somebody strays from his friends and he wants to come back to them, that he shouldn't expect to sit on the front pew and be the leader. He ought to sit on the mourners' bench for a while. That's what I'm going to do. I'm going to be supporting your position and you'll know if I'm voting with you. After I sit on that mourners' bench for a while, I hope you'll take me back into the fold."[2]

Johnson received Russell's contrition silently. "He didn't say anything,"

Russell recalled. "He just smiled." Three weeks passed before Johnson summoned Russell from off the "mourners' bench." One day while in the Senate chamber, Johnson saw Russell and called him over. "I think we ought to organize a special committee to look into the situation of the aged people, to see what can be done for them," Johnson told Russell. "I'm going to suggest that we have such a committee and that you be chairman of it." Russell politely demurred. "Well, I appreciate it very much," he replied, "but as a practical matter, you've already got a committee on aging. And I think it would be a mistake to have a special committee. . . . I'm not asking for anything to take its place. But, the fact that you would suggest that means to me that I'm no longer on the mourners' bench. And I appreciate that. I'm going to continue to show you my support." From that day forward, Russell recalled, Johnson "went out of his way to help me."[3]

Although they parted ideological company on civil rights by 1957, Russell and Johnson always shared abiding compassion for the downtrodden, the elderly, and the handicapped. While they entered politics from different backgrounds—Johnson from the hard scrabble life of the Texas Hill Country and Russell from the privileged upbringing of the governor's mansion and uptown New Orleans—both idolized the same man: Huey Long. Merle Miller said that Johnson had three heroes in his life: President Franklin Roosevelt, Texas congressman Maury Maverick, and Huey Long. "He hated poverty with all his soul," Johnson said of Huey, "and spoke against it until his voice was hoarse." When Johnson was a congressional aide, he had arranged for Senate pages to phone him whenever Huey spoke on the Senate floor. "I would go over there and perch in the gallery and listen to every word he said." LBJ biographer Robert Dallek said that Huey "excited Lyndon's imagination."[4]

Often, Russell's and Johnson's alliances were politically expedient. Their praise for each another on the Senate floor was usually standard Senate hyperbole. Nonetheless, their affection was mutual and real, even if Johnson's flattery for Russell sometimes appeared insincere. In 1958, Russell wrote a brief, gratuitous letter to Johnson, praising his majority leader for "your statesmanship and foresightedness [sic]," to which Johnson replied in a note to an aide: "Write Russell a special one. I want him to be a special Johnson man. Invite him to come to Texas this year. Ask him if there is anything he wants me to do." Several days later, Russell received Johnson's reply: "Please bring your family for a stay at the LBJ ranch because it would be very heartening for me just to spend a few days with you. If there is anything I can do to be helpful at any time, just let me know. I am a 'Russell Long man' from the word go."[5]

In turn, Russell was a true Johnson man. Johnson had been Russell's first choice for president since the campaign of 1956. In 1960 and again in 1964, Russell supported the Democratic tickets of Kennedy-Johnson and Johnson-Humphrey—despite their civil rights platforms—at his own political risk in Louisiana. His fondness for Johnson, and his confidence in the president's abilities and wisdom, often transcended the pressures of Louisiana politics. He supported his president when he could—particularly in foreign and defense matters—and opposed him only when forced to do so. Rarely did Johnson show resentment of Russell's opposition on civil rights and other social issues. A product of the Senate and a consummate politician, the president well understood the political and parochial pressures members of Congress were forced to bear. Because he was a loyal Johnson man, Russell found no joy in the occasions his convictions or home-state politics required that he oppose the president he so admired. These instances, unfortunately, occurred with increasing regularity during Russell's years as assistant Democratic leader.

When the Senate reconvened in 1968, Russell's attitude toward many of his president's programs was no more conciliatory. In fact, as Johnson soon discovered, Russell was even more determined to erect roadblocks to his programs. As Russell faced reelection in November, the year would not offer many opportunities for Russell to side with his old friend. In January, following Johnson's renewed call for a 10 percent surcharge on income taxes to finance the Vietnam War, Russell was cool to the idea. He would wait until the House sent him a bill before acting on the president's proposal, he said. "If I had to vote on it right now, I would vote against it."[6]

On civil rights, he grew more bellicose, attacking a report released in March by the President's Commission on Civil Disorders. The commission urged massive and sustained efforts to end racial segregation by creating two million new jobs and building better inner-city schools. In addition, commissioners recommended construction of six million new housing units and providing a yearly income for the poor. Russell rejected the report out of hand, charging it advocated "a turn-the-other cheek to lawlessness" and offered "little encouragement to the millions of Americans who believe the way to stop riots is to use strong methods." Later, he suggested that police should shoot looters who run from them during riots. "It might cost a few lives to be strong and enforce the law, but I don't see that we are too badly off if a few professional robbers, thieves and arsonists do lose their lives plying that kind of trade. I just don't approve of the police being weak or nambypamby when it comes down to enforcing the law against people who are trying to destroy government itself." Russell put his words into action the same month when he and South Carolina's Strom Thurmond attached anti-riot amendments to the president's landmark Open Housing Act. Russell opposed the bill, which prohibited racial discrimination in the sale or rental of housing. Nonetheless, he and Thurmond persuaded the Senate to impose criminal penalties for those who traversed state lines to incite or participate in a riot.[7]

When James Earl Ray shot and killed civil rights leader Reverend Martin Luther King, Jr., in Memphis, Tennessee, in April, Russell was careful to praise King while urging blacks to refrain from violence. "Anyone who engages in violence now is doing a disservice to the memory of Dr. King," Russell said in a speech to Louisiana labor leaders. "He had a magnificent record of nonviolent protest against things he thought were wrong—but never once did he raise his hand in violence. Nor did he ever give his approval to violence." Drawing on the experience of his father's tragic death thirty-three years earlier, Russell offered this insight:

> People asked me if I wasn't going to get even. They seemed to think I would try to strike out at anybody who had opposed my father, politically or personally. But—and I can't quite explain this—I had no urge to get even. I decided that the only thing to do was to try to conduct myself properly—to live so people would say of my father, 'He must have been a good man to have such a good son.' I can't say I've always done it, but I've tried and I've tried to continue some of the work he started—to help the poor people of our state and nation, both colored and whites.[8]

While riots erupted in Chicago and Washington, D.C, in Louisiana, protests and demonstrations were limited and peaceful. In New Orleans, several hundred black students marched on city hall and lowered the American flag to half mast, while more than six thousand black and white longshoremen walked off their jobs for a day in respect for King. In Baton Rouge, meanwhile, a peaceful group of more than a thousand black youths marched through town and swarmed the steps of the state capitol.[9]

By the time of King's assassination, Johnson had announced that he would not run again for president. The news saddened Russell. "The people of this country seldom fully appreciate a president while he bears the burdens of the presidency," Russell said. "It is only after he is gone and sometimes after he is dead, that they fully appreciate him." Despite Russell's regret, the president's retirement did little to evoke magnanimity for Johnson's latest nominee to the Supreme Court. Following the retirement of Chief Justice Earl Warren that summer, Johnson had nominated an old friend from Tennessee, Associate Justice Abe Fortas, as chief justice. To take Fortas's seat, Johnson named another longtime friend, Homer Thornberry of Texas. Almost immediately, the appointments ran aground. Labeled a "crony" of Johnson, Fortas endured intense scrutiny by southern and Republican senators. Many disliked him simply because he had been one of Johnson's chief advisers on civil rights dating back to the 1957 act. Furthermore, Fortas had been one of five justices responsible for the 1966 *Miranda* decision, which required police to inform suspects of their constitutional rights during arrests. To Russell and other southerners, despite any affections for Johnson, Fortas had coddled criminals. Under no circumstances could they explain a vote for the liberal justice to their constituents, especially during an election year.

While the president expected the nominations might run into a meat grinder of opposition from southerners, a strong promise of support from Johnson's old mentor, Georgia senator Richard Russell, was encouraging. Even before he announced Fortas's appointment, Johnson knew that confirmation would be nettlesome. The day before the president announced the nomination, he read a memorandum from his Senate lobbyist, Mike Manatos: "Russell Long classifies Fortas as 'one of the dirty five' who sides with the criminal against the victims of crime." In an election year, Richard Russell's support for Fortas meant little to Russell Long and other southerners. Judiciary Committee chairman James Eastland of Mississippi, for example, told Johnson that he would not only oppose Fortas, he would lead a filibuster against him. Across the aisle, Republicans took aim at Fortas, as well, hoping to stall the nomination beyond the fall presidential elections in hopes that a new Republican president could make the nomination. Republican senator Robert Griffin of Michigan opposed Fortas after he uncovered a potential conflict of interest. Fortas, Griffin discovered, accepted fifteen thousand dollars for teaching a law course at American University Law School. The money, however, was donated by five of Fortas's friends, whom Griffin believed might someday have interest in a case before the court.[10]

Russell's reelection campaign was at full throttle when he formally declared opposition to Fortas on July 14. Fortas, he said, had sided too often with Chief Justice Warren and justices William O. Douglas and Potter Stewart "in an almost unanimous record in favor of the criminal and against the victims who suffer from the major crimes that have been committed in this country." Two days later, Manatos reported his assessment of Russell's views in another memorandum to Johnson: "I had a long visit with Russell Long about the Supreme Court matter. He told me that he felt impelled to announce for opposition to Fortas because it is a popular posture in his state. However, he assured me he would not be involved in cloture or delaying a Senate vote. He is of the opinion there will not be a filibuster."[11]

Russell kept his word. Worried, however, about Johnson's reaction to his strong words about an old friend, Russell wrote to the president on July 18. He enclosed a clipping from the *Washington Star* in which he had elaborated on why Supreme Court justices should serve fixed terms. "You will note that I held the Supreme Court largely responsible for the major increase in crime in this country," Russell wrote Johnson. "I made this statement based on the way Justice Fortas was going thus far. I would have to vote 'No' if we were voting on whether to confirm him again. With this record well known to practically everyone in Louisiana, I would be a complete hypocrite to vote for Justice Fortas at this time." Russell added he hoped Fortas would someday prove worthy of his vote. "That, of course, is not possible between now and the time we will vote on this matter." Grasping for some note of conciliation, he closed, "I regret very much that I am unable to help you in this instance, although I wish to assure you again that it is my desire to go the extra mile with you whenever possible."[12]

In fact, while publicly opposed to Fortas, Russell supplied the White House with surreptitious advice on how to manage the nomination when it reached the Senate floor. Presidential aide Marvin Watson told Johnson that Russell had suggested that majority leader Mansfield and Vice President Humphrey should employ hardball parliamentary tactics to wear down Fortas's opponents. To break a filibuster, he counseled holding the Senate in session for at least fourteen hours a day. Furthermore, Russell passed along what inside information he had, telling LBJ aide Mike Manatos that Senator Robert Byrd of West Virginia "would not engage in a filibuster."[13]

By October, the Fortas nomination succumbed to conservative attacks. Although the Senate Judiciary Committee voted eleven to six for confirmation, Griffin and other Fortas adversaries were entrenched. They were invigorated as they launched their filibuster on the Senate floor. Soon, it was clear they could not be worn to surrender. When a cloture attempt fell fourteen votes short, Fortas mercifully asked Johnson to withdraw his name. It was a humiliating defeat for the departing president, one in which Russell found little joy for his distasteful, but expedient role.

In August, Russell overwhelmed his Democratic opponent, a little-known supporter of Alabama governor George Wallace. "I regard it as a vote of confidence in the record I've made representing Louisiana. I would think, for example, that the strong stand I took on law and order was one reason I came in so strong." Asked if his stand against Fortas helped, Russell replied, "It did. They [voters] were very much aware of what my attitude toward Fortas's nomination was." Nonetheless, Russell refused to declare his nomination a Louisiana repudiation of Johnson's policies. "I just regard it as being a vote on my record." By month's end, the Republican party nominee, a district attorney from East and West Feliciana parishes, withdrew from the race. With that, Russell was reelected by default. The confrontation he feared from his law school classmate, Governor John McKeithen, never materialized. The political hostility he endured over the previous five years from Louisiana's conservative quarter never manifested itself in a strong reelection challenge. Russell had skillfully migrated so far to the right he left no room for a challenge from a conservative Democrat like McKeithen, much less a more conservative Republican opponent. Politically, in Louisiana, he was now stronger than ever.[14]

Free from the worries of Louisiana politics, in August Russell attended the Democratic National Convention in Chicago. In the wake of Senator Robert Kennedy's murder the atmosphere was mayhem. Antiwar groups descended on the convention hall by the thousands, like moths drawn to the flame of national publicity. Expecting trouble from the protesters, Mayor Richard Daley summoned federal troops and activated the National Guard to help maintain order. Daley's show of strength had just the opposite effect. Instead of quelling the protests, the aggressive police tactics exacerbated the protesters' anger. By week's end, millions of television viewers saw horrible scenes of violence. Police brutally crushed the demonstrations. Riots erupted around the convention hall. Police arrested thousands of protesters. The whole city seemed ready to explode.

Meanwhile, inside the convention hall, the Louisiana delegation reluctantly cast its votes for Vice President Hubert Humphrey, following a brief, aborted attempt to nominate Governor John McKeithen as a favorite son. Among the Humphrey supporters was Russell, abundantly realistic about the slim likelihood that his old college friend would carry Louisiana. Russell knew that Humphrey's leadership in civil rights was anathema to most Louisiana whites. Even before he left Chicago, Russell told reporters that Alabama governor George Wallace, a segregationist third-party candidate, would capture Louisiana's ten electoral votes. Asked what either party could do to prevent Wallace from carrying the South, Russell replied bluntly, "Nothing," adding that he had known for a year that Wallace "would be the high man in Louisiana unless the major parties showed they wanted the support of the South and chose candidates who could offset his appeal." While he said that the Democratic Party had "the right to expect me to vote for" Humphrey, Russell indicated that he would do little else to help his former colleague and college friend win in Louisiana. The Senate's renowned maverick explained, "I do not plan to spend a lot of time butting my head against a stone wall." The irony of that uncharacteristically pragmatic statement seemed to elude the reporter who quoted him. [15]

The latent impact of Chicago's violence blew through the Senate one afternoon in mid-September during debate on legislation to ban sales of mail-order rifles and handguns. In Chicago, Russell lustily denounced the demonstrators as "former supporters of the Kennedys" who wanted "to show that there can't be a party without Kennedy." Now, he rushed to defend Mayor Daley when Democratic senator Stephen Young of Ohio denounced the mayor's "brutal handling" of the demonstrators. Russell strolled into the Senate chamber as Young's attacks on Daley reached their crescendo. Would Young yield? he asked. Young refused and kept talking, spurning Russell's request two more times before Russell exploded angrily. "These communist scum of the earth! I'm going to speak for America when you get done speaking for the Communists!" Wounded by Russell's outburst, Young retorted, "I speak for America as much as the senator from Louisiana." When Young finished, Russell implored him to remain in the chamber for his hour-long assault on the Chicago demonstrators. "I walked with one of those stinko mobs just to get the feel of it in Chicago. Let's face it, most of them were in college just to avoid the draft. They smelled to the high heavens. And they were just waving that Viet Cong flag." Russell rocked back and forth, waving an imaginary banner. "We love Ho Chi Minh. We love Ho Chi Minh," he mocked. Then, whacking his large stomach with both hands, he concluded, "I'm sick of seeing these young scum covering their yellow bellies with the cloth of humanitarianism." Finished, Russell invited Young to "defend those communists." Mortified, Young declined. [16]

Russell's presidential prediction was precise. George Wallace carried Louisiana and the rest of the South in the November election. Humphrey lost narrowly to former vice president Richard Nixon. It was a milestone. For the first time since his election to the Senate, Russell did not actively support his party's presidential nominee. While it did not display his characteristic intrepidity, the decision was sound politics. While, philosophically, Russell had the most in common with Wallace, as a loyal

Democrat and his party's Senate whip, he could endorse no one but Humphrey. But in Louisiana the die was cast, and Russell knew it. Wallace would carry the state, regardless of what Russell or any other popular politician did for Humphrey. For Russell, the safest political course was in giving Humphrey his obligatory endorsement and disappearing from sight. Russell's strategy was successful. He would not stand for reelection until 1974. Indeed, compared to only four years earlier, his domestic political worries were minor. His Senate politics were another matter, as Russell admitted: "I had a growing problem with Mike (Mansfield)," Russell said. "He felt like he wasn't getting much help from me. Well, I guess that's correct." Russell's problems were not limited to Mansfield. As he soon discovered, his leadership was under attack.[17]

25

A GOOD THING TO LOSE

$\mathcal{F}$OR THOSE WHO WATCHED RUSSELL for years—at times awestruck by his mental agility in Senate debate—the subject of his struggle with alcohol remains a nagging question. Was drinking responsible for the spectacular way he sometimes rode herd over his Senate colleagues from 1965 to 1969? Or, as some believe, was he merely displaying, in exaggerated form, his longtime inclination to plunge headlong into battle when persuaded of the righteousness of a cause? Did alcohol, when mixed with Russell's independent spirit, produce a sort of supermaverick? Were the pressures of being suddenly propelled into prominence and power—as Finance chairman and assistant majority leader—too much to bear? Most important, did Russell's drinking impair his effectiveness during a most crucial period of his Senate career? "It did," Russell said flatly years later. "I'd put it this way: If I had it to do over again, I don't think I'd take a drop."[1]

"I think he was just not quite ready for the spotlight and the pressures," then-press secretary Charles McBride speculated. McBride and other staff members watched helplessly as Russell wrestled with growing dissatisfaction in Louisiana over his sprouting moderation on civil rights and then with Senate discontent over his unwillingness to support much of Lyndon Johnson's Great Society program. "He was under tremendous pressure from the libs, whom after all he owed a great deal to for his whip election, to go with them on some things." Whatever course he chose, Russell could not win. In Washington, liberals assailed him for failing to give Johnson's programs enthusiastic support. In Louisiana, he outraged conservatives when he supported the president at all. With his ascension to the leadership, the prospect of becoming majority leader, and now, his committee chairmanship, Russell was the Senate's heir apparent. "He was just suddenly wrestling with all this stuff," said McBride, "having basically labored in relative obscurity for all those years." To cope with these sudden, intense pressures, Russell increasingly sought refuge in the bottle.[2]

"There's no doubt [the drinking] did have an effect on his effectiveness as a senator," recalled former aide Wayne Thevenot, who maintained that while Russell's drinking bouts were sporadic, they caused his staff members great consternation. "I think by and large, the staff felt fairly defenseless, helpless." But Russell's longtime Finance Committee aide, Michael Stern, never saw evidence that Russell's drinking impaired his effectiveness. "I never noticed it had any effect on his work at all," Stern maintained. "Even the times when he was drinking, he seemed to have a sense when it was appropriate to do it. As far as I could tell, he had a sense of not letting go when it made a difference."[3]

With Katherine more than a thousand miles away, except for the rare occasions she visited Washington, Russell was married in name only. He saw his children, Kay and Pam, only when they visited Washington or when he traveled to Louisiana on business. In almost every respect, Russell lived a solitary existence. Often, a hard day's work was rewarded with two or three strong scotch and waters with several colleagues in somebody's Capitol office. Dinner or a reception would follow, where more drinks were consumed. Before long, Russell found more than occasional solace in his drinking and the Senate's social routines.

Washington's atmosphere in the 1960s did little to discourage the senator or congressman who occasionally got ripsnorting drunk and made a scene on the Senate floor or in a Capitol Hill pub or restaurant. In the Senate were many men well known for their capacity for and love of a strong drink. Daily powwows over cocktails in numerous Capitol Hill hideaways were legendary. They were an accepted part of Washington life. When he stumbled, the errant congressman or senator always had a sympathetic colleague or two ready to take his arm and hustle him out of harm's way. The press, not known for its own moderate habits, usually looked the other way when a member of Congress drunkenly embarrassed himself in public. The unwritten rule was that reporters would write only about a politician's personal problems when they seriously affected the public performance of his duties. Even then, the press treated discussions of such drunkenness or womanizing with the utmost discretion. "When I first got into politics," political columnist Jack Germond observed, a "politician who was a notorious drunk would be described as somebody with a reputation for excessive conviviality. A politician who chased women was known as someone who appreciated a well-turned ankle. And this was the way we went at this. Everybody knew except the reader." Indeed, in the several years in which Russell's drinking was at its worst, there were less than a half dozen occasions when the press alluded to his problem. This Capitol Hill cocoon not only shielded a senator or congressman from outside scorn, it often perpetuated and exacerbated his behavior.[4]

Russell's staff was another shield. Aides often guided him from harmful situations or bailed him out of trouble when his drinking went too far. "We couldn't do much about it," Thevenot remembered. "You could try to be helpful, try to steer him away from situations that would lead into one of these drinking bouts . . . There were times when he would just disappear for hours at a time and you couldn't find him."[5]

Heredity was another factor. His father was once afflicted with the same weakness. In fact, when historian T. Harry Williams described Huey Long's behavior in his biography of the Kingfish, he could have been writing of Russell: "The habit took an increasing command over him and was most likely to grip him in times of excitement, like a campaign. Liquor had an immediate and unfortunate impact on him. It either stimulated him to words or acts of rashness, or it knocked him out." Russell's cousin William Wright agreed. "He comes from a family that drinks. His daddy drank, his cousins drank, I drank, Earl drank. All of them did. So, if there's anything that can get passed down, he got it."[6]

While the extent and causes of his problem remain open to interpretation, few would disagree that Russell's periods of heavy drinking in the late 1960s impaired his effectiveness as assistant Democratic leader. While some would argue that he was never suited for such a position, his drinking—and the erratic, boisterous behavior it provoked—only made matters worse. Friends and staff members knew that sooner or later, if unchecked, Russell's life-style would take its physical and political toll.

"Back in those days," Russell admitted, "I thought the way you ought to run the Senate was to go ahead, meet, do your business, keep them in session as late as need be, around the clock if you had to. If somebody got too much to drink, just have somebody haul him out." With years of hindsight, Russell later concluded that the Senate should never have tolerated drunkenness in its ranks. He regretted that Mansfield and other Senate leaders did not appoint a small committee of colleagues to forcefully confront him and other senators about their drinking problems. "I wish they had," he confessed. "I had a couple of friends come to me and ask me about the fact that I had had too much to drink on occasion. And I'd say, 'Well, it's not hurting anybody but me, is it? I think I can still be elected to office. So, I think I can handle my situation. I appreciate your thoughts.' Having been through what I went through, by having been embarrassed about it, knowing that it hurt my career, and having helped straighten other people out, I now would take a different attitude about it."[7]

Thankfully, by the summer of 1968, Russell's life began to change. In July, he and Katherine ended their thirty-year marriage. Katherine lived at a Nevada guest ranch for six weeks to establish the residency required for a divorce. It was a union formed in innocence and devotion. By the time it ended, Russell and Katherine were strangers. "I think they were just ships that went bump in the night," aide Charles McBride observed. In fact, Russell and Katherine had not lived in the same town for almost twelve years. "We saw Katherine two or three times a year and when she was on the scene it seemed to exacerbate [Russell's] problem," said Thevenot, who, like others who knew them both, believed that "Katherine made the fatal mistake of trying to make Russell Long into something he was not. He was not, at least at that time, the attentive, pliant husband, or the conventional human being that kept conventional hours and did conventional things." As a practical matter, Russell said that he and Katherine agreed to a divorce shortly after his 1968 election. "At the beginning of 1969, we understood that we would get a divorce," Russell said. "We were working out a settlement. She sought the divorce on grounds of incompatibility." Russell characteristically blamed himself, not Katherine, for the failure of their marriage.[8]

The divorce was not a catastrophe for Russell. To the contrary, it hastened his rejuvenation. Russell began courting Carolyn Bason, a petite, gregarious aide to North Carolina senator Sam Ervin, whom he had known for several years. Carolyn, who moved to Washington after graduating from Greensboro Women's College in North Carolina, had also worked for former North Carolina senator Clyde Hoey in her more than twenty years on Capitol Hill. In many ways, she was a fine complement to Russell. Carolyn was outgoing and curious about people where Russell was often shy and introverted. Her political instincts were sharp. The politics and personalities of Washington life intrigued her. She was the perfect companion for a politician.

When they finally decided to marry, Russell and Carolyn settled on December 23, certain Congress would be adjourned. Instead, as his wedding date approached, Russell found himself immersed in difficult conference negotiations over a huge tax reform bill. For days, as he watched the clock slowly move to the hour of his wedding, Russell kept his plans a secret from his Senate colleagues and, particularly, House Ways and Means chairman Wilbur Mills. "Most girls have to compete with other women," Carolyn later joked. "I had competition from a tax bill." Had word leaked Russell was eager for a quick end to the conference, he knew he would squander precious negotiating leverage. Mills could then have stalled for time, knowing that Russell would have to capitulate to the House or postpone his wedding. Throughout the negotiations, Russell staged an expert performance. He led Mills to believe that he would remain in conference indefinitely, even though he slipped out of one negotiating session for his blood test.[9]

At the last minute, the conference broke. Russell and Carolyn were married in a ceremony attended only by a few close friends on the appointed day at a McLean, Virginia, Presbyterian Church. The next day, Russell's office announced the wedding in a statement. While his marriage was a complete surprise to his staff and many friends, the benefits of the union were soon evident. Russell was a new man. "It was totally different," said aide Richard Dashbach. "He was this funny, sort of semi-reclusive character before Carolyn. She just totally filled out his whole life for him." Thevenot agreed. "As far as I can tell, it was a turning point, very decidedly. Just his general outlook. He seemed to be much more at ease with himself, like he'd gotten a bear off his back. She had a profound effect on him."[10]

Carolyn helped reduce Russell's alcohol consumption by several means. Shortly after the wedding, she raided Russell's Capitol office and tossed out every liquor bottle she found. "She wanted me to promise that I would not drink anymore," Russell acknowledged.

> And I said, 'I don't know whether I can keep that promise if I made it, because I've gotten in the habit.' But I said, 'I promise I won't drink to excess anymore.' . . . I knew I could control it. I had the willpower to control it, especially with her help, and she did give me a lot of help. There were a couple of times I backslid a bit, but I straightened up immediately the next day and didn't do it

again. She had a pretty good way, too, when she thought I was drinking too much. She wouldn't drink with me, neither then nor the next day or the day after that.

Almost immediately after his marriage, Russell's drinking subsided. "I drank a great deal less," he laughingly admitted, "perhaps about five percent compared to what I'd consumed earlier in life."[11]

Like his father almost thirty-five years earlier, Russell asserted control of his life. A New York journalist once marvelled at Huey's sudden triumph over the bottle, amazed that he "could alter his ways of living by act of will." Russell's friends, relieved by Carolyn's calming influence and Russell's resolve to alter his life-style, expressed the same wonderment at his sudden recovery. "Outside of being born Huey's son," observed former Lieutenant Governor Bill Dodd, "the best thing, politically, that ever happened to Russell Long was his marriage to [Carolyn]."[12]

Despite Russell's new direction, it came too late to save him from losing his leadership position. As early as November, rumors abounded that Senate liberals were plotting to oust Russell and put Maine senator Edmund Muskie in his place. The *Washington Post* gave hope to Russell's foes when it suggested in a November 14 editorial that Russell was "looking for a graceful exit from his post" to devote more time to the Finance Committee, but he "does not want it to appear that he is being ousted from his leadership post." That prompted Russell to mail letters to each of his fifty-seven Democratic colleagues, emphatically denying the paper's insinuation. "That story was in error," he wrote.[13]

In truth, Russell had indeed considered vacating the leadership, discussing the matter with his friend senator Robert Byrd of West Virginia, offering to support Byrd as his successor. When he learned of Muskie's plot to challenge him, Russell quickly dismissed any notion of turning over the reigns to Byrd. "Long's reaction," one aide recalled, "was 'OK, I'm going to run.' And for reasons as old as time, I would imagine—the thrill of the chase, the excitement of running, Long had been challenged and he had to contest it." Within days, Russell secured more than forty pledges. Muskie backed off. The effort to oust Russell seemed dead when Michigan's Philip Hart told a press conference on December 10 that liberal hopes of capturing the whip job had faded.[14]

Believing that he was assured another two years as whip, Russell and Carolyn left for Baton Rouge for the Christmas holidays. They were unaware that another challenge to Russell's leadership was brewing. On Christmas Day, Massachusetts senator Edward Kennedy—who had served in the Senate only six years and was regarded as the front runner for the 1972 Democratic presidential nomination—decided to challenge Russell. Within two days, the thirty-six-year-old Kennedy had spoken by phone with almost half of the Senate's fifty-seven Democrats. Encouraged by his initial soundings, Kennedy phoned Russell in Baton Rouge on December 27, seven days before the vote, to tell him of his decision. Russell was cordial. He welcomed Kennedy to the race, but expressed optimism that his challenge would fail.

Four days before the election, on December 30, Kennedy issued a formal statement announcing his candidacy: "With a new administration, Mike Mansfield's responsibilities will be heightened. He will need the devotion and energy of an assistant who can involve himself more fully in presenting the Democratic attitudes on the issues that come before Congress." Kennedy never mentioned Russell's drinking past or his erratic behavior. A public attack of that sort would have backfired and, in fact, was unneeded. To win, Kennedy had no need to stress Russell's problems. Those were evident. Instead, his task was simply to persuade his colleagues, especially the Senate's liberals, that he was the team player they needed to counter the new Republican president, Richard Nixon. In his statement, this message was subtle, but effective. "Not bearing the heavy responsibilities of a chairmanship of a major Senate committee, I will be able to devote whatever time may be necessary to help make the work of the Senate more effective and efficient, and to make the Majority Whip a better instrument of the will of the Democratic membership."[15]

Kennedy also boasted the support of Vice President Humphrey, a claim that Russell ridiculed. "Humphrey has long been a personal friend and from what he told me, I feel he would support me," Russell said of the defeated presidential nominee whom he had declined to actively support the previous month. "I would be willing to let him cast the deciding vote. I've had other battles for this job and Senator Kennedy's move did not surprise me." Furthermore, Russell said that Kennedy's challenge was an indication he had been voting "the way the people of Louisiana think." He added, "The extreme liberals in the Senate have not been satisfied with the majority leader or me." Nonetheless, Russell said he "welcome[d] the challenge in good humor."[16]

Like Kennedy, Russell returned to Washington and immediately immersed himself in phoning colleagues. He quickly lined up most of the Senate veterans: Eastland of Mississippi, Ervin of North Carolina, Ellender of Louisiana, Russell of Georgia, Stennis of Mississippi, and Sparkman of Alabama. Several of his original liberal supporters dotted his list: Anderson of New Mexico, Nelson of Wisconsin, and McCarthy of Minnesota. Many of his backers were committee chairman, a virtual Who's Who of the Senate Club. With such an impressive list of supporters, Russell's confidence was understandable. Even so, he knew that Kennedy was using his family's extensive nationwide contacts to influence votes. He wasted no time calling his friends around the country. As chairman of the Finance Committee, he had little trouble finding business executives willing to phone their senators on his behalf.

Confident that he had the minimum votes necessary to win, Russell and Carolyn left for New Orleans to attend the Sugar Bowl. On the eve of the vote, Russell announced he had thirty-four votes and predicted a "solid victory." On the morning of January 3, 1969, as he walked from his office to the Democratic caucus, Russell believed that he actually had only twenty-nine votes, exactly the number he needed. When the caucus convened, Russell's senior colleague, Allen Ellender, seventy-eight, and Florida's Spessard Holland, seventy-six, placed Russell's name in nomination. In a contrast of Senate generations, these elder statesmen were followed by Edmund Muskie of Maine, Henry Jackson of Washington, and Albert Gore of Tennessee, young men by Senate standards, who nominated Kennedy. Shortly thereafter, the voting began. When ballots were counted, Russell was stunned. Kennedy had beaten him, thirty-one to twenty-six.[17]

Emerging from the caucus to greet a throng of reporters, Kennedy said: "The winds of change, so evident this year, have expressed themselves. Rather than a personal victory, the significance of this action was much broader. I think it means a positive, constructive legislative program in this session." Facing the same reporters, Russell congratulated Kennedy. To some, he sounded bitter. "I don't think I could have been beaten by anyone else in the Senate." Examining his loss in vastly different terms than Kennedy, Russell explained that he had the advantage in the Senate, but that Kennedy "has supporters all over this nation. That organization goes through almost every facet of American life. Senator Kennedy has lots of friends and I have lots of friends myself. He used all the resources available to him and I used all the resources available to me." He also offered some advice to the new president. "I would suggest that Mr. Nixon ought to be very careful and watch himself in the future."[18]

By the following day, Russell displayed none of the previous day's bitterness. "When I lose a fight, if I have any regret at all it is that maybe I should have worked harder and started sooner." Any extra effort on Russell's part would probably have accomplished little. The three senators who might have helped Russell the most sat on the sidelines. Majority leader Mike Mansfield, ostensibly neutral, seemed pleased with Kennedy's election. Two influential southerners, Richard Russell of Georgia and John Stennis of Mississippi, voted for Russell, but declined to give him their wholehearted support. Without a strong signal from Mansfield and these southern leaders, Russell's candidacy sprung deadly leaks. The election had busted the solid southern bloc. Four southerners voted for Kennedy.[19]

Russell, of course, offered an entirely different analysis of his defeat to his constituents. In a prepared statement to reporters, he said: "From the day I first discovered a conflict in holding the job of majority whip and being a senator from Louisiana, I told the people of Louisiana that if the day ever came when the Democrats of the Senate insisted that as a condition of being majority whip, I would be required to vote contrary to the views of the people of my state, then they would have to find themselves another whip. In the last analysis, that is what eventually happened." Years later, Russell contended that Senate liberals would not have prodded Muskie and Kennedy to challenge him "had I been supporting their liberal agenda." He also believed his opposition of Justice Abe Fortas for chief justice incurred the wrath of some liberals.[20]

With more than twenty years' perspective, Russell's appraisal of his defeat changed little. The Kennedy challenge, Russell said

> was just more than I could have handled, even if I hadn't made any mistakes, because there's good senators, who said, "Look, I told you I'd vote for you, but I had no idea this was going to be the situation." At that time, I think [Kennedy] could have beat anybody. Most folks thought he was going to be the next president of the United States. I'd have thought that myself . . . Looking back on it, frankly, if I'd known Ted Kennedy was going to get in the race, I'd have gotten out of that race, because I felt the odds were overwhelming I couldn't win against all that, especially if Mansfield's not going to support me. From my point of view, it's the lousiest job in the United States Senate. If you're going to lose something, that's a good thing to lose.[21]

Shortly after his defeat, Russell received a letter from his old friend, Lyndon Johnson, serving his last month as president. "I can imagine that you feel pretty low about now," the president wrote. "As one who has experienced some of the vagaries of political life himself, I can sympathize. You should know, however, that you are held in very high esteem by a great many people—among them, your former colleague from Texas. And

I hope that our esteem, and your own resources of mind and spirit, will serve to take you over these bumps in the road." The new president, Richard Nixon, also wrote to console Russell. "Had his fellow Democrats not made the mistake of rejecting him for that post," Nixon said years later, "he would have been one of the most effective majority leaders in this century." Because of a combination of his drinking, stubborn political conservatism, and sometimes-reckless antics, Russell would never have the chance to prove Nixon correct.[22]

* * *

Russell's former aide Wayne Thevenot vividly remembers the summer morning in 1969 an FBI agent knocked on his door. Within minutes, the agent was firing puzzling questions to him about Russell's relationship with former Maryland senator Daniel Brewster, a Democrat defeated for re-election the previous year. The agent also wanted to know about Russell's connections with prominent Baltimore contractor and Democratic contributor Victor Frenkil. As the agent continued spurting questions at him, Thevenot began to piece together the story. Someone had alleged that Russell and Brewster accepted $125,000 each in kickbacks from Frenkil in return for pressure applied to get cost overruns approved for an underground House office building parking garage built by Frenkil's firm, Baltimore Contractors.

Thevenot knew nothing, but went directly to Russell when he arrived at his office that morning. "He sounded genuinely puzzled about what the hell it was all about." Soon, it was apparent Maryland's Republican U.S. attorney Stephen Sachs had Russell and Brewster in his sights. On August 30, 1969, the story broke. The *Washington Post* reported that a Baltimore grand jury was investigating charges that Frenkil had paid Russell and Brewster to pressure the office of the Architect of the Capitol to approve extra garage construction charges of more than five million dollars over Frenkil's original contract amount of $11.7 million. The *Post* alleged that when the government refused to pay Frenkil the additional charges, he went to Russell and Brewster for help. Frenkil had allegedly offered the senators an up-front bribe in addition to 5 percent of any money he received in any eventual settlement.[23]

At a press conference in his Baton Rouge home, Russell denounced the allegations as "cock and bull." He suggested that the grand jury had originally focused on suspicions that one of Brewster's former aides, John F. Sullivan, pilfered campaign funds. The aide, Russell charged, was hoping to avoid jail by fingering Brewster and Russell. "I know I've done nothing wrong. . . . I'd be convinced that Dan Brewster has done nothing wrong." Russell expressed confidence that "when all the facts are known I am sure I will be completely exonerated from any allegation on any sort of misconduct that may have been made before that grand jury."[24]

Russell acknowledged that he had asked Bob Hunter, his top aide, to investigate Frenkil's claim more than a year earlier after Brewster cornered him on the Senate floor. Russell said that he had agreed to help. "Knowing that Dan Brewster was in the fight of his life in an election, which he subsequently lost, I felt that this was the least I could do for a friend." But Russell claimed ignorance about the specifics of Frenkil's claims against the government, insisting that he had turned the matter over to Hunter and forgotten about it. "I have not the slightest doubt that Mr. Hunter did what was proper and nothing else. Nothing that has transpired has shaken my confidence in him."[25]

For a year, the investigation hovered over Russell like a dark cloud. "That, I think, really contributed a great deal to his general downturn in his outlook," said Thevenot, "because he saw his reputation being besmirched, for reasons that I don't think he ever comprehended." During that year, Sachs' office leaked like a sieve. Story after story appeared in the *Washington Post, The New York Times*, and other papers, repeating the allegations against Russell, Brewster, and other members of Congress. Mercifully, by the summer of 1970, Sachs's investigation was complete. On June 21, a comprehensive *New York Times* story finally removed some of the tarnish left by Sachs' well-publicized investigation. The article—the most detailed, behind-the-scenes account of the investigation—reported that Sachs prepared a forty-page memorandum to the Justice Department recommending indictments of Russell, Hunter, Brewster, Frenkil, and others, while suggesting further investigation of Representative Hale Boggs's role. But Attorney General John Mitchell— annoyed by the leaks from Sachs's office which he thought had recklessly implicated more than half a dozen prominent congressional Democrats, including House speaker John McCormick—stopped the aggressive U.S. attorney cold.[26]

On June 12, in a three-page memo to then-assistant attorney general Will Wilson, five members of the Justice Department's Criminal Division argued forcefully against allowing Sachs to proceed with the indictments. Citing "insufficient legal basis and supporting evidence to prove the charges," the staff attorneys maintained that "the investigation of this matter does not indicate that there was any conspiracy undertaken for unlawful purposes." In fact, the attorneys asserted, Frenkil's claims may "have some merit." (Frenkil was finally awarded "equitable adjustments" to his contract by a U.S. claims court in 1987.) Furthermore, the memorandum specifically exonerated Russell. "The actions by [Robert] Hunter in regard to Frenkil's claim as authorized by Senator Long were not illegal."[27]

Based on the staff memorandum, Mitchell concluded that the evidence against Russell, Brewster, and Hunter was insufficient. He ordered Sachs to abandon his attempts at hooking the two biggest fish in his yearlong investigation. Even though he reportedly wanted to indict Russell and Brewster, Sachs could never unearth evidence that the two men had agreed to Frenkil's alleged scheme nor that they had accepted money from him. Nonetheless, according to the *Times*, Sachs argued forcefully to Mitchell that the case against Frenkil was overwhelming, "assuming that all of his alleged activities were spelled out." The Justice Department's position, the *Times* reported, "is said to have been: You can indict Frenkil and, if you wish [his associates], but that's all—and you must indict and try the case without bringing into it any of the material about the political figures."[28]

With his hands tied by Mitchell, Sachs continued to pursue the case, albeit by unusual means. Employing a rare procedure, known as presentment, the grand jury submitted to the court a sealed document— essentially an indictment, without Sachs' signature. The presentment, the *New York Times* reported, charged Frenkil with exerting illegal influence on employees of the Architect of the Capitol, in addition to Russell, Brewster, and Boggs. The quasi-indictment went nowhere. Shortly after its submission, Sachs's term expired. His successor, who reviewed the case and likewise recommended Frenkil's indictment, was also constrained by the Justice Department. "The crux of the Justice Department's position," the *New York Times* reported, "is that since the Capitol architect's office never paid the $5-million claim, the Government was not defrauded."[29]

The matter had died. None of Sachs's targets was indicted, although Brewster was later indicted, but not convicted, in an unrelated bribery case. Russell was finally cleared, if not totally exonerated. As he knew well, news reports of a suspect's vindication are rarely reported with the same magnitude given the initial charges. Despite repeated newspaper stories, fed by leaks from the U.S. attorney's office, Sachs and his dogged investigators failed to uncover one shred of hard evidence that Russell had been bribed by Frenkil. "The whole thing was just a matter of them trying to make something where they had nothing," Russell asserted. Furthermore, few reporters following the story seemed to question in print why a man like Russell, worth millions from his extensive oil and gas holdings, would accept a bribe of any amount.[30]

Russell's exoneration in May coincided with the death of his longtime friend and former aide O. C. Smith, whom Russell described as "one of my closest and dearest friends." The following week only added to Russell's grief when his mother died at the age of seventy-eight. Despite his legal ordeal and personal heartaches, many friends believed that Russell greeted the 1970s a new man. The tranquility of his newfound life-style provided solace. His drinking subsided to a minimum. Indeed, Russell's former confrontational style had vanished, supplanted not with lethargy, but with a new appreciation for the potential of conciliation and compromise.[31]

26

THE WAY TO SPIKE THEIR GUNS

$\mathcal{N}$EAR THE END OF HIS SENATE CAREER, a reporter once asked Russell to name the most rewarding victory of his thirty-eight Senate years. Almost without hesitation, he supplied a surprising answer. He was proudest of his leading role in the defeat of the Family Assistance Plan—Richard Nixon's guaranteed income for every poor American family.

Nixon first proposed the idea to Congress in 1969, when rising federal welfare payments reached alarming proportions. The concerns over welfare were well-founded. From 1935 to 1960—the first twenty-five years of Aid to Families with Dependant Children (AFDC), the largest welfare category—the program had never exceeded a billion dollars a year. But by 1967, only seven years later, AFDC's yearly costs had ballooned to more than two billion dollars. In 1968 alone, the program grew an additional half-billion dollars. Furthermore, because state governments dispensed the AFDC money, benefits and qualifications for individual recipients varied widely. Working poor families with both parents present were especially penalized. Federal law did not allow such families to receive AFDC benefits. Hoping to stem the surging welfare tide and correct the government's arbitrary approach to welfare, Nixon searched for alternatives. In August 1969, he unveiled his proposal to replace AFDC with the Family Assistance Program. Nixon confidently promised an end to "unfairness in a

299

system that has become unfair to the welfare recipients, unfair to the working poor and unfair to the taxpayer."

Nixon proposed a federal income supplement as high as $1,600 a year—over and above food stamp payments—for unemployed families of four. For the working poor earning less than the poverty level, Nixon's proposal allowed the working head of a household to keep the first $720 of his earnings, and half of his income above that amount until his income reached the poverty level. In the House of Representatives, members received the plan warmly. The chairman and ranking Republican of the Ways and Means Committee, Wilbur Mills of Arkansas and John Byrnes of Wisconsin, enthusiastically cosponsored Nixon's proposal. By April 1970, the two men shepherded the bill to full House passage.

In some respects, Russell's father might have loved Nixon's plan. In the 1930s, Huey Long decried the shameful state of a nation in which almost half of its families earned less than $1,250, a wage below which would now be known as "the poverty level." To lift these Americans out of their economic despair, Huey proposed his Share-Our-Wealth program. "Every family would make not less than $2,000 to $3,000 per year upon which to live and educate their children," he pledged. Under Huey's grandiose plan, families able to work would be guaranteed "family wealth" of "around $5,000—enough for a home, an automobile, a radio and the ordinary conveniences." Like Huey, Nixon wanted to guarantee a basic income for all Americans.[1]

In Nixon's plan, Russell saw little correlation to his father's ideals. Huey Long had wanted to help those who yearned for a job. By contrast, Russell believed that Nixon's plan rewarded indolence. Giving unemployed welfare recipients a guaranteed income was ridiculous liberal social policy, he thought. His ranking Republican on the Finance Committee, John Williams of Wisconsin, was equally skeptical. Both men believed that the bill's annual four-billion-dollar price tag was outrageously expensive. Senate liberals, no more supportive than Russell, had different reasons to hate the plan. To them, the bill was stingy. Other senators believed that the White House bill was poorly drafted and impossible to administer because it left loopholes for those refusing to work.

Despite his profound skepticism, Russell dutifully convened Finance Committee hearings in late April. Three days of testimony from administration witnesses and other supporters did not persuade him that the plan would ever encourage welfare recipients to find work, one of its supposed cornerstones. By the hearing's second day, Russell sputtered in frustration, "Why don't we junk the whole thing and start all over again?" The

Russell at the 1952 Democratic National Convention. He incurred the fury of Leander Perez for casting all twenty of the Louisiana delegation's votes. (*The Bettmann Archive*)

Russell at the White House in 1965 with his former Senate colleagues, President Lyndon Johnson and Vice President Hubert Humphrey. (*Wide World Photos*)

LSU professor T. Harry Williams, whose biography on Huey Long won him the Pulitzer Prize, poses with Russell and a photograph of Huey in Russell's Washington office in 1969. (*Louisiana State University Libraries*)

President Richard Nixon attended the 1972 funeral of Russell's Senate colleague, Allen Ellender, in Houma, Louisiana. Left to right, First Lady Pat Nixon, Richard Nixon, Louisiana governor Edwin Edwards, Louisiana first lady Elaine Edwards (later appointed to fill Ellender's unexpired term), and Russell. (*The White House*)

In another Oval Office meeting in 1974, Russell talks with President Gerald Ford. (*The White House*)

Russell confers with his former Senate colleague, President Richard Nixon, in the Oval Office in 1973. Russell was one of Nixon's strongest defenders throughout the Watergate scandal. (*The White House*)

Cigar in hand, Russell discusses tax policy with his frequent conference committee adversary, House Ways and Means chairman Al Ullman in 1977. (*The Washington Post*)

Russell greets former Georgia governor and presidential candidate Jimmy Carter in June 1976. Russell's good friend, Georgia Senator Herman Talmadge, looks on. (*Louisiana State University Libraries*)

The famous Long treatment. Russell whispers in the ear of Kansas senator Robert Dole in 1975. Dole's inscription reads: "Mr. Chairman: 'I appreciate getting the word.' Thanks for your leadership, counsel and friendship." (*U.S. Senate*)

President Ronald Reagan expresses his appreciation to Russell for his crucial support of Reagan's tax reform plan in June 1986. Reagan presents Russell with a T-shirt emblazoned with the ditty Russell made famous: "Don't tax you, don't tax me. Tax that fella behind the tree!" (*The White House*)

Russell and Carolyn campaign in Beauregard Parish during the 1980 Senate campaign. (*Wide World Photos*)

Three Louisiana senators: left to right, Senator J. Bennett Johnston, Russell's successor, John Breaux, and Russell. (*U.S. Senate*)

The first Senate campaign. Russell speaks to a campaign rally in Crowley, Louisiana, in 1948. (*Louisiana State University Libraries*)

next day, Russell took his own advice. He suspended the hearings. By June, the White House remodeled the bill, but fell far short of Russell's expectations. While Nixon returned his plan to the Senate with its basic element intact—the $1,600 payment for families of four—he added a new inducement for Senate liberals. A new, lenient provision guaranteed Medicaid, food stamps, and housing assistance in addition to the guaranteed yearly income. To Russell, the White House was moving in the wrong direction if it wanted his support.[2]

Russell resumed Finance Committee hearings in July. Nixon's half-hearted overhaul had only made Russell and most committee members more resistant. "In significant respects," said Russell, "the new plan is a worse bill—and a more costly one than the measure which passed the House." Without Russell's support, Nixon's bill was moribund. Frustrated with the Senate dawdling, the president turned to a proposal from Democratic senator Abraham Ribicoff of Connecticut, a Finance Committee member. Ribicoff suggested commencing the national program after a one-year test in three areas of the country. The idea intrigued Nixon. Believing that it might be the impetus he needed, the president embraced the proposal.

Russell was unimpressed. In November, he led the Finance Committee to reject Nixon's and Ribicoff's programs. In their place, the committee substituted Russell's suggestion for a limited test run with no provision for extending the program past one year. To the watered-down bill, Russell added a one-year U.S. residency requirement for welfare recipients. Furthermore, he insisted on a "man-in-the-house" rule to suspend welfare to families with able-bodied, unemployed men. With Nixon's plan in shreds, Russell attached the emasculated welfare program to a multipurpose House-passed bill providing social security increases, veterans' pensions, and import quotas.[3]

Nixon and the liberals refused to surrender. Led by Ribicoff, they hoped to resuscitate the plan when the Senate took up the House bill in December. The Senate, however, was in no mood to plow new ground in radical welfare reform. Ribicoff's forces got even less than what Russell proposed. A two-week filibuster ended when the Senate adopted Russell's motion to purge the bill of the Family Assistance provisions. For now, at least, welfare reform was dead. Dejected, Nixon called the defeat one of his greatest disappointment of the ninety-first Congress. He vowed it was "White House priority number one" for 1971.[4]

Nixon found no new supporters in Congress the following year. Once more, his principal goal was a bust. Russell, who fought the plan with innocuous parliamentary maneuvers the previous year, now lustily attacked it with renewed vigor. He charged it would add fourteen million new names to the welfare rolls. To a group of optometrists in Atlanta, he declared that any responsible welfare proposal should remove those who "should never have been there." In April, he warned reporters at a Lafayette news conference that the bill would lure a flood of Mexican migrants across the nation's borders. "If we had a minimum wage, we'd have to post the Army at the country's borders to keep the migrants out. Why live south of the border and work for almost nothing, when you can live in the United States and get paid for doing nothing?"[5]

Meanwhile, in June, the House again embraced the plan. Ways and Means chairman Mills attached a more beneficent version of Nixon's proposal to the social security bill left over from the previous session. As before, House members overwhelmingly adopted the legislation and sent it to the Senate. To Russell, the new proposal made Nixon's original plan look frugal. The House plan guaranteed a family of four, with no income, a minimum of $2,400 a year—eight hundred dollars more than Nixon originally requested. Families of eight or more members could receive up to $3,600. Russell was appalled. "If we go the president's route, we could have half of the nation on welfare within a few years," he told the Louisiana Sheriffs' Association in August. With the promise of continued fierce opposition from Russell, Nixon smelled defeat in the more conservative Senate. Less than a month after the Finance Committee began hearings on the bill, the president asked the Senate to postpone its proceedings to consider his new economic stimulus initiative. Action on the Family Assistance Plan would wait another year.[6]

Russell launched his third year of obstructionism in January 1972, when he convened hearings on the House social security bill. From day one, he made it clear he would strongly oppose any compromise on the Family Assistance Plan. Two days into the hearings, Russell denounced Nixon for holding the nation's elderly hostage to prod Congress into passing his welfare plan. Russell told reporters that Nixon had rejected his pleas, as recently as late 1970, to separate the two issues so the elderly could receive the benefits increase they needed. "I might as well have been talking to a stone wall because the decision had been made to hold all these old people hostage to get this guaranteed annual wage for not working . . . this paid subsidy for illegitimacy. Anybody who votes for it," Russell grumbled, "ought to be voted out of office."[7]

Throughout three years of debate over Nixon's plan, Russell's opposition was as determined as his genuine desire to solve "the welfare mess."

Never once did he propose dumping Nixon's program without suggesting his own alternative. Like doctors who concurred on the scope and severity of an ailment, Nixon and Russell could simply not agree on the treatment. "[Long] was not opposed to spending more money on low-income people, but he wanted to do it in ways that preserved their incentives to work and remain or to become financially independent," recalled Michael Stern, Russell's Finance Committee aide for eighteen years.[8]

Out of this conviction emerged one part of Russell's own welfare reform program. As originally proposed, it had no formal designation and little hope of passage. Three years later, when finally enacted, the proposal—later dubbed the Earned Income Tax Credit—was the cornerstone of assistance for the working poor. It was a radical departure from Nixon's plan. Russell suggested that poor working people with income below the poverty level tax receive refunds on their earnings of up to four hundred dollars a year. "If someone doesn't work, he doesn't get the payments," Russell explained, "and that's how it should be." Nixon's men were less than enthralled. Labor Secretary James Hodgson denounced the plan as a "nine billion dollar step backward into the leaf-raking schemes of the 1930s." As with many of Russell's ideas, time would prove the best tonic.[9]

By July, Russell found himself in the peculiar position of attacking the presidential nominees of both political parties. Nixon and his Democratic rival, Senator George McGovern of North Dakota, incurred Russell's wrath for their liberal welfare policies. Earlier in the year, Russell wryly observed that it was Nixon's good political fortune the Family Assistance Plan was not law. "If we had passed that bill at that time [in 1970], Richard Nixon wouldn't have a prayer for re-election," Russell told a reporter in January. "There would have been a revolution by now—everybody quitting work to go on welfare. If that bill had gone into effect, thirty percent of the people would be standing in line to get on welfare and the other seventy percent would have been standing in line to vote you out of office." While he would vote for McGovern—"I owe a considerable obligation to the Democratic Party"—Russell made little effort to sell his party's nominee to his constituents.[10]

In late July, he returned to Washington from Louisiana declaring, "I didn't find anybody who is voting for George McGovern because of his position on this welfare thing, this guaranteed $6,500 for doing nothing." By August, he was even more candid about why he would not help McGovern. "It would be a waste of time. I think Mr. McGovern himself is probably wasting his time to try to campaign in this state. If he wants to, that is his privilege. But I think it is going to be overwhelming in this state for Mr. Nixon." As he predicted, Nixon swamped McGovern in Louisiana on his way to a record nationwide landslide victory. Years later, affirming that he had indeed voted for McGovern, Russell confessed to uttering a brief prayer as he pulled the Democrat's lever: "Dear God, please don't let this man win."[11]

The fall elections were bittersweet for Russell, who gained a young, energetic colleague in the Senate, J. Bennett Johnston. A state senator from Shreveport, Johnston's wholesome message of reform left him a few thousand votes short of election as governor in 1971. Losing to the populist Cajun congressman from southwest Louisiana, Edwin Edwards, Johnston immediately launched his campaign to challenge Louisiana's senior senator, Allen Ellender. At eighty-one, Ellender was the Senate's president pro tempore and chairman of its Appropriations Committee. Besides Russell, he was the last statewide elected official with direct ties to Huey Long. Ellender had been Louisiana's house speaker until his election to replace Huey in the Senate in 1936. In July, gallantly fending off Johnston's increasingly popular challenge, Ellender died of a heart attack. After more than twenty-three years in the Senate, Russell, now fifty-three, was at last Louisiana's senior senator.

After two years of rancorous debate, Russell's Finance Committee finally sent a welfare bill to the full Senate in July. For Nixon's purposes, the Finance Committee might as well have done nothing. Russell's bill was strong medicine to cure welfare's ills, a radical, severe departure from Nixon's idea of welfare reform. Not surprisingly, its overwhelming emphasis was on work. It would have removed 1.2 million people from the welfare rolls by offering them guaranteed, but low-paying private or government jobs while making them ineligible for food stamps. Able-bodied welfare recipients who refused to accept work would lose their benefits. States could drop families from welfare rolls, even when a man who was not legally obligated to a child assumed the role as head of the household. Those willing to work were awarded various financial incentives. Russell's jobs program included his Earned Income Tax Credit, a work bonus equal to 10 percent of wages. The bonus was extended to regularly employed low-income workers. Heads of families in jobs not covered by the federal minimum wage would be given income supplements.

The bill also addressed a problem for which Russell had doggedly pursued a solution for many years. He was infuriated when he considered the millions of delinquent, runaway fathers who abandoned their wives and children, leaving them for the federal government to support. He knew that Congress had created the Aid to Families with Dependant Children program primarily to help wives and children after the death of the father. By the 1960s, however, the program made payments to families for a wide range of circumstances—in which the father was dead, absent, disabled, or unemployed. Russell's bill would have changed that. As a condition for receiving aid, the bill required mothers to cooperate with authorities in identifying their children's fathers. As an incentive for doing this, the first twenty dollars a month collected from runaway fathers would be disregarded in determining welfare payments. "All children have the right to receive support from their fathers," Russell wrote in the committee report. "This committee bill is designed to help children obtain this right."[12]

More important to the future of Nixon's plan was another provision Russell supported in committee, as he later explained: "To keep them from coming back with something that was going to make the whole nation into a welfare state, I felt that the way to spike their guns on that would be to take all the money they estimated spending on this family program and apply that to the aged." Russell did just that, throwing his weight behind a Ways and Means Committee provision to provide a guaranteed income of $130 a month for aged, blind, and disabled persons with no other earnings. Nixon had made a similar proposal, but requested only about half of what Russell wanted. The new program was later called Supplemental Security Income (SSI). By 1975, almost six million aged, blind, and disabled persons were receiving $5.9 billion in benefits under the new program—a billion dollars more than the estimated cost of Nixon's original Family Assistance Plan proposal. "That bill took most of the aged in America out of poverty," Russell boasted years later. More important, Russell added with a sly grin, he believed that the new SSI program ultimately denied Nixon the financial means with which to finance his Family Assistance Program. In reality, SSI's creation probably had little to do with Nixon's defeat. Budgetary consequences were not yet the preeminent concern of lawmakers contemplating new federal programs. Ultimately, a shortage of votes, not money, spelled the Family Assistance Plan's demise.[13]

When debate began in late September, senators quickly became mired in the now-familiar stalemate over welfare reform. "There were thirty to forty senators who thought that welfare reform meant placing strong work requirements and work opportunities on welfare recipients," recalled then-Finance Committee aide Michael Stern. "There were thirty to thirty-five senators who felt that welfare reform meant guaranteeing a substantial minimum level of subsistence. The remaining thirty senators or so felt that either of these ideas was worse than staying with the present law. So, it was really impossible for any one position to get a majority."[14]

In fact, in the end no less than three programs were added to the same bill. This happened when no single proposal—Nixon's program, Russell's Finance Committee bill, or an alternative guaranteed income plan by Senator Ribicoff—could muster a majority throughout an acrimonious week of debate. The impasse ended when Russell supported an amendment by Virginia's Harry Byrd, the son of Russell's former Finance Committee chairman, and Delaware's William Roth to test all three programs for two to three years. "It offers us the best opportunity to lead the Senate out of the wilderness," Russell said as the Senate narrowly approved the compromise plan.[15]

Eventually, the debate produced no agreement at all. With only ten days left in the session, the Senate bill went to a House-Senate conference committee. The Senate conferees refused to accept the House-approved Nixon plan. Likewise, House conferees were as stubborn in their rejection of the Senate compromise. With mere days left in the session, both sides walked away from the negotiations. They removed the welfare section from the bill, but left Russell's SSI program intact. Russell, whose goal of stopping Nixon's program had succeeded, hailed the result as "a good bill that every senator can support." Ribicoff's assessment was gloomier. "Where we are in the entire welfare mess is that we are back where we were in August of 1969." Texas congressman Robert Price agreed, calling the final product of two years work "an emasculated, mangled and toothless shadow of the original proposal." In the end, it was Russell's role in the creation of a costly new guaranteed income program for the elderly, coupled with Nixon's own disillusionment with his plan, that spelled its demise. Nixon, Russell said, eventually confessed to him privately the program was, indeed, too costly and controversial. The president finally abandoned his Family Assistance Program. It was, he later said, "an idea ahead of its time."[16]

In many ways, Russell ended 1972 a different man. It was four years since his humiliating defeat at the hands of Edward Kennedy, who had lost the whip job two years later to Robert Byrd of West Virginia. In the time since his darkest years, Russell's life was a maelstrom of upheaval, evolution and rebirth. Katherine had divorced him, but he now was a full-time husband to Carolyn. Her calming influence was largely responsible for his transformation. While he never entirely quit drinking, he was now more temperate. He was more serene in mood and outlook. Legislative defeats and Pyrrhic victories were things of the past. As Finance Committee chairman for six years, he had become one of the Senate's most powerful forces. His command of revenue sharing, tax bills, social security and welfare reform was unrivaled. Unlike his years as assistant majority leader, Russell now derived his influence and power not from fear or intimidation, but from an ample well of goodwill and respect. For the first time in many years, Russell was happy, at peace with himself and the world.

27

HE SHOULD HAVE
BURNED THOSE
TAPES

*R*USSELL NEVER UNDERSTOOD the Watergate scandal. Why Richard
Nixon's men would burglarize the Democratic National Committee headquarters at the Watergate Hotel was always a mystery to him. "I, for the
life of me, couldn't see what [Democratic National Committee Chairman]
Larry O'Brien might have over there that might be worth somebody
breaking in," Russell later professed. "It was a hopeless situation. [Demo-
cratic nominee George] McGovern had no chance to win that race. He was
a dead duck if there ever was one. Everybody knew it was a lost cause."[1]

In its early stages, the scandal that toppled Richard Nixon's presidency
had the appearances of only a minor flap involving overzealous low-level
aides. Watergate, Nixon's press secretary scoffed, was a simple "caper."
That perception was widely shared on Capitol Hill. To many members of
Congress, the June 17, 1972, burglary—not far from Russell's Watergate
apartment—was politically insignificant. Few could fathom how a president, barreling toward a landslide victory, could benefit from information pilfered from his politically impotent challenger's camp. Like Russell, fewer still could imagine the president of the United States direct-

ing the cover-up that ultimately brought down his presidency in August 1974.

Russell genuinely liked Richard Nixon. Although colleagues during Nixon's brief Senate tenure in the early 1950s, the two men had never been close friends. In fact, in the heat of several campaigns, Russell condemned Nixon's ethical conduct, often portraying him in harsh terms. Through the years, such political rhetoric was forgiven by both men. Indeed, during Nixon's White House years, Russell and the president were often a harmonious pair. Nixon was Russell's kind of Republican, a man who understood the ways of Congress and who was willing to include its members, even Democrats, in ad hoc coalitions he formed around issues.

Often, where Nixon was conservative—civil rights, law and order, defense—so was Russell. But like Russell, Nixon displayed intriguing strains of liberalism on welfare, revenue sharing, foreign affairs, and health policy. Domestic policy adviser John Ehrlichman argued that Nixon often identified more with southern Democrats like Russell and John Stennis of Mississippi than with some Republican senators. That kinship even survived the acrimony of the Family Assistance Plan struggle. After fighting for years with Russell over his welfare plan, Nixon eventually agreed to support Russell's alternative, the Earned Income Tax Credit. Most of all, Russell liked Nixon because he was decisive and opinionated, yet always receptive to conflicting ideas and opinions. "I might not always agree with him," Russell once told a staff member, "but you know where he stands."[2]

There were also personal reasons for Russell's affinity for Nixon. When one of Russell's closest friends, his former aide O. C. Smith, was dying of cancer in 1970, Russell mentioned his condition to Nixon one day during a visit to the White House. Nixon volunteered to call Smith to help lift his sagging spirits. Shortly thereafter, Russell was warmed when he learned about Nixon's phone call to his dear friend. "That was a damn decent thing he did," Russell said. It was a kindness Russell never forgot.[3]

Therefore, it was not surprising Russell was one skeptic who initially refused to succumb to suspicions of Nixon's direct involvement in the Watergate scandal. As the Senate investigating committee, headed by North Carolina Democrat Sam Ervin, prepared to conduct hearings, Russell expressed pity for the public thrashing Nixon would receive. "I feel very sorry for him. He is going to have more revelations come out. This is just the beginning. It is not the end at all. You are going to be hearing about it this time next year, I suspect. Even though I didn't vote for Mr. Nixon, I always thought he was a good man and I still do."[4]

Even so, Russell groused that maybe Congress would finally realize the wisdom of his plan for public financing of presidential campaigns. Although passed in 1967, Congress did not activate the program until 1973. Russell believed that a publicly financed Nixon-McGovern race might have prevented Watergate by limiting the Republican party's expenditures. "It was unfortunate that the President and all his people did all within their power to keep us from putting into effect a simple little provision that would have seen that nothing like this could have happened." While he questioned Nixon's wisdom in this area, Russell left no doubt of his complete confidence in the president's integrity. In a May interview, Russell was certain that Nixon would not be impeached. The worst possible scenario, he speculated, would be the disclosure of evidence that "the president knew, or had reason to think, that the people who are his top aides were trying to disentangle themselves to get loose from the mischief they were involved in."[5]

For two months, the Ervin Committee explored the Watergate affair before a nationally televised audience. Witness after witness revealed an intricate plot among men who were more loyal to the president than the nation and its Constitution. To the committee, White House Counsel John Dean painfully described Nixon's involvement in the cover-up, including hush money to imprisoned Watergate burglars. Another White House aide, Alexander Butterfield, shocked committee members when he revealed that Nixon had taped cover-up discussions with aides. When Special Prosecutor Archibald Cox later subpoenaed those tapes, Nixon fired him.

Even as Dean's testimony drew the president deeper into the quagmire, Russell remained confident that Nixon was truthful concerning his noninvolvement. "I have never known the president to deliberately tell me a falsehood. That is more than I can say for the average politician." While Russell suggested that Nixon should release transcripts of Oval Office tape recordings—which he said might prove the president's innocence—he defended the president's refusal to do so. "He hears those tapes and, from his point of view, it confirms what he thought all the time. But somebody else hearing that would draw a different conclusion." Even so, Russell told reporters that Nixon's assertion of executive privilege regarding the tapes was a mistake. "In view of the grave damage it is doing publicly, because the public will presume—and I think correctly—that there must be something that would damage him very badly about all this if he released them, it would be to his advantage to release them, if he could afford to do so."[6]

Throughout the summer, Nixon's political health declined. Fifteen of his aides resigned. Four were indicted. Three pled guilty. In all, two grand juries were investigating the scandal, as well as four Senate committees, the House Judiciary Committee and various news organizations, including the dogged *Washington Post.* Along the way, damaging disclosures fell like rain. Another burglary of a Nixon adversary was reported. Campaign funds had been laundered. The Central Intelligence Agency, the Federal Bureau of Investigation, and the Internal Revenue Service had all been used to hound Nixon's enemies. In July, Massachusetts congressman Robert Drinan filed an impeachment motion against Nixon for "high crimes and misdemeanors" for his alleged involvement in Watergate and his secret bombing of Cambodia.

Despite a growing chorus of detractors, Russell remained loyal to Nixon. His confidence in the administration was unshaken even as Vice President Spiro Agnew was accused of income tax evasion on bribes he allegedly took as Maryland's governor. "I'm not aware of any evidence that the president violated any law or that the vice president violated any law," Russell said in August, adding that the Senate hearings were a waste of time. "I think the sooner they close it down, the better off we're all going to be."[7]

The investigations would not stop. As they intensified, Agnew's bribery scheme—unrelated to Watergate—was uncovered. In October, he pled no contest—neither guilty nor innocent—to the charges in an agreement with prosecutors by which he resigned. By now, Russell was persuaded of Agnew's culpability, and angered that the agreement provided no prison sentence. "That is not the way they have done with other people who have been in government and in other lines of endeavor and committed so-called white collar crimes of far less magnitude and which were far more excusable." Of Republican House minority leader Gerald Ford, Nixon's nominee to replace Agnew, Russell approved, if only halfheartedly, "unless they bring out something horrible against him." Former Texas governor and then-Treasury Secretary John Connally had been Russell's choice. "I just think he's a very great American."[8]

Although Nixon's administration was crumbling around him, Russell remained confident of the president's effectiveness. "I admit the president has a world of headaches. But considering all the difficulties with which that man is having to contend, I think he is doing very well." By November, Russell remained vociferous in his defense of Nixon. He called on some of the president's congressional critics to "start being fair," suggesting that some critics "issue an apology for some of the things they have said that are unfair and unkind."[9]

Russell did not serve on the Senate Watergate committee, yet he played a significant role in the unfolding national drama. The break-in and the subsequent cover-up were not the only scandals dogging Nixon. The president was now accused of vastly underpaying his federal income taxes. At the heart of the controversy were several questionable deductions, including $576,000 for donating his vice presidential papers to the National Archives and the use of his Florida home as an office expense. Nixon had also not paid taxes on his sale of some California property, arguing that it was an untaxable capital gain.

At the heart of the controversy were Nixon's papers. When he donated them in 1969, such deductions were legal. Later that year, however, Congress repealed the deduction retroactively to July 25, 1969, four months after Nixon's endowment. On its face, Nixon's donation appeared to have been legally transacted well before the retroactive deadline. When investigators discovered that the deed for the papers had been back-dated by one of Nixon's lawyers, a new scandal erupted. Hoping to settle the matter quickly, Nixon asked the Joint Congressional Committee on Internal Revenue Taxation—led by Russell and Ways and Means chairman Wilbur Mills—to rule on the deductions' legality.

Throughout the three-month inquiry, Russell strained to give Nixon every advantage. "Everything I know would indicate that he did what his lawyer and his accountant told him to do," Russell said in a Louisiana television interview. "He claimed deductions that they thought, or at least, that they advised him they felt he was entitled to take. . . . If he had put as much time on his tax returns as one of our more conscientious senators does, just working diligently, he wouldn't have much time to be president." Mills was not nearly as charitable. Even before he examined the evidence, Mills publicly criticized Nixon for taking the deductions, even if they were legal.[10]

In March 1974, before the committee released its findings, Mills, on CBS's "Face the Nation," said that Nixon would be forced to resign after the Joint Committee's report was made. Furthermore, he said that the committee's investigation would determine that Nixon owed at least $350,000 in back taxes from 1969 to 1972. Later in the day, Russell played down Mills's explosive remarks in a written statement: "I have never attempted to fix a figure on the amount of extra taxes the president may owe on his 1969–1972 returns." While the president might owe "a substantial amount of taxes," Russell declared the committee "has found no proof of fraud on the part of the president." As for critics like Mills, Russell said "anyone who attempts to fix a figure on the president's extra taxes is indulging in guesswork."[11]

The joint committee ended the guesswork in April when a staff report concluded that Nixon owed $476,431 in back taxes and interest. The largest deduction disallowed was Nixon's bequeath of his vice presidential papers. The committee's 1,120-page report also determined that Nixon should have paid $117,000 in capital gains tax on his sale of California acreage in 1970. "We will study it," Russell said hours after the staff recommendation was released, noting that the full committee would rule on its conclusions. In fact, releasing the staff report prior to a full committee vote was Russell's way of shielding himself and Mills from criticism. "I didn't want to be left in the position of having to carry the burden of what was in that report," Russell said. To avoid a slow dribble of leaks about the staff document, Russell urged its immediate release. "Let the press have it," he said he told Mills and his committee colleagues, "so that if anybody wants to give the president a break, he's got to have the guts to stand up there and be recognized and the media can ask us about why we changed it."[12]

Days later, Nixon reluctantly agreed to pay the back taxes when a separate IRS investigation concluded that he owed almost the same amount as the committee's staff had concluded. Years later, Nixon castigated members of the committee for abdicating the investigative work and its resulting conclusions to its staff. "A majority of the members were not even sufficiently concerned to go over the report or to hear my side of any major controversial issues," Nixon wrote in his 1978 memoirs. In some respects, Russell agreed, later telling reporters that he also believed the committee staff may have been too harsh on Nixon.[13]

Russell's committee report inflamed one of Nixon's most prominent defenders, conservative radio commentator Paul Harvey. On his nationwide radio show, Harvey ridiculed Russell and Mills for overstepping their bounds when the committee examined how Nixon had provided air travel for his three dogs, King Timahoe, Pascha, and Vicki. In truth, the committee merely requested manifests for Air Force One trips to Nixon's homes in Key Biscayne, Florida, and San Clemente, California, to determine the propriety of travel by family members. Harvey's criticism brought an immediate, indignant reply from Russell, who said he resented the commentator's implication that the committee wanted Nixon to pay airfare for the dogs. Russell noted that Nixon's attorneys, Kenneth Gemmill and H. Chapman Rose, were the first to raise questions about the dogs. "If I could talk dog language, I would urge that King Timahoe chase Kenneth Gemmill and H. Chapman Rose right out of the White House the next time they appear on the scene. I understand that King Timahoe, Pascha and Vicki have hang-dog looks since the unfortunate thing was blown out of proportion. It was Gemmill and Rose, not I, who invaded the dogs' privacy."[14]

As the Watergate scandal worsened, Russell remained a steadfast defender of Nixon, as did other conservative southern Democrats and a large majority of Republicans. Despite the charges and suspicions of Nixon's direct involvement, no one had yet produced the "smoking gun" to prove Nixon's guilt, Russell maintained. In an April television interview, Russell said that while the news media "have done a fantastic job of obtaining all sorts of things nobody ever thought they could get hold of, I just haven't seen where they would have any evidence to convict the president of any sort of crime."[15]

Further adding to Nixon's woes were the Oval Office transcripts revealing the president's habitual profanity. Again, Russell defended Nixon. "People get all shocked when they find out that the president used all kinds of bad language," said Russell, prone to use of strong language in private himself.

> Well, after they think about it for awhile, they come to realize that he is not the only fellow who had done that. Other presidents in the White House have used some foul language from time to time. It just hasn't been recorded and published for the American people before. Of course, there are some things that are quoted from these tapes that would appear that the president stepped over the line. He might have committed a crime. Even so, the question should be: Is that sufficiently serious enough to justify impeachment. At this moment, I don't think so.

A majority of Louisianians clearly agreed. A poll commissioned by Russell's campaign committee in late April measured Nixon's negative rating in Louisiana at 54 percent, compared to Russell's 84 percent positive rating. Despite such high negatives, almost two-thirds of the Louisianians polled did not believe Nixon should be impeached.[16]

Where the tapes were concerned, Russell sided with Nixon's close friend, former Treasury Secretary John Connally, who advised the president to burn them before they were subpoenaed. Russell remembered one White House meeting when Nixon raised the question of releasing the recordings. "Mr. President," Russell told Nixon, "as far as I'm concerned, do whatever you want about the tapes. It doesn't make any difference to me what you do about the tapes." Years later, asked if Nixon should have taken Connally's incendiary advice, Russell responded with an astonishing account of a conversation outside the Senate Dining Room with Senate

Watergate Committee chairman Sam Ervin. During a break in the hearings, Russell said Ervin confided: "You know, confidentially, he should have burned those tapes." Ervin's conviction was enough to persuade Russell. "That's Sam Ervin, the guy who's conducting the hearings, leading the charge, 'Impeach the president!' . . . If Sam Ervin thought they ought to burn the tapes, that'll be good enough to convince me they ought to burn them."[17]

House Judiciary Committee members saw matters differently. In late July, the committee recommended Nixon's impeachment on three charges: obstruction of justice, abuse of presidential powers, and trying to impede the impeachment process by defying committee subpoenas. By July 24, Nixon's days were numbered. The U.S. Supreme Court ordered him to produce additional tape recordings of Oval Office discussions subpoenaed by Special Prosecutor Leon Jaworski. Even Russell agreed with the ruling. "If the president does not comply it will hurt him very badly as Congress considers impeachment. He is in bad shape now, and any refusal would put him in worse shape." Nixon reluctantly released the transcripts, one of which revealed he had tried to thwart the FBI investigation into the Watergate burglary. With that "smoking gun" finally discovered, Nixon's presidency was over. On August 9, he ended the saga when he resigned. America's "long national nightmare," as President Gerald R. Ford told the nation, was over.[18]

From the first days of the Watergate scandal, Nixon's popularity steadily melted like ice in the sun. Friends and allies abandoned him in droves as his lies and deceit became apparent to the public. Near the end, only a small core of congressional supporters—including Louisiana Congressman Joe D. Waggonner, and senators John Stennis of Mississippi and James B. Allen of Alabama—stood with the beleaguered chief executive. Russell, perennial champion of the underdog, was steadfastly among them. Had Nixon's impeachment been brought to trial in the Senate, Russell later said, he would have voted against a conviction. As always, Russell was instinctively sympathetic when he thought a public figure was persecuted for political reasons. Senator Thomas Dodd and, to a degree Senator Joseph McCarthy, were prime examples. Furthermore, the painful memories of his father's own impeachment trial in 1929 would never leave him. Forty-five years earlier, fifteen men had rescued his father's career when they signed the famous Round Robin, a pledge that they would never vote to impeach Huey Long. In doing so, these men saved Huey and won his son's enduring gratitude and respect. In many ways, in Russell's mind, Nixon was Huey. In his own way, Russell was finally a Round Robineer.

28

PLAYING FOR KEEPS

$\mathcal{R}$USSELL NOW SURVEYED THE SENATE from his catbird seat of the Finance Committee chairmanship. In many ways, it was his domain. More than 40 percent of all government spending was under his authority. The committee he commanded held jurisdiction over a breathtaking array of federal turf: the U.S. debt, customs, revenue sharing, Medicare, Medicaid, Social Security, trade, general revenue and taxation, and tariffs and import quotas. While the Finance Committee was indeed the mighty vehicle that supplied Russell's immense power in the Senate, it meant little without the deft driving skills he brought to the job. Mastering the Senate was useless if his initiatives never passed in the House, where Ways and Means chairman Wilbur Mills ruled his committee with equally vast authority and an even firmer hand.

For years, Mills had claimed victory after almost every tax conference during Russell's chairmanship. As the House chairman, the Arkansas Democrat derived much of his might over revenue matters from the Constitution, which gives the House exclusive authority to originate revenue measures. Chairman since 1957, Mills had been the potentate of virtually every major revenue and social welfare issue that passed through Congress during his tenure. The Constitution was not his sole source of power. His personal style of running the committee made him even more formidable. In committee, he never let a bill out of his sight. He refused to establish subcommittees to consider various issues. Real power rested with the chairman only. When a bill passed through Ways and Means, Mills

316

alone held the gavel. When he took a bill to the floor, he tied members' hands with ground rules barring all floor amendments. Consequently, the House routinely approved his sacrosanct bills by wider margins.

When he carried his bills to conference with the Finance Committee, Mills was just as potent. Fearful of crossing their omnipotent chairman, House conferees slavishly voted with Mills. "If they didn't," Russell observed, "they weren't going to be on the conference again. He'd name somebody else. So, when he went in there, he had a solid majority wrapped right in the palm of his fist. I didn't have that. When I started out [managing the 1964 tax cut], I had Harry Byrd. You don't think I could control Harry Byrd, do you? He was the chairman of the committee!" By contrast, the committee which Russell inherited from Byrd in 1966 was vastly different from Mills's Ways and Means panel. Finance was a passive committee, a loose collection of members with diverse interests outmatched by the well-organized, disciplined battalion that marched into every conference with Mills. More often than not, when the dust of battle settled, most observers believed that Mills's side had prevailed.[1]

When examining tax conferences, however, the press often kept score by unsophisticated methods. Whenever Russell dropped a Senate provision from a bill, Mills was usually credited a victory, as was Russell when Mills discarded a House provision. By this simple score keeping, Mills usually won. But such a picture rarely considered the importance or value of the abandoned provision to Mills or Russell. On the Senate floor, Russell was so famous for loading tax legislation with dozens of extraneous amendments near a session's end that the measures were dubbed "Christmas tree" bills. Whenever he could, he avoided floor fights by accepting dozens of amendments to his tax bills. In return, he usually promised no support in conference. Often, when his bills were stripped of their ornaments, the remaining core legislation was roughly what Russell had originally wanted. "I don't think Russell cares very much what the floor amendments are going to be," Democratic senator Lee Metcalf of Montana said in 1971. "He knows that this is complex legislation and that it is going to be written in conference and that it is going to correspond pretty much to what the House conferees will accept." Russell agreed with that assessment. "My impression," Russell told a reporter in 1971, "is that we've been successful in persuading the House to take about two-thirds of the things we initiate. And I wouldn't expect to do any better than that, no matter who I was conferring with."[2]

Describing one conference committee, a colleague of Russell once told *Newsweek* magazine: "Long would breeze in and we'd sit around for two or three days doing nothing substantial. Then, all of a sudden, he'd start to trade. The Senate sent him laden with bounty: baubles and trinkets to dispose of when the right moment came. He seemed so damned reasonable, sitting there giving away everything. But at the critical moment, when he had the House conferees divided, he would stiffen, the ante would go up—and he would have the game won." Because Mills would not permit floor amendments to his tax bills, he often lacked the bargaining chips looser Senate rules gave to Russell. Not all of Russell's conference defeats were victories. By any measure, Mills dominated the tax-writing process. Russell, however, did not lose as often or as decisively to Mills as many assumed.[3]

Even so, to Russell the process was always rather one-sided and designed to favor Mills. By the Constitution or by tradition, the Finance Committee seemed to exist only to refine what was sent by the House, serving as the inert appellate court to its activist, domineering counterpart. For all his years in the Senate—he was now seventh in seniority—Russell hated playing this passive role. "I went to the Finance Committee not because I wanted to keep things from happening but because I wanted *something* to happen." Such a dilemma presented Russell with only one attractive option—if he could not originate tax measures, at least he could remodel what he received from Mills. This he did with increasing regularity in the early 1970s. By 1973, virtually no bill left the Finance Committee without Russell's fingerprints all over it. All year, Russell attached broad portions of unrelated legislation to minor House bills sent by Mills. "I firmly believe in what the Constitution says about the House originating revenue measures," Russell explained to a reporter inquiring about his flourishing activism. "But I haven't been able to find where the Constitution says anything about 'germaneness.' "[4]

Russell's strategy seemed successful. For much of the year, he steamed across the revenue terrain, unfettered by Mills. Russell, not Mills, was the driving force behind that year's social security benefits increase, the sweeping reform of the private pension system and the welfare benefits hikes to the elderly, blind, and disabled. Furthermore, Russell, not Mills, engineered the new regulations governing social service payments to the states. It was a bountiful year, indeed. Congress even enacted Russell's long-dormant plan to publicly finance presidential campaigns by agreeing to support the fund with a one-dollar checkoff on all federal tax returns. "They're going wild over there," complained Mills's heir apparent to the chairmanship, Congressman Al Ullman of Oregon, "adding non-germane amendments to bills, and it has to stop."[5]

While Russell's strength seemed sudden to some, he actually had embarked on the course in 1966. When he took the Finance Committee reins from Harry Byrd, Russell inherited only a skeleton professional committee staff, ill prepared to battle the more professional Ways and Means Committee. "Harry used to rely on the Joint [House and Senate Taxation] Committee staff to furnish him information, then he'd make the Treasury [Department] provide him information," Russell recalled. "He'd project the image of being very economical, but he was doing that by making the departments provide him information to pass judgment. . . . If you're going to be an activist committee, you need a staff to help you both draft legislation and help you come up with ideas." By 1973, Russell could boast more than a dozen staff experts in areas of taxation, health care, trade and welfare.[6]

Finance members were pleased with Russell and the way he ran the committee. Unlike Byrd, Russell welcomed ideas and suggestions from committee members, even the Republicans. And while Mills ruled the Ways and Means Committee through fear and intimidation, Russell mined his growing success from indulgence and accommodation. Even the committee's growing number of liberals found a friend in Russell. For example, in 1973 he created eight subcommittees. Commonplace for most Senate committees, subcommittees had been alien to Finance chairmen who historically were fierce guardians of their prerogatives. Furthermore, Russell raised no objection when the Senate's Steering Committee appointed liberal Minnesota senator Walter Mondale to his committee. He told reporters that future vacancies would probably be filled with other liberals.

One other important factor secured Russell's dominance. To many younger House members, Mills' power was excessive. He not only ruled Ways and Means, he was chairman of the Democratic Committee on Committees, which dispensed all the House Democrats' committee assignments. Thus, when Mills was caught cavorting with a Washington stripteaser, he handed his critics the ammunition they needed to expedite his downfall. In October 1974, when Washington, D.C., police stopped Mills's car near the Tidal Basin, nude dancer Fannie Fox jumped from the car and landed in the water. Several weeks later, Mills stunned his colleagues by strutting on stage with Fox in Boston. Shortly thereafter, Mills confessed his alcoholism and entered a hospital for treatment. Although he had been elected to another two-year term, Mills never recovered from the scandal. He resigned as Ways and Means chairman in the winter and retired in 1977.

With Mills deposed, Representative Al Ullman became chairman. Russell—reelected over token opposition in November 1974 to a sixth term of office—was finally senior chairman. At last, he had a chance to dominate the public debate over tax matters. His first confrontation with Ullman was crucial. Whoever won the first battle might own the momentum for years. If Russell—with twenty-two years on Finance—could not best neophyte Ullman, his stock would plummet. The committee, and its chairman, might slide into its past irrelevance.

President Gerald Ford set the stage for their first confrontation early in 1975, when he challenged Congress to stimulate the sagging economy with a one-year sixteen-billion-dollar tax cut. It was not the first time a president had suggested a huge tax reduction for economic stimulus. President Kennedy demanded the same action more than a dozen years earlier. Finance chairman Harry Byrd, who considered budget cuts as important as tax reductions, put the bill on ice until after Kennedy's death, reviving it only when Lyndon Johnson promised deep spending cuts. This time, Russell resolved the process would be different. If Ford's tax cut did not pass, no one would blame the Finance Committee chairman. In fact, as the Finance Committee began hearings on the proposal, Russell announced he wanted a tax cut twice as large as Ford's sixteen-billion-dollar request. Harry Byrd would have turned in his grave. "In the last analysis, it is an indication that the Republicans have learned something since Herbert Hoover," he told a Louisiana reporter. "In Herbert Hoover's day, every time the economy went down, he tried to keep the government spending within its income, so, he would cut government spending and that would take it down another notch."[7]

In the House, Ullman moved quickly on Ford's challenge. His committee cut individual rates by more than sixteen billion dollars and business taxes by almost four billion dollars. House liberals, however, had one major complaint. Ullman had skirted an important issue to a growing number of their ranks: repeal of the oil and gas depletion allowance, a deduction for depleted resources to spur drilling. Sacred to the oil industry, and rarely threatened by Congress, the depletion allowance allowed oil companies to write off 22 percent of their profits from drilling operations. When Ullman refused to touch the industry's treasured tax break, House Democrats did something they would have never dared under Mills. They defied the Ways and Means chairman, forcing a vote to add the depletion allowance repeal to Ullman's bill. Two days later, on February 27, the full House overwhelmingly approved the amended legislation. The measure was now in Russell's hands.[8]

While President Ford had wanted to give the nation an economic shot in the arm, Russell was eager for a massive dose. Keeping his promise to double the president's request, on March 17 he reported a huge twenty-nine-billion-dollar tax cut bill that made three major changes to the House legislation, including a one-hundred-dollar bonus to all social security recipients. To no one's surprise, the depletion allowance repeal was notably absent. "A great number of our liberal friends in Congress," Russell explained, "seem to feel the way to get more energy is to put all the energy people out of business." Russell vowed the depletion allowance would endure.[9]

When his tax bill reached the Senate floor, Russell could empathize with Ullman's humiliation. Senate liberals also vowed to kill the depletion allowance. For four days, Russell stood his ground as Massachusetts's Edward Kennedy, California's Alan Cranston, South Carolina's Ernest Hollings, and other Senate liberals struggled to add the depletion allowance repeal. The parliamentary tussle was a dizzying experience for even the most studied observer. The Senate quickly adopted three amendments offered by the liberal forces to raise oil and gas taxes by almost three billion dollars. To some, the votes signaled the Senate's willingness to curb the oil industry's treasured tax break. Nonetheless, the exercise was meaningless. Kennedy's forces were chagrined to learn they attached their provisions to the House-passed bill, while another bill, the Finance Committee's substitute version, was the measure the Senate leadership would send to conference. Any effective amendments would be attached to Russell's bill, not the original House version.

By the time this parliamentary quirk became evident, Russell and the liberals were hopelessly locked in an interminable struggle over adding the oil taxes to the Finance Committee bill. A cloture vote failed by one vote, prompting majority leader Mansfield to worry that the bill might be irrevocably caught between the stubbornness of the two powerful camps. Russell seemingly lost control of his tax bill, and in the process, had doomed prospects for the prompt passage President Ford demanded. Determined not to let the bill run aground under his watch, majority leader Mike Mansfield intervened. Russell was slightly embarrassed when Mansfield moved to return the bill to Finance Committee. Senators readily agreed to Mansfield's motion, instructing the committee to trim the bill by $3.1 billion and limit a home-buying tax credit added by the Finance Committee. Mansfield's maneuver worked. He pried the bill from Russell's hands, but only to save it from defeat.

Russell reluctantly complied with the Senate's instructions, returning the bill with the changes that Mansfield's motion had ordered. None of this meant that the debate over the depletion allowance had been settled. But now Mansfield's substitute, not the controversial oil tax amendments, was the pending business. Mansfield had cleared the air and lowered tensions. With the procedural roadblocks swept aside, the Senate overwhelmingly adopted Hollings's and Kennedy's amendment to repeal depletion for major oil companies, leaving a limited exemption for independent producers. By the time they sent the bill to conference, senators had added a host of other amendments expanding the tax cuts to twenty-seven billion dollars. The wide disparities in the House and Senate bills, Russell knew, spelled trouble in conference.

With the fast-approaching Easter recess as a deadline, the tax cut drama now centered around Russell and Ullman. Each brought markedly different bills to conference. Both men had tremendous personal pride and prestige on the line. It was Ullman's first conference as chairman, Russell's first as senior chairman—the House's David versus the Senate's tax Goliath. For his part, Russell had played tax underdog long enough. With a multitude of reporters and colleagues keeping score, one man would be cast as the loser. This time, Russell vowed, someone else would play that role.

The Sunday before the first conference session, nothing appeared to have changed. Ullman, like Mills before him, was invited to discuss the upcoming conference negotiations on ABC's "Issues and Answers." It was as if the show's producers assumed that the Ways and Means chairmanship bestowed magic legislative skills upon its occupant, regardless of his acumen and skill. Meanwhile, Russell remained on the sideline, watching at home as Ullman confidently predicted victory. "We think many of the amendments added in the Senate cannot be justified," Ullman told his interviewers. "We think there is a real danger in being irresponsible here, and doing the things that might lead to an inflationary spiral. So, many of the Senate's amendments will be cut back." Ullman took particular delight in attacking one Senate provision, the home-buying tax credit, which he derided as "not the right way to approach the housing problem." It would be dropped, he guaranteed.[10]

"If Ullman had known more about football strategy," observed *New York* magazine reporter Aaron Latham, "he would never have committed the classic coach's blunder: publicly knocking the other team on the eve of the big game. That tends to get the other side riled up." Impassioned as always by such a challenge, Russell arrived early the next morning to meet with his Senate's Democratic conferees. They included Herman Talmadge of Georgia, Vance Hartke of Indiana, and Abraham Ribicoff of Connecticut. Ullman, he said, had been mouthing off about the weakness of the Senate team. If we don't stick together, he said, Ullman and his side will completely roll over us.[11]

Later, as they assembled in the stifling heat of Ullman's cramped Capitol office, Russell needled Ullman about his television appearance. Because he had not been interviewed the day before, Russell announced that he could approach the proceedings with an open mind. Far from open, Russell's mind was already made up. He had decided he would yield nothing to Ullman the first day. "Like any good coach," Latham wrote, "he knew that if you could stop your opponent cold in the first quarter, it might break their spirit." The only acquiescence of the first day came from Ullman, who agreed to Russell's 10 percent Earned Income Credit, twice as large as the House's 5 percent version.[12]

Having won nothing from the Senate on Monday, Ullman hoped for better luck when the conference convened its second session on Tuesday morning. On this day, Ullman found Russell more accommodating. The next day's *Washington Post* reported a host of ostensible Ullman victories. Russell and his side, the paper reported, had jettisoned half a dozen amendments. Ullman was winning, or so it seemed. The catch was this— none of the amendments were ones Russell had sponsored. In truth, he could not have cared less. They were bargaining chips. He had merely thrown overboard excess baggage.[13]

Russell was very happy to toss another chip on the table that day, a compromise on an investment tax credit for new machinery. He happily agreed to increase the credit from 7 to 10 percent for two years, slightly less than the 12 percent the Senate had wanted. It appeared to be another major concession by the Senate. To the contrary, Russell actually had tucked away a provision that he ultimately considered the bill's crowning achievement. The conferees required corporations claiming the credit on large investments to contribute one-twelfth of their tax benefits to an employee stock ownership plan. Known as ESOPs, the tax incentives for stock ownership by working Americans were a modern, temperate version of Huey Long's radical scheme for sharing the nation's wealth by sapping the rich.[14]

Huey's program was never feasible because its Robin Hood methods were deemed heresy by the wealthy barons who had the ears of President Franklin Roosevelt and congressional leaders. Such tactics were no less abhorrent to the rich in Russell's day. But Russell was no radical. He was chairman of the Finance Committee, a friend of business, and a bona fide member of the Senate Club. His proposals, unlike Huey's, were not dismissed out of hand by Senate leaders. Furthermore, Russell explained, his father was a revolutionary. He wanted to divide the existing wealth among all the people. Russell saw himself an evolutionary. He merely wanted to share a portion of the nation's future wealth. For years after he inherited the idea from California economist Louis Kelso, Russell championed ESOPs with evangelical fervor. A business, he argued, would be more profitable and efficient if the employees owned the company. In the process, more Americans would share in the nation's wealth.

To Russell, the rest of the bill—the largest tax cut in the nation's history—was insignificant compared to the potential of his embryonic ESOP program. "No longer will we have a situation where three percent of the people own seventy percent of all corporate stock, and ninety percent own none of it," Russell told the Senate on March 18. "That, Mr. President, I believe, will be the great significance of this bill from the point of history, that it sets America on a road that means not just the few will own the plant and equipment in this country, but that many will own it." Forty years earlier, the words could have been Huey Long's.[15]

Following Tuesday's lunch, the conference stalled. Ullman, with firm instructions from the House Democratic Caucus to fight for total repeal of the depletion allowance, finally ran headlong into the determination and skill of Russell Long. Russell refused to budge. "Actually, Long more than refused," Aaron Latham wrote. "He went into his act. He told stories. He philosophized. He filibustered." After watching Russell's encounter with Ullman, one conferee remarked to Latham: "Trying to pin Long down was like trying to grab one hundred pounds of Jell-O." The Senate's depletion allowance provision was distasteful, he argued. It killed the allowance for the major oil and gas producers, but it was the best Russell could persuade the Senate to do. Even Ted Kennedy supported it, he told Ullman. Perhaps the chairman misunderstood the intentions of his House Democratic caucus, Russell suggested. "Just go back and tell them that Kennedy is for it and they'll love it."[16]

That suggestion produced some chuckles, but nothing more. Ullman insisted on total repeal. Russell kept chattering. "He talked so much and in so many circles that Ullman seemed disoriented, confused," Latham said. The whole debate, Russell told Ullman, reminded him of the story about the woman who went into a store to buy eggs. How, she asked the storekeeper, could he sell eggs for forty cents a dozen when the store down the street sold them for only thirty cents? Why not just buy them from the other market? the storekeeper inquired. The woman replied,

"Because he's out of eggs." The storekeeper said, "Well, if I were out of eggs, I'd sell them for ten cents a dozen." The moral of the story, Russell revealed to Ullman, was if you want something—such as oil or gas—you must pay the price, and part of the price is the oil depletion allowance.[17]

The conference was clearly going nowhere. Russell was telling stories while President Ford badgered the conferees to produce a compromise before leaving for the Easter break. All the while, Ford threatened to veto the whole thing if the total of the tax cuts was too large. A compromise was needed, which is what Representative Charles Vanik of Ohio finally proposed: Keep the depletion allowance, but phase it out over twelve years.[18]

The proposal reminded Russell of another story, this one about an Arab sheik who discovered a young man making love to his daughter. "He'd just babble about stuff that had nothing to do with taxes," one observer later told *National Journal*. "He was just wasting time. He wore everybody down." Beleaguered, Ullman finally faced the truth. He backed down. Reluctantly, he proposed continuing the independent's depletion allowance, but phasing it down, but not completely out, over several years. Russell liked the idea, but wanted to think it over. The next morning, however, Russell dashed the conferees' hopes of reaching an agreement when he returned with his answer. He rejected Ullman's offer. He would not yield one inch on the depletion allowance. For most of the morning, the stalemate appeared unbreakable until Senator Ribicoff spoke up, suggesting that the two chairmen go to lunch by themselves and try to work something out.[19]

Frustrated and exhausted, the conferees eagerly agreed to Ribicoff's suggestion and left the room. Spurning lunch, Russell and Ullman went to work. Almost immediately, Russell had an idea. Neither man was going to give, Russell told Ullman, so "why don't we just split the difference?" And with the help of Laurence Woodworth, the chief of staff of the Joint Committee on Taxation, they began doing just that, compromising or splitting their differences on the social security bonus, the house purchase credit, and the depletion allowance. By the time they reached the depletion allowance, the compromising had been so easy that even this thorny issue was no longer difficult. Ullman accepted a permanent but smaller allowance that gradually phased down until 1984. With that, the compromise was complete.[20]

Shortly thereafter, the conferees rubber-stamped Russell's and Ullman's work. The final tab on the tax cuts came to $20.9 billion. The House and Senate quickly followed suit, approving the conference report by wide margins. Having once threatened to veto the bill if it grew too expensive, Ford signed it on March 29. As the dust settled, despite considerable concession on both sides, Russell was the obvious winner. He had conceded to Ullman on a host of issues, but he had lost completely on none. He had his ESOP provision, a scaled-back social security bonus, and his Earned Income Credit. He had saved the depletion allowance and had stuffed the home-buying credit down Ullman's throat. "Ullman had managed to pare down the cost of the tax bill," Latham concluded, "but Long had retained all of the amendments about which he really cared. If you looked at the price tag, then Ullman had won the conference. If you looked only at the provisions, then Long had won." Paying grudging tribute to Russell's skills was Republican House conferee Barber Conable of New York. "The Senate stonewalled us," complained Conable who praised Ullman for his valiant fight, but added, "He was up against a stacked deck." The common perception of the first Long-Ullman encounter was summed up by Democratic Finance Committee member Lloyd Bentsen of Texas: "Russell undressed him," Bentsen declared years later. "He outmaneuvered Ullman all the way."[21]

Russell's dominance was assured. Later that year, when Ullman took the lead on energy issues by sending to the full House a measure to raise energy taxes, Russell foiled him again. The House gutted his bill and Russell bottled it up in the Finance Committee. It went nowhere. Russell frowned on another of Ullman's proposals, a House-passed tax reform measure which Russell put on hold until 1976.

For the present, Russell's conquest of Ullman swelled his growing legend for effectiveness and cunning. From this day forward, every move and statement Russell made would be scrutinized for its hidden meaning and underlying strategy. The news media treated him as legislative magician or miracle worker, quoting colleagues and Senate staff members who gushed over Russell's brilliant legislative methods. "He's the smartest man in the Senate," gushed a tax lobbyist to *National Journal.* True or not, Russell's wily ways in conference had clearly added to his growing legend.[22]

In retrospect, Russell believed that the press and his adversaries read entirely too much meaning into his actions. In truth, Russell said years later, he really was not that cunning after all. Reciting his oft-told story about the Allied Invasion of Sicily, Russell recalled that General Eisenhower "thought the way to keep the enemy from knowing what you were doing was not to tell your own troops what you were going to do. Well, in some respects I went a step beyond that. To keep my opposition from knowing what I was going to do, I didn't know myself. I'd go many times into a meeting with every intention of playing it by ear. I'd say, 'Let's just see what goes.' . . . I think many times they gave me credit for being cagey, or God knows, Machiavellian, or whatever, when as a practical matter, I didn't know precisely what I was going to insist on." Deserved or not, Russell's crafty manner and legislative prosperity brought him new glory. He was now, as *Newsweek* later crowned him, "Lord of the Manor."[23]

29

A PHLOOGIE BEATS
ANYTHING

"WE DON'T ALWAYS AGREE with Russell Long," Common Cause lobbyist Fred Wertheimer mused in 1973 to the *Wall Street Journal*, "but when he's with you, there's nobody better to have on your side." Indeed, Wertheimer's statement captured the growing Washington perception that Russell—through position, seniority, and force of intellect—was at the apex of Senate power. "When he chose to go after an issue, to rally support behind his position," remembered former aide Wayne Thevenot, "it was a beautiful thing to watch if you're experienced enough to see what was going on." By the early 1970s, "Russell Long watching" was a Capitol Hill pastime.[1]

During most crucial tax debates, Russell invariably relinquished the floor and launched out in a hunt for votes. Roaming the Senate chamber, he stalked his prey. Sighting a prospect, Russell slung his arm around his colleague's shoulder and whispered into his ear. Other times, he stood at arm's length and poked his colleague in the stomach when he made a point. "And you could just sit there and watch things start to collapse with the opposition," Thevenot recalled. "It would crumble before your very eyes." Perhaps Russell's Democratic Finance Committee colleague Lloyd Bentsen of Texas best captured the sentiment about Russell's legislative prowess: "When I see him grab someone by the arm and put his mouth to their ear and start talking, I know what's going to happen. Something's about to move to Louisiana." Republican senator Robert Packwood reflected the common Senate perspective about Russell. "He is absolutely gregariously all over you, loving you," declared Packwood, who later chaired the committee during the mid-1980s. "You cannot reject the man."[2]

When courting a vote, Russell often instinctively understood the political dynamics of a senator's decision. "Long was very candid," a liberal western senator once told Ross Baker for his Senate study *Friend and Foe in the U.S. Senate*. "You would ask him a question [on a bill on which he was an expert] and he'd probably say, 'You don't want to vote for this,' because he'd already evaluated my ideological thinking." Another liberal Democrat, an easterner, related the same attribute. "It would not have been inconsistent with my memory of Russell Long to have him sponsoring a bill—push a bill—that would favor, say, the oil and gas interests that he really cared about. But he knew that I represented a consumer state and I can hear him today saying, 'You don't want to vote for that, representing [a consumer state].' " It was this honesty, adroitness, and persistence that usually made Russell so formidable.[3]

In Senate debate, Russell possessed the rare gift of simplicity. He spoke in plain English. Always, he reduced issues to their most basic, fundamental terms. "Colleagues often walk into a meeting or a floor debate virtually cold," *Congressional Quarterly* reporter Alan Ehrenhalt wrote in 1977, "with the choice of accepting Long's explanation, which is always simple and clear, or a dissenting view, expressed in arcane economic terms. Long gets the benefit of the doubt." For example, Russell once ridiculed a plan to raise social security taxes in gradual, incremental steps as "like cutting off a puppy's tail one inch at a time to spare him the pain." The image was simple and potent. "He always twists things around backwards and they come out reasonable," marveled one consumer lobbyist in 1977. "It's a talent that he has. It's remarkable."[4]

These attributes alone were not always enough to guarantee success. When he could not win a senator on the merits, Russell was rarely above pursuing a vote with a promise to help a colleague secure a tax break his constituents wanted. "He knows the Senate is full of guys that posture a lot but have something in their closet," a veteran tax lobbyist told *Congressional Quarterly* in 1977. "Every one of them has some constituency, some interest that he has to deal with. Long knows their interests, he knows their weaknesses, and he exploits them." In 1977, *Washington Post* reporter Robert Kaiser succinctly observed, "Long cultivates the [Finance] committee the way an orchid lover cares for his flowers." During their careers, hundreds of senators were known as horse traders and wheeler-dealers. Few, however, were as candid and open about the practice as Russell. During consideration of an energy bill in 1975, Democratic senator Gaylord Nelson of Wisconsin strolled into the Finance Committee room to complain that his state's interests were not considered in a tax break for railroads. Nelson wanted relief for Wisconsin's numerous railroad-over-water ferries. "I'll be happy to give you that one without need of further discussion," Russell immediately replied, "but I expect you in exchange to vote for this next tax credit we're about to discuss."[5]

Affable, jocular, almost cuddly at times, Russell became renowned for ruling his committee with a velvet glove. If a member was intimidated by Russell, it was never the result of a direct threat. Browbeating was not his style. Russell converted colleagues—often some of the most intense liberals—by accommodating their interests when possible. Democrat Floyd Haskell of Colorado was a prime example. Although Haskell belonged to the liberal forces who demanded Finance Committee reforms, Russell faithfully came to Haskell's aid when he faced a tough reelection campaign in 1977. Russell collected thousands of dollars in campaign contributions from Louisiana oilmen and their attorneys.[6]

To win the loyalty of other committee members, Russell cheerfully shared the appearance of power by giving them key subcommittee chairmanships. Freshman Democratic senator Daniel Patrick Moynihan of New York was an expert in welfare (the architect of Richard Nixon's Family Assistance Plan, which Russell defeated). Russell, therefore, gave him the welfare subcommittee. Russell also helped Moynihan honor a crucial campaign pledge when he secured an amendment to the 1977 Social Security bill giving hundreds of millions of dollars to New York's welfare program. Sugar is vital to Hawaii, once represented by Democrat Spark Matsunaga. So, Russell gave Matsunaga the subcommittee on sugar. In most cases, such gestures were made with no hint of anticipated reciprocity. Even so, when Russell scratched a colleague's back such remittance was clearly, albeit silently, understood.[7]

As a junior Republican, Oregon senator Robert Packwood was astonished at how Russell's fairness engendered tremendous loyalty, even among Republicans. "I never had any sense of senior maternalism about, 'There, there, young man. Just wait your turn and one day you'll get to say something.' He was eminently democratic to everybody on the committee." Russell's committee colleague, Matsunaga, concurred. "He makes you feel you're helping to make the decision," Matsunaga once told

Congressional Quarterly. "Actually, he's making it." Even when a colleague voted against him, Russell did not seem to mind. Never able to hold a grudge, Russell instinctively understood that today's foe might be the next day's ally. For continued success, Russell needed friends, not wounded enemies. "No question about it," one of his liberal colleagues once told *Newsweek*, "next to Hubert Humphrey, [Russell] is clearly the most congenial man in the Senate." Even reporters who disagreed with his philosophy appreciated Russell's integrity and straightforward style. "In the Senate," National Public Radio reporter Linda Wertheimer observed in 1975, "you've got all these presidential hopefuls standing around saying presidential things, and then you've got Long, who knows how to get things done. It's not often passion, but presidential passion, guiding these other senators, but Long's passion seems real."[8]

Russell's excessive affability was sometimes mistaken for mental debility. On the Senate floor, in committee or during speeches, Russell was forceful and persuasive. In private or in small meetings, however, he often left visitors with a much different impression. Intimate gatherings usually made Russell uncomfortable. Sometimes, he seemed incapable of making small talk. When excited, he stuttered. Even when calm, he mumbled. Names, even those of longtime staff members, eluded him on occasion. Russell's junior Louisiana colleague, J. Bennett Johnston, observed this amazing characteristic on numerous occasions. "Here was a senator who could be a master out there on the Senate floor, and yet when you had some visiting firemen who would come up [from Louisiana], it was almost like he was unintelligible. He was not communicating and they were scratching their heads, because he'd be talking about something else other than what they came to talk about. And whatever it was he was talking about frequently would not be compelling, relevant, or particularly coherent." The unknowing often concluded that Russell's befuddled, awkward manner meant that he could be dismissed lightly or easily defeated. Russell's friends—and more than a few conquered detractors—knew better than to underestimate his powerful and cunning intellect. "He's a corporatist with a corn-pone exterior," consumer advocate Ralph Nader once said, noting that Russell was "never more effective than when confronted by liberals who think they are smarter than he is." Observed a *New York* magazine reporter, "he may look a little sleepy, but he isn't."[9]

One aspect of Russell's affable style was especially crucial to his legislative success. Like his father and Uncle Earl, Russell had a rare gift for storytelling. He loved to regale audiences and his colleagues with tales of his father's and uncle's legendary exploits. He relied on a vast repertoire of jokes, anecdotes, and yarns. Sometimes his stories were true. Other times, Russell conveniently inserted his father or uncle into a joke he had heard. When he gave Huey or Earl a role in the tale, the joke became even more effective and entertaining. Russell usually laughed at his own stories, often chuckling as he approached his punch line. When amused by his own humor, the sound of Russell's laughter—actually a high-pitched cackle— filled the room. As longtime aide Michael Stern remembered,

> When I first came on the Finance Committee, I laughed at Senator Long's anecdotes like anybody else. But I didn't notice any particular pattern to them. Then, I started noticing that he would typically tell an anecdote exactly when tension had built up to a point where people were starting to get testy and the atmosphere was not conducive to legislative results. And you'd see somebody might be fulminating about something, or two people might be arguing heatedly about something, and suddenly you'd sort of see Senator Long lean back and chuckle to himself and everybody got a feeling of anticipation. Senator Long was now going to tell some Uncle Earl story, or some anecdote or something. And things would quiet down, and sure enough, he'd tell that story, and everybody would laugh and the tension would go down and you could start again.[10]

When the Finance Committee became bogged down over arcane matters of the 1975 emergency tax cut bill, Russell relied on his legendary humor to break the impasse. "If every man insists on knowing what he's voting for before he votes, we're not going to get a bill reported before Monday." Some laughed. Others interpreted the remark to mean that Russell was denying senators their rights to examine legislation. Those who knew him understood the remark for what it was—a quip to break the tension.[11]

At other times, Russell used an amusing story not to break the tension, but to make an extremely effective point. Once, in Finance Committee, Russell peddled a minor break for importers of Mardi Gras costume jewelry. When he encountered initial opposition, Russell resorted to a story. He told his committee members of the poker player who won a hand, and with it, a large pot of money. As the winner began gathering his money, another player stopped him, revealing his pitifully worthless cards. "This is known as a phloogie," the man declared as he pointed to a sign on the wall that read, "A phloogie beats anything." Reluctantly, the loser continued playing until he eventually drew a phloogie. Again, his competitor prevented him from collecting the winnings, this time pointing to another sign directly behind him, that read, "Only one phloogie a day wins." When the laughter died, Russell explained the provision he wanted was "just a phloogie for Louisiana—a little one-time thing." In the hysterical laughter, no one could remember to oppose Russell's request. "I think he would have got it anyway," Republican Finance member Robert Packwood insisted, "but you so much appreciated the humor that you were inclined to give it *for* the humor."[12]

Russell may never have needed his immense arsenal of legislative skills more than in 1976, when the liberal proponents of tax reform were at their most powerful and aggressive. Tax reform had a different meaning to almost every senator. To eastern liberals from oil- and gas-consuming states, it largely meant curtailing the vast array of tax breaks afforded U.S. energy interests. To Russell, these tax breaks, or "drilling incentives," as he often called them, were essential ingredients in the nation's quest for energy independence. To the liberal reformers, oil and gas industry breaks were costly, taxpayer-financed gifts bestowed on the largest industry of Russell's home state. Such criticism always annoyed Russell. "There is nothing easier than to be a reformer from a state that does not produce gas and oil," he complained in 1977. His whimsical definition of tax reform became a popular Washington adage: "Don't tax you. Don't tax me. Tax that fellow behind the tree." To Russell, a tax loophole "is something that benefits the other guy. If it benefits you, it is tax reform." The fellow behind the tree in 1976 was the oil and gas industry—and the Senate's liberals wanted to chop it down.[13]

With Russell blocking the way, meaningful tax reform would be a daunting task. Russell had frustrated the liberals by keeping a House-passed reform bill bottled up in Finance Committee since December. The legislation imposed heavy restrictions on tax deductions for real estate investment, farming, oil drilling, and other business enterprises. Russell feared that the bill would jeopardize thousands of jobs by stifling the economy. Reformers, in turn, charged that businessmen used many of those enterprises only as shelters to avoid taxes. Russell argued an across-the-board minimum tax would achieve the liberals' goal without depressing business. "I've learned in twenty-eight years in Congress that you can't have capitalism unless you have capital. I'd hate to see the old Horatio Alger tradition become a thing of the past in America." Even the word "reform" irked Russell. "If a man said he could make a lobster fly, he'd be put in an insane asylum," Russell told the *Washington Star* in February. "But if somebody claims he can make all men angels [on this side of heaven], we call him a reformer."[14]

Russell further aggravated the liberals in April when he said that he doubted he could meet a Senate Budget Committee target of raising two billion dollars in new revenues by ending various business tax deductions. The Budget Committee's resolution was the product of a liberal strategy to obtain tax reform by exploiting new congressional budget rules which required Congress, through its budget panels, to set general revenue and spending guidelines each year. While he respected the budget rules, Russell scorned ultimatums regarding the particular affairs of his committee's domain. To him, this edict was an audacious attempt by Budget chairman Edmund Muskie to usurp Finance Committee jurisdiction. While Muskie's committee might have the authority to set the general budget parameters, Russell believed that his committee had broad latitude within those guidelines. He would not be bullied.

Russell told the Senate that Muskie's argument reminded him of late vice president Alben Barkley's second marriage. "After he had been married a while, someone asked Vice President Barkley how the marriage was going along. He said, 'It's going just great. My wife and I had an understanding before we married. I would make all the big decisions and she would make all the small decisions. So far, we've been married six months, and we haven't had any big decisions to make.' " Laughter erupted, as Russell went on to make his point. "Mr. President, the way this thing was supposed to be, I thought the Budget Committee was going to make the big decisions and the Finance Committee was going to make the small decisions. I regret to say . . . the chairman of the Budget Committee cannot find anything small enough for the Finance Committee to decide anything about."[15]

The sparring lasted four days, until Russell finally prevailed on June 21. Muskie lost on two successive attempts to force the Senate to an early debate over extension of a thirty-five-dollar personal tax credit. After the second vote, he surrendered, "I get messages pretty clearly," Muskie said. "I got two within the last forty-five minutes."[16]

Russell received mixed reviews for his role of reform adversary. To liberal columnist Jack Anderson, Russell was a "champion of the wealthy" who "allowed the rich to escape paying their fair share" at the expense of "less privileged taxpayers." The more conservative *Wall Street Journal*, however, considered Russell a hero. "Well, it looks to us as if Senator Long is distinguishing himself in protecting the economy from the tax reformers," the *Journal* said in a June editorial. "Senator Long may not be a trained economist . . . but he understands that if the Robin Hood tax reformers in Congress had their way, the net effect would be another decline in capital investment, productivity and jobs." To Russell, the debate was not about preserving special interest tax deductions, but maintaining a strong business climate. "We want people to contribute to charity, so we allow a deduction for charitable giving," Russell told *Nation's Business* in 1977. "We want manufacturers to buy new equipment, start new plants, and put more people to work, so we give them tax credits and deductions for doing those things."[17]

Russell defeated Muskie in the first round, but his victory was incomplete. The frantic way in which the Finance Committee had reported the bill to the floor outraged Muskie, Edward Kennedy of Massachusetts, William Proxmire of Wisconsin, and other liberals. On the last day of the drafting sessions, the committee had hurriedly rammed seventy-three amendments through with little or no debate or explanation. "It was evident that the members in many cases did not know what they were approving," wrote *Washington Star* reporter Lee Cohn. "They relied largely on the staff to flag questionable amendments and staff objections did block some proposals. Long was the only member who appeared to be keeping up with nearly all of the amendments. Shuffling papers and calling on his colleagues to make their pitches, he presided in the style of an auctioneer."[18]

Kennedy and his forces, joined by consumer advocate Ralph Nader, began to make headway with their assaults on the Finance Committee process. They held daily press conferences and issued press releases attacking Russell and the way he crafted the bill. The strategy worked. The outcry over the steamrolled amendments forced Russell to convene three days of unusual, postlegislative hearings on the questionable provisions to appease his critics. In the end, Russell dropped twenty amendments. More important, the liberals coerced Russell into a significant reform. Hereafter, a transcript of all proceedings would be taken. Russell took the whole episode in stride. As Nader, Kennedy, and others were castigating him for back-room dealing, the predicament reminded Russell of a story, which he told to the crowded committee room. It seems, Russell said, that a south Louisiana school board was interviewing a prospective teacher. "Some people think the earth is round and some people think it's flat," Russell said one board member told the applicant. "We want to know what you think." The teacher replied, "Gentlemen, I came prepared to teach it either way." As the laughter subsided, Russell added a pragmatic postscript to the just-enacted reforms. "I'm ready to try it either way."[19]

Finally free to consider the bill's specific tax proposals, the Senate repeatedly spurned attempts by Kennedy, Muskie, and other liberals to restore the House-approved curbs on the wide array of tax shelters. As the debate ran past the June 30 target, the Senate postponed the bill's consideration until after the Democratic National Convention. Returning in late July, the Senate handed Russell one of his few defeats. Senators sided with Muskie in extending the thirty-five-dollar personal tax credit through 1977.

Later, Russell easily staved off attempts by the same senators to send his bill back to the Finance Committee for major revisions. After losing two successive recommittal votes on August 5, Muskie grumbled, "May I say to my colleagues you kicked the biggest hole in the budget process that you could conceivably kick." Late that evening, as the debate droned on, Muskie knew that the outcome was inevitable. The Senate would side with Russell in rejecting tax reform. He surrendered the floor, saying, "I am tired of hearing my voice." On August 6, after twenty-five days of debate and more than two hundred votes, the Senate passed the tax bill forty-nine to twenty-two—the longest, most complicated tax measure to pass the Senate in two decades.[20]

In conference, the result was a mixed bag for both sides. After nine grueling day-and-night sessions, conferees raised net revenues by $1.6 billion, while extending the individual tax cuts through 1977. Many of the tax shelter curbs, while tightened more than Russell would have wanted, were far weaker than originally prescribed by the House. One provision dear to Russell made the final cut. The conference doubled the investment tax credit through 1980 for businesses contributing to his beloved Employee Stock Ownership Plans. Conferees further sweetened the ESOP provision by an extra half-percent if the deduction was matched by employee contributions. In September, both houses overwhelming adopted the conference report.[21]

Russell had largely thwarted the reform efforts, but the defeat left his liberal detractors smarting. Russell prevailed, they believed, because he ran the Finance Committee behind closed doors. Even though Russell had compromised and agreed to their demands for complete transcripts, Common Cause announced in November a campaign to remove Russell as Finance chairman. "We think the committee's procedures have got to be changed," said Common Cause vice president Fred Wertheimer. Russell's committee, said Wertheimer, was "a haven for special interest pleading" that is "uniquely unfair" compared to the workings of other congressional committees. Specifically, Common Cause and the Senate liberals wanted to decentralize Russell's power by investing greater legislative authority—

the ability to consider and initiate legislation—with subcommittees. Now that new rules for the Senate's Democratic Steering Committee called for secret votes on the confirmation of committee chairmen, Common Cause saw an opportunity. The group had helped oust Louisiana congressman F. Edward Hebert from chairmanship of the Armed Services Committee two years earlier. Its members now hoped to exploit the new procedure to defeat Russell, or at least send him a message.[22]

Russell's response to the challenge: "If Common Cause is run half as democratic as the Senate Finance Committee, it will be a great surprise to me." Republican senator Robert Packwood, an unabashed fan of Russell, was more direct in his defense of the chairman. "I think I know what the object[ion] is to the Finance Committee and, on some occasion, to the chairman. The objection is that many people who do not agree with him philosophically often lose. They lose when they have a fair fight in committee, and they come out on the floor and have a fair fight, and they lose; and they think that somehow it is because we do not have subcommittees."[23]

Russell believed that Hebert was deposed from his committee chairmanship largely because he did not aggressively challenge his rivals. Russell vowed not to make Hebert's mistake. If forced, he would compromise to stave off the challenge. Shortly before the February 1977 vote, Russell calmly promised to give Finance Committee subcommittees jurisdiction over all but the most important legislation. Overnight, the threat to his chairmanship evaporated. The secret Democratic caucus vote was forty-two to six in Russell's favor. None of the six was willing to take his opposition to Russell to the open party caucus, which later voted sixty to nothing to reelect him chairman.[24]

While Russell's power was curbed, albeit slightly, he managed to emerge with even more perceived influence. In a peculiar sense, Common Cause blessed him by furnishing the occasion to flex his legislative muscles. Remarked *Wall Street Journal* tax writer John Pierson: "Ambrose Bierce once defined a 'quorum' this way: 'In the United States Senate, a quorum consists of the chairman of the Committee on Finance and a messenger from the White House.' Times have changed since the turn of the century, when Mr. Bierce wrote 'The Devil's Dictionary.' The present chairman of the Committee on Finance no longer bothers with the White House messenger."[25]

30

THE FASTEST GUN
IN THE WEST

$\mathcal{A}$LTHOUGH RUSSELL DID NOT CAMPAIGN actively for newly elected president Jimmy Carter, he believed that he was partly responsible for the former Georgia governor's election in November 1976. As architect of the one-dollar checkoff for the presidential campaign fund—which provided $21.8 million to each candidate—Russell was proud that a Democratic nominee finally competed on equal financial footing with his wealthier Republican counterpart. "For the first time in recent years the Republicans were not able to outspend the Democrats with a deluge of money in the final months," Russell noted shortly after Carter's narrow victory over President Gerald Ford. Russell said the election proved that "we are able to remove the corrupting influence of major campaign contributions from the presidential race."[1]

While he found joy in the triumph of his campaign fund, Russell eventually derived no small amount of consternation in its product—Jimmy Carter. The man from Plains, Georgia, arrived in Washington a resolute reformer, pledged to return government to the people. He was proud of his isolation from Washington and the Congress. He bragged he had always been a Democrat, but had never met a Democratic president. Jimmy Carter, who brought an ambitious legislative agenda to Washington,

338

soon learned painful lessons about operating the nation's levers of power. More often than not, Russell was his reluctant teacher.

Shortly after the election, Carter held court at his home in Plains, where he interviewed potential cabinet nominees and talked policy with influential government and business leaders. For weeks, the little Georgia community was the center of world attention. A summons from the president-elect was a coveted prize. In time, Carter sent for Russell, who spent the night in the president-elect's home. There, he urged Carter to embrace his Employee Stock Ownership Plan approach. "I urged him to consider putting in his inaugural address the idea that we had a poor distribution of wealth in the United States and that we ought to go to work in changing it." Carter, Russell noted, disregarded the advice. "I, at least," he sighed, "had a chance to put in an oar in favor of my idea." Exactly forty-four years earlier, Russell's father met with similar presidential ambivalence when he attempted to persuade President Franklin Roosevelt of the merits of his own, more radical wealth redistribution plan. Unlike his father, however, Russell eventually proved that he had the power and influence to enact his plan, with or without Carter's support. (Carter did take Russell's advice in one important area. He agreed to nominate one of Russell's top aides— Laurence N. Woodworth, staff director of the Joint Committee on Internal Revenue Taxation—as assistant secretary of the Treasury for tax policy.)[2]

Following his inauguration, Carter unveiled his legislative program—a grandiose assortment of measures with few priorities. The new president proposed economic stimulus legislation, reauthorization of the clean air program, a comprehensive energy program, welfare reform, a new farm program, hospital cost containment legislation, reduction in water projects, housing and urban assistance, and bureaucratic reform. Breathtaking in scope, but lacking priorities, Carter's program overwhelmed Congress. Confessed one Carter aide: "We overloaded the circuits."[3]

If Carter had a priority in his early days, it was his legislation to stimulate the nation's sagging economy with a one-time, fifty-dollar tax rebate to all taxpayers. Coupled with an additional fifty-dollar bonus for all social security recipients, Carter said his program would "provide prompt spending power to almost every American." The plan, which would also raise standard tax deductions for individuals and married couples and create a public works/jobs program, was met with vast indifference in Congress. "That became a laughing stock, just a laughing stock," Russell recalled. "Surely, he could have found somebody to give him better advice. He didn't ask my advice about that type of program. He just announced it—here's what we're going to do." Although Carter had not consulted key members of Congress, the House Ways and Means Committee, under Chairman Al Ullman, promptly took up the bill in mid-February. Two days later, Ullman's panel reported it favorably to the full House with several modifications. Instead of championing a rebate for all taxpayers, Ullman's committee opted for payments to families with annual incomes of less than thirty thousand dollars. Committee members also scaled back the standard deduction increase. On March 8, the House approved the bill, narrowly turning back a Republican effort to expunge the rebate.[4]

Russell greeted the rebate with quiet contempt. "The problem with the bill is that it doesn't direct itself at the areas that are out of work—the young, unskilled, and women. Most of them don't have the skills to take a job if you could provide one." Russell convened hearings on the bill in March, shortly after the House-passed bill reached the Senate. As expected, he had strong opinions on improving Carter's plan. He adjusted the personal deductions and a House provision providing business tax credits for hiring new employees. Proving his willingness to work with his new president, Russell generously left Carter's rebate intact. Yet, he declared the onus was on Carter to persuade the Senate of its merits. "It used to be that the President or someone wanting a bill could talk to a committee chairman," Russell explained to a Louisiana reporter. "If the committee chairman thought it was a good idea, that was all there was to it." To Carter, Russell advised, "You have to talk to those troops down there." By April 14, the issue was moot. Four days before the Senate's debate began, Carter pulled the plug on the rebate. He explained that an improved economy no longer required such stimulus. To House and Senate leaders, especially Russell, Carter's abrupt about-face was frustrating, but welcome. While his instincts told him to crush the rebate, Russell had shown abundant deference to the new president. Now, suddenly Carter retreated. Remembered one Carter aide, "There was where we first got the reputation—'You can't trust these people.' "[5]

Even without the rebate, the bill Congress finally enacted had its attractive features. It extended the thirty-five-dollar personal tax credit another year and addressed the 7 percent unemployment rate with a business tax credit for new employees. The bill also simplified the tax code by adopting new flat levels for individual and joint standard deductions. As usual, Russell tucked inside something for Louisiana—a thirty-million-dollar, one-year intangible drilling cost exemption for independent oil and gas drillers.

If Carter thought the opposition to his rebate plan was daunting, it was nothing compared to the dismaying antagonism that greeted another of his proposals. His plan to cancel or reduce funding for twenty-three dam and water projects sparked outrage in every corner of Capitol Hill. These projects were the "worst examples" of "pork-barrel" politics, said Carter, who believed that members of Congress used the projects as economic leverage to win votes. The proposal blindsided most members of Congress. Not only did they challenge Carter's criticism of their projects, most suffered the double indignity of not having been consulted or forewarned. Many of them first read of the plan in the newspaper. Adding to their fury was Carter's proposal to fully fund the worthy projects in the first year. This meant scuttling the age-old practice of yearly, incremental appropriations that magnified a project's political impact. The matter baffled Russell, who believed that the president had violated a basic political rule. "He was asking for a fight when he didn't have the votes to win to begin with."[6]

With its maze of waterways, few were surprised to find Louisiana topping Carter's list with four targeted projects, including two listed for elimination. Not content to convey their fury through the floor speeches and the news media, Russell and several colleagues took their complaints directly to the White House. At a meeting with Carter's aides, Russell rose to introduce himself: "My name is Russell Long, and I am the chairman of the Senate Finance Committee." When they learned how Russell presented himself to the president's men, many reporters concluded that his introduction was a sarcastic reminder of the powerful sway he held over their proposal. In his usual modest manner, Russell dismissed that notion. "I never thought of that in terms of throwing my weight around or anything like that," Russell explained. "I just thought they'd like to know who the devil this guy was that had asked them a question about the matter." Russell said that his reason was simple and humble. "If they didn't know the guy they were explaining that to was the chairman of the Senate Finance Committee, they ought to know it. They weren't just explaining that to a passerby." Undeterred by the congressional furor, Carter held firm to his ground as Congress reduced his proposal to eliminate only nine projects and modify three. He first vowed to veto the bill, but backed down and signed it when persuaded the controversy was destroying progress of the remainder of his legislative program.[7]

For the rest of his term, Carter battled Congress over the issue. He never won. In fact, the proposal's only accomplishment appeared to have been the severe damage inflicted on Carter's congressional relations. "The controversy appeared to extend beyond substantive concerns,"

Carter historian Charles Jones observed. "The president challenged the method by which these projects were developed and funded. He was rather explicit in condemning congressional politics on this issue. Thus, members were faced with losing both their projects and their self-esteem." In his memoirs, even Carter acknowledged that the issue "was the one that caused the deepest breach between me and the Congressional leadership." Russell put it more bluntly. "It was dumb, dumb, dumb, dumb."[8]

The debacle over water projects did little to endear Carter's other programs to embittered members of Congress, as evidenced by the cool reception accorded the president's energy proposals later that year. "When I declared the energy effort to be the moral equivalent of war," Carter wrote in his memoirs," . . . it was impossible for me to imagine the bloody legislative battle we would have to win before the major campaign was over." Indeed, few questioned the necessity for comprehensive energy legislation. With oil imports increasing at alarming rates, the nation's trade imbalance was growing wider each year. The problem was unmistakable. Reaching consensus around a solution, however, was nearly impossible.[9]

Carter believed that consumption was the culprit. He urged curbing the American appetite for cheap fuel by imposing higher energy taxes. The increased revenue would go to the poor. Furthermore, the president urged greater efforts to identify alternative fuel sources. Russell vehemently disagreed with this strategy. He believed that raising the cost of drilling would drive domestic drillers out of business and result in greater imports of cheaper foreign oil. Carter's energy philosophy, Russell later told *Nation's Business*, "is an unmitigated disaster."[10]

Deceptively, at first, Carter got his way on energy matters. Congress promptly granted his wish for a new Department of Energy, to which he appointed Richard Nixon's former secretary of defense, James Schlesinger. Then, in the early months of 1977, a record cold snap depleted energy supplies, forcing wholesale closure of schools and factories. In less than a week, Congress handed Carter the Emergency Natural Gas Act. It gave him authority to temporarily allocate interstate natural gas to areas of greatest need. "Unfortunately," Carter wrote, "the almost unbelievable speed of Congress in enacting this legislation was not a harbinger of things to come."[11]

In April, after minimal congressional consultation, Carter submitted his national energy plan. It included a five-cent-per-gallon gasoline tax increase, a gas-guzzler tax on older vehicles, various conservation measures, and a reduced reliance on oil and gas as fuels with an accompanying increased emphasis on nuclear power, coal, and solar energy. Russell had minor quarrels with Carter's conservation initiatives. The rest of Carter's plan was a different matter entirely. To force down consumption, Carter proposed a variety of tax increases and controls on the oil and gas industry. Its centerpiece was a three-step "equalization tax" on all domestic production at the wellhead to bring prices to the world level by 1980. He proposed rebating all revenues to the public. In addition, the president proposed a complex collection of taxes and other provisions, all designed to encourage greater conservation by driving up energy prices.

On April 21, Carter invited Russell to the White House to discuss his energy plan. That night, the president wrote in his diary:

> I talked to Senator Long again . . . and asked him to come up and meet me later in the day, which he did. Senator Long is one of the shrewdest legislative tacticians who has ever lived. He always takes the attitude that he's innocent, doesn't quite know what is going on, and the other senators put things over on him, but that he'll do the best he can. He's a shrewd negotiator, and I like him.[12]

"I did like him," Carter insisted in his memoirs, "but I soon learned that he and the other senators from oil-producing states were busy plotting strategy to short-circuit our plans and substitute legislation of their own."[13]

Meanwhile, in the House, House speaker Thomas P. "Tip" O'Neill embraced Carter's energy program and created a peculiar Ad Hoc Select Committee on Energy. The panel coordinated activities of the five committees exercising jurisdiction over various portions of the five bills that made up the Carter program. By the August recess, House members had approved Carter's program virtually unchanged. They sent the tax portions to Russell's Finance Committee and the rest to the Energy Committee, chaired by Washington Democrat Henry Jackson.

Whether it was the calming effect of Congress's annual monthlong August holiday or the determined opposition from Russell, few would disagree that House passage was the energy plan's finest and only glorious hour. Russell hated Carter's energy tax proposals, as did a great number of Finance Committee members. When Energy Secretary James Schlesinger had appeared before the committee in August, he was shocked by the hostility the program aroused. "The weakness of the president's bill is that it requires sacrifice of Americans," Russell told him, "but does not assure them of a great supply of energy." Republican William Roth of Delaware agreed. "This is not an energy bill but a massive rip-off of the

middle class. . . . It is based on despair, no growth and higher taxes."
Republican Bob Packwood of Oregon and Democrat Herman Talmadge of
Georgia were also vocal opponents, prompting Schlesinger's vastly understated response: "I detect there may be a greater degree of skepticism in
this committee than I have encountered in other committees."[14]

To Russell, Carter was attacking the wrong problem. Conservation
efforts were laudable, but they did not address the nation's real energy
dilemma—a dependable, inexpensive domestic energy supply. Increasing
taxes on energy production, Russell believed, would only make it more
difficult for domestic drillers to explore for new sources of oil and gas. "We
have enormous reserves of conventional sources of energy—enough to
last us for hundreds of years," Russell told Schlesinger. "Long before they
are exhausted, we will have developed solar, geothermal, and nuclear
power adequate to provide for our needs forever. I certainly intend to do
all I can in this bill to encourage greater energy production."[15]

By October, the Finance Committee gutted three of Carter's most
prominent tax proposals—the wellhead equalization tax, the industrial gas
tax, and the tax on gas-guzzling cars. By themselves, the three proposals
accounted for about half the money Carter expected his energy program
would generate. As long as the House and Senate headed in opposite
directions, Carter's plan was doomed. When Russell reported the legislation to the full Senate in October, the only real revenue raiser was an
extension of the four-cent-a-gallon gasoline tax. Carter's bill was in sham-
bles. Instead of raising money, the Finance Committee bill primarily
consisted of forty billion dollars in conservation tax credits.

Throughout the summer—as support for the program eroded—the
White House was complacent, seemingly comfortable with the expectation
the Senate would ultimately discover the wisdom of Carter's program. As
late as October 16, Energy Secretary Schlesinger had appeared on CBS's
"Face the Nation" to downplay Russell's ability to put his own imprint on
the program. "When the original package went to the House, " Schlesinger told the program's panelists, "there were all these comments to the
effect that the program was being gutted or riddled and so on. Then in
August, when the House voted out virtually the entire package, everyone
said it was a remarkable triumph. I would not be surprised if we went
through the same cycle with regard to the Congress as a whole."[16]

But Russell understood the Senate better than Carter and his men. He
knew that neither his committee nor the full Senate would ever adopt the
House-passed energy program without at least some energy development
incentives. Even so, Russell wanted to help Carter achieve at least a

partial victory. He knew his best opportunity to do this rested in passing his stripped-down measure through the Senate. Then, in conference, Russell could trade off some of the conservation credits for at least one of the president's taxes. There, perhaps, he could strike a delicate compromise acceptable to both houses of Congress. Some senators were troubled by the strategy of writing wholesale legislation in conference. Even Russell admitted the peculiar nature of his scheme, conceding that "ordinarily we don't do business this way." Connecticut senator Abraham Ribicoff, however, summed up the situation, explaining, "We're trying to breathe life into something that's dead. . . . It's obvious that we are at a complete stalemate. Do you take up the issue and let it die? Or do you do something else, like this?"[17]

To succeed, Russell and his Finance Committee conferees needed carte blanche from the Senate to make the deals necessary to hand Carter some form of victory. Energy Committee chairman Henry Jackson, whose influence over the energy plan was threatened by Russell's gambit, ridiculed the proposition as a "blank check to the oil industry." Jackson had his own Energy Committee bill, which he hoped would serve as the main Senate vehicle for Carter's energy program. Afraid their jurisdictional dispute might scuttle chances for any cohesive energy legislation, Carter summoned Russell, Jackson, and other congressional leaders to a White House breakfast.[18] That night, the president described the meeting in his diary:

> Met with the congressional leaders for breakfast and we discussed almost exclusively the energy legislation. I particularly wanted Scoop Jackson and Russell Long there, so that we could have it out among a group of Democrats concerning their differences, which are very deep and personal. I thought Russell acted very moderately and like a gentlemen, but Scoop . . . was at his worst. . . . At the same time, he is supporting my position much more closely than Russell is.[19]

Jackson was not Russell's only strident detractor. Budget Committee chairman Edmund Muskie was a harsh critic. Russell's planned approach—passing the huge conservation tax credits without offsetting revenue increases—was irresponsible and a breach of the congressional budget process, Muskie charged. "We think the Senate needs to be responsible for its own action," said Muskie, "and we don't think that we should wait for a House-Senate conference." When Russell pledged to oppose any conference agreement that the president would not sign, the Senate gave him the authority he wanted.[20]

Through six days of floor debate, Russell was firmly in control. Of the forty-nine amendments adopted, only two were ones he opposed, and even those were relatively innocuous. Russell now had his bargaining chips, forty billion dollars' worth. He was ready and loaded for conference. With the Senate's blessing, he had the negotiating power he wanted. The only question remaining was how he would use his power. To a *Washington Star* reporter, Russell described his situation: "That's like being the fastest gun in the West. Every gun in town is looking for you. Everyone wants to challenge you and beat you." As he headed toward conference with the House, Russell's influence was formidable, especially if viewed from the Ways and Means Committee. To the *Washington Post*, one White House lobbyist summarized the attitude of many House members as they girded for battle with Russell: "This is Russell Long, so I know he's going to trick me out of my socks."[21]

Adding to his substantial influence was one widely acknowledged fact— President Carter needed an energy bill more than Congress wanted to pass one. But the House wanted a bill more than the Senate, which meant that the success or failure of the entire program largely hinged on Russell's willingness to compromise. "The whole conference will center on the activities of Russell Long," senior Ways and Means Democrat Dan Rostenkowski admitted. "Everybody is spooked by Long," one of Carter's energy advisers told the *Wall Street Journal*. As the conference opened its deliberations in late October, Carter promised his congressional allies he would not circumvent them to strike a deal with Russell. But even one of those supporters, seemingly eager to put the issue to rest, urged the president to do just that. "Whether it is behind closed doors or out on Pennsylvania Avenue," the anonymous congressional ally told the *Wall Street Journal*, "Jimmy Carter has no choice but to cut a deal with Long."[22]

Any hopes that Russell would launch the conference with a flurry of trading was short-lived. When the conferees convened, he was in no mood to barter. For weeks, he played the all-too-familiar waiting game. His leverage, in turn, increased with each passing day. As the first week dragged on, House conferees complained that Russell was refusing to settle tax issues until a separate conference committee—considering the nontax portions of Carter's plan—voted on price increases for natural gas. Russell, the House members grumbled, was holding them hostage until the other conferees reported a bill to his liking. Russell responded that the real impediment was the House conferees' refusal to consider tax incentives for drilling. In fact, no one really knew what kind of bill Russell would accept. At least one leading conferee, Democratic representative Thomas Ashley of Ohio, seemed to understand Russell's ploy. "If I was in his position, I guess I'd be doing the same thing," Ashley admitted, after eight days of relaxed conference negotiations failed to resolve even one major House-Senate conflict. Eventually, Russell's waiting game fatigued the House members. They were ready to compromise. Even Russell's adversarial counterpart, Ways and Means chairman Al Ullman, appeared prepared to accommodate Russell. "If we can add a couple of production incentives to satisfy the senator, I'm willing to do it," said Ullman. Despite Ullman's growing willingness to bargain, another obstacle remained. This time, Carter's men were the impediment to an agreement. To Russell's surprise, the White House spurned all attempts at compromise. Carter, still oblivious to the political realities of the situation, insisted on the House bill. Russell was perplexed. As much as he wanted to help Carter, he needed the president's cooperation to do so.[23]

"If I were in their position," Russell complained after another unproductive conference session shortly after Thanksgiving, "I'd take whatever I could get." In Russell's view, prospects for compromise were bleak. "We're as far apart as two poles. The administration has been more of a burden than a help. The trouble is when the administration people come up and offer their advice, all they do is offer us the House bill." While the White House remained obstinate, Russell's own position hardened. He would only consider a crude oil equalization tax if it were accompanied with acceptable drilling incentives. "I'm not going to vote for it without provisions to firm up production," he declared on December 7. "My view—the view of the majority [of the Finance Committee]—is that we want to see something on the production side that would justify voting for a tax."[24]

The year ended with no accord on the major portions of Carter's plan. All agreed that the White House's lobbying had been sloppy and naive. Carter had misjudged Congress. Too often, he was on the defensive. He was rarely a dynamic, influential part of the bargaining process. His efforts to rally public support for a program with little or no national constituency was a dismal failure, leaving an enormous vacuum of leadership that Russell was all too happy to fill.

Carter had tragically underestimated Russell's power and misjudged his determination to oppose an ill-advised energy plan. "He looked on Russell as an operator and did not understand the breadth and depth of Long for a while," said Russell's Finance Committee colleague, Lloyd Bentsen of Texas. "He looked at him as an oil-state senator, and Russell was much more than that." By year's end, Carter was wiser about Congress, in general, and Russell, in particular. "He wasn't dealing with a neophyte," Russell declared years later. "I'd been around for a couple of years."[25]

"Meantime," *Washington Star* columnist Mary McGrory wrote shortly before Christmas, "Russell Long appears to be running the country. It must occur to Carter that the senator from Louisiana has found a way to be president without having been elected to the job." Reflecting on his yearlong battle with the Finance Committee chairman, even Carter could not resist playfully embracing McGrory's conclusion. Months later, at a Capitol Hill Democratic dinner, the president remarked to hysterical laughter, "I came here naive, proud of myself for having been elected as the first president from the Deep South to take over the reins of the great federal government of our country—and then I came to Washington and found that Russell Long had filled that position for a long time."[26]

31

MY BEST JUDGMENT

$\mathcal{I}$T WAS AN IMPROMPTU intellectual exercise in the Senate Press Gallery which attracted a group of reporters one afternoon in 1977. At first, a clear-cut answer to the question seemed daunting—which state enjoyed the most effective representation in the Senate? Down the list the reporters went, until they came to Louisiana. "Ah, well, that's it," one journalist said. "The game's over." What they all understand, said Joan McKinney, a Louisiana correspondent who watched the game, was "in Russell Long and Bennett Johnston, Louisiana had the most effective, taking-care-of-its-own-interests delegation in the Senate."[1]

From his stewardship of Louisiana's numerous flood control and navigation projects to interstate highways and military bases, Russell cast a wide and long shadow of influence over his state's political and economic landscape. Almost singlehandedly, Russell had saved Louisiana's sugar cane industry in 1971 by preserving the crop's important price support program. Louisiana's oil and gas drillers owed much of their prosperity to Russell's eternal vigilance on their behalf. Several major industries, employing thousands of workers, were now in Louisiana simply because Russell importuned the company's executives to open a plant. Louisianians even had Russell to thank for their hapless professional football team, the New Orleans Saints. No matter what the legislation, Russell always seemed to find a way to tuck away a little something for Louisiana.

For all his popularity and acclaim—his favorable ratings now hovered around 80 percent—Russell believed such political capital was of little use unless a senator used it in constructive ways. Russell's junior colleague, J. Bennett Johnston, recalled he received high marks in a public opinion poll which was released several years into his first Senate term in the mid-1970s. "He [Russell] said, 'Bennett, that's too high. If you have this job rating that high, it shows you're not using your influence in the Senate. Because that means you're just, in effect, following the path of least resistance. A statesman, or a real senator, will be doing controversial [things], at least [he] will be spending his credibility to a greater extent than that poll would indicate.'" Indeed, Russell's philosophy of statesmanship was never tested more rigorously than when Jimmy Carter proposed his treaties to relinquish U.S. control of the Panama Canal.[2]

Ink on the 1903 Panama Canal Treaty was barely dry before Panama and the United States were bickering over control of the extraordinary, yet unfinished waterway linking the Atlantic and Pacific oceans. For sixty-three years after its completion in 1914, the two nations could not agree on the canal's sovereignty. In 1964, President Lyndon Johnson signed three treaties with Panama to forestall violence against students who raised an American flag outside a U.S.-operated high school. Russell joined a chorus of congressional opposition to Johnson's treaties. His rhetoric was bellicose. Instead of negotiating with the Panamanians, Russell suggested the United States should "fight if necessary" for ultimate control of the canal. "The sooner our country shows the world it will not be pushed around by every small nation that attempts it, the sooner our image will be raised and the sooner will we gain the respect of all people." The treaties, roundly attacked in Congress, were never ratified.[3]

By 1977, public sentiment was no more favorable to a diplomatic resolution of the canal's sovereignty dispute than in 1964. The two nations, however, had been quietly negotiating their differences since new talks began in 1970. Jimmy Carter entered the White House in 1977 persuaded that relations between the two countries would continue to deteriorate unless Congress ratified new treaties giving Panama ultimate control of the canal. In September 1977, Carter and Panamanian leader General Omar Torrijos signed accords to give Panama the waterway by the year 2000. The two men signed a separate neutrality pact guaranteeing both nations the right to defend the canal after December 31, 1999.

To many, the Panama Canal was a symbol of American ingenuity and strength. An initial Gallup poll showed Americans were overwhelmingly opposed to Carter's treaties. Even among those who correctly answered several questions about the canal and the treaties, a bare 51 percent favored Senate ratification. Constituent mail to Russell's Washington office ran overwhelmingly against the treaties. A *Los Angeles Times* reporter observed that in Louisiana the treaties "were about as popular as the income tax. Most folks wanted to turn the Canal Zone over to Omar Torrijos about as much as they would want to cede New Orleans' French Quarter to [then-Soviet leader] Leonid I. Brezhnev." For a while, at least, Russell had time to reflect on his decision. The White House asked him to keep an open mind until the Senate hearings. Out of deference to Carter, Russell and several other undecided senators kept their misgivings to themselves.[4]

The president and his aides who bungled the previous year's effort to enact their energy program showed almost none of their earlier ineptitude when challenged with winning Senate support for the treaties. This time, the lobbying effort was intense and markedly more sophisticated. The administration took many senators to Panama to see the situation first-hand. Their questions about the treaties prompted immediate and comprehensive answers. Prominent figures—including former President Gerald Ford, former first lady Lady Bird Johnson and AFL-CIO President George Meany—were mobilized to speak in favor of the treaties. The White House launched a public relations blitz which included regular briefings by Carter and his aides for local government officials, newspaper editors, and heads of civic groups.

Organized opposition to the treaties was vigorous, as well. Former California governor Ronald Reagan and movie actor John Wayne were two prominent and vocal Americans to whom the canal was a supreme emblem of American prowess and engineering skill. Turning it over to the Panamanians, argued Republican senator Robert Griffin of Michigan, would "be a dangerous step, a gamble for the United States and the security of the United States." As the public debate began, Russell, like most southerners, opposed the treaties. "Frankly, one of the reasons I was opposed to it was because the people were opposed to it. I felt that thing would be political suicide—which it was [for several senators]."[5]

Never persuaded supporting the treaties was anything other than bad politics, Russell, nonetheless, slowly moved toward Carter's camp. Divisions existed even among Russell's staff. "He, like other people, was very seriously torn about [the treaties]," remembered Russell's then-top aide, Jim Guirard. "His constituency from Louisiana was dead set against it. On the other side of the coin, he, in general terms, has the impression that through the years the foreign policy area was more or less the prerogative of the president." Influential in Russell's eventual conversion was historian David McCullough's sweeping account of the creation of the canal, *The Path Between the Seas*. McCullough chronicled not only American resolve and engineering genius, but the crude methods President Theodore Roosevelt employed to pry the Panamanian territory from the government of Colombia. Russell finally resolved to help Carter in March, after the president argued his case in a nationally televised speech. As he watched from his Watergate apartment, Russell said he turned to Carolyn. "I said, 'Well, Carolyn, this is the kind of situation where people in the position I hold ought to go with the president, even if it's not politically popular.' After all, I was chairman of a major committee and I was a Democrat. He was a Democrat. And while this thing was, politically, going to be a disaster—it was going to cost us some good senators, and it sure as hell did—when it gets that far along, if you're one of those who'll probably survive it, then you ought to go ahead and vote with him on it." On March 11, Russell placed a call to Carter from the living room of his apartment. He would support the treaties, he told the president, and he expected nothing in return.[6]

Russell's was one of a handful of crucial votes. In early February, during the first week of debate over the neutrality treaty, the White House counted sixty-two senators in favor of ratification (five votes short of the necessary two-thirds majority). Twenty-eight senators were opposed and ten undecided. Among southerners, many opposed or undecided, Russell's support would be influential. When Russell finally committed his vote to Carter, he agreed to lobby several colleagues. "There were people [Russell lobbied] who were willing to vote for it if it gave [the White House] the votes they needed," recalled Russell's former aide, Karen Stall. Those same senators, Stall remembered, told Russell they would oppose the treaties if their votes were not needed. "Without me, he couldn't have passed it," Russell said flatly, claiming he helped persuade senators Howard Cannon of Nevada and S. I. Hayakawa of California to vote with Carter.[7]

The day before the Senate vote on the neutrality treaty, March 15, Russell announced his decision. Unlike his junior colleague, Bennett Johnston, Russell bluntly admitted he would defy overwhelming Louisiana public sentiment and vote for ratification. As usual, he employed plain language and persuasive logic as he explained to the full Senate the reason for his vote:

> My best judgment is that the new treaties do serve the present and long-run strategic interests of the United States, and I will vote to ratify them. That does not make them perfect documents—or eliminate future risks—but I think the greatest risks to the United States would occur if the treaties were defeated. . . . I think we Americans can understand how we would feel if our

nation were cut in half by a canal, and with a ten-mile zone totally controlled by a foreign government. We wouldn't like it—and in fact, would not tolerate it.

Despite our enormous military power, the key to a civilized world in the future depends upon working out problems between countries without having to resort to war. . . . In my judgment, it is my duty to vote to ratify this treaty if I am to be equal to what the framers of the Constitution expected of men like me. I make this point, because I am fully convinced both by my mail as well as by the telephone calls I am receiving from my closest friends and dearest friends that my vote at this time may not reflect the view of the majority of the voters of Louisiana. [8]

As Russell expected, his vote sparked a firestorm of public criticism, kept alive by his vote a month later in favor of the second treaty to relinquish control of the canal. To this treaty, however, Russell proposed a condition. Ratified by the Senate, Russell's amendment assured the right of the United States to negotiate for a new canal with any other nation, beginning with Mexico and including Colombia. Returning to Baton Rouge shortly after the first vote, Russell faced perhaps the most friendly audience possible—a forum that included a large number of state legislators, all who understood the risks involved in voting against public sentiment. "There are times when you are going to do what's right for this country and to preserve its freedom even if it isn't popular," Russell told the sympathetic lawmakers. There were other times over the years when he believed he had voted contrary to Louisiana public opinion, Russell said, but the treaty vote was "perhaps the toughest vote I ever cast in the Senate." Other audiences were not so sympathetic to Russell's dilemma. One anti-treaty group began organizing a movement to recall Russell. [9]

While public opinion may have been against him—"I must say, it hurt more than I thought it was going to hurt"—Russell received surprising support from several of Louisiana's most conservative newspapers, even some that had opposed the treaties. "Russell Long, even if we disagree with his vote on this particular issue," the *Shreveport Times* editorialized, "is one of Louisiana's most valuable natural resources. . . . That record has got to count for something, and should not be wiped out with a single vote, no matter what the issue." Said another conservative newspaper, the *Monroe Morning World*, "Agree with him or not, Russell Long did his job, and that's all he did." [10]

After years of reflection, Russell was even more persuaded of the wisdom of his vote:

If we had not ratified that treaty, we'd have had to send troops—having built up those people to think we were going to ratify that treaty and turn that canal over to them. They were stirred up to the point that we'd have had to send troops down there. There'd have been some fighting. The hell of it is the damage to America wouldn't have been limited to Panama. Once the fighting started and the bloodshed started, all those Latin American countries [would] rise up and kick us out of the Organization of American States. They'd demand that we be expelled from the United Nations, and everywhere you go, we'd be catching hell about it. And they'd send all our ambassadors home persona non grata. . . . I think by the time it was all over, people would have said we should have ratified the fool treaty.[11]

Despite this support from more open-minded sources, Russell understood his vote would exact a political price. He was only two years from his next election and a stiff challenge from Baton Rouge state Representative Louis "Woody" Jenkins, who would charge Russell's vote was proof he had lost touch with his constituency. "I knew it would hurt a lot in the short run," Russell admitted, "but I thought in the long run it wouldn't hurt that much. It fooled me. That issue stayed alive longer than I thought. . . . In a close race, that would beat me for office." Russell also knew his popularity in Louisiana was enormous. He suspected his vote would cost him five, perhaps ten, percentage points in the next election. He was willing to risk it, reflecting on the words of Israeli leader Abba Eban, which he quoted to his colleagues before the first treaty vote: "A statesman must build a bridge between his experience and his vision, between ancient fidelities and new hopes, between echoes of the past and the call of the future." Perhaps his remark to an aide after the vote provided the greatest insight into his decision. Russell, the man who vigorously supported the Vietnam War but was later disillusioned, remarked one day, "I don't want to be an old man sending young men to war again."[12]

32

THE SAME THING
AS FERTILIZER

$\mathcal{R}$USSELL HAD NEVER SEEN A PRESIDENT stumble through his first year in Washington like Jimmy Carter. By any measure, the year was a disaster. No modern president suffered such overwhelming legislative failure in his first twelve months as Carter did in 1977. The following year had to show improvement, if only because the president's calamitous situation did not appear capable of growing worse. Fortunately, Carter's many disappointments—several of them at the hands of Russell Long—taught him much about the complexities and personalities of the legislative process. His adroitness in nursing the Panama Canal treaties through the Senate later in 1978 was evidence that he had learned something from his mistakes.

By no means had Carter acquired the Midas touch. His legislative problems were still too numerous to count. While his 1978 State of the Union address called for congressional action in a host of new areas—tax and welfare reform, civil service reorganization, and health care cost containment—much of his 1977 agenda remained bogged down in various committees. Nonetheless, the president moved into new legislative areas as he continued lobbying for the previous year's agenda. While Russell and other members of Congress had taught Carter some valuable lessons, legislative achievements would not result in proportion to his newfound wisdom. On every front, Carter's legislative path was uphill, rocky, and littered with roadblocks erected by Russell Long.

Moving to fulfill his campaign promise to make the tax code more progressive, Carter sent Congress his tax reform plan in January. The White House proposal called for slashing a handful of personal and business deductions dear to Russell's heart. One proposal, in particular, aroused howls of angry protest from businessmen. Carter wanted to end what he derisively called "three-martini lunches" by limiting deductions for business meals to 50 percent. This unpopular provision prompted one of Russell's most famous lines, delivered to reporters in 1978, "Entertainment is to the selling business the same thing as fertilizer is to the farming business—it increases the yield."[1]

From the first day, the House greeted Carter's tax proposal with disdain. The Ways and Means Committee, so willing to accommodate him during the previous year's energy debate, could find almost nothing of value in Carter's newest tax plan. Mindful of the upcoming election, a unified bloc of Republicans and half a dozen conservative Democrats made it clear that they would spurn many of Carter's tax reductions in favor of greater reductions for middle-income taxpayers. By July, after months of delay and acrimonious debate, the committee reported a bill bearing almost no resemblance to Carter's original proposal. Led by the conservative coalition, the committee cut individual rates by more than ten billion dollars and expanded many of the business deductions Carter hoped to abolish. By August, the House—ignoring Carter's looming veto threat—approved the committee bill and sent it to the Senate.

Tax reform was only one of Carter's many proposals whose fate rested with Russell during the summer of 1978. The Finance Committee had also been grappling with Carter's welfare reform proposals—too much like Nixon's Family Assistance Plan for Russell's tastes—as well as the stalled energy program, hospital cost containment, and national health insurance. "It's going to be a sight to be seen, a wonder to behold," joked Senator Daniel Patrick Moynihan of New York, one of Russell's loyal committee allies on welfare issues. "Six weeks from now there are going to be nine major conferences going on up here and Russell Long is going to be chairman of seven of them."[2]

As he did with almost every measure he received from the House, Russell went to work expanding the Ways and Means tax bill. Carter's original proposal had contained a fifteen-billion-dollar tax cut. The House increased that to sixteen billion dollars. Now, in August, Russell ruminated publicly about the likelihood of a twenty-billion-dollar tax reduction. "We needed a big tax cut and that's what [Carter] recommended," Russell told reporters in January. As he opened hearings on the bill, he made it clear he planned "to vote to cut taxes just as much as they'll let me cut them." Even the twenty-billion-dollar figure was too low, he said, adding that "if I had my way it would be a lot more than that." Russell's proposals included three billion dollars in cuts for high-income investors, further reductions in the capital gains tax, and an alternative minimum tax for the wealthy.[3]

This kind of talk, not surprisingly, drew criticism from the White House, which renewed its veto threat. The Senate's liberals, meanwhile, complained that Russell's tax cutting proposals were designed primarily to favor wealthy taxpayers. To discredit that perception, Russell countered with a proposal to expand his Earned Income Credit, the work bonus equaling 10 percent of the first four thousand dollars earned by the working poor. The strategy was partially successful. A September 8 article in the conservative *Washington Star* on Russell's proposal was headlined: "SEN. LONG MAY BECOME FRIEND TO THOSE WITH MID AND LOW INCOMES." In an article almost a week later, the more liberal *Washington Post* ignored the Earned Income Credit proposal and focused instead on other provisions that portrayed Russell's tax cutting largesse in a much less favorable light: "FINANCE CHAIRMAN CALLS FOR TAX CUT OF $3 BILLION FOR WEALTHY INVESTORS." The commotion over who would benefit from Russell's tax cutting was illustrative of the perceived paradox involved in his efforts over the years to help the poor and the wealthy all at once. "That contradictory stance—populism and protection of big business," then-*National Journal* reporter Daniel Balz wrote, "confuses Long's critics and adds to the aura of mystery that surrounds him. You can ask a dozen people about Russell Long and come away with a dozen differently shaded pictures." To those involved, the stage seemed set for another year of stalemate and inaction. A veto seemed certain. One more Carter proposal appeared destined for congressional mutilation.[4]

In mid-September, Russell gave new life to the tax plan. Announcing a sudden willingness to work with Carter, Russell said that he would seek legislation that the president could sign by trimming or eliminating some of the more excessive House proposals. To calm his critics, Russell blithely admitted that his committee had purposely bloated its capital gains tax cut to gain bargaining power with the House Ways and Means Committee. "We'll have to compromise in conference," he admitted, signaling his willingness to accede further to Carter's wishes. This talk was acknowledged cynically by the *Washington Post*. "Indeed, from early indications, it

seems that by the time the Finance panel gets through, Carter may end up
with little more than face-saving gestures," cautioned tax reporter Art
Pine. "There will be enough changes to enable the president to back away
from his veto threat, but it still won't be the kind of tax bill Jimmy Carter
could love." The probusiness *Wall Street Journal*, however, had confidence in Russell's motives. *Journal* editors applauded him for "moving his
wonders to perform on this year's tax bill, working Congress's will and
saving the administration's face" while enacting legislation "stimulating
economic growth."[5]

Meanwhile, Russell made little effort to conceal his motives. "The
House isn't going to take it the way we send it over there," he explained in
a frank interview with *Washington Star* reporter Lee Cohn in late September. "The House will talk about all we're doing for the millionaires, and
we'll talk about what we're doing for the poor that they're not doing. We're
going to compromise in conference." On October 1, the Finance Committee finished the tax bill, approving the twenty billion dollars in tax cuts
divided almost proportionately among taxpayers. Personal tax reductions
were enlarged and several business deductions were expanded beyond the
House bill. As promised, Russell increased the deduction for capital
gains—one of his admitted bargaining chips—proposing to shield 70 percent of those gains from taxes. The *Washington Post* derided the committee product in an October 1 editorial as "the Oink-Oink Tax Bill." It was,
the *Post* said, "a museum of special breaks, dodges and intensely lobbied
privileges. The mystic view holds that it is the fate of the Finance
Committee to disgrace itself from time to time to fulfill the higher purpose
of reminding the country that there is a real difference between good
legislation and bad." Indignantly responding in a letter to the editor,
Russell maintained that the bill "does far more to help the needy, the
working poor and the hard-core poverty cases."[6]

By the time it finished work on the bill, the full Senate made the Finance
Committee appear parsimonious. It bloated the tax cut package to an
enormous twenty-nine billion dollars, twice as much as the House bill.
Furthermore, the Senate decisively spurned Senator Edward Kennedy's
attack on the capital gains cut, voting to keep Russell's 70 percent exclusion by a margin of ten to eighty-two.

Carter, meanwhile, warned that "the Senate bill has a much greater tax
reduction than I can accept," but stopped short of a veto threat. If the
conferees "take the best elements of both the House bill on the one hand
and the Senate bill on the other," Carter said, "I will sign." Emerging from
a White House meeting with Carter two days later, Russell and Ways and

Means chairman Al Ullman predicted that they would resolve their vast differences to the president's satisfaction. "The president was concerned that the bill as passed by the Senate would cost far too much money, and he's right about that," Russell candidly admitted. As always, Russell explained, he was more concerned with which provisions were cut than the final bill's grand total. "I think," he said, "the president will be reasonable."[7]

As usual, when Russell and Ullman sat down to barter a compromise, they paid scant attention to Carter's wishes. In effect, they would produce a bill within the administration's general revenue guidelines and dare him to veto it. Carter needed a victory, no matter how hollow. Chances were he would sign whatever bill Congress gave him. On this, Russell and Ullman were willing to gamble. As usual, Russell came to conference loaded with bargaining chips. This bill, however, set the record. Never before had a Senate Finance Committee chairman walked into a tax conference with as many tax cuts. Unlike previous conferences, Russell began his bargaining on the first day. On most items—the Earned Income Credit, capital gains, and business deductions—he and Ullman effortlessly split their differences.

Gone were the high-minded calls for basic tax reform that heralded Carter's arrival in Washington. Even the president's simple pledge to repeal the deduction for "three-martini lunches" had been effortlessly exterminated by Russell. On November 6, Carter unceremoniously signed the bill. "We've turned around the whole thrust of what tax reform was two years ago," concluded retiring senator Clifford Hansen of Wyoming. Hansen was correct. Once more, Congress and Russell had tested Jimmy Carter's will—and Carter succumbed.

* * *

One night in June 1977, Jimmy Carter hosted House speaker Thomas "Tip" O'Neill and his wife at an intimate White House dinner. The evening was delightful and relaxing, O'Neill later told a Washington reporter. After dinner, O'Neill recalled that Carter had prodded him to reminisce about the great political figures he had known, including Lyndon Johnson and John F. Kennedy. In his famous Irish manner, O'Neill complied and reeled off several stories to Carter's amusement and fascination. In time, however, O'Neill turned the conversation to more contemporary political legends, namely Russell Long. O'Neill reminded Carter that the House had twice passed the Family Assistance Plan, Richard Nixon's welfare reform proposal. Each time when it reached the Senate, he told Carter,

Russell had stopped the program dead in its tracks. How did Carter, O'Neill asked, think he could circumvent Russell on welfare reform? "He just smiled," O'Neill recalled in amazement. "He was perfectly confident. He said, 'I can handle him.'" Jimmy Carter had many talents. Handling Russell Long was not among them. In time, the president learned how wrong he had been about Russell. Two years later, Carter would mutter to his Health, Education, and Welfare secretary, Joseph Califano: "I never can understand him. And then I never know what he's going to do—except screw me most of the time."[8]

Since his first day in the White House, Jimmy Carter had underestimated Russell, indeed the entire Congress, and was paying a severe political price for his naivete and overconfidence. "I think Russell was one who was of value to Carter and tried to help him and make him understand how the system worked and what had to be done," Texas Senator Lloyd Bentsen observed. "I think Carter developed some confidence as time went on, and he began to understand the depth of Russell." Russell's Louisiana colleague, J. Bennett Johnston, saw Carter's relationship with Congress in a more critical light. "Jimmy Carter didn't have any friends who were in Congress who you'd think of as being warm and friendly," Johnston maintained. "He just didn't have any kind of relationship with anybody."[9]

Despite the tough lessons of his first year, Carter's second year in office yielded little tangible success. He won the Panama Canal treaties and a watered-down tax bill, but little more. Like his stalled energy program, his plans for reforming the nation's welfare system were moribund. As "Tip" O'Neill predicted, Russell was a major impediment. And although his outright opposition was only one reason for the plan's unpopularity in Congress, it was certainly a significant factor.

Carter's welfare program purported to divide recipients into two categories: those expected to work, and those who could not work because of age, disabilities, or child-care responsibilities. Under Carter's plan, all recipients would receive a basic cash benefit of varying amounts depending on their family size, income, and ability to work. Carter also proposed creating 1.4 million public service jobs and incentives to spur private business to create many more. In all, about thirty-two million people would have received government checks under a program which Carter hoped would replace food stamps, Aid to Families with Dependent Children, and Supplemental Security Income.

To Russell, Carter's program was a watered-down version of Nixon's guaranteed income scheme. "While the president has insisted on some changes for the better, much of the plan and much of the thinking that went into it represent the view of those who have been in the department [of Health, Education, and Welfare] for many years, under Democratic and Republican administrations," he told syndicated columnist James J. Kilpatrick. "They are perhaps better led and a few years older—but not necessarily much wiser than they were when they served under previous presidents." While he was highly skeptical, Russell did not dismiss Carter's proposals out of hand. Instead, he suggested the government field test the program before its full enactment. "We can all agree that there are elements of the present welfare system which cry out for improvement. But before we move to a massive change in our welfare system, we must be sure that what we are doing represents a true improvement."[10]

Russell saw the welfare debate as a simple diametric difference of opinion. He believed that Carter and the liberal proponents of expanded welfare programs concluded that the poor simply needed more money. That notion infuriated Russell. He thought they simply needed work. "I really think that if you pay people for doing absolutely nothing, they vegetate—I am talking about wealthy people, too," Russell told the *Washington Star* in October 1977. Russell's distrust of many welfare recipients and the bureaucracy that coddled them ran deep. "You take a woman in Plains, (Georgia) getting welfare," he said. "She says she's been abandoned, but she's got a husband and he's earning twelve thousand dollars—and he's living there. Who would know better the real story—her neighbors in Plains or someone operating a computer in Baltimore?"[11]

Over the years, Russell's basic misgivings about the welfare system and its dependents spawned a number of innovative ideas to coerce them into jobs, including various workfare proposals, the Earned Income Credit, and employer credits for hiring the hard-core jobless. His earnest belief that government should force delinquent fathers to pay child support was the price he forced Jimmy Carter to pay in 1977 to relieve the social security system's financial crisis. When Carter proposed bolstering the rapidly depleting disability insurance fund and the old-age and survivors' trust funds, Russell balked. Only when Carter and HEW secretary Joseph Califano agreed to his "Nab-a-Dad" child support enforcement plan, did Russell agree to help the president.[12]

The result was the Child Support Enforcement Program, through which the federal government funded state efforts to locate absent fathers and force them to pay child support. When the children were on welfare, the amount of the father's child support was deducted from the family's AFDC payments. Under Russell's legislation, the government began matching welfare rolls against social security and unemployment compensation lists to locate runaway fathers. The program applied even to fathers whose children were not on welfare.

"When I was dictating this bill to a secretary," Russell told Califano during one bargaining session, "she asked me why it should be limited just to people on welfare. Her own husband had run out on her and her kids and she thought she should be eligible. So I said, 'Why not? Put it in!' And that's why the bill applies to everyone whose daddy has run away from making support payments." The program was an instant success. By 1976, child support collections had been a mere $600 million. In 1979, they grew to $1.3 billion, and had saved $596 million in welfare payments. [13]

While Russell's welfare program flourished, by the end of 1978 Carter's reform program was stalled in committee. The special House Welfare Reform Subcommittee approved it with slight changes in February 1978, but the panel's parent committees—Ways and Means, Education and Labor, and Agriculture—never acted on the bill. The following year, Carter took a different approach. In November, the House passed an administration bill that set minimum benefit levels for all welfare recipients. Still demanding work incentives instead of guaranteed cash payments, Russell refused to move the bill out of his committee. Like so many others during Carter's term, the issue died without action.

Failure of welfare reform was a symptom of Carter's inability to market broad issues to Congress and the American people. His painful attention to detail, at the expense of the big picture, cost him dearly on a number of fronts. "Lyndon Johnson," Carter's HEW secretary Joseph Califano observed, "would have said, 'Put a welfare program together that gives poor people some money and encourages people to work and keep their families together,' and left all but the key policy and political judgments to his staff. Carter read hundreds of pages of material on welfare programs and did almost everything but draft the legislation." Russell agreed. "They didn't have the support for it. They should have concentrated on doing things that needed the nation's attention at that time. In other words, you had a whole lot of ideas that you weren't going to be able to sell and he should have dropped that baggage and gone on and looked after the nation's needs." Russell, however, acknowledged his own failures. "They were," he sighed, "successful in preventing us from trying work." [14]

* * *

Congress attacked Jimmy Carter's energy plan like piranha. When they finished, the 1978 energy bill was little more than bare bones. Carter wanted to contain oil imports and penalize consumption by raising gasoline and crude oil prices by a host of tax increases. Instead, Congress killed the energy taxes. In its place, it allowed natural gas prices to rise gradually toward total decontrol, required new power plants to use coal rather than oil and gas, and gave homeowners credits for installing energy-saving devices. It was a hollow victory for Carter, but Russell was pleased. He smothered Carter's crude oil equalization tax through his stonewalling in conference committee. He had kept the liberal, oil-hating hounds at bay for another year. To perform the same feat three years in a row would be difficult. The third year of Carter's term would be his greatest challenge.

Conditions were ripe for energy taxes. Oil prices were escalating at alarming rates, almost double what they were in 1978. Rising energy costs stoked the fires of inflation, surpassing 13 percent. America was now importing almost half of its oil supplies. Meanwhile, gasoline shortages developed, rekindling bitter memories of the disastrous 1973 Arab oil embargo. By early summer, long gasoline lines had sprung up in many major cities. Another energy crisis was brewing.

Meanwhile, Carter wrestled with the difficult decision of oil price controls, set by the 1975 Energy Policy and Conservation Act and scheduled to expire in June. By law, Carter was authorized to remove controls completely, extend them, or gradually phase them out. Choosing the later course, he announced that he would partially lift all price controls over three years, beginning in June. "Each of us will have to use less oil and pay more for it," he told Americans as he predicted steep energy price increases. To deal with expected energy costs, Carter proposed a windfall profits tax to recapture the oil companies' anticipated excess revenues. Funds from the tax would go to an Energy Security Fund to assist low-income families with energy costs, construction of mass-transportation systems, and alternative energy research.

The tax was severe, subjecting some oil profits to a 50 percent tax. Once all price controls were lifted, all oil profits would be taxed at the 50 percent rate. Considering projected oil company profits—a speculated windfall of thirteen billion dollars through 1982—Carter believed that his plan was fair. "Every vote against [the tax]," he declared, "will be a vote for excessive oil company profits and for reliance on the whims of the foreign oil cartel." Making his appeal for the tax in a nationally televised speech, the president asked Americans to support his assault on Big Oil's greed. "As surely as the sun will rise," Carter predicted, the oil companies will "fight to keep the profits which they have not earned. Unless you speak out, they will have more influence on the Congress than you do."

Russell was offended by the vicious nature of Carter's attack. "The kind of speech that the president made is calculated to stir up a lot of hatred and resentment against the oil companies for crimes they have not committed," he said in an interview. "He was assuming that the public was being gouged on profits that are not being made." Russell complained that Carter had not yet learned the importance of increasing domestic production. "The first order of business ought to be to restore the one thing that has been missing from that industry for twenty years—that is, the incentive to produce. If this industry had had the incentive it needed to produce energy, the Arabs would never have been able to make any of those boycotts work." At a Finance Committee hearing in early May, Russell and other oil-state senators argued for a "plowback" provision to exempt from the tax the oil company revenues that were invested in continued energy production. "I may vote for the tax," Russell told the *New York Times*, "but I think that under the windfall provision, people who put money back into the ground to produce more energy have to have adequate incentive to do it."[15]

At first glance, a 50 percent windfall levy seemed harsh. Not to the congressional liberals. They argued that the tax was too low. The Carter plan, they said, gave special breaks to several categories of oil. Applied across the board, the House Democratic Study Group estimated that the tax was actually closer to 10 percent. "The surest proof of the plan's inadequacy lies in the fact that the oil companies haven't opposed it," argued Democratic congressman Joseph Minish of New Jersey. The oil companies were opposed, although their low-key protestations created ample suspicions to the contrary. This distrust of oil industry motives prompted opposition to the price decontrols by a small group of senators led by Democratic senator Edward Kennedy and Energy Committee chairman Henry Jackson.[16]

Russell, meanwhile, played a different game, denouncing the tax in almost apocalyptic terms. At a Finance Committee hearing in May, Russell pounced on a deputy assistant treasury secretary who explained that the Carter tax was not "the pussycat that some have suggested." Unwilling to accept the assessment, Russell assailed the hapless administration official. "Under your program, the industry can raise enough money to stay at the mercy of the Arabs, as long as you remain in government, which may not be too long," he lectured. "Did it ever occur to you that you people are flirting with the survival of freedom in this nation and on this planet."[17]

Despite his strong rhetoric, Russell was resigned to reality. He would support the tax. "One reason that we'll pass it," he said in a Louisiana television interview, "is that [from] the point of view of those of us who prefer not to have any windfall tax, if we don't pass such a tax, the president has the power to withdraw his [decontrol] plan which would mean that the producers would not receive any more incentive or any more help in producing energy than they do now."[18]

Some wondered, was Russell simply surrendering to the inevitable? Or, as some liberals suspected, was he playing Br'er Rabbit, begging the liberals to toss the oil industry into a brier patch of impotent windfall profits taxes? In fact, Russell employed both strategies. A tax was unavoidable. Russell could not hold the line forever. Knowing that, he bargained with Carter, promising help in passing the tax, but only in exchange for price decontrols. For Carter it was a risky bargain. Russell had warned that he would only help Carter to the point the windfall tax became onerous. "Having Russell Long on your side is kind of like running through a jungle being chained to a gorilla," one White House lobbyist explained of their fragile alliance with Russell. "Ain't nobody gonna bother you, but it's not an altogether pleasant journey."[19]

By June, the House Ways and Means Committee, still wary of the proposal's true severity, tightened the bill considerably while increasing the tax to 70 percent. Committee chairman Al Ullman said a strong windfall profits tax was "absolutely essential." The full House, however, weakened Ullman's committee bill, finally agreeing on a 60 percent rate. "This committee would cooperate in making any changes that are needed to get on with production," Russell told Energy Secretary James Schlesinger as the Finance Committee began hearings on the House-passed bill. Complaining about tax and environmental laws that impeded domestic oil production, Russell grumbled, "We've got to get Mr. Environment out of the driver's seat and into the rumble seat."[20]

When he finished in late October, Russell's Finance Committee weakened the House bill further. It exempted several categories of oil, including crude oil discovered after 1978. In all, the Finance Committee proposed taxing only one-quarter of the expected windfall profits from oil through 1990. Tougher than its Finance Committee, but more accommodating than the House, the full Senate—after a bitter, protracted fight from Russell and other oil-state senators—ultimately beefed up the committee bill. Russell, however, insisted on a crucial provision to phase out the tax when revenues reached a certain level, meaning if oil prices increased more rapidly than anticipated, the tax could be suspended years earlier than anticipated. This, Russell knew, would ultimately save the oil and gas industry billions of dollars.[21]

Final passage appeared certain, until one of Russell's freshman Finance Committee Republicans, John Danforth of Missouri, created temporary havoc. Danforth—with whom Russell later developed a warm relationship—came to the floor with amendments to tax production from state-owned oil wells and limit deductions for state severance tax on oil production. In all, the state coffers of oil states would lose $10.5 billion by 1990. With major state holdings, Louisiana would lose hundreds of millions of dollars. Russell was incensed. "He didn't like the idea that this new person from Missouri, who didn't really know oil, would come in here and basically force an unwinnable vote on an issue of such great importance to the chairman of the Finance Committee," remembered then-aide Karen Stall. Russell concluded that Danforth, like other oil industry antagonists, wanted to deny the industry the basic American right of making a profit. "If we had done what should have been done," Russell told the Senate, "people in the business would have made a profit. There is no doubt about it, they would have made a lot of money. What would they have done with their money? I will tell you right now, anybody in the oil and gas business, and I know a lot of them in Louisiana, is putting it back and getting more oil and gas."[22]

The situation reminded Russell of an oilman who died and applied at the Pearly Gates for entrance into Heaven. When he arrived, Russell told his colleagues, St. Peter informed the man that no room was available. It seems a population explosion was underway. The oilman would have to go below, as Russell told his colleagues:

> He asked St. Peter if he could go inside and look around a little bit to see what the place was like before he went down to the fiery furnace. He maneuvered around the streets, down those golden streets, inside those Pearly Gates, and started spreading the rumor that oil had been discovered in Hell.
>
> Well, immediately, all the wildcatters packed up and headed out. In short order, here go the guys in seismograph crews and here go the title busters and here go the lawyers; here go all the people who make a profit getting involved with those people. All headed out, just a big procession on the way.
>
> After a while, here comes this fellow headed out, with his bag packed to go down below. St. Peter said, "Hold on a minute, old friend. We have plenty of room for you up here. We have just had an exodus. You don't have to go." The guy said, "I know St. Peter, but with all those people headed down there, there might be something to the rumor."[23]

By all indications, Russell had the votes to beat Danforth. To be sure, on the morning the Senate took up the amendment, Russell, his junior

Louisiana colleague Bennett Johnston, and Finance Committee Democrat Lloyd Bentsen of Texas plopped themselves at a table in the Senate chamber. In full view, the three men made quite a show of signing more than one hundred amendments to Danforth's amendments, each suggesting a minor change in language. This public display was devised to send a powerful message. If they could not muster the votes to beat Danforth, they would tie the Senate in knots and strangle his amendments with second-degree amendments. "They'll find out what happens when they gang up against Louisiana and Texas," Bentsen told reporters with a smile. Russell agreed, laughing. "And," he added, "we'll come up with a hundred more amendments if we need to." The strategy worked. With Christmas less than two weeks away, senators were in no mood to labor through the holidays. Others, from nonoil states, were concerned about future raids on other natural resources. On Russell's motion, the Senate killed the amendment, sixty-five to twenty-eight. The full Senate adopted the bill on December 17. As approved by the House-Senate conference, the windfall profits tax was a far cry from President Carter's flat 50 percent proposal.[24]

For Carter, the bill's passage was one of the many partial victories with which he had become so acquainted. For three years, he had rarely won outright. However, his few years in Washington had educated him in the fine art of compromise and negotiation—the take-what-you-can-get-and-declare-victory school of politics. Russell was a student of that persuasion. Like Carter, his victories were rarely absolute. He, too, compromised when necessary. The difference was perception. Carter's concessions with Congress were often viewed as hollow victories because of the high moral principles he usually assigned to issues. When declaring a position, Carter often exuded the air of one who would never compromise his principles for cheap political victory. Many times, compromise appeared out of the question. But Carter often took issues to the moral brink, only to compromise in the end. In these instances, his congressional allies were frequently left stunned, angry, and embarrassed. Like Carter, Russell declared his positions vigorously. Yet, anyone who knew Russell understood that he was usually staking out a strong posture from which to bargain. Everyone knew Russell would trade, bargain, compromise, and negotiate to get the best deal he could. Such tactics were part of his legend and mystique. In the end, Russell almost always emerged with less than he originally *said* he wanted, but about what he had *really* expected.

The windfall profits tax was a prime example. The oil shortage coupled with huge industry profits made it impossible to hold the line completely on oil taxes in 1979. Carter had the power to decontrol prices, but only if Congress went along on windfall taxes. Russell could have remained intransigently opposed to the windfall tax, a popular position for Louisiana, but gained little or nothing in the process. In Russell's mind, a fair trade was possible—enormous profits in exchange for somewhat higher taxes. Like the thousands of oilmen who expected to get rich from decontrol, Russell's legislative strategy was: Yell, scream, hoot, and holler—and laugh all the way to the bank.

This strategy had its shortcomings. Many oilmen in Louisiana did not fathom the Washington rituals of compromise and concession. They understood only oil and profits. When they looked at the bill Russell helped write, they knew they would now have less of both. "Don't talk to me about Russell Long," one oilman snapped to a *Washington Star* reporter. "The guy's a traitor. He sold us down the river on the windfall tax and we're not going to forget it." In Texas, Senator Lloyd Bentsen encountered the same hostility. "I think it took years for some of (the independents) to understand it," Bentsen recalled. "They cast a broad blanket of blame." With his reelection less than a year away, a potential opponent now had two thorny issues to use against Russell: oil taxes and the Panama Canal. For a politician whose last major campaign had been more than thirty years earlier, it was a slightly discomforting thought.[25]

As former California governor Ronald Reagan easily dispatched Carter back to Georgia in the November election, Russell felt a pang of sadness. The outgoing president was a man whom Russell had genuinely liked, despite their political differences. After the election, Russell said he told Carolyn one day, "It looks like he came to Washington a stranger and he is going to leave a stranger." Carter, Carolyn reminded Russell, had tried to win his support. Jimmy and Rosalyn had even invited the two of them to a private White House dinner early in Carter's term, she noted. "Well," Russell replied, "I guess you're right. I guess that was what they had in mind." To Russell, the dinner had been pleasant, but no substitute for a pragmatic and realistic business relationship. "If I'd been in his shoes, in that same situation, I'd have gotten the chairman of the Finance Committee up there and I'd say, 'Now look, I need your help very much. I need it desperately and I'll do anything I can within reason to help you with your business, provided it's mutual. And here's what I need from you.' " Russell said had Carter approached him with that bargain, he would have gladly accepted. "If he'd put it that way, it'd been a different story." Carter, however, never proposed such a deal. "I never knew what I could count on," Russell said wistfully. "I never knew if I could count on him or not."[26]

33

THE CUSTOMERS
ARE ALWAYS RIGHT

$\mathcal{T}$HIRTY-TWO YEARS had passed since Russell won his hard-fought race for the U.S. Senate while hustling through town after town in the sweltering Louisiana summer heat. For months, he and his entourage had courted votes from the backs of pickup trucks and flatbed trailers. Drenched with sweat after each rally, Russell barely dried out in time for the next stop. Television, the infant medium, was a luxury then primarily owned by only affluent citizens. In 1948, it was no way to reach the vast majority of voters. Radio was a useful way to persuade the common man, but no substitute for life on the hustings. In those days, Louisiana politics was primarily conducted in one fashion—retail. Stirring oration, shaking hands, and kissing babies won votes. Louisianians, accustomed to their state's intense political atmosphere, wanted to see and touch their political candidates.

Much had changed since Russell's first election in 1948. Wholesale campaigns replaced the retail politics of Russell's political youth. Radio was still popular, but television was preeminent. Sixty- and thirty-second television commercials had replaced the thirty- and fifteen-minute radio speeches of a bygone era. Campaigning from the backs of pickup trucks was largely replaced by well-orchestrated rallies inside air-conditioned meeting halls and arenas. Life on the stump was a quaint relic, often performed only to provide charming "photo opportunities" for television and newspaper photographers. Meanwhile, senators and congressmen who once spent almost half of the year in their states or districts, increasingly found themselves tied to Washington and a full-time occupation. Legislative sessions that once ended by summer now dragged late into the year.

Like many politicians whose careers spanned these two vastly different eras, Russell was slow to adapt. His visits home were infrequent and rarely designed for maximum exposure. Political contacts suffered. The once-mighty Long machine was neglected and rusty, a victim of five straight elections without serious opposition. "He's so busy up there that he doesn't really know anyone down here any more," one of Russell's supporters anonymously complained to a national columnist. "He's got a lot of shaking hands to do." In an interview with *The New York Times* in 1979, Russell himself admitted as much. "My usual pattern is in the first three years of a term to stay close to the job up here and in the last three years, to step up the pace in Louisiana." In the Senate, Russell's public relations staff had primarily focused on national publications while often neglecting Louisiana media, especially those without capital correspondents.[1]

In Washington, meanwhile, Russell was a legend. In fact, a January survey of senators by *U.S. News and World Report* listed him as the most effective committee chairman and the most persuasive in debate. Several months later, in a survey of the nation's thirty most influential decision makers, the magazine ranked Russell eleventh. Back home, however, the fables of the Potomac meant little. In time, Russell's power and seniority in Washington, which always counted for so much in Louisiana, were devalued. "The first negative factor that pops into anyone's mind up here about Russell Long," wrote the *New Orleans Times-Picayune's* Washington correspondent in January 1980, "is that he's allegedly 'out of touch' with Louisiana, devoting more of his time to hobnobbing with the president and cabinet members than with the people who elect him back home."[2]

That sentiment was reflected by the number of potential opponents rumored to lust after Russell's job in early 1980. The list included Democratic state representative Louis "Woody" Jenkins, some former gubernatorial candidates—Secretary of State Paul Hardy and Public Service Commissioner Louis Lambert—and Republican congressman Henson Moore. Of that group, Jenkins was the most ambitious and scrappy. A young, ultraconservative thirty-two-year-old Democrat from Baton Rouge, Jenkins had propelled himself from obscurity two years earlier to win 41 percent of the vote against Russell's junior colleague, Bennett Johnston. With an unpopular Democratic president now running for reelection, Jenkins and others speculated that 1980 might be a tough year for Democratic incumbents. In their eyes, that meant Russell was vulnerable. "The bigger they are the harder they fall," Jenkins had crowed in the summer of 1979. "Russell Long has a lot of answering to do and a lot of explaining to do to the people of Louisiana."³

Despite Jenkins's rhetoric, Russell had much in his favor. As chairman of the Finance Committee, his fund-raising potential was almost limitless. By early spring, he reported $420,000 on hand for a potential campaign, while Jenkins struggled to retire debts of $120,000 from his 1978 race against Johnston. Furthermore, the *Baton Rouge State-Times* said that its statewide public opinion poll conducted in late 1979 put Russell's approval rating at a fairly secure 60 percent, although far below the vastly popular 70 percent he enjoyed in 1976. Russell's private polls put his personal popularity much higher than his job rating, near 80 percent.⁴

None of this meant Russell took his reelection for granted. To the contrary, he began cranking up his campaign machine by the fall of 1979, acting on the lesson learned from Johnston, who was stung by the size of Jenkins's vote. For more than a year, he had intensified his visits to Louisiana and beefed up his staff with younger, more experienced Louisiana political hands. In just six months, he had put more than twenty thousand miles on his campaign car while hitting all but four of the state's sixty-four parishes. "I expect opposition," he told reporters at his low-key campaign announcement in July. "I always approach a race as though it is the toughest race of my life." By the next week, Russell got what he expected. Jenkins and three minor candidates entered the race. By now, Russell had raised more than a million dollars. Jenkins, with little money, had only a handful of issues and the reputation as the brawler who came closer than anyone since Huey Long to unseating an incumbent Louisiana senator.⁵

Not surprisingly, Russell's Panama Canal vote was Jenkins's most effective and oft-used issue. To a New Orleans civic club in late July, Jenkins charged that Russell's vote "was cast in the full knowledge it went against the overwhelming public opinion in this state and was a deliberate slap in the face of Louisiana citizens." Russell was a powerful man, Jenkins acknowledged. "If he had been using that power to help the people of Louisiana who sent him there, I wouldn't be running against him at all. But Senator Long has forgotten who sent him to Washington."⁶

Jenkins tried exploiting other issues—Russell's role in passing the 1977 social security payroll tax increase and the windfall profit tax—but none seemed as potent as the Panama Canal. Even so, he strained credibility by blaming Russell for virtually all of the nation's economic ills. "Senator Long blames everything and everyone for inflation except for the real culprits— he and his colleagues in Congress. They say oil imports cause inflation. But the real cause of inflation is a federal government that spends more than it takes in." Jenkins maintained the cure was a balanced budget, a 20 percent income tax cut and increased defense spending.[7]

A superb and tireless campaigner, Jenkins was nonetheless doomed from the beginning by several factors. He had little money with which to air the expensive television commercials necessary to gain the needed name recognition, and then for effective attacks on Russell. President Carter—whose candidacy helped defeat enough Democratic senators to shift Senate control to the Republicans—would not be on the ballot with Russell in Louisiana's new, unique nonpartisan open primary held in September, almost two months before the November general election. Furthermore, Russell avoided presidential politics altogether, refusing to campaign for Carter, who was challenged by the Republican nominee, former California governor Ronald Reagan. "I couldn't very well campaign against Reagan," he deftly told a reporter. "He hasn't said anything yet that I disagree with." To a group of Louisiana mayors, many of whom supported Reagan, Russell argued that his reelection would assure Louisiana a forceful voice in Washington regardless of the winner. "Mr. Reagan may need me more than President Carter. If you have made up your mind to vote for Mr. Reagan, I'll give you absolution if you vote for me."[8]

On the stump, Russell, albeit reluctantly, rarely mentioned Jenkins by name. "It was very difficult for the senator" to refrain from responding to Jenkins's constant attacks, said Russell's campaign manager, Kris Kirkpatrick. Eventually, Kirkpatrick and others persuaded Russell that any response to the attacks would only give Jenkins the press attention and name recognition he badly needed. (Russell also rejected out of hand Jenkins's calls for a debate, denying him the only hope for the crucial media exposure he could not afford. "He is never where I am," Jenkins complained in late August, adding the obvious, "I think that is probably by design.") At almost every stop, Russell's message was the same: A powerful man can continue to do great things for Louisiana unless the voters turn him out of office. "I want you to know that I love this job," he often said, "and I think I know how to do it better than I did when I first got there. I think if a person's doing a good job, you shouldn't put him out just because somebody else wants the job."[9]

On one level, Russell's campaign was a sophisticated enterprise that boasted a professional staff, a highly regarded pollster, and a skilled media consultant, all fueled by more than two million dollars in total campaign contributions. On another level, however, Russell was still a creature of the bygone era. Audiences knew that he was the last of a dynasty. They often came to his rallies hoping for the rhetorical magic that seemed to have died with Huey and Earl Long. Russell did not disappoint them. He regaled them with tales of Uncle Earl. "You better keep me around," he told a New Orleans audience in June. "I once urged my Uncle Earl to retire and be a senior statesman. He told me, 'Russell, I don't want to run for governor, but who else have we got?' " Then, hanging his head in mock humility, Russell concluded by comparing the story to his own candidacy: "Who else have we got?"[10]

At most stops, Russell boasted having saved Louisiana more than one billion dollars a year by defeating Missouri senator John Danforth's 1979 amendment to apply the windfall profits tax to income from state-owned oil wells. His vote on the windfall profits tax was a necessary evil, he argued. "Half a loaf is better than no loaf at all." Often, he disarmed anger over the Panama Canal treaties by insisting that his vote was correct, but sheepishly adding, "But assume I'm wrong about that. Won't you forgive me *one* bad vote if I was wrong about that?" Jenkins's assaults on Russell as a tax-and-spend liberal often fell flat in the face of Russell's efforts to enact a thirty-nine-billion-dollar tax cut bill favored by Republican presidential nominee Reagan. In August, when Jenkins falsely charged Russell was weak on national defense, it was more than Russell could stand. This time he responded, pointing to his own distinguished World War II military record. "I think my experience fighting for this country makes me a little more qualified on matters of national defense than someone who tried to avoid the draft."[11]

The response was effective—Jenkins had escaped military service during the Vietnam War—but more important was Russell's fusillade of television commercials, augmented by a sentimental, thirty-minute documentary designed to evoke one last burst of emotion from old-time Long supporters. The successful show featured newsreel footage of Huey Long and engaging scenes of a casually clad Russell spinning Uncle Earl stories with a group of men on the front porch of a rural house. New York Democratic senator Daniel Patrick Moynihan and Republican Kansas senator Bob Dole were shown discussing how Russell had used his power and influence in Washington to help Louisiana.[12]

As election day approached, Jenkins continued his attacks on Russell,

with little result. "If I am elected," he vowed, "I will use the power of a
U.S. senator to guarantee there will never be a federal judge appointed in
this state who favors forced busing and there will never again be a vote
cast by a senator from this state for a giveaway like the Panama Canal
treaties." As long as Russell ignored Jenkins, such jabs brought scant,
ineffective press attention. Russell's game of political hide-and-seek
worked. On election day, he swamped Jenkins, polling 58 percent of the
vote to Jenkin's 38 percent. (The remaining 4 percent went to the minor
candidates.) Asked to analyze the results, Russell responded simply, "The
customers are always right."[13]

Gratified by the large percentage, Russell was gracious in victory, even
toward Jenkins. "I don't think he ran as well as he ran against Bennett, but
you got to admire a guy for trying, and that's the best thing I can say for
him." By contrast, Jenkins was bitter, bragging that he, not Russell, had
won a majority of the state's white vote. Russell, he alleged, had bought
thousands of black votes with more than two hundred thousand dollars in
payments to black leaders. "That statement is a disgrace to our democracy," Russell fired back. "I hope that this is the last time that a candidate
who is beaten by as much as twenty percent of the votes calls upon his
opponent to apologize for the fact that black Americans voted for the
winner." In truth, Russell had probably spent closer to four hundred
thousand dollars in entirely legal payments to more than two hundred black
leaders who helped transport black voters to the polls on election day. It
was a practice employed by almost every Democratic political candidate in
the state who knew that large numbers of blacks faithfully supported
Democratic candidates, but rarely voted unless prodded or transported to
the polls. To Russell and scores of other southern politicians, election-day
voter transportation had become the price of doing business.[14]

Analyzing the election, Russell admitted that the attacks on his Panama
Canal vote had worried him. "I knew it would cost me votes—and a lot of
votes—to do what my conscience told me was right about the Panama
Canal treaty," he told reporters at a postelection press conference. "I said
at the time that was the kind of vote that could cost you an election. . . . It
always seemed to me when my popularity rating was above seventy-five
percent, it was fair to challenge my own conscience whether I was really
ducking some tough votes and being an expedient politician or whether I
was doing what was best for the country."[15]

Back in Washington, assured of another six years in the Senate, Russell
watched as Ronald Reagan swamped a hapless Jimmy Carter. On election
day, Reagan's landslide victory had coattails long enough to help Republi-

cans capture twelve new seats in the Senate. The stunning victories gave Republicans control of the upper chamber for the first time in a quarter century. Russell's close friends Herman Talmadge of Georgia and Abraham Ribicoff of New York were casualties, as were George McGovern of South Dakota, Birch Bayh of Indiana, and John Culver of Iowa.

That same night, Russell's good friend senator Robert Dole of Kansas, the senior Republican on the Finance Committee, accepted a congratulatory call from Senate Republican leader Howard Baker. The Senate is ours, Baker exulted, and you are the new chairman of the Senate Finance Committee. "That's great," Dole wryly replied to the new majority leader, "but who's going to tell Russell?"[16]

34

THE FOX IN WINTER

$\mathcal{T}$O THE WORLD, Russell said his new role as ranking Democrat to Finance chairman Robert Dole would be an easy adjustment. "I didn't ask for it this way," he remarked after the sweeping Republican Senate victories of November 1980, "but I think I can enjoy serving as ranking member of Finance." He claimed his new position might actually give him a much-needed respite. "I will not be under near as much pressure," he speculated, later adding a warning to anyone expecting him to fade into obscurity. "While I will be in the minority, I expect to be part of the consensus."[1]

Old habits died hard. Russell proved this during the first Finance Committee vote of the new session—the confirmation of President Reagan's nomination of Donald Regan as Treasury secretary. As the clerk called on committee members by name, Russell answered, "Aye." Later, when the clerk asked for the chairman's vote, traditionally the last to be recorded, Russell again absentmindedly answered "Aye," a second time. Everyone, including Dole, had a big laugh. "It is just as well that I did," Russell later joked, "because Bob Dole had not had the job long enough to realize that it was his turn to vote."[2]

For Russell, adjusting to his new subjugated role was nothing compared to the frustration of struggling with the conservative economic policies of the new president. Like Russell, in many ways Ronald Reagan was a simple man who saw the world in simple terms. But unlike Russell, Reagan viewed government as a negative force in American society and a

376

primary source of America's woes. Claiming an electoral mandate for his promises to balance the federal budget, reduce government spending, and cut taxes while sharply increasing military spending, Reagan promptly sent Congress his economic proposals. Unlike Jimmy Carter's plethora of programs with no priorities, Reagan's legislative agenda was simple and compelling: Cut personal income taxes across the board by 25 percent over three years; reduce the maximum tax on all income from 70 percent to 50 percent; index tax rates to soften the bite for individuals whose incomes increase; reduce the maximum capital gains tax rate from 28 percent to 20 percent; and provide a host of other individual and business tax breaks. All the while, Reagan proposed drastic cuts in social programs—including education, housing, health care, food stamps, and school lunches—while seeking huge military spending increases.

With a slim majority in the Senate and a working majority of Republicans and conservative Democrats in the House, Reagan and his new coalition needed the support of Russell and other moderate-to-conservative southern Senate Democrats to enact his program. From the beginning, Russell was wary of Reagan's assertions about the positive impact of his economic program. He doubted that sharp tax cuts, as Reagan predicted, would spur massive individual and business investment that would, in turn, increase government revenues. Reagan's vice president, George Bush, had once called the plan "voodoo economics." Russell could not have agreed more. He believed that Reagan's proposals were simplistic, costly, and would lead to massive budget deficits. "A lot of people think we should rush this bill through," Russell said in March. "Now, that might sound good to me if I were a freshman congressman, but I've been in Washington for thirty-three years." While not opposed to cutting taxes—he had moved a thirty-nine-billion-dollar cut through his committee the previous year—Russell worried that slashing taxes by the enormous amount of $749 billion over five years was unwise. In the end, buffeted by overwhelming public approval for Reagan's program, Russell, like scores of other conservative Democrats in both houses, reluctantly bowed to constituent pressure and voted for Reagan's budget and tax cut measures. Russell's valuable support was not without its price. Tough bargaining with Reagan, Treasury secretary Donald Regan, and Dole produced a number of tax provisions favorable to the oil and gas industry. "His fingerprints," Dole said later, "are all over the bill."[3]

In a matter of months, Congress enacted almost all of Reagan's sweeping economic measures. Unlike Carter's disorganized approach, Reagan's sharply focused program was an immense legislative success. Not since

Franklin Roosevelt's first years had a president exercised such total command of the nation's economic agenda. Personal taxes were drastically slashed over three years. Billions were pumped into new military programs, while budget cuts in other areas of government were often deep and severe. But the rapture of those heady days was short-lived. By late 1981, the nation had plunged into recession. Banks failed and farms closed. The unemployment rate soared past 10 percent, while the prime interest rate climbed above 20 percent. The budget that Reagan had vowed to balance reached deficits of record proportions. The economy, dampened by high interest rates and a growing budget deficit of more than $100 billion, continued plunging downward.

In the midst of the recession, Russell called on Reagan one afternoon in late 1981 along with Finance Committee chairman Bob Dole. He hoped to persuade Reagan that his massive tax cuts were responsible for the deep recession. To proceed with the next 10 percent cut, he planned to say, would do further harm. "You might as well be talking to that wall there," Russell later recalled. "The minute I drew a deep breath, the minute he could break in, he started talking. I just didn't have a chance to say anything. He just preached away what his views about all these matters were. He just filibustered me. I couldn't get a word in edgewise from that point forward." Refusing to acknowledge that the massive deficits were to blame for the recession, Reagan chose to weather the economic storm. He continued cutting taxes.[4]

Shortly thereafter, Russell found himself again at the White House, this time in the Cabinet Room with Reagan and a group of moderate and conservative senators. All were concerned that the huge tax cuts would only deepen the recession and widen the deficit. Russell's Louisiana colleague, Bennett Johnston, was one of the first to voice his distress over the budgetary impact of Reagan's determination to enact three successive years of substantial tax cuts. "I argued for some linkage between his tax cuts and the performance of the economy," Johnston recalled. As Johnston pressed Reagan for a commitment to cancel or curtail the cuts if the economy worsened, Russell interrupted. "Bennett," he said, pointing at Reagan, "if this thing doesn't work, I should think that man right there will be the first man to recommend that it be changed." Reagan sat silent, as Johnston thought to himself, "Well, Russell, you sly old fox. You have been around here a long time. You know a lot more about this than I do." Johnston relented. Later, Russell and Johnston painfully realized the fallacy of Russell's confidence in Reagan. "That was a mistake," Russell later said of his interruption. "I should have sat back and let Reagan answer that question."[5]

Mindful that public support for Reagan was still high in many quarters of the electorate, Russell was often temperate in his criticism of the new Republican president. He gave Reagan high marks for his hands-off management style and his superior communication skills. Reagan's oft-stated desire to reform the welfare system by putting people to work was a welcome relief (although Russell strenuously opposed Reagan's cutbacks for child support enforcement program funding). In foreign and military policy, Russell was a steadfast ally. As usual, he believed in giving presidents virtual carte blanche in matters beyond the nation's shores. He enthusiastically supported Reagan's military buildup and gave his crucial support for the controversial sale of advanced radar planes to Saudi Arabia in August 1981, only one of 10 Democrats who did.[6]

Early 1982 brought little hope of quick economic recovery. Still intransigent on interest rates, Federal Reserve Chairman Paul Volker insisted on action to combat the deficit before he eased his tight grip on the money supply. Again, this prompted Russell to suggest that Reagan should postpone half of the 10 percent income tax cut scheduled for July. Firmly committed to the tax reductions, Reagan responded that he would never sign a budget "balanced on the backs of the American people." At the March convention of the Louisiana Democratic party, Russell ridiculed Reagan's assertion. "Whatever you do, it's going to be on the backs of the American people. If the only thing we had to pay was the president's salary, where would we get the money? What do you want to do, go out and ask the Ford Foundation to make a grant or a gift? The president doesn't qualify for welfare."[7]

The deepening deficit eventually forced Reagan to raise taxes by ninety-eight billion dollars, but not by delaying the tax cuts, as Russell and other Democrats had wanted. Instead, the president pushed through provisions that closed various tax loopholes and increased taxpayer compliance, including a highly controversial plan to withhold 5 percent of taxable interest and dividends on individuals depositors' savings accounts. In committee, Russell suffered his first major defeat in more than a dozen years. His amendment to raise the thirty-seven billion dollars over three years by deferring the 10 percent tax cut for high-income taxpayers was defeated, seven to twelve.

Russell, meanwhile, predicted another crisis on the horizon. He believed that Reagan's free trade policies—especially toward Japan, Taiwan, and Western Europe—were crippling vital American industries. Under Reagan, Russell saw U.S. trade barriers pummeled, while Japan and other nations threw up impenetrable barricades to U.S. products. Cheap foreign goods were essential to Reagan's fight against inflation, even at the cost of thousands of American jobs. "Free trade would be just a wonderful idea if everybody would actually practice free trade," Russell had warned in early 1980. "The heck of it is, they don't do it." Russell believed the U.S. should retaliate against trade violators. "If they are giving you the worst of it, you find some way to give them the worst of it. It is time for Uncle Sam to quit being Uncle Sap, and that we start reverting to our ancient traditions of being shrewd, resourceful, and clever Yankee traders." Such warnings fell on deaf ears with the Reagan administration. The nation's trade deficit reached seventy-five billion dollars by 1982 and headed even higher. "This nation is foolish to keep doing business with nations what won't do business with us," Russell complained, to little result.[8]

Russell's inability to influence Reagan's trade policies or limit the massive tax cuts were symptoms of a larger problem. As a minority member of the Finance Committee, albeit the ranking member, Russell's once-mighty power to dominate the nation's revenue and social agenda had been greatly diminished. Michael Stern, then Russell's top Finance Committee aide, remembers the effect of Russell's eviction as chairman.

> He seemed to be every bit as effervescent afterwards, and if there was any personal disappointment, I never detected it. What I did notice was that when he was chairman of the committee, because of the institutional role of chairman, I would go to him with all kinds of situations and problems, huge and tiny. But, when he became ranking minority member, if I would just raise some tiny issue, he would just say, "Well, whatever Senator Dole wants to do is fine with me." In other words, he no longer felt it necessary to get involved in every single thing that affected the Finance Committee.

Karen Stall, then Russell's legislative director, observed the same shift in attitude. "I think he sometimes felt frustration in that he wasn't the person [the White House] would come to to garner the votes. But overall he seemed to feel, 'Sometimes you win, sometimes you lose. This time, I'm not on top.' "[9]

For all the goodwill Russell had accumulated over the years, it meant little when Dole and Senate Republicans drafted the 1982 tax bill, which included the interest withholding provision. Time after time, Russell was excluded from the process. On almost every front, his recommendations were politely, but summarily, dismissed. "The Republicans were meeting behind closed doors for days on end," Russell complained. "They scheduled a committee meeting. We showed up and were told we couldn't come in. They'd tell us when they were ready for us." To Russell, proud of his bipartisan stewardship of the Finance Committee, Dole's new partisan system was appalling. "They had a lot more opposition than they'd have otherwise," he later noted, "if they'd invited us to participate as we'd done with them." Despite the insolent treatment by Dole, Russell found small ways to manage the isolation. Stall recalls how she once struggled with Dole's staff to obtain a tax proposal their boss planned to present at a Finance Committee hearing. "And [Long] comes in and says, 'I don't want to see it. I want to be able to go to this meeting and say, I, like all the other Democrats, have never seen this before.' " His attitude was, Stall observed, "if you want to take the rope and hang yourself, rather than get me in on the party, I think it's stupid. But why should I ask to be a part of a combine that just makes people unhappy?"[10]

"Those first two years were very partisan," recalled Philip Ufholz, then an aide to Republican senator and Finance Committee member, William Roth of Delaware. "The Republicans had been out of power for so long and won such a major victory and such a [working] majority—even [with conservative Democrats] in the House—that initiatives could just be rammed through. So, I think, the Republicans basically were very confident they could get things through. They felt they had the mandate to do it and they had an agenda and they were going to do it. They loved Russell and had a lot of respect for him, but that didn't stop them." Ufholz believed that Dole and the other committee Republicans adopted a simple guiding philosophy: "Russell's a great guy, but hell, we're in the majority now. We like that better."[11]

If Russell was down, he was certainly not out. "The fox in winter," as New York senator Daniel Patrick Moynihan called him. "Russell's been waiting and watching." His moment of revenge came in 1983, when Wisconsin Republican Robert Kasten moved to repeal the previous year's law requiring banks and other financial institutions to withhold interest and dividend tax payments from taxpayers savings accounts. The legislation had been enormously unpopular. Prodded by the banking lobby, millions of depositors flooded Congress with angry letters demanding the law's immediate repeal. Bolstered by the White House, Dole and other congressional leaders stood firm. They insisted on keeping the tax.[12]

The pressure for repeal was overwhelming, and in the Senate, Russell's shadow was seen behind almost every move to repeal it. "I'd been the loser on the issue," Russell recalled, "but I had the popular side. Every time it came up, I had the popular side all over again. I talked with some [senators] who would feel like giving up on the thing. I said, 'I don't know why you want to give up. Sooner or later, you're going to win. There's no way you can lose if you just stay at it, 'cause every time those guys cast a vote against you, it's a bad vote. It's like taking poison every time they cast another vote. If you just keep making them vote that way, after a while they're going to get sick of it.' " Russell, the cagey veteran of dozens of legislative struggles, knew when he had a winning issue.[13]

Like water on sandstone, Russell slowly, but steadily, eroded Dole's resistance. In February, Senate observers detected Russell's hidden hand when Maine Democrat George Mitchell, the Finance Committee's most junior Democrat, pushed a repeal amendment during one committee session. "Let's just say the Democrats caucused before that session," one committee member told a *Wall Street Journal* reporter with a wink. When Montana Democrat John Melcher moved to attach the repeal to a Social Security bill in March of 1983, Russell rarely left the floor during debate, rising often to support his junior colleague. Later, with Russell's behind-the-scenes guidance, Kasten threatened to bog down every important bill with a withholding repeal amendment until the Senate surrendered to public opinion. Dole knew Russell's legislative cunning was a powerful resource for Kasten. Even so, he briefly threatened to filibuster Kasten's amendment. Later, he backed down, realizing that he had, at best, only twenty-eight votes, not enough to prevent cloture or sustain a presidential veto. In the House, meanwhile, repeal opponents were also making headway, overriding the wishes of Speaker Thomas "Tip" O'Neill to force their bill onto the floor. With Russell and Kasten promising to tie the Senate in knots while House members threatened a revolt, Dole and O'Neill finally sought a compromise, a watered-down repeal that Reagan signed into law in August. Many wondered if Dole's cavalier treatment of Russell during the early years of the Reagan administration had driven Russell into his uncharacteristic battle with a fellow Finance Committee member. "I think it made it a hell of a lot easier for him to do it," speculated Russell's Democratic committee colleague, Lloyd Bentsen of Texas.[14]

To some, Russell's sudden spurt of activity was perplexing. After all, even he had once supported the interest withholding concept. "Everybody makes a mistake every once in a while," he replied sarcastically when Dole reminded him of the discrepancy, "I offer my sincere apology." More bewildering were Russell's successful efforts—over Dole's strenuous objections—for an amendment which delayed the inclusion of new federal workers in the social security system until enactment of a supplemental retirement plan for those workers. No one could remember Russell ever showing interest in federal worker issues. "It stems from last year's tax bill," one Finance Committee Democrat explained to the *Wall Street Journal*. "We were completely shut out of that. And since then, Russell has been biding his time, waiting for something to come along that gives him a chance to put a little squeeze on." In large measure, the successful spirit of bipartisanship and cooperation Russell had nurtured on the Finance Committee for fourteen years had vanished.[15]

* * *

More pragmatic than most senators, Russell nonetheless was a product of the pretelevision era. The medium that younger members used with such skill and ease was foreign to the man whose thirty-three-year Senate career was almost as old as the technology which helped usher the information age. A dynamic, persuasive orator, Russell was wary of the negative impact television might have on the Senate, the staid institution whose traditions he had grown to revere. "He truly believed that it was going to change the way the Senate did business and wasn't going to change it for the better," recalled Karen Stall, then Russell's legislative director. "He had a deep belief in the filibuster as the ultimate protection for a senator who held a minority position, and that was the bottom line." For Russell, whose first Senate speech in 1949 had been in defense of unlimited debate, television seemed a dangerous threat to one of the institution's most glorious customs. "Just let the public view a Senate filibuster," he warned the Senate. "In due course, the public will insist that we put an end to that and that we adopt a rule whereby debate can be shut off."[16]

The House of Representatives, with much more restrictive rules governing debate, had been successfully televising its proceedings since 1979. Often, however, major House debates were covered extensively on network television newscasts, while the Senate's discourse could only be described by a reporter using an artist's sketch. Sensing the lower body was eclipsing the Senate in prestige and visibility, in 1981 Senate majority leader Howard Baker began pushing the Senate Rules Committee to adopt a resolution providing for Senate television coverage. "You know," Baker told committee members, "the House and the Senate have been essentially coordinate and equal branches of the legislative department, but we are not going to stay that way if the public has free access to House

proceedings and not to Senate proceedings." Committee Democrats opposed Baker's proposal, favoring only radio broadcasts. But Baker prevailed. In a straight party-line vote in late 1981, the committee narrowly
approved the resolution Baker wanted, which he called up for full Senate
debate in February the next year. Fervently believing the cameras would
forever ruin the Senate's reputation as a great deliberative body, Russell
zealously assumed the role as television's leading Senate opponent.[17]

On the first day of debate, eager for Senate approval to begin debate on
the resolution, Baker was disheartened when he glanced at Russell's
Senate desk. "I must confess, however," he told the Senate, "that I
observed surreptitiously the deposit of three rolls of cough drops in the
desk drawer of the distinguished Senator from Louisiana, which may be a
bad sign, at least for me." Russell, who consumed honey-lemon cough
drops like candy, innocently explained that he was only nursing a cold, not
fortifying himself for a filibuster. In truth, Baker's suspicions were well-
founded. Russell may have had the cold, but it did not prevent him from
leading his Democratic colleagues, and a few Republicans, in a talking
marathon to block a vote on the resolution.[18]

"There is no doubt about it in my mind . . . when we have a television
camera in the Senate, senators are going to feel that they should be on that
camera," Russell told the Senate. "They are going to be on that camera to
the exclusion of other duties that they should be doing, not as dramatic,
not something that would come as close to getting them reelected to
office, but duties that they owe to the citizens of this country." Rules
Committee chairman Charles Mathias of Maryland disputed Russell's argument. "I do not think we are one hundred moths fascinated by the
candle of television." Baker, meanwhile, argued the Senate's obligation
was to allow the general public to view its daily proceedings. "Whether we
like it or not, we are what we are. We are elected by our constituents
to serve them according to our talents, our dispositions, our convictions. . . . We are a composite cross-section of this nation, commissioned
to debate the public's business in a public way."[19]

Baker may well have had enough support for passage of his resolution,
but he could not muster the necessary sixty votes to stifle Russell's
filibuster, falling thirteen votes short of invoking cloture. As Russell and
his forces—including Bennett Johnston of Louisiana and ranking Rules
Committee Democrat Wendell Ford of Kentucky—continued talking, Baker reached for a compromise. He agreed to return the resolution to the
Rules Committee for revision. For 1982, at least, the issue was dead. For
two more years, Baker's proposal remained only a dream. He tried again

in 1983, persuading the Rules Committee to report yet another resolution to the Senate. That year, at least, Baker never tried to bring his resolution up for Senate consideration.

Baker's announcement that he would retire from the Senate when his term expired in January 1985 raised hopes that senators would finally open the chamber to cameras as a tribute to the retiring majority leader. Once again, Russell adamantly challenged Baker's initiative, perhaps even more forcefully after he saw the partisan bickering that erupted in the House over television coverage in the spring of 1984. Until then, the House adhered to a policy of allowing cameras to focus only on members as they spoke. Panning the chamber was prohibited. But when conservative Republicans began using the House's airtime at day's end to attack Democratic policies, Speaker Thomas "Tip" O'Neill ordered the cameras to scan the chamber to show viewers that the Republicans were speaking to an empty room. The incident alarmed Russell. He worried that the Senate might one day be afflicted with the same partisan bickering if senators opened the doors to television cameras and used them as partisan tools. Baker had only a few months left as majority leader when he again tried to persuade senators to vote on his resolution. Again, Russell foiled him. Baker could not muster the votes to end the weeklong filibuster staged by Russell and his Democratic allies. The Senate would someday be televised, but not under Howard Baker's jurisdiction. "It may well be the case," historian Richard Fenno later observed, ". . . that Russell Long was trying to preserve a Senate that never was, while Howard Baker was trying to construct a Senate that never could be."[20]

35

SOME SNAP LEFT IN MY GARTERS

For all his wealth and position, Russell lived modestly. While Carolyn had helped him improve his tastes—she had discarded his comfortable but exceedingly worn furniture when she redecorated the Watergate apartment—Russell was always a man of simple passions. Neither he nor Carolyn were Washington social creatures, although Carolyn was better suited than Katherine for the obligatory capital parties Russell attended only when duty called. Most evenings, Russell forsook the cocktail hour of earlier years. Now, he went straight home after work, where he and Carolyn ate a simple dinner. When they did eat out, Russell often preferred fast food. A double hamburger from Wendy's was his favorite.

Over the years, Russell added considerable weight to his five-foot-nine frame. His exercise was limited to occasional rounds of golf, short walks around the Watergate complex, and brief swims in the pool at his Baton Rouge farm. His hair, once wiry and brown like his father's, had turned gray and thin. In thirty-six years, his conservative, Brooks Brothers wardrobe had changed little, although he no longer sported the loud neckties of his earlier years. For a multimillionaire, Russell was rarely extravagant with his money. His comfortable, modest black dress shoes had been resoled several times. His only vanity came when he posed for photographs or readied for television interviews. Always, he removed his silver wire-framed glasses and handed them to an aide for safekeeping.

At night, Russell loved to watch television. When he read, he preferred histories. His breadth of knowledge of American and world history reflected this avid interest. At times, he waxed eloquent about Senate history or the Civil War. A religious man—although he rarely attended the Methodist church to which he belonged—Russell read often from the Bible, which he always kept beside his easy chair. Many times, he quoted whole passages of Scripture from memory. In fact, biblical allusions were his favorite rhetorical device after his legendary Uncle Earl stories. More than once, he groused to a staff member that his Republican colleague, John Danforth of Missouri, an Episcopal priest, seemed unfamiliar with many of the Scriptures he knew by heart. "The Bible is his great friend and counselor," Carolyn said. "I noticed it, especially before we left the Senate. When big decisions were to be made, or he was under a great deal of stress, I'd go downstairs in the morning and find the Bible having been read sometime during the course of the night."[1]

On weekends, Russell and Carolyn often headed west from Washington on Interstate 66 to their spacious, rustic home atop Rattlesnake Mountain in the Blue Ridge Mountains near Front Royal, Virginia. Russell bought the land and a small cabin many years earlier for his solitary weekend retreats. Now, the getaway was a modest compound, including a smaller house next to the main dwelling. Making his isolation complete, Russell steadfastly refused Carolyn's entreaties to install a telephone. When the president of the United States called for him, the White House spoke first to an elderly farmer who lived near the foot of the mountain. Dutifully, the old man would climb aboard his tractor, ride up the mountain, and deliver the White House message. When in Louisiana, Russell loved to stay at the modest, white frame house he owned on several hundred acres of land southeast of Baton Rouge, not far from the city limits. To Russell's agitation, a CBS "60 Minutes" story once left the impression that "the farm," as he called it, was a palatial estate. In truth, Russell often joked that his pool was worth more than the dwelling.

As Russell grew older, his staff delighted in their boss's eccentricities. One example was his eating habits. To Russell, a meal was a mere formality to be dispensed in as short a time as possible. He could consume a hamburger, fries, and a milk shake in less than five minutes. Another source of amusement was his constant state of restlessness. At work or home, Russell was never still. Sitting at his desk, he fidgeted with whatever was before him while he rocked back and forth in his brown, leather armchair, constantly shifting his weight. Always, he fiddled with a pencil or a paper clip. Sometimes, he absentmindedly took a piece of paper before him, tore it, and rolled the shreds and chewed on them. More than one perplexed visitor left his office believing that Russell had made spitballs during their meeting. Whether he had a cold or not, Russell constantly chewed honey-lemon cough drops. Many times, he would stuff a dollar bill into an aide's hand, dispatching him to the Senate sundry shop for a fresh supply. As he aged, Russell began taking brief naps in the middle of the afternoon. Usually, he ambled over to his spacious Capitol office—"the hideaway," as the staff called it. There, he changed into his pajamas and stretched out on his large sofa. An hour later, he emerged refreshed and alert.

When he traveled, packing was a science. He believed that suitcases were poorly designed for their purposes. Even so, he improvised as best he could. Eschewing garment bags, Russell carefully packed his suits in his hard-shell luggage using an intricate method involving complicated folds, tissue paper, and hat pins. His suits always survived the trip unwrinkled. To help his staff, he prepared a four-page memorandum, "How to Pack a Bag," which included tips on traveling light and his own design for a more functional suitcase. Often, Russell packed only two or three pair of socks and underwear. At night, he washed and drip-dried the dirty garments in his hotel room.

One particular source of amusement for those around him was Russell's obsession with his socks. Like his father before him, Russell explained to the uninitiated, he had feet that perspired abnormally. Thus, he changed socks several times a day. When the mood struck him, he stopped whatever he was doing—including meetings with staff members—pulled open a desk drawer, and produced a fresh pair of socks. Other times, he wore two pair at once, especially when he traveled from Washington's cooler climate to warmer Louisiana. When he arrived at the airport, his first order of business was to remove his outer layer of stockings.

In conversation, Russell talked at a rapid-fire pace. His childhood stutter, still evident in casual discussions, made it difficult for the untrained ear to understand him. Some mistook his sometimes-unintelligible mumble as a sign of mental debility. Others knew better. "He was a fast talker," Richard Nixon conceded. "But unlike many who had that characteristic, his mind worked much faster than his mouth. I have never known anyone in either the House or Senate who could surpass him in the speed of his mental reactions on the most complex issues."[2]

To his colleagues, Republican and Democrat, Russell was a walking treasure trove of Senate history and tradition. By the 1980s, Russell was not only a legend, he belonged in the rarefied stratum of the giants of the Senate's rich and colorful history. Second in seniority only to Mississippi's John Stennis, Russell was now one of a handful of wise, elder statesman to whom younger members often came for counsel. During his early years, he had relied on his energy, humor, and intellect. Later, his position—assistant majority leader and Finance chairman—brought him power. By the 1980s, all of these attributes had melded with his seniority and universal popularity to enhance his influence among colleagues to immense proportions.

In many ways, Russell was the last of a dying breed of Senate mammoths. More and more, journalists and historians bemoaned the extinction of legislative giants like Everett Dirksen, Richard Russell, Lyndon Johnson, Mike Mansfield, Robert Kerr, Hubert Humphrey, and Paul Douglas. Decentralized and younger in age, the Senate of the 1980s was a vastly different environment from its earlier clannish era. The dignified, collegial body that Russell had entered in 1948 was now more individualistic and less respectful of the traditions and rituals of an earlier period. Running for office had changed, as well. Veteran senators could no longer depend on their power and seniority in Washington to deter challengers at home. As Russell learned in the 1980 race, the business of campaigning had drastically changed from the stump speeches and courthouse rallies of his youth. Retail politics was replaced by wholesale campaigns, masterminded by savvy, sometimes ruthless media consultants who exploited every advantage. To Russell, as pragmatic and adaptable as the next senator, the new politics made him uneasy.

* * *

On a Saturday late in February 1985, Russell and Carolyn joined a group of Democratic senators and their wives for forum at a Washington, D.C., hotel. All would stand for reelection in 1986. They had gathered to confer with several political consultants and pollsters to discuss preparations for their upcoming campaigns. What Russell heard may not have been alarming to most of his colleagues. To him, however, it was startling news.

Times had changed, the senators were told. Opponents will stop at nothing to defeat you. Their tactics will be clever, even underhanded. Some might take snapshots of you at hearings when you blink your eyes and allege you fell asleep on the job. Minor statements or votes on insignificant amendments will be taken out of context for gross misrepresentations of your record. Iowa's Tom Harkin described in vivid detail the hardball tactics he had recently used to upset incumbent Republican senator Roger Jepsen. Be vigilant, instructed the consultants. More important, they admonished, prepare to budget your time so each available minute of every day for the next eighteen months is spent campaigning. Today, they said, choose eighteen days, and mark them off. Those are the only days you will have left for rest and relaxation.

The session astonished Russell. He had not particularly enjoyed the rigors of the last campaign. Pressing the flesh in the sweltering August heat of Louisiana had drained him. Often, he complained to his staff that elections should be held when the weather and the temperatures were more accommodating to outside activities. Such vigorous hustling had been easy when he was twenty-nine, but at sixty-six Russell had little enthusiasm for the extreme physical demands of a hard-fought campaign.

Seeking another term was a question he had considered at length. Privately, after the 1980 experience, he told close friends that he doubted he really wanted another six years. "When Carolyn and I were out there campaigning in that [1980] campaign," Russell recalled, "sometimes I'd go out—I'd be making a speech in one hundred and five–degree weather in that hot, blistering sun. And she'd tell me how sorry she felt for me. I said, 'Well, the good thing about this is we don't have to run again.' " Despite that private decision, Russell batted down all rumors about his retirement. "I enjoy what I'm doing and have no retirement plans," he said unequivocally in November 1981.[3]

Such speculation was further quelled by polls that showed his Senate seat appeared to be safe. A poll conducted by the *Baton Rouge Morning Advocate* in late 1984 put Russell's personal favorability rating at an impressive 74 percent, while 58 percent of those polled said they wanted Russell reelected. Despite such strong numbers, several possible challengers loomed in the background—former Republican governor David Treen and Republican congressman Henson Moore of Baton Rouge. Together, the two men had polled 37 percent in a trial heat against Russell.[4]

Russell's armor was solid, but not impenetrable. Prodded by staff members and top supporters, Russell reluctantly began raising campaign funds. "We had a hard time talking Russell into getting that campaign going," recalled Russell's cousin and campaign treasurer, William Wright. "He wouldn't make up his mind to go and finally, we just really put him in a corner and made him start." Nonetheless, by early 1985 Russell had collected more than $800,000. His travels to Louisiana, as usual, had become more frequent. When he spoke to groups, he sounded like a candidate, vowing that the next election would return the Democrats to power and him to chairmanship of the Finance Committee. His heart, however, was never really in the effort, and so, the retreat and the startling, frank discussion had its impact. For some time, Russell had lamented that Longs always seemed to die in office. His father had died violently in office. Uncle Earl had killed himself running for Congress. Only a month earlier, in January 1985, Russell's distant cousin, Congressman Gillis Long of Louisiana, died of a heart attack. Furthermore, his senior colleague, Allen Ellender, succumbed to the rigors of his 1972 reelection campaign against Bennett Johnston. Now, Russell's own health suffered in a small, but discomforting manner. He developed glaucoma in both eyes, forcing him to wear sunglasses during committee hearings to shield his eyes from the bright television lights. By 1986, Russell's condition had worsened to the point that he affixed strips of electrical tape to his glasses, leaving only a small slit through which to see during televised hearings. Mortality weighed heavily indeed on Russell's mind as he and Carolyn returned from the campaign forum.[5]

Russell returned to the Senate on Sunday for an unusual weekend session in which Democratic senators filibustered President Reagan's nomination of Edwin Meese for attorney general. The next morning, Russell arrived at his Senate office, as usual, for a full day's work, including a surprise that would jolt Louisiana politics to its foundations. Just after three that afternoon, he summoned his administrative assistant, Kris Kirkpatrick, into his office to give him the news. He had decided, he told Kirkpatrick, not to seek reelection and he wanted to announce the decision as soon as possible. A thirty-six-year-old attorney who had managed Russell's 1980 campaign, Kirkpatrick knew Russell's decision was final. Russell had already prepared a statement, handwritten the night before on a yellow legal pad. Together, they instructed his press secretary to call a news conference of only Louisiana reporters, allowing him slightly more than thirty minutes to contact the half-dozen reporters who covered the Capitol for their newspapers.

Within minutes, word of the hastily called news conference spread like wildfire through the Senate's press galleries. Reporters for all three networks and several major newspapers dashed to Russell's office, somehow sensing the extraordinary nature of his announcement. By the time Russell looked up to read his brief statement, a horde of reporters surrounded his desk. Ironically, only two of the Louisiana reporters to whom Russell had wanted to make his announcement had been contacted. The rest were on the trail of soon-to-be-indicted Louisiana governor

Edwin Edwards, in town for a governors' conference and a meeting with Justice Department officials.

With the bright glare of the television lights illuminating the ornate office, Russell slowly began reading his statement, dispelling all the drama with his opening remarks. "After thirty-six years in the U.S. Senate, I have decided that I will not be a candidate for reelection in 1986. At that time, God willing, I will have served for thirty-eight years, and I will be sixty-eight years old. Having served in the U.S. Senate for more than half of my life, I love the institution. Even with its human frailties, it is still the greatest deliberative body in the world." Noting he was making his decision public nineteen months before the election, Russell explained, "I am making this statement at this time so that anyone interested in running for the job will have ample time to consider it and to raise funds to conduct a campaign."[6]

Paying tribute to Carolyn and his staff for their allegiance, he reserved his most emotional gratitude for Louisiana's voters.

> I want to thank the rank and file of voters—those who without any expectation of special consideration—elected to keep me in an office of high public trust for thirty-eight years. It is such voters who determine the fate of a democracy. Any candidate running a good race necessarily has close friends and enthusiastic supporters. But the outcome is usually decided by those many voters without fear or expectation of favor. The elections and the polls both demonstrate that such impartial judges of my stewardship have been most kind and considerate to me.

He did not know what he would do in retirement, he said. "But one thing I know for sure. My interest in this government and its people will continue. So long as I live, I shall take an interest in public affairs, and do my bit to sustain the government of this, the greatest free nation in history."[7]

When the reporters finally left, Russell assembled his staff to explain his decision. Many of them cried. Then, only minutes after the staff meeting, Russell's old nemesis, Senator Edward Kennedy of Massachusetts, burst into Russell's outer office. Red-faced and breathless, he had just learned of Russell's announcement. Kennedy, whose many public feuds with Russell only strengthened his personal affection for the man, demanded to see him immediately. For more than twenty minutes, they met privately while Kennedy vainly pled with his friend to change his mind.

The next day, at another hastily called press conference in Washington, Republican congressman Henson Moore announced that he was a candidate for Russell's seat. Moore's swift decision and the months of speculation that he was prepared to challenge Russell gave rise to intense press scrutiny about the "real" reason for Russell's retirement. "I think Russell Long would have lost his race with Moore," Stanley Tiner, editor of the *Shreveport Journal,* later speculated in a column. "I think Russell Long believed he would lose too, or at least knew he stood a very large chance of defeat." Others asked, Was he ill? Or, was there another more mysterious reason why a politician would renounce his claim to a prized and powerful Senate seat?[8]

The answers were not so simple. Granted, the effect of Moore's campaign had worried him, but not the aspect most observers might have assumed. After all, Russell was a man whose career was cluttered with examples of fearlessness in the face of sure defeat. For most of thirty-six years, he had been a sucker for lost causes. Never fearful of losing the election, Russell worried about the effect a punishing campaign would have on his health. "I want to leave this place on two feet, not feet first in a box," he explained to several friends. For others, he offered a similar explanation, quoting his uncle Earl, who chose not to heed his own advice about departing the scene "with some snap left in my garters."

To many observers, Russell's decision defied belief. How could someone who had tasted and enjoyed immense power and influence walk away from it so blithely, with little or no remorse? "I'd had the opportunity to serve in the Senate for thirty-eight years at that point," Russell explained five years after his retirement. "I felt I was still right on most of these issues and I felt I could do more good than somebody else would. But when a new man comes, like in [Senator] John Breaux's case, it's going to take him time to learn—learn all the people, how to get along with them and that sort of thing. But, he's also got something else going for [him]. He's in a position to take everything on as a fresh challenge." Many members of Congress had retired in disgust with the political system. Others had left when age began to take a severe physical toll. Some left for more lucrative positions in private enterprise. Few, if any, left for the reason Russell gave. "I just figured age sixty-eight would be a good age to retire."[9]

The retirement decision was invigorating. Russell had made a wise decision. He was sure of that. Free from the burdens of crisscrossing Louisiana in the summer heat, Russell could now devote his full energies to the final two years of his Senate term. He would continue to push for expansion of the dozen or so provisions he had guided into law giving tax incentives for creation of Employee Stock Ownership Plans. Sharing the wealth through ESOPs had been his passion since the early 1970s, and he was enormously proud his dogged efforts were responsible for the ten million Americans who now owned stock in the companies for which they worked. As the growing winds of tax reform threatened to wipe the revenue code clean of so-called special interest tax breaks, Russell would need all his thirty-six years' worth of legislative skills to keep ESOPs alive.

* * *

As the clamor for tax reform grew louder and the race for Russell's seat heated up—Moore was later joined in the race by Democratic congressman John Breaux and several other state officials—Russell turned to a matter of more personal importance. September 10, 1985, would mark fifty years since his father's assassination. A major documentary on Huey Long was set to premier. Once more, perhaps for the last time, the national news media would examine Huey Long's life and career. In the process, journalists and historians would draw conclusions about Long that would influence his memory for decades to come. (Years earlier, Russell had cooperated with and provided financial support to a renowned LSU history professor, T. Harry Williams, who was researching the first major, exhaustive biography of his father's life. When the book, *Huey Long,* was published in 1969, Russell was disillusioned with the product, focusing primarily on the negative aspects in Williams's generally favorable account of Long's life. It was several years before Russell acknowledged that Williams's Pulitzer Prize–winning biography had helped rehabilitate his father in the eyes of some historians.) Now, again, Russell was afforded another opportunity to remove some of the historical tarnish from his father's memory. Throughout the year, Russell granted dozens of interviews in which he talked about Huey with surprising degrees of emotion and candidness. As Huey's son, Russell knew he had a unique and final opportunity to influence his father's legacy. He devoted considerable effort to the speeches he gave in Louisiana and on the Senate floor about his father.

"I have won not just some, but almost all of my victories, by larger margins than my father ever achieved," he told the Senate on September 10. "That was in spite of a statewide media which was thoroughly unfair and constantly critical of Huey Long for the last fifty years when he was not alive to defend himself. Yet, I am convinced that much of my success, even in recent years, was because of my father." Those who knew his father, Russell contended, still rated him the most popular governor in Louisiana's history. "I will always maintain it is because those who knew

Huey Long will always remember what he did for them. Neither they, nor I, will forget the price he paid for trying to make this world a better place."[10]

By nature, Russell had never been one to hold a grudge. Years before, he had bridged the gap between Louisiana's Longs and anti-Longs. Often, he had extended hands of friendship to his father's mortal enemies, men like Congressman Hale Boggs and New Orleans mayor DeLesseps "Chep" Morrison. The old college enmities of his hard-fought race for student body president had been buried long ago when Russell courted the friendship of his erstwhile adversaries. Even Katherine, from whom he had been divorced for sixteen years, remained his good friend. Often, when in Baton Rouge for business, he dropped by her house for an hour or two of friendly conversation. In the Senate, Russell had virtually no enemies, only legislative opponents. Always kind, considerate, and armed with an easy smile and an arsenal of Uncle Earl tales, colleagues like Edward Kennedy found it impossible to dislike Russell even as they fought to bury his legislative initiatives. "They ought to sell tickets in the Senate gallery on days that Russell Long is managing a bill on the Senate floor," Kennedy said in a 1986 tribute to Long. "At the very best, they should bring in bus loads of high school classes on the days of those debates— because the young citizens who represent our future will never see a finer example of our democracy in action." But even a man possessing the most extraordinary amounts of affability and goodwill could not have been expected to act as Russell did in the summer of 1985, when he befriended the son of his father's assassin.[11]

For years, Russell had known that the son of Carl Weiss lived in Long Island, New York. A physician like his father, Carl Weiss, Jr., was an infant when the tragic events of September 8, 1935, resulted in the deaths of Huey Long and his twenty-nine-year-old assassin. The stigma attached to the incident drove Weiss's wife, Yvonne, to flee with her child to Europe for several years. When the family returned to the United States, they settled in New York, where the younger Weiss was unaware of the dreadful circumstances of his father's death until his late teens. Their paths never crossed, but Russell characteristically harbored no ill will toward his father's assassin. In fact, he once told a staff member how wrong and tragic it was for his father's bodyguards to slaughter Weiss after he shot Huey. By July 1985, as the memories of his father's life and death began to summon powerful emotions, Russell concluded that the moment for catharsis had arrived. It was time he and Weiss met.

On the morning of July 25, Russell and Carl Weiss, Jr., talked amiably for more than two hours over breakfast at a Manhattan hotel. What they discussed remains confidential by mutual agreement. Returning to Washington later that day, Russell issued only a brief statement to an intensely curious news media: "Neither of us had the power to shape the events that happened on September 8, 1935, although each of us in his own way paid a price for something he was powerless to control." (Weiss, who publicly maintained his father's innocence in the murder case, later joined other family members in calling for the exhumation of his father's body to examine physical evidence not investigated in 1935.)[12]

Content that his efforts during 1985 had admirably added to his father's reputation, Russell again turned his attention to legislative matters, the first of which was the perennial debate over televising Senate proceedings. While Majority Leader Howard Baker may not have fulfilled his dream before leaving the Senate, he had certainly made the task of Senate television much easier for his successor. As the debate over television began anew in February 1986, it was clear that the Senate's atmosphere had changed. "In talking to my colleagues in this body," said Democratic senator Albert Gore of Tennessee, whose father had served with Russell, "I sense a feeling of inevitability about television procedures." Majority Leader Robert Dole, never an enthusiastic supporter of televising the Senate, was as adept as anyone in sensing the Senate's moods. Dole understood that senators were growing tired of the annual debate. He realized that every two years, as new members were elected, the pressure for television would only grow more irresistible. With help from Democratic leader Robert Byrd, who saw the television debate as his opportunity to obtain important Senate rule changes, Dole brought the proposal to the Senate floor early in 1986.[13]

Dole and Byrd were not alone in recognizing television's destiny in the Senate chamber. Russell, too, understood that the time had arrived. "It's a classic example of when he recognized the handwriting on the wall, when it was time to give up," remembered then-administrative assistant Karen Stall. "It was guerrilla warfare and you could have continued that for a longer period of time, but he was losing people, and he knew it."[14]

Like Byrd, Russell was resigned to television's advent. In it, he saw an opportunity for the rules changes that he and Byrd believed were needed to quicken the pace of Senate procedures for a new generation of viewers. In particular, Russell wanted modifications to restrict the use of irrelevant amendments. Like Byrd, Russell was tired of debates on arms control or farm bills being commandeered by senators seeking to attach unrelated legislation. Republican Jesse Helms of North Carolina was a virtuoso of this routine, with his profusion of amendments forcing senators to take stands on conservative issues from abortion to limitations on homosexual rights. "I am willing to vote on their issues," Russell complained. "But to have to vote on various versions of that proposal on different bills many, many times during a session is really asking too much. . . . They do not have a right to have the amendment voted on every bill that passes the Senate." Byrd wanted new rules of his own, including limiting debates on motions to proceed and limiting postcloture debate.[15]

In a highly individualistic Senate, Russell's germaneness rule was a threat. "It comes down to a very simple proposition of whether or not the majority of the Senate should deny, or have the power to deny, the minority the right to offer an amendment," Republican William Armstrong of Colorado argued. By a margin of sixty to thirty-seven, senators sided with Armstrong and rejected Russell's rule. Russell may have been a victim of his own reputation for legislative skulduggery. Many suspected that Russell wanted to scuttle the entire resolution by attaching onerous rules changes that, as a package, the majority would refuse to support. In the end, the Senate approved only one of the new rules that Russell and Byrd had wanted, reducing the time allowed for debate after cloture. True to his promise to Byrd, Russell did not filibuster. Still opposed to television, he bowed to the inevitable.[16]

On February 27, the Senate voted sixty-seven to twenty-one to televise Senate proceedings for a two-month test period that summer. Satisfied with the test period, the Senate vowed overwhelmingly to keep the cameras permanently. "My fundamental objection to television," Russell told the Senate before its final vote, "is rooted in my deep concern that television in the Senate will result in an increase in political expediency at the expense of statesmanship. The nation will not be a better place for this." As Russell and others knew, only time would tell who was correct.[17]

36

CALL IT A PARADE

$\mathcal{T}$HROUGHOUT HIS YEARS as Finance chairman, Russell reserved contempt for the ceaseless liberal demands for tax reform. To Russell, reform usually meant that his adversaries were out to strip the nation's oil and gas industry of the drilling incentives he fought so hard to create. Even the label "tax reform" troubled him. "I have always felt that tax reform is a change that I favor, or if it is the other man defining reform, it is a change in the tax law that he favors." While Russell may have disagreed with the motives of the tax-reform proponents, the philosophy was not exclusively aimed at the oil industry. While Russell believed that the tax code was an appropriate tool to encourage certain kinds of activities—home ownership, charitable contributions, and certain business investments—the reformers wanted to leave most of those decisions to the free market. The tax code's primary purpose, they argued, was collection of revenue for the operation of government. These diametric views of government policy, bubbling below the surface for almost two decades, finally collided in 1985.[1]

Russell had for years derided proposals for a flat, across-the-board tax as a boon for the wealthy. "If you're rich you'll love it," he wrote of the flat-tax concept in a 1982 newspaper column, "if you're not rich, look out!" Russell believed that the clamor for tax reform stemmed from the widespread belief that the very wealthy used arcane loopholes to avoid paying their fair share. "But what constitutes a loophole is in the eye of the beholder," he contended. "I doubt that many middle-income homeowners consider their home mortgage interest deductions a 'loophole.' But how do the millions of taxpayers who do not own their own homes view this deduction?"[2]

The argument had merit, but by 1986 it was no longer simply liberals who yearned for tax reform. Two successive moderate-to-conservative presidents—Jimmy Carter and Ronald Reagan—were elected promising wholesale revision of the nation's tax code. Elected in a landslide to a second term in 1984, Reagan declared tax reform as his top legislative priority. Senator Edward Kennedy and other liberals who championed reform in 1970s were still supportive, but were supplanted by more contemporary advocates. Democratic senator Bill Bradley of New Jersey and Democratic congressman Richard Gephardt of Missouri, now tax reform's primary congressional proponents, introduced their own "Fair Tax Plan" in 1982. The Bradley-Gephardt bill sought to set flat personal tax rates of 14, 26, and 30 percent, depending on income levels. The idea attracted attention and interest from the usual tax reform quarters, but remained only a legislative conversation piece until early 1984, when Reagan directed his Treasury Department to draft a tax reform proposal by year's end. That fall, Treasury secretary Donald Regan unveiled his department's plan. It was startling in scope and staggering in the way it proposed scouring the tax code of hundreds of business and personal deductions. It recommended three personal tax rates of 15, 25, and 35 percent and established a flat corporate tax rate while eliminating a vast array of business deductions for almost every industry, including real estate, oil and gas, and timber. Worse, for Russell, the Treasury plan took aim at eliminating most incentives for Employee Stock Ownership Plans. ESOPs were dearer to Russell than any other tax provision. If he had anything to do with it, he vowed, this reform plan would not make it out of the Finance Committee.

Russell hated the tax reform plan. "I was not enthusiastic about the fundamental bill" was his understated recollection. "Basically, the bill proceeded on the assumption we ought to eliminate a great number of the [personal] deductions, simplify the code, and take the money we save by eliminating the deductions and put that into lower rates. I felt that most of those deductions served a good purpose." Russell was not the only member of Congress troubled by the proposal and its seemingly arbitrary elimination of personal and business deductions. The congressional outcry was loud. Its message was clear—the plan would go nowhere without major modifications. Cool to the proposal himself, President Reagan waited while new Treasury secretary James Baker negotiated details of a second plan with members of both tax-writing committees. After a series of negotiating sessions—attended by Russell, Deputy Treasury secretary Richard Darman, Finance Committee chairman Bob Packwood, Bradley, Gephardt, and Republican congressman Jack Kemp of New York—Baker and his men started over. Emerging again in May 1985, this time Reagan announced a plan more cognizant of political realities than the original proposal. Dubbed Treasury II, it softened the bite in many crucial areas. Russell's influence was instrumental in Reagan's restoration of ESOP incentives and most of the oil industry's prized deductions. Reagan's plan kept the flat tax rate structure of the original Treasury proposal while retaining deductions for charitable contributions and interest payments on primary residences. Reagan still wanted limits on various business tax breaks, but he also proposed more generous treatment of capital gains to encourage new investment.[3]

In May, President Reagan appeared on national television to announce the plan. Russell was pleased with the result. "Every change from the original suggestion was for the better," he said in a statement the next morning. "The president has eliminated Treasury One's worst features and substituted some better ones. . . . The debate has only begun and I have assured the president I will be among those working with him in the cause of a more just and fair tax code for all Americans."[4]

The statement was a drastic about-face for a man who had successfully fought every tax reform proposal during his Senate career. Why had tax reform's avowed enemy suddenly embraced an abhorrent idea and pledged to work for its passage? Furthermore, why would a man once known for his lust of lost causes give in so easily? Was the salvation of a few pet deductions—ESOPs and oil and gas—enough to make Russell a born-again tax reformer? The answer was twofold. First, Russell was no longer Finance Committee chairman. His fabled ability to stonewall and rout any objectionable legislation had been severely diminished when he lost the committee chairmanship. Second, Russell was no longer the Senate maverick of the 1950s and early 1960s. After years at the center of power, learning the legislative ropes, Russell had no need to fight lonely, spirited battles to get his way or make a point. Over time, his bullheaded tactics and bluster had given way to pragmatism and compromise. Skilled as anyone at sensing the mood of the Senate, Russell knew that tax reform was a game that now had unstoppable momentum. Reagan, Packwood, and now Ways and Means chairman Dan Rostenkowski, had vowed to enact the plan. If he were to save his prized ESOPs, the energy tax deductions, and the other provisions about which he cared deeply, Russell knew that he must cooperate with the tax reform proponents. As an outsider, he would have little or no influence over the final product.

Despite his conversion to the precepts of tax reform, Russell privately told staff members that he hated the idea. "I'd just as soon throw it in the trash can," he remarked to one aide. Like Packwood and several other Finance Committee members, Russell hoped that the bill would become a victim of internal House warfare. But, as he often told his staff, "When an angry mob is chasing you out of town, you might as well grab a baton, and call it a parade."[5]

In the House, crusty Ways and Means chairman Dan Rostenkowski took up Reagan's challenge, fighting passionately for his own modified plan through months of intense debate in committee and on the House floor. The Ways and Means bill differed greatly from Reagan's original proposal, including creation of a fourth, 38 percent rate for the wealthiest taxpayers and a smaller capital gains tax cut. Oil and gas fared worse under the House plan. Rostenkowski scaled back several prized industry deductions, including Russell's cherished oil depletion allowance, eliminated for all but small wells.

The House bill endured several brushes with defeat, the last of which was an attack from disgruntled Republicans who complained that Rostenkowski had excluded them from the bill-writing process. While they appealed for the president's help in defeating the measure, Reagan held firm. It was not the exact bill he wanted, but Reagan urged House Republicans to vote for it anyway, if only to keep the reform process alive. "If tax reform is killed," the president told a meeting of Republican members, "if it doesn't pass the House in any form, then there will be no tax reform." Reagan assured them that he would fight for a better bill in the Senate. He even put his list of minimum requirements in writing: lower rates, a higher personal exemption, and more tax incentives for business investment. First rejecting a Republican alternative, in December 1985 the House sent the Ways and Means bill to the Senate. Afterward, Rostenkowski toasted a hard-fought victory with champagne, raising his glass not simply to the House victory, but, presciently, "to a bumpy ride in the Senate."[6]

In the Senate, the task of tax reform fell to Republican Finance chairman Robert Packwood of Oregon. An informal, sometimes disheveled man, Packwood revered Russell. As a freshman senator on the minority side, he had never forgotten Russell's deference and generosity during his early Senate years. Packwood had admired Russell since his high school days, when he wrote a civics paper about his future colleague. "I picked Russell Long," Packwood later explained, "because he'd only been in [the Senate] a year and I didn't figure he could have done much and I wouldn't have to do a lot of research." Over the years, Packwood became Russell's student and carried a lesson Russell taught him years before: "When Congress organizes in January, you want to know where you want to be a year from September. If you know that, you know what you want to achieve, then you can structure all your thinking and organization, planning and everything toward that end."[7]

Packwood was among the Senate's most liberal Republicans on social issues. On fiscal matters, however, he was as conservative as Russell. Furthermore, he was no fan of tax reform. But like Russell, he was pragmatic. He knew how intensely the spotlight now shone on his committee. If tax reform died, it would be the Finance chairman's fault. This sentiment, *Time* later explained, became known as the "dead-cat syndrome." It meant that while few involved really loved tax reform, none could afford to have it die on their doorstep. Like Russell months before, Packwood snatched a baton and found a place at the head of the parade.[8]

Packwood quickly went to work in January 1986, trucking his Finance Committee members to a two-day retreat at a quaint country inn in Berkeley Springs, West Virginia. There, he reached out for Russell's help in crafting the delicate first draft of the Senate's plan. Why not share credit for the plan? Packwood asked Russell. No thanks, Russell replied. "I'm not trying to be co-chairman of this committee," he explained. Russell shrewdly avoided the potential snare of being tied to a specific plan early in the process, leaving Packwood to design the plan on his own. Carefully, Packwood set out to formulate his starting draft, discussing his options with every member of the committee, many of whom—including Democrats David Boren of Oklahoma and David Pryor of Arkansas, and Republicans Bob Dole of Kansas, David Durenberger of Minnesota, and John Heinz of Pennsylvania—were cool to any form of tax revision. Beyond the Finance Committee, Packwood faced potential opposition from a large group of conservative senators, mostly Republicans, who opposed tax reform until Congress addressed the nation's enormous budget deficit.[9]

By March, Packwood completed his draft proposal. Resembling the House plan in several respects, the bill dramatically shifted the overall tax burden from individuals to corporations and dropped more than six million low-income taxpayers from the rolls. Most important, and crucial to gain Russell's and other senators' support, Packwood favored leaving intact the existing tax breaks for the oil and gas and timber industries. It was a starting point, but Russell liked it, as did several other Finance Committee members who gave it their tentative support. The favorable reviews from colleagues were not without a price. While assembling this coalition of support, Packwood included some special-interest provision requested by almost every Finance Committee member.

Like Treasury secretary Baker, and Rostenkowski before him, Packwood's most daunting problem was the revenue that his plan would, or would not, produce. Reagan and Baker were bound to commitments that any acceptable plan must be revenue neutral, meaning a new tax code would produce exactly the same revenue as the current revenue laws. Any proposal that reduced net revenues would never gain the support of the large bloc of senators worried more about deficit reduction than tax reform. In March, as the Finance Committee began marking up his bill, Packwood's revenue woes worsened. Sitting next to Packwood and wearing dark sunglasses to protect his sensitive, glaucoma-plagued eyes from the glare of television lights, Russell watched as his Republican protégé was goaded by lobbyists representing almost every business interest in Washington. Committee members added almost two billion dollars a day in new tax breaks for various interests. The lower rates had been the trade-off for eliminating the multitude of tax breaks. But every new amendment restoring a tax deduction only undermined the integrity of the whole package. By early April, as the negative revenue impact reached twenty-nine billion dollars, the bill was on the verge of collapsing under its own weight. In despair, Packwood suspended the committee markup on April 18, explaining, "I think the time has come to simply reflect on the way we are going."[10]

That afternoon, Packwood and his staff director retired to a Capitol Hill bar to discuss their dilemma—how to save revenue neutrality while lowering overall rates and eliminating most special interest deductions. As they downed their second pitcher of beer, the two men hatched a fundamentally radical idea to thwart the special interest feeding frenzy. Packwood's bold plan had only two income tax rates—15 percent and 20 percent. In exchange for the phenomenally low rates—the existing top rate was then 50 percent—Packwood proposed erasing almost every deduction from the tax code. For business, Packwood's plan was not as severe. Overall corporate taxes would increase seventy billion dollars over five years.

"It was a collection of the toughest tax-reform provisions—at least for individual taxpayers—that had ever been seriously considered by any congressional body," wrote *Wall Street Journal* reporters Jeffrey Birnbaum and Alan Murray in their book on the tax reform bill, *Showdown at*

Gucci Gulch. "Packwood's plan did more than call the bluff of its members [who had feigned support of reform]; it blew them away." Five days later, the chairman called together his committee to give them the staggering news. "Any interest?" he asked after presenting its general provisions. Surprisingly, he discovered, there was. The press outcry over the way the committee had fattened the bill with a profusion of special interest breaks had shamed more than a few members.[11]

Suddenly, a simple, clean reform proposal had merit. Several senators expressed their immediate support. Others were far more cautious. Russell was among them. Such a spartan bill, he cautioned Packwood, would eventually fall apart like a suit of clothes with a loose thread. He argued that one pull to preserve even a single business or individual loophole and the whole bill would unravel. Politically, Russell believed, Packwood's plan was not feasible. In fact, as Birnbaum and Murray noted, Russell was already tugging on one of the plan's most delicate threads— Packwood's elimination of the deduction for state and local taxes, which Russell contended would result in unconstitutional double taxation. Packwood challenged his mentor, reminding him that the time-honored strategy—trading tax breaks for support—had failed miserably. "We tried that and it didn't work," he told Russell. "We tried to take care of everyone's interest in the plan, and once that was done, everyone's interest became more generic and nonregional. Now I would like to try something revolutionary and see what happens."[12]

Once again, the dead-cat syndrome was at work. The Packwood plan attracted wide, enthusiastic support. If it died, Russell eventually realized that he might be cast as the dastardly senator whose allegiance to special interests killed meaningful tax reform. It was not the note on which Russell, with less than a year before retirement, wanted to end his career. On Saturday, May 3, Russell's administrative assistant, Karen Stall, and his Finance Committee minority staff director, Bill Wilkins, met with Russell in his Watergate apartment to talk frankly about the plan and its political implications. They advised him that "these are the pros, these are the cons, but politically, it's going to happen. And if you want to have any influence over the process, you will only insure your ability to do that by being part of it." No one knew then how kindly the bill's final product would treat Louisiana's oil and gas industry or Russell's cherished ESOPs. As Russell reluctantly admitted to his two aides, he would have no influence on the outcome unless he joined Packwood's team. "I concluded, well, this thing is going to pass," Russell said later. "If it's going to pass, I'd better be with it, help shape it up to where, at least by my lights, it would be as acceptable to Louisiana as I could make it." Often Russell had quoted the late senator Robert Kerr of Oklahoma, who once said, "I'm opposed to any combine I'm not part of." Russell now resolved to join Packwood's combine.[18]

Russell ended the meeting, telling Stall and Wilkins that he would support Packwood's plan. And then, he went one step further. Now that he was on Packwood's side, he knew that he must lend his considerable influence to help bring other Democrats along with him. By 5:15 on Monday morning, Russell began working the phones, enthusiastically relating his newfound support to more than one groggy Finance Committee member. Democratic senator David Pryor received one of Russell's early morning phone calls.

"Hey, man, you weren't asleep were you?" Russell asked his sleepy colleague.

"No," Pryor answered, recognizing Russell's distinctive baritone, "I was standing here waiting for you to call."

"Well," Russell blithely continued, "I wanted to tell you, David, Senator Packwood has a bill that is a good bill, it is a fair bill, and we ought to work with him to get it passed."[14]

Russell was now an unabashed tax reform proponent, enthusiastically selling the plan to skeptical Finance Committee Democrats. By June, Russell was so supportive that he rose to promote the bill during a high-profile meeting with President Reagan and more than seventy senators at the White House. Grateful for Russell's influential help, Reagan paused momentarily to note Russell's impending retirement and to praise him as one who had "worked for economic growth and to make the U.S. strong and good and great." Announcing that he had a gift for Russell, the president produced a green T-shirt bearing the simple rhyme about tax reform that Russell had made famous: "Don't tax you, don't tax me; tax that fellow behind the tree." Russell beamed and laughed loudly as Reagan held up the shirt to the applause of his colleagues. Later in the White House press room, Russell displayed the shirt to reporters, explaining that he had coined the verse years earlier to lampoon the philosophy of most reform advocates. The poem, he quickly added, did not apply to the current bill.[15]

Packwood was grateful for Russell's assistance, although he soon discovered that Russell's vote and support had a steep price—preferential treatment for the oil and gas industry. Unknown to Packwood, while the Finance Committee met in public session to draft the bill, Russell was conducting his own closed-door sessions with a group of oil-state senators.

Meeting in Russell's spacious Capitol hideaway, the group included senators Dole, Bentsen, Boren, and Pryor, all men who worried that the bill
might put thousands of independent oil and gas drillers out of work. The
industry was already suffering a severe depression from plummeting oil
prices. Packwood's bill might be the final blow. Privately, they presented
Packwood with an ultimatum—no tax breaks for oil, no bill. They knew, as
did Packwood, that they had the votes to deliver on their threat.[16]

At issue was Russell's proposal to restore the deductibility of losses
from investments in oil ventures. Finance Committee members Bill Bradley of New Jersey and George Mitchell of Maine, who believed that the
deductions were being abused by investors with no working interest in the
oil business, were indignant. The tax break for oil and gas was simply
unjustified, Mitchell declared on the evening the committee moved toward
a final vote on the bill. Finally, Russell spoke up.

"Mr. Mitchell is a great lawyer and a great judge. He had a lifetime job
as a federal judge, and he sacrificed that to serve in the Senate. Why a man
would do that, I don't know." The remark sparked laughter in the room.
"From a legal background, a life in the judiciary, he tends to look upon this
tax law as that statue over there in front of the Supreme Court," Russell
said, pointing out the window to the court building. "They have a lady
holding a scale. She's blindfolded. She doesn't know whose weight is on
the left-hand side and whose weight is on the right-hand side. And that's
how they're supposed to decide cases over there: not knowin' who they're
helpin' and who they're hurtin'. Whoever puts the most weight on his side,
wins. To say that we ought to pass laws the way they decide cases over
there is as wrong as anything can be." Russell emphasized this point by
pounding his fist on the table. "We fellas are lawmakers. We're supposed
to know who we're helpin' and do it deliberately, and know who we're
hurtin', and do that deliberately. Now the people in the oil and gas b'ness
are the most depressed industry in the United States. If you're sittin' over
there in that court," Russell said with such force his deep voice shot up
more than an octave. "I can understand your sayin', 'I'm blindfolded. I'm
gonna treat them all the same. This fella is broke, down and out. God
knows he needs help. But the hell with him. I can't do anything about it.' If
you're a judge, that's how you'd do it. If you're a lawmaker, you'd say,
'That poor fella needs help, let's help him.' "[17]

"With that, the vigor left the drive to kill the working interest provision
exception," wrote Birnbaum and Murray in *Showdown at Gucci Gulch*.
"Bradley looked angry, but defeated. There was no use in rebutting
Senator Long—his rhetoric couldn't be matched. More important, he had

the votes." The committee approved Russell's deductibility proposal, the last major hurdle before it voted on whether to send the historic bill to the full Senate. Packwood thought, at best, he might get sixteen votes. As the clerk called the roll, however, it became clear no one was willing to oppose it. In the end, all twenty committee members voted for the bill. With Russell's substantial help, Packwood had miraculously resuscitated his wounded legislation. When it finally reached the Senate floor, tax reform had assumed irreversible momentum. On June 24, the Senate overwhelmingly sent the bill to conference committee, ninety-seven to three. "Nothing is certain in this life," Russell said after the vote. "The good Lord might call us home tomorrow, but if we're here on Labor Day, there'll be a bill on the president's desk."[18]

In conference committee, the bill once again ran into trouble. While Packwood and Rostenkowski had agreed on the bill's broad outlines, including the Senate's individual income tax rates, the two sides were soon at impasse in other major areas. Almost immediately, the special interest bickering started anew. From the first day, July 17, the House and Senate conferees were deadlocked as most members zealously guarded their state's or district's pet interests. Danforth and House conferee Richard Gephardt wanted to continue special treatment for the defense contractors that comprised a large share of Missouri's economy. Russell, Dole, and Bentsen were determined to protect the oil industry. Almost everyone had an interest to preserve. This stagnation was further impeded by a study concluding that the Senate bill, thought to be revenue neutral, would actually cost the government more than twenty billion dollars over five years. For Packwood, it meant even more partisan squabbling with Rostenkowski over how to close the widening revenue gap.[19]

By August 12, the two men were no closer to agreement than before. In fact, with nerves frayed by weeks of hard, fruitless bargaining, the two men seemed further apart than ever. At times, tempers flared as the two sides shouted at one another in bitter disagreement. "For the first time," Rhode Island senator John Chafee told reporters, "it has crept into this the view that we may not have a bill." As hopes for success slumped, Russell stepped in. "Well, it doesn't seem to me there's much progress being made here," Russell said as the room grew quiet. "We senators have a lot of confidence in Mr. Packwood, and I suspect you folks do in Mr. Rostenkowski. So I don't see why those chairmen don't just get together by themselves and come up with a proposal that we all can then consider."[20]

Russell had already made the suggestion to amenable Senate conferees in private. Packwood had passed along the recommendation to Rostenkowski, who also liked the idea. The House members, however, were unprepared. They still had their interests to protect. But because Russell had cast the suggestion as a vote of confidence in their chairman, none of the House members was willing to speak up in protest. It was a master stroke, just the kind of impetus the moribund conference needed. Astonished at the fuss over his "brilliant" suggestion, Russell humbly explained that he was simply suggesting that Packwood and Rostenkowski do what he and Ways and Means chairman Wilbur Mills had done for years—hash out many differences in private before the conference committee met.

After Russell's jump start, the pieces quickly fell into place. Within days, Packwood and Rostenkowski produced an agreement. In all, the two men agreed to shift more than $120 billion in taxes from individuals to corporations by wiping out scores of business deductions. Far from devoid of business tax loopholes—dozens of special interest breaks were preserved to win needed support—the bill was nevertheless a remarkable achievement.[21]

Early on the morning of September 18, conferees put the finishing touches on the historic bill. It was Russell's last tax conference, a detail not overlooked by Rostenkowski, who turned to Russell shortly before the vote. "Before he retreats from this chamber, I want to ask my pal and the former chairman of the Finance Committee to say a few words." With that, the room erupted into thunderous applause as the conferees rose in tribute to Russell. Later, Senator Bradley, a former professional basketball player, described the moment as "the longest standing ovation I've witnessed since Madison Square Garden." Embarrassed by the accolade, Russell looked down at his feet as he rose to respond.[22]

> As all of you know, my father served in the Congress more than fifty years ago. I was about sixteen years old when my father died. But having observed the Congress, I've always had an ambition to serve here, and I've been watching this Congress for more than fifty years, as one who hoped to serve here and then as one who served thirty-eight years in these halls in Washington.
>
> I didn't feel this way in the beginning, but I really feel this way now, Mr. Chairman, that you, Dan Rostenkowski, and Bob Packwood have brought us what is probably the best, in fact what I believe will be the best, revenue bill in fifty years.
>
> None of us are going to be entirely pleased with it. They'll be something in this bill that I'm going to have to tell people in Louisiana I'm sorry about. I wish I could have had it otherwise. But there are a great number of things in here I'm going to be bragging about along with many others.[23]

To some, Russell's statement seemed odd. How could the man responsible for creating many of the loopholes this bill abolished find such cause for celebration? As usual, Russell had accentuated the positive. He looked not at the evaporating loopholes, but at the lowered individual rates and the removal of six million low-income taxpayers from the tax rolls. Furthermore, the bill contained a generous expansion of the Earned Income Credit for the working poor and the Targeted Jobs Credit for the hard-core unemployed, both his proud creations. Most of the incentives for his treasured ESOPs had been preserved. Thanks to Russell, Louisiana's oil and gas industry had been spared.[24]

Yet, largely the bill was not to his liking. He fundamentally believed that the tax code had an important and necessary role in shaping the American economy by encouraging certain types of activity—business investments, charitable contributions, home ownership, employee stock ownership. This bill had wiped out many of those incentives, leaving a tax code designed primarily to collect revenue. Twenty years earlier, Russell would have fought such a bill with every ounce of strength and every legislative trick he knew. Now, only months away from retirement, his place in history was more important. He could not, he knew, allow himself to be remembered as the villain of tax reform. This was his swan song, his opportunity to leave the scene on a positive note. Like the legislative virtuoso he was, Russell had performed beautifully. "The ambition of my life was to serve in this Congress," he said with his usual humility, concluding his remarks to the conferees, "and after thirty-eight years, I think I'll find something else to do."[25]

Five years later—after scores of savings and loan failures, the collapse of the commercial real estate market, growing deficits, and a deep recession under President George Bush—Russell was much less sanguine about the legislation he had reluctantly helped to enact. "I felt when you take [the deductions] away and give lower rates and count on the market to make the [investment] decisions, that you cannot rely upon the money being invested in the kinds of things that you think serve the national interest," Russell insisted. "And I think I was proved right about that. You look at how the money was invested thereafter. Precious few new businesses were started. Most of the money, they took and went out and raided somebody's business and broke the company. So, it really was a heyday for the buccaneers and the pirates and the raiders. It really wasn't a good day for the people you'd hoped would build new plants and create new jobs."[26]

Finally enacted and signed by President Reagan, tax reform was an ironic swan song for Russell. Having abetted the dismantling of the tax code he had built for two decades, Russell was generous in his praise for Packwood and his Republican colleague's skill in shepherding the legislation to passage. "This is the greatest chairman the Finance Committee's ever had," Russell effusively later said of Packwood. Grateful for the praise, Packwood knew better. Years later, Russell's student borrowed a baseball metaphor to refute Russell's compliment. "He's sort of the Mickey Mantle, I was the Roger Maris. I had one great season, and he had a lifetime career."[27]

37

RUNNING FOR MY FREEDOM

$\mathcal{R}$USSELL'S DECISION TO RETIRE had sent his popularity soaring. A statewide poll in January 1986 showed an astounding personal favorability rating of 77 percent. He was now the state's senior statesman, revered and honored for almost four decades of distinguished Senate service and praised from all quarters, Republican and Democrat. Yet, Russell's sudden spurt of popularity was not prompted entirely by his impending retirement. In Baton Rouge, the state capital was a vacuum of political leadership. Democratic governor Edwin Edwards had spent most of 1985 fighting off the federal racketeering indictments which paralyzed his administration. The state's fiscal affairs were a disaster, with a $400 million budget deficit predicted for 1986. Republican and Democratic leaders, joined by a host of prominent businessmen and newspaper publishers, believed that Louisiana desperately needed strong leadership to pull out of its fiscal and moral nosedive. Wanted: a towering, respected leader to command the deference and esteem of the state legislature, while skillfully attracting new industries to replace the state's devastated oil economy. To many of these leaders, Russell was the natural choice.

Thus, beginning almost the day he announced his decision not to seek reelection, rumors flew that Russell might consider a run for governor in 1987. In truth, Russell had lusted after the office for more than forty years. To Russell, the logical progression of political ascendancy had always been to first serve as governor and then move to the U.S. Senate. Fate, in the 1948 death of Senator John Overton, had intervened. Throughout the years, the governor's office—the supreme symbol of power in Louisiana politics—had always been an enticing prospect, although less so as Russell's growing seniority afforded him greater influence in Washington. Nonetheless, Russell's sentimental side longed to hold the office his father had used to rescue Louisiana from the Great Depression fifty years earlier.

"Right now, all I'm running for is my freedom—to be a free man and do whatever I feel like doing," Russell told a group of Shreveport business leaders in February. "But after I've enjoyed that freedom for a while, I might feel like getting back in the trenches. I'm willing to think about it." Such statements only fueled speculation that Russell was ready to make the race. "I have a feeling he's going to run," Russell's colleague, Senator Bennett Johnston, told reporters in August, "because—you know—there is a certain way that a person reacts, their eyes light up, their faces are animated when they talk about certain subjects. When you talk to Russell Long about running for governor, he really gets excited."[1]

As Edwards played coy about his reelection plans, polls showed Russell and former Republican governor Dave Treen the two men the voters most wanted in the governor's office. Meanwhile, other candidates representing a younger generation waited for Russell's decision. "Russell Long is the bull who has wandered into the china shop, threatening the finely crafted ambitions of younger men," political columnist John Maginnis wrote in April. Said *Shreveport Journal* columnist Ronni Patriquin: "The groundswell for the 65-year-old Long is so great that it is beginning to look as if all the young candidates . . . gearing up for the 1987 gubernatorial campaign would be well advised to delay their plans at least four years."[2]

Hundreds of letters poured into Russell's office throughout 1986. Many of them were handwritten and heartfelt. Most were from small businessmen or average citizens pleading with him to run. The *Baton Rouge Morning Advocate,* once among his father's most robust critics, endorsed Russell's yet-unannounced candidacy a full twenty-one months before election day. "Senator Long commands respect and confidence by the voters of Louisiana," the paper said in a February 1985 editorial. "He is well known among officials in Washington, and among executives of a large number of leading U.S. industries. This state badly needs that confidence and respect. We urge Senator Long to announce his candidacy for governor soon."[3]

The prospects of a Russell Long candidacy did not delight everyone. Former governor John McKeithen, Russell's old law school classmate, shamelessly promoted his son's candidacy for governor by attacking the propriety of Russell's massive oil and gas holdings. "If the senator wants to come back and make the race, let him come on," McKeithen told reporters in July. "I don't think it's timely for the chief beneficiary of the Win or Lose Oil Company to say, 'Look, I'm your savior.' "[4]

Russell had perennially defended his inheritance of the Louisiana oil and gas leases his father and two partners had obtained beginning in 1934. The propriety of the leases, however, had always been questioned by Huey's and Russell's detractors. In all, Huey's handpicked successor, Governor O. K. Allen, signed over leases for approximately one million acres of state land to the Win or Lose Oil Company. The first lease, in Ouachita Parish, was awarded after Huey and his partners had advertised the lease only once, and then in an obscure publication. Subsequent leases obtained by Win or Lose were subject to more public and competitive bidding. "Those leases were advertised and publicly bid," argued Russell, who believed that his critics would never have raised questions if the same leases had been awarded to a less-renowned bidder. Later, the leases were sublet to Texaco, which, according to some reports, paid Huey's heirs at least sixty million dollars in revenues over the succeeding fifty years. By 1986, reports suggested that Russell had collected more than eleven million dollars in oil royalties from the investments made by his father and other Win or Lose partners.[5]

In a written statement, Russell responded angrily to McKeithen's goading.

> Many times, my political enemies have sought to find some political advantage from the fact that I inherited a royalty interest in a number of state leases as a result of my father's assassination over fifty years ago when I was a young man, sixteen years of age. . . . At this time, I am not a candidate for anything. It is apparent, however, that some would-be governors and their erstwhile supporters must think that I would be a formidable opponent indeed when they start their attack on me before I have even decided to run.

On a more personal level, Russell was stung that his old ally McKeithen would attack him to further his son's gubernatorial aspirations. Typically, Russell found a humorous way to strike back at McKeithen, once plagued by alleged Mafia connections, telling one Louisiana reporter, "I hope Huey won't be a problem for me as much as John McKeithen is a problem for Fox McKeithen."[6]

Further vexing Russell was that McKeithen's assault had fueled suggestions that Russell's efforts for oil and gas during the tax reform debate would benefit him personally. "In the present case," Russell argued, "I am not seeking to pass legislation to favor my personal interests. Instead, I am supporting legislation which I believe to be good for all Americans, and resisting proposals which would be harmful to the state which I have the honor to represent."[7]

For years, Russell was frustrated by critics who he believed did not understand the difference between a conflict of interest and, in Russell's case, a parallel interest. A conflict of interest, Russell explained, existed when a lawmaker introduced or voted on legislation designed to benefit only himself or a small group. His case, Russell believed, was a perfectly ethical parallel interest in which his personal interests and that of Louisiana's were the same. Cotton farmers, he argued, could represent cotton-producing states as part of a recognized right to have "a legislator, very much involved in the principal industries of his state, to speak up for that state or its vital industries. Were it otherwise . . . every state would be denied the right to elect those who are part of those they represent."[8]

By November, Russell tired of the constant press speculation about the governor's race. Unquestionably, he wanted to fulfill his lifelong dream to be governor of Louisiana, but not at the risk of his health. More so, as the summer turned into autumn, Russell reflected on the reasons for his Senate retirement, remembering his oft-stated dread of campaigning in the oppressive summer heat. Furthermore, he wanted more time with Carolyn, his daughters, Kay and Pamela, and his four grandchildren. He wanted to travel more. He also hoped to try his hand at practicing law again, an enticing prospect considering the number of prestigious Washington law firms ready to offer lucrative partnerships.

The demands on a governor's personal life and health, Russell wrote to himself in November, "cannot be postponed if one as successful at the polls as I have been is to leave his last elective [office] on his feet rather than in a wheelchair or a coffin. In my judgment, the job of a U.S. senator is a piece of cake compared to that of governor—and I have had the opportunity in this life to view them both at close range." In the end, Russell wrote, "It would have been different had the job been one to which I could have been appointed. But such a result is not possible and I do not favor it."[9]

On November 19, Russell ended the speculation, welling with emotion

as he told a capacity crowd of reporters at a Baton Rouge press conference that it was Carolyn who best summed up his feelings about the
governor's race. "According to her, people should know when to go. The
right time for different people varies. In my case, I had thought for years
that sixty-eight, at the end of seven terms, would be the right time for
me." Ultimately, the strong emotional tug of his rich family history
weighed heavy in his decision not to run. "My father once told my mother
that he hoped to take his name out of politics some day in honor. It has
been my great good fortune to have the opportunity that an assassin's
bullet denied to him."[10]

In Washington, as the Senate prepared to adjourn, dozens of Russell's
colleagues flocked to the chamber to pay him one last tribute. "I have
never seen Russell Long falter in his support of the common man and
woman," said Russell's close friend Senate majority leader Robert Byrd.
Democrat George Mitchell of Maine, the future majority leader, praised
Russell for having helped average people with Employee Stock Ownership
Plans. "It is the means by which working people can earn a real piece of
the American pie. And it is due to Senator Long that they have been able
to do so."[11]

Democrat Claiborne Pell of Rhode Island fondly remembered Russell's
famous sense of humor. "We have all come to look forward to those
moments when debate was most heated and when Russell Long would
break the tension and make a telling point drawing upon his endless supply
of anecdotes." Democrat Dale Bumpers of Arkansas agreed. "We need
Senator Long's sense of humor. The issues we debate here are serious
issues, but having a sense of humor lets us concentrate on the issues
rather than taking them personally. Indeed, Senator Long seems just as
young at heart today as when I first got to know him." Democrat Christo-
pher Dodd of Connecticut—whose father, Senator Thomas Dodd, Russell
had vigorously defended on ethics charges in 1967—said that Russell's
"departure from this body will leave a large void that may never be filled."
Even old nemesis Edward Kennedy had kind words. "He ranks with the
greatest senators who have ever served in this body, and we shall miss
him in the years and the debates to come." Most eloquent was Democrat
Lawton Chiles of Florida, who worried aloud that "the Senate without
Russell Long will be a reduced institution. . . . Senator Long has held a
unique place in this body. He, in fact, has been a one-man institution, spinning
plans, ideas, and reason into the mainstream of American affairs."[12]

Russell was leaving office a contented man. He had accepted a position
with one of Washington's most prestigious law firms. His successor—

Democratic congressman John Breaux—was elected in an upset over Republican congressman Henson Moore. At first, Russell was ambivalent about Breaux's candidacy. Later, he threw himself into the effort, recording an effective television commercial and stumping the state with Breaux while attacking Moore with the kind of vigor he had reserved for campaigns of a previous era. When Breaux won, Russell was gratified that a Democrat would inherit the office he so loved.

Russell's final hour as Louisiana's senior senator came at noon of January 3, 1987. That morning, a Saturday, he and Carolyn left their Watergate apartment for the Russell Senate Office Building. It was a sentimental day and Russell wanted to spend his last hours as senator in his office, on the job. There, with a few aides, Russell and Carolyn reminisced until almost noon. He was mindful that the day marked thirty-eight years and three days since he had arrived in Washington, full of ambition and vigor to fulfill his father's legacy. As the appointed hour arrived, Russell and Carolyn rose from their chairs and walked toward the door. He turned out the lights. As he began to leave, Russell remembered a small detail. He had not relinquished the key to his office. Fishing into his pocket, he produced a simple, long brass key. He clutched it for only a brief moment. As he opened the heavy wooden door, Russell paused once more. This time, he did something uncharacteristically sentimental. Before he and Carolyn walked down the shadowy corridor to their waiting car, Russell brought the key to his mouth and kissed it farewell. His work was finally done. Huey would have been pleased.

EPILOGUE

$\mathcal{R}$USSELL LONG'S LIFE AND CAREER is replete with paradoxes. Were it not for his father's fame, Russell might have settled into the life of a talented, but obscure Baton Rouge attorney and oilman. Yet, because he followed in the political footsteps of such overpowering and colorful personalities, Russell's extraordinary career and his many legislative achievements were largely overshadowed by the more exciting and legendary exploits of Huey and Earl Long. Although no member of Russell's remarkable family approached his record of legislative success and political longevity, Russell often remains in the shadows. Even his own colorful, sometimes-unorthodox style seems bland when compared to the extravagant and destructive behavior of his father and uncle.

Russell often claimed that he entered politics to restore what he saw as his father's tarnished reputation. Such historical revision was a hefty assignment, even for someone of Russell's considerable and unique talents. At best, it was a goal he could accomplish only by charting a course diametrically opposed to his father's radical ideals and authoritarian tactics. Huey's heavy-handed methods either ensured his swift downfall or were a premonition of the brief time fate had allotted him for this life. Regardless, Huey's was among the briefest tenures for a senator, while Russell's thirty-eight years of service outdistanced all but a handful of men in the Senate's history. Indeed, because he followed the antithethical path, Russell won seven statewide elections and decades of plaudits for his integrity, effectiveness, and statesmanship. But, lamentably, he did not

417

secure a measurably improved place in history for his father. Fifty-five years after Huey Long's death, the Kingfish remains vilified and detested by a majority of historians who reject what they perceive as his dictatorial methods and personal corruption. That Russell failed to repair his father's reputation had little to do with his devotion to the oft-stated mission. Rewriting this chapter in history was simply impossible; the facts of Huey Long's life are overwhelming and well-documented.

Russell's failure, however, was not complete. While lacking the power to rewrite history, he possessed the will and the way to rewrite the nation's law. Russell's legislative success in enacting a great portion of his father's "Share-Our-Wealth" program is impressive. Better suited for the collegiality of the congressional process than any member of his family— many have observed he inherited the best character traits of both parents—Russell relied on the basic blueprint of his father's philosophy to structure his own brand of moderate populism. Huey demanded immediate help for the disadvantaged, but never lived to see the fruits of his rhetorical labors. Years later, it was Russell who became a forceful, leading voice for the plight of the elderly, the disabled, the working poor, and the middle class. A generation of disabled and elderly Americans had, in part, Russell to thank for the federal benefits that eased their financial and physical pain and comforted them in their declining years.

Huey Long dreamed of reallocating the nation's wealth with a revolutionary and unworkable program to pillage the nation's wealthiest citizens for the benefit of the impoverished masses. Russell, by contrast, adopted the maxim: Politics is the art of the possible. His legislation to promote Employee Stock Ownership Plans represented a temperate and practical way to ensure that more working people share in the nation's prosperity. His fights to cut foreign aid to provide greater resources for the elderly and disabled were noble and furthered his abiding family legacy of compassion for the underprivileged. Millions of working Americans found life a little easier because of Russell's innovative efforts on their behalf—the Earned Income Tax Credit and employer tax credits for hiring the hardcore jobless.

Russell's record, however, is not devoid of failure and disappointment. While he demonstrated strong private support for basic civil rights for black Americans, he was often a vigorous supporter of segregation laws that kept those same men and women chained to their status as secondclass citizens. That he was merely reflecting his constituents' ardent opposition to integration and civil rights is small comfort to a generation of black Americans persecuted by the nation's abhorrent racial conventions.

To his credit, Russell was usually more temperate in his rhetoric and compassionate in his actions than the majority of southern politicians of his time. His support of black voting rights, the abolition of the poll tax, and increased funding for education and old-age benefits set him apart from many of the South's most odious white supremacists.

Furthermore, while decrying the failure of the welfare system, Russell often belittled and denigrated those on public assistance as lazy and insolent. Unlike today's race baiters who exploit popular frustrations over welfare fraud and affirmative action—for example, Louisiana's David Duke, the former state representative and Ku Klux Klan leader, and North Carolina senator Jesse Helms—Russell proposed numerous legislative remedies to the abuses he condemned. Usually, however, Russell seemed unable to comprehend how forcing welfare recipients into menial jobs—trash collection, ditch digging, and domestic duties—would do little to improve their lot in life. Work was work, he believed, and laziness should never be rewarded. While the sentiment is commendable, his strong rhetoric was often demeaning.

Therefore, some might conclude that Russell was little more than a rank politician who slavishly pandered to an intolerant and narrow-minded constituency. However, few, if any, legislators of Russell's era could rightfully exult in an absolute purity of mind and purpose. Even the most ardent civil rights advocates of the 1950s and 1960s occasionally surrendered their principles while bowing to constituent pressures. To view Russell only as a parochial, one-dimensional political figure is to ignore the many times he exhibited courage and ferocity throughout his career. From his loyal, yet counterproductive defense of Senator Thomas Dodd and his valiant support of President John F. Kennedy in Louisiana to his unpopular vote for the Panama Canal treaties, Russell was often oblivious to public opinion when persuaded of the righteousness of a cause.

Like his father and his uncle Earl, Russell's life was filled with promise and accomplishment, with an ample amount of disappointment and failure. While his achievements clearly outweighed his failings, Russell's promise was never completely fulfilled. Even though he was ambivalent about succeeding majority leader Mike Mansfield to the Senate's highest office, this possibility was reduced because of his drinking and his erratic behavior during the late 1960s.

In examining Russell's life, few, if any, would portray him as a grand historical figure whose presence on the national stage altered the course of history. Unlike several of his Senate colleagues—Lyndon Johnson, Richard Nixon, John F. Kennedy, Hubert Humphrey—Russell never left the

Senate's relative obscurity for larger national status. Although as chairman of the Finance Committee Russell exerted massive power over the engines of the nation's commerce and industry, his role was often so arcane and furtive that few Americans knew just how powerful and important he was to their lives. Indeed, for almost four decades, no single revenue measure passed through Congress without Russell's influence in ways significant and trivial. Rarely, however, did he introduce sweeping legislation. Instead, tax bills from the House were his vehicle for enacting new social and economic policies. His Child Support Enforcement Program, the presidential campaign fund, the Earned Income Tax Credit, and Employee Stock Ownership Plans were all attached by Russell to larger revenue measures considered in his committee.

Perhaps not enough time has passed since his retirement to adequately assess Russell Long's rightful and proper place in America's history. This responsibility is better left to qualified historians, not journalists or former staff members. For now, it may be enough to simply conclude that Russell Long was an extraordinary, honorable, and imperfect man who made a lasting and significant imprint on American life in his unique, yet quiet way.

NOTES

ABBREVIATIONS

AP	Associated Press	NS	Monroe News-Star
BRST	Baton Rouge State-Times	NSW	Monroe News-Star-World
CQ	Congressional Quarterly weekly	NYT	New York Times
CQA	Congressional Quarterly Almanac	RBL	Russell B. Long
CR	Congressional Record	SJ	Shreveport Journal
LBJ	Lyndon Baines Johnson	ST	Shreveport Times
LCAP	Lake Charles American Press	TP	New Orleans Times-Picayune
MA	Baton Rouge Morning Advocate	TT	Alexandria Daily Town Talk
MW	Monroe Morning World	UPI	United Press International
NOI	New Orleans Item	WP	Washington Post
NOSI	New Orleans States-Item	WSJ	Wall Street Journal

PROLOGUE

1. David H. Zinman, *The Day Huey Long Was Shot* (New York: Ivan Obolensky, 1963), 139–40; RBL, May 15, 1989.
2. Palmer Long; Zinman, 140.
3. AP, September 9, 1935; NOI, September 9, 1935; TP, September 8, 1935.
4. CR, August 5, 1935, 12476–77; *Minneapolis Morning Tribune*, September 2, 1948.
5. RBL, May 15, 1989; Zinman, 140.
6. RBL, May 15, 1989; Zinman, 142.
7. NOI, September 9, 1935; T. Harry Williams, *Huey Long* (New York: Knopf, 1969), 874–75.

421

8. Ibid.
9. Williams, 875; *New Orleans Item-Tribune,* September 10, 1935; TP, September 11, 1935; NOI, September 9, 1935.
10. TP, September 11, 1935; NOI, September 10, 1935.
11. TP, September 10, 1935.
12. Ibid., September 11, 1935.
13. NOI, September 12, 1935.
14. Ibid.; William Ivy Hair, *The Kingfish and His Realm: The Life and Times of Huey P. Long* (Baton Rouge: LSU, 1991), 325.
15. Ibid.
16. TP, September 13, 1935; NOI, September 12, 1935.
17. TP, September 13, 1935.
18. Ibid.

CHAPTER 1

1. Williams, 19–20.
2. Huey P. Long, *Every Man a King* (New Orleans: The National Book Company, 1933), 2.
3. Williams, 26; *The Last of the Red Hot Papas* (Baton Rouge: New Records, 1961); Harnett T. Kane, *Louisiana Hayride* (New York: William Morrow, 1941), 40.
4. Hugh Davis Graham, *Huey Long* (New York: Prentice-Hall, 1970), 15; Kane, 40; Bennett Wall, *Louisiana: A History* (Arlington Heights, IL: Forum, 1984), 258.
5. Kane, 42; Long, 9–10; Williams 43–44.
6. Williams, 51.
7. Ibid., 73, 77–80; Long, 15–18.
8. Long, 18–19; Williams, 80–81.
9. Williams, 85–87.
10. Ibid.; Long, 23–25, 29.
11. Hair, 82.
12. Williams, 120–21.
13. Kane, 47, 124.
14. Long, 41–42.
15. Ibid., 42–43, 45.
16. Forrest Davis, *Huey Long: A Candid Biography* (New York: Dodge, 1935), 82; Long, 55–56.
17. Williams, 179.
18. Ibid., 181.
19. Ibid., 186–88; Wall, 260.
20. Davis, 84.
21. Williams, 213; Kane, 52.
22. Williams, 238.
23. Davis, 91–92, 94.
24. Long, 99.
25. Davis, 91; Allan P. Sindler, *Huey Long's Louisiana* (Baltimore: Johns Hopkins, 1956), 53.
26. Kane, 55.
27. Sindler, 55; Alan Brinkley, *Voices of Protest: Huey Long, Father Coughlin and the Great Depression* (New York: Vintage, 1982), 22.

CHAPTER 2

1. Carleton Beals, *The Story of Huey P. Long* (London: Lippincott, 1935), 83.
2. Davis, 96.
3. Ibid., 105.
4. Kane, 70.
5. Beals, 120; Williams, 351–62; NYT, March 27, 1929.
6. Williams, 365–67, 87; NYT, March 29, 1929; Kane, 74.
7. Davis, 118–19.
8. Williams, 460–62.
9. Ibid., 453, 464.
10. Long, 250–51; Sindler, 76; Davis, 147; NYT, November 7, 1930.
11. Williams, 566; CR, September 10, 1985, 23225.
12. Davis, 150.
13. Long, 290; Kane, 89; Williams, 554.
14. Henry M. Christman, *Kingfish to America: Share Our Wealth, Selected Senatorial Papers of Huey P. Long* (New York: Schocken, 1985), 3–27.
15. Brinkley, 43, 44; NYT, April 30, 1932.
16. Brinkley, 45–46; Davis, 163–68.
17. Ibid., 47; NYT, October 11, 1932.
18. Brinkley, 47–48.
19. Ibid., 49–53; Williams, 583–93; Davis, 169–70.
20. Brinkley, 54, 57.
21. Ibid., 59; Williams, 628.
22. Williams, 635.
23. Ibid., 637.
24. Ibid., 638–39.
25. Ibid., 651.
26. Brinkley, 68.
27. Davis, 212.
28. Brinkley, 69.
29. Sindler, 91; Kane, 105; Williams, 736–37.
30. Brinkley, 72; Williams, 695.
31. Davis, 253; Brinkley, 81.
32. Brinkley, 203–4.
33. Ibid., 207–8; Williams, 844.
34. Williams, 859–67.
35. Ibid., 859–67.
36. Ibid., 876.

CHAPTER 3

1. MA, August 16, 1953.
2. CR, September 10, 1985, 23222; Russell was for a family friend, and Billiu was Huey's mother's maiden name.
3. RBL, February 2, 1989; McFarland.
4. RBL, February 2, 1989.
5. Ibid.

6. Ibid.
7. Williams, 101–5.
8. RBL, February 2, 1989; McFarland.
9. RBL, February 2, 1989.
10. McFarland.
11. Hair, 168.
12. RBL, February 2, 1989; Hair, 215; McFarland.
13. Undated writing, RBL Collection.
14. Dugan; RBL, May 15, 1989.
15. Palmer Long; Dugan.
16. Williams, 318–19.
17. McFarland.
18. RBL, May 15, 1989.
19. Ibid.
20. Palmer Long; McFarland.
21. RBL, February 2, 1989.
22. Ibid.
23. Stan Opotowsky, *The Longs of Louisiana* (New York: E. P. Dutton, 1960), 195.
24. Dugan.
25. RBL, February 2, 1989, May 15, 1989.
26. Dugan.
27. RBL, February 2, 1989.
28. Chinn; Dugan; Katherine Hattic Long.
29. RBL, May 5, 1989.
30. McFarland; Palmer Long.
31. Inventory of Succession of Huey Long, RBL Collection.
32. RBL, February 2, 1989, August 8, 1989.
33. RBL, February 2, 1989; Palmer Long.
34. RBL, August 8, 1989; Rose McFarland.
35. McFarland; Palmer Long.
36. *Washington Times,* February 10, 1936.
37. *Washington Herald,* February 11, 1936; *Philadelphia Inquirer,* February 11, 1936.
38. RBL, August 8, 1989.
39. Ibid.

CHAPTER 4

1. Chinn.
2. RBL, February 2, 1989.
3. Opotowsky, 196; AP, February 1, 1936; RBL, December 3, 1991.
4. RBL, February 2, 1989; Dugan.
5. RBL, February 2, 1989, December 3, 1991.
6. Ibid.
7. RBL, February 2, 1989; Chinn.
8. RBL, February 2 and August 22, 1989; Rubin.
9. Chinn.
10. RBL, August 8, 1989.
11. Handbill of J. M. Bennett, RBL Collection.
12. TP, May 3, 1938; RBL, August 8, 1989.
13. RBL handbill, RBL Collection; TP, May 3, 1938.

14. Dugan; RBL, August 8, 1989; *Newsweek,* May 31, 1948; *Washington Daily News,* May 31, 1938; *Daily Reveille,* May 5, 1938.
15. RBL, August 8, 1989.
16. RBL, August 8, 1989; Unidentified newspaper clipping, RBL Collection; *Daily Reveille,* May 12, 1938.
17. RBL, August 8, 1989; Undated editorial, *The Daily Reveille,* RBL Collection.
18. Chinn.
19. RBL, August 8, 1989; Katherine Long; Palmer Long; Chinn.
20. Michael L. Kurtz and Morgan D. Peoples, *Earl K. Long* (Baton Rouge: LSU Press, 1990), 92–99; Wall, 286–87.
21. Katherine Long.
22. Unidentified newspaper clipping; RBL to Katherine Long, June or July 1938; Diary entry, March 24, 1941, RBL Collection; Dugan.
23. Rubin.
24. RBL, August 22, 1989.
25. Rubin; Katherine Long.
26. Rubin; RBL, August 22, 1989.
27. Rubin.
28. Diary entries, December 7 and 8, 1941, RBL Collection.

CHAPTER 5

1. RBL to Katherine Long, August 12 and 14, 1942, RBL Collection.
2. Ibid.
3. RBL to Katherine Long, September 10, 1942, RBL Collection.
4. RBL to Katherine Long, September 16, 1942; Katherine Long to RBL, September 19, 1942, RBL Collection.
5. RBL, August 22, 1989.
6. RBL to Katherine Long, undated, RBL Collection.
7. RBL to Katherine Long, July 14 and 30, 1943, and September 9, 1943, RBL Collection.
8. RBL, December 28, 1989; RBL to Katherine Long, November 1943, RBL Collection.
9. RBL to Katherine Long, December 8, 1943, RBL Collection.
10. RBL to Katherine Long, March 11 and 12, 1944, December 24, 1943, RBL Collection.
11. RBL to Katherine Long, March 26, 1944, RBL Collection.
12. RBL, December 28, 1989.
13. Ibid.
14. Ibid.
15. Ibid.
16. Ibid.
17. RBL to Katherine Long, April 1944, RBL Collection.
18. Katherine Long, March 30, 1989; RBL to Katherine Long, April 16, 1944, RBL Collection.

CHAPTER 6

1. AP, June 28, 1945.
2. Gill; Hair, 298.
3. West.

4. Ibid.
5. Ibid.; RBL Collection.
6. *Life,* December 9, 1946; RBL to Conrad Manley, August 23, 1946, RBL Collection.
7. West; RBL to *Life,* December 1946, RBL Collection.
8. RBL to *Reader's Digest* and John Overton, December 1946, RBL Collection.
9. Sindler, 140; Richard B. McCaughan, *Socks on a Rooster* (Baton Rouge: Claitor's, 1967) 106–7.
10. RBL to Katherine Long, November 27, 1944, RBL Collection.
11. Sindler, 145; Gill.
12. RBL, October 27, 1988.
13. Ibid.
14. Kane, 434; Kurtz and Peoples, 11.
15. Confidential source.
16. Gill; Madden; RBL, October 27, 1988.
17. Confidential interview.
18. West.
19. RBL, October 27, 1988.
20. RBL to A. H. Perry, October, 27, 1947, RBL Collection; Confidential interview; Palmer Long.
21. Gill; William J. "Bill" Dodd, *Peapatch Politics: The Earl Long Era in Louisiana Politics* (Baton Rouge: Claitor's, 1991), 95; *NOSI,* June 29, 1960.
22. Confidential interview.
23. McCaughan, 103; Sindler, 199.
24. RBL, October 27, 1988; Gill.
25. Marshall Frady, *Southerners* (New York: New American Library, 1980), 30.
26. McCaughan, 117.
27. RBL speech scripts, undated, RBL Collection.
28. Sindler, 201; RBL, October 27, 1988.
29. RBL radio script, RBL Collection; RBL to John Overton, undated, RBL Collection; Sindler, 202.
30. McCaughan, 106–7; *Louisiana Watchman,* January 6, 1948.
31. McCaughan, 111.
32. *Roanoke World-News,* March 30, 1948.
33. Palmer Long; RBL to Francis J. Benedetto, June 19, 1948, RBL Collection.

CHAPTER 7

1. Undated notes, RBL Collection.
2. McCaughan, 121.
3. Ibid.; NOSI, May 12, 1948.
4. BRST, May 18, 1948.
5. NOI, May 19, 1948; TP, May 31, 1948.
6. BRST, May 22, 1948; Kurtz and Peoples, 7; Madden.
7. RBL, October 27, 1988.
8. *Louisiana Watchman,* June 15, 1948.
9. R. J. Caire to RBL and RBL to R. J. Caire, May 1948, RBL Collection.
10. *Minneapolis Sunday Tribune,* May 23, 1948; *Washington Times-Herald,* May 20, 1948.
11. SJ, March 1, 1984.
12. RBL statement, July 2, 1948, RBL Collection.

13. TP, July 4 and 5, 1948.
14. Confidential interviews.
15. Wilson; Gill.
16. RBL, October 27, 1988; Confidential sources.
17. TP, July 5, 1948; *Bossier Tribune,* July 11, 1948.
18. TP, July 14, 1948; BRST, July 14, 1948; *American Heritage,* November 1966.
19. *Church Point News,* July 13, 1948; TP, August 23, 1948.
20. BRST, July 17, 1948; ST, July 23, 1948.
21. TP, July 26, 1948.
22. LCAP, July 30, 1948.
23. TP, August 20, 1948.
24. A. J. Liebling, *The Earl of Louisiana* (Baton Rouge: LSU Press, 1970) 4; Confidential source; TP, August 20, 1948.
25. Earl Long letter of September 12, 1948, RBL Collection.
26. RBL, October 27, 1988.
27. TP, August 21, 1948; RBL speech script of August 16, 1948; undated RBL note, RBL Collection.
28. TP, August 23, 1948.
29. TP, August 22 and 23, 1948.
30. Radio script, August 23, 1948, RBL Collection.
31. Opotowsky, 198.
32. Ibid.
33. Anonymous campaign memo, RBL Collection; MA, January 17, 1956; TP, September 1, 1948; RBL, December 10, 1991.
34. NOSI, September 1, 1948; BRST, September 1, 1948; TP, September 1 and 9, 1948; Sindler, 215.
35. Sindler, 215–17; BRST, September 2, 1948.
36. TP, September 1, 1948.
37. Ibid.; Gill; *New Orleans States,* July 25, 1952; *Hope* (Arkansas) *Star,* August 31, 1948.
38. Sindler, 218; Radio script, RBL Collection.
39. Roland Evans and Robert Novak, *Lyndon B. Johnson: The Exercise of Power,* (New American Library, 1966), 26–27; *Washington Times,* March 21, 1985; NOI, January 3, 1949.

CHAPTER 8

1. Undated RBL speech, RBL Collection.
2. Ibid.
3. *Beaumont* (Texas) *Enterprise,* September 21, 1948.
4. Wall, 309; Gill.
5. Clinton Anderson, *Outsider in the Senate* (New York: World Publishing Co., 1970), 97.
6. Donald R. Matthews, *U.S. Senators and Their World* (New York: Vintage, 1960), 93; Fulbright.
7. William S. White, *Citadel* (New York: Harper & Brothers, 1956), 117.
8. NOI, October 11, 1948; *New York Herald Tribune,* January 9, 1949.
9. *Kansas City Star,* September 19, 1948; *Oakland Post-Examiner,* September 23, 1948; Katherine Long.
10. *New York Herald Tribune,* January 9, 1948; *Oakland Post-Examiner,* September 23, 1948.
11. Thomas Martin, *Dynasty: The Longs of Louisiana* (New York: Putnam, 1960), 191.

12. *Kansas City Star,* September 19, 1948.
13. Hair, 309; Brinkley, 77; RBL, February 5, 1990; ST, January 1, 1949.
14. RBL, February 5, 1990.
15. *New Orleans States,* January 4, 1949.
16. RBL, February 5, 1990.
17. *Redbook,* December 1951.
18. RBL, February 5, 1990.
19. White, 60–65.
20. *Tupelo* (Miss.) *Journal,* January 26, 1949; United Press, January 24, 1949; AP, January 26, 1949.
21. *Washington Star,* February 2, 1949; CBS "Meet the Press" transcript, February 5, 1949, RBL Collection.
22. *New Orleans States,* February 9, 1949.
23. RBL, February 5, 1990.
24. *New Orleans States,* March 3, 1949.
25. CR, March 2, 1949, 1717–19.
26. AP, March 2, 1949; *New Orleans States,* March 3, 1949; *Memphis Commercial Appeal,* March 7, 1949.
27. *New York Times Magazine,* April 4, 1965.
28. CBS "Meet the Press" transcript, February 4, 1949, RBL Collection.
29. RBL to Harvey Carey, February 15, 1949, RBL Collection; SJ, February 9, 1949.
30. RBL to Bill Feazel, February 15, 1949, RBL Collection.
31. SJ, July 15, 1949.
32. Ibid.; MW, July 16, 1949.
33. NOI, April 17, 1950.
34. RBL, February 5, 1990; WP, October 23, 1949.
35. *Tangi Talk,* August 13, 1949; NOI, October 18, 1949; *Redbook,* December 1951.
36. ST, January 1, 1950; MA, September 25, 1949.
37. RBL, February 5, 1990.
38. Gill.

Chapter 9

1. *Redbook,* December 1951; Katherine Long.
2. *Redbook,* December 1951.
3. Ibid.
4. Sindler, 229–30.
5. *Daily Iberian,* May 25, 1950; *New Orleans States,* May 23, 1950.
6. *New Orleans States,* April 18 and July 22, 1950; ST, July 24, 1950.
7. RBL, February 19, 1990.
8. *New Orleans States,* September 12, 1950; TP, September 11, 1950.
9. NS, SJ, and MA, September 12, 1950; NOI, September 18, 1950.
10. MA, September 15, 1950.
11. MA, January 28, 1951; *Knoxville News Sentinel,* February 15, 1951.
12. *Opelousas Daily World,* March 16, 1951.
13. James MacGregor Burns, *The Crosswinds of Freedom* (New York: Knopf, 1989), 244; RBL, February 5, 1990.
14. *New Orleans States,* June 1, 1951.
15. Merle Miller, *Plain Speaking: An Oral Biography of Harry S. Truman* (New York: Putnam, 1973), 290–91.

16. RBL, February 5, 1990.
17. LCAP, April 21, 1951.
18. *New Orleans States,* April 28, 1951.
19. ST, May 27, 1951.
20. *Time,* December 24, 1951.
21. RBL, February 5, 1990.
22. *Hearings before the Committee on Armed Services and the Committee on Foreign Relations,* United States Senate, Eighty-second Congress, First Session, Part One, Volume One, May 4, 1951, 174–77.
23. Ibid., 309.
24. RBL, February 5, 1990.
25. *Hearings before the Committee on Armed Services and the Committee on Foreign Relations,* United States Senate, Eighty-second Congress, First Session, Part One, Volume One, May 11, 1951, 668–69.
26. *Time,* December 24, 1951; RBL, February 5, 1990; George E. Reedy, *The U.S. Senate: Paralysis or a Search for Consensus?* (New York: Crown, 1986), 58.
27. Burns, 242.

CHAPTER 10

1. CR, October 14, 1949; 14507; RBL, December 3, 1990.
2. BRST, April 22, 1950.
3. Miller, 165–66; *Crowley Daily Signal,* October 28, 1952.
4. *Pointe Coupee Banner,* May 13, 1954.
5. RBL to Feazel, June 18, 1954, RBL Collection.
6. *Olla-Tullos Signal,* November 26, 1954.
7. CR, January 14, 1955, 376; TP, October 22, 1954.
8. CR, November 30, 1954, 16214.
9. CR, December 1, 1954, 16290–91.
10. Miller, 173.
11. CR, January 14, 1954, 361.
12. Ibid., 373–77.
13. *Bastrop Clarion,* January 15, 1955; ST, January 15, 1955; MA, January 15, 1955.
14. George Dixon, June 1955, King Features Syndicate.
15. Anderson, 106.
16. William L. O'Neill, *American High: The Years of Confidence, 1945–1960* (New York: Free Press, 1986), 168.

CHAPTER 11

1. RBL, October 27, 1988.
2. TP, April 8, 1951.
3. Boggs.
4. SJ, June 18, 1951.
5. Martin, 193.
6. NOI, June 20, 1951.
7. Ibid.; Kurtz and Peoples, 159; Dodd, 107.
8. McCaughan, 132; Wall, 301; Kurtz and Peoples, 160.
9. NOI, July 26, 1951; RBL to U. B. Evans, RBL Collection.

10. RBL to DeLesseps Morrison, August 30, 1951, RBL Collection.
11. RBL to David R. McGuire, Jr., August 30, 1951, RBL Collection.
12. NOI, October 16 and 18, 1951; Glen Jeansonne, *Leander Perez: Boss of the Delta* (Baton Rouge: LSU, 1977), 152–53.
13. Boggs; McCaughan, 133–34.
14. Boggs.
15. Ibid.
16. Ibid.; Dodd, 108.
17. TP, July 26, 1951.
18. NOI, October 22, 1951; NOS, October 26 and December 20, 1951; TP, October 27, 1951.
19. *American Heritage*, August 1966; TP, December 21, 1951; Opotowsky, 200.
20. Boggs.
21. RBL, October 27, 1988.
22. Sindler, 238; NYT, March 5, 1952.
23. Sindler, 241; Thomas Martin, *Dynasty: The Longs of Louisiana* (New York: Putnam, 1960), 195.
24. Feazel to RBL, January 28, 1952, RBL Collection.
25. RBL to Dodd, March 12, 1952, RBL Collection.

CHAPTER 12

1. BRST, June 1, 1951.
2. *U.S. News and World Report*, March 3, 1952.
3. NOS, March 31, 1952; ST, April 18, 1952.
4. RBL, February 19, 1990.
5. Ibid.
6. NOS, July 25, 1952.
7. Ibid., July 25 and 26, 1952.
8. Jeansonne, 190; D. B. Hardeman and Donald C. Bacon, *Rayburn: A Biography* (Lanham: Madison 1987), 363.
9. Ibid.
10. Ibid.
11. RBL speech text, RBL Collection.
12. RBL, February 19, 1990.
13. MA, July 25, 1952; BRST, July 26, 1952.
14. *Crowley Daily Signal*, July 26, 1952; *Bunkie Record*, August 1, 1952; *Jefferson Parish Times*, August 2, 1952; *Washington Evening Star*, July 25, 1952.
15. Speech text, undated, RBL Collection; *Lafayette Daily Advertiser*, August 11, 1952.
16. ST, September 9, 1952; NOS, September 19, 1952; NOI, September 21, 1952.
17. *Anderson* (S.C.) *Independent*, October 23, 1952.
18. *Crowley Daily Signal*, October 28, 1952.
19. RBL speech notes, undated, RBL Collection.
20. Wall, 308; Jeansonne, 194–93.

CHAPTER 13

1. Reedy, 18.
2. TP, July 4, 1948.

3. CR, July 23, 1955, 11785.
4. CQA, 1952, 166.
5. TP, May 14, 1952; CR, May 27 and 28, 1952, 6027.
6. CR, May 28, 1952, 6097.
7. Ibid., 6141–42.
8. RBL, February 5, 1990; CQA, 1952, 168; CR, May 8, 1952, 6144.
9. Martin, 197; *Report of the Subcommittee on Military Public Works, Committee on Armed Services,* U.S. Senate, January 2, 1953.
10. *Report of the Subcommittee on Military Public Works, Committee on Armed Services,* U.S. Senate, January 2, 1953.
11. Ibid.
12. TP, February 9, 1953; SJ, February 10, 1953; *Legislative Daily,* U.S. Chamber of Commerce, February 5, 1953.
13. *Memphis Commercial Appeal,* February 7, 1953; ST, February 10, 1953; NOS, February 10, 1953.
14. *Report of the Subcommittee on Military Public Works, Committee on Armed Services,* U.S. Senate, January 2, 1953; TP, February 19, 1953.
15. *Crowley Signal,* February 16, 1953; WP, February 18, 1953.
16. *Lafayette Daily Advertiser,* July 6, 1953; MA, July 14, 1953.
17. *Opelousas Daily World,* July 30, 1953.
18. CR, August 3, 1954, 13012; MA, August 4, 1954; *Opelousas Daily World,* August 5, 1954; Opotowski, 210; CR, June 2, 1955, 7504.
19. CR, June 2, 1955, 7505; CQA, 1955, 306; ST, June 3, 1955.
20. NOI, July 31, 1955; CR, July 28, 1955, 11785.
21. NOS, May 18, 1956; TP, May 20, 1956.
22. ST, June 19, 1956; CR, June 28, 1956, 11263, 81.
23. CR, June 29, 1956, 11400–03.
24. MA, June 8, 1957; CR, June 14, 1957, 9097–9113, 9127–29.
25. Robert C. Byrd, *The Senate, 1789–1989, Addresses on the History of the United States Senate* (Washington, DC: U.S. Government Printing Office, 1989), 627.
26. Byrd, 637; CR, February 11, 1957, 1855.
27. CR, February 11, 1957, 1856.
28. Ibid.
29. Ibid., 1864–65.
30. *Donaldsonville Chief,* March 15, 1957.
31. CR, June 9, 1959, 10302, 08; ST, May 15, 1959.
32. CR, June 9, 1959, 10303.
33. Ibid., 10316–18.
34. "Washington Report" transcript, March 18, 1959, RBL Collection.
35. RBL, February 2, 1991.

CHAPTER 14

1. Radio transcript, July 1948, RBL Collection.
2. CR, September 10, 1985, 23222; Hair, 310; Christman, xiv; *Houston Chronicle,* May 29, 1977.
3. CR, June 19, 1950, 8806.
4. RBL, February 2, 1991.
5. *Sabine* (Many, La.) *Index,* February 19, 1954.
6. CR, August 13, 1954, 14439.

7. CR, July 11, 1954, 10604.
8. MA, February 26, 1954.
9. NOI, June 30, 1954; ST, June 30, 1954; *Beaumont Enterprise,* July 6, 1954.
10. CR, March 11, 1955, 2715.
11. CQA, 1956, 393, 96; CR, February 10, 1956, 2491.
12. CQA, 1956, 396.
13. CR, February 24, 1956, 3334; MA, May 19, 1956.
14. CR, July 16, 1956, 12869, 74.
15. Ibid., 12874, 78.
16. RBL, February 2, 1991.
17. CQA, 1956, 392–97; Miller, 188.
18. ST, April 3 and 10, 1956; Miller, 189.
19. CR, July 17, 1956, 13036.
20. CQA, 1956, 397.
21. RBL, February 2, 1991.
22. *New Orleans States,* February 15, 1956; Radio script, March 8, 1956, RBL Collection.
23. TT, October 29, 1956; BRST, November 7, 1956.
24. *Labor,* May 5, 1958.
25. CR, June 25, 1959, 11936.
26. CR, June 29, 1959, 12046; RBL to LBJ, June 29, 1959, LBJ Library.

CHAPTER 15

1. Fulbright.
2. RBL, February 5, 1990.
3. RBL, February 2, 1991.
4. *Opelousas Daily World,* February 22, 1951.
5. MA, May 18, 1954; *Jennings Daily News,* May 28, 1954.
6. Wall, 308.
7. James C. Duram, *A Moderate among Extremists: Dwight D. Eisenhower and the School Desegregation Crisis* (Chicago: Nelson-Hall, 1981), 92.
8. O'Neill, 249.
9. TP, May 10, 1956; *Oak Grove-West Carroll Gazette,* May 24, 1956; *Ouachita Citizen,* May 11, 1956.
10. Undated memorandum, RBL Collection.
11. Hill oral history, LBJ Library.
12. *Lafayette Daily Advertiser,* April 10, 1957; *Algiers West Bank Herald,* July 8, 1957.
13. RBL to Stephen B. Lemann, June 26, 1957, RBL Collection.
14. CR, July 15, 1957, 11683–84.
15. *Congress and the Nation,* 1957, 1623.
16. CR, July 26, 1957, 12822.
17. NOI, August 2, 1957.
18. CR, August 28, 1957, 16213–14.
19. *Opelousas Daily World,* September 1, 1957.
20. Thurmond.
21. Robert Sherrill, *Gothic Politics in the Deep South* (New York: Ballantine, 1969), 272.
22. Reedy, 179; Douglas and Hebert oral histories, LBJ Library.
23. *Daily Iberian,* October 1, 1957.
24. LCAP, December 28 and 30, 1953.
25. CR, March 11, 1954, 3080, March 4, 1954, 2648.

26. Ibid., July 26, 1957, 12826–29.
27. *Lafayette Daily Advertiser,* October 30, 1957; MA, October 31, 1957.
28. NOI, November 4 and 19, 1957; SJ, November 8, 1957.
29. SJ, November 8, 1957.
30. RBL, February 2, 1991.

CHAPTER 16

1. *Time,* June 15, 1959.
2. Kurtz and Peoples, 214.
3. McCaughan, 168.
4. BRST, May 27, 1959.
5. Kurtz and Peoples, 216; WP, May 31, 1959; BRST, May 27, 1959.
6. A. J. Liebling, *The Earl of Louisiana* (Baton Rouge: LSU Press, 1970), 29.
7. RBL notes from undelivered speech draft, RBL Collection.
8. RBL, December 3, 1990.
9. Ibid.
10. Ibid.
11. Ibid.
12. Undelivered RBL speech, RBL Collection.
13. Martin, 219–20; RBL, December 3, 1991.
14. RBL, December 3, 1990.
15. Undelivered RBL speech, RBL Collection.
16. NS, June 11, 1959; TP, June 2, 1959; McCaughan, 172; Opotowski, 201.
17. Opotowski, 201.
18. RBL speech text, RBL Collection.
19. BRST, June 3, 1959; text of WDSU TV editorial, RBL Collection; TP, June 2, 1959; McCaughan, 172.
20. *Bogalusa Daily News,* June 12, 1959; *Lafayette Daily Advertiser,* June 14, 1959; MW, June 13, 1959; SJ, June 10, 1959.
21. *Newsweek,* June 15, 1959.
22. Kurtz and Peoples, 220.
23. *Opelousas Daily World,* June 17, 1959.
24. BRST, June 26, 1959.
25. BRST, June 25, 1959; RBL, December 3, 1990; MW, June 25, 1959; TT, July 1, 1959; ST, September 11, 1959; BRST, October 6, 1959.
26. McCaughan, 180.
27. Dodd, 55.
28. Ibid., 45.
29. *Redbook,* December 1951.
30. Madden.
31. RBL to Coushatta family, Sept. 27, 1960, and U.S. Senate newsletter, RBL Collection.

CHAPTER 17

1. CR, January 12, 1959, 502.
2. Robert Dallek, *Lone Star Rising: Lyndon Johnson and His Times, 1908–1960* (New York: Oxford, 1991), 518.

3. TP, February 3, 1960; *Jet,* March 31, 1960.
4. RBL press release, March 2, 1960, RBL Collection.
5. Ibid.
6. RBL press release, March 12, 1960, RBL Collection; *Crowley Daily Signal,* March 14, 1960.
7. *Ruston Leader,* April 12, 1960.
8. NS, April 18, 1960; AP, April 20, 1960; TP, May 3, 1960.
9. Radio transcript, June 23, 1960, RBL Collection.
10. CR, August 29, 1960, 18088–89.
11. NOSI, July 11, 1960; SJ, July 15, 1960.
12. *Opelousas Daily World,* September 18, 1960; TP, September 28, 1960.
13. RBL, May 17, 1991; ST, October 23, 1960; Nixon; TP, November 21, 1960.
14. Edward F. Haas, *DeLesseps S. Morrison and the Image of Reform* (Baton Rouge: LSU, 1974), 249–72.
15. Ibid.
16. TP, November 17, 1960; *Opelousas Daily World,* November 16, 1960.
17. RBL, May 17, 1991.
18. MW, March 19, 1961; *Franklin Banner Tribune,* March 7 and 28, 1961.
19. RBL to JFK, October 30, 1961, RBL Collection.
20. LCAP, September 13, 1962.
21. NOSI, October 24, 1962; NS, October 31, 1962.
22. *Opelousas Daily World,* October 18, 1962; MA, November 11, 1962.
23. NS, August 15, 1963, and January 4, 1963.
24. *The Progressive,* December 1963.
25. ST, February 10, 1963; NS, February 20, 1963; BRST, February 20, 1963.
26. SJ, April 17, 1963; Radio transcript, May 9, 1963, RBL Collection.
27. MA, April 20, 1963.
28. BRST, June 21, 1963; NS, June 18, 1963.
29. ST, July 23, 1963; MW, July 26, 1963.
30. RBL notes, 1963, RBL Collection.
31. *Opelousas Daily World,* July 5, 1963; Transcript, "Reporters Round-Up," Mutual Broadcasting System, July 21, 1963, RBL Collection.
32. UPI, August 23, 1963; TP, August 23, 1963.
33. *The Progressive,* December 1963.
34. RBL, August 28, 1991.
35. CR, September 11, 1963, 16796.
36. TT, August 30, 1963.

CHAPTER 18

1. TP, November 21, 1963.
2. SJ, November 23, 1963; TP, November 23, 1963; RBL, May 17, 1991; RBL to Jackie Kennedy, November 25, 1963, RBL Collection.
3. TP, November 25, 1963.
4. Reedy, 109; Miller, 357–58.
5. RBL, February 2, 1991; *Philadelphia Inquirer,* February 16, 1964.
6. *Philadelphia Inquirer,* February 16, 1964.
7. Ibid.; CQA, 1964, 531; CR, February 3, 1964, 1772.
8. *Philadelphia Inquirer,* February 16, 1964.
9. RBL, February 2, 1991; CR, February 7, 1964, 2358.

10. CR, February 7, 1964, 2358.
11. Ibid.
12. Donald W. Kiefer, *A Review of the Research on the Economic Effects of the 1964 Tax Cut, The 1968 Surtax, and the 1975 Tax Cut,* Congressional Research Service, Washington, D.C., July 1980; *Philadelphia Inquirer,* February 16, 1964.
13. CR, February 7, 1964, 2395.
14. *Saturday Evening Post,* February 27, 1965.

CHAPTER 19

1. Opotowski, 216; Katherine Long.
2. RBL, December 3, 1991; Dallek, 381.
3. Opotowski, 216.
4. CR, March 13, 1964, 5239; Miller, 369; Gilbert C. Fite, *Richard B. Russell, Jr., Senator from Georgia* (Chapel Hill: University of North Carolina, 1991), 408.
5. CR, March 12, 1964, 5059.
6. Miller, 370.
7. Fite, 407.
8. CR, April 7, 1964, 7101, May 20, 1964, 11490.
9. RBL, December 3, 1991.
10. CR, April 30, 1964, 9681.
11. LCAP, July 4, 1964.
12. BRST, June 25, 1964.
13. Ibid., July 16, 1964.
14. CR, April 14, 1964, 7903; RBL, August 28, 1991.
15. Hair, 171.
16. McBride; Dashbach.
17. CR, April 14, 1964, 7903.

CHAPTER 20

1. TP, August 22, 1964; AP, August 31, 1964.
2. *Crowley Daily Signal,* October 7, 1964; LCAP, October 14, 1964.
3. Harry McPherson, *A Political Education* (Boston: Houghton Mifflin, 1988), 44.
4. Television interview transcript, RBL Collection.
5. Television transcript, RBL Collection; *Saturday Evening Post,* February 27, 1965; RBL, May 17, 1991.
6. *Newark Sunday News,* November 22, 1964; WSJ, November 25, 1964.
7. RBL, May 17, 1991.
8. RBL, February 2, 1991; Long, 340.
9. RBL, May 17, 1991; *Crowley Daily Signal,* December 1, 1964.
10. *Alexandria Daily Town Talk,* December 9, 1964.
11. RBL, February 5, 1990; CR, April 8, 1965, 7501.
12. SJ, December 26, 1964.
13. WP, January 2, 1965; SJ, December 26, 1964.
14. *Saturday Evening Post,* February 27, 1965.
15. *Bastrop Daily Enterprise,* January 4, 1965; NOSI, January 4, 1965; ST, January 4, 1965.

16. *Saturday Evening Post,* February 27, 1965; *Birmingham Post-Herald,* January 5, 1965; *Kansas City Star,* January 5, 1965; SJ, January 9, 1965.
17. MA, January 6, 1965.
18. WP, January 11, 1965; BRST, January 18, 1965.
19. WP, January 11, 1965.
20. RBL, May 17, 1991.
21. MA, January 15, 1965; ST, January 26, 1965.
22. MW, March 2, 1965.
23. LCAP, March 24, 1965; ST, March 14, 1965; *Sabine* (Many, La.) *Index,* April 2, 1965.
24. TP, March 27, 1965; *San Antonio Express,* April 3, 1965.
25. *Miami Herald,* April 20, 1965.
26. NOSI, April 5, 1965.
27. TT, May 26, 1965; LCAP, October 22, 1965.
28. WP, June 19, 1965; NYT, June 19, 1965; *Insurance,* June 26, 1965.
29. RBL, February 2, 1991.
30. *Chicago News,* June 28, 1965.
31. McBride; Thevenot.
32. McBride.

CHAPTER 21

1. NYT, November 19, 1965.
2. WP, November 14, 1965; *Washington Star,* November 15, 1965; *Chicago News,* November 16, 1965.
3. *New York Journal-American,* November 28, 1965.
4. *South Bend Tribune* January 13, 1966.
5. CR, January 19, 1966, 595–96; *Time,* January 14, 1966.
6. Mike Manatos oral history, LBJ Library; Thevenot.
7. TP, August 6, 1964; Lyndon B. Johnson, *The Vantage Point* (New York: Holt, Rinehart and Winston, 1971), 150.
8. *Philadelphia Inquirer,* January 28, 1966; *Washington Evening Star,* February 21, 1966.
9. RBL, February 2, 1991.
10. *Los Angeles Times,* March 26, 1966; RBL, February 2, 1991; RBL press release, April 14, 1966, RBL Collection.
11. RBL press releases, July 28, 1966, September 8, 1966, and August 30, 1966, RBL Collection; *New York News,* September 27, 1966.
12. RBL, February 2, 1991.
13. *Business Week,* February 19, 1966; *Labor Weekly,* June 4 and May 14, 1966.
14. *Business Week,* December 24, 1966.
15. RBL, August 28, 1991.
16. RBL, May 17, 1991.
17. CR, April 4, 1967, 8303, 8320; BRST, April 5, 1967; NOSI, April 14, 1967.
18. NOSI, April 14, 1967; MA, April 16, 1967.
19. CR, April 19, 1967, 10208; Ibid., April 20, 1967, 10310.
20. *Washington Star,* April 21, 1967, NOSI, April 21, 1967; CR, April 20, 1967, 10310, 10313–14; CQA, 1967, 293.
21. BRST, April 24, 1967.
22. MA, April 28, 1967.

23. SJ, May 3, 1967.
24. SJ, May 4, 1967.
25. *Detroit News,* May 4, 1967.
26. Ibid.; RBL, August 28, 1991.
27. ST, May 10, 1967.
28. NOSI, May 8, 1967; *Washington Star,* May 11, 1967.
29. *Ruston Daily Leader,* May 12, 1967; ST, May 14, 1967.
30. "Face the Nation" transcript, May 14, 1967; McBride.
31. RBL, August 28, 1991.
32. RBL, January 3, 1992.
33. MA, February 21, 1967.
34. SJ, February 22, 1967; *Bastrop Daily Enterprise,* February 22, 1967; *Opelousas Daily World,* February 25, 1967.
35. Henry Hurt, *Reasonable Doubt: An Investigation into the Assassination of John F. Kennedy,* (New York: Holt, Reinhart and Winston, 1985), 269.
36. BRST, May 15, 1967; ST, May 15, 1967.
37. Transcript of May 14, 1967, "Face the Nation," RBL Collection.
38. Hurt, 272–73, 282.
39. Ibid., 278.
40. Ibid., 307.

CHAPTER 22

1. UPI, April 28, 1967; LCAP, April 28, 1967; *Beaumont Enterprise,* April 29, 1967.
2. Nixon.
3. RBL, May 17, 1991.
4. McBride.
5. ST, May 4, 1967.
6. NOSI, June 13, 1967; Tom Dodd defense memos, RBL Collection.
7. CQA, 1967, 250.
8. UPI, June 16, 1967.
9. CQA, 1967, 249; CQ, June 16, 1967, 16121.
10. CR, June 16, 1967, 16118.
11. CR, June 23, 1967, 17072; WP, June 19, 1967.
12. TP, June 18, 1967; RBL, May 17, 1991.
13. MA, June 25, 1967.
14. ST, June 29, 1967; RBL, May 17, 1991.

CHAPTER 23

1. CQA, 1967, 904–5.
2. Ibid., 906.
3. CQA, 1967, 907; *Washington Evening Star,* September 20, 1967.
4. CQA, 1967, 910.
5. NOSI, November 27, 1967.
6. CR, December 14, 1967, 36679.
7. Ibid., December 14, 1967, 36680; CQA, 1967, 916; MW, December 15, 1967.
8. CR, December 14, 1967, 36680–82; CQA, 1967, 916; TT, December 15, 1967.

9. ST, December 15, 1967; MA, December 21, 1967.
10. NOSI, December 20, 1967.
11. *Los Angeles Times,* January 25, 1981.
12. Ibid.; RBL, July 25, 1991.
13. RBL, July 25, 1991.
14. Ibid.
15. Ibid.
16. *Los Angeles Times,* January 25, 1981; RBL, July 25, 1991.

CHAPTER 24

1. Wright.
2. RBL, December 3, 1991.
3. Ibid.
4. Miller, 46; Ronnie Dugger, *The Politician* (New York: W. W. Norton, 1982), 168; Dallek, 106.
5. RBL to LBJ, September 4, 1958; LBJ to RBL, September 16, 1958, LBJ Library.
6. NS, January 18, 1968.
7. TT, March 2, 1968; NYT, April 15, 1968.
8. MA, April 9, 1968.
9. TP, April 6, 7, and 9, 1968.
10. TP, April 1, 1968; Mike Manatos to LBJ, June 25, 1968, LBJ Library.
11. TP, July 14, 1968; Manatos to LBJ, July 15, 1968, LBJ Library.
12. RBL to LBJ, July 18, 1968, LBJ Library; *Washington Star,* June 9, 1968.
13. Mike Manatos to LBJ, July 15, 1968, LBJ Library; Marvin Watson to LBJ, July 17, 1968, LBJ Library.
14. MA, August 19 and 25, 1968; *Bogalusa Daily News,* August 19, 1968.
15. SJ, August 29, 1968, and September 6, 1968.
16. MA, August 29, 1968; *Crowley Daily Signal,* September 13, 1968.
17. RBL, May 17, 1991.

CHAPTER 25

1. RBL, August 28, 1991.
2. McBride.
3. Thevenot; Stern.
4. Larry J. Sabato, *Feeding Frenzy: How Attack Journalism Has Transformed American Politics* (New York: Free Press, 1991), 31.
5. Thevenot.
6. Williams, 268; Wright.
7. RBL, August 28, 1991.
8. NYT, June 3, 1969; McBride; Thevenot; RBL, December 3, 1991.
9. CR, April 12, 1973, H 2703.
10. TP, December 24, 1968; Dashbach; Thevenot.
11. RBL, August 28, 1991.
12. Hair, 266; Dodd, 18.
13. WP, November 14, 1968; *Nashville Banner,* November 14, 1968.

14. Robert L. Peabody, *Leadership in Congress* (Boston: Little, Brown, 1976), 371; *St. Louis Globe-Democrat,* December 10, 1968.
15. Peabody, 375.
16. *Philadelphia Bulletin,* December 31, 1968; *Jennings Daily News,* December 31, 1968; UPI, December 31, 1968.
17. Peabody, 378–79; WP, January 2, 1969.
18. SJ, January 3, 1969; NOSI, January 3, 1969; Peabody, 381.
19. Peabody, 380, 82.
20. *Christian Science Monitor,* February 4, 1969; RBL, December 3, 1991.
21. RBL, May 17, 1991.
22. LBJ to RBL, January 3, 1969, LBJ Library; Nixon.
23. Thevenot; ST, August 30, 1969.
24. ST, August 30, 1991.
25. BRST, August 30, 1969.
26. NYT, June 21, 1970.
27. Department of Justice Memorandum, June 12, 1970, to Will Wilson, Assistant Attorney General, Criminal Division; *Baltimore Contractors Inc. v. The United States,* No. 272–70, U.S. Claims Court, April 30, 1987.
28. NYT, June 21, 1970.
29. Ibid.
30. CQA, 1970, 67; RBL, November 11, 1991.
31. TP, May 21, 1970; *Lafourche Comet,* May 28, 1970.

CHAPTER 26

1. Christman, 42, 109.
2. CQA, 1970, 1035.
3. Ibid., 1035
4. Ibid., 624; CQ, 1971, 520.
5. LCAP, February 16, 1971; TP, April 17, 1971.
6. MA, August 20, 1971.
7. *St. Petersburg Times,* January 22, 1972.
8. Stern.
9. MW, April 29, 1972; MA, January 4 and 31, July 13, 1972.
10. MA, January 31, 1972.
11. ST, July 23, 1972; TP, August 5, 1972.
12. CQA, 1972, 908.
13. RBL, July 25, 1991; CQA, 1971, 523.
14. Stern.
15. CQA, 1972, 910.
16. CQA, 1972, 914; RBL, July 25, 1991; Richard Nixon, *RN: The Memoirs of Richard Nixon* (New York: Grosset & Dunlap, 1978), 428.

CHAPTER 27

1. RBL, July 25, 1991.
2. Stall; John Ehrlichman, *Witness to Power: The Nixon Years* (New York: Simon and Shuster, 1982), 177.

3. RBL, January 3, 1992.
4. SJ, May 4, 1973.
5. Ibid.; MA, May 19, 1973.
6. NOSI, June 29, 1973; SJ, July 27, 1973.
7. BRST, August 8, 1973.
8. Ibid., October 20, 1973.
9. Ibid; TP, November 6, 1973.
10. TT, February 9, 1974.
11. MW, March 18, 1974.
12. NOSI, April 3, 1974; MA, April 6, 1974; RBL, July 25, 1991.
13. Nixon, 960.
14. *Beaumont Enterprise*, April 9, 1974; BRST, April 12, 1974.
15. BRST, April 20, 1974.
16. NOSI, May 18, 1974; *Houma Daily Courier*, May 24, 1974.
17. RBL, July 25, 1991.
18. NOSI, July 24, 1974.

CHAPTER 28

1. RBL, February 2, 1991.
2. CQ, September 10, 1977, 1913.
3. *Newsweek*, November 21, 1977.
4. WSJ, December 18, 1973.
5. Ibid.
6. RBL, February 2, 1991.
7. BRST, March 13, 1975; TT; February 7, 1975.
8. CQA, 1975, 99–103.
9. TP, March 5, 1975.
10. *New York*, May 5, 1975; WP, March 24, 1975.
11. *New York*, May 5, 1975.
12. Ibid.
13. WP, March 26, 1975.
14. Ibid., March 27, 1975.
15. CR, March 18, 1975, 7230.
16. *New York*, May 5, 1975.
17. Ibid.
18. Ibid.
19. *National Journal*, May 22, 1976.
20. *New York*, May 5, 1975; WP, March 27, 1975; CQA, 1975, 110–11.
21. *New York*, May 5, 1975; CQA, 1975, 110; Bentsen.
22. *National Journal*, May 22, 1976.
23. RBL, February 2, 1991; *Newsweek*, November 21, 1977.

CHAPTER 29

1. WSJ, December 18, 1973; Thevenot.
2. Thevenot; *Washington Star*, October 30, 1977; Packwood.
3. Ross K. Baker, *Friend and Foe in the U.S. Senate* (New York: Free Press, 1980), 43.

4. CQ, September 10, 1977; *Newsweek,* November 21, 1977.
5. CQ, September 10, 1977, 1906; WP, December 11, 1977.
6. WP, December 11, 1977.
7. Ibid.
8. Packwood; CQ, September 10, 1977, 1907; *Newsweek,* November 21, 1977; *New York,* May 5, 1975.
9. Johnston; *Newsweek,* November 21, 1977; *New York,* May 5, 1975.
10. Stern.
11. *New York,* May 5, 1975.
12. *Reader's Digest,* July 1979; Packwood.
13. *Newsweek,* November 21, 1977; CQ, September 10, 1977.
14. NOSI, February 21, 1976; BRST, April 21, 1976; RBL, November 11, 1991.
15. CR, June 17, 1976, 18847–51.
16. CQA, 1976, 52.
17. LCAP, June 13, 1976; WSJ, June 24, 1976; *Nation's Business,* August 1977.
18. *Washington Star,* May 28, 1976.
19. NOSI, August 23, 1976.
20. *Congress and the Nation, Vol. IV* (Washington, DC: CQ, 1976), 101; CQA, 1976, 60.
21. *Congress and the Nation, Vol. IV,* 101.
22. *Lafayette Daily Advertiser,* November 21, 1976.
23. TP, January 15, 1977; SJ, February 9, 1977.
24. WSJ, March 3, 1977.
25. Ibid.

CHAPTER 30

1. TT, November 7, 1976.
2. RBL, August 28, 1991.
3. Charles O. Jones, *The Trusteeship Presidency* (Baton Rouge: LSU Press, 1988), 127–28.
4. RBL, August 28, 1991.
5. TP, March 5, 1977; MA, April 10, 1977; TT, May 28, 1977; Jones, 134.
6. RBL, August 28, 1991.
7. Johnson, *The Absence of Power,* 159; RBL, August 28, 1991.
8. Jones, 149; RBL, August 28, 1991; Jimmy Carter, *Keeping Faith* (Toronto: Bantam, 1982), 79.
9. Carter, 93.
10. Carter, 91; *Nation's Business,* August 1977.
11. Carter, 93.
12. Carter, 98.
13. Ibid.
14. MA, August 9, 1977.
15. TP, August 9, 1977.
16. CQA, 1977, 712.
17. NOSI, October 6, 1977.
18. WP, October 27, 1977.
19. Carter, 100.
20. *Washington Star,* October 22, 1977.
21. MW, November 2, 1977; WP, November 11, 1977.
22. WSJ, October 25, 1977.

23. WP, November 30, 1977; *Washington Star,* November 29, 1977.
24. NYT, November 30, 1977; *Washington Star,* December 8, 1977.
25. Bentsen; RBL, August 28, 1991.
26. *Washington Star,* December 18, 1977; TP, August 4, 1978.

CHAPTER 31

1. McKinney.
2. Johnston.
3. TP, January 24, 1964.
4. MA, June 26, 1978; Jones, 157; Stall.
5. RBL, August 28, 1991.
6. Guirard; RBL, August 28, 1991 and November 11, 1991.
7. Stall; RBL, August 28, 1991.
8. CR, March 15, 1978, 6940-6942.
9. CR, April 6, 1978, 8997; MA, March 25, 1978.
10. RBL, November 11, 1991; ST, March 25, 1978; MW, April 30, 1978.
11. RBL, November 11, 1991.
12. Guirard; RBL, November 11, 1991; CR, March 15, 1978, 6943; Stall; Feingerts.

CHAPTER 32

1. WSJ, January 28, 1978.
2. TP, August 4, 1978.
3. WP, January 27 and September 8, 1978; WSJ, August 13, 1978.
4. *Washington Star,* September 8, 1978; WP, September 13, 1978; *National Journal,* May 22, 1976.
5. TP, September 23, 1978; WP, September 17, 1978; WSJ, September 15, 1978.
6. *Washington Star,* September 23, 1978; WP, October 1, 1978; and October 5, 1978.
7. NYT, October 11, 1978; BRST, October 12, 1978.
8. *Washington Star,* December 18, 1977; Joseph A. Califano, Jr., *Governing America* (New York: Simon and Schuster, 1981), 130.
9. Bentsen; Johnston.
10. ST, August 25, 1977; MA, August 15, 1977.
11. *Washington Star,* October 18, 1977.
12. Califano, 379.
13. Ibid.
14. Califano, 403; RBL, August 28 and November 11, 1991.
15. BRST, April 14, 1979; CQA, 1979, 613; NYT, April 15, 1979.
16. WSJ, May 8, 1979.
17. Ibid.
18. MA, June 16, 1979.
19. *Washington Star,* March 30, 1980.
20. CQA, 1979, 612; WSJ, July 12, 1979.
21. CQA, 1979, 617–20.
22. Stall; CR, December 12, 1979, 35608.
23. Ibid.

24. CQA, 1979, 626.
25. *Washington Star,* March 30, 1980; Bentsen.
26. RBL, August 28, 1991.

CHAPTER 33

1. TP, January 23, 1980; NYT, April 15, 1979.
2. TP, January 31, 1980; *U.S. News and World Report,* January 14 and April 14, 1980.
3. TP, July 30, 1979.
4. Ibid., April 24 and January 5, 1980.
5. Ibid., July 2 and 22, 1980.
6. Ibid., July 31, 1980.
7. TP, July 31, 1980; BRST, September 3, 1980.
8. TP, June 22, 1980; BRST, August 24, 1980.
9. Kirkpatrick; TP, July 13 and August 26, 1980.
10. MA, June 9, 1980.
11. SJ, June 16, 1980; TT, August 9, 1980.
12. *Opelousas Daily World,* September 7, 1980.
13. TP, September 8, 1980; BRST, September 15, 1980.
14. MA, September 14, 1980; BRST, September 15, 1980; *Beaumont* (Tex.) *Enterprise,* October 17, 1980.
15. BRST, September 15, 1980.
16. WSJ, October 7, 1986.

CHAPTER 34

1. TP, November 15, 1980.
2. MA, February 1, 1981; Speech transcript, March 13, 1981, RBL Collection.
3. TP, March 16, 1981.
4. RBL, August 28, 1991.
5. Johnston; RBL, August 28, 1991.
6. SJ, October 29, 1981.
7. TT, March 19, 1982.
8. MA, March 13, 1980; *Natchitoches Times,* November 1982.
9. Stern; Stall.
10. WSJ, March 25, 1983; RBL, August 28, 1991; Stall.
11. Ufholz.
12. *Gambit* (New Orleans), November 22, 1986.
13. RBL, August 28, 1991.
14. WSJ, March 25, 1983; CQA, 1983, 261–64; Bentsen.
15. MA, March 20, 1983; WSJ, March 25, 1983.
16. Stall; CR, February 2, 1982, 281.
17. John R. Hibbing, *The Changing World of the U.S. Senate* (Berkeley: IGS Press, 1990), 193.
18. CR, February 2, 1982, 625.
19. Ibid., 625–27.
20. Hibbing, 205.

CHAPTER 35

1. Carolyn Long, January 30, 1992.
2. Nixon.
3. RBL, November 11, 1991; TP, October 13, 1981.
4. MA, January 1, 1985.
5. Wright; RBL, November 11, 1991.
6. RBL statement, February 25, 1985, RBL Collection.
7. Ibid.
8. SJ, February 27, 1985.
9. RBL, November 11, 1991; Russell later returned $360,000 to those who contributed to his campaign.
10. CR, September 10, 1985, 23221–26.
11. Ibid., October 17, 1986, 33468.
12. RBL statement, July 25, 1985, RBL Collection.
13. Hibbing, 208.
14. Stall.
15. CQA, 1986, 45.
16. Ibid.
17. CR, July 29, 1986, S9767.

CHAPTER 36

1. Jeffrey Birnbaum and Alan Murray, *Showdown at Gucci Gulch* (New York: Random House, 1987), 15.
2. MA, July 18, 1982.
3. RBL, December 3, 1991.
4. RBL statement, May 29, 1985, RBL Collection.
5. *Newsweek,* November 21, 1977.
6. CQA, 1986, 507–7.
7. Birnbaum and Murray, 188; Packwood.
8. *Time,* August 25, 1986.
9. Birnbaum and Murray, 191–92.
10. CQA, 1986, 509.
11. Birnbaum and Murray, 210.
12. Ibid., 212.
13. Stall; RBL, December 3, 1991.
14. Birnbaum and Murray, 228.
15. TT, June 6, 1986.
16. Birnbaum and Murray, 227–28.
17. Ibid., 231–32.
18. Ibid., 231–32, 252.
19. *Time,* August 25, 1986.
20. Birnbaum and Murray, 267.
21. *Time,* August 25, 1986.
22. Birnbaum and Murray, 282.
23. Ibid.
24. Ibid.

25. Ibid.
26. RBL, December 3, 1991.
27. Packwood.

Chapter 37

1. February 25, 1986; MA, August 19, 1986.
2. ST, April 16, 1986; SJ, March 1986.
3. MA, February 11, 1986.
4. BRST, July 18, 1986.
5. MA, July 18, 1986; *Gris Gris,* November 19, 1986; RBL, December 10, 1991.
6. RBL statement, July 18, 1986, RBL Collection; *Gris Gris,* August 1986.
7. MA, July 22, 1986.
8. Ibid.
9. RBL notes, November 1986, RBL Collection.
10. NSW, November 20, 1986.
11. CR, October 15, 1986, S16339.
12. Ibid., October 15, 1986, S16506; October 17, 1986, S33463, S33464, S33468, S33444.

BIBLIOGRAPHY

ARCHIVES AND MANUSCRIPT COLLECTIONS

Johnson, Lyndon. Papers. Lyndon B. Johnson Library. Austin, Texas.
Long, Russell. Papers. Louisiana State University, Baton Rouge.
Manatos, Mike. Papers. Lyndon B. Johnson Library. Austin, Texas.
Truman, Harry S. Papers. Harry S. Truman Library. Independence, Missouri.

BOOKS

Beals, Carleton. *The Story of Huey P. Long.* London: Lippincott, 1935.
Birnbaum, Jeffrey H., and Murray, Alan S. *Showdown at Gucci Gulch: Lawmakers, Lobbyists and the Unlikely Triumph of Tax Reform.* New York: Random House, 1987.
Brinkley, Alan. *Voices of Protest: Huey Long, Father Coughlin and the Great Depression.* New York: Vintage, 1982.
Byrd, Robert C. *The Senate, 1789–1989: Addresses on the History of the United States Senate.* Washington, DC: U.S. Government Printing Office, 1989.
Congress and the Nation, Volumes I–VII, Congressional Quarterly, Washington, DC.
Congressional Quarterly Almanac. Congressional Quarterly, Washington, DC, 1949–1986.
Dodd, William J. "Bill." *Peapatch Politics: The Earl Long Era in Louisiana Politics.* Baton Rouge: Claitor's, 1991.
Haas, Edward F. *DeLesseps S. Morrison and the Image of Reform.* Baton Rouge: LSU, 1974.
Hair, William Ivy. *The Kingfish and His Realm: The Life and Times of Huey P. Long.* Baton Rouge: LSU, 1991.
Kane, Harnett T. *Louisiana Hayride.* New York: William Morrow, 1941.

Kurtz, Michael L., and Peoples, Morgan D. *Earl K. Long: Uncle Earl and the Saga of Louisiana Politics.* Baton Rouge: LSU, 1990.
Long, Huey P. *Every Man a King.* New Orleans: National Book Company, 1933.
McCaughan, Richard. *Socks on a Rooster: Louisiana's Earl K. Long.* Baton Rouge: Claitor's, 1967.
Reedy, George E. *The U.S. Senate: Paralysis or Search for a Consensus?* New York: Crown, 1986.
Sindler, Allan P. *Huey Long's Louisiana.* Baltimore: Johns Hopkins, 1956.
Wall, Bennett. *Louisiana: A History.* Arlington Heights, IL: Forum, 1984.
White, William S. *Citadel: The Story of the U.S. Senate.* New York: Harper, 1956.
Williams, T. Harry. *Huey Long.* New York: Knopf, 1969.

INTERVIEWS BY AUTHOR

Bentsen, Lloyd, September 12, 1991.
Boggs, Lindy, May 25, 1989.
Chinn, Robert, March 29, 1989.
Curtis, Carl, February 11, 1989.
Dashbach, Richard, December 19, 1990.
Dodd, William, January 19, 1989.
Dugan, William, January 29, 1989.
Feingerts, Bruce, November 3, 1991.
Fulbright, J. William, June 19, 1989.
Gill, James H., January 30, 1989.
Guirard, James, December 11, 1989.
Johnston, J. Bennett, November 25, 1991.
Jones, Theodore, January 31, 1992.
Kirkpatrick, C. Kris, September 17, 1991.
Long, Carolyn, January 30, 1992.
Long, Katherine Hattic, March 30, 1989.
Long, Palmer, April 25, 1989.
Long, Russell B., October 27, 1988; February 2, 1989; February 8, 1989; May 15, 1989; August 8, 1989; August 22, 1989; December 28, 1989; February 5, 1990; February 19, 1990; December 3, 1990; February 2, 1991; May 17, 1991; July 25, 1991; August 28, 1991; November 11, 1991; December 3, 1991; December 10, 1991; January 3, 1992.
Madden, Ragan, May 14, 1989.
McBride, Charles, December 11, 1989.
McFarland, Rose Long, July 22, 1989.
McKinney, Joan, January 6, 1989.
Packwood, Robert, December 14, 1989.
Poe, Edgar, April 14, 1989.
Rubin, Alvin, February 25, 1989.
Stall, Karen, December 20, 1990.
Stern, Michael, December 14, 1989; November 14, 1991.
Thevenot, Wayne, April 12, 1990.
Thurmond, Strom, August 10, 1989.
Ufholz, Philip, November 26, 1990.
West, Gordon, January 21, 1989.
Wilson, Justin, February 13, 1989.
Wright, William H., July 25, 1989.

ORAL HISTORIES

Aiken, George. Lyndon B. Johnson Library. Austin, Texas.
Boggs, Hale. Lyndon B. Johnson Library. Austin, Texas.
Church, Frank. Lyndon B. Johnson Library. Austin, Texas.
Hill, Lister. Lyndon B. Johnson Library. Austin, Texas.
Long, Russell. Lyndon B. Johnson Library. Austin, Texas.
Manatos, Mike. Lyndon B. Johnson Library. Austin, Texas.

INDEX

About the Author

Robert Mann has served as press secretary to U.S. senators John Breaux and Russell Long of Louisiana. In 1990, Mann was also press secretary to the reelection campaign of U.S. senator J. Bennett Johnston of Louisiana.

Before his move to politics, Mann was political writer for the *Shreveport* (Louisiana) *Journal* and was a reporter for the Monroe, Louisiana *News-Star.* He is a journalism graduate of Northeast Louisiana University.

A native of Beaumont, Texas, Mann lives in Washington, D.C.